THE Civil War LETTERS of General Robert McAllister

♣ ♣ ♣

EDITED BY JAMES I. ROBERTSON, JR.

LOUISIANA STATE UNIVERSITY PRESS
BATON ROUGE

Copyright © 1965 by Rutgers, The State University
Copyright © renewed 1993 by James I. Robertson, Jr.
New material copyright © 1998 by Louisiana State University Press
LSU Press edition published by arrangement with Rutgers University Press
All rights reserved
Manufactured in the United States of America

Louisiana Paperback Edition, 1998
07 06 05 04 03 02 01 00 99 98   5 4 3 2 1

Library of Congress Cataloging-in-Publication Data

McAllister, Robert, 1813–1891.
　　The Civil War letters of General Robert McAllister / edited, with an
introduction and new preface, by James I. Robertson, Jr.—
Louisiana paperback ed.
　　　　p.　cm.
　　Includes bibliographical references and index.
　　ISBN 0-8071-2325-0 (pbk. : alk. paper)
　　1. McAllister, Robert, 1813–1891—Correspondence.　2. Generals—
United States—Correspondence.　3. United States—History—Civil
War, 1861–1865—Personal narratives.　4. United States. Army—
Biography.　5. United States—History—Civil War, 1861–1865—
Campaigns.　I. Title
E467.1.M17A4　1998
973.7'81'092—dc21   98-24587
　　　　　　　　　　　　　　　　　　　　　　　　　　　　　　CIP

The paper in this book meets the guidelines for permanence and durability of the Committee on Production Guidelines for Book Longevity of the Council on Library Resources. ∞

PREFACE TO THE 1998 EDITION

Robert McAllister never intended to be an outstanding soldier. That is probably why he became one. Quiet, unobtrusive, devoid of ambition but filled with the patriotic fervor that can make a man a hero, he developed into a solid and dependable field commander in the Union army.

He was also one of the most prolific writers among the two million Billy Yanks in the Civil War. The publication three decades ago of more than six hundred of his wartime letters was one of the highlights of the Civil War Centennial. Reviewers were quick to emphasize the extraordinary qualities of McAllister and his correspondence. The man himself was deemed "a highly competent officer" with "a keen sense of history." That he was "one of the most assiduous letter writers ever in active service" was obvious at a glance. His writings were "the rich stuff that constitutes history . . . an exceedingly valuable contribution to Civil War history."

On the basis of sheer volume, the McAllister letters immediately joined that elite class of Civil War chronicles where reside Theodore Lyman's *Meade's Headquarters, 1863–1865* and Charles S. Wainwright's *A Diary of Battle*. Any researcher of the Army of the Potomac must consult such sources as basic reference tools in both scope and depth.

Unfortunately, the original printing of the McAllister

correspondence was a small one. In 1965 the New Jersey Civil War Centennial Commission, which underwrote most of the publication costs, was winding down its operations. The McAllister book became its farewell donation to history. Within months, the volume was out of print and commanding a premium price in the secondhand book market. Demand and cost have climbed steadily through the years.

This new edition not only will fill a longstanding need, it once again makes available the rich, incredible collection of McAllister's observations and opinions. At the same time, this compilation calls renewed attention to one of those oftentimes faceless leaders of men whose perseverance to duty sustained the Union and, in doing so, led to the United States becoming a fact rather than remaining a name.

James I. Robertson, Jr.

Blacksburg, Virginia

ACKNOWLEDGMENTS

♣ ♣ ♣

An editor's most pleasant task is to give public thanks to those whose unselfish assistance contributes greatly to the finished product. In preparing General McAllister's letters for publication, I have received aid and encouragement from many persons. My appreciation to them is nearer indebtedness.

Miss Marian Blunt, great-great-granddaughter of the General and one of my history students at George Washington University, first alerted me to the McAllister collection. A meeting followed with Miss Blunt's grandmother, Mrs. William H. Lloyd of Bethesda, Md., who for many years was custodian of the papers. Mrs. Lloyd did not merely maintain an interest in the letters; with the assistance of her daughter, Mrs. Harry W. Blunt, she had also prepared a typescript of almost all the correspondence. Her cooperation in such matters as granting publication privileges, depositing the McAllister papers at Rutgers University, and answering patiently my many queries on minute points more than qualifies "Grandmother" Lloyd for the one to whom this volume is dedicated.

The impetus for publication of the letters rests with the New Jersey Civil War Centennial Commission, especially with Executive Director Everett J. Landers, Vice-Chairman Joseph N. Dempsey, and that commission's two leading spirits, Judge David D. Furman and Earl Schenck Miers. The New Jersey Commission donated a sizable sum toward publication of the papers; Mr. Landers in particular maintained close liaison with McAllister descendants and rendered every possible assistance to me. Donald A. Sinclair, Curator of Special Collections at Rutgers University Library, was most helpful in a number of matters relative to research. Frederick P. Todd, Director of the West Point Museum, was very helpful and diligent in verifying the battle flag of the 11th New Jersey, of which a representation appears on the jacket.

Grateful acknowledgment is made to Harcourt, Brace & World, Inc., and to my friend and colleague, Allan Nevins, for permission to quote extensively from *A Diary of Battle: The Personal Journals of Colonel Charles S. Wainwright, 1861–1865.*

Many textual questions might have remained unanswered without the help of the following friends of history: Robert Bahmer, Miss Josephine Cobb and—especially—Dallas Irvine of the National Archives; Mrs. E. E. Billings of the Columbia Historical Society; Mrs. Mary Givens Bryan of the Georgia Department of Archives and History; Miss Mary V. Darcy, Executive Secretary, Massachusetts Civil War Centennial Commission; Thomas J. Harrison and James F. Kretschmann, field historians for the National Park Service; Richard Harwell, Librarian of Bowdoin College; James J. Heslin of the New York Historical Society; Hirst D. Milhollen of the Library of Congress; Mrs. Sarah Binder Moore of Philadelphia, Pa.; Mrs. Alice D. Overton of Riverside, R.I.; William H. Price of Vienna, Va.; Col. Richard Snyder, Deputy Adjutant General for the Commonwealth of Pennsylvania; Robert W. Waitt, Jr., Executive Secretary, Richmond Civil War Centennial Committee; and Francis F. Wilshin, Superintendent of the Manassas National Battlefield Park.

Final tribute must be paid to the archival care of Henrietta Baldwin, and to the cognizance of history manifested by Robert McAllister.

James I. Robertson, Jr.

McLean, Virginia
June, 1964

PUBLISHER'S NOTE

As a result of the diligence of Henrietta McAllister Baldwin and the continuing awareness of the descendants of Robert McAllister of the historical importance of this material, six boxes of family papers have been placed in the Special Collections of the Rutgers University Library. In addition to General McAllister's letters, there are many letters received by him from members of his family, miscellaneous reports, photographs, sketches, military orders, battle plans, postwar clippings and reminiscences, Henrietta Baldwin's scrapbook, and memorabilia. They are accessible to qualified scholars.

CONTENTS

INTRODUCTION ✗ 3

1. Off to War and Bull Run ✗ 27
2. Outposts at Alexandria ✗ 59
3. The Winter Ends at Yorktown ✗ 109
4. Peninsular Defeat and Promotion ✗ 148
5. From the Potomac to the Rappahannock ✗ 196
6. Camp Fitzhugh Farm, 1862–1863 ✗ 248
7. Chancellorsville and Gettysburg ✗ 293
8. "The Races Campaign" ✗ 337
9. Brandy Station Hibernation ✗ 373
10. Bloody Route to Petersburg ✗ 413
11. The Siege Begins ✗ 451
12. Lines of Endeavor ✗ 496
13. Unbuilding a Railroad ✗ 541
14. The Path to Peace ✗ 575

INDEX ✗ 621

THE CIVIL WAR LETTERS OF
General Robert McAllister

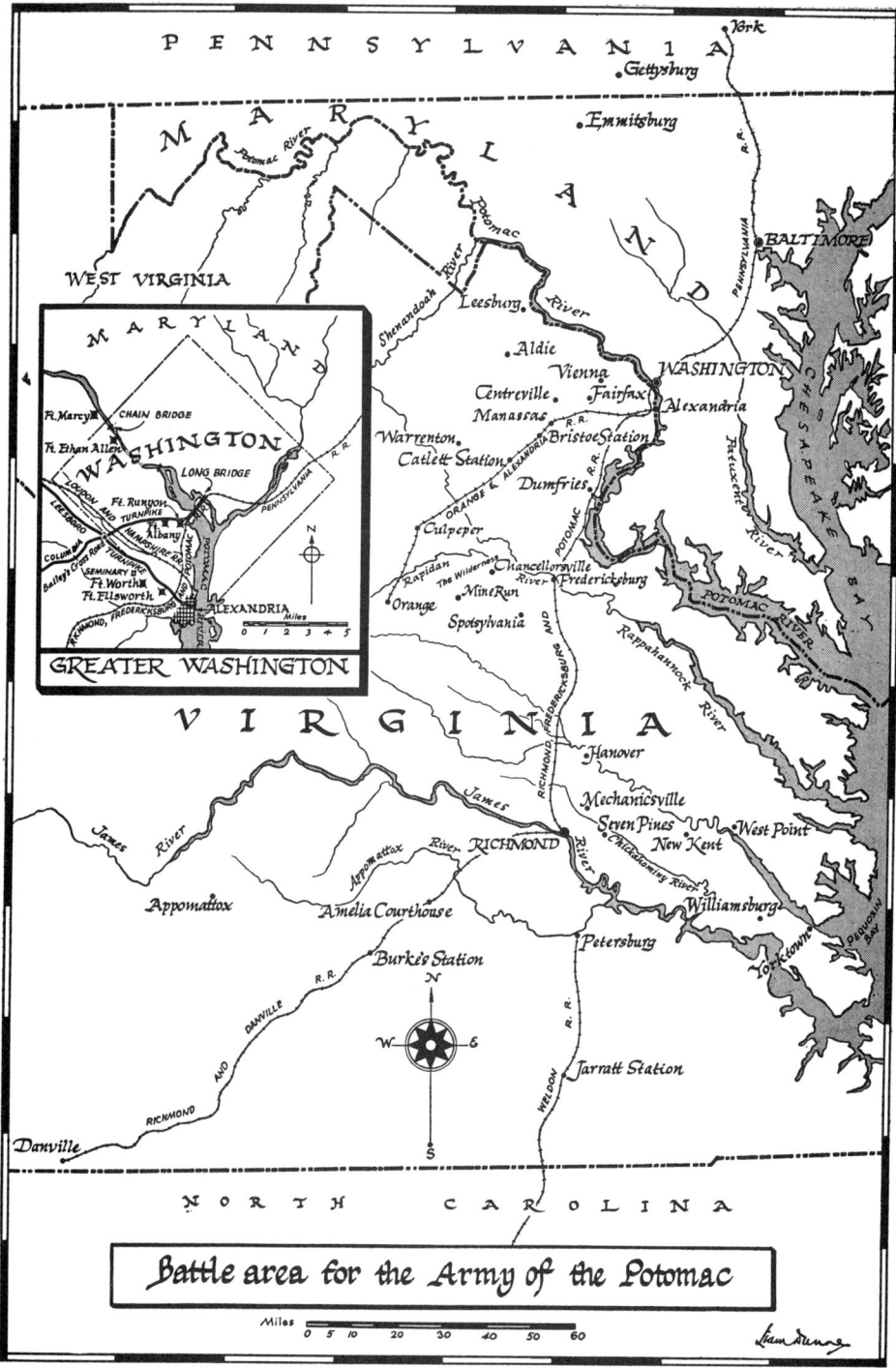

Introduction

AFTER EXAMINING the more than nine hundred Civil War letters of Robert McAllister, one might well wonder when that officer found time to fight. Be that as it may, publication of a major portion of this voluminous correspondence provides a new frame of reference for the Eastern theater of operations in general and for the Federal Army of the Potomac in particular. Yet even so large a collection of primary material might be drowned in the ever-flowing river of Civil War literature were it not for the duties and achievements of this Calvinistic fighter.

The Civil War was a soldier's war. Generals devised the strategy; corps and division commanders executed tactics by placing their units in battle position. But when the rattle of musketry began, the actual fighting and eventual outcome of the engagement rested on the men in the ranks. Valor was a deciding factor, to be sure, but so was front-line leadership. Brigade and regimental commanders could not remain behind the lines and center their attentions on maps and messages. Their places were with the troops. Their responsibilities were to inspire the men by their own bearing and to lead them into battle with demonstrative courage.

Leadership assumed a variety of forms in the Northern armies. Its flamboyant side existed in the Zouave trousers of Elmer Ellsworth and the gilt-laden coat of George Custer. The hell-for-leather fighters had no better champions than

[4] ✣ THE McALLISTER LETTERS

fiery Philip Sheridan and colorful Francis Meagher. Edwin Sumner and "Uncle John" Sedgwick were members of a venerable sect where leadership and paternalism were intertwined. Braggarts were well represented by Daniel Sickles and Judson Kilpatrick. Most numerous of all, however, were those brigadiers and colonels whose quiet efficiency and resolute gallantry ultimately proved the salvation of the Union.

Robert McAllister belonged to that noble class. As second-in-command of the 1st New Jersey Volunteer Infantry Regiment, colonel of the 11th New Jersey in the III Corps, and brigade commander in the elite II Corps, he participated in every engagement of the Army of the Potomac save South Mountain and Antietam. He was twice wounded and three times promoted for heroism on the battlefield. His regiment distinguished itself at Chancellorsville and Gettysburg. His brigade anchored the Federal center in the Wilderness, was the first to pierce the Confederate line at Spotsylvania's "Bloody Angle," and saved an entire wing of the army at Boydton Plank Road and again at Hatcher's Run. Yet few memoirs and commentaries of the period mention McAllister's name.

Outside his own corps he was virtually unknown. His diary-like official reports, sprinkled throughout the 128-volume *Official Records of the Union and Confederate Armies*, have heretofore escaped the searching eyes of historians. Today, in the state that McAllister adopted and ably represented in the field, the more colorful personalities of Phil Kearny and Judson Kilpatrick dominate historical attention. The officer whom soldiers affectionately called "Mother McAllister" has become as well "New Jersey's Forgotten General."

Time is an unfortunate eraser of memory. The years have clouded recollections of this epitome of the Scotch Presbyterian warrior. Nevertheless, one writer who knew McAllister intimately has explained both the neglect and the value of his Civil War career.

> General McAllister was not a brilliant officer, as the world uses that term. He had none of the nervous vehemence

of Kearney, none of the dazzle and dash of Sheridan. In the heat of the fiercest battle he was as cool and calm as on parade. Plain and unpretending, indifferent to the dignity and apparently unconscious of the privilages and claims of rank, with a temperament which nothing ever disturbed, he seemed, at the outset, to many who did not know him, destitute of every essential of a commander; and there is no doubt that for a time he suffered in the estimation of some of his superiors, as well as of his own command, from the excessive simplicity of his carriage and the utter absence of that sort of bluster which for awhile passed current in the army and among the people for genuine courage. Indeed, the more thoughtless and reckless among his own regiment, seeing him live soberly and simply, and laboring incessantly to improve the morals as well as the soldierly efficiency of his troops, were wont to grow jocular, around the camp fire, over his more homely peculiarities. But when the hour for fighting came, and the battle had been joined, neither officers nor men —neither his superiors nor [his] subordinates—cared to remember that they had ever thought of him otherwise than proudly.

Not a soldier of the schools; slow, perhaps, to apprehend and practice upon nice military rule, he yet had what is better than all the knowledge of the books—perfect and entire fearlessness, joined with the sturdiest tenacity of purpose; and these, making him a leader and so an inspiration to his followers, gave him success in the most desperate and exhausting straits, and secured him a place, by common voice, among the "fighting Generals" of the war.[1]

Even General Daniel Sickles, who sought far more praise than he granted, stated in an 1890 letter: "McAllister was as good an officer as New Jersey sent to the war, and that is saying a great deal." [2] However, Robert McAllister's roots lay in Pennsylvania—among a family ruptured by the approach of civil war.

1. John Y. Foster, *New Jersey and the Rebellion* (Newark, 1868), 833–34.
2. Daniel E. Sickles to Josiah Kitcham, July 15, 1890, in typescript-scrapbook compiled by Henrietta McAllister Baldwin (and in possession of Mrs. Harry W. Blunt, Bethesda, Md.), 76. Cited hereafter as Baldwin MS. This bound volume of over 300 pages was the culmination of several years' labors by Gen. McAllister's younger daughter.

[6] ✷ THE McALLISTER LETTERS

His great-grandfather, Hugh McAlister (the surname originally possessed only one "l"), emigrated from Scotland to America via Ireland in 1730 and settled in Perry County, Pennsylvania. His son, Hugh McAllister, II, married Sarah Nelson and fathered eight children before leaving to fight alongside George Washington in the Continental army. The last child of that marriage was William, born in 1775. William grew up at "Hugh's Fancy," the family homeplace in the Lost Creek Valley section of Juniata County. In 1802 he married Sarah Thompson, and from this union came nine children.[3]

The fifth child was Robert, born June 1, 1813. Even in infancy he displayed the repugnance toward intoxicants that became so integral a part of his mature makeup. A common custom of that era was to massage ill babies with whiskey. "But Robert could never stand it," his mother recalled. "He always grew white and sick from such treatment. He seemed to have a natural antipathy to intoxicating liquors in any form or used in any way."[4]

Farming occupied most of Robert's adolescent years. He was devoted to his father and performed year-round labors on the McAllister farm. The boy's education never passed the elementary level—a shortcoming Robert regretted and which is readily apparent in the grammar of his Civil War letters. In 1835 an uncle bequeathed him twelve hundred dollars. When later asked why he did not use the funds to further his education, McAllister replied matter-of-factly: "Father needed the money and I loaned it to him."[5]

On November 9, 1841, the twenty-eight-year-old McAllister married Ellen Jane Wilson at the Mercersburg home of her brother.[6] The bride, orphaned at the age of fourteen, had been raised by various relatives. She was an industrious

---

3. The children of Robert and Sarah Thompson McAllister in order of birth: Jane Thompson, Nancy, Hugh Nelson, Thompson, Robert, Elizabeth, William, a son who died unnamed, and George Washington. J. Gray McAllister, *McAllister Family Records* (Easton, Pa., 1912), 5–6.
4. Baldwin MS., 4.
5. *Ibid.*, 5.
6. A copy of the marriage certificate is in McAllister's pension claim file, Record Group 15, National Archives.

and energetic girl, in many respects older than her years. Moreover, she shared the McAllisters' strong Presbyterian bent. The newlyweds spent several months at Hugh's Fancy before moving into a two-storied brick home on the farm. The residence was a gift from Robert's father. Here were born the couple's two children: Sarah Elizabeth (1843–1935) and Henrietta Graham (1845–1924).

Robert and his older brother Thompson continued to assist their father in the management of the vast McAllister tract. Between these two brothers was a closeness stronger than mere kinship. A mutual cord binding them together was a love of the military. Prior to 1839 Thompson had organized and become captain of an artillery company of fifty Juniata County men. Robert, one of its charter members, also later became captain of the unit. "My brother Thompson and I," Robert sadly reminisced years later, "spent a great deal of time together, studying military tactics, were always connected with military companies, and were both fond of drilling. Little did either of us think that the time was coming when our swords would be drawn against each other."[7]

Proved leadership, and the ability to command respect, brought Robert McAllister steady promotion through the ranks of the Pennsylvania militia. From captain of the "Juniata Troop" of cavalry that he organized, Robert advanced to major and quartermaster of the "14th Division of Uniformed Militia" and ultimately to brigadier general of the 1st Brigade in that division.[8] Even though militia service was sporadic and consisted principally of paper work and drill, McAllister gained experience that was to prove of value to him during the days of civil war.

Meanwhile, by 1847 farming had become an unprofitable occupation for the McAllisters. Robert and his father decided to begin railroad constructing, since the Pennsylvania Railroad was then spreading its iron tentacles across the Keystone State. The father-son combination submitted the low bid for a section of construction opposite Thompsontown and,

7. J. Watts de Peyster, *A Sketch of General Robert McAllister* (cited hereafter as de Peyster, *Robert McAllister*) (New York, 18—), 5.
8. Baldwin MS., 6–8.

in November, 1847, received the contract. The sudden death of his father a month later did not prevent Robert from fulfilling the contract on schedule.[9] Success in this initial venture brought additional construction jobs on the Pennsylvania, as well as work contracts with the Sunbury & Erie at Northumberland, and the North Penn at Jenkintown and Shimersville. Expanded operations led McAllister to form a partnership with financier T. Harkins Dupuy.

In 1854 Dupuy & McAllister Company obtained the contract for the rail junction of the North Penn and Lehigh Valley lines at Bethlehem. Because of this lucrative contract the McAllister family left the Lost Creek Valley home that it had occupied for thirteen years and moved to Bethlehem. Robert and Ellen lived at the Sun Hotel; Sarah and Henrietta attended and boarded at the local Moravian Seminary.

Dupuy & McAllister next combined with the New York firm of Rutter & Brothers for construction of the Van Ness Gap tunnel on the Warren Railroad near Oxford Furnace, New Jersey. The Warren Railroad consisted of only eighteen miles of track between Hampden Junction and Delaware Bridge; yet it was under perpetual lease to the prosperous Delaware & Lackawanna Railroad. In 1857, with work on the tunnel proceeding satisfactorily, McAllister moved his family from Bethlehem to Oxford Furnace. Three years of boarding had made the whole family eager for a residence of their own. McAllister purchased an old stone house near the firm's office, and his wife quickly converted it into a comfortable home. The children especially liked the beautiful rolling country of western New Jersey. Henrietta McAllister wrote a half-century later:

> Immediately in rear of the house was a pleasant, rocky, wooded hill with a romantic brook which flowed on through our yard. An open space in front of the house was designated "Glen Ellen Park" in honor of Mother. Beyond this was the

---

9. By the terms of William McAllister's will, the farm was divided equally between Thompson and Robert. The former took the half containing the old homeplace; Robert assumed ownership of the half on which his home was situated.

temporary track of the Delaware & Lackawanna R.R., which was in use till the tunnel would be completed, and beyond the track were the store and offices of the firm and the shanties of the workmen, and beyond them rose a beautiful hill. . . . The whistles, the going and coming of the men, and all connected with the work soon became interesting to us. Events proved that this little house with all its deficiencies and inconveniences was our happy home for five years.[10]

Depression struck the nation in the autumn of 1857. When the Delaware & Lackawanna, indebted to McAllister's company for more than $36,000, could not meet the monthly payroll of the 300 laborers, the situation at Oxford Furnace became critical. Several of the older workers remained loyal to their employer. "Our old hands," McAllister wrote on Christmas Eve of that year, "wished us to continue the work, said they would not ask for any cash payment till next Spring, and at the same time offered us all the money they had . . . but of course we did not accept their kindness, not knowing when we could pay them." [11]

Such devotion was far from unanimous. Lack of wages brought unrest. Numerous fights broke out around the construction site, and a boardinghouse belonging to the firm was left in embers. McAllister survived through the financial assistance of such friends as Lucian Wilson, and through the economizing measures of a new partner, George B. Wiestling. Work was resumed in January, 1858; the Van Ness Gap tunnel, completed in 1862, became an important feature on the Lackawanna's main line between New York and Scranton.[12]

McAllister missed the dedication ceremonies. Spasms of unrest that coursed through the nation in 1860 became convulsions of war in April of the following year. The national upheaval was no better exemplified than in the schism of the McAllister clan. Members of the family gathered at the old homeplace in January, 1860, for their regular reunion. Yet

10. Baldwin MS., 10–11.
11. *Ibid.,* 11.
12. The tunnel remained a part of the Lackawanna's main line until the turn of the century, when the railroad constructed a new and shorter route to Scranton. Portions of the original roadbed are still used for freight service.

hot tempers (a family trait) and angry words racked the assembly. Several years previously Robert's favorite brother, Thompson, had moved to Covington, Virginia. Ironically, he too had gone into railroad contracting; and while Robert was superintending a tunnel on the Lackawanna, Thompson was overseeing the construction of a tunnel for what became the Chesapeake & Ohio. But the two brothers shared no common ground in political beliefs. Thompson violently defended Southern rights and principles, while Robert argued just as vehemently for the Union. The reunion dissolved among heated verbal exchanges; the two brothers departed enemies.

Following the Confederate bombardment of Fort Sumter, both Robert McAllister and George Wiestling stumped Warren County, New Jersey, on behalf of the Northern war effort. One morning toward the end of April, 1861, McAllister walked into the firm's office, where Wiestling sat poring over a ledger.

"Mr. Wiestling," McAllister began, "we have been making our war speeches, trying to inspire others with patriotism, thrown our flags to the breeze, and urged men to go to war. I think it is time one of us said, 'Come, boys,' instead of 'Go.'"

Wiestling thought for a moment, then replied: "General, you are the military man of this firm."

"Yes, I am," McAllister acknowledged. "That means that I shall go. Well, my country is dear to me and I will do all I can for her. Will you take care of my interests here?"

"Yes, to the best of my ability," Wiestling promised.[13]

With the reluctant approval of his wife, the forty-seven-year-old farmer and contractor prepared to enter active military service.

McAllister first considered joining the forces of his native Pennsylvania. There influential friends, plus his former commission as brigadier general of militia, would have placed him in good standing for high command. But local inducements in New Jersey prevailed. McAllister organized an infantry company, gave it the county name "Warren

13. Baldwin MS., 13–14.

Guard," and became its captain. The company marched enthusiastically to the state rendezvous camp at Trenton. It arrived too late to be included in New Jersey's first contingent of three-month volunteers. The Warren Guard then spent several impatient days in drill and in anticipation of Abraham Lincoln's second call for troops.

The President's new request came on May 3, 1861; however, it bore an unexpected proviso. New Jersey was asked to furnish three regiments—not for three months' service, but for three years or the duration. Scores of recruits at Trenton's Camp Olden promptly went home. Those of the Warren Guard who agreed to the terms became the nucleus of Company C, 1st New Jersey Volunteers.

Governor Charles Olden was well aware of McAllister's prior service with the Pennsylvania militia. He asked the short, slim officer to help organize and train this first of New Jersey's three-year regiments. McAllister agreed, with the understanding that he was to be the regiment's colonel. He entered upon his training duties with customary industry and conscientiousness. But during this interim Olden was subjected to strong pressure to name William R. Montgomery, a semiretired Regular Army officer then living in Pennsylvania, to the post of colonel of the 1st New Jersey. In a long conference with McAllister, the Governor asked him to take the lieutenant colonelcy of the regiment. Montgomery was certain to win quick promotion to brigadier, Olden explained, and McAllister would be his natural successor as head of the 1st New Jersey.

McAllister was disappointed at this turn of events. At the same time he admired and respected the experienced Montgomery. "I will accept the place under Montgomery," he told Olden, "but under no one else." [14] Olden quickly made the assignments to command.

The 1st New Jersey reached Washington in June, 1861, and joined the military forces that shortly would fuse into the Army of the Potomac. In time this army became the nation's

---

14. Henrietta McAllister later stated: "There never was any trouble between Col. Montgomery and Lt. Col. McAllister—every thing was harmonious and in time they became warm friends." See *ibid.*, 15, 18.

idol. Yet incompetent leadership—and Robert E. Lee—brought it costly misfortune. "Its story is a sad one," one soldier stated, "for it was always better than its commander, and marched and fought, endured and achieved, rarely animated by victory." [15]

The army's first battle was a horrible case in point. After garrison duty at Alexandria and Vienna, Virginia, McAllister's regiment rushed to Centreville. The men arrived in time to cover the Federal retreat from the debacle at Bull Run. McAllister always insisted that his regiment was instrumental in saving General Irvin McDowell's dispirited forces from total defeat. The 1st New Jersey spent the next eight months on outpost duty at Alexandria's Episcopal Seminary. For McAllister the significant event of this period—and one of the hardest blows to morale he suffered during the war—came in August, 1861. Montgomery received the expected promotion to brigadier; but without explanation the colonelcy of the 1st New Jersey went to Alfred T. A. Torbert, a former Regular Army officer and twenty years McAllister's junior. Only a keen sense of duty prevented McAllister from resigning from the service. For a time he sought command elsewhere; but officers were then so numerous, a popular story ran, that Lincoln threw a club at a dog on Pennsylvania Avenue and hit five brigadier generals.

McAllister checked his pride and remained with the 1st New Jersey. Winter inactivity ceased in March, 1862, when the regiment and the rest of Philip Kearny's brigade moved out and occupied Centreville. McAllister's troops were the first to reach the former Confederate field headquarters. A month later the regiment was at Yorktown with the invading army of General George B. McClellan. As part of William B. Franklin's division, the 1st New Jersey participated in the May 7 action at West Point, Virginia, then was an advance element in the snail-like progression toward Richmond. The regiment's christening in a major battle came June 27 at Gaines's Mill. McAllister had temporarily as-

---

15. W. P. Derby, *Bearing Arms in the Twenty-seventh Massachusetts Regiment* . . . (Boston, 1883), 297.

sumed command from the ailing Torbert. His unit fought gallantly but lost 159 of its members. Fortunately, its activity in the remainder of the Seven Days' Campaign was confined to a minor role in the engagement at Glendale.

Long-awaited promotion came to McAllister while the Army of the Potomac sprawled in neutrality at Harrison's Landing. Late in June Governor Olden named him colonel of the 11th New Jersey. When McAllister arrived in Trenton the following month to take command of the newly formed regiment, he beheld with despair a mob of recruits characterized by filth, disorganization, and general lack of discipline. McAllister set to work immediately to improve the regiment's appearance and conduct. Companies made regular trips to the bathhouses; drill and inspections filled daily training schedules; in true McAllister fashion, regulations repeatedly and explicitly forbade the presence of intoxicating spirits in camp. This last-named restraint proved the most difficult to enforce. Consequently, "some poor slave of appetite" continually resided in the guardhouse.[16]

In August the 11th New Jersey united at Washington with other elements of the Federal army. The new regiment was "looked upon with something like contempt by the older regiments from its own State, owing to its youthful *personnel*, the average age being about seventeen." Members of veteran units twitted "McAllister's boys" in the course of the latter's bridge-guarding duties at the battle of Fredericksburg and during the winter months at Falmouth. McAllister never ceased efforts to improve his regiment. His labors were rewarded in May, 1863, when the scarred but still determined Army of the Potomac moved into the Wilderness to do battle again with Lee's Confederates. The 11th New Jersey was a segment of Sickles' III Corps. Its dual responsibilities in the abortive battle of Chancellorsville were to form a new line because of the rout of the XI Corps and to hold off "Stonewall" Jackson's onslaughts. Severe fighting continued for two days. The 11th New Jersey's losses far outnumbered those of

16. Thomas D. Marbaker, *History of the Eleventh New Jersey Volunteers* . . . (cited hereafter as Marbaker, *11th New Jersey*) (Trenton, 1898), 3–4.

any other regiment in its brigade. Nevertheless, its valor was exemplary, and the conduct of its colonel won universal praise. "Thenceforth," a member of the regiment asserted, " 'McAllister's boys' became a title of honor." [17]

Gettysburg came close to being the ruin of both the "boys" and "Mother McAllister." A degree of foolhardiness marked Sickles' July 2 decision to advance his corps from the Little Round Top area to the Emmitsburg Pike. With flanks unguarded, and virtually alone in the open, the III Corps caught the full fury of General James Longstreet's assault. The 11th New Jersey fertilized the Peach Orchard with human blood. More than 140 of its members were killed or wounded. Among the first to fall was McAllister, who was struck first by a musket ball and then by a shell fragment.[18]

He was borne to the rear with blood streaming from his leg. In a field hospital the regimental surgeon pleaded with him to take a little whiskey as a stimulant. McAllister steadfastly refused. Finally the doctor surreptitiously spiked a glass of milk that McAllister drank. "He was heard afterward," one soldier recollected, "speaking in terms of praise of the milk given by the Gettysburg cows." [19]

McAllister asked that his wound be reported as "slight" so as not to alarm his family. Yet Ellen and Henrietta McAllister were not deceived. They enlisted the aid of Belvidere banker Israel Harris and attorney David Dupuy and set out for the battlefield.[20] The party proceeded as far as Philadelphia, where they discovered McAllister en route to Belvidere under the care of a doctor. By covered wagon, ferry, and

17. *Ibid.*, 71.
18. According to regimental surgeon Edward F. Welling, McAllister received "a wound of the left leg, above the knee, a little below the thigh, the ball passing around the femoral artery and just missing it and coming out behind, and also another [wound], a slight shell wound of the right foot near [the] big toe." Affidavit of Dr. Welling, Feb. 24, 1885, McAllister's pension claim file.
19. Marbaker, *11th New Jersey*, 152.
20. In 1862 Mrs. McAllister and the two daughters had left Oxford Furnace, New Jersey, and moved into a more comfortable home seven miles distant in Belvidere. Henrietta McAllister thought Belvidere "an unusually attractive place because of the culture and character of its people." She added: "We became much attached to them because, during all our anxieties for Father while he was fighting the battles of his country, they were so patriotic, interested and friendly." Baldwin MS., 19.

rough railroads, the crippled Colonel eventually reached his home.[21]

Three months of recuperation followed, during which time McAllister gave his older daughter in marriage. He hobbled back to the army early in October, took part with his regiment in the Mine Run Campaign, and spent the ensuing winter at Brandy Station. Alternating between regimental and brigade command helped him to pass the months of monotony. In the spring of 1864 the Army of the Potomac began the final drive against Lee's forces. Long lines of Federals moved across the Rapidan into the Wilderness—and vicious fighting. Six weeks of uninterrupted campaigning left gaping holes in the army. McAllister dramatically summarized this warpath in a letter to a compatriot.

> It was one battle day and night and night and day. No cessation, no cessation. Often we wished for the darkness to close around us that we might have rest, but alas, with the darkness came not the rest so ardently desired, but work, fight and march. The flash of the rifles and muskets, as well as the cannon, together with the fiery paraboles of the fuses and bursting missles of the mortars would illuminate the heavens all around the battle field. Then the night struggles were frequent and arduous, and at times again we often wished for the return of the morning, but its return brought no change from the toils of working, marching and fighting. Our thinned ranks told us the sad story of the deadly conflict through which we were passing. The long lines of graves told the stranger the direction of our marches and the dispositions of our battles. At each morning roll-call, fewer and fewer numbers responded to well known names.
>
> Where are they? The reply came from newly made graves.[22]

The white-haired Colonel passed his fifty-first birthday while fighting gallantly with the II Corps in this campaign. He received a slight wound in the Wilderness, recovered in

---

21. Accounts of McAllister's trip home and of his family's journey in search of him are in Baldwin MS., 22–26.
22. McAllister to J. Watts de Peyster, undated letter, *ibid.*, 77.

time to lead his men against the "Bloody Angle" at Spotsylvania, and commanded part of the Federal force that stormed the Confederate works along the North Anna River. The 11th New Jersey providentially missed participation in the Federal massacre at Cold Harbor. McAllister fought the last ten months of the war from the trenches in front of Petersburg. Three skirmishes and four battles each added laurels to his military reputation. He was breveted brigadier general for conspicuous conduct in the October 27, 1864, engagement at Boydton Plank Road. McAllister and his brigade saw limited action in the conclusive Appomattox Campaign. On July 22, 1865, McAllister's name was included in a long list of brigadiers appointed "Major General of Volunteers by Brevet" for "gallant and meritorious service." [23]

Many officers chose to remain in the army and pursue postwar military careers. However, McAllister felt that "a soldier's life in time of peace is too inactive to my liking, and it would be the last vocation I would choose." [24] In June, 1865, he returned to Belvidere, New Jersey, and looked into a number of job possibilities. His first endeavor—part interest in a Mississippi cotton plantation—ended in financial ruin. Meanwhile the General had made the acquaintance of Robert L. Kennedy, a New York financier who spent his summers in Belvidere. Kennedy at that time was negotiating for complete control of the Ironton Railroad Company, which consisted of hematite ore mines at Ironton, Pennsylvania, and a railroad that snaked sixteen miles from Ironton to a junction at Coplay with the Lehigh Valley. The company badly needed an efficient general manager. Kennedy approached McAllister, who surveyed the company's holdings and promptly accepted the offer.

That the Ironton Railroad firm achieved high success in the postwar years was due in no small part to the energy and careful control exercised by the new general manager. Ini-

23. U.S. War Dept. (comp.), *War of the Rebellion: A Compilation of the Official Records of the Union and Confederate Armies* (Washington, 1880-1901), Ser. I, Vol. XLVI, Pt. 3 (cited hereafter as *OR;* unless otherwise stated, all references will be to Ser. I) pp. 860-61, 1259, 1309.
24. Baldwin MS., 32.

tially McAllister boarded at the American Hotel in Allentown, Pennsylvania. He daily made the fourteen-mile round-trip to his office, and on weekends he journeyed twenty miles to Belvidere to be with his wife and younger daughter. In 1870 the family left Belvidere and moved to Allentown.[25]

Henrietta McAllister (who married attorney Johnson Baldwin in 1873) wrote of this period:

> Father and Mother enjoyed their life in Allentown. They liked the people and the people liked them. Father was one of the public spirited men of the place. Whenever there was a Republican procession, or a military parade, they must always have him in command. . . . The years passed on with the ordinary variations of health and sickness, bad business years and good ones, but with no striking changes in their lives. [Sarah McAllister Lloyd], living in Germantown, came frequently to see them, usually bringing some of her children with her. Every two years I came from Pittsburgh, bringing my children with me for a visit of six to eight weeks. The number [of children] increased with the years, but there never seemed to be too many for either their home or their hearts.[26]

Henrietta's reminiscences omitted one significant event of this period. Late in 1870 a very ill Thompson McAllister left his Covington, Virginia, home and sought medical treatment in New York. Not since 1860 had Robert had any contact with his Confederate brother; but the deep affection of earlier years overcame estrangement. Robert and Hugh Nelson McAllister met Thompson in New York. They enjoyed a warm reunion marred by the doctor's pronouncement that Thompson's illness was fatal. The brothers bade farewell to one another, aware of the literal nature of their good-bys. Three months later Thompson died peacefully in his sleep.[27]

---

25. For three years the McAllisters occupied a suite at the American Hotel. In 1873 McAllister purchased a home at the corner of Walnut and Fifth streets. There the family lived during their stay in Allentown. *Ibid.*, 37–38.
26. *Ibid.*, 38–39.
27. J. Gray McAllister, *Sketch of Captain Thompson McAllister, Co. A, 27th Virginia Regiment* (cited hereafter as McAllister, *Thompson McAllister*) (Petersburg, Va., 1896), 26–27.

For sixteen years McAllister served as general manager of the Ironton Railroad Company. He was also one of ten commissioners appointed in 1876 by Governor John F. Hartranft of Pennsylvania to select a site and design for a new mental institution to be constructed in southeastern Pennsylvania. The commission's efforts culminated in the network of cottages erected at Norristown. The labors of over sixty-seven years soon began to tell on McAllister. He and Robert Kennedy sold the Ironton firm in February, 1882. A year later, at the insistence of his partner, McAllister and his wife Ellen moved to "Erlenbach," Kennedy's imposing home in Belvidere, New Jersey. Henrietta recalled: "The mansion was large and delightful, with broad verandas, commanding beautiful views of the surrounding country." [28]

McAllister spent five years of happiness on this eighty-acre estate. Local friends and Civil War veterans beat a steady path to visit the McAllisters at Erlenbach. The General rarely missed services at the First Presbyterian Church. The genuine friendliness of townspeople, and the continuing generosity of Kennedy, brought McAllister great contentment in those twilight years. Suddenly, one setback followed another. Kennedy died in 1887, and the liquidation of his estate forced the McAllisters to take up residence in the Hotel Belvidere. At the Christmas season of 1888 McAllister suffered a severe stroke. The attack left his right arm paralyzed and his health permanently impaired.

McAllister finally consented to ask the Federal government for a pension.[29] By then Bright's disease had complicated battle wounds and effects of the stroke. McAllister's petition for total disability was rejected; the government instead awarded him fifteen dollars monthly.[30] In the summer of 1890 financial problems from without and physical problems from within pressed heavily on the aged warrior. General J. Watts de Peyster, a close friend to McAllister, then wrote a strong letter to the Commissioner of Federal Pen-

---

28. Baldwin MS., 40–41.
29. His attorney in these proceedings was his son-in-law, Johnson H. Baldwin.
30. See pertinent papers in McAllister's pension claim file.

Robert and Ellen McAllister posed for these photographs sometime in the late 1850's.

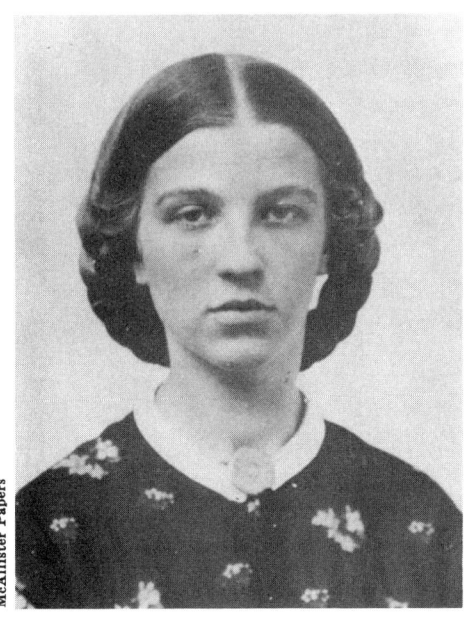 

Sarah (left) and Henrietta McAllister, from photographs made in 1862–63

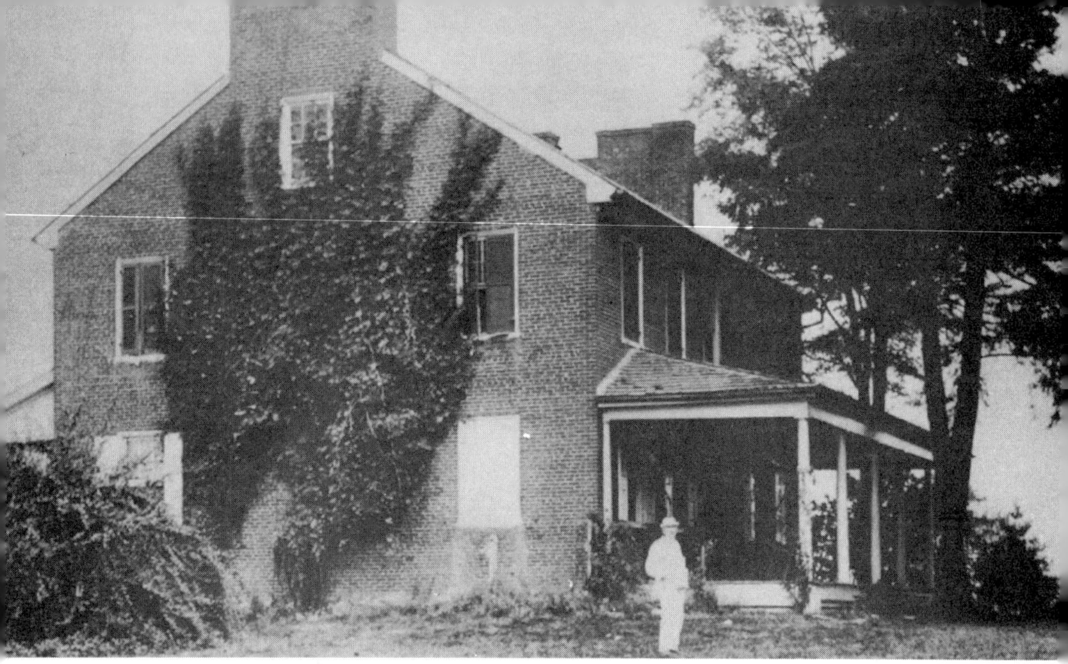
McAllister Papers

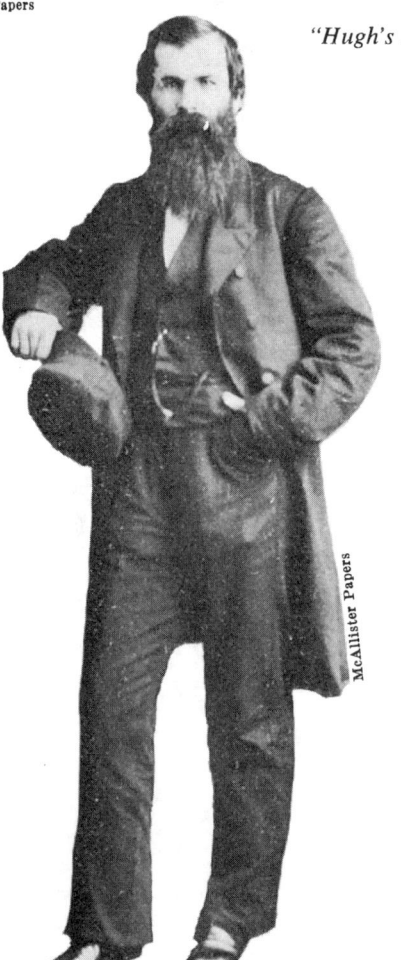

"Hugh's Fancy," ancestral home of Robert McAllister

McAllister Papers

George B. Wiestling, McAllister's business partner

University of Virginia Library

Everett Landers

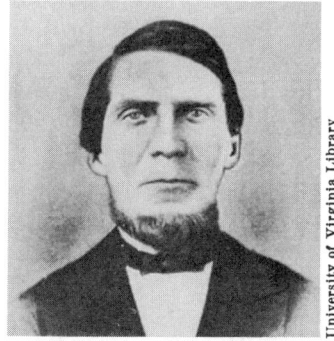

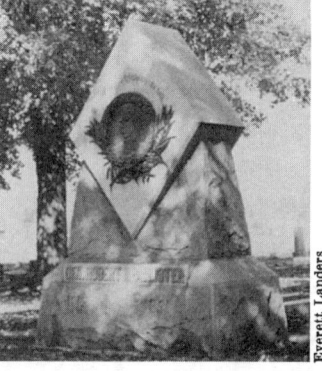

Above: *Capt. Thompson McAllister*
Army of the Confederate States of America
Brother of Robert McAllister

Below: *Robert McAllister's grave*
Belvidere, New Jersey

sions. De Peyster urged a full pension for McAllister. He recounted McAllister's many deeds in the war, avowed that his disability was a direct result of the rigors of military service, and concluded: "If there is a man and soldier in the United States who deserves all that the country can legally or equitably accord to him, it is the broken in health and crippled Major General Robert McAllister." [31] The petition was again denied.

Ellen McAllister, in precarious health herself, did all she could for her husband. Yet in mid-February, 1891, the General's condition took a decided turn for the worse. Members of the family hastened to Belvidere. "Just as the town clock was striking the twelve strokes which closed the day on Monday, February 23d 1891," McAllister died at the age of seventy-seven.[32]

In his last years McAllister had acquired a strong dislike of military funerals. On one occasion he had stated that he wanted "no brass bands at my funeral, nor firing over my grave." The family at first tried to adhere to his wishes. Plans were announced to hold simple burial services in Allentown, Pennsylvania, where McAllister years before had purchased a cemetery plot. A delegation of Belvidere citizens immediately called on the widow. "General McAllister's war record was identified with New Jersey," they pointed out. "His body ought to rest in New Jersey soil. It is all wrong to take it out of the state." [33]

Ellen McAllister finally acquiesced. Elaborate, semimilitary services were held in Belvidere. From the First Presbyterian Church the coffin—draped with the tattered flag of New Jersey's 2nd Brigade—was borne to Belvidere Cemetery and buried after numerous eulogies.[34] On May 30, 1894, an impressive monument purchased by the citizens of Belvidere was dedicated over the grave of McAllister.

His achievements in the arenas of the Civil War did not

31. J. Watts de Peyster to Green B. Raum, Aug. 2, 1890, *ibid.*
32. Baldwin MS., 48; McAllister's pension claim file. Cause of death was ambiguously given as "intestinal nephritis." Ellen McAllister died in 1905 at the age of eighty-eight.
33. Baldwin MS., 49–50.
34. See *ibid.*, 50–51, 152–217.

[20] ✕ THE McALLISTER LETTERS

go entirely unnoticed during the epidemic of recollection writing subsequent to the conflict. Several veterans praised his valor;[35] others called attention to the high standards of Christian character that he manifested.[36] One brigade commander who fought beside McAllister in the last year of the war summarized him well—even though failing to spell his name correctly.

> MacAllister is a character truly original. From what I have related of his services in front of the enemy, the reader would doubtless be led to imagine him as hard fighters are generally represented—still young, with loud voice, fierce mustache, lofty step, etc. Nothing could be further from the truth. McAllister is a good *pater familias*, having passed his fortieth year. His voice is soft and calm; never, never on any occasion is it raised to the pitch of an oath or anything resembling it. Not only is his mustache not twisted, but his face is as closely shaven as that of an honest pastor. Everything about him has the air of simplicity and modesty. His habits are those of an anchorite. A temperance man, he never touches liquor of any kind, not even beer. Tolerant as to others, rigid for himself, he preaches by example only. His staff had full liberty to use moderately the liquors he refused himself. . . .
>
> As punctual in his religious habits as he was sincere in his belief, he had Protestant religious services regularly on Sunday at his headquarters. The most pleasant attention we could pay him was, on that day, to listen to the sermon of his chaplain.
>
> His habitual kind-heartedness for the soldier did not affect his discipline. When he personally intervened in a punishment, he seldom failed to accompany it with a reprimand, the tenor and tone of which recalled to the culprit the scoldings he had received from his mother in his childhood. So that the soldiers among themselves called him affectionately "Mother McAllister." But when the day of battle came, the mother led on her children as a lioness her cubs. Because

---

35. For example, see Andrew A. Humphreys, *The Virginia Campaign of '64 and '65* (New York, 1883), 86; de Peyster, *Robert McAllister, passim;* Baldwin MS., 18–19, 58, 81.

36. For example, see Marbaker, *11th New Jersey,* 276; Foster, *New Jersey and the Rebellion,* 834.

he was a most exemplary man, McAllister was none the less the most energetic soldier.[37]

The truest testimonial to McAllister was not so elaborate. Contained in a private letter from John Y. Foster, its worth lies in the fact that it was a sincere tribute to a sincere man. McAllister, Foster stated, was "the simplest minded, bravest, most conscientious of all the men from New Jersey who achieved distinction in the war. He went forward in the path of duty, all unconscious of self, because *every natural impulse compelled him to do so*, and it was this genuineness and simplicity that made him the conspicuous figure he was." [38]

Robert McAllister's keen sense of history is apparent in every facet of his Civil War letters.

Military activities notwithstanding, he scarcely permitted a day to pass without sending at least a few lines to his wife, to his daughters, or to all three of his loved ones. McAllister wrote a majority of his letters either before breakfast or just prior to bedtime. Occasionally he began a letter at dawn and added intermittently to it throughout the day. Similarly, he sometimes started a letter at night, adjourned to his bed to rest, and resumed the communication the following morning. In his writings he took pains to note such items as troop movements, camp life, conversations with general officers, morale, weather, the condition and inhabitants of occupied territory, army religion, the health of soldiers, plus almost exhaustive accounts of the engagements in which he participated. When he had no news to convey, McAllister passed along rumors then current in camp.

His long, purely military discussions possessed comparatively little interest for his feminine addressees. No doubt commentaries on marches, battles, and siege lines left Mrs. McAllister and the girls dumbfounded. But McAllister was

---

37. Régis de Trobriand, *Four Years with the Army of the Potomac* (cited hereafter as de Trobriand, *Army of the Potomac*) (Boston, 1889), 707–8.
38. John Y. Foster to Henrietta Baldwin, June 15, 1888, Baldwin MS., 144–45.

not merely writing to his family. References to the traditional righteousness of the Union cause, recurrent speculations on what historians would say of particular events, the detail of his narratives, and his constant insistence upon the preservation of his papers suggest that McAllister in truth was addressing his letters to posterity.

McAllister's correspondence lacks the incisiveness of Theodore Lyman's remarkable letters; it possesses no penetrating insight into high command such as characterizes Charles Wainwright's voluminous diaries; nor do its faint traces of humor classify it with the entertaining recollections of John D. Billings and Henry Morford. Rather, the value of the letters lies in their continuity, comprehensiveness, vivid descriptions, and strikingly personal touches.

McAllister displayed a cold attitude toward Confederates. He never accepted the thesis that the South was seeking peaceful independence, not the overthrow of the United States. Likewise he habitually underestimated the fighting qualities of "Rebel" soldiers. Federal defeats he attributed to internal weaknesses rather than any external brilliance on the part of his adversaries. Significant too was McAllister's almost total indifference to the Negro race. He abhorred slavery, but he never considered himself—even after the issuance of the Emancipation Proclamation—as fighting for human freedom. The preservation of the Union was in his mind the sole issue of the war. The only mentions of Negroes in the letters are McAllister's references to camp servants and to colored units that his brigade relieved in the Petersburg trenches.

A strong advocate of Christian morality, McAllister was prone to write excessively on spiritual matters. But he generally did so after recounting some instance of wickedness— such as a group of rowdies converting the brigade chapel into a dance hall. His asceticism tended to make him a colorless individual, and no doubt many were the soldiers who called him "Mother McAllister" in tones other than complimentary. Yet a warm and human side of the man appears in his letters. Unrestricted pride in his regiments, unbounded joy at the birth of his first grandchild, sincere compassion for the sick and wounded, deep remorse at the deaths of comrades, and genuine affection for most of the officers and men with whom he served—all reveal McAllister as a sentimental and quite interesting figure.

For military students McAllister's letters have special value. His detailed descriptions of campaigns are midway between the broad perspectives of field commanders and the restricted views of foot soldiers within the ranks. He wrote only of the immediate stage of conflict where his own troops were performing, but he did so with such minute and graphic detail that in many instances maps of these sectors of battle are unnecessary. Postwar commentators who examined McAllister's letters termed them "perfect guides" and "exhaustive in regard to the operations in which he participated." [39] Moreover, McAllister's eloquence proved a triumph over faulty grammar and inconsistent spelling.

Bits and pieces of his massive correspondence have made their way into print. John Y. Foster obtained use of some of the letters for his thick and hastily compiled *New Jersey and the Rebellion*. Thomas D. Marbaker gained access to the letters in the preparation of his *History of the Eleventh New Jersey Volunteers*. . . . Both authors quoted at length from the letters—and both authors plagiaristically incorporated a few into their respective texts. Edward K. Gould extracted part of McAllister's narrative on Chancellorsville for his biography of General Hiram G. Berry. The New York *Citizen* printed a number of McAllister's official reports in its 1871 issues. With the help of his daughter Henrietta, and relying on his letters, McAllister prepared a summary of Spotsylvania for the Century Company's *Battles and Leaders of the Civil War*.[40] For the most part, however, the huge collection remained unpublished and unused.

McAllister always hoped that the bulk of his letters

39. *Ibid.*, 85, 132–33.
40. McAllister's daughter handled most of the details relative to the article for *Battles and Leaders of the Civil War*. Henrietta inherited her father's meticulous care of historical documents. Just before McAllister completed his article, she wrote: "I understand the 'Century' people are better than most publishers about returning manuscripts, &c. However, I don't propose to trust them with anything but *copy*." Henrietta Baldwin to McAllister, Oct. 1, 1887, Robert McAllister Papers, Rutgers University (cited hereafter as McAllister Papers).

would someday be published. Toward that end he bequeathed three hundred dollars, which descendants deposited in a Pittsburgh bank. In 1902 Mrs. Henrietta Baldwin asked Daniel Sickles to write a foreword for the anticipated volume of letters. On December 12 of that year the old General replied:

> Your request would have been complied with long ago, had I not mislaid your address.
> I have great pleasure in paying a just tribute to the memory of your honored father, General Robert McAllister. His service under my command in the Third Army Corps, was conspicuous for every soldierly accomplishment. I was always sure of the execution of any order given to him. A regiment soon acquires the character of its commander. McAllister's regiment, like himself, was always trustworthy, as will be seen by anybody who reads the reports of Chancellorsville and Gettysburg.
> At Gettysburg, where McAllister was twice wounded, his regiment lost 154 killed and wounded, out of 275 present. Major Kearney, the only other field officer present, was also seriously wounded. All the captains were either killed or wounded and the regiment fell under the command of Lieut. Schoonover, a gallant young subaltern, who made the final report of the part taken by the regiment in the action.
> General McAllister was a Christian soldier, whose devotion to the flag and the Union will always be cherished by every officer and man who served under him or with him. I am glad to know that you are about to publish his war-time letters. Every statement he makes can be depended upon for its accuracy. Such contributions as these to history will be welcomed by every historian. I shall be glad to have a copy of your work.[41]

Nevertheless, commercial publishers showed no interest in the letters. An attempt by some members of the family to get the letters privately printed ended in failure. Other of the McAllister descendants considered the correspondence too personal—and too critical of certain Civil War generals—to

41. Daniel E. Sickles to Henrietta Baldwin, Dec. 12, 1902, Baldwin MS., 148.

be made public. Undaunted, Mrs. Baldwin devoted the remaining twenty years of her life to the letters. She carefully traced in ink most of McAllister's penciled communications, added some explanatory notes garnered from postwar conversations with her father, and put together a thick scrapbook on the General and his descendants. Meanwhile McAllister's three-hundred-dollar bequest lay untouched, save for twenty dollars withdrawn to purchase a storage trunk for the letters. In that container, and for nearly half a century, the papers passed from one generation to another. Their publication now is a literary highlight of the Civil War Centennial.

In the course of the Civil War Robert McAllister addressed more than nine hundred communications to his family. Some letters are no more than two- or three-sentence notes; others are practically verbatim repetitions of letters sent earlier to either Ellen McAllister or one of the daughters; and a number of letters treat only of personal and historically insignificant matters. Such superfluities notwithstanding, published here, intact or in part, are 637 of McAllister's personal wartime letters and battle accounts.

Every care has been exercised to preserve the flavor of McAllister's writings. The faulty sentence structure and misspellings have for the most part been retained. In the case of proper names, the initial misspelling is included; subsequent references to persons have been corrected. A number of minor alterations performed were little more than what is expected in modern-day copy preparation. For example, periods have replaced dashes at the end of sentences; overly long and complicated passages have been converted into series of shorter, more intelligible sentences; paragraphs have been employed for changes in subject matter. Necessary punctuation marks, as well as natural connecting words that McAllister inadvertently omitted in the haste of writing, have been added. Repetitious material, unimportant treatises on religion, passing references to friends and neighbors, and complimentary closes have been omitted for the sake of continuity.

The scope of McAllister's letters demanded unusually extensive documentation. Albeit Civil War buffs may find many footnotes unnecessary, the initiate into this fascinating field of history will at least have the option of pursuing further places and events mentioned in the correspondence.

At the 1894 dedication of the McAllister monument in Belvidere, John Foster predicted: "History will give him a bright page on its rolls, and a grateful country will appreciate his services and revere his memory." [42]

History has been slow in acknowledging this soldier, and the nation has been tardy in honoring his memory. But now, through his letters, Robert McAllister enriches history and honors himself.

42. *Ibid.*, 185.

1

Off to War and Bull Run

LIKE MOST of his younger compatriots in that war's first spring, McAllister did not envision a long contest. One pitched battle, he was certain, and the Rebels (he never elevated them to Confederates) would promptly sue for peace. This belief in a short war explains why most of the men in the Warren Guard company that McAllister led to Trenton's Camp Olden balked at enlisting for three years. Fortunately, patriotism surpassed practicality, and the first three-year regiment quickly took shape. McAllister expected to be its colonel because that post had unofficially been promised him. When the colonelcy went instead to William R. Montgomery, McAllister agreed to take second-in-command on the assumption that Montgomery would soon move up to brigadier status.

As lieutenant colonel of the 1st New Jersey Volunteer Infantry Regiment, the middle-aged construction engineer accompanied his unit to Washington, thence to outpost duty across the Potomac at Alexandria and Vienna, Virginia. The eagerness by day to see action and the false alarms by night from imaginary enemies kept enthusiasm high and nerves raw.

Then, on a hot Sunday in July, 1861, occurred the disorganized battle near Manassas between what amounted to little more than two armed mobs. McAllister and his 1st New

[28] ✣ THE McALLISTER LETTERS

Jersey took no active part in the melee. Their task was to act as rear guard at Centreville for General Irvin McDowell's routed force. As stated in his letters home, McAllister was certain that the calmness and steadfastness of his New Jerseyans had been principal factors in the safe withdrawal of the Federals from the field. He attributed defeat to poor military leadership and the North's general unpreparedness for war. Moreover, as is evident throughout this first group of letters, the conscientious Colonel felt several of his fellow officers to be more interested in personal glory than in national victory.

♣

(McAllister's daughter Henrietta to her sister Sarah, who was in Philadelphia attending a finishing school)

"Glen Ellen," April 30, 1861

My very dear sister,

I received your letter a few days since and was very glad to get it. I write now principally to tell you that Father is raising a company to go to the war. They will tender their services to the Governor but may not be accepted. Last night there was a military meeting at the Oxford Furnace Store. It was quite enthusiastic. There is about $1000 subscribed for the equipment of volunteers and support of their families when they are gone. John I. Blair [1] subscribed $500 of this money.

On Thursday night they had a fine meeting in Belvidere. Their fund is about $1500. John I. Blair also gave $200 to them. Father said to tell you the country is on martial fire. Twenty-three persons have volunteered their services here and I understand about forty-five from Belvidere. Probably both companies will unite under Father's command. George Brewster [2] and Harry Warner [3] are very patriotic. They

1. Blair was a leading figure in the mineral industries of eastern Pennsylvania and western New Jersey. He was one of the founders of Scranton, Pa., as well as the man for whom Blairstown, N.J., was named. *The Biographical Encyclopaedia of New Jersey in the Nineteenth Century* (cited hereafter as *N.J. Biographical Encyclopaedia*) (Philadelphia, 1877), 566–67.

2. On May 22, 1861, Brewster joined the 1st New Jersey as a sergeant. Rapid promotion to captain followed. He was killed in action at the battle of Gaines's

said that if the people did not show energy raising a company here by last night, they would go somewhere else and join.

We feel very sorry to have Father go and put himself in danger, on his and our account. But we must remember that our country is in danger and other people have to let their friends go, and we should have enough patriotism to do the same. If Father's services should be accepted, he will manage to go and see you before he goes.

We are all pretty well. Mary Leger has gone away to get married, and consequently we have no girl. If Father goes away, we don't know that we can get one. You must excuse my writing with a pencil, but I did not find a pen. We all send much love.

Hennie

(*Robert McAllister to his wife*)

Trenton House, Trenton, May 3d 1861

My dear Ellen,

We are all in doubt here as to what will be done with us. The four Regiments have left, and the Governor's Proclamation [4] this morning, saying that he has no orders for any more troops, dampens our feelings very much. We fear that we may be sent home, but will know this afternoon. The Captains of the 5th Regiment [Militia] now here will call on the Adjutant General [5] this evening and learn what we are to do. Some think that we will be put in camp for drill until we are wanted. Others think that we will be ordered home. If the latter, our Company is broken.[6] If the former, we will be satisfied for a short time. But not

---

Mill. New Jersey Adjutant General's Department (comp.), *Record of Officers and Men of New Jersey in the Civil War, 1861–1865* (cited hereafter as *N.J. Record*) (Trenton, 1876), I, 76.

3. Henry C. Warner enlisted in the 1st New Jersey along with Brewster. He too attained the rank of captain, but survived the war. *Ibid.,* 69, 70, 76; II, 1347.

4. Lincoln initially asked New Jersey to furnish four regiments for Federal service. Enough men responded to make eight full regiments. Gov. Charles Olden at this time was beseeching the government to accept the four additional units. Coincidentally, the President's second call for troops came on May 3—the date of McAllister's letter. *OR,* Ser. III, Vol. I, pp. 142–43, 150.

5. New Jersey's wartime Adjutant General was Col. Robert F. Stockton, Jr. He "had many good qualities to reform the wretched militia system of the State," one writer stated, "yet for actually organizing troops in regiments and brigades he was inexperienced [in 1861] . . ." George A. Townsend, *General Alfred T. A. Torbert Memorial* (cited hereafter as Townsend, *Torbert Memorial*) (Wilmington, Del., 1922), 14. See also Foster, *New Jersey and the Rebellion,* 17n.

6. McAllister's company incurred such high battle losses that in January, 1864, it officially ceased to exist. James P. Snell (comp.), *History of Sussex and Warren Counties, New Jersey . . .* (cited hereafter as Snell, *Sussex and Warren Counties*) (Philadelphia, 1881), 82.

for long, as all want to be at the seat of war. I will write you this evening when I will know something in regards to it.

My call down here was to accept the post of Colonel in the 4th Regiment, which left the night I came down and, of course, I was too late for it.[7] It was the Governor that wanted to give it to me, but under the circumstances I would not have accepted. There was trouble—and is still trouble among them in Bordentown. One company fought their captain. They elected one of their captains (Capt. Baker)[8] to the post. Not much is known about him and he will have a hard time of it.

Our 5th Regiment promises well—a better set of men all around. I know not who will be elected to the command; some think my chances are good, but I don't pretend to know. If we're not now mustered in, it will never be a Regiment. Pennsylvania will receive one half of our troops in less than two days. The trouble lays in our Legislature. They want—i.e., the Democrats want—to make political capital out of it. David Smith [9] is a Secessionist and goes against the support of the troops.

If I go home I will not want my trunk. If we organize, I will run up, so you need not send my trunk.

Love to all, not forgetting Mrs. Wiestling,
Your Affectionate Husband
Robert

Trenton House, May 4th 1861

My dear Ellen,

Our prospects for being mustered in are some better than when I wrote you yesterday, though there is nothing positive yet. We talk of going into the barracks here just vacated by the 1st Regiment. When all things are right, I will run up home—but can't now.

Col. Scranton [10] has been quite ill. He came home from New York very sick, but is now recovering. . . .

---

7. Matthew Miller, Jr., served as colonel of the 4th Militia during its three-month tour of duty. *N.J. Record*, I, 53.

8. Probably Isaac H. Baker, who commanded what became Co. H of the 1st New Jersey. *Ibid.,* 91.

9. David Smith, a resident of Oxford Furnace, represented that district in the state legislature. See George W. Cummins, *History of Warren County, New Jersey* (New York, 1911), 102.

10. Lt. Col. Charles Scranton served as an aide-de-camp to Gov. Olden until the January, 1863, expiration of his term. *N.J. Record*, I, 9; Snell, *Sussex and Warren Counties,* 81.

OFF TO WAR AND BULL RUN ♣ [31]

State Arsenal, Trenton, May 6th 1861

My dear Ellen,

We are here encamped in these barracks, enclosed by the State Arsenal on one side and a heavy stone wall on the othr side.[11] All around the inside of which are temporary barracks made for sleeping and large sheds for eating. We have no cooking to do; everything is prepared for us. Although I say we, I have not slept here yet as it is not safe for me to do so. I am still at the Trenton House in town, about one mile from here. We are all in doubts as to what we will do. We will know today or tomorrow. I fear trouble if we are asked to enlist for three years. Not more than one half will go and we can't compell them to do so. I don't think it makes much difference, as the war can't last long. Such an uprising of the Northern people never was heard of in the annals of history. The South must cave in.

Col. Scranton is sick today, but I don't think he is dangerous. It will be some time before he is well. . . .

I think the children had better go back to school, and I will try and see them before I leave for the seat of war—if I leave at all. Tell Mr. Wiestling [12] that I want him to let each have fifty dollars to pay for the tuition and board. . . .

We are now in the service of the State, and I fear we can't get into the United States service unless we tender for the 3 years instead of 3 months. It will place me in a bad position. I am willing to go, but the men will not. A day or two will decide it.

Brother Thompson is in the Rebel army.[13]

It is raining hard; bad time for parading. I am getting acquainted with various men who I find very agreeable. Why don't you write me? . . .

---

11. Camp Olden, the state's first training encampment, was "south of Trenton, near the Delaware and Raritan canal, and opposite the State prison." Its first residents exhibited more enthusiasm than neatness. An officer who arrived there with a new detachment noted conservatively of other recruits drilling: "Their uniforms had not been issued to them and their rags were fluttering in the breeze just as ours were. It was not what might be called an encouraging sight . . ." Camille Baquet, *History of the First Brigade, New Jersey Volunteers, from 1861 to 1865* (cited hereafter as Baquet, *First Brigade*) (Trenton, 1910), 6, 353–54.

12. George B. Wiestling was McAllister's business partner.

13. In March, 1861, and at his own expense, Robert's brother Thompson organized an infantry company in the Covington, Va., area. This unit, known as the "Allegheny Roughs," became Co. A, 27th Virginia, Stonewall Brigade. Thompson McAllister was its first captain. McAllister, *Thompson McAllister,* 15.

Trenton House, Trenton, May 14th 1861

My dear daughter Sarah,

. . . You no doubt are anxious to know how I am getting along in Military Matters. I have not yet been appointed colonel but still think my chances good. The requisition for the two Regiments have not arrived but is expected every day. As soon as it is received, these two Regiments will be formed and the field officers either elected or appointed. The latter I think most likely. And while I am not sanguine of success, I have reason to believe I will get it—either Colonel or Lieutenant-Colonel. But you had not better say much about it as it might be a failure, you understand. . . .

Col. Scranton is now getting quite well. He and Mrs. Scranton talk of leaving for home tomorrow. I will remain here a few days to see this Regiment organized. I have no company here now. About 20 of the men are mustered into other companies; the balance are at home. Only about two of the Belvedere companys staid. The rest would not go for three years. Out of seven companies here, only four are permitted to go. The other three had to be abandoned—in fact are now abandoned. Many other companies have since offered their services, but all are rejected. Our men have got an honorable discharge, but still they ought to have staid. I done all I could but they would not go into it for three years, except those that are here. . . .

Trenton House, Tuesday evening, May 14th 1861

My dear Ellen,

Things have not changed since I left home on Saturday. No requisition for troops yet, but expected any day, after which there will be a stirring time till the Regiment moves. I stand as I did before: the Governor says prominent, but he does not know whether he will have the power to appoint officers until the requisition comes. . . . So all is in darkness yet. I will write every day. . . .

Trenton, Monday Night [May 20, 1861]

My dear Ellen,

The Governor sent for me today and told me that he wished to appoint William Montgomery [14] colonel and me lieutenant colonel of

14. William R. Montgomery was born in New Jersey in 1801 and graduated from West Point in 1825. Meritorious service in the Mexican War brought him brevet promotion to lieutenant colonel. However, in 1855, while in command of

the 1st New Jersey Volunteers. He said that Montgomery has seen 40 years of service in the United States Army but was thrown out of his post by the Administration on account of his Republican proclivities. They want him to get a post here, for he will soon be appointed by the General Government to brigidere general. The Governor said that he wanted me behind him to take his place, that I would certainly be the colonel, and that in this way I could get my hand in and arrive at the post aimed at. After considering the whole matter, I consented; and the appointments are now made.

My friends think it is the best thing I could do. They are all highly pleased with the appointment and think my prospects ahead are good. I am perfectly satisfied, as I have one who is fully competent over me, and I will learn more under him than from anyone else.

Many other officers would give me a handsome sum for my position. If an inferior man had been placed over me, I could not have a chance of rising in rank. Parisen [15] is out altogether. His character would not stand the test. I will be mustered into the United States service tomorrow morning. I no longer will be my own master and, of course, will be underpaid. . . .

Excuse me for not writing more, as I must sleep some. . . .

Trenton House, Trenton, Wednesday, May 22d 1861
My dear daughter [Sarah],

You have no doubt seen by the papers that I am appointed Lieutenant Colonel of the 1st Regiment, New Jersey Volunteers. . . . But *confidentially,* we have three applicants for chaplain, but as yet no Presbyterian. I cannot promise your friend, Rev. Smith,[16] but I would like him to come up here and I will do all I can to get him

---

Fort Riley, Kan., Montgomery was court-martialed and dismissed from service "for appropriating a portion of the Military Reserve" at Fort Riley "to the uses of the Pawnee Association for a town site—he being interested in that association." Efforts in 1858–60 to have Montgomery restored to command were many and futile. On May 21, 1861, Gov. Olden appointed him colonel of the 1st New Jersey and classified him as a man of "some thirty years' service [but] still in the vigor of life." Montgomery's compiled service file, Record Group 94, National Archives; *OR,* Ser. III, Vol. I, p. 248; *N.J. Record,* I, 68.

15. The only individual by this name who served in a New Jersey unit was Samuel H. Parisen. He became a lieutenant in Co. C, 1st New Jersey, in May, 1861, and served in that capacity until his May, 1863, dismissal from service. *N.J. Record,* I, 76.

16. The Rev. Charles A. Smith was principal of Philadelphia Collegiate Institute for Young Ladies, where Sarah McAllister was then enrolled.

appointed chaplain. And I think I can do a good deal. . . . I can introduce him to the Colonel, go with him to camp, and introduce him to the officers. . . . Give Mr. Smith my kind regards and tell him I will expect him . . . and hold the place open for him. . . .

Trenton House, Thursday Morning, May 30th 1861

Dear Ellen,

Brother Nelson [17] has been here and gone. I consulted him in regards to my will and had it written. I will tell you all about it when we meet. You are in any event left well off, so that there will be no difficulty in you having all the comforts around you.

I am kept very busy and time flies rapidly. I calculate to go into camp tomorrow.

I would like you to send me down another pillow and a couple of sheets, or perhaps more pillow cases. Two pillows and I can do without bolsters. My bed will be 2½ feet wide. I could double the sheets, or you could cut them to suit. I believe I would rather have them come down to the floor. Our bed will be two feet from the floor. We put our beds on camp stools. Upon the whole, rather comfortable, & comfort will come good. . . .

Table cloths is just what we want. Our table is 2 feet, 3 inches wide, and we can make it any length we desire by adding table to table. We will have not less than six to dine and may have a dozen. So you see we want table cloths, towels, napkins, &c. Send immediately on receipt of this by express. Do write often. I don't know when we will leave here. . . .

Camp Olden, Monday Morning, June 3d 1861

My dear Ellen,

Saturday, the first day of June, was my birthday, making me forty-seven years of age. I concluded to move into camp and take up my quarters here. Saturday night was my first night in the tented field in this campaign. I slept very soundly on my two-foot bed. Not much

17. Hugh Nelson McAllister (1809–1873) was Robert's oldest brother. He maintained a law partnership in Bellefonte, Pa., with James Addams Beaver, who shortly became his father-in-law. For some of Nelson McAllister's many homefront activities on behalf of the Union, see J. W. Muffly (ed.), *The Story of Our Regiment: A History of the 148 Pennsylvania Vols.* (hereafter cited as Muffly, *148th Pennsylvania*) (Des Moines, Ia., 1904), 30–38, 42.

OFF TO WAR AND BULL RUN ♣ [35]

like the six-foot one at home. The Sabbath dawned in all its buety. We had no drill save the reveille and roll call until church time. Then we formed by companies and marched to the grove, where our Chaplain, the Rev. Yard,[18] delivered a very appropriate address—which was merely an introduction. He is a Methodist preacher. We like him very much.

I went to town according to previous arrangements and took dinner with the Rev. Dr. Hall[19]—Presbyterian, Old School, First Church—and brought him out. At four o'clock he gave us an excellent sermon. In the evening we had a prayer meeting. I find that our Regiment has a large religious element in it and we can have large prayer meetings. . . .

I am boarding at a farm house close by. They are a very fine family: one single daughter and several married—pretty and educated—quite a pleasant place. It is quite a favor that I get in there. Col. Montgomery and I will board there until we commence cooking on our own account. I have been thinking of arranging with them to board you for two weeks and have you to come down. Come down at any rate and stop at the Trenton House and I will have you comfortable. . . . I know not what our stay will be here, but think it will be short and we may as well be together while we are so close.

Col. Montgomery is not here and I have the whole command—in fact, have had it from the beginning. We expect to get our uniforms this week. Then we will look like military men. . . . I am very busy and have hardly time to write. . . .

Camp Olden, 1st Regiment, 1st Brigade, N.J. Volunteers
June 6th 1861

My dear daughter [Sarah],

Why don't you write me? Not a word from you. Why is it so? Henrietta does much better. . . .

You may think it strange that we are the 1st Regiment. Well, I will explain it to you. Those Regiments that went in the first call went only for three months and are called *militia,* while we three-year men are called *Volunteers.* In fact, it is Regulars under another name.

18. Robert B. Yard served as chaplain of the 1st New Jersey until his Mar. 7, 1864, resignation from service. *N.J. Record,* I, 68.
19. The Rev. John Hall was one of the most noted and respected Presbyterian ministers in New Jersey. See his *History of the Presbyterian Church in Trenton, N.J.* (New York, 1859).

Don't call us the 5th Regiment any longer or you will not be able to keep up with reports correctly. . . .

I have written for your mother to come down and spend a week here soon. I will let you know when to come up, which will be before we leave. I have got a five-gaited horse which you would like to ride. I would let you ride him when you come up. He is perfectly safe, a fine up-headed anamel—goes off as a military horse should go. You and I could take a ride through Camp Olden. Would not that be nice? But as you have not a riding dress, you can't do it. You must appear in good style, for we are all dressy here. . . .

Headquarters, Camp Monmouth, 1st Brigade
1st Regiment, June 30th 1861

My dear Ellen,

We got along finely with our Regiment except the delays usual in transporting large bodies of troops. We were delayed some three hours in Philadelphia, first waiting for the cars, and then taking refreshments prepared for us by a committee of ladies appointed for that purpose by the citizens for all Troops passing through the city.

We had one man who broke his arm by falling asleep and leaving it hang out of the window, and one that was hurt by an accedental discharge of a musket a little before arriving in Baltimore. We had loaded all our muskets to be prepared for the worst; and had an attack been made (by the citizens of Baltimore), we would have returned it with compound interest.[20] For all seemed to have a fixed purpose to fight if they had done so.

We arrived in Washington on Friday morning about 3 o'clock and marched into quarters. The officers were put up at Willard's [Hotel]. We took a wash and breakfast; and then Major Hatfield[21] and myself with a detail of men came out here about one mile from town around ten o'clock yesterday and in two hours had our camp all staked out. We had the regiment here in good time, and soon our tents were all up. Once more we looked like a camp. We were looked upon

---

20. On Apr. 19 a secessionist mob in Baltimore had assailed the 6th Massachusetts as that regiment passed through town en route to Washington. Four soldiers and twelve civilians were killed in the street fighting.

21. Allegedly the first man from New Jersey to enlist for a three-year period, Maj. David Hatfield died at Elizabeth, N.J., July 30, 1862, as a result of wounds received at the battle of Gaines's Mill. His own reminiscences of army service are in Baquet, *First Brigade,* 411–36.

by surrounding camps with admiration, as our tents look so much better than those around us.

We are in sight of some seven or eight camps, all looking beautiful, in the distance. My quarters are close by Mrs. Pierce,[22] who lives in a splendid mansion with beautiful grounds. A highly respectable family with large wealth, all the members are highly educated and accomplished, and as kind as any one can possibly be. The Major and I have taken dinner with them; we were invited to tea. Staid all night and was asked to take our breakfast with them this morning, which the Major did, but I declined as I had so much to do. Mr. Pattison [23] is a son-in-law married to the only remaining daughter. He is also an accomplished gentleman of large wealth—a Southerner but an out-and-out Union man. Though slave owner, &c., he is a military man at that. We are very comfortably situated. If you come down here and we are at this camp, I can no doubt get you in this family, where you would have me in the same yard. But, as water is scarce, they talk of moving us to another place. Tomorrow will decide. It is thought that we may remain here for some time, but all is uncertainty. Will write you often. Love to all. . . .

Camp Monmouth, 1st Regiment, 1st Brigade, N.J.V.
July 6th 1861

My dear daughter Sarah,

I receive no letters of any account from home. What is the matter? I have so much to do that I can't write often.[24]

Troops are moving over the Potomac River every day. We expect an order to move very soon but are not positive as to the time. You may look for stirring events daily. All are on the alert. The forward movement is the all-absorbing topic. . . .

22. The Washington city directories for the 1853–65 period list only one lady who fits McAllister's description. This was Mrs. Mary A. Pierce, a widow who ran a boardinghouse on the west side of 1st Street between B and C streets.

23. Comprehensive efforts to identify this gentleman failed. Maj. Hatfield was probably referring to the same man when he wrote in his diary on June 30, 1861: "Our camp ground is owned by a slave owner; has some thirty slaves. The house in which he lives is within a stone's throw of our camp." Baquet, *First Brigade,* 413.

24. McAllister neglected to mention that on July 3 the 1st, 2nd, and 3rd New Jersey Regiments marched in review past the White House and to the admiration of President Lincoln. "I am happy to say," wrote Maj. Hatfield, "that the First Regiment was the largest one out by odds and their marching the best." *Ibid.,* 7, 413.

Camp Monmouth, 1st Regiment, 1st Brigade, N.J.V.
July 10th 1861

My dear daughter Henrietta,

You see by this letter that we are still at this place. But a report says we will cross the river very soon, though no official notice of it yet. But Genl. Mansfield [25] told me yesterday it would be in a few days. Our men are anxious to cross and take part in the grate strugle for the Union, Constitution, and law. If the news would come for a forward movement tonight, I don't think we would have a sick man in camp, although many are complaining now. Such is the anxiety of our boys to get forward to meet the Rebel forces.

Col. Montgomery has not yet arrived, though I have been expecting him today.[26] It is possible I may have to fight the first battle without him. If so, I will do the best I can—trusting in God for guidance and success. I have thus far got along very well, and every day experience gives me more ability to command. . . .

I have not received but one letter from your mother. It was directed by friend Wiestling. We get more than two hundred letters per day in our camp, and yet I get none. And as to funds, I don't hear about them, let alone get them. I don't know what I will do if I don't get some money. I will have to reduce our fare to hard bread, as we will not have the wherewithal to purchase the comforts of life. I have called at the express office, but no package for me. . . .

Camp Monmouth, 1st Regiment, 1st Brigade, N.J.V.
July 11th 1861

My dear daughter Sarah,

I wrote your sister yesterday and, having a few moments, thought I would drop a few lines to you. I have written to your mother, yet have received but one letter from home before today, when I received one from Alice,[27] making a total of two letters from home. But I will excuse you all on the grounds that you have many business cares.

Yesterday I received a notice from Genl. Mansfield that I was

---

25. Joseph K. F. Mansfield commanded the cumbersome Military Department of Washington, which included portions of Maryland and Virginia in addition to the city itself. *OR,* II, 607.

26. Montgomery was then recuperating at his Bristol, Pa., home. While in training at Camp Olden, he had fallen from his horse and fractured a rib. See Montgomery to J. F. K. Mansfield, July 4, 1861, Montgomery's service file.

27. Alice R. Dick was Mrs. Ellen McAllister's niece. She later married Dr. Edward F. Welling, a surgeon in both the 3rd and the 11th New Jersey.

appointed Field Officer of the Day and to report to him at 6 o'clock. I got ready, mounted my charger, and in full trim was off to the city. Before I got there, there was a tremendous storm of wind, driving the dust in the streets so that I could not see one foot before me. But down Pennsylvania Avenue I went at a canter. Arrived at Willard's, got my horse into comfortable quarters, and looked at my watch, which told me it was just six o'clock. The storm continued and rain followed. I must be punctual.

I went up past the White House, arrived at Genl. Mansfield's quarters, and reported myself for duty. "Order: Go out among all the camps in the District east of 14th Street. Call at this office at 9 o'clock tonight and a guide will be furnished you who will conduct you to all the camps."

Down to Willard's I went. I took supper and at 9 o'clock I was on hand amidst a furious thunder storm, rain pouring down and lightning flashing in all quarters. Soon my guide was on hand and off we went amidst the storm and darkness of the night. From camp to camp we went—challenged by sentries, returned the countersign, admitted, called out the guard and inspected them, gave orders & instructions to all around, bid good night, and off to another camp. The rain ceased; night became more pleasant, and upon the whole I had a right pleasant time of it.

After journeying on for hours in this district—riding many miles and becoming satisfied that all was right, I came home. Found our own camp all right except for an alarm, when all got under arms in line of battle because of the firing of sentry guns at something more in imagination than in reality. Went to bed and slept soundly for an hour or two when "Crack, crack" went the guns again. I jumped out of bed, put on my clothes, took my sword, and in less than five minutes our Regiment was in line of battle—waiting for something in the shape of an enemy. But of course nothing of the kind appeared. Daylight soon dawned, reveille beat, and the business of camp day commenced.

The alarms, though false they be, serve a good purpose to acustom our men to fall in in double-quick time. We have company drill in the morning, battallion drill at half past nine o'clock, target firing by the right wing before dinner, target firing by the left wing after dinner, battallion drill at 5 o'clock, and dress parade at six. So you see we are all kept busy, and I think improving. . . .

Mail just arrived; a letter from home, sweet home, from loved ones left behind. . . . I need not tell you that letters are welcome here to the heart of one whose home is in a tent, overspread by two large cherry trees, where I am now writing. Well write often, for I long to hear.

Tell Mr. Wiestling I have not yet been able to see his brother John. Time would not permit it, and I have found but few Pennsylvania Regiments here. I think they must be off from us. But I will hunt him up. Tell him to write me where his regiment is located. The Rhode Island Regiment is close by, but I have not yet been over to see the members. They are an A Number One regiment.[28]

We expect to leave here in a day or two, cross the river a short distance from Alexandria, and encamp alongside the three-months New Jersey Militia. This will not suit our boys, as they want to push on into the heart of the Old Dominion. When we move and after we land on the other side, I will write your mother all about the place. . . .

Camp Monmouth, 1st Regiment, 1st Brigade, N.J.V.
July 11th 1861

My dear Ellen,

I have just received a dispatch from Genl. Mansfield to be ready to march tomorrow morning at nine o'clock. We cross the Long Bridge [29] and receive orders. I don't know where we are going. I will write you as soon as I can after receiving the information. All is quiet in camp, but in a few hours all will be on the move. . . .

28. The 1st Rhode Island had reached Washington late in April when the city was virtually defenseless. Its commander was Col. Ambrose E. Burnside. The Rhode Islanders—most of them of high social standing—were recognizable by their gray trousers, blue flannel shirts, and scarlet bedrolls. "When men like these leave their horses, their women, and their wine," one of Lincoln's secretaries observed, "it is hard to set any bounds to the possibilities of such an army." Augustus Woodbury, *A Narrative of the Campaign of the First Rhode Island Regiment* . . . (Providence, 1862), 18–73; Margaret Leech, *Reveille in Washington* (New York, 1941), 68.

29. The Long Bridge crossed the Potomac River at the lower end of 14th Street. The dilapidated guard buildings around the structure evoked strong ridicule from their occupants. When one company was finally relieved from guard duty at the bridge, reputedly "the rats in and about the old buildings stood on their hind legs in line at 'attention' as the boys filed by." Sheldon B. Thorpe, *The History of the Fifteenth Connecticut Volunteers* . . . (hereafter cited as Thorpe, *15th Connecticut*) (New Haven, 1893), 26–27.

Camp Trenton, Virginia, July 13th 1861

My dear Ellen,

I write to inform you of our safe arrival at this place, Beck's Mill,[30] five miles from Washington. We arrived in good time last evening, put up our tents, and all is right. So you see we are now on the sacred soil of Virginia—poor soil at that. This is a most miserable and forlorn place as any man need wish to see. But as we will not stay here very long, it don't make very much difference. We are to be pushed forward whenever and wherever needed as the program is carried out. We are in sight of a railroad leading from Alexandria to some place I don't know but leading to our enemies.[31] Will write you this evening. . . .

This is certainly a very healthy place—all woods, and high up in the hills. Direct your letters as before to Camp Trenton. All these camps are called Trenton. The whole seven New Jersey regiments are in this neighborhood but not together. . . .

Headquarters, 1st Regiment, N.J.V., July 13th 1861

My dear Ellen,

All is in motion. I have just received orders from the headquarters of Genl. Runyon,[32] now at Alexandria, to march at six o'clock this morning. It is now two o'clock. We leave our tents and baggage here and take with us two days' rations. We take the railroad at this place and go to Vienna, about fourteen miles from this camp. We can't go all the way by railroad car, as the track is torn up. We may remain at Vienna, as is said in our order, and we may advance, which is the most likely. I hardly know what to take with me as reserve baggage, but will think and decide.

Col. Montgomery was here this evening, but went back to Washington. I have sent him the dispatches and expect an answer before we move. The orders are for him to take command of the two Regiments, the 1st and 2nd New Jersey. The 3rd is gone; it left this eve-

30. Most military maps of the period designate this place as "Roach's Mill." It lay a mile southwest of the present site of Washington's National Airport. See J. G. Barnard, *A Report on the Defenses of Washington* . . . (cited hereafter as Barnard, *Washington Defenses*) (Washington, 1871), Plate 1. See also Baquet, *First Brigade,* 7, 414.

31. The Loudon & Hampshire Railroad (over which McAllister and his men rode the following day) connected Alexandria with Leesburg and points westward.

32. Brig. Gen. Theodore Runyon of New Jersey was in command of the Washington defenses both during and immediately after the Bull Run Campaign.

ning. But I don't think Col. Montgomery will be able to go. His rib has not united yet, and he can't ride on horseback. McLean [33] is also sick. If neither of them are present, the command of the two regiments devolves on me. I hope Col. Montgomery will be in the neighborhood. I have had but a few minutes' conversation with him, he being surrounded as usual by everybody.

The flag presentation by California to our troops took place in the meantime.[34] You will see all about it in the paper. It would have been a splendid turnout if it had not been for the sudden call for troops. But as it was, only a part of our Regiment and a part of the 2nd were present.

Direct your letters as usual, only put 1st Regiment, Three-Year Volunteers, and all will be right. . . . I don't know where I will write you from again, but most likely Vienna. . . . Keep up your courage and let us trust in God. . . .

Vienna,[35] Virginia, July 17th 1861

My dear daughter [Sarah],

We have arrived here in safety. Our train was the first that has passed over the road since the firing on the Ohio troops at this place and the burning of the cars.[36] The wreckage is to be seen at every turn. The secessionists have all cleared out. We are now in sight of Fairfax Courthouse. The Rebels have abandoned that place and gone down to Manassas Junction, where we expect to fight them if they don't run again. I think they will make a stand at that place. . . .

33. Col. George W. McLean commanded the 2nd New Jersey until his December, 1861, resignation from service. *N.J. Record,* I, 102.

34. The "California Regiment" was a popular and misnamed unit. Its members came largely from Philadelphia and New York; its colonel was Oregon senator Edward D. Baker. Moreover, the contingent was not a regiment but two battalions of 800 men each. In the autumn of 1861 the two battalions were consolidated and redesignated the 71st Pennsylvania Infantry.

35. Vienna lay eighteen miles by road southwest of Washington.

36. McAllister was referring to the June 17 skirmish between elements of the 1st Ohio and 1st South Carolina. The Confederates loosed an unexpected fire on the Ohioans' train as it rounded a curve a mile east of Vienna. No sooner had the Federals deployed for action than the panicky railroad engineer fled with his train back to Alexandria. Thus stranded, the 1st Ohio suffered casualties of 5 killed, 6 wounded and 9 missing. Confederate losses are unknown. *OR,* II, 124–30.

Camp Vienna, July 18th 1861

My dear Ellen,

I wrote yesterday on our arrival here, since which I have slept none. We lay on our arms all night, expecting every minute to be attacked, but the morning dawned without the enemy appearing. Had they come, the position of our lines and pickets here was such as to have enabled us to defeat double our number. We are expecting soon to see the firing at Manassas Junction. How long we will remain here I know not. I am very well but very tired. . . .

Vienna, July 18th 1861

My dear daughter [Sarah],

I have written two short letters since our arrival here, but I could not give you any particulars for the want of time. You no doubt are anxious to know about this place, as it will be noted in the future history of our country.

There are not more than one-fourth as many houses in Vienna as there are in Oxford Furnace—one store, a blacksmith shop, and a hotel. The last two were abandoned by their former occupants, and I am now sitting and writing this letter in the parlor of the hotel, which is a large fine room and well furnished, carpeted, cushion chairs and handsome sofa, table and large looking glass. We use the room as our headquarters. All the rooms are used by our officers. The beds are comfortable things for us poor soldiers who have come here without our camp equipment. We have neither tents, cooking utensils or baggage; all were left behind. Our privates brought 48 hours' rations with them; the officers brought nothing. We do the best we can in getting army provisions and have a large range in the kitchen to cook with, and also some table furniture. In a word we are keeping hotel. Though our supply of provisions are scarce, we have all the customers we want.

The Loudon and Hampshire Railroad runs past this place. The burnt fragments of the cars, burnt sometime since, are lying right here by the window of the hotel. We were on the first train that has come this distance. On the last few miles, we had two companies out in advance of the train. Had the Ohio regiment done the same, they never would have been fired on by that masked Rebel battery. We have daily trains here now to receive and send our mail.

When the Secessionists were encamped here, the Union families had to leave. Now those families are coming back, and the Rebels have cleared out. Part of us are quartering in their houses; the balance of our men lie out on their arms. I was out all of last night expecting an attack. . . . We don't think there is so much danger now.

Here come two good horses captured by Capt. Birney [37] today. Their riders fled and left their horses and fixtures, so we have got horses. Our own horses will be here tonight. Two of these horses belong to Capt. Alfred Lay,[38] formerly of Genl. Scott's staff but now a captain in the Rebel army. The third belongs to a Rebel spy, a ringleader of the Rebels here. These men—Capt. Lay, George Winter, and a Dr. Williams—were the principle men in bringing down the battery that was so destructive on the Ohioans in the railroad cars. Unfortunately the men escaped and have gone to Manassas Junction to fight us there, but our boys there are ready for them. We anticipate a big fight at that place.

Manassas Junction is from fifteen to eighteen miles from this place. If we can be spared from here, no doubt we will have our hands in that fight. You already know that Fairfax Courthouse is in our possession. The Rebels left there yesterday morning. It is but two or three miles from here. Cars have just arrived with telegraph poles. We will soon have an office at this place and be able to communicate with the world.

I have forgotten to say that Col. Montgomery is with us now. He is not able to ride on horseback, but he can be of great use to us in planning.

Our boys are all eager for the fight, ready to go anywhere the fighting is to be done. We have the pluck and the nerve amongst our boys. . . . It is reported here that we have a force of 70,000 men at Manassas Junction. The Rebels are concentrating all their forces at that place. No doubt but there will be a big fight. You will have the result before this reaches you. Look out for stirring events. . . .

Vienna, July 19th 1861

My dear Ellen,

We are still here and constantly under excitement. Our outpost was attacked last night, but the cowards that done it fled. We were

---

37. William Birney was the first captain of Co. C, 1st New Jersey. He later became colonel of the 4th New Jersey and emerged from the war as a brevet major general. *N.J. Record,* I, 11, 76, 182.

38. McAllister erred on this man's first name. The officer in question was George W. Lay, an 1855 graduate of West Point who served successively on the staffs of Gens. Winfield Scott (USA) and Milledge L. Bonham (CSA). *OR,* I, 654; II, 478, 520; Douglas S. Freeman, *Lee's Lieutenants: A Study in Command* (New York, 1942–1944), I, 704, 722.

soon under arms and ready for them. We were called out twice by our pickets firing. By mistake one of our men was shot by one of our sentinels, but we think he will recover.[39] He is a member of Capt. Birney's company, a stranger to me, and not one of our Oxford Furnace men. We don't get much sleep.

Flying reports have come in from our advance forces near Manassas Junction in which five or six hundred of our men are killed by a masked battery. But is not official and we don't like it. I hope to have it contradicted before this reaches you. . . . We are only about fifteen miles from Manassas Junction and think it strange that we don't hear the firing. Taylor and his regiment are there.[40] The 1st and 2nd New Jersey are here—much against the wishes of our boys. Even though we have a great deal to do yet, we want to be with the advance. Our position is considered dangerous. But to be in the war is all we desire. . . .

Headquarters, Vienna, Sabbath Morning
July 21st 1861, Half Past Nine A.M.

My dear Ellen,

I wrote you a hasty note upon receiving marching orders; but as we have to wait until the companies we have sent out on scouting expeditions last night return, I have a spare moment.

All is bustle and excitement in preparing to move to the conflict. We have to march, as there is no railroad and we have not even baggage wagons. We leave knapsacks and trunks all here to be sent down to Camp Trenton. I take but little with me. My best uniforms, and some articles which I have never had on, are all in the trunks and will be sent down today to our camp at Beck's Mill. . . . I go with but little marks of an officer.

You will hear of the battle before this reaches you. All our New Jersey troops will be in it. If spared, I will write you at the first opportunity; but having no tents or quarters, I may not be able to write. We have but this day's provisions with us. I intended to hold church services today, but war has no Sabbath.

Now, my dear Ellen, bear up. Pray for my temporal and eternal welfare. . . . May God help you all; and if we never meet again on earth, may we all meet in another and better world. . . .

39. Pvt. John Biedeman of Co. C was discharged from service in November, 1861, for "wounds accidentally received near Vienna, Va." *N.J. Record,* I, 77.
40. Reference here is to Colonel (later General) George W. Taylor and his 3rd New Jersey.

[46] ✗ THE McALLISTER LETTERS

Fort Albany,[41] Arlington Heights, July 23d 1861

My dear Ellen,

I now drop you a hasty note to inform you that I am here and well, my health never better. You have seen an account of the battle —a terrible disaster. I feel sad. We did not reach the field, although we had forced marches, until the battle was over. But we were in time to cover the retreat. Our Regiment has done noble service to our country—saved thousands of dollars worth of property and many lives. We were more in danger than many of those in battle. Our regiment has got and is receiving a great deal of credit.

We forced our way through the retreating columns, formed a line of battle, and protected the retreating forces. We were the very last to leave the battlefield, and we were in danger of being cut all to pieces. Will write you a long letter today telling all. . . .

We are now in this fort and will most likely be here for some time. . . .

Fort Albany, opposite Washington
Wednesday, July 24th 1861

My dear Ellen,

I commenced a letter to Mr. Wiestling yesterday, but found it impossible to finish it. This morning I commenced it again and had written but a few lines when a call to arms aroused me. I closed just where I was, without having told half my story, and buckled on my armor. The danger was not so great as reported, and we have a lull in camp again. One half of our regiment are out throwing up breastworks to screen us from enemy shots so that we can protect the battery at . . . Arlington Mills. I have no doubt but that the enemy is approaching and will ere long attack us in order to get at Washington.

Let the country wake up and assist us in rolling back the tide of battle and all will be well.

I find that we are getting a great deal of credit for the noble stand we took in trying to force our troops back to form a line of battle and defend our country. I have not seen the paper to any extent, but we are informed that mention is favorably made of our Regiment. I am writing a history of our doings on that dark and fatal day. This is the

---

41. Fort Albany stood just east of the intersection of present-day Glebe Road and Columbia Pike. For a good description of its works, see Warren H. Cudworth, *History of the First Regiment (Massachusetts Infantry)*, . . . (cited hereafter as Cudworth, *1st Massachusetts*) (Boston, 1866), 68–70.

letter I refer to. Tell Mr. Wiestling I will as soon as possible continue my account of this whole matter, or rather so far as our Regiment was concerned. Time does not permit me to do it as I would like, as there are so many interruptions. . . .

I have just had a call from John I. Blair, James Blair Wildrick,[42] Mr. Harris,[43] and a number of other Warren County friends. They staid but a few minutes. Their time was precious.

I will now state that I shall never forget the night I spent at Centreville. After trying in vain to rally our forces, we marched on and through Centreville and formed line of battle on a hill with our right resting on the road along which the Rebel army would advance to attack us. We expected Col. McLean's Regiment would be up to assist us. But here we learned that they too had retreated.[44] On looking around in the dark, we discovered that we had two regiments near by, but no artillery or cavalry. We prepared for battle, expecting every minute to have an attack. We waited in silence.

After an hour or two we discovered that these regiments were moving. We went to them to learn what was up. They told us that they had orders to retreat.[45] We thought this very strange, as Genl. McDowell had ordered us to make a stand. They all retreated and left us alone. The Colonel ordered me to march down to the village and post my men on both sides of the road leading towards Manassas Junction, so that if an attack was made we could give them a raking fire. The Colonel and Maj. Hatfield rode off about three miles to see Genl. McDowell.[46] I was the only commissioned officer on the ground,

---

42. Wildrick was the son of a former congressman and brother of a man who had been offered command of the 1st New Jersey at that unit's formation. *Portrait and Biographical Record of Hunterdon and Warren Counties, New Jersey* (cited hereafter as *Biographical Record of Warren County*) (New York, 1898), 434–35.

43. Israel Harris was cashier of the Belvidere Bank and a close friend of the McAllister family.

44. By sundown of July 21, Federal army commander Irvin McDowell reported, "the condition of our artillery and its ammunition, and the want of food for the men, who had generally abandoned or thrown away all that had been issued the day before, and the utter disorganization and consequent demoralization of the mass of the Army, seemed to all who were near enough to be consulted . . . to admit of no alternative but to fall back" from Centreville. *OR*, II, 321.

45. These two regiments were the 8th New York, under Lt. Col. Julius H. Stahel, and the 29th New York, under Col. Adolphe von Steinwehr. Both regiments were in the brigade of Col. Louis Blenker, who reported: "At about midnight the command to leave the position and march to Washington was given by General McDowell. [My] brigade retired in perfect order . . ." *Ibid.*, 425.

46. See *ibid.*, 438; Baquet, *First Brigade*, 416.

Adj. Henry [47] having been sent to bring back Col. McLean and his regiment.[48]

All was now still as death, save the groaning of the wounded in the hospitals close by. One hospital was in a church, and the other in a dwelling house. Our Surgeon, Dr. Taylor,[49] went and amputated limbs and attended the sick. All the other surgeons had left with their own troops for fear of being taken by the enemy. During this calm, our troops, overdone, lay down on their arms and fell asleep. Of the sentinels that I put out, several also fell asleep. I sat on my horse, expecting an attack any moment. It was a *sad and sorrowful* night, a night that I shall never forget.

During this time, Dr. Taylor came to me and said, "Colonel, come in and see these poor fellows, many of whom are officers."

I replied, "I am alone and know not the moment we will be attacked. To go in and see the wounded might destroy the whole command."

About 2 o'clock in the morning, Maj. Hatfield returned and said that Col. Montgomery had ordered us to retreat. We did so in good order.[50] The hardest task that I ever performed in my life was to leave the wounded behind, but to get them away was impossible. No wagons were available; and were we to stay, we would all be cut to pieces.

Dr. Taylor came to me and said, "Colonel, will you let me stay with the sick and wounded? All the other surgeons have left. I can't think of leaving them here to die."

"I should like to do so," I replied, "but you will be taken prisoner. Besides, we may want your services within an hour. But whatever Col. Montgomery says will be all right."

"Where is the Colonel?" he asked.

"Half a mile ahead of us," I said.

He rode on, saw the Colonel, and got permission to stay. I bid him goodby, I suppose never to meet him again, as reports say the

---

47. William Henry, Jr., who joined the 1st New Jersey as adjutant, was mustered out of service in June, 1864, as colonel. *N.J. Record,* I, 68.

48. According to Maj. Hatfield, Montgomery searched diligently for McLean and his 2nd New Jersey. Finally Montgomery "learned that they had marched to Centreville, when Colonel McLean showed the white feather and swore that he was not going to have his men killed. So he wheeled his regiment about and . . . marched back two or three miles to a point near Germantown and there halted for the night." Baquet, *First Brigade,* 416. See also *OR,* II, 438.

49. Edward F. Taylor had become surgeon of the 1st New Jersey on June 25.

50. McAllister oversimplified this rearward march. "A drenching rain had set in," one New Jersey soldier recollected, "and the march back to camp was accomplished through Virginia mud, which has the reputation of being the most exasperating material to deal with in the world." Baquet, *First Brigade,* 8.

hospitals were bombarded and burnt to ashes a very short time after we left.[51] The cruelty of the Rebels to our wounded has no parallel in history.

We now fear that the Doctor has been put to death.[52] If not, he will be a prisoner for a long time. Poor fellow, I feel sad at the thought that he has been treated thusly. God forbid that it is the case. I still hope that it may not be so, but we all fear the worst. Has not Dr. Taylor acted a noble part? Will not history record the noble deed?

Ex-Governor Newell [53] from New Jersey was here today. I gave him all these particulars. He thinks the world of the Doctor. He is a relative of the Governor's wife, and very highly and respectably connected.

Yesterday a flag of truce to procure the wounded and dead went up with nice comfortable wagons to bring them home, but the hardhearted Rebel villains refused to receive them and they had to return.[54] *What a blot on Southern history!* But this will tell in our future battles.

Love to all. I am tired and must go to bed. All is quiet. . . .

1st N.J. Volunteers
Fort Albany, July 25th 1861

Friend Wiestling,

In writing to you yesterday I had to stop short, as the cry was: "The enemy are coming." But it turned out to be only a troop of horse. Fire was exchanged and they disappeared.

The right wing of our Regiment have since been engaged in throwing up breastworks at the Arlington Mills, some three miles out

---

51. On the morning of July 22 Confederate Gen. Milledge Bonham's brigade briefly occupied Centreville. Bonham and his regimental colonels reported the capture of huge amounts of stores, but made no mention of fires anywhere in the Centreville area. *OR,* II, 519, 521–32.

52. Taylor received a parole from the Confederates and returned to duty three weeks later. For an absurd account of his "treatment" while a prisoner, see Baquet, *First Brigade,* 345.

53. New Brunswick-born William A. Newell was a physician and U.S. congressman prior to his election in 1856 as governor of New Jersey. For at least twenty years he was regarded "as the most prominent and influential leader" of New Jersey Republicans. *Cyclopedia of New Jersey Biography* (New York, 1923), I, 229–31.

54. McAllister displayed unfounded prejudice here. The large number of prisoners taken by both sides at this first major battle of the war—when neither side was equipped to handle prisoners in any great numbers—led to a brief but successful exchange program.

from the river at a road and railroad crossing, where we are planting a battery to sweep the road. We hope the North will pour down her troops so that before long we may take up our line of march to Centreville and Manassas Junction and regain what we have lost.

No retreat should have been ordered at Bull Run, for the day was ours. The enemy were whipped. The men fought brave enough, but we have too many cowardly officers. Yet we have very many brave ones who did credit to our arms.

Sabbath morning, July 21st, the 1st and 2nd New Jersey Volunteers were encamped at Vienna. Col. McLean commanded the 2nd New Jersey. Being Lieutenant Colonel of the 1st Regiment, I commanded that unit, as our Col. Montgomery outranked McLean and thus had command of the whole.

The roaring of artillery announced the opening of the battle of Bull Run. Three of our companies were absent on reconnaissance and had not returned when orders came from Headquarters for us to move up to Centreville. We were soon on our way and moving rapidly toward the scene of conflict. We passed Germantown, the artillery sounding louder and louder. Some miles on this side of Centreville, we met a gentleman who said all was right, that the enemy were driven in toward Manassas Gap. On we went, feeling elated. After awhile the artillery ceased firing. We then knew that the battle was decided; but which way was the question.

Soon the sad story was told by the confused masses of the retreating army. We determined to do what we could to stop the panic. We threw our columns across the road, appealed to their patriotism, to their honor, to the Flag, and urged them to return and help us fight the battle. But the panic was so great that our appeals were for the time unheeded. We then charged bayonets and stopped the stampede, letting only the wounded pass on.

We turned into our ranks about five hundred of the stampeders, then marched through their retreating columns. We drew our swords and pistols on men and officers who would not willingly turn back. The whole scene beggars all description; and yet, strange to say, our officers and men were all cool. We marched through those retreating columns with a firmness which astonished all who saw the Regiment —and which has since been the topic of universal praise. Had I time, I could give you some singular instances, several of which were amusing even amid the sad spectacle around us.

A civilian with a broad-brimmed hat and pale as death came riding along at a rapid rate. I ordered him to halt. Very much agitated and frightened, he said, "I am a civilian and must pass on."

"No, you cannot pass," I replied. "My orders are to stop everybody, and you are included in that number."

He then said, "I am a bearer of dispatches to Washington and must pass."

"You cannot pass till this panic is stopped," I answered, "for everyone who passes helps to increase the stampede."

"Here are my papers," he said, pulling them out of his pocket at the same time. "Look at them."

I replied, "I have no time to examine papers now. Wait until we are through with this job and we will consider your case."

He again implored me in pitiful tones to let him through. Pointing to Col. Montgomery, I said, "There is my commander. Go to him."

He went to the Colonel and had some conversation with him. Montgomery, disgusted with the man's cowardice, raised himself up in the saddle and exclaimed at the top of his voice: "Let that man go!"

I did so, the stranger put spurs to his horse and made the very stones of the pike fly behind him. That man was no other than Russell, the corespondent of the London *Times*.[55]

In contrast to this gallant Englishman, I saw a lady to my left—I am ignorant of her name—sitting quite calm and unconcerned in a buggy amid the throng of soldiers, civilians, horses, mules, wagons, ambulances right side up and wrong side up. The Colonel said to her, "Madam, are you not afraid?"

"No, Colonel," she replied. "I feel perfectly safe."

Cheer after cheer went up for us as we advanced, and solemn promises were made on the part of the stampeders that they would fall in our rear if we advanced through them and formed line of battle. Others cried: "Go up yonder hill and you'll get it! You will be cut to pieces!" Still others encouraged us with hopes that we would save their retreat and bear the brunt of the battle.

The stampede was now stopped and we were on the summit of a hill. Col. Montgomery had a conference with Genl. McDowell and urged the propriety of making a stand on the heights of Centreville—throwing up breastworks, holding the position, and not retreating to Washington. The General consented and ordered him to take his command to the other side of Centreville and form his lines for defense. We passed Centreville and took up a position on the hill with our right

---

55. William Howard Russell, a conscientious and dandified Englishman, was the Civil War's first field correspondent. His own account of the meeting with McAllister contrasts naturally and drastically with McAllister's version. William H. Russell, *My Diary North and South* (Boston, 1863), 458–59.

resting on the road along which the enemy would have to come. But when we had accomplished this and were ready for battle, we found that our 2nd New Jersey Regiment had retreated. Two regiments under the command of Col. Blenker were the only troops left besides our own Regiment.

Col. Montgomery sent for McLean's regiment (the 2nd N.J.V.), and we waited in silence. Stillness reigned over that valley. Not a sound was heard save the groans of the wounded and dying in the hospitals not far distant. Our Surgeon Taylor was busily engaged amputating arms and legs. . . .

Having placed pickets out to give the alarm, the men laid down on their arms. Col. Montgomery and myself began to look around to see what was going on. We had a consultation with the colonel of a New York regiment—one of those under the command of Blenker, and we concluded to fight and stand by each other. We returned to our regiment. An hour passed away in silence. We then thought we heard something. On examination we found that our neighboring troops were moving off and that we alone would be in possession of the field. Now came the question: what are we to do?

We concluded to take another position around the lower hospital and across the road along which the Rebels would have to come. We reformed in the new position but left the road clear. Yet we so arranged our forces as to sweep the road with a raking fire in case the cavalry came. I . . . waited in silence. Col. Montgomery and Maj. Hatfield left to call on Genl. McDowell, who was two miles off, to learn why Blenker's two regiments had left us alone, and to find out what was to be done.

After sitting some time on my horse in silence—the men having nearly all fallen asleep, I passed over to the left wing on the other side of the road in order to throw out additional pickets. One of our captains asked me if I knew the danger we were in.

"Certainly," I replied.

"Why don't we retreat?" he then asked.

I told him my orders were to hold this position and that I was going to do it.

"We may as well surrender at once," he said, "as we will be cut to pieces."

I told him we would never surrender and that we would give them a tremendous fight.

I then returned to my position and remained there until Maj. Hatfield returned and informed me that we had to retreat. Our orders were given in a low tone, almost a whisper.

Before we moved off I sent a messenger to inform Dr. Taylor of our orders to retreat. The Doctor came to me and asked permission to remain with the wounded . . . He asked where Col. Montgomery was. I told him he had not yet returned, but that he was likely to be ahead of us and we would meet him. We did, and consent was granted. This is the last we have seen of that noble martyred man. The cruelty of the Rebels as seen on the field of battle causes us to have great fears concerning Taylor's fate. No exchange of prisoners can take place, as we do not regard them in any other light than as rebels. So the President informs Ex-Governor Newell, who has been trying to do something in this case.

As we marched from Centreville, we had our rear column in a condition to defend. Cavalry was what we most feared. After marching several miles we reached the rear of the retreating column and thus protected them until we arrived at Fairfax, when we took a more advanced position for some miles. Afterward we formed protection for a battery and reached this place about 2 p.m. Monday, worn out and terrible hungry. We had not eaten anything for thirty hours save a dry piece of bread when we were in line of battle at Centreville. Almost all that time we were on duty. Our horses had nothing to eat and no time to eat. Worn out by fatigue, many of our men sank down on the roadside and could not even be forced along. They lay all night in a pelting storm. The ambulances had all left. Remember that all wagons save twenty or thirty had left us; and of those, the drivers had cut loose their horses and ridden off at great speed.

Had it not been for our regiment, an immense number of wagons would have been left along the road and would now be in the hands of the enemy with all the stores they contained. We saved the Government a large amount of property. When we went up, parts of the road were literally covered with picks, shovels—in a word, with everything belonging to an army. When we came back, nearly all was picked up, owing to our having stopped the retreat and the security the soldiers felt after we had passed them.

I have forgotten to tell you that our friend, Adj. Henry . . . is a good and brave officer. He acted in a whole manner bravely and very cool. In fact, we have no fear of any of our Oxford friends. You can rely on them.

I do contend that we—i.e., all the army—ought to have formed at Centreville according to Montgomery's idea. Had that plan been pursued, we would be in possession of it yet.

A great many claim the credit of protecting the retreat and being the last to leave the field. But it is all in the imagination, *for we* *were the very last to leave Centreville.*⁵⁶ In confidence I tell you that when our Colonel called on Genl. McDowell, he could not be found. He had retreated without giving us orders to retreat, and we would have been left to be cut to pieces had we not accidentally discovered that Col. Blenker was retreating. You see it stated that Blenker's command saved the retreat, and yet we were in Centreville two hours after Col. Blenker left.

I have now given a fair, unvarnished statement of the whole matter, but have been so much interrupted that I fear it will be uninteresting. . . .

Camp Princeton—opposite Washington
July 26th 1861

My dear Ellen,

I have just finished a letter to Mr. Wiestling that was written at intervals and constantly interrupted. A part of it was written on my knee, as my tabel had been taken down preparatory to our moving here to this camp. This place has been occupied by one of the New Jersey three-month regiments—now gone home—and was thought to be a better location than the one we had at the fort. This position is halfway between Fort Albany and Fort Runyon. I do not like it as well as the one we have left. But still it will do. I fear the fever and ague; as yet it has not been unhealthy, but the sickly season has now set in. . . .

As to news, you are far better posted than I am. You have the New York papers, which are so far ahead of all the other papers that a man knows nothing if he does not read them. In the first place, we don't get them until the day after they are published—and hardly get them at all. When we do, we have not time to read them. Although they are full of blunders and misstatements, yet it is only from them that we can get anything reliable. Our Washington papers know nothing until the news has passed around the world and come back. Then it is published for something new.

I don't think Washington will be attacked at all. Little will be

56. Col. Blenker closed his official report of the Bull Run Campaign by stating: "I have read since so many reports in newspapers, where many a commanding officer pretends to have been in the very rear with his brigade or regiment in the retreat, that I am obliged to repeat in the most absolute terms that, according to my order, all regiments, artillery, and stragglers had passed my arrière guard at Centreville and the last artillery at Fairfax Court-House, and that the brigade under my command not until order was received by General McDowell marched across Long Bridge into Washington." *OR,* II, 428.

done on either side until fall, when our army will be swelled to a tremendous size and will be well-drilled. Then we will take up our line of march and see Centreville again. We have with us plenty of cavalry and artillery, without which we can't do much. There will be no failure the next time. Let the people and the press leave Genl. Winfield Scott have his own way and don't hurry him until he is fully ready, and you will not hear of a defeat.

The truth is, in the battle at Bull Run the Rebels had more than three to one to our troops, besides being protected by their breastworks and a first-rate position. They acknowledge a loss of three thousand.[57] Ours is, as you see, lessening every day. It is positively said that the enemy retreated. Truly a strange battle! . . .

Our men are getting paid today. This is the first money we have gotten. We, the field officers, will get ours, they say, tomorrow. . . .

I wrote Mr. Wiestling today that I have lost some of my baggage, which is now in the hands of the enemy. The articles are about as follows: my fine large shawl, India rubber blanket, woolen blanket, a new pair of gauntlets never worn, two pair of gloves, several shirts, Henrietta's portfolio with letters and papers, military books, army regulations, Hardee's *Tactics*,[58] my large printed Bible with a whole lot of countersigns—and what is more than all, your ambrotype and Henny and Sarah's dagguerrotypes.

The reason I took them along was because as I was leaving Vienna, I thought I would get wounded or sick. I would then long to see you, and it would be a comfort to see all your likenesses if I could not see you in person. So now, dear, you will be gazed upon by those notorious Rebels. I want you all to get them taken over again and send them to me as soon as you conveniently can. . . .

It is better to lose my baggage than to lose my head. My first campaign has been of use to me. . . .

Camp Princeton, July 27th 1861

My dear Ellen,

I have been thinking a great deal about you and the children, home and friends, and feel as though I would like to ask for a fur-

---

57. According to official National Park Service figures, the Federals at Bull Run sustained 2,708 killed, wounded, and missing out of 35,732 who took part in the battle; Confederate losses were 1,982 of 31,810 engaged. Cf. *OR,* II, 327–28, 568–70.

58. William J. Hardee's *Rifle and Light Infantry Tactics* was the most popular military manual of the time. Thousands of inexperienced officers, North and South, pored over its stilted language in an effort to learn their new profession.

[56] ✗ THE McALLISTER LETTERS

lough for a few days and go home. But I can hardly indulge in that pleasure, for it will depend on many circumstances. I will not ask for one until we are completely settled and have no prospect of a march. In fact, if there is a prospect of a march, I could not get a furlough, nor would I want it. . . .

We are getting this dirty, filthy camp cleaned up, and we are now looking better.

Large numbers of troops are pouring into Washington. Regiment after regiment are crossing the Long Bridge to this side, showing that the government is at last waking up to a sence of duty. No doubt we will have troops enough this time to gain a victory.

Our regiment stands A Number One in the estimation of all who know the facts. Notwithstanding Col. Blenker and Col. Evinstein [59] claiming the credit of being the last to leave the field, the truth is now becoming known and our regiment has the honor. Congressman Stratten [60] paid us a visit yesterday and said that in the Senate, I think it was, we were handsomely noted by some of the speakers. And he also said that tomorrow the New York *Herald* will have a very favorable notice of our Regiment.[61] . . .

You ask me where Taylor's regiment was at the time of the battle. Like the 1st and 2nd N.J., it was on the reserve list. But it was stationed at Fairfax and, I suppose, was not ordered to move at all. We all think it very strange that Genl. Runyon had 15,000 troops on the reserve way up here, and that not one of them was ordered down.[62] Had our whole Brigade been together as it ought to have been, under the command of Col. Montgomery and brought into action, we think all would have been right.

Why these blunders, we know not. But the results have been very disastrous. Had our 2nd Regiment alone come up and stood beside us,

59. On the retreat from Bull Run, Blenker had detached Max Einstein and his 27th New York to guard the Centreville headquarters and hospital. *OR*, II, 427.

60. John L. N. Stratton represented the Mount Holly district in the Congress.

61. Not everyone in the army shared McAllister's confidence in the reportorial accuracy of the *Herald*, especially its coverage of the Bull Run affair. A captain in the 26th New York wrote in late July: "The New York *Herald's* account of the battle is a most egregious burlesque." John S. Applegate, *Reminiscences and Letters of George Arrowsmith* (cited hereafter as Applegate, *Arrowsmith Reminiscences*) (Red Bank, N.J., 1893), 57.

62. One embittered infantryman declared that Runyon's force performed no more service in the battle "than the Queen's Guard in London." However, Runyon and his 5,752 men had dutifully obeyed McDowell's July 17 order to remain within the defenses of Washington. *OR*, II, 304, 309; Henry N. Blake, *Three Years in the Army of the Potomac* (Boston, 1865), 30; Foster, *New Jersey and the Rebellion*, 55–57.

we would have held Centreville without a doubt. And the retreating troops might possibly have been brought back in time to have saved us from being cut off. But Providence has directed it otherwise, and it is all for the best.

The 2nd and 3rd New Jersey Volunteers are mortified that they were not along to share in the honors of the 1st Regiment. Col. McLean, reaching Washington much sooner than other New Jersey troops, boasted at Willard's of what he had done. But the facts were known, and he had to shut up. Notwithstanding all this, he had a piece published complimenting the 2nd for their gallantry on that occasion and for their services to the Government in saving property. But it soon appeared that he led the advance in the retreat, and everybody has become perfectly disgusted with him. His own men and officers have petitioned to have him removed. . . . McLean disobeyed orders, and the facts will be inquired into. . . .

I think it is unlikely I can get leave of absence. Things point that way now. Camp life such as we have is very hard and laborious. We perform a vast deal of labor. Last night the men were again called out by an alarm that the enemy were coming. As usual, it was false. Day and night we are on the lookout. Work, work—drill, drill—form, form—is all the go. Sunday, Saturday, and every day. . . .

Remember me kindly to sister Elizabeth and to my friend John T. Dick. I hope his health has improved. Tell them to make themselves at home. It is nice for you to have them with you during these exciting times. . . .

Camp Princeton, Tuesday Morning, July 30th 1861

My dear Ellen,

I have nothing in particular to communicate. All seems to be a lull in camp. We know but little as to what is being done in organizing our regiments into brigades, and who are to be our several commanders. I think Col. Montgomery will be appointed a Brigadere General. But over what troops, I know not. I fear that the New Jersey Regiments will be separated and have no state distinction. This we are all much opposed to, but we have not the fixing of these things. I don't want you to write to President Lincoln. It will do no good—and will certainly do me harm. So, dear, don't you do it. I think he is doing all he can, and blame should not be cast on him, nor on the Administration. But confidentially, I think we have a miserable lot of generals. This I dare not say outside. That McDowell was drunk on the day of the battle of Bull Run, I have no doubt.[63] These things will be rectified now that a thorough reorganization is going on.

Our men fought very bravely at Bull Run, but there did not seem to be anyone to give orders. A stand could undoubtedly have been made at Centreville, and should have been made. It would have been worth millions of dollars to our Government had it been done. With Col. Montgomery as the commander, it would have succeeded. And if all our regiments had been there together, we would have made a stand creditable alike to ourselves and to our country. . . .

63. The North badly needed a scapegoat for the humiliation at Bull Run, and McDowell was selected. A month after the battle, Russell of the London *Times* quoted a "general officer" as saying: "There are thousands of people who this moment believe that McDowell, who never tasted anything stronger than a water-melon in all his life, was helplessly drunk at Bull Run. Mind what I say; they'll run you into a mud-hole as sure as you live." Russell, *My Diary North and South*, 499–500.

2

Outposts at Alexandria

IN THE AUTUMN of 1861 the greater Washington area was "half city and half camp. The wide extent of vacant lots, where scarcely a house was to be seen, was occupied by the tents of the infantry, stretching like an outer girdle upon all the neighboring heights."[1]

Yet many people felt that the Army of the Potomac was living too much up to its title. It seemed glued to the river for which it was named, rather than on the offensive for which it was created. McAllister was but one officer who fidgeted impatiently. He yearned for action; he daily expected his 1st New Jersey to be part of a grand, forward movement; and he interpreted each of a dozen skirmishes between pickets as the overture to a mighty battle.

But one week of monotonous inactivity followed another. McAllister's exasperation assumed caustic overtones. When his wife failed to purchase watches for herself and daughters as speedily as McAllister requested, he devoted unnecessarily long passages in several letters to the subject until the watches were duly obtained. Resentful at not being given command of the 1st New Jersey, McAllister sought the help of influential friends in gaining the colonelcy of another regiment. He was critical of his brigade commander, Philip Kearny, and his immediate superior, Alfred T. A. Torbert. He thought

---

1. De Trobriand, *Army of the Potomac*, 77.

ill of the latter's being absent so much from the regimental camp at Alexandria's Fairfax Seminary—even though such absences automatically placed McAllister in command of the 1st New Jersey.

Thus, he whiled away this five-month period by writing lengthy letters to his family, drilling his men, inspecting picket lines, reading military tactics, and rededicating himself through prayers and church services to the Omnipotent Being whom he adored.

♣

Camp Princeton, August 5th 1861

My dear Ellen,

This is, I suppose, the last letter I will write from this camp, as we have orders to move to Cloud's Mill,[2] said to be about four miles from Alexandria out from the river towards the enemy. Whether the object is to get into a more healthy location, or to advance on the enemy by degrees, I don't know. By some mistake the teams are here to move us, without our knowledge of the intention. Having no notice of it, we are not ready and may not leave until tomorrow morning.

It now appears that the three New Jersey regiments are thrown into a brigade and are to have a horse troop, also an artillery battery, &c.[3] Ah, this is just what we wanted. But I am sorry to say it is thought that Carney[4] is to be our Brigadier General instead of Col. Mont-

2. Cloud's Mill was a Federal outpost on the Little River Turnpike, midway between Alexandria and Annandale. See Applegate, *Arrowsmith Reminiscences*, 60–64; Baquet, *First Brigade*, 418.

3. The brigade then consisted of the 1st, 2nd, and 3rd New Jersey, Battery G of the 2nd U.S. Artillery, and Co. G of the 2nd U.S. Cavalry. *OR*, V, 15.

4. Philip Kearny, New Jersey's most distinguished Civil War soldier, entered the Civil War with possibly more military experience than any other participant, North or South. He lost an arm in the Mexican War, yet rushed to Europe and joined the French army, then campaigned from Algiers to Italy. One writer described him as "all flame and color and ardor, with a slim, twisted streak of genius in him." A French officer remarked that Kearny "went under fire as on parade, with a smile on his lips." A thorough soldier, he required as much of every man who served under him—"tolerating no evasions, making no exceptions, accepting no excuses." *OR*, Vol. LI, Pt. 1, p. 434; Foster, *New Jersey and the Rebellion*, 69, 804–22; Bruce Catton, *Mr. Lincoln's Army* (Garden City, 1951), 32.

gomery. If this is so, Col. Montgomery will resign and leave us alone, for which I would be very sorry. The Colonel, however, may be appointed brigadier general for some other brigade—from Pennsylvania, most likely. . . . A day or two will decide the matter. In any event, we will lose the Colonel from our regiment. But how I would like him to be our Brigadier General so that I could have his counsel and advice. . . .

If you don't get any letters for a day or two, don't be disappointed, as moving changes everything. Direct your letters to Alexandria instead of Washington. . . .

Camp Edgehill,[5] Va. [August 6, 1861]

My dear Ellen,

I have but time to say we arrived here last evening after a hard and hot day's march in which many of our men gave out. All the New Jersey regiments are encamped near us. We are here in the yard of a comfortable residence belonging to a Mr. Irwin,[6] now a Quartermaster in the Rebel army. The family, negroes included, fled about the time our troops took Alexandria. After the Ohio Regiment was fired into at Vienna, a few rowdies from a Michigan regiment came back into the house and destroyed the furniture. They broke almost everything, including a marble-topped table broken in two, &c. It was a terable wreck of property.

The blacks are actually in want of something to live on. They are glad to do our washing.

We are in the most advanced post of our army and, of course, are liable to attack at any moment. But we have a first rate, elevated position and can repel a much larger force. If we were more secure, I would like you to come and stay with me. We could have a nice room with a fine mahogany bed, washstands, &c., or at least what is left of them. Yet in view of constant alarms and you being so easily excited, I don't know that it would be right for me to have you come. But we will see. . . .

I would suppose that the Irwin family are among the F.F.V's.[7]

5. Camp Edgehill was situated on an eminence known as Munson's Hill. Because of its forward position and proximity to the Confederate lines, it was known also as Camp Advance. See Baquet, *First Brigade,* 418; Willard Glazier, *Three Years in the Federal Cavalry* (New York, 1873), 39.

6. Probably Capt. W. H. Irwin, who served as asst. quartermaster of the 11th Virginia. F. L. Brockett and George W. Rock, *A Concise History of . . . Alexandria, Va. . . .* (Alexandria, 1883), 41.

7. First families of Virginia.

We are about 8 miles from Mount Vernon and 8 from Fairfax. . . .

Henrietta, my dear daughter, enclosed you will find a piece of Miss Irwin's composition which Mr. Yard handed me and desired that you and Sister should see it. . . . This paper, as well as cancelled notes, were lying all over the floor from numerous drawers pulled out and broken up. Shame on those soldiers. . . .

1st Regiment, Camp Edgehill, or Camp Advance
August 9th 1861

My dear Ellen,

I have just finished a letter to Mr. Wiestling, referring to the *Tribune's* article of the 7th, which I want you to read. It shows how annoying these newsmongers are and how far from the truth they get.[8] Such are well calculated to mislead the minds of the people.

I really don't know what to say about you coming here in this exposed position amid such constant excitement. We are called out under arms almost every night by alarms of sentries firing. Last night gunfire was exchanged on the outposts. It is true that if we are permitted to remain here, it will become more safe. But . . . I can't leave camp for an hour on account of our position. Yet get everything ready; and if things change for the better, I will write you. We have two ladies—officers' wives—in the camp now. They are quite genteel, respectable, and refined. . . .

Meade [9] is not with me now. He has left. He was very worthless and lost many of my articles, including the beautiful knife Mr. Wiestling and Mr. S. T. Scranton [10] gave me which I valued very much. I only learned it was gone when we had a prospect of a fight. When we moved from Camp Monmouth to Camp Trenton, Meade

---

8. The New York *Tribune* for Aug. 7, 1861, reported in an unsigned story (p. 5): "It is rumored that Colonel Montgomery, not having obtained the appointment of Brigadier, and feeling that he is too far advanced in years for the active field duties of Colonel, will resign his place. Should this occur, as we trust it will not, we learn that a general stampede of the line officers, who have little confidence in other field officers, may be expected, unless his place should be filled by an officer equally competent." As McAllister reported in subsequent letters, this "rumor" appeared to consist of more propaganda—circulated in the hope of helping secure the promotion of Col. Baker to Col. Montgomery's position—than truth. For a similar opinion of the *Tribune's* field reporting, see Russell, *My Diary North and South,* 497–98.

9. Meade was the first in a succession of body servants employed by McAllister.

10. Seldon T. Scranton was a business associate and close friend of McAllister.

took it out of the tin box and put it in his pocket unknown to me, and got drunk and lost it. Of course someone got it. I was not aware of the fact for a month afterward. Meade said he knew nothing about it, but I have positive evidence and he finally owned up and told me as stated above. I forgot to say to Mr. Wiestling that I wished him to buy me another one and charge me with it. I ought to have one by all means. . . .

Camp Advance, August 10th 1861

My dear Ellen,

You need not feel badly about the *Tribune* correspondence in regard to our field and staff officers. The contradiction will appear in today's paper. The strongest kind of letters have been written by Genl. Montgomery in my favor, paying the highest compliments to me as a gentleman and as an officer, fully competent to take the command of the regiment and by all means worthy of promotion. He has written two such letters to the Governor and has no doubt of my being promoted. All the field and staff officers, and many of the line officers, are my warm and personal friends. Some of the line officers prefer ease, pleasure and liberty to go when and where they please. They get drunk as often as they wish without being noticed. They neglect to see that their men are provided for, and they try to throw the responsibility of any want and neglect on the field officers.[11]

These men have laid a deep plan to get Col. Baker,[12] one of the three-month colonels, to fill Col. Montgomery's place. He is just the kind of man to suit them. He is not a military man and is not a gentleman. He is a low politician of Democratic side. His heart is not in the cause; he now says that we must compromise, that we can't conquer the Rebs. This then is my competition. You can judge what he is by the fact that he has spent part of the days in this camp treating these men for their votes and supplying them with good brandy, &c. He is a mean, low, contemptible man and a disgrace to the service. What I will do if he is appointed is another question, but we don't mean that he shall be. We can and will head him off, so rest easy.

11. At this time, the observing de Trobriand stated, Federal soldiers "had everything to learn, drill, marchings, service, discipline, and very few non-commissioned officers to instruct them, even supposing the officers capable of doing it, which was rarely the case. . . . There were a great many men, but few soldiers." De Trobriand, *Army of the Potomac,* 84.

12. Henry M. Baker had served as colonel of the 2nd New Jersey Militia. *N.J. Record,* I, 28.

[64] ✗ THE McALLISTER LETTERS

That piece in the *Tribune* is part of their program. They had to manufacture these lies in order to carry it out. We are all disgusted with their duplicity. They now say that it is not me they are opposed to, but that they fear Capt. [William] Henry will be appointed major. They don't like him at all, simply because he knows more than all of them put together. I will keep you posted on these and all other matters. . . .

We don't get a single good night's sleep—constantly waken up by the pickets firing. Camp life is a very hard life. . . .

Camp Edgehill, Monday Morning, August 12th 1861

My dear daughter Henrietta,

I have as usual but a few minutes to write before breakfast, having been up since reveille and around at roll call to the companies to see if all are at their posts. And I have also been to see the sick. . . .

An order came from Headquarters yesterday to be ready, that the enemy were advancing from the direction of Mount Vernon. We soon had all our telescopes and glasses out to see them, as we have a fine view of the surrounding country from this place. No enemy made their appearance, so Capt. Birney and myself mounted our horses and rode in that direction to see and hear the enemy. But we learned nothing. We called at Genl. Howard's [13] headquarters and were very well and handsomely received.

I found the General a very pleasant man, as well as a religious man. He is a Colonel but acting as General, commanding four regiments composed of three Maine and one Vermont regiment. They were in the battle at Bull Run and did very well.

While we were there, it began to rain and the storm continued for a time. After it slacked off a little, we started back. Other officers tendered their gum coats. It was very dark, and we had no sooner started than it commenced raining again. But on we came, not knowing at all times whether we were on the right road. We found a creek that we were compelled to ford. The water, very high, was roaring like a cataract. We concluded to go back and get a light. We failed to get one, so we came back again, plunged our horses into the creek, and

13. In June, 1861, Oliver O. Howard had resigned his post as professor of mathematics at West Point to accept the colonelcy of the 3rd Maine. He was to lose an arm and gain a major general's commission in the course of the Civil War. His command at this time consisted of the 3rd, 4th, and 5th Maine, plus the 2nd Vermont.

reached this side in safety. We were challenged time and again by our sentries, gave the countersign, passed them, and reached home very wet at a late hour. We concluded that there was no approach of the enemy, so I laid down and slept very soundly and now feel very bright, ready for the activities of the camp and field. . . .

On Saturday afternoon I went out with Capt. Birney to reconnoiter. We passed all our lines beyond the cross roads and went on towards Fairfax—in fact, went to within six miles of Fairfax and but a very short distance from the Reb pickets. Had we now advanced to the top of a hill (which we had a notion to do), we would have been on their pickets. But we turned home, concluding that we had gone about as far as it was safe. Yesterday a troop of cavalry went out in the same direction but found no signs of the enemy. We can't think that they are advancing at all, yet we have no doubt but that they are fortified and ready to receive us.

Sentinels are those men placed immediately around the camp. They never sit down but must always be on the alert. Pickets are different. We send them out miles from camp on roads and crossings. They are placed three together. One will always be on the lookout while the other two are resting so as to give early information as to the movements of the enemy. These scouts go out in the country between the enemy pickets and ours. They are liable at any moment to meet the enemy scouts. Then a contest may occur. . . .

Here comes an order detailing me for Brigade officer of the day, so I must close. . . .

Camp Edgehill, August 13th 1861

My dear Ellen,

I have but a few moments to write. I have been in the saddle all night, acting as Officer of the Day in this Brigade and going around amongst the pickets. So I feel rather tired to commence the arduous duties of the day. And now we have the trouble of moving again today, so we are all preparing to pull up stakes and march back one mile towards Alexandria to a most splendid place for an encampment —the grounds of a very large Episcopalian Theological Seminary, deserted now, of course.[14] It has plenty of water, splendid grounds, and

14. The Protestant Episcopal Theological Seminary, where McAllister was to spend the first winter of the war, was founded in 1823. The school closed at the outbreak of civil war, "and the faculty and students fled to join the Southern army." The "Fairfax Seminary," as it was popularly called, became both a Federal outpost and a field hospital. William A. R. Goodwin, *History of the Theo-*

finely furnished rooms in the building, if we desire to take them. Our other Jersey regiments are moving ahead of us and may monopolize the best of everything.

The 15th New York is now camped on the grounds but will leave in a day or two. Many of their officers have their wives with them, living in the building with all the comforts of home. We can get boarding for you in the building. In a word, come whenever it suits you; or at least get ready and I will write after getting there and tell you all. I think the children ought to come with you. This place is in sight of Alexandria, and Washington can be seen from the top of the building. . . .

Camp St. John, August 15th 1861

My dear Ellen,

I wrote you a few lines this morning when I got up, which by the way was . . . too late for the mail. And now before retiring to bed, I will write you again.

I told you that the calomel I took opperated very well and I have not had a chill today. Before retiring, I will take a dose of quinine. I have no doubt but that I will be all right in a day or two. . . .

We have a good deal of sickness, principally chills and fever. [Henry] Warner and Lieut. [George] Brewster are both under the doctor's care. We have a large home, belonging to one of the professors, which we use as a hospital. There are quite a number of beds in it. Our sick are as comfortable as can be expected under the circumstances. . . .

I have a comfortable room in this, the main building. I have a fire kindled in the stove, for it is quite cold. . . .

Henrietta asks me if we are the most advanced regiment. We were so when at Edgehill; but since we came down here, we are all about on a line. But all notwithstanding, all of the New Jersey regiments, some of New York, as well as some of Maine, have moved down on this line. We hold all the ground we had, and our scouts go over all this territory every day and occupy it at night. Four companies of our regiment are detailed for this duty for every twenty-four

---

logical Seminary in Virginia . . . (New York, 1923), I, 218–39; Julia S. Wheelock, *The Boys in White* (New York, 1870), 33; Fred C. Floyd, *History of the Fortieth (Mozart) Regiment, New York Volunteers* (cited hereafter as Floyd, *40th New York*) (Boston, 1909), 71.

hours. Their headquarters is Edgehill; they occupy the Irwin home. Over this district or county the Brigade Officer of the Day has to travel night as well as day, visiting all these pickets. These officers are chosen from the Lieutenant-Colonels and Majors. One half of them are on Court Marshall at Alexandria; consequently, this duty comes on a very few of us very rapidly. It was getting wet on this duty that upset me.

You ask me if I have got any pay from the Government. I wrote you that we had been paid for one month and eleven days—to the 30th of June. July, of course, is due us. I am not certain that we will get any more before the last of this month, when we will be paid for two months. I am not in any want of money. . . . We can buy nothing on this side of the River, and I don't go on the other side very often. I have been to Washington only once since I crossed over, and that was to see Brother Nelson. . . .

I now have the good news to tell you that our Dr. Taylor has arrived here. He is now in camp, and is not at all well. He has the chills and fever and is looking badly. We are all very much rejoiced to see him. He is now on a parole; whether he will return is not certain, but I don't think he will. . . .

Camp St. John, Monday Morning, August 19th 1861
My dear Ellen,

I wrote you that I was sick, but I am now getting better. On Saturday I was again field officer of the day. The exposure, together with the loss of sleep, caused me to feel badly yesterday. But I have no chills and, I think, but little fever this morning. I feel quite well and have concluded . . . not to go on field duty again until I am entirely well.

It is raining now every day. I don't know when we have seen the sun. We have two hundred men sick from chills and fever. Of course, many of them are but slightly ill, and I may say none of them are in danger. Yet sickness cuts down the strength of our Regiment very much. It helps the grumbling, for it gives the men food to work upon. And all camps have their grumbling.

We occupy these buildings for hospitals. . . . If the buildings could be cleaned up, we would not have more than half that number sick. Dr. Gordon [15] is sick; Brewster and Warner are better; and I

15. Charles C. Gordon served as a surgeon in the 1st New Jersey until his February, 1863, discharge from service. *N.J. Record,* I, 68.

will be well in a day or two. Dr Taylor is not here now . . . but he can't re-enter the service. So we will have to get another physician.

Now, dear, I don't know what to say about you coming here. Genl. Montgomery, I find, is opposed to ladies coming here and talks of issuing an order prohibiting them from coming. . . . But the idea is this: in case we were attacked, what would the ladies do? Where would they go? Who would attend to them? I don't believe myself that we will be attacked at all, although at the top of this building we can see the enemy at work. . . .

But if you can come, stop at Willard's, hire a carriage, and tell the driver that you want to come to this Regiment encamped at this Seminary near Alexandria. Most of the drivers knows where it is, as they are out every day. You will have to get a pass from the Provost Marshal. Mr. Willard will see to getting it for you. . . .

Headquarters, 1st Regt., N.J.V., near Alexandria
August 20th 1861

My dear Ellen,

Our sick have accumulated so much that we are beginning to take all the furniture out of these rooms and turn this large building into a hospital. So I move into another wing of this same building, where I have got a good comfortable room. When you come, we can have it to ourselves. . . .

A report last night says that the enemy have crossed the Potomac and have destroyed our communication with the North. If this is the case, you can't get here. Neither can this letter get to you. But we don't believe the report at all. These reports are heard every day. . . .

I am going to have the chills today. I feel it now. Half of our officers are sick, as well as nearly one half of our men. The Campbells [16] are the only ones from Oxford that have not got the chills. Brewster and Warner are better. I thought I was better but find it was a mistake. . . .

Camp at the Alexandria Seminary, August 22nd 1861

My dear Ellen,

. . . I have been sick but am better this morning. Yesterday I had a very heavy chill followed by raging fever. I took calomel pills

16. Samuel and William Campbell of Co. C were both mortally wounded at the battle of Gaines's Mill. *Ibid.*, 78.

and have opperated very well and feel much better this morning. I expect to be well in a day or two. Our sick are nearly all getting better. The sun has at last made its appearance. We have had a long hard time of it, and it has nearly ruined our Regiment.

Last evening Col. Montgomery told me that an order had come from Headquarters that we had to move again—down to Alexandria, as it is thought we cannot hold our position. This seems to me very strange. I can't think that we are in any danger at all. I have been out all over this country for miles, and I do not find the enemy pickets any closer to us than they have been. On the other hand, they have taken some of them farther back. . . .

As to my promotion to Col. Montgomery's place, I have the strongest assurances from official quarters that all is right. I may be disappointed, but think not.

That piece in the *Tribune* of the 7th was written by Lieut. Evans,[17] a coward who resigned after the Bull Run battle, and who never was a friend of mine. . . .

Headquarters, 1st Regt., N.J.V., August 25th 1861
My dear daughter Sarah,

This is the Sabbath. I am sorry to say that we hardly know when it comes, as we have so many duties that we can hardly distinguish it from other days of the week. Today, however, we had a nice service in an Episcopal church belonging to this Seminary. We also had communion. A few of us partook. It was quite solom. Next Sabbath afternoon we are to hold a larger service, in which members of other regiments are to participate.

Inclosed you will find a lock of my hair, which I send for your mother, though she may soon be here. I still thought it best to send it, as I have it now and it might get lost. . . .

We have two Rebel prisoners here who were taken yesterday evening in a skirmish. Some cavalry belonging to us went outside our pickets as usual, and a captain belonging to one of the New York regiments accompanied them. As they were riding, some Rebels in a cornfield fired on them and killed one of our men, shot the captain's horse, and took the captain prisoner. On the other hand, our men took two of them prisoners. This was in sight of their pickets. You will see it all in the papers.

17. Augustus O. Evans resigned Aug. 5, 1861, as a lieutenant in Co. I. *Ibid.,* 94.

In one of these rooms, before this struggle broke out, roomed two brothers by the name, I think, of Conrad. They were students here, preparing for the ministry. Both joined the Southern army against the wishes of their father, who forbade that they should ever come home, as he was a strong Union man. After the battle of Bull Run, both brothers *were found dead, locked in each other's arms*.[18] A sad story. We hear of many students here who joined the Rebs and who lost their lives at that battle. The loss of life on their side was immense.

I feel better today and am getting quite well. Colonel—no, General—Montgomery has gone to Washington. I suppose he will be back today. He will not be with us long, as he has got his General's commission—and a good one it is, dated back to the 17th of May last.[19] Those officers who have served their country faithfully have that honor conferred on them so that they can outrank the upstarts. So you see our Genl. Montgomery will have command over many others when it comes to the question of rank.

I am not certain but have every reason to believe I will soon be promoted to Colonel. Everybody says so and has shown assurances to that effect from the Knowing Ones. Notwithstanding the plot against me, I knocked Col. Baker higher than a kite. I laid him low, so he is out of the way. If I don't get the promotion, it will be given to an experienced army officer. . . .

Headquarters, 1st Regt., N.J.V., August 28th 1861
My dear daughter Henrietta,

The reason I have not written the last two days was because I have been out with the whole Regiment on picket duty and hourly expecting an attack. The place was at the junction of the old Leesburg road with the Seminary road, about one mile or a little more from here. I have been on duty night and day for two days and will continue for 24 hours longer. I came in to change clothes and will leave in a few minutes. I will leave a note on this table for your mother, if she comes.

18. The two brothers were Holmes and Tucker Conrad, sons of a prominent Martinsburg, Va., attorney. The incident of their unusual deaths is basically as McAllister described it. See James I. Robertson, Jr., *The Stonewall Brigade* (Baton Rouge, 1963), 43.

19. Montgomery's promotion to brigadier was announced Aug. 24; two days later he became military governor of Alexandria. Montgomery's service file; *OR*, Vol. LI, Pt. 1, p. 455.

I am getting quite well, but this hard duty and loss of sleep may cause another relapse.

We may not be attacked, but it looks like it. Yet we say let them come! We are ready for them. We will not let them come down this far. . . .

Camp at Seminary, August 30th 1861

My dear daughter Henrietta,

You have not been receiving your daily letters from me as usual because . . . for three days I have been on laborious picket duty. Our whole Regiment was at the junction of the Leesburg and Seminary roads. This is not the junction of the new Leesburg turnpike, for that is called Bailey's Crossroads. It is one mile farther out towards the enemy. . . . Our junction is nearly all woods except for an open space—like an old field—at the forks.

The other morning, news came in that the New York pickets were driven in at Bailey's Crossroads and that the enemy were advancing on us. Our Regiment was ordered out to fight them. All able to bear arms, myself among that number, started for the scene of action. We had with us two pieces of artillery—twelve-pounders—and about 40 horsemen. We took up a line of battle and waited the approach of the enemy. Col.—or Genl.—Montgomery was in command a part of the time and, in his absence, I had the command. We staid there three days and three nights and it rained almost constantly all that time. A good portion of that time we were stationed in line of battle.[20] When we were not so formed, we rested under trees and in bush houses.

These huts or houses are built of bushes and, when it don't rain, are rather comfortable—especially when we lay pine tops on the floors. This is considered rather healthy. But when it rains hard, we get about as wet indoors. Water comes through and we often leave our bough houses to seek shelter under a tree. After nightfall we can't have a particle of fire, for that would tell the enemy where we are and they would fall on us right and left. So you see what a fine

---

20. For details of skirmishes that occurred at this time, see *OR*, Vol. V, pp. 119–22; Vol. LI, Pt. 1, pp. 37–39; James H. Stevenson, *"Boots and Saddles": A History of the . . . First New York (Lincoln) Cavalry* (cited hereafter as Stevenson, *"Boots and Saddles"*) (Harrisburg, 1879), 49; "Civil War Letters of William J. Reichard," *Proceedings of the Lehigh Valley County Historical Society*, XXII (1958), 150.

time we had picketing in the forest of Old Virginia and watching for the Rebs. . . .

We kept patrolling the roads with some men and receiving reports every hour. The enemy, however, have not advanced, and Washington is safe yet. . . .

Camp Fairfax, Fairfax Seminary, Virginia
September 10th 1861

My dear Ellen,

Last evening I received your letter written on the 1st from Philadelphia. I had not heard from you since you left here. Genl. Montgomery told me of your passing through Scranton and calling on him. I felt very lonely and dull after you left and could not help but wish I was home. I do think you will have to spend more time with me if we remain any time at one place. The truth is, this is a miserable way to live. But I do it because I love my country and its institutions, and am willing to sacrifice much—even life itself—to sustain our glorious country and the best Government in the world.

Lieut. Tolbert [21] of the Regular Army has been appointed to Genl. Montgomery's place in our Regiment. I have been treated badly in this manner. Still, I would rather he was appointed than Lieut. Col. Tucker.[22] I will treat him well, of course. Torbert is engaged to be married to a niece of Genl. Stockton's, and all that influence—including Col. Halstead's—was thrown to him.[23]

I have not determined what course I will take. I can't very well get out of the service with honor at the present time, as we expect to have a battle every day and I shall not be found retreating to the sound of the enemy's cannon. But the time may come when I will let

---

21. Alfred T. A. Torbert was twenty-eight years old at the time of his appointment as colonel of the 1st New Jersey. His comparative youthfulness, plus the fact that he had had but five years of military experience, led McAllister to believe that his own claims for the colonelcy of the regiment had been unjustly bypassed. Henrietta McAllister termed Torbert's appointment "one of the hardest blows Father ever received." Baldwin MS., 18.

22. Isaac M. Tucker, then lieutenant colonel of the 2nd New Jersey, succeeded to command of that regiment following the December, 1861, resignation of Col. McLean, *N.J. Record,* 102.

23. Here McAllister was exhibiting exaggerations so often a by-product of hurt feelings. In 1866 Torbert married Mary E. Curry, "the only daughter of a merchant farmer" near Milford, Del. His biographer gave the impression that the two did not become engaged until after the war. Stockton's subordinate, N. Norris Halsted, served as an aide-de-camp to Gov. Olden until January, 1863. Townsend, *Torbert Memorial,* 55; *N.J. Record,* I, 9.

them have my commission. This is strictly confidential. I will act prudently and not rashly in the whole matter.

Genl. Montgomery wants Capt. Birney and myself to get leave from Governor Olden or Governor Andrew Curtin [of Pennsylvania] and form a regiment in one or both of these states. We will see more about this in a few days, but we will most likely advance on the enemy and will have to remain as we are at present.

Maj. [David] Hatfield is sick. Except for Adj. [William] Henry, I am the only field officer here. I have been interrupted almost constantly since I sat down to write this letter. All is bustle and confusion as usual. . . .

Headquarters, 1st N.J. Regt., September 11th 1861

My dear Ellen,
. . . Maj. Hatfield is sick and confined to his bed. The whole duty devolves on me, our new colonel not having arrived here yet. I have not fully decided what I shall do, but I can't under the present circumstances do what I would like. As we expect every day to meet the enemy, it would not do for me to resign. All will depend on how I am treated by the young Colonel. The position of Lieutenant Colonel is more pleasant than that of Colonel, and in many ways preferable. But that is not the question involved in this matter.

We will receive our pay one of these days. Then I will send you money to buy Sarah a handsome watch. If possible, Henrietta may also get one.

We have got the cleanest camp on this side of Washington. This is so stated by all who have seen these camps. The Sanitary Committee [24] has been here and given us credit for the cleanest camp in the Army. . . .

Headquarters, 1st N.J. Regt., September 16th 1861

My dear Ellen,
I received two letters from you last night. I am sorry that in them you implicate everybody in my not being appointed to Col. Mont-

24. Established in 1861, the U.S. Sanitary Commission was an outgrowth of several women's relief agencies. Its basic goal was to do for the soldiers what the government did not do; and toward this goal it became famous for caring for wounded, improving camp hygiene, staging charity fairs, and providing food and shelter for disabled troops.

gomery's place. Now one request: keep cool. I can manage it all right. Don't you write to Governor Olden or anyone else here on the subject, or I will be dissatisfied. It will do more harm than good. I know who are my friends and will know more by and by. I am not going to do things rashly. I am placed in a situation where I must be careful how I act.

As to my character being injured by Kearny's arresting me, that is all moonshine—nothing to it. He is arresting officers every few days.[25] But more on this subject later.

Enclosed you will find $250 which I send to you to buy watches for Sarah and Henrietta. . . . I would much rather that you keep one of the watches and, if I live, I will buy Henrietta a watch in a few months. Now I wish this carried out without failure. It is my intention to buy each one of you a watch, and you ought to be considered first. If I die, you can keep it in remembrance of me. So you take one of these two and Henrietta can have one soon. . . .

Headquarters, Camp Seminary, September 16th 1861
My dear Ellen,

. . . We have moved our camp back in front of the Seminary, where we were at first when we came here. It is much the best place of the two.

Since you left, we have had two deaths in our Regiment.[26] The corpse of one of the soldiers was sent home. The body of the other was taken to Alexandria to be sent by express, but the express company would not take it unless it was enclosed in a metallic coffin. We sent an order down to buy one in Alexandria. It costs about forty dollars to send a corpse home without a metallic coffin. To get one is rather expensive; the money has to be raised in the Regiment. The last time, we raised about one hundred dollars to bear the expense. The men are very liberal. When the money was raised, they were to

---

25. One officer wrote of Kearny: "His severity, sometimes brusque, often eccentric, at first made him unpopular. But the men soon saw he was less indulgent to the shortcomings of officers than to theirs . . ." J. Watts de Peyster, *Personal and Military History of Philip Kearny, Major-General, United States Volunteers* . . . (cited hereafter as de Peyster, *Philip Kearny*) (New York, 1869), 204. See also *ibid.*, 206, 210; *History of the Third Pennsylvania Cavalry . . . in the American Civil War, 1861–1865* (Philadelphia, 1905), 12–14.

26. The only member of the 1st New Jersey listed as dying in the period in question was musician Daniel H. Brower. He succumbed Sept. 6 to typhoid fever. On the day after McAllister's letter, Pvt. George Wannan of Co. H died of consumption and was buried in Alexandria. *N.J. Record*, I, 72, 78.

get a metal coffin; but they could not purchase one and so bought a mahogany coffin and sent the body on in that.

You need not be uneasy about the money I loaned to persons in camp, for I have got it all back and you now have it. I don't lose as much as you would think. You don't understand camp life or you would not say so much about my loaning money. A man that would not pay back on payday what he had borrowed from a friend would be looked down upon and would ruin himself forever in camp.

Maj. Hatfield is still very ill with fever. We hardly expected him to recover, but he is now a little better and we have hopes for him. He had the best constitution of any officer amongst us. He had never been sick, but he is weak enough now. . . .

Tell Sarah to cool down her passions relative to my not getting the appointment of colonel. I don't want any of you to write to the Governor on the subject. I will attend to all that, for you can only play smash and injure me. . . .

Headquarters, 1st N.J. Regt., September 19th 1861

My dear Ellen,

I was most disappointed in not receiving a letter from you last night. Write every day.

My health is improved and I am getting quite well.

Our young Colonel has gone home and I am again in command. This is quite pleasant and agreeable.

I know the informers who worked against my appointment. It was the Stockton clique, in order to advance their own interests and designs by working with Kearny against Genl. Montgomery and his friends. The battle still rages against our old Genl. Montgomery. . . .

Headquarters, Camp Seminary, September 30th 1861

My dear daughters,

You have seen in the papers that our pretended advance on the enemy's lines on Saturday by our Brigade was taken for a reality by the enemy. They retreated without firing a shot, except a few rifles. Our line on the right, hearing of our advance and the enemy's retreat, went forward and acquired Munson's Hill.[27] Night came. We had no

27. For some weeks ominous Confederate works had peered down from Munson's Hill on the Federal positions. Kearny, determined to remove the menace to his troops, led a reconnaissance in force against the eminence. The Con-

dinner and no blankets, as we had not intended to remain after dark. Except for four companies of our Regiment detailed as pickets, our Brigade remained in position.

It was a queer move, for it was not intended to advance our lines. But the enemy heard that we were moving our whole force and thus commenced a retreat. They no doubt expect us to follow them to Bull Run again. But in this they will be disappointed, for we will hardly commit that blunder again—at least I hope not. Yet we are going to advance somewhere soon. You may look for stirring news, for our army will be put in motion any day. . . .

Camp Seminary, October 1st 1861

My dear Ellen,

I don't know where you are but thought I would write you and let you know that I am well.

If you have not stopped at Philadelphia and bought those watches, I want you to *go right down and attend to it*. I hope you will listen to me in this matter.

I am well and getting along finely. We are to be ready at a moment's warning. We expect the enemy to strike somewhere but can't tell where. There is something in the wind.

Lieutenant. Col. Tucker is under arrest by Kearny. I condemn Kearny for doing it. I have no sympathy whatever with the young aspirant. He did not do the fair thing with me, but now he calls me in for counsel and advice. Kearny will soon have all of our officers under arrest. Some are always in that fix. Yet he now treats me decently. . . .

Headquarters, Camp Seminary, October 5th 1861

My dear Ellen,

I have just come out of prayer meeting, where our little praying group have been assembling. I feel very tired, having been very much engaged all day. . . .

---

federates withdrew hastily. The "works" at Munson's Hill, a New Jersey officer wrote disgustedly, turned out to be "of the most absurd character." Cannon were nothing but logs cut and daubed with black paint. "The whole thing has been a grand humbug and bugaboo!" James F. Rusling, *Men and Things I Saw in Civil War Days* (cited hereafter as Rusling, *Civil War Days*) (New York, 1899), 199; Stevenson, *"Boots and Saddles,"* 51–52. Cf. Adam Gurowski, *Diary* (Boston, 1862), I, 101; de Peyster, *Philip Kearny*, 208–9.

We are drilling every day in the hardest kind of style—men carrying their knapsacks to prepare them for long marches. I acted as Brigadier General today and gave the commands. I got along very well and was mightily complimented. Tomorrow Lieut. Col. Tucker takes his hand at it, and the next day I take the command again. This is with the 1st and 2nd Battallions that he drills as a Brigade—going through all the evolutions of the line. On Monday and Saturday Col. [George] Taylor commands the 3rd and 4th in the same way. Genl. Kearny commands the whole four battallions. I like it very much, and it is such an advantage to me in studying military tactics. You may ask where Col. Torbert is. He went to Washington today; but if he had been here, I would still have drilled, as Genl. Kearny wants all of us at it. I must say that Col. Torbert is the best drill officer that I have yet seen. There is not a man in the Division that can begin to drill with him. Kearny is nowhere beside him.

I am studying very hard and spend but few idle moments. I don't read the papers for want of time. You know more about the war movements than I do, except those immediately around here. I want you to subscribe to any paper you think proper for the children. The *Times* is a good paper. I prefer a good daily paper to the light trash. . . .

I met with a little misfortune last night. After retiring and falling asleep, I waked up with my bed on fire. A spark from a candle must have caught it as I was tucking in the clothes around me—while the candle was sitting close by on a camp stool. No damage was done except holes burnt through the comforts, the new one among the rest. I sent one to Alexandria today to my washwoman to mend, and tomorrow I will send the other two. I have just been thinking that they will not look very well. If you would make one or two nice ones, not too wide, and send them to me, I could give the other ones to the soldiers. But I can do with them if you can't conveniently make new ones. I was not burned in the least. Having the blanket next to me kept the fire off me. . . .

Headquarters, 1st N.J. Regt., Camp Seminary, Virginia
October 7th 1861

My dear daughters, Sarah and Henrietta,

. . . We, as you are aware, have had no battle yet. The enemy has moved back two or three miles, making the field over which we ride very large. It takes me five or six hours to go round our outposts.

I told you that we have had no battle yet. On the other hand, some of our friends and neighbors have. Col. Taylor's son [28] is here on a visit. He and Dr. Cox [29] rode out to see our outpost pickets. Then they took a notion that they must make an excursion towards the enemy lines. They took with them eight men as bodyguards and also a company—in case they got in a tight place they had to defend. After having travelled less than a mile, Dr. Coxe and Taylor (being in the advance) discovered the enemy close on their front.

Dr. Coxe exclaimed: "For God's sake, don't shoot me!"

The Rebs said, "Halt, then."

"We are halted," Dr. Coxe replied.

Yet the mule on which the doctor was mounted was determined not to be taken prisoner. Then, just as the doctor said he would give himself up, the mule wheeled around and ran. Taylor's horse followed. The Rebs fired at them and at the men on foot. Three of the latter were wounded, but the doctor and Mr. Taylor were not hit by the balls—though one went through Taylor's cap.

One of the privates in the bodyguard will lose his arm, and I don't know that any of the three wounded will ever be able to do service again. Rather a dear pleasure excursion, we think. Dr. Coxe is always getting into these scraps.

I have nothing new to communicate to you, as we have not fought any battles yet. But we scared the enemy back from Munson's Hill and Mason's Mill, even though the New Yorkers get all the credit for it, as usual. They have three newspaper reporters here on the grounds, and a part of our Division are New Yorkers. Of course they do everything according to the reporters' stories. But the fact is: the advance movement was made by our troops, and the enemy, seeing us, retreated. Taking the hint, the New Yorkers came out and marched into the forts after we had driven the Rebels out. Fort Mason was taken by the 4th New Jersey Regiment before the New Yorkers got there. Our Jersey boys drove the enemy out twice. The enemy force at the other fort retreated before our army got to them, so we of course had no fighting to do. I have no doubt but that we will have a forward movement soon. . . .

I wrote to your mother several times to come home by Philadelphia and buy the watches, but she did not do so. I then wanted her to go down and see you and attend to it. I don't know that she will. I want to buy you a watch and chain, and also one for your mother.

28. This was young Archibald S. Taylor. See *Biographical Record of Warren County*, 500–1.

29. Lorenzo L. Coxe was surgeon of the 3rd New Jersey.

I wanted you all to have them as keepsakes—bought with money I earned in my country's service—to remind you that I love my country and am willing to fight for it. . . .

Headquarters, 1st N.J. Regt., October 9th 1861

My dear Ellen,

The knowing ones say we are to move on Friday towards Aquia Creek to attack the enemy on the left flank. As to the certainty of this, I can't tell; but I think it very possible. There is to be a grate and grand movement of our army very soon. You will hear stirring news. . . .

Headquarters, 1st N.J. Regt., Camp Seminary
October 10th 1861

My dear Ellen,

I have just returned from Washington, where I went today in company with Maj. Herbert,[30] who was on a visit here. Genl. Montgomery was along and we acted as his aides. We intended to call on Simon Cameron but found him absent. We called on the President but found him too busy to see us, he being closeted with Secretary [of the Treasury] Salmon P. Chase. We called on Adjutant General Lorenzo Thomas, but he was not in. Our object in seeing Cameron was to get him to appoint me colonel in some regiment, if there was a vacancy. But he was not at home. However, I have written to Brother Nelson to work that card. We also called on Genl. McCleland,[31] but he was away. New Jersey has to raise two more regiments, and my friends are at work to get me appointed colonel of one of them. I very fortunately met a number of the very men from New Jersey I wanted to see: Maj. Alison,[32] Mr. Striker [33] (who is said to have more influ-

30. Charles M. Herbert was a state disbursing officer and quartermaster.
31. A 34-year-old native of Philadelphia, George B. McClellan had graduated second in the West Point class of 1846. He was a highly successful railroad executive when the Civil War began. McClellan wasted no time in returning to the army. In June-July, 1861, he won a series of miniature victories in the hills of western Virginia. These successes, coming at a time of Northern reverses elsewhere, led to his appointment late in July as supreme commander of all troops in and around Washington. McClellan skillfully reorganized the scattered units into the tightly knit Army of the Potomac.
32. Thomas S. Allison was head of New Jersey's Military Pay Department.
33. A delegate to the 1861 Peace Conference, Thomas J. Stryker then resided in Trenton. In 1867 his son William became the state's adjutant general.

ence with the Governor than any other man in the State), Genl. Paryne,[34] and our congressman, Perry.[35] All of them have promised me their support.

I will write to the Governor on the subject. So will Genl. Montgomery; and my constant friend, Maj. Hatfield, will do all he can for me. The Governor still is said to be my friend. He would have appointed me in preference to anyone else but for a systematic misrepresentation, as well as falsehoods, put forth not by our men but by those seeking the post and their friends. Yet my chance is still thought to be good. If Col. Charles Scranton would do the right thing with me, he could help me in this matter. I am satisfied that last time he did not do what he could and should have don. If he had heard some of our friends talk about it, he would have waked up. . . . If I had gon to Trenton, talked in person with the Governor, and told him the truth as to these false reports, I would today be Colonel. I hope you are not railing out against the Governor. I beg of you to say nothing.

As for Mr. Dick: I wish you to tell Mr. Wiestling to send him $100 and charge me with the same. Mr. Dick said in his letter that he needed this amount. I sympathize with Mr. Dick and his family, for I see so many families around here in the same condition—formerly wealthy, but now with everything taken from them or destroyed. We must not be so selfish as to let our friends thus suffer. Send on the draft, by all means; don't delay it. . . .

I bought a first-rate field glass today for fifteen dollars. It is an indispensable article on the field of action which I will carry with me whenever I ride out. I have got a thick, warm uniform coat, lined, walled, and plain, and calculated for the field of operations. It is not as good a mark to shoot at as the full dress coat, which I will not take with me. They have all cost me much money, but I had to have them. . . .

We have not moved yet but are expecting the order daily. I don't know where we are to go or anything about it. But a grand movement is on foot. . . .

Camp Seminary, Virginia, October 13th 1861

My dear Ellen,

. . . Yesterday I was Field Officer of the Day and was out all day. I made some changes—advanced the center line of our pickets

---

34. Lewis Perrine served from 1855 to 1865 as quartermaster general of New Jersey.

35. Nehemiah Perry represented the Newark district in the 37th Congress.

towards the enemy lines. After doing this, I went down to our left to visit at Edsall's Hill the companies of the 3rd New Jersey stationed there. I also extended our pickets down to the Orange & Alexandria R.R. I was making my way back to the Little River Turnpike to visit our pickets on the center of our line, whom I had ordered to advance. One of our lieutenants, Tantrum,[36] was accompanying me. Passing through a thick wood, we heard firing and felt satisfied that it was our pickets and the enemy engaged in daily conflict. We started at full speed through the woods, soon reached the pike, and up it towards the enemy's lines we went.

My war horse, Charley, full of speed, seemed to know that something was wrong. He pushed forward rapidly until we met a few of our cavalry retreating at full speed. I stopped them and inquired what was wrong. They replied that the enemy fired upon them, &c. I ordered them back, and up the hill we went. There we met the pickets retreating. I asked why they did not stand their ground. They answered that the enemy in a large body was flanking them. I then collected our forces at the foot of the hill where they said the enemy was coming.

The enemy was not on hand. I rode up to the top of the hill and found our men in line of battle. We had now about fifteen men, independent of four horsemen, but our numbers were increasing. I got out my glass and discovered what they called the enemy—which looked to me very much like our own soldiers scattered all around. I now determined to send out patrols. But on looking around, as is usual on such occasions, our horsemen I found to be gone. Lieut. Tantum, as brave an officer as I would want, knew what I wanted and started off towards the enemy alone. I also sent forward the scouts in the same direction.

All of them returned in a half hour. They informed me that the "enemy" were the Cameron Riflemen,[37] who went out scouting, made contact with the Rebels, and had to retreat towards our lines, leaving their dead and wounded on the grounds. A messenger was sent to me, asking assistance to collect the casualties. I granted it. We then moved up the pike and they advanced down the hill in scouting order. We reached the ground where the battle was fought and found three dead and several wounded, but no enemy. They had retreated, if there were any—of which I have some doubt. After examining the matter, questioning our own men and the Cameron Guards, I really fear that the

36. Lt. William H. Tantum of Co. B became captain of the same unit in August, 1862. He served in that capacity for the remainder of the war. *N.J. Record,* I, 73.

37. "Cameron Rifles" was the nickname of the 68th New York.

deadly fire was from our own men. But I have not said so publicly.

One thing is against this view of the subject—there were only about 5 or 6 of our men, and the guards say that they found 3 dead and 6 wounded. It is not likely that our squad could do much fatality in one volley. But the enemy were in the neighborhood, and it is probable they came down the pike, fired, then retreated, and, as is charged, fired from the cornfield.

I returned home at dark, having been in the saddle all day. My horse had had nothing to eat, and yet he came home kicking up his heels and squealing. He is a noble anamel, and never seems to tire. I often ride him day and night, and he is always the same.

I went to bed last evening expecting to start out at one o'clock to visit the pickets. But I was roused up in the middle of the night with a message that I was not to go, as we had orders to be ready to march at daylight, and that I must report at half past four this morning at Kearny's headquarters, which I did. I got orders to go out on a line of pickets and notify them to be ready to fall in with their regiments as we advanced. I did so. But it was all a false alarm, and we were left the privilege of having the balance of the Sabbath to ourselves. The order came from Genl. McClellan, who thought that the enemy were going to make an attack on our right flank. . . .

I see all around me ruin and desolation—families of wealth who can hardly get the necessaries of life. *Oh, the desolation of war.* You may well thank God that your lot has been cast in a land of peace and plenty. . . . We may soon have to move from here. Let us pray God for protection through this dark hour of our Country's history. . . .

Camp Seminary, Virginia, October 16th 1861

G. B. Wiestling, Esq.

Dear Friend,

I am writing you this morning of a skirmish that seven men on our outpost pickets had with the Rebs yesterday morning. . . . Jordan Sibley's [38] funeral took place today, and his remains were laid in the grave. His bravery is the theme of conversation on every lip. We concluded to pay him more than the usual honors to a private, and all of the Regiment not on duty turned out for the services. We performed the funeral in real military style—the band playing, &c.

From the Sergeant in command of that picket post I learned the

---

38. Pvt. Jordan Silvers of Co. A was the only Federal fatality in the Oct. 15 affair which McAllister was about to describe. *N.J. Record*, I, 72; *OR*, V, 238.

following facts. A little to the left of the Little River Turnpike, about one mile in advance and in sight of our pickets, is a heavy piece of woods. The enemy's cavalry are posted in these woods. One horseman was in the habit of coming out into the pike and throwing up his sword, as much as to say: come, if you dare. Our seven men took position in the cornfield extending on both sides of the road and finally shot him. Then came about 40 Rebel horsemen at full speed. Our boys fired and, they say, emtied nine of their saddles. Among those that they killed was the Lieutenant who led the cavalry. We have his blanket and sword with his name on it.

Jordan Silvers was surrounded by three of these horsemen who jumped the fence. He killed one of them and did not have time to reload. He was in the act of drawing his bayonet on one of the others when he was shot by a pistol ball that passed through his arm, entered the body, went through his heart and out the other side of his body. Two of our men besides him was either killed or taken prisoner. Their names are Donly and Nickales,[39] both from Elizabeth. One cap was found with a bullet hole through it, which is proof that one more was killed. That was Donnelly. Nichols was seen to fall; but his being killed is not certain. The other four men escaped and retreated to their posts. It was a fatal skirmish, but it was the best skirmish fight that we have yet made. Our men have certainly fought with unusual bravery.[40] . . .

Today our men were ordered out to drive the enemy from those woods. But when we were all ready to start, the order was countermanded, so we all attended Silver's funeral. It is possible that we may go out tomorrow, but I don't know. The enemy are very bold here. The time for fighting has come, and you will hear a grate deal of such work.

If you look on your map of the seat of war and pass your eye along the Little River Turnpike, you will see what is called Benton's Tavern.[41] A little to the side of it is this battleground. We can see

---

39. Pvt. James Donnelly of Co. A was discharged from service shortly after this engagement. Pvt. Alphonso I. Nichols of the same company served out his three-year enlistment. *N.J. Record,* I, 70, 71.

40. The one official report of this Oct. 15 action is in *OR,* V, 238. "These skirmishes," stated one writer, "were only important in so far as they trained the men to vigilance and celerity of movements, though they undoubtedly gave a spice to the otherwise dull and monotonous life of the camps." De Peyster, *Philip Kearny,* 209.

41. Benton's Tavern was located on the south side of the intersection of Little River and Columbia turnpikes. It was approximately seven miles west of Alexandria. See *The Official Atlas of the Civil War* (cited hereafter as *Official Atlas*) (New York, 1958), Plate VII.

along the pike for about two miles, or nearly that. The road must be nearly one hundred feet wide. Corn fields lay right and left, and woods to the right and left of these fields. In these woods are concealed the enemy. They can slip along this road without being seen and make a dash on our pickets. Company A has the advance post on this pike, and Company F is about one mile in the rear on the same road. They are to advance forward when they hear firing. Yet this fight was all over before they could get there. Company F is the one in which Warner is a lieutenant. He was crazy to be in the fight. Had he been there, he would have fought like a lion.

Did I tell you that he and William Henry took a ride out to the crossroads? They kept going and took several shots at the enemy until they were in time fired upon.

Lieut. E. G. [George] Brewster has been promoted to a captain to replace [William] Birney, who has been assigned as a major to the 4th New Jersey. Oxford Furnace men are doing well. . . .

Tell Mrs. McAllister that she must excuse me from writing to her when I write you. If you think it proper, you can show her your letters. In fact, I write to you all as a general thing. I generally write you the accounts of our doings in the way of marching and fighting, &c. . . .

Headquarters, 1st N.J. Regt., October 17th 1861

My dear Ellen,

I have not wrote you for two days because I have been writing to Mr. Wiestling, who no doubt will show you the letter. . . .

I have nothing new to communicate at present. I was down to Alexandria and saw Genl. Montgomery. He has moved into new quarters. I don't mean his office and headquarters but rather his residence—for eating and sleeping, &c. I can assure you that it is fine—large parlors handsomely furnished, bedchamber, bathing rooms all complete, kitchen and cooking utensils—just as the Secessionists left it. The General could entertain you now, if you came.

I am urging him to apply for a major generalship, which he will do as soon as Secretary [of War] Cameron gets back. I hope he will get it.

We have delightful prayer meetings now, three or four nights a week and well attended. There is quite an interest. Two will be baptized this coming Sabbath. I hope you all will continue to pray for the outpouring of God's holy spirit upon us, *for oh how we do need it.* How thoughtless are the multitude around us.

I wish you to send me in the package of blankets two pairs of suspenders, good and strong. I have got a good warm coat and am getting a good vest made. I also got a couple of pairs of shoulder straps. You know you were so annoyed at mine being so faded, so I am all right now. It is right to have them nice, as that is the first thing looked at to tell one's rank. . . .

(*Next morning*) Dear Ellen, A stormy night. Rain poured down in torrents. It stopped this morning. I am Officer of the Day for this Friday and am just getting ready to go out.

Sad news has just come to camp. The Sergeant Major of the 4th New Jersey lost his life last night.[42] He advanced beyond our line of pickets. After scouting for some time, he was returning by another route. He came up to his own pickets, was challenged, but did not give the countersign. The pickets opened fire, and he was killed. . . .

Camp Seminary, Sabbath Morning, October 20th 1861
My dear wife,

I came off Brigade Officer of the Day duty yesterday morning quite sick. After making out my report and returning from Genl. Franklin's Headquarters [43] (where Genl. Kearny sent me on business), I went to bed and staid there until noon. I feel much better and will soon be well again. . . .

Oh, the distress caused by this wicked rebellion. Amongst the most wealthy families all around me, devastation and ruin are everywhere. . . .

Any clothing you and the Misses Scranton think proper to send will be thankfully received. . . . Blankets are the most needed of anything else. One blanket is all the Government allows a soldier. How they're supposed to keep warm is a mystery to me. Comforts will do, but they are not so convenient to carry. While in camp, they are first-rate; but if they get wet, they are not like a blanket—they do not dry so well. Undershirts always come good, drawers the same. Let the ladies do their duty and they will save many a poor soldier's life during the coming winter. If we advance—which we will do, of course, we will have no tents and only what we can carry. We will

42. *N.J. Record,* I, 183, erroneously gives Oct. 28, 1861, as the date when Sgt. Maj. Thomas S. Bonney of the 4th New Jersey was killed on picket duty.

43. William B. Franklin, who graduated first in the West Point class of 1843, was a sober and serious Regular Army officer. He was then in command of a division composed of the brigades of Kearny, Henry W. Slocum, and John Newton. *OR,* Vol. V, p. 16; Vol. LI, Pt. 1, pp. 461, 466.

have to lay on the cold, damp ground, so you see the necessity of warm clothing. I fear that the advance will be thrown into cold weather. If so, it will be very hard for many to endure the cold unless we go down south. . . .

Camp Seminary, October 21st 1861

My dear Ellen,

. . . I feel much better this morning. My fever has left and I can move around with ease. I think I will go down to Alexandria today and do a little business and see our old friend, Genl. Montgomery.

This morning is quite cool. There is talk of us moving this week. . . . Maj. Hatfield is now here and takes his place today. . . .

If you have not sent my things yet, I wish you would include one dozen white cotton gloves. They cost me twenty-five cents a pair here, and only cost about ten cents at home. . . .

Camp Seminary, October 22nd 1861

My dear Ellen,

I wrote you this morning, telling you I was drawing up a furlough to go home. Col. Torbert and Genl. Kearny both signed it and sent it up to [General] Franklin. He returned it to me, saying that all the furloughs sent up for the last several days to Genl. McClellan have been returned without his signing them, and that it was useless to continue sending them. This is in view of an onward movement. They want all hands, and we will all have enough to do. I was not too much disappointed, for I did not leave myself think that I would get the leave of absence. But, dear, I could not help thinking what a delightful time I would have had with my family and friends. . . .

1st Regiment, N.J.V., October 23rd 1861

Sarah and Henrietta, my dear daughters,

. . . We are still here but expect every day to move. No furloughs are now granted. Everything indicates a forward movement. I have no doubt but that you will hear of stirring battles and hard fighting before many days roll around.

I have been sick and off duty for a few days, but am now well again and on duty. The weather is wet and damp. I had hoped to get a furlough, come to your city, get you both, and then run up home and see your mother. Would it not have been delightful! But though I asked for only five days, I could not get it. You may ask why I did not seek a furlough sooner. I could not because a portion of that time I was in command of the Regiment, and also because Maj. Hatfield was home sick and did not resume his post until Monday. I have had a hard and busy time, yet now I get along easier. But when we advance, then comes the tug of war.

In regard to William Lloyd,[44] tell him that as soon as I get command of a regiment I will get him a post of honor. I do not have the forms right now; besides, there are so many applications for everything in the shape of an office. I think I can do something for him by and by. . . .

Camp Seminary, October 25th 1861

My dear Ellen,

. . . We are all quiet here. News of the enemy crossing the river has reached us, but we don't know of its correctness. If true, we will have fighting without advancing. . . .

We had a very heavy frost here this morning. In fact, it is nearly as cold here as at home.

I have the Rev. Dr. Baird [45] with me. He was sent out by the Young Men's Christian Association of Philadelphia to ascertain the spiritual wants of our army. We are commencing a new organization here called the Havelock Association. Its object is the promotion of religion in our army. It originated with the Doctor and myself during the first visit he made here and while we were lying in bed in our tent. I have no doubt but that it will be the means of doing a great deal of good. I will write you more in regard to it, and you will soon see about it in the papers. . . . We hope soon to see these organizations all through the army. . . .

We have just learned that Genl. Stone has had to retreat across

44. This was the beginning of closer ties between the McAllister and Lloyd families. In August, 1862, William H. Lloyd was commissioned an officer in McAllister's 11th New Jersey. His brother, Wilson Lloyd, married McAllister's daughter Sarah the following year.

45. The Rev. S. J. Baird was one of the first agents of the U.S. Christian Commission. See Lemuel Moss, *Annals of the United States Christian Commission* (Philadelphia, 1868), 103, 602.

[88] ✼ THE McALLISTER LETTERS

the Potomac River and that it is more than likely we will have to move today.[46] . . .

       1st N.J. Regt., Camp Seminary, October 29th 1861
My dear daughters,
  Enclosed you will find three Geranium plants which you will place between the leaves of some book. The two large ones are from the flower garden at Mount Vernon. A party of our officers, in company with Dr. Baird, visited that sacred place last Saturday. I could not go, as I was Brigade Officer of the Day, so the Doctor presented me with these two large leaves. I told him that I would give them to my daughters. The small leaf was presented to me the same day as I was riding towards our outpost pickets in company with my particular friend, Dr. Paul,[47] a very excellent and witty gentleman on a visit here. We called at a Mrs. Richardson's,[48] a member of the F.F.V. from whom I have received a greate deal of kindness. Mrs. Richardson is an accomplished lady—but at heart a Secessionist, having two sons in the army of our enemy. But, notwithstanding this, she is remarkably kind to our officers and soldiers, many of whom have enjoyed the family's hospitality. I have often been invited to dine and to take tea, but time would not permit it. One night, while on duty, I staid at their house. I frequently call when I pass by. . . .
  The Mount Vernon plants I call Union, and the little delicate plant I call Secession. I hope it will soon be smothered by the grate overpowering plants of the Union. . . .

        Camp Seminary, October 31st 1861
My dear Ellen,
  It is now nearly bedtime. A few hours more and this month is gon from us, never to return. What a sad thought. I feel gloomy this

  46. An expedition on the upper Potomac by forces under Gen. Charles P. Stone ended in an Oct. 21 disaster at Ball's Bluff. Among the 921 Federal casualties were Senator Edward Baker, a grandson of Paul Revere, and a son of Oliver Wendell Holmes. The Ball's Bluff debacle led to the formation of the Congressional Joint Committee of the War to investigate this and other blunders of the military.
  47. Dr. J. Marshall Paul, Sr., of Belvidere had retired from the active practice of medicine. He was then an industrious elder in the same Presbyterian church which McAllister attended. Snell, *Sussex and Warren Counties,* 516.
  48. Probably Mrs. Johanna Richardson, the widow of Frank Richardson of the Alexandria area. She is the only widow listed in the extant city directories of that era.

evening from the fact that I have not received any letters from you since the beginning of the week. I fear that you are sick. . . .

We are still here but, as usual, expecting to move very soon. This was Muster Day with us. Review, inspection, and muster takes place preparatory to making out payrolls so that we can receive our pay for the last two months. We expect to get this in a few days. When I receive mine, I will send you, if I am spared, $250 at least. With this you can buy Henrietta's watch, silverware for your table, or anything you choose. . . . You will only have a watch to buy for Henrietta, as she already has a splendid chain. When that is done, I will have fulfilled a promise I made to you long since and also to the children to buy each of you a watch. I particularly desired it now, as I wish to give each of you a lasting keepsake. I did not come to the army to make money. I wish to share with all of you what little funds I may thus get for my services to the United States.

I wrote you this morning that a box came. On opening it, I found that a lid on one of the cans had busted and spilt the tomatoes out on the clothes. Beyond a few stains, it did but little harm. The comfort is very nice; indeed, everything is. All will come in good during this cold winter. . . .

I would have been pleased to have had you see our parade today. Genl. Franklin's whole Division—infantry, cavalry, and artillery—made in all about 8,000 troops.[49] It was a splendid sight. We are all drilling very hard. We have Brigade drill every day. I study military tactics and drill all the time. There is so much to learn and so much to do. Our Regiment stands A Number One in drilling. . . .

Don't direct your letters to Lieut. Robert McAllister, but to Lieut. Col. Robert McAllister. There is no Lieut. McAllister here. . . .

Camp Seminary, November 2nd 1861

My dear Ellen,

. . . Today I was relieved from my anxiety over your being sick by receiving a letter from you dated the 31st of October. It was the first I have received from you since the one you wrote me on leaving for Philadelphia. I didn't know anything about your trip to the city, nor that you bought yourself a watch. The children wrote me that. Sarah's watch is a perfect beauty. She is perfectly delighted with it. I am glad that she is so well pleased.

49. The consolidated morning report for Nov. 12, 1861, listed Franklin's division with an aggregate strength of 11,400 men. *OR,* V, 16, 650.

I received Henrietta's photograph, which I think is very good. I also received your ambrotype. I think it is much better than the one you sent me sometime since. . . . I have you, Sarah and Henrietta all standing up before me, looking right at me while I am writing this letter. When I look at you all, it reminds me of home sweet home, but the sweet voices are not there. I know not when I shall enjoy that pleasure—perhaps never. But let our united prayers go up to God day by day for the presivation of our lives, and for our meeting again and enjoying each other's society. But if He wills it otherwise, may we meet in another and better world, where there will be no parting. . . .

I would like it very well if Col. Scranton would use his influence to get me appointed colonel. I have some friends at work, and I think I will get an appointment. But I don't know. Governor Olden says I have done my duty faithfully, that he is perfectly satisfied with me as a gentleman, Christian, and as a military man, and that he holds me in high regard. He had directions from the War Department to appoint Army officers, if they could be had, to command regiments. He said that after the volunteer officers got experience that could only be had in actual service, he would not overlook their claims. I have now been in service six months, and I think I ought to know something. Well, if Governor Olden doesn't appoint me, Governor Curtin will—after I have met the enemy and resigned this post, if I live. Curtin has written Olden on the subject. This is confidential. Keep cool and say but little and all will be right. . . .

Camp Seminary, November 8th 1861

My dear Ellen,

In the morning I will receive my pay for the last two months. Then I will enclose in this letter $250, from which I wish you would buy yourself a handsome gold chain and Henrietta's gold watch. The balance of the money is at your disposal. Buy clothing for yourself and the children. . . .

I did not write you this morning. I came off field duty and did not have time. We are drilling hard and studying military tactics. I have gotten a grate deal of credit for my performance in the evolutions of the line—Brigade drill. There are no troops that drill better than ours.

Tomorrow afternoon a party of us officers are to take a ride over to Mount Vernon and visit that estate. It is about seven miles from here. We will take a look at the tomb of Washington, &c. . . .

Our men are sending home a grate deal of money. It takes about $35,000 to pay a regiment for two months. The men send about one half of it home. This is a grate relief to your county. It makes money more plentiful with you and relieves many families from want that would otherwise suffer. You ought to be thankful that you are all in a county of peace and plenty. There is a grate deal of suffering here amongst the few remaining citizens.[50] This war is desolating this land. Virginia is now reaping the bitter fruits of her treachery. Oh, how foolish she acted in taking a part against this government. This generation will not get over it. . . .

Camp Seminary, November 11th 1861

My dear Ellen,

I received today a letter from you dated the 9th. I find that most of your letters come through now in two days, which is quite an improvement. I did not write you this morning as I was very much engaged. I lost my horse and was out hunting him. The circumstances are as follows:

I went down to church in Alexandria and hitched my horse under Genl. Montgomery's shed. The General insisted on my putting him in the stable. I said to let him stand where he was, it being a comfortable place. After church I took tea with the General, and my horse broke loose and started for home. I got on one of the General's horses and rode after him. But I lost all trace of him after I reached the edge of town. I knew he would run home if he was left alone. I came home, but no horse was here. Two of our teamsters went out after him, but returned about midnight without him.

This morning I called on Genl. Franklin, who told me to take as many of the cavalry as I wanted and go around among the camps. I did so; and after two or three hours' search, I found him carrying the Colonel of the 16th New York Regiment,[51] who was busy drill-

---

50. A few months earlier Gen. Hiram Berry observed: "Alexandria . . . was under martial law. Houses deserted, stores untenanted, and grass growing in the streets, gave the place a general appearance of delapidation, making it indeed a fit nursery [for] secessionists." Edward K. Gould, *Major-General Hiram G. Berry* (Rockland, Me., 1899), 52. The "delapidation" grew worse. See William S. Lincoln, *Life with the Thirty-fourth Massachusetts Infantry in the War of the Rebellion* (cited hereafter as Lincoln, *34th Massachusetts*) (Worcester, 1879), 27.

51. Colonel of the 16th New York was Thomas A. Davies. The quartermaster of the regiment, to whom McAllister referred a few lines farther on, was probably William H. Davies. Frederick A. Phisterer (comp.), *New York in the War of the Rebellion, 1861 to 1865* (Albany, 1912), III, 1913.

ing his regiment—and Charley with his head up as proud as Lucifer. The Colonel was highly pleased with him. He said he was glad I had found him but sorry he had to lose him, for he considered him a noble horse.

Charley was walking his way home, I learned, and if left alone would have come home. But the Quartermaster of the 16th New York happened to be on the road, caught him, and took him home with him. All was right with Charley, and nothing was broken on the saddle or bridle.

I would as leave have lost $500 as to have lost Charley. He is one of the finest horses in the Brigade. Genl. Kearny would give me most any price for him. He will ride up to the mouth of cannon, stand any amount of firing, and keep time to the music on the march. When the band strikes up, he fairly dances. He stands any amount of hard riding. I would not part with him on any account.

Our camps are all rejoicing over the glorious news of our army in South Carolina.[52] Tonight's report says that Charleston is taken. That is too good, I fear, to be true. At any rate, our boys are all rejoicing over it. We need victory to cheer them up. . . .

I sleep very warm and comfortable. I have not had any fire in my tent yet. I want to get used to the cold. Our privates all have fires in their tents and are very comfortable. They are not suffering at all. If we were settled down to stay for the winter, we could fix ourselves comfortable. But we are expecting to move every day, and most likely we will go without our tents. This is the reason why I don't have fire. . . .

My time is wholly taken up. I have no doubt but that you feel lonely. If you would rather go to boarding, why do so. But everything is in so much uncertainty as to my movements that I think it best for you to remain as you are for the present. . . .

Camp Seminary, November 13th 1861

My dear Ellen,

I had not time to write you this morning, as we have had a busy day. We had a drill in the morning and a review in the afternoon of

---

52. On Nov. 7 a Federal armada of fifty ships under Flag Officer Samuel F. DuPont blasted its way into Port Royal, S.C. The capture of this important harbor midway between Charleston and the mouth of the Savannah River gave the Federal navy an ideal deep-water base for its Atlantic blockading operations.

Franklin's Division. The cavalry and artillery were not with us. We numbered about thirteen thousand. It was a splendid sight. But tomorrow we are to have about twenty thousand. Genl. McClellan is to be present and, I suppose, the President. . . .

Our New Jersey troops compare well with our neighbors, the New Yorkers.[53] We think that we are better drilled than they are. We are drilling all the time and ought to be good at it. Yesterday I drilled the 1st and 2nd Regiments as a brigade and acted as Brigadier General. I got along first rate without a mistake. Troops performed well. I can drill a brigade as well as a Brigadier, and better than some of them.

You need not make and send me any more comforts, as I have three mended up very nicely—unless you wish me to give them to the soldiers to keep them warm. None of them are suffering yet. Most of them have two blankets and all have fires in their tents.

Hold on; here comes an order. What is it? "Kearny's Brigade takes the field tomorrow at 11 o'clock, [General Henry W.] Slocum's at 11:30 [General John] Newton's at 12, and cavalry and artillery at 12:30." This is for tomorrow's grand review. You see by this how slow large bodies move. We have the right of this army, and New Jersey will have to stand an hour and a half from the time we get on the ground till all the rest are there.

Another order from Genl. Kearny. What does it say? "Three cheers for the Union, just as Genl. McClellan comes on the ground, to show our willingness to take the field against the enemies of our country." Well our boys will give it with a will, for they are fond of yelling. I do think these reviews are grate bores, a grate adieu about nothing—or rather a long time to do nothing. We all have to appear in our best bib and tucker, white gloves, &c.

Today I saw a few ladies on horseback. They are a scarce artical in these diggings. I suppose they belong to an officer's family. Many of the New Yorkers have their wives and daughters with them. . . .

Brewster was thrown from his horse as he mounted to go over to Mount Vernon. However, he was not hurt very much, for we rode over that evening. But the next morning he felt worse. He applied for a furlough to go home but was refused. I have no doubt we will leave here soon to engage in the deadly strife. I will write you as soon as I know we are going. Everything points that way. . . .

53. The New York "neighbors" were the 15th, 16th, 18th, 26th, 27th, 31st, and 32nd Regiments. Late in October a member of one of these units wrote his home-town newspaper: "Kearney's New Jersey brigade is not far from us and they have an excellent reputation." Applegate, *Arrowsmith Reminiscences*, 109.

[94] ✕ THE McALLISTER LETTERS

Camp Seminary, November 15th 1861

My dear Ellen,

. . . Genl. Montgomery has been very sick with bilious colick. Mrs. Montgomery has come and is attending him. He is better today and there is hope of his recovery. I went down to see him today.

We are to move onward very soon. I'm going to try for a furlough to go home for seven days. Genl. Kearny and Genl. Franklin both say that they will do what they can to get it through, but it will in all probability be defeated by Genl. McClellan—as nearly all are now.[54] I am going to try to do it anyway. If I am ordered away before the furlough runs out, they will telegraph me and I will return at once. . . .

Our grate review came off yesterday and a very fine one it was.[55] Our New Jersey troops got the praise in appearance and marching. We are well drilled. There is no doubt but that we will need this for the future battlefields.

I want to go down to Mount Vernon tomorrow but may not be able to get off. Col. Torbert is sick; he has a terrible cold. He is looking miserable. I don't think he will be able to stand a campaign. My health is now very good. . . .

Camp Seminary, November 17th 1861

My dear daughter [Sarah],

. . . Yesterday was quite cold. This morning it has moderated and is quite pleasant, with the appearance of rain. . . .

I am glad that Slidell and Mason are caught.[56] These ringleaders are the ones that ought to suffer, not their poor deluded following. . . .

I did not get to Mount Vernon, as I wrote Henrietta I would.

---

54. On the previous day, and unknown to McAllister, his two daughters wrote no less than McClellan himself and requested a furlough for their father! They described eloquently and at length his faithfulness to duty and personal sacrifices since entering military service. "We did not intend to encroach upon your time by a long letter," the two girls concluded, "but before closing we would wish you 'God speed' in all your noble efforts to save our Union." Sarah and Henrietta McAllister to George B. McClellan, Nov. 14, 1861, McAllister's compiled service file, Record Group 94, National Archives.

55. Maj. Hatfield's diary entry for that date reads: "Grand review to-day by General McClellan, 12,000 troops in the field. We were under arms from ten o'clock in the morning until 3:30 P.M." Baquet, *First Brigade,* 421.

56. Confederate diplomats James M. Mason and John Slidell were en route to Europe when they were forcibly removed from a British ship, returned to the United States, and imprisoned. This "Trent Affair" produced a serious but short-lived diplomatic crisis between the North and England.

On the day we arranged a party to go, it rained and stormed all day. The next day that we set apart for the pleasure excursion, it stormed again. So I have been disappointed in my intended visit.

You speak of the review of our Division. It came off in fine style. It was a magnificent sight—about 13,000 troops. Our New Jersey Brigade, it is said, performed better than any of the others. As to the truthfulness of this, I cannot say, as I was an actor in the scene and, of course, was busily engaged.

We have all sorts of rumors here as to where we are going. Many think we will go down south; others say that we are to go to Fortress Monroe and advance from there towards Richmond;[57] others say that we are to advance on this old and well-fortified-by-the-enemy route through Manassas and, of course, through the battleground of Bull Run. This is the very worst way we could go. Some few think that we will stay here. I do not coinside with this last view, for I am satisfied that we will move from here. Everything indicates it. There is no doubt in my mind but that we will have a grate deal of hard fighting to do and that very soon. Our troops are prepared for it.

I have just returned from church where I heard a very good sermon by the Rev. Proudfit, a son of Dr. Proudfit.[58] He is the Chaplain of the 2nd New Jersey. Our chaplain, Mr. Yard, is sick. We think we have the best chaplain of any of our regiments. He has done a grate deal of good here. We have religious meetings four and five nights a week. We have some very interesting prayer meetings, though at one time our meetings were so badly attended as to be discouraging. But God has blessed our feeble efforts, and we are happy to say that some are anxiously enjoying the way of salvation. . . .

Camp Seminary, November 19th 1861

My dear Ellen,

We had some rest from drill this evening and, in fact, all afternoon, as we were getting ready for the grate review tomorrow at Bailey's Cross Roads. You will see it in the papers. This is to be the largest we have yet had. It is said some seven divisions are to be present—from 30,000 to 100,000 troops. I think the first number is

---

57. Army rumors traveled amazingly fast. McClellan's first—and supposedly secret—memorandum relative to a peninsular campaign came forth during the latter part of November. George B. McClellan, *McClellan's Own Story* (New York, 1887), 202–3; William Swinton, *Campaigns of the Army of the Potomac* (hereafter cited as Swinton, *Campaigns*) (New York, 1866), 70n.

58. Chaplain Robert B. Proudfit was the son of John Proudfit, a well-known New Jersey cleric.

the nearest, for we will not have room for any number beyound that. It takes a large piece of ground to hold even 30,000 men. . . .

Maj. Hatfield's father is now here on a visit. I had a pleasant ride with him today out towards the outposts. He and all the family have been and are warm friends of mine. I find I have a grate many true friends in New Jersey, even though I did not get to be Colonel. . . .

Camp Seminary, November 20th 1861

My dear Ellen,

I returned here to camp last night very tired from the grate review of our troops. And a grate one it was, such as this continent has never seen. It was a larger army than Genl. [Winfield] Scott ever commanded or reviewed—60,000 soldiers all splendidly equipped, with knapsacks and blankets, haversacks and canteens—all ready, if necessary, to advance into the enemy's country.

About 1 p.m. the President and Cabinet, Genl. McClellan and staff arrived. This was announced by the roar of artillery. They then commenced reviewing the troops, who, instead of the usual presentation of arms as the officers passed, took off their hats. Cheer after cheer went up that made the valley resound with the din of human voices such as these hills and valleys had never before heard. The whole plain, far beyond what the eye could reach, was covered with one dense mass of human beings and horses. The reviewing officers and their staffs passed by at a fast canter. Yet it took them more than an hour to pass the troops, though we were closed in massed formation by divisions—one regiment ocqupying only a length of two companies, and the ballance of the regiment in the rear and facing to the front.

After this was over, we marched by column of divisions past the reviewing officers, who were stationed about three-fourths of a mile on the line of march from the point where our Regiment was standing. We marched by in fine style, our Brigade on the right. Column after column, regiment after regiment, brigade after brigade, thus passed in review. About three-fourths of a mile after passing the reviewing officers, we halted, took some refreshments, remained about a half hour, and then started for home. When we came away, this large army had not more than half passed the reviewing officers.[59] . . .

59. The Nov. 20 inspection of the Army of the Potomac was characterized as "the largest and most magnificent military review ever held on this continent." While the general effect of the review was imposing, a Maine soldier recollected

This fine display took place at Bailey's Cross Roads, about 2½ miles from here on the plain below Munson's Hill. The fort on the hill, being ocquipied by our own people, looked down on the splendid sight. Carriages and citizens were there in large numbers. Miss Taylor,[60] daughter of the Colonel, was the only lady on horseback and cut quite a spling. . . .

Camp Seminary, November 22nd 1861

My dear Ellen,

Enclosed you will please find a Geranium stem which I got at Mount Vernon yesterday. I wish you to take good care of it, plant it in a pot, and cultivate it with all care and attention. I got it from the garden planted by Washington. It was given to me by the old negro who went with Genl. Lafayette to the tomb of Washington when the General went to commune with his old friend in that solom place. The negro's story of the affair was that he did not know what Genl. Lafayette said, but that he had a long talk with Genl. Washington. These large leaves are from a bush brought by Genl. Lafayette and presented to Washington. The large enclosed stone I picked up on the shore of the river at Mount Vernon. The small pebble is from Washington's tomb. The small berries are from the outside.

I was accompanied by Adj. Henry, Lieut. Warner, and Corp. Campbell [61]—an Oxford [Furnace] party. We had a delightful time and a beautiful day. . . .

Camp Seminary, December 4th 1861

My dear Ellen,

It is now half past nine o'clock. I have to retire soon, as I must be up and start for Benton's Burnt House in the morning by 4 o'clock with two companies. One company is there now. The enemy are

---

that the affair was also "bewildering and fatiguing to the troops." Earl S. Miers (ed.), *Lincoln Day by Day: A Chronology, 1809–1865* (Washington, 1960), III, 78; Edwin C. Bennett, *Musket and Sword* (Boston, 1900), 38. For other descriptions of the review, see Stevenson, *"Boots and Saddles,"* 63–65; Newton M. Curtis, *From Bull Run to Chancellorsville* (cited hereafter as Curtis, *Bull Run*) (New York, 1906), 80–82; E. M. Woodward, *Our Campaigns* (Philadelphia, 1865), 71–72.

60. This young lady was either Caroline or Elizabeth Taylor, the two daughters of the 3rd New Jersey's commander.

61. Cpl. William Campbell served with the 1st New Jersey until his death from wounds received at Gaines's Mill.

pressing hard on our lines. They attacked us day before yesterday, killed 2 of our men and took 12 prisoners, while we killed 2 of theirs and took 3 prisoners. They came on our men unexpected and took them by surprise.[62]

I am going to take command of these companies and all the pickets—about eight companies in all, but scattered along our whole line. At Benton's we will have three companies, as this is the point where the enemy are pressing hardest. This house is on the Little River Turnpike. I will remain out there three days and nights.

I don't know what is up; something is in the wind, as large bodies of troops are collecting here. Genl. [Edwin V.] Sumner's whole division is now alongside of us. The whole country is one grate camp. . . .

Benton's Burnt House, Fairfax County, Va.
Friday, December 6th 1861

My dear Ellen,

I had a comfortable night's sleep on the soft side of a board and feel quite rested this morning. The weather is fine and not near so cold as it was.

No enemy have made their apperance since they took our men prisoners. I hardly think they will come now, as we are preparing for defense. If I have luck, I will finish my fortification by tomorrow. It is a rifle pit in the form of a half moon, with a ditch on both sides. It is situated on this beautiful spot close by the ruins of this house where the Benton family of F.F.V.'s so long resided. I write this letter sitting on the stump of one of the beautiful shade trees, now cut down, which surrounded this beautiful residence for miles around. Now all is a pile of ruins. The apple orchard was cut down to make a barricade to block a sudden charge of cavalry. Fine large boxwood, ten feet high, which adorned the garden, were cut down to make bush houses for our soldiers. Outhouses which escaped the fire have been all torn down to build kitchens and stables for our camp. Oh God forbid that this desolating war should ever reach our beautiful North. How thankful you ought all to be that you are not in the midst of it.

62. On December 2 a body of Confederate cavalry temporarily broke the Federal picket lines just to the west of the position held by Franklin's division. The routed pickets were members of the 45th New York, and strong evidence exists that they were intoxicated at the time of the attack. Total Federal losses were 1 killed and 14 captured; Confederate casualties numbered 3 killed and 2 captured. *OR,* Vol. V, pp. 451–64; Vol. LI, Pt. 1, p. 49.

The waving of that signal to the Rebels when they charged on the Cameron Rifles and fired on our pickets, which was done from these windows by Miss Benton, caused most of this destruction and no doubt will shake them up. It is indeed a beautiful place; land rather good.[63]

Miss Kniten and Miss Dupuy, in company with Mr. Dupuy, came up and took dinner with Capt. Rairison of the 2nd Regiment on Wednesday.[64] He met them when we were on the road to Mount Vernon. Miss Bell was with them. Maj. Hatfield and I thought it strange that Mr. Dupuy did not have a carriage and take them comfortably as well as decently. They were all on foot. I asked them all to take dinner with me today and have prepared for them. But here I am on the outpost and can't go in and receive them. This is a sample of a soldier's life for you. However, Maj. Hatfield is going to attend to them, as is Adj. Henry and some other officers. . . .

Camp Seminary, December 11th 1861

My dear daughters,

. . . Thursday morning at 4 o'clock I took two companies out to Benton's burnt house to prevent a surprise by the enemy. I staid four days and built a rifle pit and breastwork. We can defend the place against five times our number. It is first rate for defense. The enemies' scouts were pressing on our lines, but we cannot think their main body is moving on us. If so, all the better for us. They were very bold at this place—took 12 of our men (New Yorkers) prisoners and killed two. . . . The men were some on sentinel duty; others were roaming around very casually; and the Rebel cavalry made a dash and took them prisoner. One or two of our sentinels thought that they were our cavalry and presented arms to them and of course were taken. The alarm was given, but it was too late to catch them. They will not catch our boys asleep now. We are all on the alert and ready for them.

Yesterday evening I had a very pleasant horseback ride with Mrs. Little [65] of your city, and also Mrs. [Bernard] Peters, the wife of

63. For other references to this tavern, see Francis C. Adams, *The Story of a Trooper* (Washington, 1864), 219–20, 223.
64. The party calling on Capt. Henry O. Ryerson included attorney David A. Dupuy and his daughter Eliza.
65. Mrs. Amos R. Little's husband was co-owner of a large dry goods store on Philadelphia's Chestnut Street.

[100] ✗ THE McALLISTER LETTERS

the Editor of the *Saturday Evening Post*. Mr. Little is a well-known merchant in your city. Their husbands were with them, called at our camp, and were introduced to me by one of their number, a Mr. Evans,[66] also from your city, who had been introduced to me earlier by Mr. Dupuy. We rode out as far as Cloud's Mill. Night coming on, we returned. I expect them back tomorrow, when, if time permits, I will accompany them to the outposts. They are good riders, and it is pleasant thus to roam over this *sacred* soil. . . .

Your mother writes me that she has purchased a splendid watch and chain for Henrietta. Now take good care of your watches and wind them up regularly. And look out for pickpockets when on the street and in cars, or you will soon be missing your watches. We now have a whole family with gold watches! . . .

Camp Seminary, December 11th 1861

My dear Ellen,

. . . You and Mr. Wiestling ought not to delay too long looking for a house in Belvidere, as you may not get the one you want unless you look for it soon.

What you saw in the paper relative to the change in the appointment of army officers has not yet become a law.[67] It is but a proposition, but it is thought that it will be passed by Congress. If so, I will be promoted very soon, being the senior Lieutenant-Colonel of all the three-year volunteers. All our officers will be promoted. The President appoints, but it is in the regular line of promotion.

Col. Montgomery goes home today.[68] He says he will try for an active command and will have a talk with Governor Olden as to my claims. If he gets an active command, I want to be with him.

The weather is very warm here and perfectly delightful. Col. Torbert is in Washington again, and I am in command. He no doubt is working for promotion, as he is said to be tired of us all. The whole Regiment is down on him. The other day two poor soldiers, unable to do duty, came from the hospital. They were not attentive enough.

---

66. Probably G. H. Evans of the Christian Commission.
67. McAllister was referring to McClellan's remedial measure of organizing boards of examination to assess the ability of field officers then in service. See Oliver O. Howard, *Autobiography* . . . (New York, 1907), I, 168; Allan Nevins, *The War for the Union* (New York, 1959–1960), I, 277–82.
68. From Dec. 13, 1861, through Jan. 2, 1862, Montgomery was listed as being on "sick leave." Montgomery's service file.

Torbert flew into a passion, rode over them, and trampled them down.[69] Now, of course, the men are down on him. . . .

Camp Seminary, December 12th 1861

My Dear Ellen,

. . . I feel sad this evening from the fact that an order has come for us, and the whole Division under Genl. Franklin is to turn out tomorrow afternoon to witness the execution of a poor soldier.[70] He has been condemned to be shot. I know not the person or the circumstances connected with the case, but no doubt the sentence is all proper and right. But I do not wish to be a witness at his execution. I feel for him, yes, and pray for him. . . . Gladly would I be far away from these sad and solom scenes which we are ordered to witness tomorrow. To absent myself is not military and would cause remarks. I would love to see a pardon granted if it could be at all consistant with good discipline.

Your box has arrived, but I have not seen it yet. I will if spared get it in the morning. The men were all pleased with your gloves and thank you and Mrs. Scranton for them. Mrs. Sidgrave[71] of Philipsburg has knit and sent a pair to each of us field officers that are very nice. The ladies of Philipsburg sent Capt. Mutchler's company[72] a pair for each member. . . .

Camp Seminary, December 14th 1861

My dear Ellen,

This is Saturday evening. The bustle & excitement of the week are gone, and very soon we will pass over the threshold to the begin-

69. No proof exists of such misconduct by Torbert. On the other hand, New Jersey's wartime historian asserted, Torbert during the winter of 1861–62 "devoted himself to the work of drilling and disciplining the regiment for active service, and soon advanced it to a state of proficiency which enlisted the warmest encomiums from General Kearney and others." Foster, *New Jersey and the Rebellion*, 826.

70. On Dec. 13, 1861, just north of the Seminary, Pvt. William H. Johnson of the 1st New York Cavalry became the first man executed in the Army of the Potomac. For the details of his crime and punishment, see Adams, *Story of a Trooper*, 245–48; Stevenson, *"Boots and Saddles,"* 68–70.

71. Mrs. Charles Sidgraves was the wife of a prominent Shippensburg political commentator. See his *Warren County Politics: A Reminiscence* (Easton, Pa., 1898).

72. Co. D of the 1st New Jersey was under the command of Valentine Mutchler, who later became major of the 11th New Jersey.

ning of another week—which may, for ought we know, be our last. How many in camp at this time are looking for a way to the North, to their pleasant homes—longing to be there in the bosom of their families and friends. Yes, my thoughts often roam to my mountain home rendered delightful by your presence and the sweet voices of all the members of our family, collected around a peaceful fireside, who have so often cheered my drooping spirits. . . .

Col. Torbert has gone to Washington today and will not be back till tomorrow morning. We have in our camp a lieutenant colonel, cousin of Capt. Brewster, who is visiting him.[73] He was with Genl. [Nathaniel] Lyon when he fell [at Wilson's Creek], and he has been in a number of those skirmishes in Missouri. He tells many matters of interest . . .

I feel exceedingly bad that I did not call at the T. H. Dupuy's. I had intended to do so. But you know that I did not get to Washington until after 12 o'clock on Saturday night. At 9 o'clock on Sunday morning I called to see the children, went to church three times, and called at Dr. Harris's.[74] So my time was wholly taken up. . . .

Camp Seminary, December 15th 1861

My dear Ellen,

. . . After the usual morning dress parade and inspection, I went to church. I heard about half of Dr. Camp's [75] sermon, commencing at 10 o'clock; then came an excellent discourse at 11 by the Rev. Mr. White,[76] Presbyterian preacher from Trenton. At 3 o'clock I heard the latter part of Rev. Proudfit's sermon. And this evening at half past 6 I heard another most excellent address by the Rev. Mr. White. . . .

Today I received your letter of the 12th. Your uneasiness as to something happening to me is not real. All is quiet here on our lines. I have never had better health, and I have been very comfortable. The weather is not cold but very pleasant; in fact, it has been delightful. Whether the quietness in our lines is the calm that precedes the

---

73. Probably Col. Robert B. Mitchell of the 2nd Kansas. See *OR,* III, 56, 67, 70, 83.

74. A well-known Philadelphia physician, Dr. John Harris accompanied his wife to Washington when she went to minister to the army on behalf of the Ladies' Aid Society of Philadelphia.

75. Norman W. Camp was chaplain of the 4th New Jersey.

76. Ansley de Forest White was pastor of Trenton's Second Presbyterian Church.

storm, I know not. As to our further movements, I am completely in the dark. But time will soon tell the story. . . .

We have a grate many visitors from the North. I have made the acquaintance today of Mrs. Joseph Trimble & Mrs. Robert B. Potts, both of Camden. They are connected with the aid association [77] and have sent to our hospital quite a number of articals. They express themselves as highly delightful with everything here. They and Rev. Whiteman [78] were at dress parade this evening. All spoke in the highest terms as to the appearance and drill of our Regiment. They were particularly pleased with our closing with prayer. Our men do look very well and can perform well.

If we stay here much longer, I will write for you to make me a visit. The matron in the hospital [79] will furnish your quarters for sleeping, and you will of course board with us. These Camden ladies are with her now. She is very ladylike, kind, and obliging, and she will make you very comfortable.

Your box came all right. The chickens were very good; the cake I have not tried. The comfort and blankets came just in the nick of time. My waiter, Thomas Ellsworth, has left me, and I have another man in his place. Thomas had his own blankets and took them with him. I gave this new man, Joe, my coarse blanket and one of the oldest comforts, so that fixes him up. Those you sent take their place.

I have had a letter from brother Washington acknowledging the one I wrote to Mother. . . .

Camp Seminary, December 17th 1861

My dear Ellen,

. . . Some of our religious meetings are very interesting. Religious duties, feelings and interest are on the increase in our New Jersey regiments. May your prayers and ours go up to the thrown of God day by day for the outpouring of His holy spirit upon us. We so much need His presence in camp to bear us up against the tide of irreligion that is rolling over us like a mighty wave. I feel a grate responsibility resting upon me here when I see so many of our soldiers

77. This was the Ladies' Aid Society of Philadelphia, which faithfully delivered packages and encouragement to the men in the army.
78. The Rev. Charles Whitehead, a native of Perth Amboy, N.J., was then serving as chaplain of the New York City Hospital. See *N.J. Biographical Encyclopaedia,* 277.
79. In an unpublished portion of his next letter, McAllister referred to the matron as "Miss Barcliff." The name is probably misspelled.

going down to distruction regardless of the profession they have made, the training they have received at home, and, above all, apparently in defiance of the many prayers that have gone up in their behalf. Oh, what a world of sin this is, and how we trample God's holy hand under our feet.

A scouting party of six men and officers went out from our picket lines manned by the 2nd New Jersey. The advance guard, seeing a force of cavalry coming towards them, hollowed to the others in their rear, who had stopped at a pond to catch some geese. But the latter did not hear them and were taken prisoners. The advance wheeled and escaped, so the enemy ended up with both the men and the geese.

Genl. Kearny has left for home today to improve his health. He has been, and is, now in a doubtful condition. Some think that he will never be able to return to duty. Genl. Montgomery went home for the same purpose, but he is to be back in 20 days. He is recovering rapidly. I do wish you would go down to Bristol and see him. He and his family would like this very much. The General is such a warm friend of mine. . . . He is going to see Governor Olden to get me out of this Regiment. . . .

Camp Seminary, December 21st 1861

My dear Ellen,

. . . I had a few little things to attend to in Washington, so I got a pass and went over there. After finishing up all I had to do, and having considerable time left, I mounted my horse and went out to call on my friends, the Pattersons. Col. Patterson was not at home, but Mrs. Patterson and Mrs. Pierson were.[80] Both of them received me kindly and cordially. Mrs. Patterson had a very bad cold and was quite hoarse. She had a nice repast served up for me and had what I have never gotten since I left home—the kind of milk you give me that has all the light stuff on the top. That is what we don't get around these diggings. They take off all the light stuff, then mix it with water and, after all that, call it cream.

Col. Patterson is in New York helping to fix out their naval ex-

---

80. Carlisle P. Patterson, popularly called the father of geodetic coast survey, was the owner of "Brentwood," a vast estate that extended from the present Gallaudet College campus to 3rd Street, and from Florida Avenue to Patterson Avenue. Mrs. Eleanor Brent Pearson was the widow of Joseph Pearson and the mother of Mrs. Patterson.

peditions. He is very anxious to go in command of one of them. But Mrs. Patterson is opposed to it and thinks he can do more good where he is. You know he has taken all the soundings along our coast, has made all their surveys, and knows just what vessels are needed in their expeditions. . . .

Both Mrs. Patterson and her mother have given me a pressing invitation to dine with them on Christmas and spend the evening. I accepted the invitation on condition that I could leave the Regiment, as I would be in command at the time. Since my return here, I have been thinking I cannot do myself the pleasure and will probably have to decline. I will write a polite note to that effect. The reason is that they don't dine till 5 o'clock. I could not come home after dining and spending the evening. Having the command, it will not do to stay away at night. . . .

The news today from the line is cheering, also the news from McAll's Division on the upper Potomack.[81] This morning I saw in the Baltimore papers that Franklin's Division had all moved forward. This is a mistake, for we're all here yet, and there is no talk of our moving that I know of. . . .

Camp Seminary, Christmas Evening, 1861

My dear Ellen,

Another Christmas has come and is now almost gone. What grate reason we have to thank a kind Providence for His protecting care over us during the past year. When we look back and see the dangers we have escaped, and think how God has preserved us in the midst of these dangers, our hearts ought to go up with grateful acknowledgements to Him for His mercies. . . .

This is my first Christmas in camp and far away from my family and the endearments of home and old friends. As I stated to you, I had a very pressing invitation to spend the day with my particular friends, the Patterson family. But as I was in command of the Regiment, I considered it best to remain on the ground. I also had an invitation to a submarine ball—an underground ball. In Fort Taylor, now called Fort Worth (the fort we Jersey boys built),[82] is a large

---

81. On Dec. 20 Gen. George McCall's division of Pennsylvanians fought an engagement at Dranesville, Va., with Confederate cavalry under Gen. J. E. B. Stuart. The Southerners withdrew after a short but spirited fight, and the Federals claimed the victory. OR, V, 473–94.

82. Forth Worth stood two and a half miles west of Alexandria on the Little River Turnpike. A week after the 6th New York Artillery was transferred there,

bombproof magazine, two hundred feet long and perhaps twenty feet wide, in which the officers of the 3rd New Jersey are having a ball tonight. It is said to be a splendid affair.

Quite a number of ladies are invited and expected, but most of them are Sesesh. I suppose they are going it swell at this time. . . . Col. Taylor is like me as to our young men being so intimate with Secessionist ladies. He thinks their object is to get information to convey to the enemy. But our improved system of signals will prevent communications across the lines.

I wish you, family, and all in Juniata a Merry Christmas and Happy New Year. Give a grate deal of love to Mother, Washington's family, and lots of love to all my friends. Forget none, and tell them for me that I fondly hope that their influence and weight will be thrown in support of this war and our laws and Constitution. Without these, property or life is worth nothing. I would add that one man at home sympathizing with Rebellion is doing more harm to our cause than if they and ten more were in the Rebel army fighting against us. What is wanted now is True Patriotism. The man who doesn't give hearty support to our bleeding country in this day of our country's trial is not worthy to be a descendant of our forefathers, and he ought to be denied the protection of our laws and shipped at once to South America, where they will have a government that suits them.

My prayers are that every friend I have will stand up for our country and place his dependance on God. . . .

Camp Seminary, December 27th 1861

My dear Ellen,

. . . I have nothing new to write. Everything is quiet in our camp, and we are fixing up for winter. But Genl. Franklin says that we are not going to stay here this winter—notwithstanding all the apparent preparations. . . .

Tell William Banks [83] that I wish him a grate deal of happiness in the matrimonial world, and that I think he and all young active

---

one of its members wrote home: "Here we are encamped on a side hill, outside the work, the mud about eight inches deep, very little to eat, and plenty of work. If you could just look in upon us now, and see how I live, you would scarcely believe your eyes." *"More Than Conqueror," or Memorials of Col. J. Howard Kitching* (cited hereafter as Kitching, *Memorials*) (New York, 1873), 31.

83. William Banks was McAllister's nephew and a native of Mifflintown, Pa.

men ought to be in the army to help us put down this wicked and unjustifiable rebellion. Our country and property is worth nothing if we don't, nor will life be secure. We will be held responsible before God if we don't do our part in helping to transmit this boon of civil & religious liberty down to succeeding generations. Our glorious institutions are likely to be destroyed; will we not help to save them? Our house is on fire; shall we stand by and watch it burn and not raise a helping hand to pute it out? . . .

Patriotism, hast thou fled with the sound of the cannon at the fall of Fort Sumpter, when the Star Spangled Banner was lowered in the dust? Oh no, the sound of Sumter's cannon is still ringing in our ears and has already kindled the martial fire in millions of our people and caused a half million to fly to arms to save our land. If we fall, another half million will take our place. And if nasty England pokes her nose into our private quarrel, we must make war a business and lick her along with the rebel South, and then make Canada ours. Our cry should be: "To arms! To arms! Go forth and falter not in this hour of our country's trial!" . . .

Camp Seminary, December 29, 1861

My dear Ellen,

. . . The report about an artillery battle turns out to be all a hoax from beginning to end. The enemy were not at Poplar Church at all.

Mrs. Harris [84] was here yesterday and returned to Washington last evening. She is doing good work in the army. Is it not strange that a delicate lady as she is could stand it so well? It shows the necessity of *exercise*.

I think we will have a battle before long. Exactly when, I don't know. . . .

84. Mrs. John Harris, "an extremely delicate . . . woman of culture and fine address," volunteered at war's outset to become first field representative of the Ladies' Aid Society of Philadelphia. She performed outstanding work in the field and elicited praise from McAllister in several of his letters. See also Robert to Nelson McAllister, undated letter, McAllister Papers; L. P. Brockett, *Woman's Work in the Civil War* (Philadelphia, 1867), 149–60; George G. Meade (ed.), *The Life and Letters of George Gordon Meade* . . . (cited hereafter as *Letters of George G. Meade*) (New York, 1913), II, 144.

Camp Seminary, Va., December 29th 1861

My dear Ellen,

I wrote you a few lines this morning; but I was very much hurried, as I had to eat breakfast and have dress parade and inspection—all before 9 a.m. After this I attended church and heard an excellent sermon by Rev. [George R.] Darrow, the Chaplin of the 3rd Regiment. At 3 p.m. I heard another sermon by Rev. Proudfit, Chaplain of the 2nd. This evening, at half past 6, our Regiment has its meeting. Mr. Yard is home on a furlough. Mr. Darrow or someone else will preach for us. We always have a full house in the evening. Our priviliages for divine service and religious meeting are most excellent here. If we always could have such priviliages, how I would like it. When we move from this place, we will not be so well off. But oh! How hard it is to get persons to make good use of these golden opportunities! How prone we are to wander away—far away into the pattern of sin. We have many instances here where members of churches have gon far on the road of ruin, and to all appearances will everlastingly seal their fate. Oh! How much we need your prayers, and those of all good Christians! . . .

The Tattoo has now been beat, and very soon our camp will be in the arms of sleep. A sad thought has just crossed my mind: this is the last Sabbath of the year. Yes, this Tattoo has just reminded me that the Sabbaths of 1861 are no more. They are numbered with the things that are gon and past. And sad indeed must be the thought to us all, especially when we reflect on the idle Sabbath days we have spent, the blessed priviliages we have trampled under our feet, and the deaf ear we have turned to the warning voice that has come to us in language that can not be misunderstood. . . .

You ask me to pray for you. Do you suppose that I would forget one so near and dear to me? No, it cannot be. I could not be a Christian if I forgot to pray for own dear family and friends. A Christian can not live without prayer. . . .

3

The Winter Ends at Yorktown

IF IMPATIENCE or enforced inactivity had been fatal maladies, Lieutenant Colonel McAllister would have succumbed at Alexandria in the war's first winter. The new year brought daily rumors that McClellan's colossus, the Army of the Potomac, was going to shake off the cobwebs of inertia and move southward toward Richmond. McAllister faithfully accepted every such report. Although the mighty army remained sprawled along the banks of the Potomac, he continued his daily hopes and expectations of an offensive.

In February Ellen McAllister spent several days at Fairfax Seminary with her husband. But the weather spoiled the visit. Continual rains turned the camp of the New Jerseyans into a sea of mire. The "Sunny South," McAllister complained, consisted of "mud, mud." He freely criticized the backwardness of northern Virginia, never seeming to realize that the war of which he was a part had wrought Virginia's miserable appearance.

The long-awaited advance came in March. Kearny led the New Jersey Brigade in a move on Centreville, and a company from McAllister's regiment had the honor of being the first Federals to enter the former Confederate stronghold. McClellan's army then began embarking at Alexandria for an invasion of the Virginia Peninsula. At first it appeared that McAllister's brigade would remain behind as part of the

Washington defenses—a possibility that ran counter to the troops' preference and good morale. Three weeks of anxious waiting followed. "We are drilling, drilling," McAllister moaned, "and I am sick and tired of it."

Then came orders for the New Jersey regiments to board ships. By mid-April, as part of General William B. Franklin's division, the 1st New Jersey was at Pequosin Bay, just south of Yorktown. McAllister looked forward to the one grand battle which, he was certain, would end the war. His belief that McClellan was "destined to be one of the greatest men of the age" was not shared by all his contemporaries. Of the campaign about to begin, the gossipy Washington bureaucrat Adam Gurowski wrote: "Would God that all this ends not in disaster. If it ends well it will be the first time success has crowned such transcendent incapacity." [1]

♣

Camp Seminary, Va., January 1st 1862

My dear Ellen,

Genl. Kearny returned today. You know that he has been absent on furlough for some time on account of bad health.[2] He has returned some improved but not well. He gave a dinner party today, at half past 4 p.m., to which I was invited. I hesitated about going, but in military circles an invitation is binding and you can't decline.

Genl. Kearny lives in Bishop John's house, close by this place.[3] The family are Secessionists and left house and everything in a hurry.

---

1. Gurowski, *Diary*, I, 197.
2. Kearny was sickly all his life, a fact he effectively masked by seemingly boundless energy. "Days of constant exposure and activity were often succeeded by sleepless suffering," his biographer stated. "He aged terribly during the short period of his generalship . . ." De Peyster, *Philip Kearny*, 222. See also Baquet, *First Brigade*, 422.
3. An Alexandria resident once described the Rt. Rev. John Johns, Bishop of Virginia, as "genial, lovable, and strong mentally, as befits a father in the church." His home was situated just down the hill from the Seminary. It was "an elegant mansion, supplied with all modern improvements, and from which a beautiful view of the surrounding country was had." A New York cavalryman stationed there added: "This mansion, with its grounds laid out with such good taste, was the property of a bishop, who had strayed from his flock when the war began, and gone down South, where 'his sympathies' were to assist Mr. Davis in setting

It is, as all the houses near here, handsomely furnished. Genl. Kearny met us at the door, ushered us into the parlour, and introduced us to Genls. [William B.] Franklin, [Samuel P.] Heintzelman, [William H.] French, and [O. O.] Howard. Some of our colonels were present—but not Col. Torbert, for he had gone to Washington. Colonels [James H.] Simpson, [Isaac M.] Tucker, [William B.] Hatch, and the senior captain of each regiment, together with a senior lieutenant from each regiment, were there. Capt. Brewster was among the number. Although not a senior captain, he is a favorite of Genl. Kearny's. In all, there were eighteen of us in uniform, including Genl. Kearny's staff.

Now you know the party; and I think I can hear you and the ladies say—womanlike—what had you on the table? In the first place, in the center stood a large frame more than three feet high, around which was twined evergreens stuck full of lighted candles. On top of this was a horizontal wheel in the form of a fan, moved around by the heat from the burning candles.

And now the courses: first, oyster soup; second, chicken; third, roast turkey; fourth, venison; fifth, Irish custards; sixth, apples, nuts, &c. Then we adjourned to the parlour, where tea was served us by waiters. In addition to all this, there were wines. Genl. Howard and I did not partake of them, as we are total abstainers. Genl. Howard is as strict in everything as I am. When the subject came up of my not drinking wine to the health of the others, and drinking to their health with water, Genl. Howard looked right over to me and said: "Gentlemen, look at Colonel McAllister and see how healthy he is, showing clearly the value of temperance."

Genl. Howard is about as healthy as I am, and that is healthy enough for any lady.

I found these generals very pleasant and sociable in conversation, and all treated me remarkably kind. I was very well satisfied that I went. . . .

January 2nd 1862

My dear family,

New Year's Day is over and we will go into hard drill, which by the way is improving very much. Even my horse Charley takes up

---

up his new government and developing the glories of human slavery." Mrs. Burton Harrison, *Recollections Grave and Gay* (New York, 1911), 37; Adams, *Story of a Trooper*, 196–97. See also Mrs. Judith W. McGuire, *Diary of a Southern Refugee during the War* (Richmond, 1889), 47; *History of the Twelfth Regiment, Rhode Island Volunteers, in the Civil War* (cited hereafter as *History of the 12th Rhode Island*) (Providence, 1904), 264.

the time of the music and marches forth very dignified and certainly very proud. When starting for drill, he kicks up his legs and squeals. Off he goes towards the line of march, keeping time to the music of the band—with his head held up, of course. He seems to know almost all the orders, and he is ready to strike for his place either in front or alongside the column as the case may be. When we are ready to come in from the field and the call is given for the drum and bugle corps to take their positions in front of the column, he knows as well as I do that we are going home. He throws up his head and kicks up his heels and acts warhorse-like, looks at the head of the column as his place, and cuts all kinds of pranks until he gets to his position. Then he is satisfied, having all the drum and bugle corps at his head. . . . You no doubt think I am vain with regards to my horse. But he is such a noble fellow that I thought I must tell you about his military pranks. . . .

Camp Seminary, January 4th 1862

My dear Ellen,

. . . This is the coldest night we have yet had in Virginia. The ground is all white, sleet and snow together. It has blew up quite cold for this climate. . . . I am sitting very comfortably in my tent by my little camp stove. I have as yet been able to keep warm at night, but I can't keep fire at night. The stove is small and of sheet iron. It burns and heats rapidly, but soon dies out. Such a stove as the one in our house in Juniata would be worth ten of these. We would not always have to be putting in wood. But when we moved we could not take so large a stove with us. So this is the kind that suits camps. Unless the weather gets much colder, I can get along very comfortably.

Gen. Kearny called here on me today and paid his respects. He complimented me very highly for the able manner in which I handled the Brigade yesterday. He was not present, but he had reports from his aides, who acted as my aides. Others present appear to have reported me very favorably in my playing Brigadier General. Genl. Kearny said that they reported to him that I was so perfectly calm and cool and gave orders as if I was accostumed to it. I replied that I could have done a grate deal better had I known beforehand that I was to take the command. . . . Our Brigade is the best drilled on the Potomac. All admit that to be a fact. That speaks well for us Jersey boys.

We had a Havelock Association [4] meeting this evening. I was there part of the time. Before the meeting closed, the Mayor of Trenton [5] came in. He said he would call at my quarters tomorrow morning. The 9th Regiment left today to join Genl. [Ambrose] Burnside's expedition.[6] . . . I think that our whole army will move in a week or two. . . .

Benton's Burnt House, January 7th 1862

My dear family,

I am here at the old place amongst the ruins of the old homestead of one of the F.F.V.'s. Dreary and desolate it is. My headquarters is in a small outhouse—one used, I presume, for an office, perhaps to barter in human flesh. . . . But the desolating hand of war has laid all around me a heap of ruins. The handsome mansion, barn and outbuildings, fences, and all have shared alike the fate of the destroying hand. The yard in front of the house, with its fine trees and garden, with its beautiful boxwood and flowers, are all demolished. . . .

I came out here yesterday and will remain for three days. It is possible I may stay for a week. One of us field officers now have to remain out here and take command of all the outpost companies. If the enemy advances, we will commence the battle and try and hold our position until we can be reinforced from the camps.

The ground is covered with snow, but it is not more than one inch thick. The weather is cold enough to keep it from melting. A continuous freeze is here, but still it is not uncomfortable for our pickets. They lie in bush houses, as they all do out from this station, and you would be surprised how comfortable they are. They have large fires, and in their pine thickets the wind can't get at them. . . .

4. This society of the 1st New Jersey was organized for the "moral and religious improvement of its members." Chaplain Yard was its first president; Sgt. Jethro B. Woodward served as secretary. See *Havelock Association Constitution and Circular Letter* (Philadelphia, 1861).

5. William R. McKean was then mayor of Trenton.

6. For a personal account of the regiment's action in the Roanoke Island campaign, see J. Madison Drake, *The History of the Ninth New Jersey Volunteers* (cited hereafter as Drake, *9th New Jersey*) (Elizabeth, 1889), 21–54.

Headquarters, 1st Brigade Pickets
Saturday morning, January 11th 1862

My dear Ellen,

I am still here at the Benton ruins. We came out here on Monday and will be relieved on Monday next. We now stay a week at a time. Our turn will not come again for 9 weeks, long before which time we will move forward. So I suppose this is my last picket duty at this place. We have had a cold, wet time while here. . . . Now all the frost is gone and the roads are very bad, which will be against our advancing at present.

The Paymaster is now at camp paying off our Regiment. I don't know whether they will come out here and pay or if we go in, or perhaps they may not pay those of us who are here. But I can get my money most any day and will send you the two hundred spoken of in my last letter. . . . You will desire and also prepare to carpet and furnish your house in Belvidere. You will want to fix it nice. You ought to go down to Belvidere and measure your rooms and see what you want. Keep both of your girls, as you will need them. I would rather you keep house so that if I get sick or wounded I will have a home to go to where I will be comfortable.

Belvidere is one of the most pleasant towns I know of, and I think it will suit you very well. You can buy your milk and ice and have it brought to your door. The society is equal to any town of its size; and if I should not live, it is about the best place you could make your residence. I have often thought of buying a lot in or near that place and building there. . . .

Few men have lived a more stirring and active life than I have. As you well know, when the reverses of 1857 came, I did not sit down and fold my arms and despond and make no effort. I kept up my spirits and labored the harder. Our trouble of '57 done us all good. I think we are all better for having seen that day, so on that score I have no regrets. I shall always remember our friends of that dark day, some of whom were almost strangers to us. To Lucian Wilson I owe much.[7] He was a *true* friend. . . .

Camp Seminary, Va., January 14th 1862

My dear Ellen,

Yesterday evening, on my return home from a long week's picket duty, I received a letter from you dated the 9th. Although we had

---

7. Wilson was a friend of long standing who resided in Juniata County, Pa.

Brig. Gen. William Montgomery

Maj. Gen. Philip Kearny

Maj. Gen. Alfred T. A. Torbert

Maj. Gen. Gershom Mott

MCALLISTER'S IMMEDIATE SUPERIORS

Members and camp of the 1st New Jersey, Fairfax Episcopal Seminary, Alexandria, Virginia, January, 1862

very cold and wet days, I have stood it very well and, thanks to God, my health is remarkably good. . . .

We are all in the dark as to our movements, or whether we will move at all. I have no doubt but that we will—and very soon. Genl. Kearny told me last evening that we would all move within ten days, though he was not certain as to where or how. It is thought we might move down and brake up the Rebel lines. We would have had a forward movement before this if Genl. McClellan's health had been good.[8] It is now supposed that we will have to move without him. I would be very sorry if this were the case, for I have grate confidence in him and want him to lead our army to victory. . . .

Camp Seminary, Va., January 19th 1862

My dear Ellen,

. . . I wrote to Mr. Wiestling yesterday morning. I told him that the Hutchison family were here singing.[9] There has been quite a mess kicked up in regard to it. It is as follows.

They got permission from Genl. McClellan to sing in all our camps. They crossed the Potomac River and held their first concert in our church. Dr. Oakley,[10] who you have seen and who has but one idea—*preserving democracy,* said at our dinner table just before we went into the church that if the Hutchinsons sang abolition songs they would be hissed. Maj. [David] Hatfield replied that such would not be permited. Dr. Oakley then said that he would not go to the concert.

Having charge of the affair, Maj. Hatfield went into the church before I did. The concert commenced and all went on smoothly. Our boys were highly delighted. Dr. Oakley soon came in. The Hutchinsons then sang a song giving a history of the grate rebellion. A question was asked in the song: "And what caused all this?" The answer was: "Slavery." This was the end of the concert, and the Hutchinson family sat down amid raptuous applause, mingled with a few hisses.

One of the hisses was from Dr. Oakley. Maj. Hatfield, perhaps not knowing that I was by that time there, got up, said that he wanted

8. On Dec. 20 McClellan had fallen ill of typhoid fever, and for a time grave doubts existed of his recovery.

9. The Hutchinson family were "popular abolitionist minstrels from New Hampshire." The Washington *Star* howled at their using army camps as "arenas for political pow-wowing." The song to which McAllister referred two paragraphs farther was a musical version of John Greenleaf Whittier's abolitionist poem, "We Wait beneath the Furnace Blast." Leech, *Reveille in Washington,* 122, 126; Burton J. Hendricks, *Lincoln's War Cabinet* (Boston, 1946), 287.

10. Lewis W. Oakley was a surgeon in the 2nd New Jersey.

no more hissing, and added that if there was more, he would put the transgressors out of the house. At this, Dr. Oakley rose and in a loud voice said, "Begin with me!"

Maj. Hatfield replied that there were enough men in the 1st Regiment to restore order. I then rose, raised my hand, and ordered all to be seated. At the same time, Mr. Hutchinson rose and commenced a new song. All became quiet. His daughter then sang alone, and everyone was mightily delighted. After this, everything passed off quietly, and I supposed that all was right.

Then, to my surprise, the next morning I was called over to Genl. Kearny's Headquarters to give testimony in the case. Other witnesses had also been examined. A paper then made its appearance from the General, stating that I had done wrong in not putting Maj. Hatfield and Dr. Oakley under arrest, as I was the senior officer present. Genl. Kearny then ordered the two gentlemen under arrest.

All officers present say that I done right. Both sides of the question unite in this. Yet Kearny, looking at it from a military point of view, told me that I done wrong. Well, to sum up the whole matter, an order has made its appearance from Genl. McClellan revoking the order giving the Hutchinsons permission to sing in our camps and ordering them on the other side of the river. Nine-tenths of our officers and men are sorry, as they wanted to hear them sing again. The affair has made some excitement; of course, the newspapers will have a grate deal to say about it, in which I may be handled badly as well as others. But, if an attack is made on me, my course will be defended in the *Tribune* and *Times*. There will be a grate many wrong statements relative to this affair. . . .

I am satisfied that the course I took was the only wise one for me. All say that I am right. Oakley and Hatfield are the lions of the day, though they are now caged up. . . .

I will have a talk with Genl. Kearny when he is in a good humour and get him to recall that sensure of me. But, as all say, it don't amount to anything. . . .

Camp Seminary, Va., January 22nd 1862

My dear daughters,

I received Henrietta's present to me, a sleeping cap, which is just the thing for picket duty and bivouacking. It will come in all right very soon, as we will move forward in a few days towards the enemy's line. . . .

You ask me whether we have tents on picket. No, dear daughters, we do not. I had my quarters with some officers in one of Benton's outbuildings—once a milk house, which fortunately had a fireplace and was not consumed in the conflagration that destroyed the mansion. Some of the men were in other outhouses, and some were in the tobacco barn on the Dangerfield farm.[11] But the majority of men bivouacked in bush houses, built of pine bushes with a big fire in the center and a hole in the roof for the smoke to pass out. You would be astonished at how comfortable they can make themselves in these bush houses, and especially in the woods. Of course the water gets in and the wind passes through, but still it is a protection. You know that soldiers don't have many comforts in times of war, especially on a march.

We all expect to move in a few days towards the enemies' lines. The whole army will be put in motion and you will hear some stirring news. The news of the battle at the mountain pass in Kentucky, near Somerset, is but the beginning.[12] Soon, very soon, the loud roar of cannon, and the firing of musketry and small arms will reverberate through the valleys, along the plains, and echo and reecho from hill to dale, from valley to mountain, from the Potomac to New Orleans— such as this continent has never heard. This, we hope and pray, will crush forever this wicked rebellion. Mourning will go up in many a household, but our country must be saved, cost what it will. I fondly trust that our gallant boys will stand the fire and brave the storm of battle, and that God may extend His protecting arm over and around us in the hour of trial. . . .

We would have moved before this had not the roads been so bad. Rain, rain, every day. The roads are in terrible condition. We have some snow but not much. This Sacred Soil is very muddy soil.

Here comes a letter from your mother. She is to be in Washington on Saturday night. I will meet her there. If you go to the Walnut Street Station, you can see your mother and ride with her to the Baltimore depot and tell her I will meet her at the Washington depot, though I have already written her to that effect.

Mrs. [John] Harris was over here one day last week with a Mrs. Ingham [13] from your city, and a married daughter whose name I don't now recollect.[14] . . .

11. The Dangerfield farm was adjacent to the Orange & Alexandria Railroad and three miles south of the Benton tavern. *Official Atlas,* Plate VII.

12. On Jan. 19 Federal forces under Gen. George H. Thomas routed Confederate Gen. Felix K. Zollicoffer's army at the battle of Mill Springs (or Logan Cross Roads), Ky.

13. Mrs. John Ingham was the wife of one of Philipsburg's most successful businessmen.

14. The married daughter was either Mary I. Hamlin or Emma I. Spettigue. See *Biographical Record of Warren County,* 294–95.

The roads are so bad that traveling is out of the question. I think that it is possible we may move before your mother comes. But tell her to come on to Washington or Alexandria. . . .

St. John's [Camp] Seminary, Missionary Room

My dear daughters,

Your mother and I are nicely ensconsed in this building. It is the library belonging to this Seminary. The room we occupy is the Missionary Room. The grate difficulty is that your mother don't like the stained glass; but as I have been without glass for so long, I think it is quite an improvement and can't see the objection to any kind of glass as it is all an improvement on the almost opake canvass of our tents. I laugh at your mother and tell her that it is too much style for her. . . .

It is raining almost every day and we have mud without limit. This prevents us from getting around. Your mother has not been in camp, though it is only a few rods from here to our tent. The condition of the roads prevents us from moving forward and may for some time to come. . . . I have sent you a picture of the camp and the Seminary which I think is very good. You can have it nicely framed. I will get mine taken on horseback, if the weather clears up. . . .

Camp Seminary, Va., February 10th 1862

My dear daughters,

We received Henrietta's nice letter yesterday, and we are glad to hear that you are both well. Your mother is enjoying herself as much as could be expected under the circumstances. Owing to the mud, it is next to impossible to step outside the door without plunging into it ankle deep. And there is no prospect of its drying up, as we have rain nearly every day. We cannot get around without a grate deal of trouble. The roads are in an awful condition. It is next to impossible to haul any kind of load. We can hardly get enough wood to burn, or forage for our horses. . . . We have heard of your frozen roads and good sleighing, particularly in New Jersey, and wish we had it here in exchange for mud, mud, of which we are so very tired.

I will send you photographs of your mother and me, taken separately and together. We had them made in Alexandria. They will be finished this week by Benjamin, who takes them in the very best style. He is from New Jersey and is making two or three hundred dollars a day.

There is an Episcopal preacher in Alexandria who would not pray for the President of the United States, leaving that part of the prayer out. This has given grate offence to the Unionists and our army. Today he not only omitted this prayer but also prayed for President [Jefferson] Davis and the so-called Southern Confederacy. This could not be borne. The guard took him right out of the pulpit to the guardhouse. He was followed by his daughter and a portion of his congregation.[15] It has caused grate excitement. These Secessionists are too insulting to be tolerated in our community. . . .

(Postscript by Mrs. Ellen McAllister)

My dear daughters,

I will tell you how the 1st Regiment come to church, also the 2nd and 3rd. The 1st Regiment are very near the church. I heard the band play. On looking out, your father told me it was the 4th Regiment coming to church with the band playing in front. You remember Mr. Camp that you seen at Camp Olden? He is the chaplain, Episcopalian, and high church enough to be in the steeple. . . .

The regiments here are highly favored in having the Seminary for a hospital. It is very comfortable. Every room is carpeted and has a stove in it. It has been a source of gratitude to our poor sick soldiers. There was a citizen from New Jersey visiting here. His foot doubled under him and he broke his ankle. I seen him in the hospital yesterday. He broke it two weeks ago. Since then I seen another poor fellow very ill with typhoid feaver. He died last evening. Another is very ill.[16] My friend Woodward [17] is sick but not much. He is the only man from the 1st Regiment sick. The whole Brigade have the use of the

---

15. "One of the most violent outrages committed upon a clergyman of the [Episcopal] Church took place in St. Paul's Church, Alexandria, Va., Feb. 9, 1862, when the Rev. Dr. [Kensey J.] Stewart, rector of the church, during the Litany, was ordered by an agent of the government to say the prayer for the President of the United States. Dr. Stewart proceeded without paying any attention to the scandalous interruption; but a captain and his soldiers, who were present in the congregation for the purpose, drew their swords and pistols, intruded into the chancel, seized the clergyman as he knelt and was about to begin the petition to be delivered from all evil and mischief, etc., held pistols to his head, and forced him out of the church, and through the streets, just as he was, in his surplice and stole, and committed him to the guard-house of the 8th Illinois Cavalry." Joseph B. Cheshire, *The Church in the Confederate States* (New York, 1912), 172-73.

16. Pvt. Jonathan Totten of Co. D, 3rd New Jersey, died Feb. 8 of typhoid fever. Two days later Pvt. Isaiah Brighton of Co. I, 4th New Jersey, died at the Seminary from measles. *N.J. Record,* I, 163, 221.

17. Jethro B. Woodward was a sergeant in Co. D of the 1st New Jersey.

hospital. They have an excellent Matron in the hospital. Men do the nursing. She makes delicasies for the sick and looks after there wants generaley.

The soldiers expect to move as soon as the roads are fit. To move now would be madness. Your father and I went to Alexandria on Wednesday in an ordinance wagon and we were very near upsetting several times. You have not the least idea of the roads until you seen them. If you hear of anyone in a hurry for us to move, tell them to come to Virginia and see the roads. . . .

Camp Seminary, Va., February 21st 1862

My dear daughters,

. . . We were startled this morning by seeing it announced in the papers that among the bodies on their way from Ronoke Island is that of Capt. Joseph Henry.[18] None of us knew of his being either wounded or killed until we saw this morning's announcement. Some of us still think it may be a mistake, but I fear that it may be true. None of his friends have heard a word from him since the battle of Roanoke. His brother started right on to Washington to hear more and, if true, to go on North. His family will be grately distressed.

As to our friend Genl. Montgomery, he is all right. Those charges have been shown to be false, and he has been fully acquited by Genl. McClellan and others in authority. As to that man who was said to have frozen in the stable, it now appears he died in consequence of having drank too much liquor. He could not have frozen by the side of a large fire, and besides, he had gotten up in the morning and drank water freely and then laid down and died. All other of the charges against Genl. Montgomery are alike false. Tell my friend, Dr. [Charles A.] Smith, that he don't know Genl. Montgomery, or he would not suppose for a moment that the charges are true. The cause of these complaints was other mens' ambitions leading them to try and get at the General's situation.

We have nothing here but mud, mud, rain, and some snow. But they are talking strongly of moving somewhere—most likely up towards Manassas or perhaps around it. A report today says that 2,000 Rebels have come into Annandale close by our pickets. Tomorrow morning 8 companies from this Brigade go out to look for them. If they are there, we will all go out and stand them a battle. But I think the report is a mistake.

18. Henry was killed in the fighting of Feb. 8, 1862. *OR*, IX, 80, 99; Drake, *9th New Jersey*, 44, 385–86.

February 22nd. Telegrams here last evening to William Henry from Oxford Furnace and from Col. Charles Scranton confirm the death of Capt. Joseph Henry. The funeral will take place on Sunday —tomorrow, or at least they think so. I have no doubt but that he fought bravely and then died fighting gallantly for his country. . . .

Camp Seminary, Va., February 27th 1862

My dear Ellen,

. . . We have orders to be ready to move at a moment's warning. We are to take but little baggage. I will take my valise, trunk, and just what I will most need. Tomorrow we will have muster and I rather think that we will move the next day. . . .

I heard this evening—but don't know as to the truth of it—that we have met with a reverse up the river in Banks's Division,[19] which was the cause of Genl. McClellan coming over in such a hurry. I hope it is not true. We will all feel sad if it is the case. . . .

Camp Seminary, Va., March 1st 1862

My dear Ellen,

. . . I am rejoiced that the rumour about Genl. Banks's defeat was not true, though we know nothing of the particulars. But we were requested to say to our Regiment that it is false. I have no doubt as to our moving very soon. Everything looks like it.

Last night was a very cold night, and the ground is now frozen hard.

They have become very strict and a person must now have a recommendation to get a pass. An order came last night forbiding any passes to be granted to officers or soldiers, except in extreme cases, either to Washington or Alexandria. So you see something is ahead. Mrs. Osborn [20] and Mrs. Hatfield are anxious to get over the river. You went at the right time. . . .

---

19. Maj. Gen. Nathaniel P. Banks commanded the upper Potomac region, with headquarters at Frederick, Md. At this time he had pushed southward into the Shenandoah Valley in an effort to clear that area of any Confederate threat to Washington.

20. This was the wife of the Rev. Henry S. Osborn, who was pastor (1859–64) of Belvidere's Second Presbyterian Church. Snell, *Sussex and Warren Counties,* 543; Baldwin MS., 246. McAllister mentioned Mr. Osborn throughout his Civil War letters.

Camp Seminary, Va., March 3rd 1862

My dear Ellen,

. . . We are still waiting orders to move forward. In a conversation with Genl. Kearny last evening, he said that there is no doubt as to our moving immediately. He thinks it is a mistake that we have not moved sooner. If Banks is successful, he says we will go right on.

I wonder what has become of Mr. Wiestling. Have you seen him yet? I think it is strange he is not here. The Rev. Dr. Abbot,[21] the traveler and historian, gave us a very interesting lecture in the church last evening on the signs of the times. The house was crowded. Dr. Oakley & Gorden were present, though a part of Rev. Abbot's speech relating to our own country was more objectionable to them than the Hutchinsons were. Yet they did not hiss.

There is no disguising the fact that our army is becoming more and more opposed to slavery every day. And those that will not see it will soon find themselves in the background. I never saw anything like it. Rank proslavery men who came here are now the other way. . . .

Camp Seminary, Va., March 4th 1862

My dear Ellen,

Why don't you write me? Not a scrape of a pen from you since I left. What is the matter? I fear you are sick. If so, let me know. Judge Casey [22] can write, if you ask him.

We are still here but all is in readyness for a move when the word comes. . . .

Mrs. Hatfield left for home yesterday. Poor creature, I pity her. So do all of us. Her heart is broken. She loves her husband, but he is so cross, cold and ugly to her. It is a subject of remark by all the men. Your friend, Dr. Welling, is very sick with the measels. He is suffering very severely. . . .

21. John S. C. Abbott was a Congregational minister and historian. He first achieved literary fame with his biography of Napoleon. His best-known theological study (among fifty-five published volumes) is *Practical Christianity*, which appeared shortly after Abbott's visit to the army camps.

22. Joseph Casey, a member of the U.S. Court of Claims in Washington, became chief justice of that tribunal in 1863.

The Winter Ends at Yorktown [123]

Camp at Burk Station on the Orange & Alexandria R.R.
March 9th 1862

My dear Ellen,

I received your telegram yesterday, but am sorry to say that it was out of the question for me to meet you in Alexandria. I have command of the Regiment. However, Col. Torbert came on last evening; yet he is much worse now and in bed. I think he will go back to camp on Tuesday.[23] . . .

I feel so sorry about Mother. I had hoped that I would yet see her in this world, but I suppose she is now no more.[24]

You have no doubt seen Mr. [Wilson] Lloyd. I was just starting out when he came to see me. I had no time to talk with him. I referred him to you. I don't know but that he might be desirable as our son-in-law. Nor do I know that I will have any objections. If he is steady and has good business habits, he will be rich one day—or can at least make a good living. But I could say nothing, as I was taken by surprise and wanted to know more. Do as you think best. They ought not to be in too grate a hurry. I will write to Sarah on the subject as soon as I can get time. . . .

Centreville, Va., March 11th 1862

My dear Ellen,

Here we are in this noted village without firing a gun. By order of Genl. Kearny, I sent forward a scout yesterday morning—one corporal and three privates—to get in the rear of the Rebel forts. I soon received another order to push forward one company, which I did. Then came another order to advance a whole battalion and so on, and soon all was moving up this way. The first company arrived here before any other troops, and the honor of reaching this place first belongs to us—our Regiment.[25] The enemy have all gone; and from reliable information, they have left Manassas and are fortifying at Gordonsville, where I suppose they will make a stand.

23. A few days later McAllister reported Torbert's "being unable to ride on horseback on account of rheumatism." *OR,* V, 538.

24. McAllister was sadly correct in his presumption. His mother, Sarah Thompson McAllister, died Mar. 7, 1862, at the age of seventy-nine.

25. In a Mar. 10 dispatch, Kearny stated: "This morning I occupied at 12:30 p.m. Centreville with a detachment of the First Infantry . . . I was without orders, but necessarily found my self occupying the country in advance of all the columns, as a necessary precaution for my own flanks . . ." *OR,* Vol. LI, Pt. 1, p. 550. See also *ibid.,* V, 539; Baquet, *First Brigade,* 16; de Peyster, *Philip Kearny,* 252–53.

I was worn out from want of sleep and proper food, but last evening I had a very polite invitation to quarter at Dr. Alexander's,[26] which I did. I had a good supper and a good night's sleep, and now I feel ready for anything. Where we will go now we know not.

The enemy's fortifications here are immense. Thousands of lives would have been lost in taking them. This is a sheet of paper I received from Miss Alexander—Sesesh, of course, but very kind to our troops notwithstanding.

This is a beautiful morning. Everything looks bright. . . .

Fairfax, Va., March 12th 1862

My dear daughters,

You have seen by the papers that we have taken this place, Centreville & Manassas, the enemy having left on our approach. We took but one prisoner and one Sesesh flag, a large amount of ammunition and some flour. The enemy left in a grate panick. If we had been a little sooner, we could have overtaken their retreating columns.[27]

Our Regiment was the last to leave Centreville at the Bull Run retreat and the very first into it on this occasion. The Jersey Brigade came off with honor. Had it not been for Genl. Kearny, the advance would not have been made so soon. I was in command of the Regiment and had advanced as far as the crossroads—the old Fairfax Road and the Braddock Road, just below here. On Monday morning I received word to push forward a scout to get behind the forts at Centreville. This I started. Then came an order to advance a company. This I done, with horsemen following to report to me every three-fourths of a mile that they advanced, and I in turn reported to Kearny. The next order I had was to advance the whole Regiment, and on we went. But by the time I was fairly on the way, our first company was in the town. When I reached there about half past 3 p.m., I was very tired, having lost so much sleep. I had a comfort-

---

26. The home of Dr. Robert Alexander stood on the west side of the Warrenton Turnpike (now US 29), midway between Centreville and the Bull Run battlefield. In addition to the 57-year-old physician, the family included his wife Elizabeth, two daughters in their twenties, and two teen-age sons. Data supplied by Francis F. Wilshin, Superintendent, Manassas National Battlefield Park.

27. This assertion is incorrect. Gen. Joseph E. Johnston's withdrawal from Centreville was unhurried and characterized by a needless sacrifice of matériel. Moreover, the Federal advance was so slow that Johnston "would have had ample time to remove from the Manassas area the last pound of provisions and the newest trunk of the most recent volunteer." Freeman, *Lee's Lieutenants*, I, 139–41; Anon., *Battle-Fields of the South* (London, 1863), I, 233.

able night at Dr. Alexander's, a very pleasant family. I then received an order to return to this place, where we have a large army collected to go somewhere.

The Taylor [3rd New Jersey] Regiment was on our left some miles away. They went forward to Manassas but are back now. We could have gone to Manassas before any of them, if we had been permitted to do so. But my orders were to stay at Centreville until further instructions. This I did.

I have lost my spectacals and have grate difficulty in seeing to read and write. I want you to buy a pair, which you can get for 75 cts. or a dollar, and send them to me. . . .

Fairfax, Va., March 13th 1862

My dear Ellen,

. . . I am very well and have got rested from the fatigues of the march and exposures. We do not know what is to be done but are awaiting orders. Genl. McClellan's headquarters are here—as well as all his staff, which is a big cavalcade. I met them when I came down from Centreville, halted, formed lines, presented arms, struck up the band, and our boys gave him three harty cheers. Genl. McClellan seemed to be pleased.[28]

I understand that they had a council of war yesterday, and last evening the General was reviewing troops by moonlight.[29] So I suppose they have decided on some immediate action. We have an immense army here, thousands on thousands.[30] The telegraph is now here and I suppose we will soon have a post office. But direct your letters to Alexandria until further notice. . . .

Camp Seminary, Va., March 15th 1862

My dear daughters,

. . . The enemy fled in haste (from Centreville), thinking no doubt that the whole Potomac Army was at their heels. Yet in fact

28. According to Maj. Hatfield, McClellan "took off his hat and smiled very pleasantly." Baquet, *First Brigade,* 423.
29. See Floyd, *40th New York,* 131; Samuel L. French, *The Army of the Potomac from 1861 to 1863* (New York, 1906), 39–40.
30. On Feb. 28 McClellan reported that 86,199 of the 185,420 men in his army were stationed in the Fairfax-Arlington-Alexandria area. *OR,* V, 732.

there was none but part of our Brigade, and we drove the whole Rebel army. Thirteen of our Lincoln Cavalry charged on 150 of the Rebel infantry and drove them back in dismay. They ran and reported that we charged on them with 5,000 men. Genl. Kearny says that it was the finest cavalry charge he ever saw.[31]

We staid at Fairfax Court House until last evening. Then came an order to come down here for the purpose of taking transports down the river this morning. Where we know not. . . .

It is a fact beyond dispute that the Rebels did not bury the dead of our army at Bull Run. Some were not buried at all. And it is also a fact that they boiled the flesh off of some scouts and made dippers out of bones. One of these vessels was found with the inscription on it: "This is the skull of a fine Yankee." Then followed the motto of Virginia: "Sic Semper Tyrannis." [32] These inhuman and savage barbarities has disgusted the whole army—in fact has abolitionized it. All the men are now opposed to slavery. . . .

Camp Seminary, Va., March 15th 1862

My dear Ellen,

Important events that will form part of the history of our country fly thick and fast around us. After the Rebels fled with dismay and disorder from Centreville and Manassas, we were ordered back to Fairfax Court House. Up till yesterday evening, we knew nothing as to where we were going. Genl. [Edwin] Sumner was in advance of the army near Brentsville. We supposed that we would be pushed forward in that direction. But all at once came an order to pack up and come here. We suppose that we are to take the boats for some place south. We expect to leave here in an hour or so. Some suppose we are going to reinforce [General] Burnside, but my own opinion is that we are going to Acquia Creek, up it as far as possible, and then march towards Fredricksburg and meet the enemy in that direction. But there is no telling.

We arrived here last night about 1 o'clock tired, wet, hungry, and sleepy. I came into this missionary room, got out my army trunk,

31. Seventeen members of the 1st New York Cavalry participated in this March 9 charge against Confederate pickets at Sangster's Station. Kearny watched the assault with unconcealed enthusiasm and termed it "one of the most brilliant he had ever witnessed." Stevenson, *"Boots and Saddles,"* 80–81.

32. Especially in the first year of the war did each side accuse the other of gross but untrue barbarities.

made my bed, and went to sleep supperless. I rested well, feel refreshed this morning, and will after finishing this hunt up something to eat.

Everything here looks forlorn and desolate since the troops left. I have just built a fire in your stove and am getting warmed up. This room reminds me of you and your stay here with me, but these pleasant scenes are now numbered with the things of the past. . . .

Camp Seminary, Va., March 17th 1862

My dear Ellen,

I wrote you yesterday morning from Alexandria that I expected to go down the river today, that we were under orders to that effect, &c. Last evening the order, so far as cook's rations were concerned, was revoked. It is said we will not go for a day or two or perhaps more. I think the want of vessels is the cause of it.[33] [General Samuel] Heintzelman's Division are geting on the transports now, and the road between here and Alexandria is lined with more troops than they can get on board in two days. As they are not very well protected from storm, and as we are in our old good quarters, it is most likely they will be shipped first.

I am sorry you did not stay here a few days longer. I could have seen you more. I saw Mrs. Harris today. She was here and said that she urged you to stay, as she was satisfied I would be down here again. . . .

I don't think we are leaving Virginia. I have made arrangements to leave all my surplus baggage in Alexandria at Dary & Harmon, corner of Prince and Royal Streets. Enclosed you will please find their card. It is marked 2 trunks and 2 boxes. If anything happens to me, you will know where to get my belongings. They would not be safe here as there is no guard. This firm we deal with are good Union men, in whose hands the baggage will be perfectly safe. . . .

Genl. McClellan has his headquarters here now. His wife and family were here today. He escorted them to Alexandria, and I saw them bidding adieu to each other. Mrs. McClellan held her husband's hand a long time.[34] . . .

---

33. The real answer lay in getting 121,500 men, 14,592 animals, 1,150 wagons, 44 artillery batteries, 74 ambulances, pontoon bridges, and tons of supplies aboard 389 steamers, schooners, and barges. *OR,* V, 46.

34. Bidding farewell to his wife, the former Ellen Marcy, was but one of countless chores McClellan performed that day. See *ibid.,* Vol. XI, Pt. 1, pp. 9–13.

[128]   ✗   THE McALLISTER LETTERS

Camp Seminary, Va., March 22nd 1862

My dear Ellen,

This is Saturday morning and we are still here. It has been raining hard ever since I got awake. I slept on the floor of my tent rolled up in a blanket, and was very comfortable. . . .

Ten or twelve thousand troops shipped out yesterday, and a thousand more are ready to embark. It may be several days before we get off, though we may start very suddenly. We are looking for it daily.

Genl. Montgomery is going to leave Alexandria. He has been assigned to Annapolis, Md. Why this change I know not. The General was desirous of leaving Alexandria—but for the purpose of going into the field. He wanted active duty. I have not seen him since this arrangement was made, but I can't think that he likes the change. If I were him, I would rather be in Alexandria than in Annapolis. . . .

Camp Seminary, Va., March 23rd 1862

My dear Ellen,

. . . We are still here and may be for some days—some say a week. Heintzelman's and FitzJohn Porter's Divisions have gone, and there seems to be as many troops waiting to embark as ever. We are likely to be the last. Genl. Franklin told some officers of this Division that we would probably be about the last to get off, but that we would have the hardest work to do. . . .

Camp Seminary, Va., April 2nd 1862

My dear Ellen,

. . . It is thought that we will get off this week somehow. But as our whole Division leaves as a fleet, we will be in Alexandria two or three days longer. Genl. McClellan goes with us.[35]

The cry against Genl. McClellan is all wrong.[36] His plans are now being carried out everywhere. Victory after victory is the result. Why do you condemn him? He is destined to be one of the greatest men of the age. Shame on the *Tribune* to take the stand against him

35. On April 1 McClellan departed for Fort Monroe aboard the steamer *Commodore. Ibid.,* V, 60, 63.
36. Several newspapers, especially Horace Greeley's New York *Tribune,* were highly critical of the slowness of McClellan's military preparations. See Warren W. Hassler, Jr., *General George B. McClellan: Shield of the Union* (cited hereafter as Hassler, *McClellan*) (Baton Rouge, 1957), 52.

that it does! I do wish you would throw it up and take in its place the New York *Times*. I have quit reading the *Tribune;* it has lost its circulation in the army.

They talk about Genl. [Henry W.] Halleck in the West doing so & so. He is a grate man, but he is acting under Genl. McClellan, who is in telegraphic communication with him all the time. I know it is said that Genl. McClellan has nothing to do with the West, but that is not the case. Rely upon it that Abraham Lincoln and Genl. McClellan are together in this matter and are destined to be among the world's grate men. The trouble is, we have too many designing politicians.

Maj. Hatfield is under arrest. The circumstances are these: We had Brigade drill yesterday; the Brigade was divided into two units, with the whole under command of Col. [James] Simpson. I had command of the 1st Brigade—1st and 2nd Battalions, with Maj. Hatfield in command of our Regiment, the 1st New Jersey. Col. Simpson has a squeaky voice. As usual, some of the boys laughed at him. Simpson got angry, rode up to Maj. Hatfield, and in a very arbitrary and insulting manner reprimanded him for not keeping his men quiet.

The Major was not where the laughing occurred. He asked Simpson, "Do you mean to insult me? I don't take your insults."

After Simpson had talked very abusive to the Major, he rode back to where Col. [George] Taylor and Capt. [James M.] Wilson (Genl. Kearny's aide) were standing. A few words passed between them. Simpson then rode back to the Major and asked him if he had said that he would not take his orders. The Major replied, "No, I do not take your insults."

Then Col. Simpson put him under arrest. Simpson is very easily excited and gets very angry. But the fact of the matter is that Simpson has disliked the Major ever since our advance, because of the piece that appeared in the paper giving the Major the credit for reaching Fairfax first. Simpson afterwards met him in Genl. Montgomery's office and abused the Major to the astonishment of all present. Now both Maj. Birney and Maj. Hatfield are under arrest. They are to be tried today. . . .

Camp Seminary, Va., April 4th 1862

My dear daughters,

. . . I write in grate haste to inform you that the program is changed—that Genl. McDowell's corps (ours) is not going down the

Potomac River. We have orders to move up to Manassas Junction and on along the Orange & Alexandria R.R. A portion of our army goes today and the ballance tomorrow. . . .

Camp on the banks of Cedar Creek
Catlett's Station, Va., April 7th 1862

My dear Ellen,

We left the Seminary on Saturday about 1 o'clock, took the cars, and arrived at Bristoe Station. We staid all night and yesterday came to this place. It is two miles below Warrenton Junction. We are repairing the railroad as we go.[37] All the bridges were destroyed, but we have them all rebuilt up to this place. This is Cedar Creek, and the R.R. bridge here is 100 feet long. We expect to have it rebuilt in a day or two. I have not had my horse yet. He came by the road. Our teams must have traveled very slow, or else got lost, for we have not seen them yet.

The rascally Rebels have torn up the track for miles and bent the iron rails so as to make them useless for relaying. We can't get more supplies without the railroad. I can't tell you whether we shall leave here today or not, but I am satisfied that we are on the *onward to Richmond route* now. We will soon meet the enemy, unless they run (which I don't think they will).

I am sitting on a block of wood beside a fire, but I am cold and chilly. . . .

Catlett Station, Va., April 7th 1862

My dear daughters,

We left camp on Saturday at 1:30, took the cars, arrived at Bristoe Station at 9:30, and encamped for the night. Yesterday—Sunday—at 2:00 we left for this place, seven miles distant. We did not reach here until late last night, having to wait upon the completion of a bridge across a little creek. We pushed the car containing our baggage by hand a part of the way. Then a locomotive came and relieved us and brought our baggage until another burnt bridge stopped us. We left our baggage, moved forward to this place, and

---

37. One of the better accounts of this expedition is in Adams, *Story of a Trooper*, 320–23.

pitched camp without blankets, provisions, or anything that makes life comfortable. The men had their rations in their haversacks, and their blankets, overcoats and shelter tents on their backs. I had rolled up my cloak in the blanket roll, and of course it was in the car back to the rear.

There are but few houses in this country. Fortunately an Irish railroad family was living here. They got up a pretty good supper and made me a bed on the floor. . . .

We are encamped on the bank of Cedar Creek. The creek at this place is 100 feet wide and has a very high bridge which the Rebels have, as usual, burnt down. It will have to be rebuilt before we can advance, as we must have the railroad to carry our supplies. This, however, will be done in a couple of days. Besides burning the bridges, the Rebels have torn up the tracks for miles. We will rebuild the railroad, whip them in the bargain, and reach Richmond—those of us that may be spared. . . .

Catlett Station, Va., April 8th 1862

My dear daughter Henrietta,

This is a point on the Orange & Alexandria R.R. We arrived here on Monday evening and have expected to move on. But it commenced raining on Monday noon and has been raining, snowing, and sleeting ever since. The ground has been and is covered with snow. It is very cold and disagreeable. Our camp is very muddy. Mud six inches deep will give you an idea of it. Neither horse nor man could walk well in it. I wish that some of these "Onward to Richmond," anti-McClellan people were here to taste some of the beauties of our advance. We make our beds on top of mud. Water and mud are the order of the day. We don't know what it is to be comfortable. Instead of beautiful green fields and singing birds, which was to charm us on our march in this land of Dixie, we have mud, snow, and rain to frown upon us in this strange land called the Sunny South. But we are making history and must not complain. . . .

It has now commenced snowing very fast, and it looks as though we will have a very deep snow. . . .

I must tell you how I am writing. Mr. Yard and I have a little S tent.[38] In front of this we have a large fire and have the front of the

---

38. This was the popular Sibley tent, modeled after an Indian tepee. See Edwin W. Stone's mistitled recollections, *Rhode Island in the Rebellion* (Providence, 1864), 1–2, 246–47, for pointed comments on this type of shelter.

tent open. This does very well and gives us a little heat when the wind is favorable. But every little while the wind switches; then it and the snowflakes shake hands and come in together to visit us. Our feet are in the mud and our eyes are filled with smoke. Such is the condition during the writing of this letter. . . .

Catlett Station, Va., April 11th 1862

My dear daughters,

I wrote you each a letter telling you about the terrible storm of rain, snow and sleet we had here in the far-famed Sunny South. The storm is over and the sun shines once more. The snow is gone except on the mountains. They are still white and look beautiful in the distance. It is still very muddy. The ground was frozen this morning, but it is getting warmer and I hope we will have some pleasant weather.

Our men have stood it better than could have been expected under the circumstances, though quite a number have become sick.[39] We will leave here today or tomorrow and move forward about three miles beyond Warrenton Junction to a road leading to Fredericksburg, where the enemies' scouts are prowling around. Our bridge here progresses very slowly. I don't know why it is not pushed more rapidly. The track will have to be relaid all the way to the Rappahannock, as the Rebels have destroyed it all. This section will soon be done. If the bridges were completed, we could cross the cars and haul the iron. All the old iron was heated and bent so as to be useless for relaying. . . .

This is beautiful country—land badly tilled but much better for cultivation than lower down. Farms are very large and there are but few houses. The F.F.V.'s do not live very nice and have but few comforts around them. Few carpets are on the floors of these poorly furnished houses, and the ladies are not nearly so accomplished as in the North. In fact, they have been standing still for the last twenty years. They prided themselves on family, and worshipped slavery, and fancied that they were superior to all creation. We in the North have made rapid advances in refinement, education, and everything that is calculated to raise the scale of civilization and religion.

And now the pride of aristocracy is passing away for the want of

---

39. For hardships associated with this campaign, See Curtis, *Bull Run*, 91–93; Frederic Denison, *Sabres and Spurs: The First Regiment, Rhode Island Cavalry* . . . (Central Falls, R.I., 1876), 59–61.

wealth to support it. Their slaves are running off and they are all ruined. Buildings and fences are destroyed; war and famine are both upon them. What is to become of them I don't know. But one thing is certain: they must change their whole system. There will soon be no slaves in Virginia. They are either leaving their masters, or their masters are leaving them. . . .

Alexandria, Va., April 13th 1862

My dear Ellen,

You will no doubt be surprised to find us here. We are ready to embark for Yorktown. We get on the boat tomorrow, perhaps in the morning. We received the order Friday evening, left Catlett Station, and marched to Bristoe Station, where we arrived about 12 o'clock. We laid down tired, supperless, and tentless in the open air and enjoyed a few hours of sleep. Reveille was at 4 o'clock. We marched to Fairfax Court House. Arrived there at about 5 p.m., scratched up a kind of supper, slept in a bush tent, and this morning at 5 o'clock we resumed our march and arrived here about noon. We have encamped for the night and tomorrow we will embark.

All of Franklin's Division is with us, including artillery and cavalry. It is the flower of our army. The grater part of our Division is pleased with the change, as they have but little confidence in Genl. McDowell. They have not forgotten the Bull Run defeat. And besides, Genl. McClellan desires this Division to go with him.

I understand that Kearny's Brigade leads the advance to Richmond. This is what he so much wanted. If Yorktown is not taken before we get down, we will be right in it. But keep up your spirits. God can protect me there as well as here. . . .

We will no doubt have some hard fighting, but the Rebellion will soon be ended. The finishing stroke will be along the York and James Rivers in this state. . . . If I should not live, you are in comfortable circumstances. That is what thousands of widows and orphans cannot say. We ought to thank God for his goodness to us. If my life is spared, I will be home before long. . . .

One thing I had forgotten to tell you. You heard me speak of the Alexander family at Centreville. Yesterday, as I was passing through there, I called and found the whole family in tears. Their father and husband was no more. He had died very suddenly a few hours before I reached there. I sympathized with them and left. Such is life; we are all passing away. . . .

Alexandria, Va., April 14th 1862

My dear Ellen,

I wrote you last night that I supposed we would be off before this time, but it seems now that we don't go for a day or two. It appears that Genl. Franklin has gone down the river to consult with McClellan, and it is said that we will not start until he returns. Wednesday or Thursday is fixed for our departure. Yet as movements in military matters are very uncertain, I cannot make any calculation. . . .

Tuesday morning, April 15th. Nothing new this morning; things progressing slowly toward embarkation. Our wagons are now going on the transports. I think we will go aboard tomorrow.

One of our men was shot last evening. He with a comrade was out of camp without leave of absence. When coming home, either them or some others were breaking into a house. A sentinel fired at the housebreakers, and this man of ours was shot through the thigh. His limb will have to be amputated. He says that they were standing in the street watching the housebreakers when he received the ball. One thing is certain: he had no business out at that time in the evening. In fact, he had no leave of absence whatever. They were up to no good. I have but little sympathy for him. We have so much trouble keeping the men in camp.

You have asked me how I am treated by Col. Torbert and others. I am treated very well. The Colonel is quite pleasant with me now. He dare not be anything else. I have too many friends for him to take a stand against me. . . .

Camp Seminary, Va., April 16th 1862

My dear Ellen,

. . . I will have to retire soon tonight, as we are to leave in the morning. We embark at 10 o'clock. Whether we will sail tomorrow or not I can't tell, but I suppose we will. I will write you on board the boat, if I can, but it is most likely I will not have time. I will do the best I can in the way of writing, but you must not expect to get letters regularly now. It may be a number of days before you hear again from me. So, dear, don't be uneasy if you don't hear from me often. If I get sick or hurt I will if possible write to you to come on, for I want you to nurse me. You are right in having all of your traveling dresses ready for any sudden call, so that you can start at a few minutes' notice. . . .

The Winter Ends at Yorktown

1st Regt., N.J.V., April 17th 1862 4 a.m.

My dear Ellen,

We are on board the *Hero,* an old North River boat. We are very much crowded. The officers will have good quarters, though I have not seen them yet.

We are going to the neighbourhood of Yorktown and expect to be in the fight very soon. All of Franklin's Division is embarking. Our Regiment is all on the *Hero.* I am very well—feel first rate. My horse Charley is sick. He is either foundered or has a bad cold or distemper. It is very hot today. . . .

On board the *Hero,* 3 miles below Alexandria
Friday, April 18th 1862

My dear Ellen,

We embarked last night, came down here and anchored, where we are laying till the Division fleet arrives, which will be today. We are on the *Hero.* The 2nd Regiment, with Genl. Kearny and staff, are on the *Elm City.* The 3rd are on the *J. A. Warner.* The 4th is on the *Arrowsmith.* These are all here in the fleet, besides many others. When we all get together, we will look very formidable. The weather is very pleasant. We hope it will continue so till the end of the journey I have a very comfortable berth.

My horse, I think, is a little better today. I fear it is distemper He will not be fit for use for some days. We have a case of measles on board and they are about to send him ashore, so a number are writing letters to be sent home by him. . . .

Aboard the *Hero* in the Pequosin River
April 20th 1862

My dear Ellen,

. . . We have had a pleasant trip down here. Last night we lay at the mouth of the York River. We sailed down here this morning. We came up with the fleet all laying and waiting for us. Col. Torbert has gone on a little boat to the *Mystic,* Genl. Franklin's quarters, to see what is to be done. There are various conjectures and rumors, but we will know nothing deffinent until we begin to camp. The plan of execution will no doubt soon begin. . . .

It is now storming and raining rapidly. I hope we don't disembark today or commence tomorrow morning. I don't believe in Sunday work. We have never marched on Sunday when it has been of any advantage to us. We came down from Fairfax Court House on Sunday, expecting to come right on board the boats. Instead of doing so, we lay in the hot sun at Alexandria until Thursday afternoon. On our last advance, we marched from Bristoe Station to Catlett Station on the Sabbath in order to hurry up matters. Then we lay there almost a week, turned around and came back. The longer I live, and the more I see of the world, the more I am convinced of the wickedness of working on the Sabbath day—either in peace or war.

Oh, how necessary religion is to war. . . . I am perfectly disgusted with the profanity in the army, owing in grate measure to the profane language of our officers, but few of whom are or ever have been Christians. In fact, they dislike to be where the Gospel is preached. . . . It is hard to have religious services with such an irreligious crowd. What poor mortals we are. The greater the danger, the less preparations are made for death.

My horse has been very sick. I have succeeded in getting a passage through him, and he is now a little better. I fear he has the lung fever. But he will get over it, though I will not have the use of him for some time. . . .

On board the *Hero,* April 21st 1862

My dear daughters,

I have written fully to your mother as to our movements. Our mails are very irregular, but I will write, hoping you will get it some time. . . .

The first day's sail from Alexandria was exceedingly pleasant, the day fine, and the water scenery beautiful. The Potomac is a magnificent river. The land scenery is not by any means interesting. We came down to the mouth of the Rappahannock and stopped for the night. We lost the ballance of our fleet. They started off and left us aground. Saturday morning dawned and the boat started. The day was cloudy but pleasant. Passing Smith's Point and Windmill Point, the water scenery was most beautiful on our left. No land could be seen on our right. The land was so distant that you could but see the green trees in outline, and that added much to the beauty. The water is fresh for about forty miles below Alexandria; then it tastes of salt.

I spent most of my time on the hurricane deck so that I could better see the scenery.

About 3 o'clock it commenced raining. Now we heard the booming of heavy cannon. Some said it was a battle; others thought that it was practice.[40] It finalley ceased. I learned yesterday that it was a battle in which numbers were killed on both sides, but which accomplished little.

At 8 p.m. we were down to the mouth of the York River. We threw out anchor and stopped for the night. The storm continued all night. I retired and slept soundly. In the morning we hauled up anchor and started downriver and came up with the fleet laying in the Pequosin Bay, about five miles from the York River. Here we threw out anchor and lay all through the Sabbath. We had services on the boat. . . . This day, Monday, the storm has not abated. I don't know that we will move today. When we do move, we will go back to the York River and go up and under fire to Gloucester, opposite Yorktown. The object of this is to effect a flank movement. We are expecting a very hard battle, which may commence any day—or any hour. We are to lead the advance to Richmond. . . .

Hero, Pequosin Bay, April 22nd 1862

My dear daughters,

I have written either you or your mother almost every day, though the letters did not start out until yesterday. Our letters are taken to a shipping point and then go by a mail boat to Fortress Monroe. We have not received any letters or papers since we left Alexandria. Direct your letters to Washington. As soon as the postmaster finds out our position, he will forward them to us.

It has cleared off, and the sun is shining beautiful. On deck it is delightful. As I told you, we will go back to the York River and from there to Gloucester. . . . It is my opinion that Genl. McClellan has his headquarters quite close to the enemy's lines and is very diligent in pushing on our attack. He is placing siege gun after siege gun in position. On Saturday night, after the men had worked all day and retired for the night, the General sent a party of soldiers in advance of the guns to a woods. The enemy, not knowing this, also sent their men to take possession of the woods, so they could shell our boys.

---

40. This was probably the artillery exchange mentioned in *OR,* Vol. XI, Pt. 1, p. 350, and in Oliver W. Norton, *Army Letters, 1861–1865* (Chicago, 1903), 71.

Along they came. Our boys opened fire; the enemy retreated in double quick time and did not stop until they got to Yorktown.[41] So you see, Genl. McClellan is wide awake.

Last night we heard their guns. These skirmishes take place every night. The enemy is trying to prevent McClellan from planting his guns. But this they can't do.

I have just learned that we go up the York River this evening, and disembark in the morning near Gloucester. Heavy batteries are there.

8 p.m. An order came this evening to put our men on shore here in order to rest them, as we are so much crowded on board. We put off five companies; in the morning we will disembark the rest and clean out the boat. This new order convinces me that McClellan is not quite ready yet to commence the attack. . . . The report of McClellan having taken two batterys is a mistake. He did take one; but as he did not wish to bring on a general engagement, he withdrew his men with a severe loss. When the proper time comes, it will be all right. . . .

Hero, Pequosin Bay, April 22nd 1862

My dear Ellen,

. . . I have information now that we will go up the river this evening and commence landing at or near Gloucester tomorrow morning. And I judge that the grate battle will commence at the same time, so that fire will open from river to river. Some of the largest batteries are at Gloucester. We have gunboats to assist in attacking them. We will have to charge them, no doubt. If we beat the enemy here, as I have no doubt we will do, the war will be ended.

Adj. Henry was put under arrest this morning. It will not amount to anything, and no doubt he will be released before we get into action. It was one of Genl. Kearny's fits that caused it. Maj. Hatfield is still under arrest; but the courtmartial, I understand, acquitted him. The verdict has not been made known to him. No doubt it will be before we go into an engagement. . . .

I do not think that there is any alteration of our movement, as it is most likely that Genl. McClellan is quite ready. The story that he took two batteries is a mistake. He took one with a severe loss and

41. The details of this skirmish are in John H. Rhodes, *The History of Battery B, First Regiment, Rhode Island Light Artillery* . . . (Providence, 1894), 80.

gave it up, as he was not quite ready to bring on a general engagement. One of his aides lost an arm and died today from the effects of it.[42] . . .

On Shore, Pequosin Bay, April 24th 1862

My dear daughters,

. . . If you take up the large map of the state of Virginia and look below the mouth of the York River, on the right side going down, you will see a bay. The proper name is Pequosin, but on many of the maps it is not named at all. This bay is not of much note. It is said that there has never been a steamboat in it until our army came down. It is a grate place for small sailboats engaged in the oyster business and also in catching clams. But it is now full of steamboats—large and small crafts—so that the harbor at New York is nothing compared with it. Since I cannot count the boats, I cannot tell you how many are now laying here. The native Virginians look upon the scene with astonishment. This little obscure bay now becomes a place in history, for the events transpiring here will be read with interest in our future history.

Our divisions are all on the shores of the bay for health and exercise, as we were very much cramped for room on the boats. We are only waiting for orders to move up the York River, which will take place as soon as Genl. McClellan is ready to commence the attack. We are to land below Yorktown, as I said before, and turn the enemy's flank, recross the river and get in the enemy's rear. We hear the big guns every hour, day and night. McClellan fires to prevent the enemy from completing their works; the enemy fires to prevent us from completing ours. The Berdan Sharpshooters [43] are doing good work for us. They are out in front of our lines and almost under those of the enemy. As soon as the Rebel gunners show their heads above the breastworks, they are shot down. They are really afraid

42. Lt. Orlando G. Wagner of the Topographical Engineers was the officer wounded in the Apr. 17 engagement. "Poor Wagner, of the Topags," McClellan wrote his wife, "lost an arm this afternoon by the bursting of a shell; he is doing well, however." *McClellan's Own Story,* 125, 311.

43. Organized by Hiram Berdan, the nation's top marksman, the Berdan Sharpshooters were officially designated the 1st and 2nd U.S. Sharpshooter Regiments. Members of these units were crack shots with their Sharps rifles; they quickly came to be revered by one side and feared by the other. For a history of these regiments' wartime service, See C. A. Stevens, *Berdan's United States Sharpshooters in the Army of the Potomac, 1861–1865* (cited as Stevens, *Berdan's Sharpshooters*) (St. Paul, Minn., 1892).

to load their guns. In this way McClellan is able to build his works and also prevent the Rebels from building theirs.

We are on the northeast side of this bay. The ground is very level like that around Trenton. Rather fine farms would be here, if cultivated in our Northern style. But, as you are aware, they are far behind us in everything. No pumps, only well buckets—and not let down by a windless but by a ballance pole. The well buckets are not made of staves and iron hoops, but of boards in the form of a boy's rabbit traps—nailed together with an iron bale on the top to fasten it onto the perpendicular pole that is attached to the ballance pole. These miserable containers for drawing water do not hold as much as one of our small wooden pails do. Everything is on the same scale, but the farms are large, and this land is good.

The owner of this 600-acre farm where we now are is Mr. Wynne.[44] He has three sons in the Rebel army, a large number of negroes (the most miserable lot of creatures I ever seen), and the women driving ox carts. He has two daughters, said to be rather nice. They play and sing in a sort of way. Mr. Wynne, his darkies say, was always saying that the Yankees could not come here to disturb him. So the evening before our army arrived, he was still consoling himself with the sweet idea that the Yankees could not come to disturb him. He said so with *a prefix to Yankees*. In the morning he got up from a sweet night's slumber to find the bay covered with our fleet and the Yankees as thick as blackbirds all over the bay. He swore and sank back in his easy chair, almost wishing he was out of this world. I see him every day, and he is one of the most woebegone men I have ever seen. However, he was kind to me and invited me into his house. But I was in a hurry and did not go in. If I stay longer and I have time, I will call and see the family. I forgot to tell you that they grind their corn and all grain by an old-fashioned hand mill turned by the slaves.

Close by here we have another neighbor by the name of Crockett.[45] They are a good and true loyal Union family. . . I have looked around to find some wild flowers or some strange plants or leaves to send you, but I could find nothing that you had not seen.

Our boys go out fishing for oysters and clams, all of which we get near our camp. I walked up to Crockett's today for a good drink

44. Owing to the fact that several "Wynne" families then inhabited the semi-isolated Pequosin Bay area, positive identification of this individual could not be made. The best wartime map of the area (which took its name from the Indian word for "mosquito") is in *Official Atlas,* Plate XVIII, Map 1.

45. Like the Wynnes, the Crocketts were abundantly scattered throughout the area. For other Federal accounts of civilians in the Pequosin Bay region, see Adams, *Story of a Trooper,* 359–63, 372.

of water. A doctor belonging to some regiment was hauling a cartload of oysters with Mr. Crockett's cart. He dumped them in Crockett's yard at the woodpile and ordered the negroes to build a fire. One of our officers asked him for a few oysters. He replied that he had none to spare, as he had invited some friends up to dine with him. Who the doctor was I don't know, nor do I care. He ordered all around him —the guard, the negroes and all—as though he was Lord of all Creation. I came to the conclusion that he was both selfish and fond of oysters and, as they did not cost him anything, he would have a grate mess of them.

I had a talk with an old negro today, a very old man who told me that he remembers well when Yorktown was besieged in 1781. He does not know how old he is, but he does remember that event. He also tells some amusing stories as to the sayings and doings of the Rebels. They were bragging about what they would do to the Yankees when we came down here—how they would whip us, &c. . . . What they did do was run away and leave their fortifications and a large number of good winter huts.

I am writing on my knee as I have neither table, chair, or stool. These were comforts and conveniences that we had to leave behind in our advance movements. . . .

Pequosin Bay, April 26th 1862

My dear Ellen,

The want of ink causes me to write you with a pencil. Our boat, the *Hero,* has gone down to Fortress Monroe to get a supply of fresh water and coal. She left yesterday and has not returned yet. This morning there has been some very heavy firing up along the lines towards Yorktown. . . . It commenced at 5 o'clock and now, at 7:15, it has very nearly ceased. This firing is an every day occourance. . . .

I do not think Genl. McClellan is ready to open the ball yet, nor do I think he will move until he is completely ready. His object is to bag them all.[46] Some think there will not be much hard fighting, but the indications are that there will, and that the contest will be a hard one.

46. McClellan, wrote a sympathetic biographer, "was a circumspect man with a tendency to magnify difficulties at times, and [at Yorktown] he hesitated to take what he considered to be an unnecessary risk of serious defeat." Yet, the same writer confessed, "had he launched an immediate all-out attack with the forces then with him, it is probable that McClellan could have carried the enemy's position." Hassler, *McClellan,* 88.

Sabbath Morning. Our transport has returned from Fortress Monroe. The Colonel says we will go aboard this evening and move off on Monday. . . .

The weather is wet, cold, and rather disagreeable. A number of our men are becoming sick—measles, colds, chills and fever.[47] My health is good, for which I ought to be thankful. I am able to stand a grate deal of hard campaigning.

My horse is getting well and he will be fit for use before long. I have not had him on shore yet, though most of the horses are landed. I thought it best not to bring mine as the weather is so uncertain. He was very comfortable on board after the other horses left and he could lie down.

The firing yesterday morning was a battle.[48] Our boys drove the enemy from a battery and spiked their guns. I have received no letter yet nor has anyone. . . .

Pequosin Bay, April 27th 1862

My dear Ellen,

. . . It is a pleasure for me to write you, although it would be more pleasure for me to receive a letter from you. One of the gratest pleasures I have enjoyed since our seperation has been our corrispondence. By this mode of communicating, we are able to know what each other is doing. To one like myself, far from home, it is a gratification beyond discription. But I have been deprived of this since our embarkation. I have not received a single letter from anyone. . . . *Oh, how I long for a letter.* It is now ten days since I heard from any of you.

We are still on shore and will not, as I said this morning, go on board this evening. When we do depends on Genl. McClellan. When he is ready and gives the word, the grate ball will be opened; and the roar of artillery will exceed anything this continent has ever witnessed. We have an immense number of heavy guns now in place. More are being put into position. The enemy have their big guns ready for action. Soon, very soon, the action will take place. . . Our troops

47. The army's medical director reported only a small incidence of sickness at this time. Malaria and typhoid fever were the most common complaints. *OR,* Vol. XI, Pt. 1, pp. 181–82.

48. This was a skirmish near the mouth of the Warwick River and involving a portion of the 1st Massachusetts. At day's end, however, McClellan reported "no firing on either side that amounts to anything." See Cudworth, *1st Massachusetts,* 148–53; *OR,* Vol. XI, Pt. 1, pp. 382–85; Pt. 3, p. 123.

are all in good spirits and sanguine of success. But we all calculate on hard fighting. . . .

Let it not be said that ambition, much less gain, induced me to leave my pleasant home, with a family dear to me, with all its comforts and pleasures, to live in the midst of the torrent of War. No, far from it; for the largest salary paid to army officers would not be an inducement for me to leave all these blessings—to turn my back on home, friends, society, and all that makes life pleasant in a Christian community. No, you and my friends know that I was, and am, actuated by a pure love of country. I have no regrets as to the course I have taken. God is blessing our efforts in this, our country's cause; and soon peace will be restored to our now distracted country. . . .

Pequosin Bay, April 28th 1862

My dear daughters,

Having a few moments to spare, I thought I would write you a few lines. We are still here on the farm of Mr. Wynne. I suppose Genl. McClellan is not quite ready for action or we would not be here. . . . There is more or less constant firing along the lines. However, we are too far below them for their shots to reach us; and, of course, we take no part in this, as we are to act at the proper time in a diffirent place. . . .

Our men are in fine spirits and very confident of victory. . . .

On Saturday night Genl. McClellan sent 6,000 men and throwed up rifle pits within pistol shot of the enemy breastworks. The enemy knew nothing of it until morning. Then they began to shell, but our marksmen stood behind and popped away.[49] The Yankees are a full match for the Southerners. . . .

This country has nothing of any kind in it. In fact, it is destitute of everything that is nice and comfortable. . . . I do not see a single flower in *Massa* Wynne's garden. I was in their parlor yesterday, and I will tell you how it was furnished: plain walls, no paper, no carpets, chairs like those in our kitchen, an ordinary dining table with a few books on it. This is all except a very handsome piano. The contrast is very grate. This is a family of the F.F.V.'s. While I was there, the pet lambs and little negro children ran through the entry. They have a large number of slaves, though the grownup men are all out throwing up fortifications for the Rebels to stand behind to shoot at us Yankees.

49. See *OR*, Pt. 3, p. 465.

And yet there are those in the North who cry out in favour of returning the runaway slaves—who cry "Peace! Peace!" when there is no peace. The blood of thousands who have and will fall in battle will cry out against these *poor miserable polititions*. I am happy to say that I know of no one in the army so low as to favour the return to Bondage of these fugitives from labour. . . .

Camp Windfield, Pequosin Bay, April 29th 1862

My dear Ellen,

I was highly delighted to receive by last night's mail a large number of letters—thirteen in all. One came from Mr. Wiestling, one from Brother Nelson, two or three from the children, one from Alice [Dick], and the rest from *my dear Ellen*. All received a harty welcome. Send on your letters.

We are still here but may be moved into action at any hour. Yet I don't think we will move for a day or two. McClellan is not quite ready yet. He is taking every precaution to make sure work when he commences the attack. He will, I have no doubt, bag them. He is planting batteries of the largest siege guns to bear on them. We have firing night and day, but as yet the Rebels have done little damage to our side.

Today I expect to ride up towards our lines in the direction of Yorktown. We can go up and have a fair view of the enemy and their works. McClellan is up there, very busy in planting artillery and making preperations to storm the enemies' works.

. . . I don't intend that Thompson shall ever get anything from my estate in that Covington & Ohio R.R. matter, if it can be helped—fighting, as he is, against me and my country.[50] . . .

I don't want you to shut yourself up in the house and not visit. I will be depressed if you do. Go out, visit, enjoy yourself—that is my sincere wish. If you don't, you will loose your health. Now I beg of you to do as I said. Whether I am sick, wounded or dead, don't shut yourself up. Save your health for your own sake and for the children.

This is the first warm day we have had since we came here. . . .

50. Both Thompson McAllister and his son (Robert's nephew) William had fought at the first battle of Bull Run. William continued in service with the Confederate army; Thompson took charge of home guard in his Covington, Va., home. McAllister, *Thompson McAllister,* 11–13. 15, 18.

The Winter Ends at Yorktown

Pequosin Bay, May 1st 1862

My dear daughters,

We are still at this place and do not know but that we may remain a few days longer. We are no doubt waiting till Genl. McClellan is fully ready. When he does move, he will move with some purpose. We had no cannonading yesterday. All was as quiet as a Sabbath day in a Christian community. But this morning some batteries opened and kept up a brisk fire for some half hour. All is quiet now. We suppose that the enemy discovered our boys planting a battery right under their noses and undertook to shell us out. This is the cause of most of the firing that is now done. Still the Yankees are successful in planting our guns so that McClellan has a good strong line of batteries right in front of theirs. . . .

Some think the Rebels may retreat from this position. But I do not think so. They must fight here or the Rebellion is at an end. We have the intelligence of the capture of New Orleans. Some of us fear that the news is too good to be true.

I have received a letter from Mr. Eshelman, a young man who was once a clerk in our Virginia operations. He writes from Ohio, having escaped from Secessia with difficulty. He spent some time last winter at your Uncle Thompson's in Covington. He writes that your uncle is an out and out Secessionist and that the whole family are very bitter—that Thompson commanded a company at the battle of Bull Run—that his son Willie was also there—and that they both escaped unhurt except for Thompson receiving a little scratch and Willie getting a bullet through his canteen. . . . He also stated that Willie was with [Stonewall] Jackson and supposed that he was at the battle of Winchester.[51] Mr. Eshelman added that Thompson was in the iron business with Thomas Steams, making iron balls and cannon to shoot Union men with. This same Steams has two sons in the Union army with Genl. McClellan—to be shot at by these very balls. And you know that Thompson has a brother in the same army. I am disgusted with Thompson, and *all friendship has ceased.*

This Eshelman has four brothers, two fighting on the Union side and two with the Rebels. The two on the Rebel side are now prisoners. One was at Fort Donelson in the Illinois regiment that was almost cut to pieces. The other brother is in McClellan's army. Here in this short letter we find three families represented who are fighting on both sides. It is painful to think of. . . .

---

51. On Mar. 23 Confederate Gen. Thomas J. ("Stonewall") Jackson suffered his worst defeat in a battle at Kernstown, just south of Winchester, Va.

Pequosin Bay, May 3rd 1862

My dear Ellen,

... This is a beautiful morning, the most pleasant we have yet had. I feel very well. My health is remarkably good. ... News from all parts of the country is bright for the success of our arms. One good battle here will settle it. Mr. Edge,[52] the correspondent of the London *Times,* had a conversation with Genl. Wool [53] yesterday. The General told him that Fort Macon [54] was in our possession, that Burnside was most likely knocking away at Norfolk,[55] and that Beauregard was retreating from Corinth.[56] All of this is glorious news for us. Things are certainly looking bright. Yet we don't know what is before us. ...

Ship Point, May 4th 1862

My dear Ellen,

By this heading you will see that we have moved. However, it is only across the creek, or an arm, of Pequosin Bay—about two miles from where we were before.

Genl. Kearny has left us and Col. Taylor takes his place as Brigade commander.[57] It is rumored that he will be appointed Brigadier General. I hope he will get it. He is a grate favorite with Genl. Kearny. Col. Torbert is pushing his claims very hard. Some think they will both be appointed. It was also rumored that I would be named Colonel in the 3rd Regiment. ...

---

52. Frederick M. Edge, an English journalist, was then special correspondent for the London *Morning Star.* Difficulties with McClellan notwithstanding, Edge was a staunch Unionist.

53. Maj. Gen. John E. Wool then commanded the 10,000-man garrison at Fort Monroe.

54. Fort Macon, which guarded the inlet to Beaufort, N.C., surrendered on Apr. 26 after a month's siege.

55. Burnside was still campaigning in North Carolina and was not to return to Virginia until late June.

56. Following the Apr. 6–7 battle of Shiloh, Tenn., Gen. P. G. T. Beauregard and his Confederate army fell back to Corinth, Miss. Federal forces laid siege to the city late in April, but on the night of May 29–30 Beauregard adroitly escaped with his forces.

57. Kearny left the New Jersey brigade on Apr. 3 to assume command of the 3rd Division in Heintzelman's III Corps. Col. George W. Taylor of the 3rd New Jersey was promoted to brigadier and assigned to fill the vacancy created by Kearny's transfer. *OR,* Vol. XI, Pt. 3, pp. 129, 133, 215.

Yorktown, Va., May 4th 1862, 7 a.m.

My dear Ellen,

We arrived here at 6 a.m. and anchored. . . . We are still aboard the *Hero*. We will no doubt push forward after the enemy. It is not worth my while to give you the particulars, as you will have them before this reaches you. I have not been on shore yet, but I understand that the Rebels have left all their large siege guns, camps, a large amount of flour, &c. The Rebels are said by deserters to be very much demoralized. The fall of New Orleans and Fort Macon has had a depressing effect on them, and I cannot see how they will hold out much longer. But we think they will make another stand here.

God seems to be fighting our battles and giving us victory after victory. Unless the enemy turns this into a gurillar war, it will soon be over—and, if spared, I will be home. . . .

4

♣ ♣ ♣

Peninsular Defeat and Promotion

Following the Confederate evacuation of Yorktown, McClellan dispatched Franklin's division to West Point in a thrust aimed at turning the left flank of Johnston's army. The move failed, owing to a combination of Federal slowness of advance and Confederate adroitness of withdrawal. The May 7 delaying action by Confederates at West Point marked McAllister's baptism into battle. In the short fight he and his regiment performed creditably. Yet, as was almost natural for a man in his first battle, McAllister wrote of the West Point action at such length that the magnitude and importance of the action lost their true perspectives.

The 1st New Jersey was one of the lead elements in McClellan's advance up the Peninsula. With Colonel Torbert incapacitated for most of the campaign, McAllister was at the head of the regiment. The Federals crept westward as far as Seven Pines. There Johnston's Confederates delivered a savage assault over muddy fields, and the Federal invasion moved no farther. McAllister's role during this engagement was that of guarding bridges across the swollen and strategically valuable Chickahominy River.

In spite of the setback at Seven Pines, McAllister remained convinced that Richmond would shortly fall and take down with it all of the "wicked rebellion." In true McClellan fashion, McAllister criticized Secretary of War Edwin Stanton and "anti-administration" men for asking more of the Army of the Potomac than it seemingly could give. McAllister also spent this month of immobility before Richmond in describing the countryside, accusing Confederates of atrocities, and mentioning skirmishes at various points along the Federal lines.

Robert E. Lee's sudden assault on the Federal right at Mechanicsville caught McClellan, McAllister, and most of the Union army by surprise. In the ensuing Seven Days' Campaign, the 1st New Jersey participated only in the battle of Gaines's Mill. The regiment's losses were heavy. Unfortunately, McAllister wrote no detailed account of his role in this costliest of Peninsula contests. He might have written at length on the recent campaign while the defeated Federal army lay jammed on the bank of the James River; but promotion and a new assignment occupied his thoughts.

If nothing else, the Peninsular Campaign convinced the heretofore overconfident Colonel that the Civil War was to be neither short nor easily won.

♣

Yorktown, Va., May 5th 1862, 11 a.m.

My dear daughters,

Before this reaches you, you will have heard the news of the evacuation of this Rebel stronghold. Our army is in full possession of all the navy siege guns, ammunition, a large amount of produce, &c.

They have taken us by surprise in leaving before a grand battle could take place. We did not know of their retreat until the Sabbath morning, when we were ordered on our old *Hero* with horses, rations, forage—in a word, with everything needed for a campaign. Then we came out and anchored for the night. We started at dawn today and came to this place, where we are now laying and waiting for orders. We expect soon to either land or go up the river. Large bodies of cavalry and artillery started from the front of the works in pursuit of the enemy. Heavy firing has been heard up the river. . . .

I have not been on shore, but there is no doubt that this place is strongly fortified. Why they left is best known to themselves. They no doubt feared that they would be surrounded. Our army would all much rather that they had stood a fight, as we could have taken them all prisoners and ended the war.

7 p.m. I have just returned from the town. It is a most miserable dilapedated place. The Rebels have left a large number of Torpedoes fixed in the ground so that when stepped on they would explode.[1] We have lost one or two men today killed in this way. This is barbrous and a cowardly practice. The fortifications are very strong—far superior to those of Manassas and Centreville. Had they not evacuated, we would have lost a grate number of men. Enclosed you will find flowers and leaves from inside the fortifications and Yorktown.

They have been fighting up the river all day. The Rebels have made a stand. We took three of their batteries and afterwards lost them. We could not hold them, for our force was too small. . . .

We leave here tonight and go to West Point, Virginia. It is said we will have a fight. It is positively stated that Richmond is in our hands. If so, short work will be made of the Rebellion. . . .

Yorktown, Va., May 6th 1862

My dear Ellen,

I wrote you last evening that we were going up to West Point this morning. We were up and started; then an order came to wait here for further instructions. So here we are at 7 a.m. We seem to be acting as the reserve and may move to any point at any time.

I heard this morning that our boys whipped the enemy last evening. But I also heard the sad intelligence that one of our New Jersey regiments in the 2nd Brigade was badly cut up by being led into an ambush.[2] . . .

---

1. "Land torpedoes," or booby traps, were the invention of Confederate Gen. Gabriel J. Rains. Although Rains had used the weapons with great success during the campaigns of the 1840's against the Florida Seminoles, Confederate officials soon came to regard the "torpedoes" as inhuman and ordered their use stopped. *OR*, Vol. XI, Pt. 3, pp. 509–12, 517, 608; Michael Hanifen, *History of Battery B, First New Jersey Artillery* (hereafter cited as Hanifen, *1st New Jersey Artillery*) (Ottawa, Ill., 1905), 15–16; James Longstreet, *From Manassas to Appomattox* (Bloomington, Ind., 1960), 79, 660.

2. On May 5, the day after Johnston had abandoned the Yorktown line, part of McClellan's pursuing force collided with the Confederate rear guard at Williamsburg. The resulting battle was savage, confused and, by day's end, inconclusive. Of four New Jersey regiments engaged, the 8th suffered heaviest losses: 35 killed, 122 wounded, and 4 missing. *OR*, Vol. XI, Pt. 1, pp. 450, 487–88.

West Point, Va., May 7th 1862

My dear Ellen,

We had a pleasant ride up the river yesterday and arrived here about 4 p.m. Tuesday. We made a reconnaissance by gunboat around the shore, threw a few bombs into the woods, and late in the evening commenced disembarking. [General Henry] Slocum's Brigade came on shore first. We did not commence till 9:30 p.m. It took us nearly all night to get ashore and carry our traps a half mile from the shore to this place. The enemy did not try to prevent us from landing, but they kept up a fire on our pickets all night and killed one lieutenant belonging to Slocum's Brigade and one or more privates.[3] It was said that Genl. Lee had last night a force of 30,000 troops within 2½ miles of us.[4] We slept none and were under arms, expecting an attack, at 4 a.m. It is rumored that the Rebels left about 2 o'clock this morning. Had they attacked last night with 30,000, we would have had only about 13,000 men. . . .

West Point, Va., May 8th 1862

My dear Ellen,

I have not been able to write you for the last two days, owing to my being so closely engaged. I have not slept any for two nights. We had a battle yesterday, fought all day, and staid on the battlefield last night. Sleep was out of the question. I have grate reason to thank God that my life has been spared and that I have come out of the battle unharmed, though balls flew thick and fast around me. . . .

During the night after we got here, we were ready for action. No real engagement took place, though we were prevented from having either rest or sleep. We were put under arms before day the next morning (Wednesday). It again calmed down and the pickets reported that the Rebels had all retreated along the road that night as if they were leaving this part of the country. Scarcely had this become known when heavy musketry fire was heard up in the woods that skirted a very large field which came down to the river and in which we were camped.

Our whole Division was under arms in a very few minutes. Sev-

3. This action occurred on the night of May 6–7. One picket on each side was killed, and two other Federals were captured. *Ibid.*, p. 615.
4. McAllister erred here. Gen. Robert E. Lee was not then in command of the Confederate army. Rather, he was serving in the anomalous capacity of "military adviser" to President Jefferson Davis. The Apr. 30 return for Johnston's army showed about 56,500 men present for duty. *Ibid.*, Pt. 3, pp. 479–84.

eral regiments were thrown into the woods, and the ballance of us drew up in line of battle together with the artillery. We hade every reason to believe that the enemy were in large force, which afterwards turned out to be true. They now had more than three to one of us.[5] The 15th, 31st & 32nd New York, together with a Maine regiment, now moved into the woods and the battle commenced.[6]

The firing was very rapid. The Rebels retreated up the hill through a very thick forest with a grate deal of fallen timber and in places underbrush and green briars—in fact, everything that could be in a forest to obstruct the march. It was made even worse by deep ravines, marshes, and creeks extending into the main land. All these formed good natural fortifications for the enemy. There they had a battery as well as rifle pits. In a word it was a very strong place for them, and they had many advantages over us.

On, on went our regiments, driving the Rebels before them but at a considerable loss of life on both sides. Soon they reached the arm of a river with a considerable depth of water. Here the enemy's reinforcements came pouring down upon our boys, cutting up our regiments to a considerable extent. These regiments had to retreat, followed by the enemy, down to the edge of the woods. Had they come further, our batteries would have played into them and we would have moved our whole force against them.

There now was a pause. Our troops rallied with some additional ones, and the battle again commenced. But the Rebels had the best of us. Our whole army was now threatened. The artillery opened into the woods, and the gunboats began throwing shot and shell.

I had forgotten to say that Col. Torbert was detailed as Officer of the Day and was not with us in these movements. He had charge of a large force, 8 companies from each regiment, which left only six companies in our Regiment. I was in command of them. After acting with the main body of the army, we were sent to protect one of the batteries.

The artillery fire soon ceased. Genl. Newton came along and asked me to lead my Regiment into the woods in support of the 31st and 32nd New York and Goslin's Zouaves.[7] They had retired, having twice been beaten back. Their retreating was endangering our army.

5. This ratio is exaggerated. McAllister stated that the Federals had 13,000 men in position at West Point. Yet Confederate Gen. W. H. C. Whiting's division—the only one involved in the attack—numbered but 6,545 troops. *Ibid.,* p. 483.

6. The regiments in support of McAllister's men were the 18th, 31st, and 32nd New York, plus the 5th Maine. *Ibid.,* Pt. 1, pp. 615–16.

7. Col. John M. Gosline commanded the 96th Pennsylvania. For Newton's orders to McAllister, see *ibid.,* p. 624.

In a few minutes my men were in readiness, and we started towards the woods. I marched in advance of them, came up to the edge of the woods, and held a consultation with Col. [C. E.] Pratt, now acting Brigadier General, as to our movements. He told me to detail one company as skirmishers in our advance. Before this I had detailed two companies to move across the marshes & ponds. In a moment the line was moving into the woods in splendid order—and to the admiration of the forces held in reserve.

We had advanced but a very short distance when they opened fire upon us. I ordered my men to lay down. In a few minutes came the order to charge. On we went and crossed a worm fence. The enemy, seeing us, commenced retreating a little, which gave a good chance for our skirmishers, who were pelting away in fine style. But it prevented our advancing. My Regiment dropped down and a portion of it commenced firing with the skirmishers. On looking around I found that we were the only regiment, except the skirmishers, which had crossed the fence. All the others had stopped at the fence, which was a very grate protection to them.

I went to the officer in command of the whole—Col. Pratt of the 31st New York—to know the cause of the change in the attack plan. He informed me that he had orders not to advance beyond the fence, but to hold it to the *death*. By this time the enemy had given way. I drew my Regiment back to the fence. There we lay that evening and night. It gave us a chance to bring off the dead and wounded, which we did to some extent. Some twelve or fifteen we did not get until yesterday morning. Strange to say, I had none killed and but three wounded—those very slightly. At the close of the evening, all the troops were relieved except us. Our whole Brigade was brought out.

At dawn we were ordered to advance. We pushed on over the battleground, passed some eight of our dead, and soon found that the enemy had retreated during the night and left the field to us. Thus ended my first battle.[8] We were then ordered back to here. I suppose we will only stay overnight and then push forward.

Our Regiment has got a grate deal of credit for the manner in which the men went into action and conducted themselves while under fire. Genl. Franklin says we done what the 32nd New York and Gosline's Zouaves could not do: we held the fence.[9] The Regulars

---

8. For other accounts of this action, see Baquet, *First Brigade,* 427–28; Kitching, *Memorials,* 61–64; de Trobriand, *Army of the Potomac,* 213–14; Freeman, *Lee's Lieutenants,* I, 193–99.

9. In his official report Franklin made no mention of the gallantry of the 1st New Jersey. *OR,* Vol. XI, Pt. 1, pp. 614–17.

said that we advanced into the woods in the style of Regulars. Col. Torbert spoke highly of me to Genl. Franklin and his aides, and I am told they were perfectly delighted.

I must say the men behaved nobly, and all were as cool as it is possible for men to be under such circumstances. The wounded men were in Capt. Brewster's company. Adj. Henry was with me and acted well, as he always does. Permit me to say that I was unusely cool and calm and had perfect control of myself and the troops. But, dear, it was God that controlled, guided, and protected us, and we ought to give Him thanks. . . .

Franklin will move forward today. McClellan is coming up quite close. . . .

Friday evening, May 9th 1862

My dear Ellen,

I was so tired last night that I could not write or think well, or I would have given you a better discription of the West Point battle. It was Newton's Brigade that went into the fight, and you can very well see the honor conferred on the 1st New Jersey by reinforcing them when the other regiments retreated. Col. Pratt said that if he had had our Regiment at first that these other regiments would not have retreated as they did. We fought Texas Rangers, Alabama troops, Tennessee troops—and the Hampton Legion from South Carolina,[10] which is amongst their best troops. They had two divisions while we had but one.

A man living near the battleground says that they lost a large number, and that the enemy says they killed 500 of our men. Some 40 dead bodies of the enemy are said to have been piled up in one place. The killed, wounded & missing on our side is thought to be 150 men. Mr. Yard saw 40 dead bodies after they had been brought in. Poor fellows, how I pity them—far from home and all their comforts.

I have just learned that Genl. Heintzelman is killed,[11] also Capt.

---

10. The South Carolina aristocrat, Wade Hampton, organized the Hampton Legion shortly after the outbreak of war. It originally consisted of 6 infantry companies, 4 cavalry companies, and a battery of artillery. During the Peninsular Campaign it was a part of Gen. James Longstreet's division.

11. Although his losses at Williamsburg were very heavy, Gen. Samuel P. Heintzelman escaped personal injury.

Wilson and Lieut. Bernard,[12] aides to Genl. Kearny. They, of course, were not with us in the battle.

Fighting is going to be hard. We will be in it very soon, but this Rebellion must be put down. . . .

Kent County Courthouse, Va., May 12th 1862

My dear daughters,

. . . We are in pursuit of the enemy. We are following them day by day. Our camp fires are in sight of each other. Where they camp one night, we camp the next. We have now stopped here until the whole division gets up, which I think will arrive today. We have only ours and the 2nd New Jersey Regiments here.

We came on to assist Genl. [George] Stoneman, who is in the neighbourhood. After joining him, he would not let us go back. We have thus been leading the advance.[13] Our cavalry have had several skirmishes, with some loss. We can't advance much farther without fighting again. The enemy are disputing every inch of the ground. We are expecting a hard battle when we reach the Chickahominy River. I can't write much now. I have scribbled this letter at five or six places along the road, sitting on stumps or on the ground. . . .

Kent County Courthouse, Va., May 12th 1862

My dear Ellen,

I am now sitting in the courthouse on the Judge's bench and occupying his chair of honor.

The morning after the West Point battle we went into camp and rested. The next day we were ordered to come out and meet Genl. Stoneman, McClellan's advance. We done so. Although our order was to return to Franklin's division, Genl. Stoneman saw the enemy in front and would not consent to our going back. . . . If the enemy knew how small a force we have here, they no doubt would attack us. Success would be in their favour. But by night we will be strong enough for them.

12. Capt. James M. Wilson and Lt. William C. Barnard were both killed at Williamsburg. See Kearny's report, *OR*, Vol. XI, Pt. 1, p. 493.

13. On May 8 Franklin dispatched two New Jersey regiments and a four-gun battery to guard the wagon trains of cavalry commander George Stoneman. *Ibid.*, Pt. 3, p. 162.

This is rather a pretty country. As is generally the case in Virginia, the buildings are all very poor. Most all of the inhabitants have gone. Oh, what a courthouse this is! It is the meanest kind of building. It must have been built in King George's time. When we approached this place, the Rebel rascals burnt the jail and a large storehouse filled with corn. (The jail was full of corn also.) The Rebels destroy everything as they retreat so that we can't get the good of it.

It is now thought that we will get to Richmond soon. We are now only thirty miles from it. Fifteen miles from here is the Chickahominy River, where the Rebels are fortifying to receive us and where they are making their last-ditch stand. . . .

Our men are in fine spirits and anxious to be led on. . . .

Banks of the Pomonkey River, May 13th 1862

My dear Ellen,

I wrote you yesterday from New Kent and had an opportunity to mail it. Last night after dark we got an order to march. When everything was in readiness, we came to Cumberland on the banks of this river. Then we marched about five miles from Cumberland up here to what is called the White House property. It is a very large and handsome property belonging to Genl. Lee of the Rebel army.[14] This property came to Mrs. Lee from the Custis side of the family. Genl. Lee . . . was here yesterday morning, as well as his army. In fact, their pickets were in sight this morning. But I think they have fell back.

We are within twenty-five miles of Richmond and are in the neighbourhood of the place where it is said the Rebels will make a stand. We are pressing steadily on them. If they stand at all, I think they must soon do it. . . . Their army is very much demoralized. Deserters come in daily to us. They all say that . . . their cause is now perfectly hopeless and the very best thing for them is to lay down their arms and end this unholy war. I am completely disgusted with Brother Thompson and his son William. I can never have any regard for them again.

14. The White House and its 4,000 acres were the property of William Henry Fitzhugh ("Rooney") Lee, one of three sons of Robert E. Lee. The estate was bequeathed to him by his maternal grandfather, George Washington Parke Custis. Fire gutted the house in June, 1862. Douglas S. Freeman, *R. E. Lee: A Biography* (New York, 1933–34), IV, 386; Francis T. Miller (ed.), *The Photographic History of the Civil War* (cited hereafter as Miller, *Photographic History*) (New York, 1911), I, 275, 315. See also Richard F. Fuller, *Chaplain Fuller* (Boston, 1863), 256–57.

We will stay here today and most likely tomorrow. We are still acting in conjunction with Genl. Stoneman. Our Brigade has not got up with us yet. We are far in advance of all our army. In fact, we have the enemy in our rear, unless they have slipped out this morning. But our situation is a safe one on account of our being on the banks of the river and near the protection of the gunboats.[15] We are also well supplied with artillery. I hear cannonading now, but don't think it will amount to much. . . .

I have just learned that in the battle of West Point we had 50 killed and 135 wounded and missing.[16] Some of the wounded who were numbered among the missing were killed on the Rebels' retreat. Such is the savage foe we have to deal with.

Since writing the above, I have taken a ramble over this Lee property. It is much the finest tract of land I have seen in Virginia. I was told today that there is 10,000 acres in it. It is a son of Genl. Lee, a colonel in the Rebel army, that lived on it. There are three brothers, all in the army. I am in favour of confiscating all their property and hanging them besides. The buildings here are nothing extra. The yards are large but not handsomely improved. The house is new. . . . We have the Stars and Stripes floating from the housetop and a gunboat laying in the river in front of the house with its guns pointing towards it.

Wednesday morning. We were under arms at 2 o'clock this morning, with everything packed and expecting an attack. We thought we might have to retreat until reinforcements came to our aid. We have in this advance but 6,000 troops all told, and it was ascertained yesterday that the enemy had 30,000 in front of us. But daylight has come and we have not been attacked and don't think we will be today. Before night we will have reinforcements. . . .

This is hard business. We sleep very little, as we are up by 2 or 3 every morning and sometimes march all night. . . .

Pamunkey River, Va., May 15th 1862

My dear Ellen,

I wrote you yesterday morning that our situation was then rather critical, as reinforcements had not arrived. But I am happy to say

---

15. The gunboat *Currituck* was then patrolling the narrow Pamunkey River. *OR*, XI, Pt. 1, pp. 637–38; Bennett, *Musket and Sword,* 48.

16. The 1st New Jersey had the lowest casualties (3 wounded) of any of the six regiments involved in the fight. *OR*, Vol. XI, Pt. 1, p. 618.

that cloud has passed away. The enemy have retreated and our pickets occupy the hill in front of us. . . . Reinforcements are now coming up rapidly, and I suppose we will all advance very soon. . . .

A reliable report came in last night that a number of Rebels have come in and given themselves up. They were in our rear, and we passed them the other night while they lay concealed in the woods They lay there until almost starved; then seeing the impossibility of getting through our lines, they came in last night and gave themselves up. . . .

Camp at White House, Va., May 18th 1862

My dear Ellen,

I wrote you a hasty note yesterday, stating that we had just received orders to advance. After having all packed and mounted my horse, I received an order that we would not go. After an examination as to how much baggage each officer had, we were dismissed and again pitched our tents and cleaned our camps. This beautiful Sabbath morning finds us still here. . . .

Genl. McClellan had his headquarters at this White House for a day or two. Yesterday he moved his tents about a mile further in advance.[17] He is now up on the hill looking down upon this vast army. No doubt his plans are all laid for a forward move. I presume we are waiting for McDowell and Banks to get ink in the right place before we start.[18]

You knew Wilson, Kearny's aide, and Barnard, also an aide. They were both killed in the battle of Williamsburg. Wilson fell dead with a musket ball in his head; Barnard lived about fifteen minutes after he was hit. All he said was: "They shot me." Poor fellows, they fell in their first engagement. Kearny does not get the credit that he deserves for that engagement. He is now perfectly idolized by his command. Since the battle he can't go out without being cheered. There can be no doubt as to his ability to command. Taylor is not liked. He is the most unpopular man or officer I know, and all hope that he will not be assigned to our Brigade. He is not the man for us.

17. On May 16–18 McClellan used the White House as his headquarters. On the 19th he moved to Tunstall's Station. *Ibid.,* p. 24.

18. McDowell was at Fredericksburg with the largest of the Federal corps —38,000 men. His duty was to defend Washington against a threatened attack from the Shenandoah Valley by Stonewall Jackson. Banks, who commanded the Shenandoah Department, was then advancing southward up the Valley in quest of Jackson.

Col. Torbert has written a letter to the Governor on my behalf for a colonelcy in one of the regiments with a vacancy. . . . There are now three vacancies. The 3rd, 6th, and 8th New Jersey are all without colonels. The 8th is not vacant yet, but it is thought that Johnston cannot live.[19] . . .

I think that Belvidere is just the best place you could possibly live. I would rather live there than any place I know of. There are many other places you may think of; but when you get there, you would not like it at all. When I get home you will be contented. You really ought to be now, as you have so many comforts. . . .

On the York and Richmond R.R., May 19th 1862

My dear Ellen,

I wrote you yesterday morning . . . telling you we were about to start. We got up at 3 o'clock, packed up, and at 4 were ready to start. We left the White House about 5 this morning and reached this place, about five miles distant, at 9 a.m. Here we pitched tents. I suppose we will move forward tomorrow, but I am not certain. Franklin's and [William F.] Smith's Divisions came up today. Stoneman's Brigade, with whom we acted until we reached the Kent Courthouse, is now about four miles in advance of us. He has had scouts within eight miles of Richmond without meeting much opposition. Various reports are in circulation as to the intentions of the enemy. One report is that they are leaving Richmond and will not fight. The other is that they are concentrating in large force and will give us battle—and also that they outnumber us. If this is so, and I fear it is, *McClellan is not to blame*. He wanted all of McDowell's Division, which ought not to have been refused him. But it was done by [Secretary of War] Stanton. The President then stepped in and said that McClellan must not be interfered with.

Genl. Kearny was this morning down at Cumberland, but no doubt he has come up to the White House. Other troops are advancing on other roads. This army moving is a most magnificent sight such as this continent has never seen. What a history will be written of this Rebellion for the benefit of succeeding generations! Long lines of artillery and cavalry and infantry move along over hill and dale, carrying with them the destructive weapons to put down this wicked rebellion and teach the Southerners with force what they would not

---

19. Col. Adolphus Johnson remained at the head of his regiment until his March, 1863, resignation from service. *N.J. Record,* I, 366.

learn in time of peace—that governments are not so easily broken up, and that God requires obedience to law and order. . . . History will do justice to those who are thus so actively engaged in this restoration of our government to its original purity, to the blessings of millions yet unborn.

It is probable that the enemy are fortifying at the Chickahominy swamps. If they are, I think that McClellan will get around them and they will be compelled to take a new position. I have every confidence in Genl. McClellan. The New York *Tribune* has lost nearly all circulation here owing to its unjust attacks on the General. It has now changed its course—but too late for its own benefit. I hope you take the *Times*. Our Rev. Mr. Yard is a reporter for that paper. Look at his letters. He has written one that will place our Regiment in its right place in the West Point fight.[20]

. . . *Tuesday morning, May 20th 1862.* I am well and never enjoyed better health, though many of our men are falling sick. At a time when we want every man, our ranks are being considerably reduced. . . . The roads are bad; and when it rains, it is very hard to get supplies brought to us. We are now leaving the river. As the railroad bridges are not yet repaired, we have to depend on wagons. I hardly think we will move from here today. . . .

Tunstall's Station, Va., May 20th 1862

My dear daughters,

We left the White House yesterday morning at 4 a.m. and had a pleasant march to this place, about seven miles nearer Richmond. We are the advance of the main army, but Stoneman's Brigade is several miles in advance of us. We see but very little of the enemy, though we are but eighteen miles from Richmond. What they are up to we can't tell. Genl. McClellan is taking us to our right in order to turn their left flank, so I guess McClellan will work over our card well. We all like him very much and say it is a shame the way he has been abused.

We will most likely stay here today to await our supplies. They have to be moved from the White House by wagons over very bad roads. . . .

20. At West Point, Mr. Yard wrote, "the line was as firm as a division in its column at a review. Not a man flinched. Lieutenant-Colonel McAllister, when the enemy broke, bravely pursued them some distance . . . This firm and determined movement decided the result." Foster, *New Jersey and the Rebellion,* 73n.

You ought to have seen this army move off yesterday morning. It was a most magnificent sight. The morning was beautiful and bright; and as you cast your eyes towards Richmond, you could see the long lines of cavalry, artillery, and infantry moving slowly along. The weapons of war glittered in the sunlight, making the wheatfield look more like blades of steel than of wheat. . . .

I think we will have a hard battle before we get to the capital of the Rebels. It will be their last struggle. That we will triumph I have no doubt, but many brave troops will fall before reaching Richmond. . . .

The country here is very fine. It is much the best part of Virginia I have yet seen, though the land is not well cultivated and the buildings are not good. . . .

            12 miles from Richmond, Wednesday, May 21st 1862
My dear Ellen,
    . . . Today the morning was pleasant. At first we advanced very slow, owing to our pioneers having to mend the road in many places. But the latter part of the march was rapid and the day exceedingly hot. Our men fell out all along the road. After we stopped here, they all caught up and we have pitched tents for the night.[21] (The men have their little shelter tents.) Our wagons have not yet arrived and, of course, we are sitting down in the woods waiting for them. Before it gets too dark, I thought I would write you this letter. It is now after sundown. Mr. Yard is making some sketches, at which he is very good, and I am writing to my dear Ellen.

The enemy have not shown themselves to us today. But there was a little skirmishing out here yesterday evening with Stoneman's advance.[22] The Rebels have now left. About twelve miles up is what is called the Bottom Bridge, across the Chickahominy River. Last evening our forces reached that place and the enemy set fire to the R.R. bridge. Our artillery fired on them to prevent it. [General Silas] Casey's Division, and also [General Darius N.] Couch's Division, are there—and I think Kearny too. We are making a flank movement on their left and will no doubt take them where they least expect it. But this must not become publick, as there is an order forbidding any

---

21. The men of the 1st New Jersey marched only seven miles that day, but they did so without rations. Baquet, *First Brigade,* 430.

22. A small-scale artillery duel followed the May 20 seizure by Federals of Bottom's Bridge. *OR,* Vol. XI, Pt. 1, pp. 25, 645–48.

officer from communicating any knowledge of this kind. . . . The enemy are making a stand about six miles from Richmond and along the Chickahominy, from which we will have to drive them. I think that McDowell will join us,[23] but I fear that he is rather a slow coach. He ought to be here now.

Good morning, dear Ellen. After I quit writing last evening, I fell asleep on my good big blanket you were so kind to get me in Washington. . . . I slept very well and feel first rate this morning. . . . This is a beautiful morning. The sun is bright and the air is balmy.

Our wagons arrived in the night, and we have had a comfortable brackfast. The grate trouble in advancing without water and without railroads is the trouble of getting our supplies along. Our horses are half the time without feed. You at home know but little of their difficulty. My horse has gotten entirely well. I am now using him. . . .

Col. Torbert treats me well and wrote a strong letter to the Governor in favour of my appointment to colonel. All is pleasant. . . .

Camp at Cold Harbor, Va., May 22nd 1862

My dear daughters,

I last wrote you from the White House property. We left there on Monday morning and came about five miles on this side near Tunstall's Station and camped. Tuesday afternoon we took up our line of march and came seven miles further. Wednesday morning we started and reached this place yesterday evening. I think we will not remain longer than to get up our supplies.

This place is called Cold Harbor from an Indian once having froze to death here.[24] There is no water of any kind but wells and springs. We are out from all streams. We are getting very near the Chickahominy, where it is reported the enemy are in large force to

23. On May 17 Sec. of War Edwin Stanton ordered McDowell's corps to join McClellan's army. *Ibid.*, p. 28.
24. McAllister's statement as to the origin of the name "Cold Harbor" is, to say the least, novel. A number of stories exist about the name. One is that it was a corruption of "Cool Arbor"; other and more popularly accepted beliefs are that the spot was once a stagecoach stop which either served cold sandwiches to passengers or else offered unheated shelter for the night. Robert W. Waitt, Jr., to James I. Robertson, Jr., Jan. 7, 1964. See also Adams, *Story of a Trooper,* 481; Alfred S. Roe, *The Ninth New York Heavy Artillery* (Worcester, Mass., 1899), 96n.; Charles S. Wainwright, *A Diary of Battle: The Personal Journals of Colonel Charles S. Wainwright, 1861–1865* (cited hereafter as Wainwright, *Diary of Battle*) (New York, 1962), 401.

attack us. Another day's march will bring us face to face with them. Then we will help to decide between Northern courage and Southern chivalry. That we will beat them I have no doubt. But in the contest we will lose many valuable lives. Then this war will be over, and this wicked Rebellion will be at an end.

We have passed some good farms; still they are not in the good state of cultivation as are our Northern farms. This farm that we are on is all sand, even though it is high-laying land. It is a grate place for raising sweet potatoes and melons, &c. We are in the advance of the main army, though Stoneman is ahead of us with his cavalry and some artillery. As he moves forward, so do we. On we go from day to day. We have now only twelve miles more to go to reach Richmond. But of course the hardest part is yet to come.

Our men are all anxious to go into Richmond. They desire to fight them and put an end to the war. We have grate faith in the skill and bravery of Genl. McClellan and are willing to wait or move as he says, satisfied it will be for the best. . . .

I have just learned that the enemy's pickets have appeared in front of our lines, which shows that they are going to contest the ground. We are to move as soon as we get in our supplies.

Enclosed you will find a picture of the field & staff officers drawn by Chaplain Yard. I asked him to draw it for your benefit. He has a good deal of taste in that way. . . .

Camp at Cold Harbor, Va., May 22nd 1862

My dear Ellen,

I have not received any word from you for three days. The last ones were written by Alice. I feel very uneasy about you. Do write, or have Alice to write me how you are. . . .

We have had a quiet day and rested from the fatigue of yesterday's march. We are only stopping to get up supplies. Though it is 9 p.m., we have no order for moving tomorrow. Judging from the circumstances, I am inclined to think we will.

Friday morning. It now appears that a reconnisense was made yesterday. Our troops advanced to within four miles of Richmond and returned without seeing the enemy. Many rumors are afloat that they are leaving Richmond. Other reports say that they will fight. But if we can get within four miles of the city, we can easily shell them and they can't make much resistance. . . .

Camp at Cold Harbor, Va., May 24th 1862

My dear Ellen,

Your welcome letter of the 21st came to hand this morning as I was at brackfast. I was hartily rejoiced to find it was from you, as that alone was sufficient to tell me you were getting better. On reading it, I found that you were sitting up, which was the best news I could get. . . .

If possible, I love to walk out alone in the calm of evening, away from the noise of the camp. Then I think of home and its endearing charms and wish a thousand times I were there—or could see you for only an hour. God grant that we soon meet around our pleasant friends. . . .

We are still here. Yesterday Stoneman threw some shells across the Chickahominy to feel out the enemy, but he did not get a response. . . .

1 p.m. I can get you no news of any importance. Mr. Edge, corrispondent of the London *Star,* has just returned from McClellan's Headquarters, which are close by here. He could not get any news. They communicate nothing, and the Press can get nothing.[25] All will be kept in the dark until after we get into the city. . . .

Camp at Cold Harbor, Va., May 25th 1862

My dear Ellen,

I closed my letter to you yesterday in a hurry, informing you that we had orders to hold ourselves in readyness to move at a moment's notice. We got ready, but the order was countermanded in the evening. The cause of it was a skirmish one of our Michigan regiments had with the enemy on Dr. Gaines'[26] farm, about four miles from here. We captured twenty-three prisoners, besides the wounded, and left on the field that many dead. We either killed, wounded or took them all prisoners, so that it was a total defeat for the whole party.[27]

---

25. McClellan apparently had little patience with battlefield correspondents. Another newspaperman who fared even worse than Edge was George A. Townsend. See his *Rustics in Rebellion* (Chapel Hill, 1950), 71–82.

26. Regarded by Federals as a "rank secessionist," Dr. William G. Gaines was a well-to-do physician who lived at Powhite and owned the mill bearing his name. Following the June 27 battle at Gaines's Mill, Gens. Lee and Longstreet spent the night at the doctor's home. Stone, *Rhode Island in the Rebellion,* 105; Robert W. Waitt, Jr., to James I. Robertson, Jr., Jan. 7, 1964.

27. McAllister was referring to the May 24 skirmish near New Bridge. Confederate losses were 18 killed, 26 wounded, and 34 missing, while Federal casualties numbered 3 killed and 17 wounded. McClellan tersely reported:

They were the Louisiana Bushwackers, such as we had to attack at West Point. They are real sharpshooters. I seen them yesterday. They looked hard. We had two men killed and seventeen wounded.

We are now going to move at 8 o'clock this morning to take up our position on the right of the line, coming around on the north side of Richmond. We now seem to be taking our place in the line that is to move forward on Richmond. I don't know where McDowell is, but I have confidence in Genl. McClellan doing right. He will finaly conquer the Rebels.

Yesterday evening Mr. Yard and I rode over to Dr. Gaines' plantation. It contains twelve hundred acres and is beautiful, even better than Lee's White House farm. The grove of trees around the house is the finest I have ever seen. The flower garden is most beautiful. . . . I forgot to say that Dr. Gaines was all packed up and partly loaded when Genl. Stoneman's advance guard reached his dwelling. This put a stop to the Doctor's packing, and he is now under guard at his own house. . . .

New Bridge, 8 miles from Richmond, May 27th 1862

My dear Ellen,

. . . Yesterday we received an order to be ready to cross the Chickahominy at a moment's notice, that we were to leave our tents and baggage behind, and also the men their knapsacks. Each man was to take a blanket roll and three days' provisions in their haversacks. We got ready for the ball to open and expected to cross last evening and commence fighting on our march to the city of Richmond.

Shortly afterwards the order was countermanded. On inquiry I find that in the baloon assention [28] of yesterday morning a large Rebel force was seen moving towards the center of our line at Bottoms Bridge. An attack seemed inevitable. Our orders were to cross and flank the enemy. The Rebels did not attack us, so the order was revoked.

We are still daily looking for a move and know not when this long-looked-for hour will come. There are in our own camp, as well as in the Press, differences of opinion as to a battle. . . .

"Fourth Michigan about finished Louisiana Tigers." *OR,* Vol. XI, Pt. 1, pp. 651–66.

28. Wartime aerial reconnaissance made its debut in the Civil War with the hydrogen-filled balloons of Prof. T. S. C. Lowe. See David Donald, *et al.* (eds.), *Divided We Fought* (New York, 1952), 58–59.

Now, dear Ellen, I have a word to say to you. I am here in this grand army, an army such as has never marched on this continent. As an officer and soldier I intend doing my duty to my country and pray God that He will enable me to discharge all the obligations devolving on me. . . . But some must fall and give their lives as a sacrifice on our country's altar. If my dear and loved family should be deprived of their head, mourn not for me. Remember that we all have to die. . . . Put your trust in God and ask Him to bear you up in your affliction. . . .

New Bridge, Va., May 29th 1862

My dear Ellen,

I have been much disappointed in not receiving any letters from you for two days. If I do not get one today, I will feel badly. . . .

We have not had an order to cross the river yet, but may very soon. It seems to be very quiet now. Genl. Porter's victory was complete and resulted in the capture of a large number of Rebels commanded by Howell Cobb of Georgia.[29] These prisoners say that our men fight beyond anything they have ever seen or heard of. In a ride last evening to Mechanicsville, we met quite a number of prisoners coming in. They were wounded and lying in the ambulances. At Mechanicsville I saw a nice mansion house standing in a beautiful grove of trees through which so many of our cannon balls went, completely riddling the house. One struck the brick chimney and knocked a hole through it. The reason Stoneman fired so much at the house was because the Rebel sharpshooters were in the house and on the roof picking off our men. They had to leave in a hurry. . . .

It is but five miles from Mechanicsville to Richmond, but the enemy were just across the creek. I have seen them plain. They have batteries planted on this side and most likely on the other side too. So we are looking at each other for the present. But this will not last long, as we will cross and march to Richmond. This is beautiful country, the finest I have seen in Virginia.

We have all run out of postage stamps and can't get them. I will not put on the last one I have. Send me some as soon as you receive this and don't forget.

29. On this date Gen. FitzJohn Porter's division dislodged Confederates from Hanover Court House and sent them retreating eleven miles westward to Ashland. Georgia's Howell Cobb was not involved in this action. The fighting was with the Confederate brigade of Gen. Lawrence O. Branch. *OR,* Vol. XI, Pt. 1, pp. 33–35, 680–85, 740–42.

Banks' defeat will not retard our onward march.[30] But to say the least, it was bad management—not on his part, for he done well and made a masterly retreat. But somebody is to blame. As for McDowell, he will delay coming until we fight the battle. He is a very slow coach. He is acting indipendent of Genl. McClellan. It is a perfect outrage. If they would let McClellan alone, we would long before this have been in Richmond. . . .

Camp on the Chickahominy, May 31st 1862

My dear family,

Long before this reaches you, the news of the terable battle of this day will have gone to you by telegraph.[31] We were not in the engagement, for the attack was made on the left of our lines and not on us. I do not know the troops engaged but think Genls. Heintzelman, Sumner, Keyes, and Kearny. These troops had crossed the river some days ago and, we understood, were attacked. The battle commenced about 1 p.m. and did not close till 8 this evening. We have no intelligence relative to it yet, as it has just ceased. It continued long after dark, a very uncommon occourrance. I say it was terable for the roaring of artillery and musketry was more terrifick than I have yet seen or heard. It was rapid and constant. Very many valuable lives have been lost this day. As soon as I get any intelligence that is reliable, I will write you. We think the battle will be resumed in the morning and that it will become general along the whole line. . . .

Camp on the Chickahominy, June 1st 1862

My dear Ellen,

. . . we had orders to be ready to cross the river by daylight. The morning dawned and we were all ready to move. The artillery passed down towards the river and remained ready for action. But

30. Stonewall Jackson's forces routed Banks's army at Winchester on May 25 and drove it from the valley. Banks suffered 3,500 casualties and so incalculable an amount of stores that Confederates thereafter referred to him as "Commissary" Banks.

31. At Seven Pines Johnston ceased his retreat and launched a full-scale attack on the Federal left. By late afternoon the mauled corps of Heintzelman and Erasmus Keyes were about to break. Fiery Edwin Sumner and his corps then rushed onto the field "with almost the impact of Blücher at Waterloo" and saved the day. Nevins, *War for the Union*, II, 122–23.

no order came for us to move. About 8 o'clock the firing commenced on our left wing (where the battle raged yesterday) on the other side of the river but lower down.[32] There was little cannonading but the musketry was very rapid and lasted for more than two hours. We had no firing here except the artillery shooting across the river at the Rebel wagon trains that were passing and repassing all day. This afternoon they kept up a considerable fire from their batteries.

About noon came an official dispatch that we had whipped the enemy and drove him back. This was good news for our boys, who began to cheer hartily. About 3 p.m. came another dispatch from Genl. McClellan saying that we had drove the enemy at every point with grate loss to them, that all our troops except Genl. Casey's Brigade had done nobally,[33] that our loss was considerable, and that Franklin's & Porter's Divisions should not cross the river until further orders but to complete the bridges, &c.

We ought to thank God for this victory. The fighting was very hard and the outcome for awhile very doubtful, for Casey's Division faltered and retreated. At this critical time Genl. Kearny came rushing in, charged and fired on Casey's men, turned them back, fought like a tiger, rolled back the tide of victory, and saved the fortunes of the day.[34] Genl. Kearny is a real go-ahead man and makes a good general. . . .

Tonight we hear heavy cannonading on the James River. I think our gunboats are working their way up to Richmond. If they are successful, Richmond will soon be ours. . . .

Monday morning, June 2nd. There is a very heavy battle now going on in the vicinity of Richmond. We only know it by the cannonading we hear. It has been going on since daylight, and it is now 7 a.m. and still continuing. We undoubtedly must be held as a reserve or for some importat purpose. We may be moved any minute. . . .

---

32. The day after Seven Pines (or Fair Oaks, as the battle is often termed), Confederates made a weak assault farther to the south and were easily repulsed. See Alexander S. Webb, *The Peninsula* (New York, 1885), 97–117.

33. McAllister was referring to the noon dispatch of McClellan to War Secretary Stanton. After hard fighting, McClellan reported, his men "drove back the enemy at the point of the bayonet, covering the ground with his dead. . . . With the exception of Casey's division [our] men behaved splendidly." *OR,* Vol. XI, Pt. 1, p. 749.

34. Maj. Hatfield verified the fact that Kearny's troops fired into Casey's men when the latter "gave way unaccountably and disunitedly." McClellan was high in praise of Kearny's gallantry in the battle. Baquet, *First Brigade,* 431; *OR,* Vol. XI, Pt. 1, pp. 39, 749, 751.

Camp on the Chickahominy, June 2nd 1862

My dear Ellen,

I wrote you this morning. Since that time I received a letter from Sarah telling me that you are much better. . . . This is the very best news for me that I could get. . . .

The fighting I spoke about this morning ceased about 9 a.m. In the middle of the afternoon it commenced again and continued for an hour or more. It was in the direction of Richmond. It may have been in and along the James River. No one here seems to know anything about it; and, of course, nothing official is known. We know but little of the battle of Saturday and Sunday except what I have told you—that we were successful and drove the enemy at every point. Losses were heavy on both sides. I fear it is very heavy on ours. Had McClellan had his own way, without being so much hampered by anti-administration men together with Stanton, he would have long since been in Richmond. Those that talk and condemn everything are not the ones that are willing to come and do the work. That we can get to Richmond I have no doubt, but look how our men have to fight from day to day.

Tuesday morning, June 3rd. . . . Our Regiment goes on picket duty today, so I shall be engaged. This duty is not as dangerous as it was. Our artillery are firing at intervals through the day, dropping shells across the river, and it has caused the Rebel pickets to fall back and not be so bold as they were.

Our paymaster, Maj. Allison, is here now paying the troops. He will pay us tomorrow, as we are on picket duty today. I can let you have $250 out of my March and April pay. I will send you a check either to your bank in Belviere or to one of the New York banks. . . .

Camp on the Chickahominy, June 5th 1862

My dear daughter Sarah,

I am not certain that you are in Philadelphia. But as you and Henrietta both wrote me that your mother was much better and that you would return to school on Monday, I have no doubt but what you are in the city.

We are still at this place, building bridges preparatory to crossing the river. Genl. Smith's Division crossed today. One hundred and twenty-five of our men were detailed this morning as a fatigue party to work on the bridge. As soon as they got there, the Rebels opened their batteries on them. Immediately our artillery responded. Then we witnessed quite an artillery battle.[35] The firing was quite brisk for awhile. Then our pieces in this camp were run out and commenced firing. The Rebels retreated. Had they returned the fire of our guns, their shells would have come right into our camp. But their attention was directed to other batteries, so we could see the whole battle. I have not yet heard as to the number of killed and wounded.

We are living right under the guns of the enemy. Unless the firing assumes the proportions of a battle, we don't pay much attention to it. Day before yesterday a shell came right into camp and fell right between Col. Simpson's and Maj. Birney's tents. It did not burst and fortunately done no one any harm. We often find them whizzing overhead.

I was out on picket duty day before yesterday and the night following. Our whole battalion was out and I had command. We were on this side of the creek, and the Rebel pickets were on the other side quite close to us. In the evening it commenced raining and continued to pour down in torrents all night and the next morning. It was expected that the enemy would attack us that night, so we had to be on the alert. I visited the pickets at 11 p.m. Adj. Henry and an orderly took the left wing, and I took the right wing. We had a time of it. It was pitch dark. We got off the line and then got lost. We felt our way back, succeeded in finding the line, went along it safely, and returned to the woods where our reserves were. We were wet through to the skin.

We had difficulty in finding our tent but got into it at last. It was too short. The Adjutant said we would either have to leave our heads or our feet stick out. I proposed to draw up our feet and have both head and feet indoors. In this way we rolled ourselves up in blankets. Yet as the ends of the tent were open, it began to blow in on our heads. I then covered up with the blankets and fell asleep. . . . In the morning I got awake and found it was raining very fast and blowing hard. The water had run under us. Henry was still fast asleep, enjoying his delightful bed. It seemed almost impossible to get him up. At last I hollered out, "Adjutant, you will drown! The water is rushing under you!"

He scratched open his eyes, saw his condition, and concluded that it was not so pleasant after all.

We called our servants to get our horses, summoned our orderlies, and went on our rounds. Stopped at Mr. Sidney's [36] barn, where

---

35. See *OR,* Vol. XI, Pt. 1, pp. 45–46, 1000–2.
36. McAllister stopped at a building on the farm of either E. Sydnor or William B. Sydnor. The two farms were adjacent to one another and situated

we also had a reserve, to get out of the pouring rain. After awhile we rode back to the woods. But our tent was too wet to go into. Blankets and all were completely saturated. Our men all had bush houses that of course leaked. So we stood under the trees until about 10 o'clock, when we were relieved by another regiment. We got home here between 11 & 12 o'clock, having had no brackfast and our clothes all wet.

This is a very poor discription of picket duty on this peninsula in front of the Rebels. It may give you an idea of active service in the field.

I must tell you a good anicdote that occoured on the banks of the Chickahominy. Our men were cooking coffee. The Rebel pickets hollored out: "Are you making coffee?"

"Yes," was the reply.

"Is it real coffee?" the Rebels asked.

The answer again was yes.

"Will you give me some if I come over?"

Again he was told yes.

"But," he asked, "will you let me come back?"

The reply was yes.

So over came the Rebel, drank a cup of coffee, ate some biscuits, and then said he would have another cup, which was given to him. He then decided that he wouldn't go back at all, so he gave himself up and was brought up to the General's quarters. . . .

Camp on the Chickahominy, June 6th 1862

My dear Ellen,

I wrote to you and Mr. Wiestling yesterday morning. After I wrote you, we had an artillery battle. The loss on our side was one man wounded and two horses killed. The enemy retreated and let the bridge-building go on. We leave this morning and move camp & baggage to Mechanicsville, about 2½ miles up the river, to relieve a brigade that is now stationed there. Smith's Division, which is part of our army corps, crossed over the river at New Bridge yesterday. Why they did not go up to Mechanicsville on this side I don't understand. I suppose it's to prevent a flank movement of the enemy.[37] . . .

---

midway between Cold Harbor and Mechanicsville. *Official Atlas,* Plate LXXVII, Map 1; Adams, *Story of a Trooper,* 489.

37. On June 5 McClellan reluctantly sent a division north of the flooded Chickahominy to reinforce his right flank, which was militarily isolated by the stream. *OR,* Vol. XI, Pt. 1, p. 46.

At this time all seems very quiet. I have no doubt but that we shall have a splendid triumph of our arms very soon. I think the Rebellion is nearly played out. . . .

Mechanicsville, Va., June 6th 1862

My dear daughter Hennie,

I wrote your mother last evening and this morning and told her that we had orders to come to this place. Our old camp was three miles below here. We are on the same side of the river; but as it has a grate bend above here, we are only about 4½–5 miles from Richmond by road. In one of my former letters to your mother I spoke of this little town and how Genl. Stoneman's advance fought the Rebels here and how his artillery knocked the houses to pieces.[38] Some of them are perfectly riddled. Cannon balls have went clear through them. In the best house in the village is a room in which one of Stoneman's shells busted, tearing everything to pieces. From the rooms and roof of this house the Rebel sharpshooters were trying to pick off our men when Stoneman unlimbered his guns and demolished the town. That made the enemy fly in such a hurry that they did not have time to destroy the bridge. So you see we have one bridge to cross on our way to Richmond.

The enemy are quite close here as they were down the river. They are looking right at us and we at them. We have just our Brigade here, with four pieces of artillery pointing right at the Rebels. We are on the extreme right of the army, unless Genl. McDowell is somewhere that we don't know of. It is possible that the Rebels may try and flank us. But if they do they will not find us asleep. Besides, we think we have a good position. It appears that we have come up here to relieve Bartlett's brigade [39] and do picket duty for a few days. . . .

We are in a nice grove of trees close by this village, a beautiful spot but the dirtiest place I have ever seen. Language could hardly give you a picture of it. It was a Rebel camp until Genl. Stoneman sent the cannon balls flying through here. The trees as well as the houses show the marks of them. We are cleaning it up and hauling the dirt and filth away and will soon have a very nice camp. When we came here, the 96th Pennsylvania Regiment was encamped on it.

38. See *ibid.*, pp. 657–58; Kitching, *Memorials*, 67.
39. Col. Joseph J. Bartlett was in temporary command of a brigade composed of the 5th Maine, 16th New York, 27th New York, and 96th Pennsylvania.

But some of our regiments, I am sorry to say, don't police as much as they should. The 96th squatted down right on top of the Rebel dirt, a thing you won't get the 1st New Jersey to do.[40] We police first and pitch tents afterwards. The 96th Pennsylvania had a large sick list. No wonder. I am sick now looking at the filth.

June 7th. . . . I was up a little after 3 to be ready in case the Rebels attacked us. But they did not come. They tried this place the other day; Maj. [William] Hexamer played on them with his battery and caused them to retreat. The rascals had the very cannon they took from [General Silas] Casey's Division in the battle of last Saturday. The Major dug up some of the balls and seen the marks. So we were fighting against our own pieces. As a general thing we can throw shells farther than they; but we can't when they have our guns. . . .

Mechanicsville, Va., June 8th 1862

My dear Ellen,

I wrote you and Henrietta yesterday and explained how we came here and what for. All as yet has been very quiet, except for a little firing along the line. But somehow or other there is an impression that the Rebels will attack us today, probably because they usually choose the Sabbath to fight us and partly from other indications. Musketry and cannon fire has been heard along our lines during the night. One thing I am sure of: Genl. McClellan will not commence a battle on Sunday, for he is opposed to it. But of course, if attacked he will defend. That is his duty. . . .

I took a ramble through the now desolated houses and yards in this village. All these houses are pierced with cannon balls. I have not seen a single inhabitant still here. I saw in the paper yesterday that this place was to Richmond what Germantown is to Philadelphia —a place for the wealthy who live and do business in the city, but leaving the impression on the minds of the people that it is quite a considerable place. There are not more than a half a dozen houses in it. One church, a small building that would compare with one of our school houses, a carpenter and blacksmith shop, several ice houses, and two or three stables sums up the whole town. It is a very pretty place and once had some nice yards. . . .

---

40. Maj. Hatfield noted: "The ground was perfectly filthy. We set about to clean it up; there must have been at least fifty loads of dirt." Baquet, *First Brigade,* 431.

Mechanicsville, Va., June 9th 1862

My dear Ellen,

... Yesterday passed off very quietly, though it was expected we would be attacked. Three Rebels came to our pickets yesterday morning and gave themselves up. Capt. [Valentine] Mutchler brought them in. Two of them are from Louisiana and the other one from this state. They said that half a pound of flour and a half a pound of meat is all the rations they get. They also say that if we don't attack them for ten days, the whole Rebel army will have to give up for want of provisions.[41] These seemed like very intelligent men and say that there are many more who would like to come over if they could get off and get through our lines. They knew nothing about the evacuation of Corinth and say the whole cry is: "Defend Richmond!" They also say that they have two heavy siege guns opposite us and have the range of our camp.

Last evening one of our pickets run across the river on the bridge and exchanged with the Rebel Major a New York *Herald* of the 6th for a Richmond paper of the 7th. When the Major opened up the paper, he exclaimed that Corinth had been evacuated and remarked that he had not heard a word of it before now. They are kept in perfect ignorance of their defeats.

Mrs. Harris is here in the neighbourhood. I called on her last evening. She will be here today, then return to White House, where she makes her headquarters. I do not know when we will advance but suppose soon. ...

Mechanicsville, Va., June 13th 1862

My dear Ellen,

I was not able to write you my usual letter yesterday as we had to move our camp at daylight, owing to the enemy having shelled us. About 5 p.m. they opened their two siege guns right into our camp. Several shells busted right over our heads. But God protected us and not a man was hurt. We formed our lines and moved away a little piece from the woods; then our batteries opened on them. After about an hour's firing they stopped and all was quiet again. This morning we came over to these woods but are no further from the enemy. They don't know that we are here and will not likely get the range. If they commence again, they will most likely fire at the old camp.

---

41. For more on the destitute condition of the Confederate defenders, see *Battle-Fields of the South,* II, 112–17.

We are getting some heavy pieces in place and perhaps today will open on them. Then we shall have a brisk time of it. The enemy is showing themselves strong at the upper bridge, and it is thought that they want to make a demonstration on us. We have planted our cannon, taking the range of the two they have, so that if they attempt to cross we will be ready for them.

Our regiment goes on picket this afternoon and remains out twenty-four hours. I will be in command. The Colonels of the regiments on picket duty always act as Officers of the Grand Guard. The commands of regiments devolves on Lieutenant Colonels. . . . It is possible that we may cross the river soon and push for Richmond. McClellan was here yesterday, looking around. . . .

Camp Advance, Mechanicsville, Va., June 16th 1862

My dear Ellen,

. . . My last letter was written at Meadow Bridge, 1½ miles above here, where we were on picket duty. Our position was a dangerous one, and I did not sleep any that night. All our Brigade was under arms, for an order came in the middle of the night that the enemy had crossed above us and were flanking us. If attacked, our Regiment on picket duty was to hold out and not give way until reinforcements came. Our reserves would come out in support of the pickets instead of the pickets falling back on them. The other regiments of our Brigade moved out to our right and formed lines of battle. During the night we planted a twelve-pounder brass piece and threw up a breastwork on the railroad and turnpike at Meadow Bridge. . . . But the day dawned and no enemy made their appearance.

On the Sabbath morning the sun rose in all its magnificent splendor and witnessed the movements of the two contending armies. Yet I am happy to say we had no battle. The enemy was not to be seen, and you know that Genl. McClellan never commences battle on God's holy day. About 9 a.m. our Regiment was relieved and we came into camp. . . . Friday, Saturday and Sunday were exceedingly hot. I suffered much from heat on Saturday. Last evening it rained, and it has been cool ever since.

Our camp is in a beautiful woods like the one we were shelled out of in the village. We still keep our camp fires burning there so that the enemy can shell away as long as they please and do us no harm. They can throw shells here as well as there, but we are so nicely concealed under this shady grove that they don't know where we are. Our boys don't mind the shells much now. We are getting used to them. One throwed at Co. K coming home yesterday fell behind them, bounced over their heads, but done no harm.[42]

I am sorry to say we had two deaths in our Regiment yesterday —dysintery and typhoid fever.[43] Poor fellows. They came to serve their country and have done it nobly. But here, far from home, with no kind friends to soothe their dying pillow, they pass off the stage of action with none really to feel their loss here. It is a solemn duty that devolves on our Government to see that the wives and families of these deceased soldiers are cared for. We have not had many deaths in our Regiment. Only three are now with these two buried on the Peninsula. We have a large sick list, but none are dangerously ill. Our other Jersey regiments have lost more than we have. Our army is greatly reduced by sickness. This climate is not healthy. . . .

Adj. Henry was bitten by a snake the day after the battle of West Point, but he was soon well again. He was not very ill from the effects of it.

When you receive this letter, buy and enclose in your reply a necktie. Send it at once. I have to wear paper collars. They are too low to use as a stock; besides that, the perspiration ruins them. The neckties are the only thing used by the officers. Get a neat black one, or one as dark as you can—and the sooner the better.

If I get a tie, I can get along even if I don't get the undershirts, though I need them badly. There is no chance to get anything here. We all expect to get new clothes when we get to Richmond by having them sent to us.

We are all quiet here today. Not a single shot has been fired. We regret the loss of so many wagons and stores by Steuart's Rebel cavalry.[44] It was a bold dash by him and shows the necessity of McClellan having a larger force to protect our rear. And yet there are those in the North who cry out: "Why don't we get to Richmond?" If McClellan had rushed on, as some designed, his army

42. On June 16 Col. James H. Simpson of the 4th New Jersey reported: "A [Confederate] battery, situated about midway between the Mechanicsville Bridge and the Meadow Bridge, opened for the first time yesterday morning with shell, two of which were thrown, one toward a foraging party of cavalry, the other toward a company of the First New Jersey Volunteers, returning from picket, and which unnecessarily exposed itself." *OR,* Vol. XI, Pt. 1, p. 1057.

43. The two soldiers were Pvts. John O'Neil of Co. C and Henry Spohn of Co. K. *N.J. Record,* I, 78, 100.

44. McAllister was referring to Confederate Gen. "Jeb" Stuart and his cavalry, who made a June 12–15 reconnaissance all the way around McClellan's army and returned to their lines with 165 prisoners, 260 horses, and many captured arms. Stuart's report of the affair is in *OR,* Vol. XI, Pt. 1, pp. 1036–40.

would have been cut to pieces. He is moving *slowly but surely,* though I think his force ought to be much larger. However, I am willing that he should direct us, guided, I have no doubt, by a higher power. . . .

Camp near Mechanicsville, Va., June 18th 1862

My dear Ellen,

. . . We have orders to pack up and leave. We will probably go tonight or in the morning. There has been a grate many movements of troops today, indicating something of importance. There was heavy cannonading down the river today somewhere near our old camp. I think a forward movement will take place tomorrow. The fate of Richmond will be decided very soon. If I am spared to get through, I will get a furlough and go home. If I am wounded, I want to go home. If killed, I will be sent home. We hope for the best. . . .

We have many rumors here. One is that Fort Darling is taken by our gunboats and the Stars and Stripes are now floating over it.[45] This wants confirmation. I fear it is too good to be true. We heard firing there yesterday. If it is true, Richmond will soon fall into our hands. Other stories this evening say the Rebels are evacuating Richmond. This I don't believe, for prisoners and contraband agree that they are determined to make a hard stand. Their preparations for it confirm these statements. But, of course, their case is hopeless. They must give up sooner or later, yeald obedience to our Government, and stop this bloody war. . . . I would not be surprised if a number of them don't give themselves up when we go forward. A portion of them are sick and tired of the Rebellion. And well they might be, for half of them don't know what they are fighting for. One of the prisoners said in my presence that he was satisfied they were fighting for nothing less than despotism of the worst kind. He was quite intelligent.

I think Thompson and his son Willie are in [Stonewall] Jackson's army, if they are living. I want nothing to do with him or his family. He has acted badly when he could have done otherwise and been a man and a *patriot*. But no, he has all this disgrace so that he and Lydia [46] could own a few miserable slaves and be ranked No. 1 in

---

45. This rumor was untrue. Fort Darling stood atop Drewry's Bluff on the James River. Its garrison successfully withstood one Federal assault in May, 1862, held out against a second attack in May, 1864, and remained defiant until the April, 1865, evacuation of Richmond.

46. Lydia Miller Addams was the first of Thompson McAllister's three wives.

Virginia society—miserable society, kept together by the labour and sale of slaves. . . .

One thing I meant to mention before I started on this campaign: I borrowed $25 from Genl. [William R.] Montgomery and intended sending him a check on Riggs & Co. Bank in Washington. But I can't find out where he is. The money is there for him. If anything happens to me, he has my receipt for it. . . .

Fair Oaks, across the Chickahominy, June 19th 1862

My dear Ellen,

I wrote you last night that we had marching orders but did not know our destanation. We started this morning and just arrived here. Forces are collecting here for the final move on Richmond. I think it most likely that we will move in the morning. Before you get this, you will have the news of the surrender of Richmond. . . .

I find that we are right close to the battlefield of May 31-June 1. Last evening, close by this place, there was a skirmish of considerable magnitude.[47] The enemy made the attack to drive us away, but our artillery opened on them in such power that they were driven back with a grate loss, supposed to be four or five hundred, while we had but one man killed and ten or fifteen wounded. We have just got the information that Fort Darling is now in our possession. This is a grate advantage to the taking of Richmond. The battle last night will cause dismay in the enemy's ranks. All helps the final result.

Alice [Dick] wishes my advice as to your taking a trip to Shippensburg or Juniata. I am perfectly willing that you do so. Go any place you like. Had you not better go to Bethlehem or some one of the summer resorts for your health? In those agricultural neighbourhoods they will all be so busy. I would rather you remained in Belvidere until we get to Richmond, when I will get a furlough and go home. If this should not take place soon, you need not wait. . . .

Camp near Fair Oaks, Va., June 20th 1862

My dear daughter Sarah,

I received your letter yesterday evening after our arrival here. We left our camp near Mechanicsville yesterday morning, went down the river on the other side, and crossed on the bridge called New-

---

47. The details of this June 18 reconnaissance by the 16th Massachusetts are in *OR*, Vol. XI, Pt. 1, pp. 1060–63; Fuller, *Chaplain Fuller*, 261–63.

berry's Bridge. We marched two miles from the river and camped here near the ballance of our Division. It was said last night that the grand movement to Richmond would be made this morning. But up to this time—now evening—nothing of importance has occoured beyond skirmishing, which we more or less have every day. . . . I think we are now in such a position that an attack cannot much longer be delayed. We are looking for it hourely.

We are in Taylor's Brigade, Slocum's Division, Franklin's Corps. Col. [George] Taylor has been made a Brigadier and has our Brigade. Kearny has been made a division commander. He was taken from us and has now no less than fifteen regiments under him. He is about one mile to our left and ready to pounce on the enemy at the word go. He is turning out remarkably well and is considered a most excellent general. He has certainly done good service, both at Williamsburg and at Fair Oaks.

This forenoon I visited the Fair Oaks battleground. This end of the ground is about eighty rods from our camp. I was all over the ground. The matters of interest were pointed out to us. Mr. Yard and Maj. Hatfield were along. Why it is called Seven Pines I cannot tell. As a general thing, this is pine country. No doubt some farm was called that from a cluster of trees. The reason it is called Fair Oaks is that a few acres near this is covered with oak timber. A plantation with good buildings near these oaks became a place of resort from Richmond. It was called Fair Oaks when the railroad made a station there. The battle is now called after it in prefference to the battle of Seven Pines.

This country is three-fourths woods, low and swampy—in a word, a most miserable, forelorn looking place. Where the battle was fought was so wet they could not use artillery. So the battle on Sunday was fought with small arms. It was the most rapid and terrifick firing I ever heard—one continuous roar all the time. I know you have seen discriptions of the battle, so I will refer to the appearance of the battleground.

Graves are everywhere to be seen. Men were buried on the ground where they fell. Our Union soldiers all have head and footboards with their name, company, and regiment on them. The ground is very low and wet for graves. The Rebels are buried in piles with no marks or boards but simply the raised ground showing that something was buried there. You may think this is hard; but you must remember that the battle was fought on Saturday and Sunday. The Rebels had possession of the ground all Saturday night and Sunday morning. A portion of the ground—part of Casey's camp—was in

[180] ✕ THE McALLISTER LETTERS

their possession until Monday morning. They had the [railroad] cars running all the time. Yet they left near 3,000 of their dead on the ground. The bodies swelled up and began to decay. When we drove them back and got possession of the ground, our men were buried first. By the time our men could attend to the Rebels, their dead bodies were in a very unpleasant condition to do anything with. I saw a place where about twenty of them lay in two square rods. They were piled up and a mound of earth thrown over them. In Casey's camp, now occupied by the 5th and 6th New Jersey, there are a grate many graves of both Union men and Rebels. The smell arising from these badly buried men, and from the dead horses, is very unpleasant. It will undoubtedly produce sickness. But I suppose the idea is that we will move forward soon. We are not on that ground and have none of those difficulties.

In an open field I was shown a chimney where the brave Jeff Davis hid his precious self during a part of the battle.[48] I suppose it became too hot for him and he retreated. The 8th Alabama came out of Richmond on the Sabbath morning in white shirts and pumps. You know this is the crack Rebel regiment got up by the governor of that State and composed of the very elite. They moved forward on our troops and were driven back by the 5th and 6th New Jersey. In their retreat they ran into a Michigan regiment that fired a volley into them, mowing them down. Then they went in another direction and run against another of our regiments, and another volley was poured into them. All were either cut down or taken prisoners until there is nothing left of them.[49]

There is no doubt that the loss of the Rebels was two to our one.[50] Where one of our men lay dead, there were two of them. But the slaughter on both sides was terable. . . . When I contemplate the destruction of life in this contest, I feel that I am willing to sacrifice anything to catch Jeff Davis & Co.—the leaders of this wicked rebellion—and have them pay the penalty of death and be buried as many of our poor soldiers are buried, just rolled into a hole with nothing to mark the spot.

48. Throughout the battle President Davis—accompanied by Gen. Lee—was either riding along the lines or quartered with Johnston in a small house on Nine Mile Road. Charles Marshall, *An Aide-de-camp of Lee* (Boston, 1927), 57.

49. McAllister was probably referring to Col. John B. Gordon's well-disciplined 6th Alabama, which suffered 385 casualties out of 650 engaged in the battle. See John B. Gordon, *Reminiscences of the Civil War* (New York, 1904), 26–27, 55–59; *OR*, Vol. XI, Pt. 1, pp. 41, 817–20, 835–26.

50. Confederate losses at Seven Pines numbered 6,134 men; Federal casualties were 5,031. *OR*, Vol. XI, Pt. 1, p. 762; Freeman, *Lee's Lieutenants*, I, 244.

Saturday morning. Quiet still continues along our lines. . . . This morning is beautiful, but I think it will be a hot day. If I live to get to Richmond, I will get a furlough; if not, I will get your mother to come and see me. . . .

Camp near Fair Oaks, Va., June 21st 1862

My dear Ellen,

. . . There are now no signs of a forward movement. We are throwing up earthworks all along the front, doing heavy picket duty, and building roads and bridges preparatory to a grand movement. We may be kept at this work for some time. . . .

The enemy are very close by; our entrenchments are just in front of them and our men are lying all over this ground, which is swarming with flies. However, our Brigade is not on this ground. Our position is not as nice as I would like it to be. It is rather low and swampy. The country is not near so nice as that we just left on the other side of the Chickahominy. That is a beautiful country around Mechanicsville.

I would like dearly to go home. However, as we are now situated, it is out of the question. . . .

I did procure an armor vest. But it is too heavy, too warm, and inconvenient to wear in this hot weather. I may put it on some time. I did not have it on at West Point. There are different opinions about them.[51]

John Sweny [52] is living, but he has been sick and is in the hospital at the White House and not much better. Capt. Mutchler has written to his father. . . .

Camp Lincoln, Fair Oaks, Va., June 22nd 1862

My dear Ellen,

I have time to write you but a line this morning, as the mail will soon start. I am quite well, for which I am thankful to God and trust I acknowledge His loving care over me.

  51. Sutlers and private dealers made earnest efforts to peddle to soldiers metal chest plates guaranteed as "iron-clad life preservers." Such accouterments never became popular—except as frying pans for cooking rations. Francis A. Lord, *They Fought for the Union* (Harrisburg, Pa., 1960), 145–46.
  52. Pvt. John Sweeney of Co. D deserted at Trenton while on an April, 1864, veteran furlough. *N.J. Record,* I, 82.

As you see by the papers, we have skirmishing all along the lines every day. Yesterday afternoon there was quite an engagement, and last night another one. Our Brigade was not in either of them. We formed the third line and have not yet done any picket duty. That is why we have not got into the skirmishing. When the grand move will be I don't know. You know more from the papers than I can tell you.

A grate deal of sickness is in the army. The climate is bad for us, and there is no help for us. Yet I am willing for McClellan to have his way. Success is sure. . . .

Fair Oaks, Va., June 23rd 1862

My dear Ellen,

. . . Yesterday, the Sabbath, was one of the quietest days I have ever witnessed in camp. It was very warm and the men staid in their tents. The enemy did not annoy us—not a gun fired by them. I think I heard two shots from our side. All was so quiet we did not know we were in the midst of war. Last evening we had a delightful prayer meeting in front of my tent and some appropriate remarks by Chaplain Yard. It now looks a little like rain. If it rains much it will be bad for us in this low ground. But still it will cool the atmosphere and make it more pleasant.

I have a chance to send a messenger to the White House today, and I will see if my shirts that you were to send by express are there. . . . I want those undershirts bad and would like to have two nice fine woolin overshirts that would be decent. These that I have are so rough and coarse. We cannot use white shirts as we cannot get them washed. In camp we often pull off our coats, so you can see the necessity of a nice shirt that is fit to be seen in. . . .

Col. Torbert is sick but not very bad.[53] I hope he will be well when we move forward. . . .

The enemy lost heavily in the skirmish on Saturday night. Our loss is very light. The enemy no doubt are trying to get at our stores, as they must be in need of food. But our lines are too strong for them; they can't brake through them. We have three times more men now on the reserve third line. . . .

53. At this time, one writer asserted, Torbert "was down with Chickahominy fever [malaria] and could hardly stand on his feet . . ." Townsend, *Torbert Memorial*, 21. See also R. F. Stockton, *Memorial Address . . . at the Service Held in Memory of . . . A. T. A. Torbert* (Trenton, 1880), 5; George T. Stevens, *Three Years in the Sixth Corps* (New York, 1870), 73–75.

Fair Oaks, Va., Tuesday morning, June 24th 1862

My dear Ellen,

We had an order at 4 a.m. to be under arms, ready to march. We immediately got ready and are now waiting for further orders. We had a bad thunderstorm last night. Just before it commenced, heavy firing was heard a short distance from here on the left. It is possible this call to arms may have arisen from that firing. It is all quiet now. But they may open fire again at any moment. A report last night said that the enemy had fell back a mile or more and that we were advancing our pickets. If so, we have to support them. Yet it is very hard to tell anything about it. The enemy find they cannot brake through our lines. What their next dodge will be I can't say. Perhaps they will fall back a little and get us to follow them and then make a bold stand to defeat us. Time will determine. But McClellan is wide awake for them.

Had you not better ask Mr. Wiestling to come down to Belvidere until he is well? He would be near a doctor.

Lieut. Ettringham [54] was shot by one of our own pickets, as the paper stated. I ordered him out to visit the pickets He got outside our lines before he was aware of it and was then fired upon. But the ball, though close to his face, did not hurt him. . . .

Fair Oaks, Va., June 25th 1862

My dear Ellen,

Yesterday was a day of battle. Fighting was principally on the left, and Kearny's and [Major General Joseph] Hooker's Divisions did most of the hard fighting as the pressure was the heaviest there. Our line here was undisturbed. We were ordered out to act as reserves for [General Israel B.] Richardson's Brigade and were not in the fight. The battle commenced in the afternoon and continued all day long. We came in at dark. Our lines on the left were advanced from one to two miles, and the enemy was trying to push these lines back all night. Though dark, firing continued at intervals all through the night. Now it is morning, the sun is just up and the battle has again commenced at the same place.[55] So we will undoubtedly have a

---

54. Lt. Joseph B. Ettringham of Co. H resigned from service in September, 1862. *N.J. Record,* I, 91.

55. On June 25 Federals attacked at Oak Grove (or King's School-House) but were driven back after all-day fighting. *OR,* Vol. XI, Pt. 2, pp. 96–97, 787–88.

warm time. I think that McClellan will only hold the ground we have and get his big guns in place. Then we can send shells to Richmond. This ground is very low but the ground gained is much higher. . . .

A report says that [FitzJohn] Porter's Division crossed at New Bridge yesterday to our right. If so, we will advance on the right to get a beautiful hill which McClellan is anxious to place his guns on.

In the fighting yesterday the 19th Massachusetts lost 44 men. They advanced, the enemy lay in ambush; then the Rebels rose and delivered a deadly volley, cutting the Massachusetts boys down. There was a Lieut. Warner, a splendid young man, shot through the head.[56] I saw his body when it was brought past our Regiment. . . . It now seems that our loss along the whole line may amount to 1,000 killed, wounded and missing. . . . The noble and brave are the most likely to fall.

As the 19th Massachusetts was advancing yesterday, they heard a voice up in a tree saying, "Save your friends." Their Colonel [Edward W. Hinks] looked up and saw a lot of Rebels in the trees. He immediately ripped out at them and gave the order to fire. Down tumbled two Rebels. Lieut. Warner was shot by these rascals. This trick of the Rebels in battle—"Don't shoot your friends"—as well as the white flag deception, are both completely played out, and many a Rebel has to bite the dust for these past deceptions. Our men pay no attention to these ruses; on the other hand, knowing the deception, they fire most desperately.

We were drawn up in battle array yesterday on the Fair Oaks battleground, of which I have spoken before. . . . A very short distance from where I stood is a white oak tree in an open space. Under this tree General Pettigrew was taken prisoner by our boys in that Sunday battle.[57] One of these days I will send you a leaf from this tree.

9 p.m. All is now very quiet along the whole line. Not a gun is to be heard. Why this unusual quiet I can't tell. . . .

11 a.m. [*June 26*] We have now fallen back to our old lines. Nothing was gained yesterday, only that we have shown the enemy that they can't brake our lines. McClellan has ordered that there must be no more skirmishing and picket firing. He evidently intends to invest the city, starve them out, complete the surrender, and save life. If so, we may not have to do much fighting. . . .

56. In this action the 19th Massachusetts lost 11 killed and 40 wounded. Among the dead was Lt. Charles B. Warner of Co. H. *Ibid.*, p. 37; *History of the Nineteenth Regiment, Massachusetts Volunteer Infantry* (Salem, Mass., 1906), 80–84.

57. Confederate Gen. Johnston J. Pettigrew fell wounded during the battle of Seven Pines. He believed his injuries to be mortal, refused assistance to the rear, and thus fell into Federal hands.

Fair Oaks, Va., June 27th 1862

My dear Ellen,

A short time after I finished my letter to you yesterday, heavy firing commenced on our right at or near Mechanicsville.[58] It continued until as late as 9 a.m. It was the most terrifick firing I have ever heard, so far as artillery is concerned. It was a continuous roar, small arms not anything like the Fair Oaks battle. Stonewall Jackson attacked [General George] McCall's Division and a heavy engagement took place. McCall drove the enemy for four miles, took cannon, a quantity of ammunition, and gained a complete victory. But this morning at 5 o'clock they opened battle again and it has raged as it did yesterday morning.

We are now ordered up to support Porter's Division but don't think we can get there in time to be of any benefit to our army. I did not sleep any last night. Our Regiment was on picket duty, and it was by far the most dangerous duty yet performed on picket. We protected a large working party of 600 men while they were throwing up earthworks. This was accomplished before daylight and not over fifty feet from the enemies' pickets and right under the guns of two of their earthworks. Our orders were given in whispers. . . .

Camp Lincoln, Fair Oaks, Va., June 28th 1862

My dear Ellen,

Yesterday was a terable day for us—one of the hardest fights of the war. I took my Regiment into battle. I am unhurt, though thousands of balls passed close by and over me. Thank God for His protective care of me. But I have to record the loss of nearly half of our Regiment. The brave boys fought to the last. We were the last to leave the field, and crossfires hurled death and destruction all around us. I was there among the brave fellows and we were forced to leave. I seen them all out of the woods, and we were nearly all captured.

Capt. Brewster is killed; he fell dead.[59] Corporal [William]

58. The wounding of Johnston at Seven Pines led to the elevation of Lee to command of the Confederate army. Utilizing the theory that the best defense is an offense, Lee on June 26 launched an all-out attack on McClellan's isolated right flank. The failure of Stonewall Jackson's brigades to arrive on the field as scheduled contributed to the Confederate defeat at Mechanicsville. Lee nevertheless renewed his offensive the following day at Gaines's Mill. His troops finally smashed the Federal lines after some of the most vicious fighting of the war.

59. George Brewster went down while "fighting bravely," McAllister officially reported. *OR,* Vol. XI, Pt. 2, p. 439.

[186] ✕ THE McALLISTER LETTERS

Campbell is killed and I suppose Sam [60] is too, as he is reported missing. What is worse than all, the enemy has possession of the ground and we can't get the bodies of these brave defenders of our country's cause. Many wounded are on that ground. I will, if spared, write you all about it. Oh! How badly I feel! Maj. Hatfield is wounded but will recover.[61] He fell in the early part of the engagement and was carried back to the rear. He is all right. We were not supported and could not hold our position. Inform the [Seldon] Scrantons and friends.

The 3rd Regiment is cut up as badly as we are—perhaps worse. The 2nd Regiment had only four companies in the fight.[62] Col. [Isaac] Tucker was killed; Maj. [Henry] Ryerson was wounded and is a prisoner. The 4th Regiment's officers are all killed, wounded or missing. The whole regiment is lost.[63] We are going to move and perhaps fight again. Goodbye, my dear family. . . .

Camp near City Point, James River, July 1st 1862
My dear Ellen,
I have not written you since the letter I wrote you on Saturday, the day after the terable battle [at Gaines's Mill], in which our Brigade lost fully one half of its number in killed, wounded and missing.[64] The loss of the 4th Regiment has reached a very high figure. Only about eighty of them are left. Our loss is not as large as first estimated, as many that we thought were lost came strolling in later. It is about 180 men. Though large, it is a wonder to me that it was not three times as many—standing as we did for one and a half to two hours under a storm of lead and hail. The equal of it has not been seen on this continent.

60. Sgt. Samuel B. Mutchler of Co. D served out his three-year enlistment. *N.J. Record,* I, 79.
61. Hatfield died July 30 from the effects of his wounds.
62. The 3rd New Jersey suffered losses of 215 men; the 1st New Jersey had 159 casualties; and four companies of the 2nd New Jersey lost 113 men. *OR,* Vol. XI, Pt. 2, p. 40; Baquet, *First Brigade,* 319.
63. McAllister did not exaggerate here. The 4th New Jersey sustained 585 losses, including 437 missing. On July 4 Gen. [George] Taylor, the brigade commander, stated of the regiment: "All the account I can give of them is that but one officer, wounded, and 82 men have rejoined my command." *OR,* Vol. XI, Pt. 2, pp. 40, 438, 604. For memoirs of battle by members of this regiment, see Baquet, *First Brigade,* 361–62, 393–95.
64. In August, 1861, the New Jersey Brigade had numbered 2,800 men. The battle of Gaines's Mill removed from its ranks 1,072 men killed, wounded, or missing. *OR,* Vol. XI, Pt. 2, p. 40; Baquet, *First Brigade,* 9. Cf. Townsend, *Torbert Memorial,* 21.

I would write you a long letter, but we have orders to form a line of battle. So I will just add that I came out of the action untouched, thanks to Him who watched over me. Last night I was under fire again and not hurt.[65] We have one or more battles every day. The like of it has never been witnessed. We are now on the James River. We have lost in these late engagements 20–30,000 men. The slaughter among the enemy is terable. They fight like tigers. . . .

Adj. Henry is not hurt. Poor Brewster is no more. I fear William Campbell is killed and also Samuel. They may be taken prisoners. . . .

Outpost Picket, James River, July 8th 1862

My dear Ellen,

I came out here yesterday as Grand Brigade Officer of the Day with a detail of 700 men from the 2nd and 3rd Regiments. We had been throwing up a redoubt during the night. Our men are nearly worked down and worn out by fatigue and picket duty. Col. Torbert is and has been very sick,[66] Hatfield is wounded and, I suppose, gone home, and Adj. Henry is not well and poisoned at that, so that I have really all the duty to do—Colonel, Lieutenant Colonel, Major, and all. If my health gives way, I will not be able to stand all of this duty. My health has been very good, but I expect the chills and fever to take hold of me soon in this sultry and unhealthy climate. But we will hope for the best.

I long to get home but do not see how I can have that privilege. Col. Torbert will go if he can get a sick furlough—which, I suppose, he will. Mr. Yard is sick and goes with him. If I am to do all the work and all the fighting as Lieutenant Colonel, they may soon have my commission. For I feel that it is unjust. The official reports give me credit in the battle [of Gaines's Mill], and well they may. I think Col. Torbert gets more than is due to him. Genl. Taylor says that Col. Torbert had nothing to do with the hard-fought battle of Gaines's Mill, or Friday's battle at Woodbury's Bridge; and in his report Genl. Taylor gives me full credit and says that I staid with my Regiment in the woods to the last and spoke in the highest terms of my conduct.[67]

---

65. The brigade filled a breach in the Federal lines late in the June 30 battle of Glendale. Though its fighting was minor, the unit's timely arrival on the field was providential for McClellan's successful retreat. *OR,* Vol. XI, Pt. 1, p. 66; Pt. 2, p. 163.

66. See *ibid.,* Pt. 2, p. 440.

67. Taylor wrote: "Colonel Torbert being unwell, the regiment was led by Lieutenant-Colonel McAllister, and well sustained by his presence and courage." *Ibid.,* p. 438.

So do they all. You will get the Newark *Advertiser,* in which our Jersey troops get full credit. Their corrispondent [68] was on the ground and noting everything, so I subscribed to it for six months. I paid for it so that you can be more fully posted up on our Jersey boys.

We have a strong position here. If the enemy attack us, we can cut them all to pieces. If we are not attacked, we will most likely remain here for some time, and it is not likely that there will be any fighting. I have no warrant for saying this; yet it is not only my own impression but the general opinions among our "Knowing Ones." . . .

I have had the strongest assurance from Maj. [Charles M.] Herbert that Governor Olden would appoint me Colonel of the 11th New Jersey Regiment. He says it is a fixed fact and that I would be called home any day now. Since then I have heard nothing. It is possible that more wire pulling must be done. But one thing I do know: if Governor Olden overlooks my claims again, he will have my commission and I will go home and enjoy the comforts of home and family. I have shown to the country and the world that I am no coward, and I have sacrificed a grate deal for my country. I can resign much better now than I could before I fought in the recent battles. I have been in the service for fifteen months, a longer period than I expected to stay. But we will see what Olden will do. There are plenty of chances of promotion—in fact, too many, as so many of our brave officers have fallen. . . .

Harrison's Landing, Va., July 8th 1862

My dear daughter Henrietta,

I have just received one of your nice letters written to me the 5th of July, for which I am much obliged. The battle of Gaines's Mill was fought the 27th of June. I wrote your mother the next morning and I see that you have not yet received it. Before that, you have my letter giving you a history of all the battles until we reached this river. The one at Gaines's Mill (or, as it was called, "the one before Richmond") was when we all fought so hard and where our Brigade lost so heavily. Although we could not call it a victory, it was the means of saving our army. Had not our Brigade fought as they did under one of the most grueling fires ever recorded, and stood as tried veterans, the enemy would have reached the bridge and crossed that night. Our army would have begun a retreat unprepared, the teamsters would have taken a panick, and our army would have been cut to pieces.

68. For field correspondent A. D. Fowler's dispatches of this period, see Baquet, *First Brigade,* 82–85.

We done nobely. It is so recorded in the official reports and so regarded in military circles.

It was the hardest-fought battle of the war. Most battles have some pause in the showers of balls. But not this one, which was one continuous roar of musketry unprecedented in past history. We had to fight our way to the river. It was one battle after another, sometimes with artillery alone, and sometimes with small arms. It was a hard time. But we whipped the Rebels in every engagement and were thus enabled to march on.

Now Hennie, understand that this large army was stretched out for miles and that the rear guard have the fighting to do. This guard was changed, sometimes one portion and sometimes another. In this guard we had a very large section of artillery. On Monday and Monday night our Brigade was on the rear when we were attacked on all sides. We were under arms all day and all night, though, strange to say, our Brigade did not get into the actual fight. But at nightfall we were called forward to assist Genl. Kearny and charge the enemy at a proper time. We hurried on amidst a shower of balls and then laid down to be ready for the charge. The balls passed over our heads. After a hard struggle the Rebels went back into the woods, the officers trying in vain to rally them. We could hear them distinkly. They would cry out: "This way, 2nd Georgia!" "This way, Alabama!" "This way, Louisiana!"

We give three hearty cheers and this frightened the Rebels. We heard them say in answer to the officers' commands: "Rallying is played out! Don't you hear the Yankees cheering?" Others said: "They have got reinforcements. There is no use now trying to get them. They can whip us!"

Now, dear daughter, this cheering done grate good. It saved us fighting another battle which, I can assure you, we had no wish to do. In the middle of the night we resumed our march towards the river. This was a dark night for us. We expected to be attacked on all sides and calculated that many of us would never reach our destination. But God saved us from another battle. There were several battles fought that day and a grate loss of life on both sides.

We must have lost near 15,000 men in killed, wounded and missing during our retreat. The enemy puts their loss at 30,000.[69] There were desperate scenes. The reason that the enemy lost so

---

69. McClellan's army suffered 8,651 of its 15,849 casualties during the retreat from Gaines's Mill to Harrison's Landing. Total Confederate losses during the Seven Days' Campaign numbered almost 19,000 men. *OR,* Vol. XI, Pt. 2, pp. 24–41, 973–84.

heavily was that they did not regard life if they could only accomplish their object. They massed their troops against a given point in order to brake our lines, and our artillery mowed them down. They used the Napoleon plan; but notwithstanding this, we could whip them. Yet many a Northern house is made desolate by these desperate strugles. . . .

I have now seen more hard fighting and more campaigning than most officers and soldiers that make the military a business. You may ask how I felt under fire. I did not think of fear, but I was fully aware of the danger and knew not the moment I might be struck down. The Major [Hatfield] fell in the beginning of the action, and everything then devolved on me. I rode in but found that I could not get along in the woods with a horse. I dismounted, sent my horse to the rear, and acted on foot. I went all along the line through showers of balls, but strange to say, not one struck me. God protected me through that dark hour and enabled me to do my duty to my country. After I got out of the woods and went down through balls and shells to the place where our reserves were, I sank down perfectly exhausted from heat and fatigue. I never felt so weak in my life. At one time I thought that I would fall into the hands of the enemy or be shot down, as whole platoons fired at me. Dust and gravel were thrown over and around me from the balls striking at my feet. How I escaped is a miracle! Many of our men were shot down or taken prisoners at this time.

Lieut. [William] Tantum is not wounded or taken prisoner. He was on the sick list and not present in the action. The first accounts of battle are not correct, for the reporters on this occasion got their casualty lists in the hospitals. But few of our wounded ever reached there. They were carried back from the field and left. The enemy fired into the hospital and some of those in it were killed or taken prisoner.

We formed a new line of battle near the bridge, but night came on and the enemy did not dare attack us again. After resting awhile we crossed over and went into camp.

The Rebels got one of your nice neckties. The last two you sent me were just the thing. . . .

Harrison's Landing, Va., July 10th 1862

My dear Ellen,

. . . Col. Torbert has got a hard attack of fever and has gone home. I have all to do. If I brake down, I don't know what will become of the regiment. My health is still good except for diarrhea which prevails all through the camp, owing in part to bad water. But I feel quite well. We have a grate deal of picketing to do and fortifications to build. The enemy cannot drive us from here. Our position is a very strong one. They have already fell back and don't bother us much now. I do not think there will be fighting for some time to come.

I am very much obliged to Mr. Knighton [70] for his interest in me and especially for his prayers. I wish Mr. Wiestling would read him my letter giving an account of the battle, if he thinks it proper to do so. Tell him his friend Meves of the 3rd Regiment was killed.[71] He was a good, clean man and highly regarded. Capt. Tunis's son [72] was not killed but wounded. Warren County has suffered considerably. All fought well and Warren ought to be proud of such soldiers. . . .

Maj. Hatfield fell very soon after we got into the woods. He will get well, but the ball going $\frac{1}{16}$ of an inch lower would have killed him. Capt. Mount [73] is badly wounded but will get well. I would like to tell you more, but time will not permit. . . .

Harrison's Landing, Va., July 12th 1862

My dear Ellen & family,

I am in receipt of your letters daily now. The mails are coming regularly. I received a letter from you this morning dated the 9th and was astonished to hear that you had only then received my letter written on the morning of June 28th, the morning after the battle. I have written you almost daily since. . . .

Reports here from Trenton say that I am to have command of the 11th Regiment, but I have not gotten any official notice of it yet. If it is so, I suppose I will soon be home. If it is the case, I will tele-

---

70. Frederick Knighton, soon to become chaplain of the 11th New Jersey, emigrated to America from Derby, England. Following his 1847 graduation from the Princeton Theological Seminary, he became pastor of Oxford Furnace's First Presbyterian Church and remained in that capacity until 1873. He was known as "a thorough classical scholar and distinguished mathematician," but his constant penchant for reading was to prove a great source of annoyance to McAllister. *Minutes . . . of the Synod of New Jersey of the Presbyterian Church . . .*, LXV (Trenton, 1888), 39–40.

71. Capt. Charles Meves of Co. A, 4th New Jersey, was killed in action at Gaines's Mill. *N.J. Record,* I, 184; *OR,* Vol. XI, Pt. 2, p. 987.

72. Probably Cpl. Daniel W. Tunis of Co. H, 2nd New Jersey, who was discharged in September, 1862. *N.J. Record,* I, 137.

73. John D. P. Mount resigned Feb. 8, 1863, as captain of Co. I, 1st New Jersey. *Ibid.,* 94.

graph you to meet me in Philadelphia and the girls to come along too.

We have nothing of particular interest in camp. Everything is very quiet. A report has just come in that we are to move 9 miles up the river, but I don't know where it come from. We have a grate deal of sickness. . . .

Harrison's Landing, Va., July 14th 1862

My dear Ellen,

I wrote yesterday that I was appointed Colonel of the 11th Regiment.[74] I have been congratulated all around. Genl. Kearny wrote me a complimentary letter. Col. Torbert is sick in Philadelphia. Maj. Hatfield is wounded and at home. No field officers are here in the Regiment except Adj. Henry and myself. I find there is difficulty in getting away under these circumstances. I will stay a few days longer; then, if Taylor don't let me go, I will carry my request up to [Generals] Slocum and Franklin. I wrote the Governor that I wanted some three weeks at home before I take charge of the 11th New Jersey, and I spoke of the necessity of my leaving here soon.

I have just finished a letter to Capt. Brewster's brother at Naglesville, telling him all I know about his brother's death. This is in answer to a letter I received from the brother today.

I am very well, but we have a grate deal of sickness here. You have no idea of it.[75]

Mrs. Harris is at Harrison's Landing doing all she can. I saw her yesterday.

I have not got the shirts yet. Don't send me any more. I have today written to Alexandria to Davy and Harmon to send my trunks and box on to Belvidere, so you can look out for them. Many of the clothes will come in handy while I am in Trenton. I forgot to tell you that on our march and fighting I lost my note book and yours, Sarah's, Hennie's, and Mr. Wiestling's degarytypes. All fell in the hands of the Rebels. I did not loose much besides this and my field glasses. Yet I came off safe myself, for which we ought to be thankful. . . .

---

74. McAllister's commission as colonel of the 11th New Jersey was dated June 30, 1862. Baldwin MS., 94.

75. For discussions of the widespread illness then prevalent in the army, see Warren Lee Goss, *Recollections of a Private* (New York, 1890), 73; Bennett, *Musket and Sword*, 74; John G. B. Adams, *Reminiscences of the Nineteenth Massachusetts Regiment* (Boston, 1899), 38.

Harrison's Landing, Va., July 17th 1862

My dear Ellen,

I am still here. After I received my commission as Colonel of the 11th Regiment, I called on Genl. Taylor and showed him my commission and Governor Olden's letter. I saw that he did not like my going away; but of course he could not stop it. Governor Olden unfortunately said that as Col. Torbert was sick and Maj. Hatfield wounded, I might have to stay until Col. Torbert returns. This Genl. Taylor took hold of and no doubt will use it against my going for some days. I called on Genl. Slocum and told him about it. He said that as a matter of course it was my right and that I would have to be relieved. He said that I should write to Capt. E. Sparrow Purdy, Asst. Adj. General, and that it would all be right. I have just done so and sent it up to Genl. Taylor. He will be compelled to sign it and send it up until it reaches Genl. McClellan. Then an order will be sent for my discharge. It may have to go to Washington and be signed by Secy. Stanton. . . .

I have just come off of picket duty. Between doing picket duty and building forts, we are kept very busy. Half of our officers are sick. Warner has been quite ill but is now getting better. I think the sickness is not on the increase and we will soon have a turn for the better. My health is still good, but the hot weather has caused me to lose flesh. Clothes that were too small before fit me now. . . .

Harrison's Landing, Va., July 18th 1862

My dear Ellen,

I have today received two letters from you and the girls dated the 14th and 15th. They came through quicker than my letters, which are delayed very much at Fortress Monroe.

I wrote you that I have my commission as Colonel of the 11th Regiment. The Governor has fulfilled his promise to me. I forgive him for the past, and all is right now. A grate many persons worked hard for that post, but he held it back for me. Lieut. Colonel [Stephen] Moore is said to be a first rate man. I have no doubt of it from what I have heard from diffirent persons. He will be able to take a grate deal of labour off of my shoulders. The Governor wants me to stay until a field officer takes my place. So does Col. Torbert, who wrote me from Trenton and congratulated me on my appointment. I will give him the credit of writing a strong letter to the Governor for me. . . . I think as Governor Olden did: I have earned the promotion.

I sent in a paper yesterday for an honorable discharge from my present position, and I hope soon to have it back approved. Then I will—field officer or no field officer—go right on to Philadelphia. . . .

Harrison's Landing, Va., July 21st 1862

My dear Ellen,

It is now evening and I have not got my paper relieving me from command sent back to me yet.

I am getting along very nicely here. I have not had it too hard for the past few days. We have got a very pretty camp now—have built pine houses to protect the men from the scorching rays of the sun. We have the camp cleaned every day, and all the dirt and filth is covered. I see no other camps so pretty and clean. The health of the men is improving, though our sick list is very large. None are in a very dangerous condition. We have not had a death since we came here.[76] We regularly get supplies for the men and they are moving along nicely.

Col. Torbert has not returned yet; but no doubt he will very soon, as he is improving. We have a grate many men in the North that ought to be here. They went home on sick pretense without a furlough. Many men here are denied that privilege on account of those rascals. They ought to be drummed out of any city and town, treated with scorn, and tried for desertion. . . .

Harrison's Landing, Va., July 22nd 1862

My dear Ellen,

I have not yet got permission to leave. My paper has not returned. They seem to want to keep me here. Still, I hope for the best.

One of our brave boys died last night,[77] and I have just returned from the funeral. He escaped unhurt in battle but soon fell a victim to abcesses. . . .

Dr. [Edward] Welling, your friend, received a commission today

---

76. McAllister oversimplified the situation. It is true that no member of the 1st New Jersey died at Harrison's Landing during the three weeks he was there. Yet in that same period 7 members of the regiment died of wounds received at Gaines's Mill, 2 died while home on sick furloughs, and 5 others succumbed to disease before the end of July. *N.J. Record,* I, 72–100 *passim.*

77. Pvt. John W. Kirby of Co. D "died on march from Harrison's Landing to Newport News, Va., July 21, '62." *Ibid.,* 81.

as Surgeon in my new regiment, the 11th New Jersey. He is quite elated. . . .

Harrison's Landing, Va., July 24th 1862

My dear Ellen,

I am still here under the slow process of red tapism. Genl. Taylor has not done the right thing in holding back his approval to my application for so long. Then when he did approve it, I was told that the quickest way to get home was to resign. But I had my paper sent up as it was, and it has not yet returned. If it returns approved all right, I will soon be on my way home. But if it is returned disapproved, I will send in my resignation. . . .

5

♣ ♣ ♣

From the Potomac to the Rappahannock

McALLISTER got his leave, went to New Jersey, and organized a regiment. In mid-August, he returned to the scene of war. This time he was a full colonel; behind him marched the youthful-looking and newly organized 11th New Jersey, which had been recruited from all across the state. The troops reached Washington, crossed the Potomac, and entered the hubbub of military preparation. "Everything wears a warlike aspect," one of their compatriots noted: "long lines of troops as far as the eye can reach, immense trains of army baggage, and hundreds of cannon are moving in all directions. There is nothing but military movements to be seen or heard of here." [1]

The regiment's first duty was to guard vital Chain Bridge, the westernmost of the three Potomac crossings into Washington. After General John Pope's army limped back from defeat at Second Bull Run, McAllister moved his men to Alexandria's Camp Ellsworth—almost in sight of the spot where the 1st New Jersey had spent the previous winter.

For McAllister these autumn months were a time of trial and tribulation. First was the arduous task of polishing his more than 900 recruits into a fighting unit. The process was

---

1. David Craft, *History of the One Hundred Forty-first Regiment, Pennsylvania Volunteers, 1862–1865* (hereafter cited as Craft, *141st Pennsylvania*) (Towanda, Pa., 1885), 12.

slow and always fatiguing. Joy over a long visit from his wife Ellen and daughter Sarah turned into despair when Sarah fell ill at Alexandria of typhoid fever. To add to the Colonel's despondency, the chaplain of the 11th New Jersey proved a far cry from the religious zealot that McAllister had expected.

Yet the hardest blow dealt the new Colonel was the removal from command of General George B. McClellan. McAllister saw no valid reason for McClellan's dismissal. And because he doubted the ability of McClellan's successor, Ambrose E. Burnside, he envisioned no bright future for the Army of the Potomac.

McAllister wrote a long, detailed account of his brigade's march to Fredericksburg. As early as November 28 he predicted that a Federal attempt to carry the heights of Fredericksburg could but result in disaster. During the December 13 battle the 11th New Jersey guarded the Virginia end of one of Burnside's pontoon bridges. The regiment thus escaped the wrath of a defeat that bordered on a massacre.

♣

Headquarters, 11th Regiment, N.J.V.
Trenton, N.J., August 14th 1862

My dear Ellen,

The bearer of this is Rev. Janeway,[2] who you heard me say was to be chaplain of our Regiment. He has declined and is going up to see Mr. Knighton and, at our request, offer him the position. You will please show him attention. . . .

Trenton, N.J., August 14th 1862

My dear Ellen,

I find it impossible for me to go home today. I had intended to go last night but could not and do justice to the organization of my

2. The Rev. John L. Janeway had served as chaplain of the 3rd New Jersey Militia during the first months of the war. In September, 1862, he became chaplain of the 30th New Jersey. *N.J. Record,* I, 40, 920.

Regiment. We have to complete the organization tomorrow, it being the last day alowed for that purpose. I don't want to be behind the other Colonels. They are pushing hard to be the first [to the front]. We still want some [more] men. I am hoping for the best.

... I fondly hope that your health is improving and that you will be well enough to spend a few days with me before I leave. It is said that we leave very soon—perhaps the first of next week. I suppose we will go to Annapolis and the camp of instruction. If so, I will have to go on and then get a furlough to come back and settle my tunnel business. All is hurry here now

Mutchler [3] is our Major. [William] Henry is Major of the 1st Regiment. I could not get Mr. Wiestling in [the 11th New Jersey], as this arrangement was done without my knowledge. ...

Willard's Hotel, Washington, D.C., August 27th 1862

My dear Ellen,

We got off very nicely on Monday morning and arrived here about 11 a.m. yesterday. We had a very pleasant trip and no accidents whatever.[4] At Baltimore we were detained for awhile—from 2 until 7 a.m. The Major and I had to call on Genl. Wool [5] at the Eutaw House for orders, which we received. We took a comfortable brackfast and came on here in a fast train. We overtook our regiment and came with them here. I called on Genl. Casey [6] for orders, which were to march over the Long Bridge and encamp at Camp Seward near Fort Albany, about 2½ miles from here and a little above where we camped after the retreat from Bull Run.[7]

It is a beautiful place and has *good water*. It gives a most magnificent view of the city and the country, and it is said to be very healthy. You and the children must certainly visit me while we are here, which will be for some time.

---

3. Valentine Mutchler had formerly been captain of Co. D, 1st New Jersey.

4. For Capt. Philip J. Kearny's contrasting, critical account of the train ride to Washington, see *Historical Magazine,* Ser. 2, Vol. VIII (1870), p. 184.

5. Aged John E. Wool then commanded the military department in and around Baltimore. See *OR,* Vol. XII, Pt. 1, p. 3; Pt. 3, pp. 319–20.

6. After his disappointing performance at Seven Pines, Silas B. Casey was ordered to Washington and assigned the duty of "receiving and encamping troops as they arrive in the city from the several States." *Ibid.,* Pt. 3, p. 568.

7. Of the move to Fort Albany a sergeant in the 11th New Jersey recalled: "The streets of Washington being very dusty, and the day extremely warm, this first march resulted in a number of sun-strokes." Marbaker, *11th New Jersey,* 7.

I am glad to hear that you are so much better. I hope it will continue and that you will soon be well. I expect to ask for a leave of absence soon to visit you and to settle up the tunnel business. I met Judge [Joseph] Casey, who, hearing of my arrival, came to the depot to see me. He inquired very particularly for you, having heard of your illness. He says that Mrs. Casey has also been quite ill, and that he will call on me at the Regiment soon.

Maj. Herbert [8] starts for home this evening. He was, as he always has been, a grate help to me. . . .

Fort Marcy,[9] Va., August 30th 1862

My dear Ellen,

Yesterday morning at half past two I received an order from Genl. Casey to proceed at once to Chain Bridge. A Connecticut regiment and a Pennsylvania regiment accompanied us.[10] On reaching Chain Bridge, we found that a portion of the floor had been taken up, as fears were entertained of a tirade by the enemies' cavalry. However, it was soon replaced and we came over here to assist in protecting this fort.

Troops are pouring in rapidly; and from the appearance of things, we are likely to have a battle. Heavy firing has been heard all morning in the direction of Centreville. It has ceased now. We don't know the results. I understand that Genl. McClellan is out there.[11] If so, all will be right. If McClellan can hold the enemy in check out at Centreville, we will have nothing to worry about here. If not, the war scene will be on this line of fortifications. The way things look now, such will be the case. You know much more than I do, as we have not had the papers since we came to this fort.

We have one company in the fort and the rest outside. But if attacked, we will all go inside. All seems to be confusion and raw

---

8. Maj. Charles M. Herbert, the quartermaster of Trenton's Camp Perrine, had accompanied the regiment from that training camp to Washington.

9. Recently restored by the National Park Service, Fort Marcy overlooks Chain Bridge from the Virginia side of the Potomac. For detailed plans of its wartime appearance, see Barnard, *Washington Defenses,* Plates 7 and 8, pp. 45–47.

10. The two regiments were the 14th Connecticut and 127th Pennsylvania. *OR,* Vol. XIX, Pt. 1, pp. 767, 782.

11. What McAllister heard was the second day's fighting at Bull Run between the armies of John Pope and Robert E. Lee. McClellan, then back in Washington, was about to take command of the city's fortifications. *Ibid.,* Vol. XII, Pt. 3, p. 807.

troops. Our General is Doubleday of Fort Sumter notoriety.[12] He is a Colonel but acting as our General. I like his appearance very much. . . .

Fort Marcy, Va., Sunday, August 31st 1862

My dear Ellen,

After Mr. Wiestling left yesterday, a heavy and hard battle was fought up about Manassas or Bull Run. The cannonading was very rapid. It lasted until 8 o'clock at night. We don't know what the result is; but we have reason to think that we have gained a victory, as we see no stragglers or fugitives coming along.[13] The battle in the forenoon was a decided victory for us. I am in hopes that Jackson got a good drubing. We will soon have news.

I feel better this morning and think I will soon be well. We are getting all our camp fixings here and will soon be comfortably fixed. This location is an undoubtedly healthy one—good water and very hilly. Tell Mr. Wiestling it is now thought that Capt. Campbell, now Lieut. Colonel of the 15th New Jersey, is killed.[14] I am sorry to hear it, as he was a noble and brave man. If it is true, Mr. Wiestling might stand a chance to get the post. . . .

Fort Marcy, Va., September 2nd 1862

My dear Ellen,

We had quite a rain last night,[15] and this morning is cool. I am quite well and we are getting our camp fixed up pretty well. It was a

12. This was an inaccuracy which McAllister corrected in a subsequent letter. The man in charge of the Fort Marcy defenses was Col. Thomas D. Doubleday of the 4th New York, a brother of noted Gen. Abner Doubleday. *Ibid.*, p. 726.

13. "The next day," Sgt. Thomas Marbaker wrote, "Pope's shattered and defeated forces marched by us, and as regiment after regiment filed past, with tattered battle-flags and soiled and bloody clothing, the majority of us, perhaps for the first time, began to realize what war really meant." Marbaker, *11th New Jersey*, 8–9.

14. Edward L. Campbell had been a captain in the 3rd New Jersey prior to his appointment as second-in-command of the 15th Regiment. *N.J. Record*, I, 697.

15. It was in this same rainstorm that Gen. Philip Kearny died in action at the battle of Chantilly, twenty miles south of Fort Marcy.

very rough piece of ground, hilly and full of stumps and brushes right beside the Fort. New troops are coming in rapidly. All the spaces between these forts are filling up to make a solid line of defence which, I suppose, is called the second line of defence and will continue as such unless our main army is driven back here. This event will hardly take place.

There has been hard fighting in [General John] Pope's and part of McClellan's army. The loss of life is heavy. We have nothing definent yet.[16] Our troops fought gallantly, but as usual the Rebels got heavy reinforcements when they were driven back. Yet I think we can hold the Centreville line of fortifications until our army can be suficiently reinforced to advance. "Onward to Richmond" is a hard road to travel. Those that condemn McClellan ought to try it themselves. We must hope and pray for the best.

I have no fear for the safety of Washington. It is supposed that the Rebels may make the attempt to cross here at the Chain Bridge, but we are preparing for them. The river is very low and can be crossed any place above here. But there are fortifications on the other side of the river that are also ready for the Rebels. . . .

Fort Marcy, Va., September 5th 1862

My dear Ellen,

You no doubt have all sorts of rumors as to our doings. We here hear many things relative to our Regiment being cut up in battle which has no foundation. We have had no fighting yet, though the excitement around us is at times considerable. I do not think that the enemy will attempt to get across here. They may try it higher up the river, as the water is very low and they could cross almost any place with cavalry & infantry, but not with artillery. I doubt, however, that they will attempt it; for if Jackson did try it, we could easily take him prisoner. So we may all rest easy.

Col. Doubleday, acting Brigadier General, came here last evening under a grate state of excitement and ordered me to be ready for action—that the enemy were in sight and before dawn this morning we would be attacked. The necessary preparations were made, and in

---

16. The Second Bull Run Campaign was a disastrous setback to the Union cause. In addition to more than 14,000 casualties, Pope's army left behind "all the bright hopes with which the Union forces five months earlier had begun their advance on Richmond." Nevins, *War for the Union,* II, 180.

the evening I had my men drawn up in line of battle. I addressed them and told what they had to do in case of attack. It had a good effect. They seemed fully ready and willing to fight. I think the Regiment a good one. All we want are good arms and a chance to drill. The enemy made no appearance, and I don't think they will.

Hennie asks me what kind of fort this is. It is rather a small one, and the last of this line of fortifications on this side of the river.[17] It is also in a very strong position and could be made a very strong fort. There is no water in it; and, of course, it is not calculated to stand much of a siege. But the ground around it is good for defence. It is outside that we expect to do a grate deal to repel the enemy. The river is close by, and the Leesburg turnpike passes the Fort. The whole country is now covered with troops. We have some heavy guns in the fort. One heavy siege gun was hauled up and put in place day before yesterday, and a mortar gun came yesterday. There are some seven or eight guns in it now. Some of these are capable of doing good execution if well handled. But I am inclined to think the gunners know but little about their business. Eighteen or twenty of them are my own men, who of course are very green in gunnery. I have not seen anything in the others that shows skill, and I don't think any of them have ever been in action.

Our Genl. Doubleday is not Doubleday of Fort Sumter fame, but a brother. I think he is brave but not of much experience.

Fort Ethan Allen is a very large and fine fort on the next hill below, in sight about ½–¾ of a mile from here and nearly opposite Chain Bridge.[18] This is a fort that can be defended and is capable of standing a long and heavy siege. It no doubt is intended to be the fort for the defensive line.

Our Regiment has already been favorably noticed and stands well. It has got the credit of doing more than it has done. Genl. Doubleday thinks the world of us. He says he can depend on us and especially on the officers. So, you see, it is a good thing to have a name.

I have done as you said and put on my flannel bandage. I thank you for the string. After all gets settled down again—as it will soon, I will get a furlough and go home. . . .

17. The semiliterate Simeon Drake of Co. D, 11th New Jersey, wrote of Fort Marcy: "it is a nice place. i like it well e nuff so far But thear is no thing for to by hear with out going a cupple of miles." Simeon Drake to his wife, Sept. 4, 1862, Simeon Drake Papers (cited hereafter as Drake Papers), Rutgers University.

18. Fort Ethan Allen lay a mile southeast of Fort Marcy alongside present-day Glebe Road in Arlington. Barnard, *Washington Defenses,* Plates 7 and 19.

Fort Marcy, Va., September 6th 1862

My dear Ellen and family,

I receive your letters regularly—only one day after writing date, which makes us quite close together and certainly very pleasant. All is quiet on our lines and, as I said before, we will soon settle down. Before long, I no doubt can get a furlough and go home. I do not anticipate the fighting that some do until we again advance.

I had a call last evening from John McClay, Dr. McClay's son, from Greenvillage, Franklin County. He belongs to the 123rd Pennsylvania Regiment, lying right alongside of us. He is quite a nice boy, 17 years old, and a private. He tells me that he was at Tuscarora Academy and that nearly all the students old enough enlisted and are now in the army. He took tea with me. I am sorry to say he told me that Capt. John T. Dick [19] was killed in the battle of Saturday last. Like Capt. Brewster, his body was left on the field in possession of the enemy. He speaks positive as having seen some friends who were in the battle who say that Capt. Dick showed himself a brave officer. Your sister will be distracted. Poor woman, she will be distressed. . . .

Fort Marcy, Va., September 6th 1862

My dear Ellen,

Since writing you this morning, I have received orders to move bag and baggage to Fort Lyon near Alexandria. We have sent for wagons and will go down tonight. It is in sight of our old camp ground at the Seminary.

The 15th New Jersey also goes to the same place. We are to be in Heintzelman's Corps. I don't know who will be our Brigadier General. . . .

Willard's Hotel, Washington, D.C., September 9th 1862

My dear Ellen,

We have moved to Fort Lyon.[20] We came down from our camp on Sabbath afternoon and now have most of our tents and baggage at

---

19. Dick, who was captain of Co. H, 107th Pennsylvania, fell in the Aug. 30 fighting at Bull Run. *OR,* Vol. XII, Pt. 2, pp. 388–89.

20. Fort Lyon was situated one and a half miles southwest of Alexandria on the Telegraph Road. Next to Fort Runyon, it was the largest of the twenty-three forts in the Potomac defenses. An 1863 explosion in one of the magazines virtually demolished the fort. Barnard, *Washington Defenses,* Plate 2, pp. 14, 19–20, 35–36; Delavan S. Miller, *Drum Taps in Dixie* (Watertown, N.Y., 1905), 65.

Fort Lyon. We are to be attached to Heintzelman's Corps and Grover's Division (formaly Hooker's Division). I like Grover very much.[21] He stands well as an officer and a soldier. Heintzelman's Corps, you know, is one of the very best in the army. We are not yet brigaded but will be in a few days.

I came here today to get new arms and have effected a change. . . . There seems to be but little excitement relative to Jackson's advance into Maryland.[22] I have no doubt but that Jackson will be defeated in his plans. McClellan has got hold of the army again and all will be right.

I will write to Mr. Wiestling and, if he thinks it best, we will have to settle up all our accounts. But I still expect to get home soon. . . .

Camp Advance, near Fort Lyon, Va., September 12th 1862
My dear Ellen and family,

We are still here, all quiet and all well. A flying rumor came last night that Genl. Burnside had a hard battle day before yesterday and was defeated.[23] But it wants confirmation. I don't believe it. The Secessionists of Alexandria raise all kinds of reports to dampen our ardour. But we don't take their unfounded reports until we have them confirmed from reliable sources. I am still hopeful that all must come out right and this wicked rebellion must be put down. I agree with Sarah & Hennie: God will do for the best. And though we are passing through a sore trial, and our nation is suffering a terable calamity, our government will yet stand before the world in all its former grateness as a tower of strength—teaching rebellious spirits in all nation that governments and their power come from God. . . .

On the day I was in Washington, Maj. Herbert and I rode out to call on our friends, the [Carlisle] Pattersons & Mrs. [Joseph] Pearson.

21. Maine-born Cuvier Grover was a professional army man who had distinguished himself on the Peninsula and at Second Bull Run. In spite of a lifetime devoted to the military, Brig. Gen. Grover was an easygoing commander whom all soldiers "learned to love and respect." Martin A. Haynes, *History of the Second Regiment, New Hampshire Volunteers* . . . (cited hereafter as Haynes, *2nd New Hampshire*) (Manchester, N.H., 1865), 46, 100–01.

22. On Sept. 5 Stonewall Jackson's corps crossed the Potomac and entered Maryland. The remainder of Lee's army followed close behind in this first Confederate invasion of the Middle Atlantic States. Excitement in Washington at that time seemed to be more over McClellan's restoration to supreme command in the field.

23. The rumor was false. Burnside, then commanding the right wing of the Army of the Potomac, reported no action on Sept. 10. *OR,* Vol. XIX, Pt. 1, p. 416.

I found them all well and need hardly tell you that I met with a warm reception. Mrs. Patterson & Mrs. Pearson took me by both hands, held them tight, congratulated me on my return, and added that they had never forgotten me in their daily prayers. They then said: "Oh! How delighted we are to see you! You must stay all night and give us a history of your trials!" . . .

Col. Patterson had heard of my being in town and had hunted and sent all around to find me. He heard of my passing through with my Regiment and spoke of it as being a very fine one. I never met with such kindness. They are grate Patriots—all for the Union, with their heart and hand in it. When things settle down, you and the children must come and visit, and we will call on the Pattersons and Caseys.

If I continue [staying] here, I can get board right near to my tent. We are camped right before the door of an old family, F.F.V., relatives of Commodore Brooks of Revolutionary renown.[24] He built a very plain and comfortable house. Some officers' wives boarded there last winter. So get well, come down, and stay with me awhile. We will have some old-fashioned chitchat, and Sarah and I can have a few nice rides. . . .

Camp Advance, Va., September 13th 1862

My dear Ellen,

. . . I have written two letters to Mr. Wiestling to which I have received no answer. I directed them to Oxford. I also received one from S. T. Scranton, urging a settlement and desiring that it should be made immediately, even if I could not be there. To this I consented and have written to both Mr. Wiestling and Mr. Scranton to that effect. I still think . . . I will get home on furlough, but I think it best to let Mr. Wiestling and Scranton close up the books. So tell Mr. Wiestling to go ahead and do the best he can.

I wrote Mr. Wiestling a strong letter to send to Governor Olden to appoint him to a field post as soon as a vacancy occurs in this

---

24. McAllister was referring to the descendants of Revolutionary War hero James Brooks. A Massachusetts soldier stationed in the Fort Lyon area was probably describing the same residence and occupants when he wrote: "Close to our front is a small, unpainted house, occupied for a while last winter by Colonel [Thomas] Meagher and his wife, but now tenanted by a low down white and his family, who claim to be Union." Lincoln, *34th Massachusetts*, 36. See also Foster, *New Jersey and the Rebellion,* 820–21.

or other regiments.[25] I have not heard that he has received it. His brother John told me that he was coming on here. I have been looking for him daily. . . .

We have had some rain and the day is quite cool. I have not heard any war news. I don't know whether we shall be here long or not. . . . Tell Sarah that William Lloyd is a most excellent business man and is making a very good military man. Anything I put in his hands is sure to be attended to. Our Quartermaster [26] was hurt, and I was about to appoint Lloyd to his place. . . .

Camp Advance, Va., September 14th 1862

My dear Ellen,

I have been so much engaged this morning that I had not time to write you before the mail left. . . . I called to see the Roberts family [27] yesterday. They treated me very kindly. I can get boarding for you and the girls with them, if you will come. This I wish you to do as soon as things settle down. We are moving today near to the Roberts's and will likely settle down there for some time. We will be much nearer Alexandria and right on the Fairfax turnpike, not far from the Seminary. We are going into a new Brigade but the same Division (Genl. Grover's). The new Brigade is composed of our Regiment, the 120th New York, 33rd and 34th Massachusetts—all new like ourselves, and to be commanded by the senior Colonel. I am not certain this is not to be myself. If so, I will have my hands full to organize it. However, it is only a temporary arrangement.

I wish we could have the Sabbath to rest. We are always moving on Sunday.

Mr. Knighton has arrived in Alexandria but has not got out here yet. He is not as rapid as he would have the army to be. . . .

25. On Nov. 28, 1862, Wiestling accepted appointment as colonel of the 177th Pennsylvania Militia. He held that post until his August, 1863, discharge. Records of the Adjutant General's Office, Commonwealth of Pennsylvania.

26. Quartermaster Garret Schenck remained with the 11th New Jersey until June, 1864, when he resigned to accept a commission in another unit. *N.J. Record*, I, 542.

27. The A. M. Roberts family that befriended McAllister (see his letter of Oct. 4, 1862) had extensive holdings in the vicinity of the Episcopal Seminary. Mr. and Mrs. Roberts also became noted for their tender care of Federal sick and wounded. See Lincoln, *34th Massachusetts*, 43, 59.

Camp Grover, near Alexandria, Va., September 15th 1862

My dear Ellen,

I have but a few minutes to write you. I told you yesterday that we were moving. We got all moved nicely and will soon have a nice camp.

Col. [George D.] Wells of the 34th Massachusetts outranks me, even though I am acting Brigadier. I don't care about it, as it is only a temporary arrangement and I would have a grate deal of hard work to perform. Besides, I wish to make my own Regiment a model one and wish to give it my whole attention. I am better satisfied as it is.

I am on a General Court Marshall to meet today to try Capt. Hill.[28] I don't know the charges. I will have to go in a few minutes. I am kept very busy.[29]

Mr. Knighton was in town last night and this morning. He don't appear to me to be in any hurry whatever, notwithstanding his commission in our army. . . .

Camp Grover, Va., September 16th 1862

My dear Ellen,

Last evening I received two letters, one written by you and the other by Sarah. So Hennie is gone to school. I will miss her very much in our corrispondence. It is right that she now finishes her education, and I hope she will have good health to enable her to do so.

Well, the tide is turned: victories are on our side.[30] Tell Mrs. Dr. Paul that we are right—McClellan is the man for the times. I am full of hope, notwithstanding the dark cloud that has been hanging over us. The further north the enemy can get, the better we can whip them. Providence is directing all things. . . . Let us not be so quick to condemn our best men. Mr. Knighton can't run down McClellan

---

28. The charge against Capt. John T. Hill of Co. I was apparently minor. In April, 1863, he was promoted to major of the 12th New Jersey. *N.J. Record,* I, 575. See also Marbaker, *11th New Jersey,* 34, 357–58.

29. Indeed, the Colonel was so busy that he forgot to mete out punishment to two soldiers he caught operating a whiskey still. On the other hand, he continually strove to better the appearance of his regiment. As Pvt. Drake observed: "The cornel [Colonel] give orders that every man in the regiment shuld have there here cut as short as it could be cut, so it meaks me look rether wild." Marbaker, *11th New Jersey,* 11; Simeon Drake to his wife, Sept. 20, 1862, Drake Papers.

30. On Sept. 14 McClellan's pursuing forces gained a hard-earned victory over a portion of Lee's army at South Mountain, Md. Yet on the following day Stonewall Jackson's Confederates seized Harpers Ferry and its Federal garrison.

in the army as he has done at home. The feeling here is all McClellan. Pope & McDowell is nowhere.

Things will soon settle down, as I told you. You and the children must come and make me a nice visit. Get yourself ready to travel and about October you come out here. . . .

The weather is beautiful but rather dry. The healthy season is now near at hand. . . .

Camp Grover, Va., September 17th 1862

My dear Ellen,

I have only a few minutes to write you my usual morning letter. I received your kind letter of the 15th last evening and rejoiced that you are getting so well. . . . I look for a letter every evening. It is a grate comfort to me to get letters from home.

Our temporary brigade is broken up. Our Regiment (the 11th New Jersey) and the 120th New York is under my command at present and will most likely remain so until we are brigaded, which is delayed for some cause or other. Something is pending. Something is to be decided, after which we will be brigaded. We have orders to be ready to march. . . . Heintzelman's whole Corps is under orders—new and old troops to move at a moment's notice. . . .

I must go to our Court Marshall. We were in session yesterday and got through with one case. We will have business for a long while. If we move, the Court will be adjourned. I have my hands full commanding two regiments, the Court Marshall, together with the duties of my own regiment. But my health is good and I can get along very well. . . .

Camp Grover, Va., September 18th 1862

My dear Ellen,

We are still here. No further orders have come except to be in readiness to move at a moment's notice. They were fighting in Maryland all day yesterday.[31] I don't know the result. We will have news

31. McClellan's all-day, piecemeal attacks at Antietam Creek failed to crush Lee's invading army. The 23,100 casualties made Antietam Creek the bloodiest one-day battle of the Civil War.

this morning. Our movements depend no doubt on the results of the Maryland battles.

Dowd [32] and Wiestling has given up the sutling business. It is a mistake on their part. They have lost a splendid chance to make money. But if Wiestling desires it, it is all right. . . .

Camp Grover, Va., September 19th 1862

My dear Ellen,

As usual, I have but a few minutes to write you. We are still here but are all in readiness to move. We have got our new arms at last. They are not what we wanted: the Springfield rifle musket. But we have got a new Austrian rifle for our flank companies and the Springfield smoothbore, buck-and-ball musket for the eight center companies.[33] It is now thought that the musket with buck and ball is after all the best arm in the service. I am satisfied with this arrangement. . . .

I think all will settle down quietly before long. Then, if spared, we will have the blessed privilege of seeing each other. . . .

Camp Grover, Va., September 21st 1862

My dear family,

Sabbath has dawned upon us once more in peace and quietness. Beyond the order to be in readiness . . . we have no orders. After inspection we will have divine service and prayer meeting in the evening. . . .

McClellan has done well—gained a decided victory, saved Washington, Maryland, and Pennsylvania, and given the Rebels a hard stroke. But, as usual, his enemies will still cry him down. How splendidly his men fought under him, compared to what the troops did under Pope. . . .

32. Olney B. Dowd, a New York merchant, and George Wiestling, McAllister's business partner, had apparently collaborated in a venture to sell supplies to the soldiers.
33. The same rationing of Springfield and Austrian muskets was used for other regiments. See *History of the 12th Rhode Island*, 10; A. W. Bartlett, *History of the Twelfth Regiment, New Hampshire Volunteers* . . . (cited hereafter as Bartlett, *12th New Hampshire*) (Concord, 1897), 28.

Camp Grover, Va., September 21st 1862

My dear daughters,

I have not had time to write you since you went to the city. This is the Sabbath, and it has appeared more like Sunday than we have had since this Regiment came out. We have been moving on the last two Sabbath days. All was bustle, and there was no time for devotional exercises. Besides, Mr. Knighton has only been with us a week. We had service at 10 a.m. and prayer meeting this evening. Both of them were largely attended and delightful. We have a large religious element in this regiment and I think good work can be done here. Mr. Knighton has entered on his duties and, I think, will please the men very well. He has done well today. I find his voice is much better adapted to outdoors speaking than in a small room. In fact, it is very pleasant to hear him speak in the open air. . . .

I like Genl. Grover very much. He has given me the command of two regiments. The 120th New York is a new regiment and a very good one.[34] So you see I am playing Brigadier General. But it is only for a short time—until some arrangement is made that the General is looking for. However, I hope we will get a good Brigadier General and one that knows his business. . . .

Our 1st Regiment and old Brigade has, I see, been in another engagement under Franklin and has lost heavely again. They are very much reduced.[35] Unless they get recruits, they cannot go into many more engagements. A brave regiment, a good fighting Brigade, noble fellows—how they have fought and how they have fallen.

I am very pleased with our Regiment. They drill well and learn to do picket duty very fast. Indeed, they learn everything fast, but our details are so large that we have but little time to drill. We have a heavy picket to furnish and a very heavy detail to dig rifle pits.

Lt. William Lloyd is quite taken with his duties and makes a good officer. I like him very much. He takes hold of everything with a will and has the making of a first rate officer.

If I am spared, I calculate that I will have a tip-top regiment, comparing well with the very best regiments in the field. And I think most of the men will fight well. . . .

---

34. The 120th New York, known as the "Ulster Regiment," had been mustered into service three weeks earlier. Its colonel, George Henry Sharpe, recruited the unit from around the Kingston area.

35. At Antietam the 1st New Jersey lost only 2 killed and 17 wounded. However, its casualties at Second Bull Run three weeks earlier had been 9 killed, 126 wounded, and 204 missing. *OR*, Vol. XII, Pt. 2, p. 260; Vol. XIX, Pt. 1, p. 195.

Camp Grover, Va., September 27th 1862

My dear Ellen,

I have written you every morning. I hope you get them regularly. Yesterday morning I enclosed a copy of the letter I sent to Mr. Archibald.[36] I have no doubt but that he will see we get justice done us. His influence is grate. I had a notion to write John I. Blair, but I have not done so. If he is the patriot he pretends to be, he can hardly take advantage of us when we are fighting for our country and could not get home to settle in this trying hour of our country's history. William E. Dodge [37] will no doubt put his foot on any attempt to defraud us out of our just dues, for it is ours. The work was finished in time according to contract. But there will be no trouble. . . .

This is a beautiful morning—weather a little cold but very fine and quite dry. . . I fear that we are going to lose our Genl. Grover, for which I am very sorry. He is only a Brigadier and acting as a division general. Now Genl. Sickles has come back. He outranks Genl. Grover and will have the command until a division general is appointed. I like Grover very much. We have got along so nicely that I am pleased with my situation. Grover is so pleasant and so kind. He is an excellent officer, brave, and he has distinguished himself. Sickles is the man that killed Keyes. I hear he is brave, but that he has poor discipline in his brigade.[38] . . .

Camp near Alexandria, Va., September 28th 1862

My dear daughter Sarah,

I received last evening from you a welcome letter dated the 26th. It did not come by slow coach. Better still, it was dated and care-

---

36. James Archibald had been chief construction engineer on the Warren Railroad when McAllister was superintending work on that line's Van Ness Gap tunnel. Unpublished letter, McAllister to his wife, Sept. 25, 1862, McAllister Papers.

37. William E. Dodge was one of the foremost merchants and financiers of his day. His offices were in New York. See *National Cyclopaedia of American Biography,* III (1893), 174–75.

38. Daniel E. Sickles, one writer summarized, was "always in some sort of crisis, be it financial, legislative, sexual, or homicidal." When Sickles discovered his wife having an illicit affair with Philip Barton Key, he murdered the son of the author of the national anthem—and then won court acquittal on grounds of temporary insanity. At the outbreak of the Civil War the flamboyant New Yorker organized and took command of the Excelsior Brigade. A prewar U.S. congressman, Sickles became a stormy postwar diplomat. W. A. Swanberg, *Sickles the Incredible* (New York, 1956), 110.

fully written so I could read it right straight along without a single guess. . . .

We are still here and still under marching orders. When you and your mother come, I have a nice place for you to board—provided I am at this place. And I have another nice place for you to visit out here in the country: Mrs. Shoot's,[39] a strong Union lady and one of the First Families. She goes in for the President's proclamation [40] and all, though she was a large slave owner. But most of her negroes have run off. . . .

Genl. Daniel Sickles is now our acting Division General in place of Genl. Grover, for which I am very sorry. I liked Genl. Grover very much. He was a good and brave officer. . . . But this arrangement will only last until a Major General is appointed. Then I think it is likely that Grover will get it. At least I hope so.

This Daniel Sickles was the one who killed Key in Washington some years ago. He has got credit for doing a grate deal more fighting than he has ever done. New York corrispondents have cracked him up where the credit for fighting was justly due to other brigades and regiments. But so it is. Well, we will wait and see. I suppose we will soon be brigaded. Into whose hand we will fall is hard for me to tell. . . .

Camp near Alexandria, Va., September 28th 1862
My dear daughter Henrietta,

It gives me grate pleasure to write you. I would do so much oftener but my time is so wholy ocqupied that it is with difficulty I get time to write my daily home-letters. These I do not wish to dispense with, as it is the daily record of all my doings which may be of grate benefit to you hereafter. The enemy have gotten all the pocket diaries that I kept. In fact, this is the only safe plan. I hope Sarah and you will carefully file away these letters.

This is the Sabbath. Stillness reigns in camp. Beyond picket duty and extra daily duty, nothing is doing. After inspection we had divine service. Soon we will have dress parade and close with an evening prayer, which we all so much like. At the close of the day, when the bulk of our toils in camp are over, and as the shades of evening are

---

39. McAllister was probably referring to the widow Shooter, on whose property Fort Ellsworth stood. See *Official Atlas,* Plate LXXXIX, Map 1.

40. On Aug. 22 Lincoln issued his preliminary Emancipation Proclamation.

thrown back from the western horrizen and night is closing in on the departing rays of the sun, and the calm evening breeze fans the thousands of soldiers that inhabit the tented fields, and all seems quiet—oh! what a fit time for a whole regiment, standing at dress parade, to uncover their heads and, in the attitude of prayer, to raise their harts to God . . .

We have a good deal of sickness in our camp. Measels are prevailing.[41] We have not had any deaths yet.

Your Uncle Nelson commanded a company of Pennsylvania Militia to the Maryland line. Mr. Wiestling was the Colonel. Well, Uncle Nelson is a good patriot and shows that he don't only talk but acts. I don't know whether your Uncle Washington came out or not. I suppose he would wait until the enemy got up to Juniata. . . .

Camp Ellsworth, Va., October 1st 1862

My dear Ellen,

I have not had any letter from you for three days. I wrote you every day except Tuesday, when we were moving to this camp.

We moved to this place yesterday. It is right at Fort Ellsworth, overlooking Alexandria.[42] It is a beautiful place at the outskirts of the town, and with a fine view. The cause of our coming here is that near here they have a large camp of about 15,000 troops—convalescents, recruits, paroled men, and stragglers. Some of them require guarding, which we are ordered to do. It will take about 100 men for guard duty. This detail is small compared to the detail we had that was so large we could not drill. Now we can have battallion drill. Otherwise, I would rather not have come here. As we were before, we had three companies on picket and 100 men in trenches. Besides, we have almost 100 men sick. The measels are running through my Regiment.

I am invited to attend a party this evening at Genl. Sickles's and requested to take with me any officers that I may think proper. I will tell you all about it tomorrow. The General is very pleasant with me, but I still prefer Genl. Grover. . . .

---

41. When authorities learned that 300 members of the 34th Massachusetts had never been exposed to measles, they promptly quarantined the entire regiment until the epidemic subsided. Lincoln, *34th Massachusetts,* 43–44. See also Theodore F. Vaill, *History of the . . . Nineteenth Connecticut Volunteers* (Winsted, Conn., 1868), 22.

42. Fort Ellsworth was situated atop "Shooter's Hill," a mile west of Alexandria alongside the Little River Turnpike (now Virginia Route 236). See Barnard, *Washington Defenses,* Plate 3, pp. 9, 12, 20.

[214] ✗ THE McALLISTER LETTERS

Camp Ellsworth, Va., October 2nd 1862

My dear Ellen,

We got a mail last evening and I was delighted to receive three letters from home . . . I also received one from Col. Wiestling, the first for a long time. I am glad that he has gotten up to Oxford, but fear it is too late to save the interest on our stock—if it was in danger, as alleged by S. T. Scranton. I hope, however, he may be able to fix it all up and also that there may be no hard feelings existing between the parties hereafter. . . .

There is a Lewis family, nice and highly respectable, living right here by the camp.[43] I became acquainted with them last year when we encamped on this ground previous to embarking for Yorktown. I will see them today and ask for boarding. I have no doubt but that I will get it. Mrs. Jones, whose husband is an officer now in the hands of the Rebels, boarded there up until a few days ago. She was an accomplished lady and he a splendid man. The Lewises look to be very nice and clean. They have a piano and can play it. If I don't get boarding for you there, I will try someplace close by. If not there, we will go up to the Roberts's. . . .

The weather is so fine now. It will be delightful. . . . I have more time than I have heretofore had or may have again, for we may move before long. But you come and stay until I move. . . .

Camp Ellsworth, Va., October 3rd 1862

My dear Ellen,

. . . I applied for boarding at Mr. Lewis's. Mrs. Lewis thinks she cannot take any more boarders—her girls have all run off, &c. But she said that she would see if she could get a girl. If she can, she will take you. So the matter stands. However, I will fix it. You tell me when you can come on. You must spend some time in Washington. I will meet you at Willard's.

Enclosed you will please find my invitation to Genl. Sickles's reception. In compliance with it, I started with my military friends and arrived at the General's Headquarters. The General received us very handsomely and kindly. Soon we were ushered into a large room in a house close by his tent, where we partook of a handsom repast, or refreshments, which we all enjoyed very much. It was not a dinner but

---

43. Contemporary maps of the Alexandria area show neither the Lewis farm nor the A. M. Roberts estate, which McAllister mentioned again several lines farther along.

mearly refreshments don very nicely indeed. After this we spent some fifteen or twenty minutes in conversation, than had a leave-taking and departed to our several camps. Of course, it did not equal Genl. Kearny's in style, for Kearny got things up *Tip Top*. All seemed much pleased. Capt. Hill enjoyed it very much.

Enclosed is the photograph of Genl. Kearny and Genl. Hooker. Kearny's is good; I never seen Hooker to know him. . . .

Camp Ellsworth, Va., October 4th 1862

My dear Ellen,

I think I have close by a nice place for you to board—only about forty rods from this Headquarters. It is the home of A. M. Roberts, who owns a mill and a fine farm. He himself is a Jersey man; his wife is from western Pennsylvania and an accomplished lady. They are an exceedingly pleasant family. They have been keeping boarders—officers and their wives—and are full at present. But they think they will have a room for you and Sarah in a week or two. . . . Col. Pratt of the 31st New York boarded there for a long time last year with his wife. . . . They will let me know in a day or two, but I am satisfied it will be all right. . . .

Camp Ellsworth, Va., October 8th 1862

My dear daughter [Henrietta],

I am in a grate hurry but concluded to write you if it should be but a line. Your mother and Mrs. Lloyd [44] are here enjoying themselves. I got boarding for them at Mrs. Roberts's, a very nice place close by. We were at Mount Vernon yesterday and enjoyed ourselves very much.

Mrs. Lloyd talks of going home tomorrow, but I hardly think that she will get off. I think Sarah had better come down and spend a week. I would like for you to come too, but it would not do for you to leave school now. . . .

Camp Ellsworth, Va., October 14th 1862

My dear daughter Hennie,

Your mother is quite well and enjoying herself. She is sorry she is not at home to receive Mrs. [Joseph] Casey. You call and see her

44. Mrs. William Lloyd of Philadelphia was the mother of Wilson Lloyd, Sarah's fiancé.

without fail and tell her all. Your mother talks about going home the last of next week, but she will not if the weather remains favourable.

So you are getting after the Rebels in your state. I hope it will be the means of stirring up the lukewarm and then the indolent out to fight for this country—instead of their passing judgement on the brave and good men who are doing all they can for the country. Let them shoulder their muskets and help in the cause, and they will be of some use in their day and generation. These are trying times. It is the duty of every man to be up and doing. Our country's call is loud, and all ought to respond. . . .

Camp Ellsworth, Va., November 3rd 1862

My dear daughter Hennie,

Your sister has been quite sick with typhoid fever, but she is now better. Your mother and she intended to leave for home today, but the doctor thinks it better that she remain for a day or two so she will be better able to travel. She has not been out of the bed for several days but will be up today.

We are still here at Camp Ellsworth. Most of the troops have moved forward. No doubt you will soon hear of fighting. . . .

Camp Ellsworth, Va., November 8th 1862

My dear Ellen & family,

I received Sarah's letter written on your arrival home last evening. I was glad to get it, as I was somewhat uneasy for fear you would both take cold in that cold car. . . . I am rejoiced that you both stood it so well and arrived safely. I fondly hope you will be none the worse for your trip.

We have had no good weather since you left. First it was cold and blustry. Yesterday it snowed all day. The ground is all covered with snow two or three inches deep, and this morning it is moderately cold. Mrs. [Edward] Welling and Mrs. [A. M.] Roberts are congratulating you on having had good weather to travel as well as a pleasant time while here. Mrs. Welling would have left yesterday, but the storm prevented it. . . .

Well, we are under marching orders again. Orders came last night to get shelter tents and be ready at a moment's warning to move to the front. We made out the recquisitions and are preparing for it.

We may not go, but we are to be prepared for any immergency. The army in force has gone forward. I suppose we are fighting now. A considerable number of troops went by here after you left, but none have passed for the last two days. We are in a bad condition to move —so cut down by sickness. We buried two more of our men yesterday.[45] One of them was getting well and walking around the day before he died. He eat one of these abomable *pies,* sickened, and died. How provoking. I wish there was not a pie to be had. No wonder the pie dealers are ordered away. They ought not to be alowed to come near us. I have forbiden the sutler to sell them. . . .

Neither Lloyd nor Hill are back. Nearly all our officers are either away or sick. We are in as bad a fix as can be for moving. . . .

Camp Ellsworth, Va., November 9th 1862

My dear Ellen & family,

. . . We are still here, though under marching orders. We may not go at all. I think it is probable we may not. We have had a grate deal of fun about the chimneys—teasing our officers as to how they were going to take them along, and how much transportation they wanted. It falls the hardest on Col. [Stephen] Moore, as he had his tent all lined with boards and is very comfortable. In fact, he has made a house inside and has a tent outside. But shutting out the light makes it rather gloomy. The Colonel pretends he don't care, but that is only put on.

Dr. Byington [46] has a long face. He and Mr. Knighton are the "Onward to Richmond" men when there was no probability of our going. But they are not so anxious now. Mr. Knighton shuts himself up in his own tent and does not seem to take any interest in anything. He does nothing but read and, I would calculate, he is not suited for his post. I hope he may improve. He is loosing what little popularity he had, which was never very much. He thinks it is hard that he can't rail out against our officers as he likes. I am real sorry that I ever appointed him. Dr. Byington, the best friend he has, says he can't do any good here. The truth is that Mr. Knighton is but a Bookworm. This is all confidential. I wish nothing said about it. I can't think he

---

45. Pvt. William W. Tuttle of Co. H, 11th New Jersey, died Nov. 6 of typhoid fever; Pvt. Reading Chafey of Co. I died in camp the following day. *N.J. Record,* I, 574, 578.

46. Edward Byington served as assistant surgeon of the 11th New Jersey until his March, 1863, resignation. *Ibid.,* 542.

likes it here. He has left our mess and joined the Doctor's. They don't want him. He is about as lazy a man as I ever saw.

One reason he left us is that he don't want to do our catering and to lay in our supplies. This is the chaplain's business in all Colonels' messes. I took him in through courtesy, and he has not appreciated it. In other words, he has treated me badly. But leave it go. As long as he is disposed to attend to the good work in which he is engaged, I will uphold him. But I fear he is not disposed to do his part. . . .

Camp Ellsworth, Va., November 10th 1862

My dear Ellen,

. . . The snow has all gone here and the weather has become more mild. I think it has somewhat settled. We are still here; our orders are to march no further but to be prepared.

We see by yesterday's Washington papers that Genl. McClellan is recalled and ordered to Trenton.[47] What this means we can't say. But one thing is certain: it is putting a damper on our army and will do mischief. Capt. [Isaac H.] Baker, 1st New Jersey, who is on his way home to recruit, told me last night that the news of McClellan's recall is like a wet blanket thrown over his regiment's spirit. But I am satisfied that Genl. McClellan will yet come out right. He has many bitter enemies. Time will tell the truth. . . .

Camp Ellsworth, Va., November 11th 1862

My dear Ellen,

This is a beautiful morning, more like summer than winter. I am very well.

Nothing is new here except a general dislike and regret in the army that Genl. McClellan is removed. I fear the consequences of such a move. It will work evil and be no good at such a time as this.

Mrs. Welling left yesterday. Mrs. [Stephen] Moore and family are living in camp. We all board together. It makes it more pleasant— the cooking is much better done. . . .

47. Owing to McClellan's inactivity following the battle of Antietam, Lincoln on November 5 removed him from command and assigned Gen. Ambrose E. Burnside to head the Army of the Potomac.

Camp Ellsworth, Va., November 12th 1862

My dear Ellen,

Last evening I received a very nice and well written letter from Sarah, dated the 10th. . . . I am pleased to learn from it that you are so well and that Sarah is getting well fast. I hope soon to hear of you both being fully recovered.

I wish you would write to Mrs. Roberts. They all inquire so frequently and kindly for you. They called on me last evening and continue to show themselves very friendly.

We buried two more of our men—one yesterday and one the day before.[48] Two or three more will die. The disease runs into typhoid fever. Col. Wells's Regiment is the same way.[49] I hope we will not have so much more sickness now. The worst is over. It has been very severe on us.

Some troops are still going up on the [railroad] cars. I have no doubt but hard fighting is before them. Burnside must move forward to satisfy the country, even if it should sacrifice our army. Whether we are sufficiently ready or not, I fondly hope he will be successful. He will be if we attack Richmond from other points in connection with this. If not, I fear the results. I do not know the plans. I hope they are well laid and that all may prove right.

I feel for Genl. McClellan. He was a safe man; and if he got into difficulties, he could get us out. He knew that; Pope did not. Burnside is a good man, but he is to be tried on a large scale. If he fails, the results will be disastrous . . .

Camp Ellsworth, Va., November 13th 1862

My dear Ellen,

I received the carpet bag and its contents last night just before going to bed. The carpet will be a first rate thing. The aples are excellent and will do me a long time, if they keep. . . .

We have a church in town for a hospital.[50] We took out the pews

---

48. Pvts. Peter Jones of Co. B and Benjamin McDonald of Co. D died Nov. 9 and 11, respectively, from "remittent fever." *N.J. Record*, I, 550, 557.

49. According to the regimental historian of George D. Wells's 34th Massachusetts, more sickness at this time was being feigned than felt. Lincoln, *34th Massachusetts*, 53–56.

50. All Alexandria churches were eventually converted into hospitals. See Miller, *Photographic History*, VII, 234–35; Cudworth, *1st Massachusetts*, 292; Wheelock, *The Boys in White*, 18–19, 60.

and have bedsteads, gas light, and heater. So we will have the sick as comfortable as circumstances will permit.

Enclosed you will find a copy of the letter I wrote to Mrs. Harden. Her son was the first member of my Regiment that died.[51] You were at the funeral. The body was taken home. She wrote a most excellent letter to our regiment which I thought required an answer. Capt. [Dorastus B.] Logan's company was very much pleased that I wrote to her. The Captain read the letter to the company. . . .

The weather is beautiful. Miss Moore [52] is enjoying the daily rides. Of course, being the only young lady in camp, she receives a good deal of attention. I find that Mrs. Moore being here makes it much more pleasant. Our cooking is so much better done. . . .

Camp Ellsworth, Va., November 15th 1862

My dear Ellen,

Last evening I received Sarah's nice long letter of the 13th. She is doing well now in writing. I hope she will continue. . . .

So you see by the papers that Burnside give a reprimand to an officer for merely saying: "We might as well give up."[53] I think the General is right. We did not come here to give up. Give up after we have lost our brothers, fathers, and sons in this desperate struggle? The blood that has moistened this soil cries out against it. Our brave men, cripple for life, tell us as they wheel along our streets: "Never give up!" The beautiful, interesting boy that you seen and talked with at the Seminary with both feet amputated tells you: "Never yield to the unprincipled foe!" The base rascality of the Rebels, practiced from the braking out of this wicked rebellion—whose wickedness is looming up before the civilized world—tells us "Never! Never give up the Ship of State!"

We are making history. The eyes of the world are upon us. We must do our duty. Live or die, our country, through the blessing of God, must be saved. . . .

51. Cpl. John S. Harden died Oct. 19, 1862, of "congestion of [the] brain." *N.J. Record*, I, 573. A copy of the letter that the Colonel wrote Mrs. Harden is in the McAllister Papers.

52. Lt. Col. Moore had two daughters, Clarissa and Josephine. At this time both were under nine years of age. J. M. Van Allen, *History of Bergen County, New Jersey* (New York, 1900), 573.

53. McAllister was repeating the fabrication of some newspaperman. As a matter of fact, after receiving command of the army Burnside "wept like a child" and for days afterward was "the most depressed man" in camp. *Letters of George G. Meade*, I, 325.

Fairfax Courthouse, Va., November 16th 1862

My dear Ellen,

Orders have come to our General Carr [54] to move forward and join the Division under Genl. Sickles without delay. . . . Our army is moving on; Sickles will not likely go forward without this Brigade. It is a very large and fine Brigade.[55] So we are in for it. We will not stop long in one place. I will write you as often as I possibly can. . . .

I like this place very much and also Genl. Carr. He is very kind and makes it very agreeable for us. I am not certain we will remain in this Brigade, but at any rate we will be in Sickles's Division.

We have just received orders that Genl. Siegle [56] will take our position and also one at Fairfax Station. We go as soon as he arrives here tomorrow or the next day. . . .

Fairfax Courthouse, November 17th 1862

My dear Ellen,

Here we are in what appears to be our home for awhile, unless some unexpected military changes takes place. We are the only regiment here. We are to have a piece of artillery, though we have none now. One of our Brigade regiments are at Fairfax Station, one is at Centreville, we are here, and three more are at points of equal importance. We are all watching Stuart's cavalry, who are daily expecting to visit us.[57] We are on the lookout. We have just the excitement that we want. Two companies daily go on picket at important points, waiting for our visitors and to fight and give the alarm of their approach. So look out for news. . . .

I wish Sarah was here. What a splendid time we would have riding over this fine, healthy country. It is just the place for her, just

---

54. A native of upstate New York, Joseph B. Carr carried a decade of militia experience into the Civil War. From his initial position as lieutenant colonel of the 2nd New York, he rose unspectacularly but steadily to brigade command. Like McAllister, he was an unpretentious officer who preferred to do his duty fully and quietly. The best biographical sketch of Carr is in New York Monuments Commission (comp.), *Final Report on the Battlefield of Gettysburg* (Albany, 1902), III, 1351–53.

55. McAllister's brigade consisted of the 1st, 11th, and 16th Massachusetts, 2nd New Hampshire, 11th New Jersey, and 26th Pennsylvania. Although this was an unusually large number of regiments in one brigade, the aggregate strength of the unit was only 1,900 men. *OR,* Vol. XIX, Pt. 2, p. 197.

56. Maj. Gen. Franz Sigel was in command of the defenses in and around Fairfax Court House.

57. Confederate cavalry chief Jeb Stuart and 1,800 of his horsemen had just returned from a bold raid on Chambersburg, Pa.

enough excitement to please her and her father. I found a saddle in strolling around last evening; so whenever she is ready, tell her to come on and we will have a splendid time of it. . . .

                  Wolf's Shoals Ford, Occoquan River, November 19th 1862
My dear daughter Henrietta,

My engagements have been such that I could not write you as I wished to do. I am on my way towards Richmond with that portion of my Regiment fit for duty—there being over 200 sick and unfit for duty. (We have lost twelve by death.) I think we will be more healthy now. Our men are in fine spirits.

Last Saturday night we were ordered to march to Fairfax Courthouse and report to Brig. Genl. Carr of Sickles's Division. After we arrived there and got settled down, Carr got orders to come here. We are waiting here now to get up our supplies, after which we no doubt will move on to Fredericksburg and try and get to Richmond. With what success, time will tell.

This is a Brigade of veterans from Israel Richardson's old Division—real fighting material. We have now with us only one battery: the 2nd Maine, but tomorrow we will be joined by the 2nd Massachusetts and very soon by two or three other batteries. The 26th Pennsylvania Regiment now belongs to us, but I think it is to remain at Centreville. . . .

I wish you to call at my tailor's, Stock's,[58] and tell them to send my uniform home to Belvidere. If I want it, I can get it from there. It will be useless to me here—only end up in the road and forgotten. Mr. Lloyd bought me a blanket and sent it to Stock's to go with my uniform. Send that home too. . . . I am on the forward move. . . .

                      Wolf's Ford, Occoquan River, November 19th 1862
My dear Ellen,

. . . We have halted here to get up our supplies, both rations & forage, and we may remain a part or all of tomorrow. We don't know positively, as no other regiments have yet joined us. Why, I cannot say. I suppose all is right, or will be soon.

    58. Charles Stocks & Co. of Philadelphia did a thriving wartime business in supplying tailored army uniforms.

Some of our officers & men left behind have come up; but far too many are staying back. Two hundred men are sick. Two have died since we left,[59] making twelve that have died in the regiment. Lieut. [John V.] Anderson has resigned on account of bad health. His resignation [of November 14] has been accepted. I have written to Governor Olden nominating Lieut. [William] Lloyd to fill the place. I expect his appointment very soon. Col. Moore is not with us, being detailed on the Court Marshall still in session in Alexandria. Capt. [Philip J.] Kearny, Capt. [Theodore] Stagg, Lieut. [William S.] Provost, and Lieut. [Orrin B.] Fausett are all sick at Mr. Roberts's. Capt. Stagg took sick a few days before we left. Capt. [John H.] Grover is detached on fortifications duty. However, I have asked that those detailed on other duty be relieved. Mr. Knighton is still behind. He don't show much of the "Onward to Richmond Spirit" since our orders came to move. As to Genl. McClellan's removal, nothing is said to Mr. Knighton about it.

I am sorry to say that a furlough is now out of the question, and it is also useless to send me a box at this time. Hold it back until I write you to send it. If my uniform and blanket have not been sent, don't have them sent here. I can do without them very well. . . .

Wolf's Shoals Ford, Va., November 20th 1862

My dear Ellen,

I wrote you last evening and have mearly to say that I am well. We are still here and may move today. Teams are passing in grate numbers, but I have not seen any troops yet. I suppose that they have gone by some other rought. . . .

Wolf's Shoals Ford, Va., November 21st 1862

My dear Ellen,

We are still here in a terable rain storm. It rains all the time, with mud similar to last year. It is unpleasant all around. Chaplain Knighton came wading along last night and arrived very wet. This is his first lesson in campayning. His onward-to-Richmond propensities

---

59. Pvt. John C. Sharp of Co. H died Nov. 18 of heart disease; Pvt. John H. Tronton of the same company succumbed to typhoid fever the following day. *N.J. Record*, I, 574, 582.

are down to the freezing point. He looks down in the mouth, much to the amusement of our officers. Quartermaster [Garret] Schenck came in with Mr. Knighton, looking like a drowned rat. Well, we have good laughs to cheer us on our tedious journey.

I don't know whether we will go on or not today. It matters but little, as there is no comfort here. Still, I get along with more comforts than others because I have had some experience and have become accoustemed to hardships. Our men have stood it well, but I fear they will soon become sick. If the weather was clear, we would be all right. . . .

Wolf's Shoals Ford, Va., November 22nd 1862

My dear Ellen,

The rain storm is over and the weather is not cold. But the roads are very bad, with holes deep in mud. We are likely to remain here for some days, so we will try and fix ourselves somewhat comfortably. We are doing pretty well. I have a stove in my tent, and the boys like their shelter tents very much. I have laid on the ground since I started, but today I will fix a whiteoak or pine mahogany bedstead such as you seen me have in my tent at Camp Ellsworth. For the time being, that will be more comfortable.

Sickles's other Brigades are coming up. Some of them arrived last evening and are encamped over the river to our rear. We are in the advance, and my regiment is the most advanced. Sickles arrived last night. Genl. Carr paid quite a compliment to our regiment by saying that the reason he placed us in the advance was that we are the most reliable and he could trust us to be on the farthest and most exposed pickets.

I don't know what our movements mean, but we have changed base. Tell Mrs. Dr. Paul that it is well this was not done by our favourite, Genl. McClellan. Had he made the change, *it would have been called a defeat*. The contemptuous scorn would have curled on thousands of lips in derision of his plans to save our noble army. I am not saying that this new plan is not all right; no doubt but that it is. But I don't pretend to know anything about it. I follow the plans laid down by others. As a good soldier, I will do my duty without a murmur, trusting in God to save our country.

We get no papers here—no news of any kind. It is the best place to spend a life in solitude I ever saw, remote enough for anybody. The houses of the inhabitants are not much larger than our wall tents and not half as comfortable. This is the most miserable, out of the way, forelorn looking country I have ever seen. The farms consist of a few acres cleared or partly grown up. Old cleared ground and a cow or two is the wealth of the farmers. The people don't live but stay. Children don't wash at all. . . .

Wolf's Shoals Ford, Va., November 22nd 1862

My dear Ellen,

I wrote you this morning; but having another opportunity of sending a letter to Alexandria, I thought I would drop you a line or two. I have not received any letter from you for two days. We have now no regularity in our mails. But we will have soon, I think, as our Division is coming together now and things will work better.

We have just got the news of the death of Genl. Patterson.[60] He shot himself through the heart last night. I have not heard any causes given for it. I suppose it was mortification at his failure at not holding a position he had at or near Washington. He retreated, and afterwards half of his men advanced and drove the enemy. . . .

Wolf's Shoals Ford, Va., November 23rd 1862

My dear daughter Henrietta,

. . . We crossed the river at this ford on Thursday, our boys wading through the water on the shoals. The water was quite shallow then, but it has rained since and the water is much higher. We were in the advance of the whole Division. The ballance of the Division got here yesterday.

Night before last, Genl. Patterson shot himself. He was in command of the 2nd New Jersey Brigade, who are encamped about 1½ miles in the rear of us. The cause that induced Genl. Patterson to do it I do not know—though it was said that it was owing to his mistake in not taking Warrenton Junction when he could have so easily taken

60. Brig. Gen. Francis E. Patterson died Nov. 22, 1863, from an "accidental" pistol wound. He had commanded the 6th and 7th New Jersey during the Peninsular Campaign. Patterson was evidently a heavy drinker, for a chaplain once noted that he failed to do his duty at a critical time because "he had admitted an enemy into his mouth which had stolen away his brains." Cudworth, *1st Massachusetts*, 236; Rusling, *Civil War Days*, 285–86; James E. Smith, *A Famous Battery and Its Campaigns, 1861–1864* (Washington, 1892), 86.

it and immortalized his name. He was not regarded as a good officer in this Division, though I knew but little about him. . . .

Wolf's Shoals Ford, Va., November 23rd 1862

My dear Ellen,

This is Sabbath evening and we are still in the wilderness. The weather has become cold, but the roads are drying to some extent. We had preaching today around a log fire and had quite a large congregation. Mr. Knighton's sermon was very appropriate, and I trust that it will do some good. His text was 1st Corinthians, 15th Chapter, 25th verse.[61] Our service today reminded me of the service we had on the shore of Pequosin Bay last summer. You remember me writing you about our preaching and prayer meeting on the sea shore. We have prayer meeting tonight on the same spot.

This is truly a wild place—nearly all woods, very hilly, and quite romantic. Wolf's Ford Shoals, or Wolf's Shoals Ford, or, as the inhabitants call it, Wolf's Run Shoals, takes its name from the shallow water at this place, just where Wolf's Run enters the Occoquan River. It is a place where the wolves came in time of high water to cross the river. This is the place where part of our army came across. There was no bridge and we had to wade. It does not look like a river now, more like a large creek. But both Bull Run and Cedar Run, where we went last March, enter into this just above this ford. Cedar Run is quite large—or was when we camped on its banks last spring, and Bull Run is quite a stream.

Things look much as if we are preparing for a long march. We have orders to make out recquisitions for everything wanted for our men, including an extra pair of shoes for each man. Well, what the plan of campaign is I cannot tell. One thing is certain: campayning in winter is and will be terable on our men. But I am willing to do what I can to put down this rebellion. The advocates of winter campayning ought to be here and take their hand in it, instead of setting besides their warm fires in comfortable houses and talking about what this and that General ought to do, and condemning our best and bravest men.

I am happy to say that God has thus far spared me, continued my health and strength, and enabled me to endure the cold and fatigue of this hard, exposed life. In fact, I feel very well, ready for anything. . . .

61. "For he must reign, till he hath put his enemies under his feet."

On the March, Aquia Creek, Va., November 27th 1862
My dear Ellen,

Tuesday [day before yesterday] morning we left our camp at the Occoquan, marched twelve miles, and reached Dumfries after dark. The day was cloudy; but it did not rain, and it was a good day for marching. The wagons had a hard time of it.

After pitching our tents, it commenced raining and rained all night. We had started at 8 o'clock yesterday morning, came within one mile of Acquia Creek, and stopped for the night. The night was cold. Our wagons stuck behind in the mud. The road was terable— hub deep in mud. I slept in a bush house. It was rather cold but I got along pretty well. I had nothing to eat. I sent out and bought two turkeys for three dollars. We had supper on one and brackfast on the other. We resumed the march at 7 o'clock this morning. We crossed the creek on round logs, or chopped down trees, that we laid across the stream, came about two miles, and are now waiting for the Division to come up. I am the second regiment in the advance. Tomorrow I will take the lead. We will get nearly to Fredericksburg tomorrow. We expect to fight there. Our men are standing it well. We have nearly 600 men and are the largest regiment in the Brigade. We stand well.

This is Thanksgiving Day. I wish we could all be together. I hope you will enjoy yourself. . . .

In the field at Potomac Creek, 6 miles from Fredericksburg,
November 28th 1862
My dear Ellen,

I wrote you yesterday while sitting on a stump. After resting at that place we passed our old New Jersey Brigade. They came out to the road to meet us, and my old Regiment gave me a warm reception —three harty cheers. Most of the officers, as well as many of the men, came running up to shake hands. It was truly gratifying. Mr. Knighton said he was mighty pleased with it. It looked well and was highly creditable to me. We passed them, passed through Stafford Court House, and came on here to the banks of this creek and encamped for the night. We have no orders as yet for the day, but I understand we are to move about ½ mile from here. We are now in sight of Hooker's Grand Army,[62] which is to be our destination.

---

62. Burnside had divided the Army of the Potomac into three Grand Divisions. William B. Franklin commanded the Left, Joseph Hooker the Center, and Edwin V. Sumner the Right. *OR,* XXI, 84, 761–62.

Our Quartermaster is sick. I have appointed Lieut. Lloyd to his place. He is mounted on a horse and does splendidly. He is a most excellent business man. I expect his commission as 1st Lieutenant to come soon. We have not had any mails yet. My health is very good, notwithstanding the fact that we are sleeping without tents. . . .

Camp in the field opposite Fredericksburg, Va.
November 28th 1862

My dear Family,

As we came along, and stopped to rest, I would set down and pencel a few lines to you to keep you posted. Now we have arrived here and, for the first time, have our tents up, a table to write on, stove and fire, and feel quite comfortable. I have concluded to write you an account of our march to this place. . . .

Saturday, November 15th. Got an order to prepare for a forward movement late in the previous evening. Received an order to move immediately and report to Genl. Carr at Fairfax Courthouse. Sent the order around to the company commanders to be ready to move by 2 a.m.

Sunday morning, November 16th. Cold November winds blew furiously. Cold winter seemed to be right upon us. The thought of going out from a very pleasant and exceedingly comfortable camp to dwell in the shelter tents for a winter campaign was not very pleasant. And to go with a delicate regiment with 200 on the sick list and nearly 100 more unfit for duty, owing to the measels and the unhealthy location of our regiment, made it worse. I need not describe to you some long faces. I would rather turn on the smiling ones at the prospect of a change and at the thought of soon seeing the enemy, when and where they could show their patriotism. . . . For myself, I had nothing to say, but a determination, by the help of God, to do my duty. . . .

At the appointed time—2 a.m., the line was formed reaching clear across our camp ground. The men turned out much better than I expected. Many that had just left the hospital were found in the ranks. All being ready, I gave the order "Forward, March!" Then we started off in fine style. The night was cloudy; but as it was moonlight, we moved along nicely. However, we did not move fast. We arrived at Fairfax Courthouse about 9 a.m. I reported to Genl. Carr. He mounted his horse and showed us where to camp, where he wanted me to dig rifle pits, &c. Our men soon fixed up their shelter tents quite snugly and, strange to say, were quite pleased with them.

Monday, November 17th. Cleaned camp and felt quite at home. But at 9 p.m. I received orders from Genl. Sickles to march towards Wolf's Ford on the Occoquan River. The next morning, *Tuesday, November* 18th, we struck tents and marched to Fairfax Station. There we waited orders. It now comenced raining quite fast. About 3 p.m. the 2nd New Hampshire Regiment came up and also Genl. Carr & staff, together with Osburn's Battery [63] and a train of wagons. The New Hampshire regiment led off, followed by the battery and the wagon train. We brought up the rear. Night came on. It was raining quite hard, very dark, and the roads were muddy. When within two miles of the Ford, we halted and turned into a field, stacked arms, and soon had large blazing camp fires burning all around us. The railroad ties came in very good and certainly very handy. I have no doubt those fires that night saved both health and life, as our boys were able to dry out their clothes before retiring. We got out our tent and pitched it—just one for all the Field and Staff. We had a cup of coffee and some hard crackers and all laid down in this tent. We had plenty of blankets, was very comfortable, and slept very soundly. We awoke the next morning refreshed and ready for the march.

Wednesday, November 19th. Morning came, dull and raining. I had a cup of coffee and hard crackers. At 8 a.m. we started. After marching two miles, we reached the ford called Wolf's Ford Shoals. There we were before a heavy redoubt and long rifle pits commanding the ford. It is a position of grate strength, and the enemy a year ago threw up these earthworks, thinking no doubt that we would come along. But we went other roughts and they abandoned them. This is called a river, but it is what we call a creek, though in high water it no doubt looks like a small river. We went up past the rifle pits and the redoubt and went into camp. We threw out pickets for safety, not knowing but a dash of cavalry might be made upon us at any hour. Here we rested and remained until Tuesday morning, November 25th.

On Monday [November 24] I took a ride with Capt. Hill, Adjt. Schoonover,[64] and a number of other officers to post ourselves as to the lay of the country. During our ride we came across an old lady who was very much distressed about our soldiers taking everything from her. She did not know whether she was in favour of the Union or

63. Capt. Thomas W. Osborn commanded Battery D, 1st New York Light Artillery.
64. John Schoonover, shortly to become McAllister's second-in-command, left the teaching profession for the army. He was wounded three times. McAllister's subsequent letters testify to his courage and dependability. See also Marbaker, *11th New Jersey,* 349–51; Foster, *New Jersey and the Rebellion,* 298; Snell, *Sussex and Warren Counties,* 87–88.

against it, but she was opposed to the war and wished it stopped. She said they were all very poor and were getting worse and worse every day, they did not know how they would live, &c. I asked her what the general feeling as to the war was.

"Well," she said, "I will tell you. I hear them say that they will fight until every man is killed, except one, and he is to run so his life will be spared to replenish the race."

I need not add that this raised a laugh. At another house where we stopped, and seeing a grate number of children, we asked the father how many children he had. He replied that he did not know exactly but thought he had about seven.

This country is sparsely settled, poorly cultivated, and the inhabitants look miserably poor. Poor miserable houses, dirty children, and pitch pine is about all they seem to raise. The truth is: they are now starved. Add to this poverty an unusual amount of ignorance and you have a faint discription of what the inhabitants, including F.F.V.'s, are like along the valley of the Occoquan River. I will mearly add that we had a very pleasant and profitable ride, returned home with a good appetite, and enjoyed a very plain meal more than we might a finely got up dinner at home. I then went out, drilled my regiment, and came in very tired. I retired early, expecting a good night's sleep. But I had just fell asleep when an orderly road up to my tent with an order to move by 7 o'clock the next morning. Cooks had to be wakened, the day's rations cooked, and three days' uncooked rations put in the wagons. The camp was soon all in a bustle. I did not sleep much.

Tuesday, November 25th. Reveille at 4 a.m. Brackfast over, we packed up and loaded wagons with what we had. One of our teams had gone to Washington the day before for our regiment's express matter. Maj. [Valentine] Mutchler had gone by order of Genl. Sickles to bring back from the convalescent camp all men fit for duty. So I was the only field officer left.

All being ready, we started: 1st, cavalry; 2nd, artillery; 3rd, ammunition trains. Then came the 11th Massachusetts, 11th New Jersey, 2nd New Hampshire, followed by Osborn's Battery, &c. The line included Genl. Sickles's whole Division, except two regiments of our Brigade left at the Ford as a guard. We marched rapidly. The day was cloudy, but it did not rain. On we went, stopping occasionally to rest. The country became better as we advanced. Night closed in upon us very dark. Still we continued the march long after dark. The men were tired but done well.

As we raised the hill overlooking Dumfries, and to the grate joy of our tired soldiers, we could see the camp fires of our advance guard burning brightly but still at a distance. On we went with renewed energy, and with the pleasant prospect of stopping for the night. We passed Dumfries, an old dilapidated place with a mill and a few houses, forelorn and desolated. Now we arrived at the mill. A creek had to be crossed. There was no bridge, only a foot log. To pass all our men over it would take till morning. Into the water our boys went, and over the creek we landed. We reformed on this side, marched to the place for camp, stacked arms in line, unslung knapsacks, hunted up rails, and soon the whole field was illuminated with blazing fires. Our wagons were behind, so the Field and Staff had no tents. (The men had their shelter tents.) We made a cup of coffee and had a few crackers. This constituted our supper. We were about to retire on the cold damp ground and without shelter when the wagons arrived. I need not tell you that there was joy among us. We got a tent out, pitched it, spread out our blankets, and was soon asleep. But the rain soon came pouring down, running under tents and blankets.

Wednesday, November 26th. Reveille at 4 a.m. It was still raining. At 7 a.m. the line formed, our regiment being further in the advance than the day previous. On we went, roads terable beyond discription. Teams were sticking fast, with a number of mules and horses stuck in the mud holes. We had to stop several times to let the teams keep up with us.[65] Finally we stopped for the night. It had now quit raining. The cold north wind told us of the comforts of home and of our unprotected and exposed position here. . . . The beautiful, bright, and comfortable camp fires counteracted the cold and chilling winds that blew over and around us. Our wagons were now behind. No tents existed for the officers tonight, and all were most out of provisions. We built a bush house with a big log fire in front, sent out and bought two small, poor turkeys for three dollars, cut one of them up, and stewed it. With fingers for forks, we had our supper and relished it as a Godsend to those in need.

I called on the General and told him that our men were out of provisions and that our Quartermaster was sick and far to the rear. He told me to appoint an acting quartermaster and let him go back and hurry forward the provision wagon so that we would be able to start by 8 o'clock the next morning. I came back to camp, wakened Lieut. Lloyd, and appointed him acting quartermaster. He mounted a horse and rode off. About 3 o'clock in the morning he arrived with

---

65. For other accounts of the hardships of this march, see Rusling, *Civil War Days,* 284–85; John W. Storrs, *The "Twentieth Connecticut": A Regimental History* (Ansonia, Conn., 1886), 38–39.

one team and a small quantity of hard crackers.[66] These were given out to the men. At dawn of day another wagon arrived with some pork, and the men had brackfast. We had our other turkey with a cracker apiece. But the turkey divided among so many did not amount to much for anyone. This was our Thanksgiving brackfast.

Thursday, November 27th, Thanksgiving Day. We resumed our march, and on we went through mud and swamps. Only one regiment was in advance of us. After crossing a creek and marching about 2–3 miles, we waited for the teams to get up. We found ourselves within two miles of our old 1st Brigade. Some of our officers went forward to call on them, and soon lots of the boys were down to see us. They give us a harty welcome. They said that they were keeping Thanksgiving and had cooked some things trimmed up to their best. Again we started and were not long in reaching the 1st Brigade. There the 1st Regiment give me a warm reception. I told you of this in one of my former letters. Many were the warm greetings I received that day from old friends, not only in the 1st Regiment, but officers in all the four old regiments. It brought my mind back to the days of the campaign on the Peninsula. . . .

On, on, on the Brigade marched, passing along a road lined with troops. We soon reached Stafford Court House, a dilapidated looking place. We waded through mud, marched about three miles, and turned into a field and camped for the night. We built a bush house, as the night was somewhat cold and no wagons were up. We had a cup of coffee and one cracker apiece. Maj. Henry and Adj. [Peter D.] Vroom [Jr.] of the 1st N.J. Regiment called to see us. They supped with us on our scanty meal and left. We retired and slept soundly. Wagons arrived during the night. Our horses had nothing but stale oats to eat. But they succeeded in getting a little corn fodder.

Friday, November 28th. Got orders to move. My Regiment led the column. The day was pleasant; and after traveling a few miles, we came up with the rear of Hooker's camps, passed through them, and, about 2 p.m. reached this place and pitched our tents. We have a nice, comfortable camp alongside of a pine woods near Falmouth. I have laid out my camp nicely. My tent is pitched here in the grove, and the Privates' tents are in the field. A wide avenue leads to my quarters. Pine trees, just planted, are on either side of the avenue, making our camp look beautiful. And if we remain here a short time, it will go ahead of all the camps around us.

66. The standard army bread ration of the time was known as "hardtack" or "seabiscuits." The cracker was rectangular in shape, almost unrelenting in texture, and oftentimes wormy in content. Bell I. Wiley and Hirst D. Milhollen (eds.), *They Who Fought Here* (New York, 1959), 52, 56–57.

We are the advance of Sickles's Division, but Genl. [Edwin V.] Sumner's Grand Army Corps are in the advance of us, reaching to the [Rappahannock] River. We are eight miles in advance of my old Brigade. Our pickets talk across the river with those of the enemy. What the program is I know not. But one thing is certain: we must lose an immense number of men if we have to cross the river here, as the enemy are well fortified on the other side. They have five chances to our one. *The time for crossing has gone by.* The enemy have had time to strengthen their fortifications. Who is to blame—whether any person—I am not able to say. God grant it may all be for the best. Perhaps it is, for it may not be the object of our army to cross here. Better heads and abler minds than mine are guiding our opperations. My prayer is that they succeede.

I hope to have time to ride down to the river and take a look at Fredericksburg—perhaps tomorrow, if I am spared. Then I will describe it to you.

I visited our old Brigade yesterday and took dinner with Mr. Yard and Col. [Mark W.] Collett, now commanding the 1st Regiment. It was like home. Col. Torbert was not at home. Dr. Welling was with me. We had a pleasant ride and time. Dr. Taylor was there. Seeing him reminded me of old Bull Run times. . . .

Camp in the field opposite Fredericksburg, Va.
November 29th 1862

My dear Family,

We are now in front of the Grand Army and in sight of Fredericksburg, where I suppose we will soon have a battle—though, I confess, I don't know anything about the campaign. But I do know that we are right in front of the Rebel army. I have my tent up and stove in and am once more as comfortable as circumstances will admit. My health is most excellent. It could not be better. We have now but little sickness. Our men are becoming healthy. . . .

We have no mails as yet. Through some misunderstanding at the post office in Washington, mail has not been sent to our Brigade. But I have written and all will soon be right again. *I long for your letters.*

I am going on inspection. Monday we are to have a review of Hooker's Grand Army Corps, so we are preparing for it.

Enclosed you will please find Genl. McClellan's farewell address,[67] which I want you to keep for me. . . .

67. See Hassler, *McClellan,* 330.

Camp before Fredericksburg, Va., November 30th 1862

My dear Ellen,

This is Sabbath morning and the last day of the month. . . .

The cars have come whistling through here. Now our supplies will come without so much hauling by wagons. I have not received a single letter since I left Fairfax Courthouse. We have not had a mail, but we live in hopes that we will have one soon. . . .

The health of my Regiment is now good and improving rapidly. I sent down for a large number of our convalescents in the straggler's camp, but I have only received 18—healthy men that those young surgeons excused. They can pitch quoits, run, hop and jump, eat all their rations, and swear; yet these good for nothing surgeons [excuse them from duty].[68] That whole camp is a fraud on the Government and ought to be broken up.

Col. Moore is still on the court marshal and lives with his family in a tent now in the convalescent camp. It is another perfect outrage to keep him there when our regiment every day is expected to fight. The truth is: he likes it and, I fear, does not want to brave the storm of battle. He could get returned if he would make the application. His hitherto patriotic family are pleading with him to stay where he is. They even go so far as to tell him to resign. I fear that he has not got the pluck. If he does not come on at once, he will stand very low in the regiment.

Capt. [John H.] Grover is a coward. He got himself detailed on fortification work so that he would not have to come. But I will work him. Capt. Kearny is still sick. So is Capt. Stagg, besides a number of officers sick and detailed around Alexandria. Five more are on recruiting service. But one thing: we have the real fighting boys here. . . .

Camp before Fredericksburg, Va., December 1st 1862

My dear Ellen,

I have time but to write a few lines. My health is first rate and I am in good spirits. I am about starting down to visit my old regiment. I look for rain; still I think I will go. Dr. Welling is to accompany me. This old Regiment and Brigade are in our rear some seven miles.

---

68. McAllister's low estimation of army physicians was an opinion shared by many Civil War soldiers. Field surgeons of that day labored under numerous handicaps, not the least of which was a large number of incompetents among their ranks. A penetrating summary of army surgeons is in Bell I. Wiley, *The Life of Billy Yank* (Indianapolis, 1952), 129–32.

I send you this morning the sheets with my account of the campaign. I have nearly another sheet ready and will send the ballance soon.

I got my blanket and drawers last night. . . . I hope you have my new suit of clothes by this time. I have all I want here. . . . No pay yet, nor any prospects of any. . . .

                        Camp at Falmouth, Va., December 5th 1862
My dear Ellen,

. . . We are still here, but the General says we may move any day or hour. . . . Capt. Kearny has arrived. He got pretty well and came down on a visit and leave of absence. He is very anxous to join his regiment. He will in all probability be detained by a Higher authority than that which detailed him. He applied for a pass this morning to return. I signed it; but it was returned, asking me if I wanted him to go. I answered no, but wished him to return to Alexandria, get discharged [from the hospital], and return immediately. It is so arranged. I hope soon to have Capt. Kearny with us.[69] Lieut. Col. Moore, Capt. Grover, and [Lieutenant John] Oldershaw like their positions so well that they will not ask to be relieved. But I have nocked that. They will receive an order in a few days to rejoin their regiment. . . .

On Wednesday I received a mail—five letters from you and two from Henrietta—the first I have received for over a half a month. I know I could not have received one half of your very welcome letters. . . .

It does not suit a man with a family to be in the army, especially to be all the time campayning. For almost one year I have been on the go all the time. Oh, how I long to retire and spend the few remaining days of my life at home with my dear family. God grant that I may soon be permited to do so, that peace may be restored to our most distracted and bleeding country. . . .

    69. Philip J. Kearny, a cousin of "Fighting Phil," remained with 11th New Jersey until his death in August, 1863, from wounds received at Gettysburg. However, at the time of McAllister's letter he was far from satisfied with his army duty. "I would just as lief, and a little rather, go in some other Regiment," he stated in a Dec. 9 letter to his brother. "Ours is, by no means, the best that has left New Jersey. Our men are not of a high standard, either socially, morally, or physically. Already two hundred and fifty are unfit for duty. Our officers, with but few exceptions, are mechanics . . . and our Colonel (though I believe him an excellent man) as a Colonel is very inefficient and unpopular with the men." *Historical Magazine*, Ser. 2, Vol. VII (1870), p. 186. Col. John Schoonover wrote a strong rebuttal to Kearny's published letter. See *ibid.*, Ser. 3, Vol. I (1872–1873), p. 123.

Falmouth, Va., December 6th 1862

My dear Ellen,

... Franklin's Grand Army Corps has moved, but where I don't know. Some say to Belle Plains. It is rumoured that we move soon. Indications are that we will. I am looking for orders to that effect every hour.

Yesterday it commenced raining in the morning, and in the middle of the afternoon it commenced snowing. It snowed rapidly all afternoon and part of the night. This morning the ground is covered with snow from two to three inches deep. It is now the middle of the day and the snow is melting. I think that it will nearly all go away today. I hope it will, as it makes it so unpleasant for the soldiers in their shelter tents. Nearly all are without fires. Winter campaigns are very hard on the men—in fact, on all of us. The ladies of the North could not do a better thing than to knit mittens for the soldiers— thumb- and one-finger mittens. We have had no pay, can't buy them, and the Government don't provide this artical of comfort. I wish we had some for this regiment.

I would not advise the ladies to furnish articals of comfort for the convalescents & straggler's camp. A large portion of those men are more able to do duty than thousands of men here at the front, on whom the safety of the country depends. That convalescent's camp is a fraud on the Government and, as it is conducted, an outrage on the good and brave men that are here on the front, battling for our country. We have many men from this regiment now playing the rascal—or playing sick, as we call it. We hold them in low repute and call some of them cowards. Don't lavish your money on that quarter.

The Grand Divisions of our army numbers about 65,000 men, and yet we have only 40,000 here.[70] Some of the others are sick and no doubt unable to do duty, but a large number are playing sick, eating full rations, and . . . careful to hide away when sent for. That camp is as large as ever, though the sickly season is now past. Thousands of them look fat and hearty, leaving those of us here to fight for them and us too. I am disgusted with it and hope it will be broken up—the sick taken to hospitals and the weak put on duty. It has become a place for the cowardly, lazy & indolent soldiers . . .

70. On the trimonthly army return, dated Dec. 10, 1862, Burnside's three Grand Divisions numbered 201,855 present and absent, and 128,927 present for duty. This would indicate that 72,928 men were absent from the army for one reason or another. *OR,* XXI, 1121.

Falmouth, Va., December 7th 1862

My dear Ellen,

We have not moved today and may not for several days, though the indications are that we will move very soon. . . . It is very cold, ground froze hard. It did not thaw today. Tonight it will freeze much harder. But still we get along and are as comfortable as could be expected—indeed, more so. Some of the men have made chimneys at the end of their shelter tents. Some have none and do without fire. But they say they are comfortable. Some have fires outside of their tents, and some roll themselves up in blankets and stay all they can in their tents. The Adjt. and I have a little stove and are rather comfortable. I sleep on the ground as it is warmer than to be hoisted on a narrow bedstead. I have plenty of blankets and can sleep warm. . . .

Falmouth, Va., December 8th 1862

My dear Ellen,

About the middle of the day I received the mail and two letters from home—one written by Henrietta and dated the 4th, the other written by you and not dated at all. This has given me a grate deal of uneasiness. It speaks of Sarah being so very ill.[71] It is one you wrote in pencel. Henrietta speaks of her being so much better, having a relish for food, &c. On looking at the postmark, we cannot tell whether it is 3 or 5. Mr. Knighton said that it was a 5. This convinced me that she was worse instead of better, and that the prospect of her recovery was dark.

I immediately stated the case to Genl. Carr and asked him for a furlough. He said to draw up a furlough for five days and he would sign it. I did so and he endorsed it and recommended it very strongly. I then got leave to visit Sickles in person. As I was dismounting from my horse, I met our old friend, Col. [George H.] Sharpe of the 120th New York. I told him my troubles. He expressed a grate deal of sympathy and accepted an invitation to accompany me around. We called on Genl. Sickles. He said I could not get a furlough and declined to sign it. I told him how hard it was to have a struggle between duty and family, and that married men should not be in the army. He said that if I were in or around Alexandria, there would be no difficulty; but we are here at the front, &c. He advised me to go to Genl. Hooker and see his Adjt. Genl., which I did, Col. Sharpe accompanying me.

71. Sarah McAllister was still suffering from the effects of typhoid fever, contracted when she and her mother visited the Alexandria camp.

We called on Col. Joseph Dicoson.[72] He spoke of the difficulty in granting these furloughs but said that he would introduce me to Genl. Hooker, which he did. The General received me handsomely. I stated my case to him. I found him a man of feeling, a gentleman in every sense of the word. He told me that I ought to go home, but that he had not the power to grant me the furlough for five days. But he said he would give me leave to take it up to Washington. He gave me a pass for three and a half hours to go there. If it was not approved, he pointed out, I would have time to come back. However, he added that we would move in five days and that I would hardly get it passed.

After talking over the whole matter, we concluded to telegraph you as to how Sarah is and be governed by the return answer. I road to the telegraph office and sent you a message. . . . If she is better, I will not attempt to go home. If she is worse, I will try, though it is surrounded with difficulties.

I am delighted with Genl. Hooker. He is a perfect modle of a gentleman. I shall not soon forget either him or Genl. Carr for their kindness towards me in this matter. I don't wonder that Hooker is so much loved by all that know him. To know him is but to love him. . . .

Morning has come but no news from home. I am anxiously looking for an answer. . . . We are constantly expecting orders to move. But where we don't know. If we cross here, we will have a hard battle. If we move further up or down [the river], we cannot expect to cross without fighting. . . . We have some pretty sick men here. But the health of the regiment is much better than it was. . . .

Falmouth, Va., December 9th 1862

My dear Ellen,

I was grately rejoiced this evening to receive your telegram telling that Sarah was out of danger. It was truely good news for me. I was thinking all day about her and very uneasy. . . .

We have just now got marching orders. It is now nearly bedtime. We are to have four days' cooked rations with us, sixty rounds of cartridges, and to be ready to move tomorrow evening at sundown. We strike our tents at 3 o'clock tomorrow afternoon. Where we are going I don't know. I would not be surprised if we marched down to Aquia Creek and then go on transports, sail down to the York River, and then up to West Point—our old ground—and take the condemned

72. Hooker's very dependable adjutant was Lt. Col. Joseph Dickinson.

Chickahominy rought. Time will tell. We may go down this river and cross below. I can't think that we will move across here. The loss of life would be terable. I do not think it is or has been the intention of our commanders to cross here. This is undoubtedly only a faint. But a day or two will determine. I will gather up all my letters you and others have sent me . . . and send them to you. I will now retire after reading the last chapter of Revelations and offering up an evening prayer. Good night.

Wednesday morning, December 10th. Had a comfortable night's sleep and feel ready for a march this evening or night, as the case may be. But we will not move until night. I am still in the dark as to where we are going. I now think we will go down this river and cross below. What obsticals we will meet with I am unable to tell, but that we will soon have fighting I have no doubt. . . .

In the field below Fredericksburg, Va.
December 11th 1862

My dear Ellen,

The ball is opened. The battle commenced at 3 o'clock this morning. As yet it has been almost entirely artillery.[73] We are soon to cross on the pontoon bridge that we are building. I expect to be in the fight with my regiment before night. God grant that we may all do our duty. You will have the news of the battle before this reaches you. Recollect that we are in Sickles's Division. It is going to be a big fight. . . .

Pontoon bridge, 2½ miles below Fredericksburg, Va.
December 13th 1862

My dear family,

I wrote from the field day before yesterday. Yesterday we expected to cross at Fredericksburg; but for some cause unknown to us,

73. A tremendous artillery duel on Dec. 11 preceded the great infantry battle that occurred two days later. Recalling the action on Dec. 11, a New York officer wrote: "All day and throughout the following night the earth shook with the thunder of the heavy artillery, the flash and roar of the guns on Stafford Heights were answered by flash and roar from Marye's Heights and the adjacent hills, while the fiery trail of the deadly shells in the air and the devouring flames consuming the doomed city on the plain lent a terrible sublimity to the scene." In an effort to calm nerves made ragged by the fusillade, the men in the 11th New Jersey struck up impromptu choruses of "The Star-Spangled Banner." Capt. H. Seymour Hall in Kansas Commandery, M.O.L.-L.U.S., *War Talks in Kansas* (Kansas City, 1906), 189; Marbaker, *11th New Jersey,* 24–25.

we were delayed till evening and then brought down here last night in the dark and guarded these bridges for regiments of our brigade.[74]

The battle has commenced and is now raging. It is more artillery than small arms, though both are engaged. There is every appearance of a terable battle. We are in line ready to cross the bridges as soon as called on. The firing has slacked a little now, but it has not stopped. Soon it will commence again. The ambulances are going over to bring back our wounded, which no doubt are many, judging by the number that are going. . . .

We are now throwing across another bridge to take over large seige guns. I have no doubt of terable hot work today and tomorrow. We have only two regiments of our army corps across, and we go next, I think. God grant us success and protection is my prayer. Keep up your spirits under any circumstances. If I am wounded, come to me if possible. I understand that there is now some arrangement in which officers wounded are taken to places where their families can come and attend them. But if possible, get me home, the place above all others for me. If I fall, my remains will most likely be sent to you. Inter me as you think best, either in Belvidere or Juniata—the latter, if you would rather. . . .

On the battlefield 4 miles below Fredericksburg, Va.
December 14th 1862

My dear family,

I wrote you yesterday when at the pontoon bridges, immediately after which a terable battle was fought on the left and right of our lines. The cannonading was most terrifick, small arms not so rapid as some other battles I have seen, but a grate deal of skirmishing. Our dead and wounded are quite numerous. I remained at the bridges all day and night. Consequently, I was not in yesterday's battles, as they continued all day long and long after dark. It was thought that today (the fourth day since the battle commenced) would be the hardest of all. But up to my writing it has not been so, though we have had considerable firing both by cannon and skirmishers. We are now on the front line and send two companies at a time out as skirmishers. We have already sent to the front six companies, which have been under fire. They are relieved every two hours.

74. Pictures of the bridges that McAllister's men guarded are in Miller, *Photographic History*, II, 91; IX, 193.

Our boys have done splendidly, officers and all.[75] Capt. Hill lost one man. Capt. [Luther] Martin had one killed and five wounded.[76] These two companies [I and D] were the first that went out and had the hardest fighting. Lt. [Edward D.] Kennedy done well—stood right up to the mark. Capt. Hill is a fine officer. In fact, I can't but praise all that have been tried.

We are now on the battleground of yesterday which was taken and lost and again retaken. We hold it now. Jackson is said to be in our front. I hardly think there will be much more done today. We will hold this ground and tomorrow morning the battle will be renewed with increased force. This ground will be the scene of a terable battle by the rising of tomorrow's sun. Firing has almost ceased. We are bringing in the wounded, and I just now saw the body of Christopher Graham, shot through the head. He lives near Trenton. We will bury him here on this spot. . . .

I do not see that we have gained much more by all our fighting here than a foothold on this side of the river. The enemy are strongly fortified, a line of batteries on the crest of a line of hills in our front, with woods at that. While the enemy is covered, we are on this flat, cleared land. They can see us; we can't see much of them to drive them out of their strongholds (some five miles in length). It will have to be done at a tremendous loss of life.

Our army never fought better. They don't think of giving way. I have confidence in my regiment. They are in good spirits and ready for the continuation of the fight. My attention has just been called to a long line of Rebels at the edge of the woods to our left. Our Belviderers are all living. A man by the name of Nelson from our town and another by the name of Davis are both wounded but not dangerously.[77]

Camp near Falmouth, Va., December 17th 1862
My dear Ellen and family,

You will no doubt be surprised to see the date and place of this letter. I wrote you from the battlefield on Sabbath evening and also on Monday. After holding the front line and fighting with our skirmishers for twenty-four hours, we were relieved and brought back to

---

75. For praise of the steadfastness of the 11th New Jersey at Fredericksburg, see *OR,* XXI, 379–80, 383.
76. Total casualties in the regiment were 3 killed and 4 wounded. *Ibid.,* 134.
77. Pvts. Edward D. Nelson and George Davis of Co. D both survived their Fredericksburg wounds. *N.J. Record,* I, 556.

the second line to protect a battery. This was on Monday morning. This was the fifth day's fighting. But the fighting was much less on Monday than on any one day since the battle commenced. Our picket lines were completely quiet, especially on the center where we were. In the afternoon a flag of truce went over to ask leave to bury our dead left in the hands of the enemy on Saturday. This took place in sight of where I was with my regiment, but more to our left.

An officer in the Rebel army inquired for me. He was either a Colonel or a Brigadier General. He was told that I was in command of the 11th New Jersey. He seemed to be aware of the fact and said that he knew me like a book. It must have been either Thompson or one of the McDonalds.[78] He did not send his compliments. Small loss. However, this was Jackson's force that was in front of us and with whom we were fighting. Thompson and his tribe are, I think, with Jackson.

At 10 o'clock that night we had orders to form. We were marched across to this side of the river and bivouacked for the ballance of the night. I soon found that not only our Division, but all of the center, was falling back. We lay down and had just got to sleep, when down came the rain in a perfect torrent, wet us all through, and put out our fires. I got up, though some slept through the storm. About noon we were ordered back to our camp here. What is to be done I don't know. What all this move means I can't tell. But we have had too much to do. To go and take those hights would be to sacrifice too much life. I am satisfied that it would cost us 50,000 lives. It is positively stated that we have already lost 10,000 men.[79] I made up my mind that, to take it, many of us would have to bite the dust. I am not prepared to praise or condemn those in command. Time will tell us all.

I am proud of my regiment. It is all that I could ask; a braver set of men I don't want. It is a real fighting regiment. I will write you all the particulars. One of our wounded men have died.[80] He died a brave man. . . .

78. Robert's brother Thompson was still commanding the home guard at Covington, Va. The only McDonald of any rank then in the Confederate army was Col. Angus McDonald, an aged but colorful lawyer-Indian fighter-soldier from the Shenandoah Valley.

79. Federal losses at Fredericksburg totaled 12,653, including 1,284 killed. *OR*, XXI, 142.

80. Pvt. John H. Williamson of Co. D died of wounds received in the battle. *N.J. Record*, I, 558.

Falmouth, Va., December 19th 1862

My dear Ellen,

I have just received three letters from home. . . . I am perfectly satisfied with your arrangement about the money. It is perfectly safe in U.S. Certificates—interest paid regularly and in gold. . . . I have not got my pay yet. It will soon amount to one thousand dollars. Muster day must soon be here. I have not much money, but I can live. The Brigade commisary supplys us with food; it will come out of our pay. So we are all getting along on plain diet. A little money will go a grate way with us. . . .

I am here on three days' picket duty. I came out yesterday and will be relieved tomorrow. I have command of all our Brigade pickets —three regiments. It is a responsible job. But, by the help of God, I am able for it in any immergency, fight or not fight. But Johnny Reb has not shown themselves yet. All is quiet.

No doubt a grate deal is said about our retreat from Fredericksburg. Let me tell you that it is well we got out of that place as well as we did. Had we remained on that flat another day, we would have been butchered and our army would have been distroyed. We would not have been here today. I am still a McClellan man, but Burnside done well in getting us out of that place. We lost heavily as it was, but nothing to what it would have been had we stormed those hights. Who is to blame I don't know. . . .

Falmouth, Va., December 22nd 1862

My dear family,

I wrote you from the picket outpost on Saturday amidst the cold and chilling blast of winter—the coldest I have experienced yet. However, it was dry and we got along as well as could be expected. I am now in camp again, seting beside a comfortable stove. Our men are washing themselves and their clothes, all of which is much needed. We had no time to wash after our advance and battle until we were ordered out to picket duty. It will not be our turn to go on picket again, as we staid there three days and we have a large number of troops to do it.

I do not know what is in the wind, but we will most likely move somewhere soon. One report says to the James River, another that our Division (Sickles's) is to go to Alexandria to the defenses of Washington. But I don't believe it. It is true that that is our proper place, and Sickles coming away was through a mistake. And after getting here he was ordered back to Genl. Heintzelman. But there was some informality in the order and it was not returned—Sickles wanting to take part in the battle of Fredericksburg.[81]

All sorts of rumors exist about resignations at Washington. I hope that William H. Seward has not resigned.[82] He is the very best man we have and we want him where he is. I am not in favour of changes. They result in no good, or at least, they have not.

I think Burnside done well to get us back on this side of the river. But whether he is responsible for putting us there will soon be known. It was a *terable slaughterpen* to take troops into. And when I saw it, I never expected to get out alive. The retreat was done handsomely without any loss, for which Burnside deserves a grate deal of credit. McClellan should not have been removed. Our army was never in a better condition. They fought like tigers—as brave troops as ever composed an army. They moved up against those batteries with a heroism unequeled in the annals of warfare. . . .

Falmouth, Va., December 23rd 1862

My dear Ellen,

. . . I have been wishing to have time to give you a history of our doings from the time we left this camp and moved towards Fredericksburg, crossed the river, took part in the battles, and returned to this place. I will copy my report to Genl. Carr, which will give you and the children an outline of our movements. But you must not leave it to be published, as it would bring me into difficulty—though you can, if you choose, read it to friends.[83]

---

81. In a letter of Dec. 28, a New Jersey officer serving on Sickles' staff commented: "General Sickles and part of his staff went up to Washington yesterday. . . . I suspect that he is working for his *Major Generalship,* and doubtless he will get it. He is one of those industrious, indefatigable, unconquerable men, that never leave a stone unturned when their mind is once 'set'; and such men usually accomplish whatever they undertake." Rusling, *Civil War Days,* 292.

82. Sec. of State Seward was then under such heavy fire from Radicals in Congress that he submitted his resignation to Lincoln. The President refused to accept it. See Hendrick, *Lincoln's War Cabinet,* 331–46.

83. McAllister's official report of the Fredericksburg Campaign is printed here because it escaped publication in the *Official Records,* it provides a comprehensive account of the 11th New Jersey's action in the battle, and it illustrates the rough grammar of official dispatches before they were edited for publication. McAllister's congratulatory order to the regiment is printed in full in Marbaker, *11th New Jersey,* 28–29.

Headquarters, 11th Regiment, N.J.V.
Camp near Falmouth, Va., December 17th 1862

Capt. L. Benidict
Asst. Adjt. Genl.
1st Brigade, 2nd Division
3rd Army Corps

 Sir,

 According to your order in regard to a detailed account of our movements since my regiment left this camp, I have the honor to report as follows.

 According to orders from Genl. Carr, our line was formed at 7 A.M. December 11th 1862, and in a half an hour the Brigade was formed and moved towards the river. Halted on a hill overlooking Fredericksburg. Here we remained till evening, when we received orders to bivouack for the night. 7 o'clock next morning we were moved towards the river and halted. 3 o'clock P.M. we were then ordered to move back by the left flank. After passing Genl. Burnside's Headquarters we were halted and moved by a circuitious rought towards Franklin's Pontoon Brigades. Halted in the woods and ordered to bivouack. Had got comfortable fixed when I was ordered to move my regiment down to the river to guard the uper pontoon bridge. We marched down, lay at the bridge, detailing a guard, with orders to let no one cross without a pass from a General officer. Here we remained until 7½ o'clock A.M. December 14th, when we received an order from Genl. Carr to cross over, which we did and took our position in the second line of battle close by the main road leading down the river. In less than an hour we were ordered to move forward and relieve the 26th Penna. Vol. in the front line of battle. Shortly after we were in line we were ordered to send two companies to relieve the 26th Penna. Vol. pickets, or skirmishers. I at once ordered my two flank companies, commanded by Capts. Martin & Hill. They obeyed and deployed, moved forward handsomely under a gauling picket fire alike creditable to themselves and their respective companies. The men never flinched but fought with the courage and coolness of old soldiers. A grate deal of credit is due these officers and men. In two hours we relieved these companies by Cos. A & B, Capts. [William H.] Meeker and Kearny, who also went in to it with both will and courage. They acquited themselves with honour and are deserving of praise. When they were in two hours the firing ceased. And we relieved every two hours during the afternoon and night. In my visit to the pickets during the night I found them watchful and when the Adjt. visited them later they were also very attentive and are deserving of credit. All these companies proved themselves highly satisfactory to myself and trust that their conduct will meet with your approbation.

December 15th 7 o'clock A.M. we were relieved and fell back to the position we had on the morning of the 14th with orders to protect the battery in front of us. 10½ o'clock P.M. we received orders from General Carr to move back in the road after which we marched across the river with the Brigade and bivouacked for the night. December 16th received orders to fall in and follow the 2nd New Hampshire and in the evening arrived at this camp.

Below you will please find the list of casualties.

Respectfully
Your Obedient Servant
R. McAllister
Col. Comdg. Regt.

List of Casualties December 14th 1862

Names	Rank	Co.	Remarks
Christopher Graham	Private	I	Killed
John Williamson	do	D	Killed—New Brunswick
George Davis	do	D	Wounded—Barcastle
George Burnett	do	D	Wounded slightly—Livinston
Edward D. Nelson	do	D	Wounded slightly—Belvidere
Peter Burk	do	D	Wounded severely—Newark
Warren Green	do	I	Killed—shot through the head—Newark
			In addition to the above we have one man missing—making a loss of eight in all

(Continuing his letter of December 23 to his wife)

My dear Ellen,

Had it not been for the soft and loose ground receiving the balls, our loss would have been five times what it was. Some of our men fired sixty rounds. The loss was in the first two companies that went in. The firing was then by far the most rapid, and the loss of life shows it. Lt. [William] Lloyd was acting quartermaster and, of course, was not in the engagement.

I was in command of the Regiment in line of battle and was not in the skirmish, though balls occasionly came across to us. Dead bodies—killed the day before—were laying thick in front of our men. It was indeed trying on our boys, but they stood it like men. . . .

6

Camp Fitzhugh Farm, 1862-1863

"THERE IS not near the inthusiasm in the army that we had when Genl. McClellan had the lead." So wrote McAllister in the weeks of despondency that followed the battle of Fredericksburg. The 11th New Jersey spent the winter of 1862–63 amid sickness and low morale at Camp Fitzhugh Farm near Falmouth. Save for a twelve-day furlough home in late January, McAllister was constantly with his regiment and noting the small events of winter inactivity.

He declined to attend a New Year's party given by General Sickles; and with obvious disgust he described the tipsy condition of one high-ranking guest who had difficulty returning home. The Colonel and his New Jersey troops then took part in the inglorious "Mud March." McAllister shared the army's disappointment in the failure of the expedition. However, he was not as outspoken as the New Jersey artilleryman who remarked: "I feel that I have been through Virginia from top to bottom. If the hellish state was sacred, after this it will be sanctified, for damned if we are not all sacred, living monuments of Virginia mud." [1]

Typhoid fever, an ever-present menace in all Civil War camps, struck hard that winter in the tents and huts clustered around Falmouth. Several members of the 11th New

---

1. Hanifen, *1st New Jersey Artillery*, 42–43.

Jersey succumbed to the disease. McAllister fortunately escaped an attack, though a severe case of diarrhea prostrated him for a week in February.

His letters home during this period treat also of the shortcomings of the regimental chaplain, who McAllister felt was "of no earthly use to us here"; of personal incidents within the ranks of the regiment; of Peace Democrats and their antics in New Jersey; and of preparations for the spring campaign.

April, 1863, opened on an optimistic note. President Lincoln came down to Falmouth and reviewed an Army of the Potomac that, under the careful scrutiny of new commander Joseph Hooker, had strengthened organization and regained morale. McAllister's letters reflect the high note of optimism on which the army poised before a westward march to the Wilderness—and a crossroads known as Chancellorsville.

♣

Falmouth, Va., December 28th 1862

My dear Ellen,

I received a nice letter written on Christmas day from Hennie this morning, in which I was rejoiced to learn that Sarah was still mending very rapidly and that you were well and all enjoying yourselves. . . .

Col. Birney [2] called here yesterday and we took a ride to Falmouth. We watered our horses in the Rappahannock and rode down the river shore for several miles, along the line of our pickets. We looked at the Rebels on the opposite side and in the streets of Fredericksburg. Our pickets do not fire on each other. They can talk across the river. Our pontoon bridges are all taken away and hauled back, I understand, to Belle Plain. What is to be the next movement I know not. Our army is in a very good condition—not demoralized—but all are tired of war. Yet they will fight to the last. . . .

2. A former major in the 1st New Jersey, William Birney had just assumed command of the 4th New Jersey. *N.J. Record,* I, 76, 182.

Falmouth, Va., December 30th 1862

My dear Ellen,

... Mails are now coming regularly and are received in from three to four days, which is a grate improvement. But it will soon all be deranged again. We are once more under marching orders. We are to be ready at twelve hour's notice ... but where we are going I don't know. Some think we are going to Alexandria. Others think we are going down on the Peninsula again, which I think is probable. If so, I can't go home at all. If we go to Washington, I will try for a furlough. I am exceedingly anxious to get home a short time. My desire to see you all is very strong. ...

Capt. Hill is a little better; Lloyd is also better. His furlough application has not come back yet. Hill's has not been sent up. I have directed it be done. Lloyd and Hill are very much reduced and ought to be at home. We are having quite a number of deaths—typhoid fever and colds settling on the lungs. These winter campaigns are very hard on the men. Shelter tents and cold storms do not agree well and will kill a grate many men.

My health has been very good. I have not even had a cold untill now. I have a slight one and do not think it will amount to much. I will soon be well again. ...

Falmouth, Va., January 1st 1863

My dear Ellen and Family,

I wish you all a happy new year and may God spare you to see more. How good He has been to us all to spare our lifes thus long amidst so many dangers in this dark hour of our country's history—to see the light of this beautiful new year's day. Not a cloud is to be seen—calm and beautiful as a summer morning, but not quite so warm. ...

I wrote you the other day that I was not well. I feel much better now and think by tomorrow I will be entirely well. Capt. Hill is much better; Lt. Lloyd is also better. His furlough has not yet come back. I do not know why it is delayed.

Genl. Sickles had a reception today to which, with other officers, I was invited. However, I concluded that it was better for me not to go, as I was geting well and quietness was all I wanted. So I staid at home in my tent, writing letters, &c. The reception was quite a fine afair.[3] A number of Generals—Hooker among them—were there. I

---

3. Sickles, who always "did things in grand style," hosted a New Year's Day "open house" for his officers. "The champaign and whiskey ran in streams,"

sent my compliments and regrets. The truth is, I did not like Sickles's treatment of my application for a five days' furlough to see my sick and, as I feared, dying daughter. While Genl. Carr & Hooker treated it so kindly, Genl. Sickles had not, however, forgotten the circumstances. When Col. Moore presented my compliments and regrets, Sickles immediately inquired how my daughter was, &c. I think perhaps his conshins troubled him a little, but perhaps not. His memory is good and he remembered it. One thing is certain: I have not forgoten it.

Col. Sewel [4] of the 5th N.J. Vols. got so drunk at the reception today that he fell off his horse this evening while passing our camp and to the grate amusement of our boys. Of course, he takes the ground that "officers ought to have a little." Brigadier Genl. Mott [5] and others were with him; but our boys making so much fun over the drunken officer caused Genl. Mott to clear out. So Sewell's comrades tried to get him along. But he was rather a slow coach, and an ambulance was brought to take him home. No doubt he will be made a Brigadier General yet. Oh! When will our war powers awaken to a full sense of their duty and strike from the rolls all officers grate or small that will thus bring disgrace on the posts of honor that they hold and make brutes of themselves in the eyes of those who they command? . . .

We have not heard of moving since the order I told you about in my tent. Mr. Knighton has been crazy to get to Alexandria to see his wife. I have at last succeeded in geting him a three-day furlough,

---

de Trobriand recalled. "I wish I could add that they were used in moderation; but the truth is that the subaltern officers, attracted by the good cheer, partook of them so freely that it was not to the honor of the uniform nor to the profit of discipline." De Trobriand, *Army of the Potomac*, 398. The full details of the daylong affair are in Swanberg, *Sickles the Incredible*, 165–66. For the highly contrasting manner in which the enlisted men spent New Year's Day, see James J. Reeves, *History of the Twenty-fourth Regiment, New Jersey Volunteers* (hereafter cited as Reeves, *24th New Jersey*) (Camden, 1889), 24.

4. William J. Sewell had emigrated to America from Ireland in 1835. He served as colonel of the 5th New Jersey until July, 1864. Breveted a major general at war's end, he then became a member of Gov. Parker's staff. He closed out his public career by representing the Camden area in the New Jersey Senate. Foster, *New Jersey and the Rebellion*, 836–38.

5. Gershom Mott, frequently mentioned throughout McAllister's subsequent letters, was a native of Trenton who had served admirably in the Mexican War as a lieutenant in the 10th U.S. Infantry. He returned to civilian life and held a number of jobs before the outbreak of civil war. One of the first men from New Jersey to tender his services to the Governor, Mott was appointed lieutenant colonel of the 5th New Jersey. From that post he slowly rose in rank to brigadier general. No question was ever raised as to his valor; it was his ability that at times created doubts. *N.J. Biographical Encyclopaedia*, 442–44; Foster, *New Jersey and the Rebellion*, 822–26.

and he has gone. I have no doubt that he will overstay his time by at least three days more, and it will be but a very short time until he will send in his resignation. He is so completely tired of the service. He says no one knows anything about our difficulties as soldiers until they come out, that he has had wrong views, &c. He is not in his place here.

When he came to us, we had a considerable religious element in our regiment—prayer meetings regularly, &c. We may well ask where they are now. Now we have the prayer at evening dress parade, but that is all. I have done a grate deal to bring out the regiment on Sabbath day to hear him preach. But he does not know how to interest soldiers, and it has become a very uphill business. I told him the other day that we ought to have prayer meeting. He promised to do so, but that was all that was done. He keeps in his tent and pours over his books. He is a real Bookworm.

I have been told by Col. [Stephen] Moore that Mrs. Knighton looks careworn. This no doubt is owing to the fact that the Oxford congregation has not come up to their promise to pay her the salary due. Not a cent has been paid, our Government has not paid us, and Mr. Knighton has not got a cent to live on. This is hard. He has borrowed from Mr. Steuart [6] and will, I suppose, borrow again from him. He will soon be relieved, as the Government is to resume payment. But we are not to be paid for the last two months. I will only get at the coming pay 2½ months; the other two months will come at some other payment. Well, if we get that much, it will be a grate relief to our soldiers & their families.

All I have said about Mr. Knighton is confidential. Don't whisper it out of the family. . . .

Falmouth, Va., January 3rd 1863

My dear Ellen,

We are all in a bustle preparing to move camp about 2½ miles from this place where there is more wood and water, both of which are very scarce here. I have not been well for two or three days but am geting better. I thought it best not to make my bed on damp ground tonight, so I stay here until morning, then go over. . . .

This is beautiful weather—not very cold and no rain or snow, all of which is good for us. . . .

6. John Stuart was an elder in Belvidere's Second Presbyterian Church. Snell, *Sussex and Warren Counties*, 543.

CAMP FITZHUGH FARM, 1862–1863 ♣ [253]

Camp on the Fitzhugh Farm,[7] Va., January 6th 1863

My dear family,

The mail bag came round sooner than I expected so I have only time to write a few lines. I am pretty well, still attending to my duties, but have a bad case of diarrhea. I hope to be better soon. Lloyd is better, anxously wanting his furlough, which is hanging free. Hill is better and in the same fix. Lt. Kennedy is quite sick but not dangerous. Lt. [Aaron] Van Cleve, I do not think, can live. His father is here attending to him. They are from Trenton. We have a grate deal of sickness. . . .

Fitzhugh Farm, Va., January 7th 1863

My dear Ellen,

. . . We had a splendid review day before yesterday in Stoneman's Corps. Remember it is Hooker's Grand Army Corps composed of two or three corps. Genl. Stoneman commands our corps, in which is Carr's Brigade, Sickles's Division. You recollect that I was with Stoneman in the advance for several days when on the Peninsula until we reached the Chickahominy. He is a good officer, and this review was splendid. If the Government would only pay the troops, all would be right. Men are discouraged that their families are in want and, of course, have no hart to work or fight. I hope we will all soon be paid. . . .

Fitzhugh Farm, Va., January 9th 1863

My dear Ellen & family,

I write you every day, even if only a line or two. I feel quite well this morning. If I only had something I could eat that would not hurt me, I would be well. Our cooks fry entirely too much for health. I got a pound of butter yesterday from a sutler. I paid sixty-five cents for the pound. The commisary does not keep the artical, and you know how hard it is for me to do without butter. Send us some in your box of nice things I am looking for. Col. Moore is going to have a box sent. The Colonel & I are alone in the mess; so if you send a box too,

---

7. In 1752 Thomas Fitzhugh had laid out an immense estate four miles northeast of Fredericksburg. Both Sickles and Gen. Hiram Berry used the home as a headquarters that winter. By the end of the war the mansion was in ruins. *Official Atlas*, Plate XXXIII, Map 1; Cudworth, *1st Massachusetts*, 334; Rusling, *Civil War Days*, 293; Gould, *Hiram G. Berry*, 235.

we will live. Put in a few donuts. They are considered quite a treat here. If I can't eat them myself, I can return the compliment of some of my friends who are always ready and willing to share there boxes with me. I like donuts myself; but as I am now, I dare not eat them. I feel now that in a day or two I will be all right again. A bottle of Jamaca Ginger would be good for me. I have a bottle in my trunk at Mr. Roberts's, but that is not here. . . . I have nothing with me but a pair of sadle bags and my small hand trunk, which is all I can carry. So if the Rebels get all I have, they won't get much except blankets and pistols. . . .

Our boys are fixing up in this new camp very nicely. All or nearly all have built huts, covered by shelter tents, with a nice little fireplace in them. In fact, they are first rate, and the men are now more comfortable than they have been since we left our comfortable camp at Fort Ellsworth. Col. Moore and I have just one wall tent, and we have a nice little stove in it that Mrs. Roberts give me as a present. Recollect that we have not got two tents put together, as we had at Alexandria, but just one of them for both of us. Of course we are hampered, but we get along very comfortable and, when we move, we have but little to lumber up with. The object is to keep the army in marching order—to be ready in a moment's notice to pull up stakes and march. I suppose by the time we are all comfortable fixed, we will have orders to move. But this is the fate of war. . . .

No pay yet and another set of rolls are made out. . . . I pity some of the wives of our poor soldiers.

Mr. Knighton got a three day's furlough and left on the last day of the year. We are now up to the 9th and he has not made his appearance yet. When men & officers get furloughs and then violate their obligations, it prevents those of us who are perfectly willing to act up to the very letter of a furlough from geting away. This very thing may prevent me from geting my furlough. I worked hard to get this furlough for Mr. Knighton. . . . He does no good here. He is entirely out of place. . . .

Fitzhugh Farm, Va., January 11th 1863

My dear family,

. . . I am quite well today and feel ready for duty. One of our Sargeants died last night of typhoid fever.[8] He was a good man from

8. Sgt. William L. Foster died Jan. 10. In the period September, 1862–April, 1863, twenty-one members of the 11th New Jersey succumbed to typhoid fever. *N.J. Record*, I, 549; Marbaker, *11th New Jersey*, 54.

the state of Indiana. He has a brother here as a Lieutenant.[9] Our regiment is improving in health. Lt. Lloyd has gone home on 20 days' furlough; he left this morning. He is pretty well and in a few days will be all right. Capt. Hill & Lt. Kennedy have not received their furloughs yet, but no doubt they will very soon. Both are a good deal better. Lt. Van Cleve is a little better, but his case is very doubtful. He has his furlough but is not able to leave. His father and brother are both here. They are very respectable people.

We have had considerable rain, and the roads are very muddy. Genl. Carr tells me that we will likely move very soon. The restlessness of the people of the North will not permit this army to lay long here. So we must go on, no matter what it costs in life or money. Our regiment are now so very comfortable; and if permited to remain a short time, our men would become healthy. But if we are to brake up this comfortable camp and expose our men to storms and bad roads and weather after so much sickness, we must loose heavily—even if we should not get into battle at all. But we will do our duty, come what may. . . .

I wish you to send me the woolen night cap that Henrietta knit for me. It is just the thing for bivouacking and laying out of doors. . . . Mr. Knighton is not back yet. What does he mean? . . .

Fitzhugh Farm, Va., January 13th 1863

My dear Family,

I have but time to write a line. I am just going out on inspection. Genl. Stoneman is to take a look at us this afternoon. I am quite well now and hope to continue so. We still have deaths in our regiment, though not so much sickness as usual. In fact, all new regiments are suffering that way. Deaths are more numerous than they were on the Peninsula. . . .

Fitzhugh Farm, Va., January 14th 1863

My dear Family,

. . . We have all sorts of rumours in camp regarding moving. It is thought by some that we will cross at the old place, Fredericksburg, but as to this I cannot say. I have but little doubt, however, but

9. Reuben Foster was a lieutenant in Co. F, 25th New Jersey.

that we will soon move against the enemy. If so, I hope we will be more successful this time and trust that God will throw His protecting shield over and around us and grant us success in our efforts to put down this wicked rebellion.

I am looking for my box with as much anxiety as a school girl. The fact is: something good to eat will be a treat.

Sarah, you don't know how the whole army loves Genl. McClellan and longs for his return. I am honest in my conviction when I say that he is the man for the times. I have nothing to say against Burnside. I think he is a good man.

Mrs. Harris is in the neighbourhood. I expect a call from her today or tomorrow. . . .

Lieut. Van Cleve is geting better and will, I think, soon be able to go home. His father is nursing him faithfully. . . .

Mr. Knighton is not back yet. He stands a good chance of being dismissed from the army and loose all his back pay, now amounting to over five hundred dollars. He has not written a single word to us. I don't know what to do. His absence will be discovered; and if I keep it a secrete longer, I will be rolled up Salt River. The effect on the men is bad. . . .

Fitzhugh Farm, Va., January 14th 1863

My dear daughter Henrietta,

. . . I am always highly delighted to receive letters from you, and it gives me pleasure to answer them. But you know that my duties to my regiment, the daily corrispondence home, together with my business letters, takes up all my time. Contrery to my wish and inclination, I am compelled to write but few other letters. But I will do the best I can.

As you are aware, we have moved our camp to this farm and have fixed ourselves up nicely. Our men have all built little huts and covered them with their shelter tents, and all have fire places in them. The men are very comfortable—more so than we have been since we left Fort Ellsworth. But I don't think we will be left to enjoy it long. Rumors are flying thick and fast relative to our moving. . . . My own opinion is that we can't stay here long and that we may move any day.

This army can't lay here all winter, even if its removal should cost the lives of one half of our army. Little do the people of the North—living in fine houses, laying back in there easy chairs in heated rooms or beside blazing coal fires, reading the sensation newspapers, and at the same time condemning this General and that one, this move and that move—know of the suffering in our army—suffering by cold, wet, and disease that are carrying down thousands of our brave men to an untimely grave. Little do they know of the work of moving an army, and the difficulties to be encountered. All the men in the army, who a short time ago were at home speculating, come out now and acknowledge that they knew nothing about it, and that there views are entirely changed. I wish all such could come and try there hands. It would be a holesome lesson and would teach them wisdom and stop a grate deal of this complaning at home, as well as lessen the dissatisfaction in the army. Oh! When will we learn wisdom? . . .

I suppose you have seen Lt. Lloyd. He went off in such a hurry that he did not say goodby. Capt. Hill has not got his furlough yet, nor has Lt. Kennedy. . . .

Fitzhugh Farm, Va., January 16th 1863

My dear Ellen,

For the last twenty-four hours my spirits were up to a high degree with a fair prospect of geting home on leave of absence of twelve days.[10] Genl. Sickles encouraged it and thought that there was no doubt of my geting it through. But by the time it got up to Genl. Stoneman's, an order for moving Hooker's grand army made its appearance. Of course my leave could not thus be granted at this time. Though this order has not reached here yet, it will. We are to move tomorrow morning, the 17th. . . . I understand that Hooker's Corps moves up the river and crosses. . . .

Mr. Knighton has come back after being absent for fifteen days. Nothing will be said about it, but the effect on the regiment is very bad. . . .

Fitzhugh Farm, Va., January 17th 1863

My dear Family,

I wrote you yesterday that we had marching orders and that we would move this morning. Our movement is postponed till tomorrow

---

10. On Jan. 14 McAllister requested a ten-day furlough. Sickles wrote an unusually long letter in support of the application. See McAllister to J. M. Dickinson, Jan. 14, 1863, and Sickles to McAllister, Jan. 14, 1863, McAllister's service file.

at 1 p.m. We are all to be ready then, though we may not move at that time. I am satisfied that we will move very soon. Something is on the carpet. . . .

This day is beautiful but a little cold. It froze last night, but it is pleasant today. We have a large number of sick men. . . .

Fitzhugh Farm, Va., January 18th 1863

My dear Family,

I wrote you yesterday that we were to march at 1 p.m. today. It is now 12 o'clock and the movement has been postponed until 1 p.m. tomorrow, when we are to march as calculated for this day. I have no doubt but that we are to go up the river and cross above Fredericksburg, take the enemy by the flank, and have fighting to do. Why the postponement I am not able to tell. I suppose we are not altogether ready. Our movements are dependent on others. Time will determine.

The weather is fine but cold. It will be chilly to lay out. But we must take our chances and do our duty as good soldiers.

I have talked to Mr. Knighton about not having more preaching and prayer meeting in our camp. I done it kindly and told him we are all to blame and that we must be better hereafter. He is somewhat stired up to a sence of his duty, and we had a very pleasant little meeting last evening back of this camp, in the woods beside a very pleasant fire. Our Chaplain seemed to be what he always ought to be —warmly enlisted in the good cause. We are to have another one this evening and also a service today, which will take place around the graves of two of our soldiers who died in the hospital last night with the typhoid fever.[11] We have now lost forty men by deaths in our regiment.

The mortality is even worse in Col. Sharpe's regiment, the 120th New York. They have over 100 sick in the hospital and buried two yesterday. So it is with all the new regiments. I don't think the deaths on the Chickahominy begin to come up to what we have among the new troops. The old regiments fair better—but little sickness and very few deaths among the old soldiers. I tell you this country is not healthy. I have not now over one half of my officers & men on duty. *This is winter campayning.* But we must do the best we can.

Genl. Carr is now home on a furlough. I hope he will be back before we have a battle. I have confidence in him and don't think

11. The two soldiers were Pvts. James Dever of Co. D and Bingham Cartwright of Co. H. *N.J. Record,* I, 557, 573.

much of Col. Blisdale,[12] the Colonel commanding our Brigade. He drinks a little too much for me. Genl. Carr told me that he would come right back if there should be a move, even if he had not been home one hour. . . . All his staff are with him. Capt. [LeGrand] Benedict, his Adjt. Genl., is geting married. Won't they all have a nice time of it? But we want them all here. They are good officers, and I can depend on them. . . .

Had I made my application for leave a few days sooner, I would have got it through. But it is well I did not, as they would have telegraphed me, and I would have come right back. If they had not done so, I would have felt badly to be absent when my regiment moved. . . .

We have no smallpox in our regiment now. The company that we had in Alexandria had some. . . .

Fitzhugh Farm, Va., January 19th 1863

My dear family,

Our orders to move at 1 p.m. today (Monday) have again been put off until tomorrow at 1 p.m. For what cause we know not. Some think we will go without doubt tomorrow; others think it very doubtful. That we are to cross the river is no secret. That is the object. Our baloon is up almost all the time when the weather is favourable, and no doubt a good watch is kept on the enemy, their work, and movements. I hope that Genl. Burnside knows exactly what he is doing and that we may be successful this time. But God only knows what is before us.

The weather is fine but it is very cold, especially at night. Our men must suffer terably to bivouack, and many of them will suffer very much. Genl. Carr has not got back yet, but I hope he will before we go into action. . . .

You know Frank Sargeant, who was in Genl. Montgomery's

12. Of all the officers with whom McAllister served, the one he liked least was unquestionably Col. William Blaisdell of the 11th Massachusetts. A native of New Hampshire, Blaisdell in 1841 enlisted as a private in the 4th U.S. Infantry. Nine years later he left the service with the rank of sergeant. He became a prosperous businessman and was instrumental in organizing the 11th Massachusetts. Hampered constantly by chronic bronchitis and subjected to frequent coughing spells, Blaisdell nevertheless proved so capable and energetic an officer that on several occasions he was recommended for promotion to brigadier. Blaisdell was obviously brave; yet—as McAllister's letters indicate—he was ambitious to a fault. Blaisdell's service file, National Archives. See also Massachusetts Adjutant General (comp.), *Massachusetts Soldiers, Sailors and Marines in the Civil War* (cited hereafter as Mass. Adj. Gen., *Massachusetts Soldiers*) (Norwood, Mass., 1931–35), I, 737.

office and who I talked of making an Adjutant if I had got the Colonelcy of the 10th Regiment. You know he said if I would do something for him he would stand by me. I have appointed him 2nd Lieut. [of Company G] in my regiment. I am looking for him every day. . . .

January 20th. We are all in a bustle, geting ready to move forward.[13] We will be on the roads in an hour. Looks like rain or snow. Good By, God bless you all. . . .

Camp in the woods above Falmouth, Va.
January 22nd 1863

My dear daughter,

. . . I wrote you the other day that we had orders to move. We started on Tuesday the 20th at 1 p.m., marched about two miles, and halted to let Genl. [William] Franklin's Army Corps pass us. Night came on; it commenced raining and was very dark. We then got orders to return to our old camp. We went back. Our tents had all been taken down, but our men soon had their shelter tents over their old huts and fires kindled in the fireplaces. Then they became somewhat comfortable. But my tent was in the wagon, and it was too dark and rainy to fix it up. I lodged in one of the line officer's tents that had not been taken down. I laid down to sleep with some dozen or more officers, fell sound asleep, rain poured down in torrents, our tent leaked, and I wakened up and found that I was laying in water. I got up and set by the fire for awhile, then laid down again and slept soundly.

Morning came, and with it an order to take our position in column. Many of us started without having brackfast, rain pouring down still in torrents. We marched on through mud and water, through fields and woods, men plunging in over their shoes at every step.[14]

---

13. At this time, Gen. Darius N. Couch wrote, Burnside "tried to regain the confidence of the army" by crossing the Rappahannock a few miles above Fredericksburg and striking Lee's left flank. This "effort to redeem himself" proved Burnside's end. The army floundered in rain and mud, the advance turned into "perfect folly," and Burnside shortly thereafter relinquished command of the army to Gen. Joseph Hooker. Robert U. Johnson and Clarence C. Buel (eds.), *Battles and Leaders of the Civil War* (cited hereafter as Johnson and Buel, *Battles and Leaders*) (New York, 1884–87), III, 118–19.

14. Gen. A. Seth Williams, writing to his daughter with no small degree of exaggeration, stated of the roads around Fredericksburg: "It is solemnly true that we lost mules in the middle of the road, sinking out of sight in the mud-holes. A few bubbles of air, a stirring of the watery mud, indicated the last expiring effort of many a poor long-ears." Milo M. Quaife (ed.), *From the Cannon's Mouth: The Civil War Letters of General Alpheus S. Williams* (Detroit, 1959), 159.

Artillery and wagons were stalling and sticking fast all along the road. Men were falling out—more stragling than I ever seen on any march. Everybody was wet through to the skin, cold and chilly. We arrived here about 3 p.m., fixed ourselves as comfortable as we could under the circumstances, made big fires, and the men pitched their shelter tents. We got a light "A" tent for Col. Moore, the Adjutant, the Major, and myself. We made a large fire before the tent. Rain continued in torrents. We all bunked in and slept soundly till about 5 o'clock this morning, when we heard the three guns that sounded like signal guns. I suppose that they were from the side of the enemy. We all thought that the battle was opened. It is now evening and we have heard nothing since.

We are still here. We have sent our regiment to make roads. It is almost impossible to move wagons or artillery. What they are going to do I don't know. I fear that the storm will be against our move. But it may be against the enemy as well as ourselves. . . . We are all in the dark as to our movements. We know nothing about what is doing outside.

There is not near the inthusiasm in the army that we had when Genl. McClellan had the lead.[15] There is a feeling of doubt hanging around everyone, officers & men. I am sorry to see and hear it, but there is no disguising the fact. I am still for McClellan but not opposed to Burnside. I think Burnside is a good man and I want him to have the harty support of all the army. I would like also to see the administration & the army have the full support of all at home—more encouragement and less fault-finding. . . .

Camp Fitzhugh Farm, Va., January 24th 1863

My dear family,

The terable condition of the roads, and the utter impossibility of hauling artillery, ammunition, and provisions, made it necessary for the army to halt before it reached the river and build corduroy

---

15. One of the army's chroniclers stated more positively: "It would be impossible to imagine a graver or gloomier, a more sombre or unmusical body of men than the Army of the Potomac a month after the battle [of Fredericksburg]. And as the days went by, despondency, discontent, and all evil inspirations, with their natural consequent, desertion, seemed to increase rather than to diminish, until, for the first time, the Army of the Potomac could be said to be really demoralized." Swinton, *Campaigns,* 256. See also Howard, *Autobiography,* II, 347–48; Craft, *141st Pennsylvania,* 46; Blake, *Three Years in the Army of the Potomac,* 159–60.

roads to get back. We are now all in our old camps. Burnside's not to blame for not advancing, for it was out of the question to advance.

I am well, will try for a furlough, but don't know whether I will get it. . . .

Camp Fitzhugh Farm, Va., February 9th 1863

My dear Ellen & family,

Sarah & I arrived in Philadelphia about half past 8 p.m. We went to Mrs. Lloyd's and found Lt. Lloyd ready to start. . . . I arrived here in camp yesterday evening and found all as usual. This Brigade and another part of the Division had a tramp up the river and destroyed two bridges.[16] They were in that snow storm and had a hard time of it. But they accomplished their object. The cavalry done the work. The infantry supported them and acted as a reserve. . . .

It is terably muddy; roads are impassable. We have an inspection today by Genl. Carr, now in command of the Division. I must get ready for it. Stoneman is the chief of cavalry. . . .

Camp Fitzhugh Farm, Va., February 11th 1863

My dear Ellen & family,

I wrote you yesterday and had my letter ready for the mail. George Ribble's [17] furlough came and I sent it with him, as you will get it much sooner than by mail. Dr. Young [18] has resigned and gone home. We are trying to get Ribble to fill his place. I have written a strong letter in his favour. Dr. E. Byington has written to his father [19] and Dr. Clark [20] of your town to do all they can for him. . . . Dr.

16. McAllister was referring to a Feb. 5–9 expedition sent out to destroy the Orange & Alexandria Railroad bridge spanning the Rappahannock River. Confederates thwarted the attempt. Owing to bad weather, Mott reported, the march was "one of the most severe . . . that any troops have ever been called upon to perform." *OR*, Vol. XXV, Pt. 1, pp. 7–9; Marbaker, *11th New Jersey*, 37–40.

17. George T. Ribble was asst. surgeon of the 11th New Jersey.

18. Asst. surgeon Edwin B. Young resigned from service on Feb. 5. *N.J. Record*, I, 542.

19. Dr. Roderick Byington, the father of one of the 11th New Jersey's surgeons, was a highly respected physician, a strong advocate of temperance and public education, and a ruling elder in Belvidere's Second Presbyterian Church. Snell, *Sussex and Warren Counties*, 508–9.

20. Dr. Samuel Clark maintained a large medical practice in Belvidere. See *N.J. Biographical Encyclopaedia*, 250–51.

Ribble is more competent than most young medical men are that have graduated. He has certainly done his duty here and deserves promotion. I think a grate deal of him.

Genl. Hooker's recent order leaves us one field officer and two line officers.[21] Two men out of every hundred have furloughs, not exceeding ten days. Lt. Col. Moore has left this morning with a leave of seven days, together with one line officer and one man from every company. Col. Moore's business required his going home at this time. Yet seven days is but a short furlough. I found twelve very short. Time flies so rapidly. I was fortunate in geting mine before this order came out limiting leaves of absence to ten days. Col. Moore asked for ten but only got seven. From this I judge we will move soon.

The 9th Army Corps, Burnside's old Corps, have all gone.[22] The last Division left today. They are no doubt going south, either to North or South Carolina. All were glad to get off. All prefer going south to remaining in this poor, miserable, forlorn, unfortunate state. I would not be at all surprised if we were moved from here and sent south.

To advance on Richmond from here, I think as I have always thought, is a fruitless task. But we may cross and try our fortunes of war once more with our faces towards the coveted city.

McCall's old Division [23] have gone, it is said, to Washington to take the place of some nine-months men in the fortifications, so that these short-lived regiments may have a chance to show their bravery before they leave the service. A good idea. We three years men have a long tug before us. We have to fight first, last and all the time. It was a grate mistake ever to muster nine-months men. But it was done for the best. Our troops are cheerful and in good spirits. No demoralization about them.

Saturday, February 14th. What I had written you thus far was

21. On Jan. 26 Hooker succeeded to command of the army. Restoring morale was his most pressing problem. Some 85,000 men were absent from the front, and desertions in January averaged 200 per day. Hooker promptly began a liberal granting of furloughs; later, when Lincoln issued a general proclamation of amnesty, large numbers of deserters voluntarily returned to the ranks. *OR*, XXI, 1005; Mason W. Tyler, *Recollections of the Civil War* (New York, 1912), 75.

22. Beginning Feb. 6, Gen. William F. Smith's IX Corps left Falmouth for Newport News. The last of the three divisions moved out of the Falmouth defenses on Feb. 10. *OR*, XVIII, 149.

23. Gen. George A. McCall's Pennsylvanians were not noted for cleanliness or model behavior. When these men reached Washington, a Connecticut recruit asked in horror: "Could these blackened, bearded, tattered, begrimed veterans who swooped down upon the slop barrels of the cook houses 'like the wolf on the fold' . . . be the army of the Union?" Thorpe, *15th Connecticut*, 21.

interrupted by the calling of an agent representing the Sanitary Commission. He was a very gentlemanly man whose business was to get all the facts relative to the regiment: encampments, marches, bivouacs, picket duty, sentinel duty, fatigue duty, water, food, &c. I have answered a hundred questions.[24] He says it will form a part of the history of this war. Before he was through, our state agent came, whose business it is to get a list of deaths and discharges, as well as desertions. A record is kept in the State Department. This is done monthly. This prevented me from having my letter ready for the mail that day.

That night I took sick—a terable diarrhea accompanied by severe pain, and also a chill followed by fever. Until now I have been in bed, taking medicine, and am doing very well. I am now able to set up and write this. I am better every way and think in a day or two I will be ready for duty. Our Brigade is now out on picket duty. I was to have command of it, had I been able to have gone out. . . .

Camp Fitzhugh Farm, Va., February 15th 1863

My dear Ellen,

. . . I am still confined to my bed except when I go back to the sink. I am now seting up to write this letter. I am no worse. The Doctor thinks I am better, though I have still some fever. All I want is cold water. I think of Peirson's Spring, as well as you. My boy Henry attends me very well. He stays with me night and day. The Doctor thinks he will soon have the fever broke and then I will get well. Don't be at all uneasy about me, as there is no danger attending my case. . . . I get along better than you think I do. But I must confess it is not equal to your Hospital. . . .

Camp Fitzhugh Farm, Va., February 17th 1863

My dear Ellen,

. . . I feel better today than I did yesterday. The irritation of my bowels still continues. You know that is the weak place with me and I have to be so careful. The fever has left me but I still cannot eat anything of any account.

24. Actually, field representatives of the U.S. Sanitary Commission were then seeking the answers to 180 different questions. William Y. Thompson, "The U.S. Sanitary Commission," *Civil War History,* Vol. II, No. II (June, 1956), p. 48.

It began to snow last night, has snowed all day long, and shows a fair prospect of continuing. I cannot write any more. . . .

Camp Fitzhugh Farm, Va., February 21st 1863

My dear Ellen & family,

I am happy to inform you that I am a grate deal better. I feel like a new man—no fever and diarrhea considerable checked. I feel that I will soon be able for duty again. I walked out this morning and enjoyed the delightful balmy breeze. The sun is shining beautifully, the spring birds are singing, and our Brigade Band is playing. The notes are carried along on the morning breeze, cheering up the hart of many a sad one thinking of home, sweet home. These delightful sounds are mingled with the more stiring sounds of the bugle coming from the banks of the Potomac Creek. These, together with the rolls of the drums, tell us that the preparation for war still goes on and that the time of battle will come . . .

Camp Fitzhugh Farm, Va., February 22nd 1863

My dear Ellen & daughters,

Dr. Ribble returned last evening with a whole lot of good things from you to me, for which I am very much obliged. If I was well, how I would enjoy them. As it is, I can taste a little of some of them. Those nice cakes broken in tea is about all I can eat now. But I hope soon to be able to do justice to the ballance of the things.

I am geting better but slowly. I have no fever, only a continuance of diarrhea, which seems hard to control. I stay in bed a good deal and keep as quiet as I can do under the circumstances. . . .

We are in the midst of a terable storm. It commenced blowing and snowing last night, some time before midnight—a real northeast storm. It has continued up to this time, 3 p.m. Snow is about a foot deep, and it is very cold. It takes all we can do to keep warm. Wood is now geting far off—all cleared away since we came here. Roads are in a terable bad condition. We can hardly drag a team through the mud. We are now cuting too many of our beautiful trees left for the protection of our camp. Cutting them is a matter of necessity to keep from freezing. Thus, with what the men carry from a distance and what little the extree teams haul, we are enabled to get along. . . .

I believe we have had more snow this winter here on the Rappahannock than you have had on the Delaware. Yesterday, I wrote you, was such a beautiful day and now a terable storm! We will not let any of our men suffer, but it takes watching. I am down on winter campaigns. . . .

                    Camp Fitzhugh Farm, Va., February 23rd 1863

My dear Ellen & daughters,

I feel much better today, although the diarrhea is not altogether stoped. But I hope it soon will be. The ground is covered with a thick coat of snow. It is very cold, a real Northern winter. Yesterday was the 22nd and the Sabbath. As it was, they intended to have a grand review. But the storm prevented it, so everybody was glad to remain indoors. . . . So all the 22nd we had was the salutes fired by the artillery. The sound went out over the camps amidst the raging storm, telling us that it was [Washington's birthday]. Had it not been for the salutes, I would not have thought of the day.

The box has not arrived and never will now. We went down to Aquia Creek for it, but it was not to be found. We was told there that a number of boxes had been opened on account of the contents decaying. I suppose mine was one of them. Don't send any more unless ordered. . . .

                    Camp Fitzhugh Farm, Va., February 24th 1863

My dear family,

. . . I am much better today and feel as though I am geting well and think I will soon be on duty again.

You spoke of a letter coming to me from Trenton. That reached me. It was a bill for $20 for Mr. Knighton's coat. He has neglected to pay for it; and in case of a failure to pay, they look to me because I said it would be all right. I presented it to our chaplain and give him to understand that it ought to have been paid long since, that I calculated he would see to it at once. He took the letter, said that he would answer it at once, but added: "I have no money now."

You know he has sent all his money home, keeping nothing to live on. He is too niggardly mean to be an officer in any post in the army. His meanness has killed him here. . . . I have lost all confidence in Mr. Knighton and can't help it.

The ground is still covered with snow—so much so that we can't drill or do anything out of doors. . . .

        Camp Fitzhugh Farm, Va., February 25th 1863
My dear Ellen & children,
 . . . I am much better and will soon be fit for duty, for which we ought to be thankful to God. . . .
 The ground is still covered with snow, though it is melting some today. We are laying here very quiet. We can't drill for the snow and mud; I have nothing to read, and I don't know anything that is going on even in the Army of the Potomac. There is something wrong in regard to the papers, but we don't know the cause. Some say it is a strike among the newsboys; others say that Hooker's order restricting one newsboy to a division is not enough.[25] No one boy could do the work of distributing papers to a whole division. This has caused the newspaper men to draw off altogether. Be that as it may, we suffer by it and all here are in perfect ignorance of what is going on. . . .
 Our man Fitzer [26] from your town got a furlough. His time has expired and there is no word from him. I fear that he has deserted. He is a rascal. I wish you to ascertain quietly if he has been home— or if he is at home now. If so, we will have him dead or alive. There is a man to be shot soon for desertion. One from our regiment is to have his head shaved, the letter "D" branded on his skin, and drummed out of camp in the presence of the whole Brigade.[27] If Fitzer deserts, he will fare as well. Let me know about him. Do it all quietly, or he will get timid of it and clear out. I have looked upon him for some time with suspicion. He had by his cunning worked himself in as ammunition teamster at Division Headquarters—a very lazy position. He is a very lazy man. We have reason to think that he don't care about his wife and that he may not be there at all but gone

 25. In an effort to tighten army security, Hooker restricted visitors' permits and asked Sec. Stanton to take positive action against those newspapers that continued to reveal aspects of the army's condition and movements. *OR*, Vol. XXV, Pt. 2, pp. 153–54, 239, 269–70. Cf. Reeves, *24th New Jersey*, 27.
 26. Pvt. Jonathan R. Fitzer of Co. I, though demoted from corporal in November, 1862, served in the 11th New Jersey until his May, 1865, muster from the army. *N.J. Record*, I, 576.
 27. McAllister was probably referring to Pvt. Daniel Doremus of Co. K, who was dishonorably discharged Mar. 18, 1863, at Falmouth. *Ibid.*, 581. The proportion of desertions in the 11th New Jersey during its first year in the field was "not greater than that of many other regiments," its historian stated. He added that "no regiment was without its quota of the second class—the weak-kneed and faint-hearted." Marbaker, *11th New Jersey*, 111.

[268] ✗ THE McALLISTER LETTERS

in some other direction. He took with him all his blankets, &c. They say at Division Headquarters that they will have him, cost what it will. . . .

Camp Fitzhugh Farm, Va., February 26th 1863

My dear Ellen,

. . . I am geting well and will soon be ready for duty again, for which I am thankful to God. Today it has rained all day, but the ground is still covered with snow. Snow and mud is the order of things here, with no prospect of improvement.

The 2nd New Hampshire is going home on leave of absence for 30 days. This is an old regiment belonging to our Brigade. I am sorry to loose them. I don't suppose that they will ever join us again, but no doubt will recruit and be asigned to some other corps. And yet I do not know such about their object in going home.[28] . . .

Don't you give up your New York daily paper. Keep that by all means. That is our history, more interesting to us than all others. I wish I had time to read as you all have. How I would enjoy it. But I must study military works and can't carry books with me. I must always be in light military order. . . .

Camp Fitzhugh Farm, Va., March 1st 1863

My dear Ellen & family,

This is the Holy Sabbath Day. I have hardly left my tent—have been reading some tracts, &c. I find it is near mail time and I quit reading to write you. This is one of my greatest enjoyments. I did not write you yesterday . . . because I took a short ride on horseback and on my return was so tired that I lay down to rest and fell asleep. When I got awake the mail had gone. I have road for two days and expect to take a longer ride tomorrow, if I feel as well as I do today and the day is favourable. . . . Last night and this morning it rained quite fast; but it has since cleared up and is now very windy, which will dry up the mud very fast. It would be a blessing to us to have good roads once more. . . .

28. On Feb. 26 "one of the most important movements" in the history of the 2nd New Hampshire occurred when the entire regiment went home on furlough. The unit rejoined the brigade shortly after the battle of Chancellorsville. Haynes, *2nd New Hampshire,* 128–31.

I am about promoting Lt. Lloyd to a captain. I have written the letter to Governor Parker [29] nominating him. He will soon have two bars on his shoulder. He has the making of a good officer and is worthy of promotion. He is geting up fast. I have a number of promotions to make and have a spirit of competition for the honours. I have got Capt. [John H.] Grover dismissed from the service for absence without leave.[30] It is his place that Lt. Lloyd is to fill. A number of my line officers have to resign on account of bad health. They can't stand campayning at all. Some of them look miserable, just mear shadows. Don't be uneasy about me; I will soon be all right again. . . .

Camp Fitzhugh Farm, Va., March 3rd 1863

My dear family,

I rode over yesterday to the Lacy House [31] on the river bank by Fredericksburg to see Mrs. Harris. She was very kind and gave me a large loaf of homemade bread, which I brought back with me. But we can now get bread without much difficulty, as we have a Brigade bakery. The Lacy House is a very large mansion, and Mrs. Harris has it for her Headquarters with two other ladies, all engaged in the good work of dispensing to the sick and needy. They are doing a grate deal to relieve the suffering. Mrs. Harris looks real healthy—very diffirent from what she once did. I met there the Surgeon from Col. [James A.] Beaver's regiment,[32] the 148th Pennsylvania of Couch's Division, about three miles from here. I would like to see Col. Beaver. Perhaps I will ride over in a few days.

My ride yesterday done me good, but I feel very tired today from the fact that I am examining some officers & sargeants in tactics

---

29. Joel Parker was New Jersey's "War Governor" and served another gubernatorial term beginning in 1872. "In the despatching of troops he was second to none in the country, and for his solicitude for the welfare of all who went into the field he received and merited much public commendation as well as private appreciation." *N.J. Biographical Encyclopaedia*, 135–36.

30. Grover was discharged by special orders dated Mar. 9. William Lloyd succeeded him as captain of Co. F. *N.J. Record*, I, 563.

31. Also known as "Chatham," the Lacy House stood on the northern bank of the Rappahannock immediately opposite Fredericksburg. Both Burnside and Sumner used it as headquarters before its conversion into a field hospital. *Official Atlas*, Plate XXV, Map 4; Johnson and Buel, *Battles and Leaders*, III, 107; Andrew E. Ford, *The Story of the Fifteenth Regiment, Massachusetts Volunteer Infantry* . . . (cited hereafter as Ford, *15th Massachusetts*) (Clinton, Mass., 1898), 241–42.

32. Surgeon of the 148th Pennsylvania was Uriah Q. Davis. For the sad state of health of the regiment during this period, see Muffly, *148th Pennsylvania*, 166–67.

and have been at it most all day. I will not promote anyone until I examine them thoroughly. But it is very tiresome to me now. Tonight I have a school of the Captains. It meets two nights every week. I am bringing our officers right up to the mark. Col. Moore has the 1st Lieutenants, Adjt. Schoonover the 2nd Lieutenants, and we have Company schools for the Non-Commissioned officers. We are all wide awake to tactics. . . .

Camp Fitzhugh Farm, Va., March 4th 1863

My dear Ellen,

. . . I am continuing my examinations. I have our Sargeant on hand now. I suppose I have asked him four hundred questions and am not more than one half through. He answers very well. I think he is worthy of promotion. He is a real student. His name is Banister.[33] I have quite a number of candidates; and if I give them all as thorough an examination as I am giving Sargeant Bannister, I don't know when I will be through. . . .

We are having terable wind storms here; the wind is blowing rapidly. . . .

Camp Fitzhugh Farm, Va., March 6th 1863

My dear Ellen,

I did not write you yesterday, as I took a ride and the mail was gone before I returned. . . . I am geting along well. I have not yet reported for duty, as I want to get strong and able to stand rough wagons and hard knocks. We are not doing much, so I concluded to get entirely well before reporting for duty.

I called yesterday on Mrs. Benedict, wife of Capt. Benedict, Adjt. Genl. to Genl. Birney. He was formally Adjt. Genl. to Genl. Carr. He is a young man that I have taken a fancy for, and he has been very close to me. He has been married but a short time to a young lady from Troy, New York. They live in a tent beside his office—two tents together—and look to be very comfortable. She complains a little of being cold, at which I do not wonder. It is hard to keep warm in one tent with one little wood stove. It must be worse in two tents. She seems highly delighted and, like Sarah, enjoys camp life very much. She is getting ready to ride out on horseback when the

33. Sgt. George H. Bannister of Co. D was promoted to lieutenant in June, 1863. *N.J. Record*, I, 555.

weather permits. . . . She is a nice little pleasant lady, quite girlish, and she enters into military society with a harty will.[34] We have quite a number of ladies here. All or nearly all have come in lately. Mrs. Genl. Farnum, Mrs. Genl. Graham [35] and a lot of Colonels' and Captains' wifes make up the female society. Some of them keep the roads warm riding out these few fine days. We always have one or more officers to accompany them. They dress handsomely and, of course, are much talked about.

Genl. Sickles had a grand party on last Sunday night in which they had a grate time. These ladies were all present and all the Generals, including Genl. Hooker. Each lady got a lock of Genl. Hooker's hair, which made quite a shearing of the old gentleman's head. I will write you more again on the subject. I will have to close to examine another Sargeant.

Here comes my box at last. I will open it and stop a little while. I have opened and examined it. Turkey and chickens spoiled, some roten apples, some good; mince pies pretty good, fruit cake good, dried fruit all good; shirts somewhat dampened by decaying apples; butter a little tainted, don't know how it will do; canned fruit, of course, is good.

Many of the things will come in very good and will be of grate value to us. . . . I will divide some of the things with Drs. Byington and Ribble. . . .

Camp Fitzhugh Farm, Va., March 9th 1863

My dear Ellen,

Adjt. Schoonover is going home on furlough, and I requested him to call on you and leave these papers. You will ask him to stay all night and show him attention. He will have Fitzer arrested. . . .

This is a beautiful day and I feel quite well. I have not been on field duty yet, though I am able to do duty. I have been busy in exam-

---

34. "Her presence," one officer wrote of Mrs. LeGrand Benedict, "was hailed by the chivalrous officers of Berry's staff, who racked their ingenious brains to devise contrivances that would add to the comfort of her habitation and the pleasure of her novel experience." Gould, *Hiram G. Berry*, 241.

35. Mrs. Farnum was the wife of Col. J. Egbert Farnum, temporarily commanding a brigade. A year earlier, Hooker reportedly was "very sweet on Farnum's wife." Mrs. Graham was the wife of Brig. Gen. Charles K. Graham. A Catholic chaplain who paid a courtesy call on the two ladies exclaimed: "How fresh and balmy the air felt when I got outside!" Wainwright, *Diary of Battle*, 17, 162; William L. Lucey (ed.), "The Diary of Joseph B. O'Hagan, Chaplain of the Excelsior Brigade," *Civil War History*, VI (1960), 407.

ining officers. We have our school progressing regularly and find all are studying military tactics. They show a grate improvement in drill. Our regiment is now up to others in drill and will not stand aside for any of them. We can drill or fight as the case may be. The health of the regiment is good; boys in fine spirits, no demoralization here, ready for anything.

We are geting up a preamble and resolution and will have a meeting of our regiment tonight. Tell this at home and make the Copperheads hide their faces. You will see them.

There is to be a big weding in the 7th New Jersey Regiment on Thursday night. A Capt. Hart is to be married to a lady in Washington. The bridesmaids and a lot of ladies are to accompany the bride to camp to be married. General Hooker is an invited guest, and they are to have a big time all around. This information I got from Andy Robinson [36] of your town, who dropped in a little while ago on a call. Andy can tell all about it, for I think he will be there. He is to call again . . . in a day or two.

Camp Fitzhugh Farm, Va., March 11th 1863

My dear Ellen,

Mr. Freeman, the Adjutant's clerk, leaves for home on a furlough. He will be in Belvidere for a few hours and will call and leave this letter with you. I told you we were to have a meeting last evening in favor of a rigorous prosicution of the war, against the resolution of the State Legislature at Trenton and denouncing severely the *Copperheads* of the North.

The meeting came off handsomely and evinced a grate deal of enthusiasm showing that our regiment is sound to the core. The preamble and resolutions which you will see published in all the papers (Belvidere *Intelligencer* included) will tell you what we have done.[37]

---

36. Andrew Robeson was a member of a prominent Warren County family. His brother James achieved local fame as a courtroom attorney.

37. Prompted by Lincoln's Emancipation Proclamation, the heavily Democratic New Jersey legislature in March, 1863, passed a resolution urging the Congress to meet with Confederate commissioners "for the purpose of considering whether any . . . plan may be adopted, consistent with the dignity and honor of the national government, by which the Civil War may be brought to a close." This seeking of "peace-at-any-cost" aroused a storm of indignation among New Jersey regiments. The 11th and 24th Regiments quickly issued counterresolutions denouncing the action of the state legislature. Francis B. Lee, *New Jersey as a Colony and as a State* (New York, 1902), IV, 75; Foster, *New Jersey and the Rebellion*, 278–79; Reeves, *24th New Jersey*, 31; Rusling, *Civil War Days*, 298.

I hope it will make some of the Copperheads hide their heads and crawl back into their old holes and not dare hereafter to insult the army now fighting for the life of our country. . . . The whole thing went off fine. The preamble and resolutions were unanimously passed and ratified by the Regiment—not a dissenting vote. Republicans & Democrats all went in for them. . . .

I am very well and ready for duty. The ground was partly covered with snow last night. This morning the sun is out and the snow is melting. What kind of weather have you in the North? . . .

Camp Fitzhugh Farm, Va., March 12th 1863

My dear Ellen,

. . . Our Regiment and Brigade are out on picket duty. I did not go as I thought it would not be prudent for me to do so, the weather being so very changeable. Had I have went I would have been in command of the Brigade. But as it has turned out very cold and disagreeable, it is better that I remain indoors and not expose myself. . . .

The big wedding has come off today in the 7th New Jersey.[38] I have just heard from them. Genl. Hooker and other Generals are in attendance. I hear the band playing from here. Capt. [Daniel] Hart, the groom, is from Philipsburg in your county. I do not know whether the bride is or not. Ten ladies accompanied her from Washington yesterday. I suppose they are having a good time of it all around in the Regiment—officers of all grades as well as the privates. It is the officers of that regiment that give the entertainment and pay the expenses. The novelty of the thing causes a considerable excitement. My friend Genl. Carr thinks it is proper and right and says that he likes to see the weddings in camp. You know he could not go to Washington, as officers are prohibited from going there. So the bride came to Capt. Hart, and the officers of the regiment proposed to have a big wedding.

You ask me why I don't apply for the Brigadier Generalship. In the first place, I have never had a very grate anxiety to get the post.

38. The groom was Capt. Daniel Hart of Co. E, 7th New Jersey. Various accounts and opinions of the field wedding are in de Trobriand, *Army of the Potomac*, 425–26; Craft, *141st Pennsylvania*, 52; David S. Sparks (ed.), *Inside Lincoln's Army: The Diary of Marsena Rudolph Patrick, Provost Marshal General, Army of the Potomac* (cited hereafter as Patrick, *Inside Lincoln's Army*) (New York, 1964), 221; Gould, *Hiram G. Berry*, 241.

I often thought that Genl. Taylor would have been a greater man if he had not been a General. But be all that as it may, there is no chance now. The President has nominated far more than can or will be confirmed by the Senate. Col. Torbert, Col. Birney, Genl. Carr, as well as a lot of others, are still hanging fire. I have no doubt that if my life is spared and I continue in the service, I will have a chance of acquiring that high position and will receive it on my own merit, which is far better than to get it from friends constantly working for it. I am not affraid but that I can fill the post with credit. . . .

Fitzer has returned—says he was sick, &c. . . .

Camp Fitzhugh Farm, Va., March 15th 1863

My dear Family,

Last evening I received Ellen's letter dated the 11th. It came through much sooner than usual. Inclosed you will please find a small piece of paper which Capt. [William] Meeker took from a tree yesterday as we were passing out to the pickets. It was nailed up on an aple tree as a notice to the passing soldiers that the inmates sold pies and the other articals thus named. I send it as a specimen of spelling to you for to have a good laugh. Whether the proprietor is one of the first families of Virginia or one of our Northern hustlers I don't know, but I rather think he is a Virginian.

Now about the big man and big shoes that Sarah took such an interest in.[39] The shoes arrived and I gave them to him as a present from my daughter Sarah. He was highly pleased and thanked her and her father hartily and said that he would never forget her or me for our gift, that he would do his duty faithfully in camp, on the march, on picket and in battle—all of which he has done and, I have no doubt, will do again. I paid Capt. Lloyd for them, so it is Sarah's present. I told him at the same time that my daughter had a pair of stockings for him but that the box had not arrived. He thanked me over again. My box not coming, I spoke to Mrs. Harris and she gave me two pair that were just the thing—too long for anyone else. So I brought them and gave them to him. He was as usual very thankful for them.

39. A note by Henrietta McAllister in the McAllister Papers states that a member of the 11th New Jersey with abnormally large feet aroused Sarah's sympathies. When Sarah learned that no army-issue shoes would fit the man, she waged an arduous search in the Belvidere area until she located a suitable pair. The soldier, a member of Co. F, was seriously wounded at Gettysburg. See McAllister's letter of Dec. 11, 1863.

McAllister Papers

Camp of the 11th New Jersey at Fitzhugh Farm, Virginia, 1863. Sketches by Sgt. Smith of McAllister's regiment

Col. McAllister's headquarters at Fitzhugh Farm as drawn by Sgt. Smith in March, 1863

Maj. Gen. Daniel E. Sickles

Miss Helen Gilson in her nurse's uniform

After my box came, I decided that Sarah's big man had a good supply, so I gave them to another big man (in Capt. [Dorastus] Logan's company) who was delicate and very needy. But he was not half as thankful for them as Sarah's man. Mrs. Harris gave me a pair of stockings, the tops of which was red, white, and blue, to give to the bravest man on the battlefield at Fredericksburg. This was hard to decide, but I at last gave them to a man in Company D. Your white ones of the same character I gave to Capt. Hill's company to a man that was very gallant in that engagement. Mrs. Harris was very particular to have the name of the man and the account of the gallantry that he displayed so that she could send it to the lady in Philadelphia who knit the socks, as she would keep a record of them and it would become a matter of history. . . .

Camp Fitzhugh Farm, Va., March 21st 1863

My dear Family,

Until last evening I had been six days without letters from home. But I am happy to say that from last night's mail I had the pleasure of receiving two. . . .

We have snow and rain here about every other day. The ground is covered now with snow. The weather has been cold. . . .

I am sorry to say that we are losing Dr. E. Byington. You know that his father was urging him to go home and that, very much against his will, he wrote me a letter on the subject which I enclose to you. Knowing all the facts, and his being a real and personal friend, I was compelled against my own wish and the interest of my regiment to sign and forward his application. It has returned approved. I now suppose we will get some good for nothing doctor like [Henry M.] Fagan. All regret Byington leaving. He stands very high and is liked by everyone. It is a perfect shame to take him away.

I am going over to the Christian Commission [40] this afternoon to get papers and tracts. One of there agents was here and is not only willing but anxious to supply us. I showed him Steuart's [41] letter to

---

40. Organized by evangelical ministers and laymen, the U.S. Christian Commission was the central agency for soldiers' relief. Its 5,000 members held more than 77,000 prayer meetings and distributed to the troops more than 2,500,000 Bibles and hymnals. The best summary of its material contributions is Charles J. Stillé's *History of the United States Christian Commission* . . . (New York, 1868).

41. George H. Stuart, president of the Christian Commission, later declined two invitations to serve in the cabinet of President U. S. Grant.

Miss Gill.[42] He says it is all right and he will see that we are supplied. He wants no money and says that all subscriptions ought to go to the Society in Philadelphia. We are perfectly willing to pay for our papers and tracts. This gentleman's name is George E. Street.[43] . . .

Camp Fitzhugh Farm, Va., March 25th 1863

My dear Ellen & family,

I have a few minutes before going on to drill to write you. . . . I hope your box will arrive soon, as we are very likely to move in a few days. Then you will hear from us in the way of fighting and battles. My regiment is in fine spirits and in good health. We stand well. Genl. Mott offered two regiments in exchange for us. Genl. Mott commands the 2nd New Jersey Brigade. But General [Sickles] said to him that it would be very nice to have a full New Jersey brigade but that he was not disposed to accept the offer as he was well pleased with the 11th New Jersey. Though that is a New Jersey brigade, I don't want to go there. We are very comfortably fixed here and will get all the credit we deserve. . . .

I will send you a paper, the Monmouth *Democrat,* in which you will find a letter written by one of our orderly sargeants telling how happy and contented our men are. Then you will see another letter from the 29th with a doleful picture. Their not geting rations is not true; if it is true, it must be the quartermaster's fault. Just look at the contrast in the two letters. . . .

Genl. [Joseph B.] Carr's wife has come on. She is a nice lady, very kind & polite. I called on her this morning. . . .

Camp Fitzhugh Farm, Va., March 26th 1863

My dear Ellen,

The notes of preparation are going on for a speedy move. We shall soon pull up stakes and be once more on the march. I now believe we will cross the Rappahannock once more. But I am ignorant

42. Sarah A. Gill of Newark served as a field nurse through most of 1863. She apparently was related to a Belvidere neighbor of the McAllisters'. Unpublished letters, McAllister to his wife, Apr. 2, 1864, and Sarah Gill to McAllister, July 19, 1864. McAllister Papers.
43. For George E. Street's account of religion in McAllister's command, see Moss, *Annals of the U.S. Christian Commission,* 399–400.

of the plan. We are now ordered to reduce the baggage to the lowest notch. I will keep you posted as to our movements. . . .

We have a magnificent camp—archways sprung over the streets as we enter them and also between the privates' tents. They excel in beuty anything I have ever saw. They are made of evergreens. Each company tried to excel the other in tasts and beuty. The name of the company is also suspended in the circle of there arches. There are all styles of architecture and on a large and extensive scale. The boys have also sprung two arches over the avenue leading to my Headquarters. One is at the door of the tent, and the other is at the road entrance. My pavement along this avenue is a carpet of beautiful evergreens. Our camp is the admiration of all the camps in the neighburhood. Strangers gaze at this camp scene with wonder, and you ought to see how proud our boys are of it. If time will permit, I will have a drawing made of it and send it to you. . . .

Mrs. Benedict came with Mrs. Carr. She is a fine looking girl. Riding on horseback is the general amusement. I spent last evening with the General, his lady, and Mrs. Benedict. They are all from Troy, New York. They are coming down to see our camp. . . .

Camp Fitzhugh Farm, Va., March 27th 1863

My dear Ellen & family,

Enclosed you will find a nice patriotic letter written me by a Mrs. E. A. Smith, who has a son in my regiment. We all admire the letter and I read it to the regiment. I wish we had more of that kind instead of the poor miserable dishartning letters—to get my poor boy home and out of the army and signed by a hart broken mother. This letter done me good and ought to be published. You can show it to our friends. . . .

Those resolutions have brought the 11th New Jersey into notice and have done good. We are congratulated from all quarters. Every officer in the regiment got a copy of *The Evangelist* containing Dr. Speer's [44] sermon. I enclose it with the other papers. . . .

I have not yet got the picture of our camp but expect to get it if we are not hurried away too soon. Everything points to our moving in a few days. . . .

---

44. Samuel Thayer Spear was one of the foremost Presbyterian ministers of that day. In addition to serving as pastor of a New York City church, he also headed a program for using the wealth of larger churches to aid smaller congregations.

[278] ✕ THE McALLISTER LETTERS

Headquarters, 11th Regt., N.J.V.
Camp near Falmouth, Va., March 24th 1683

Mrs. E. A. Smith
Madam,

Your very kind and patriotic letter of the 17th was received in the due course of the mails and its contents noted. These are the letters we want in the army. They breathe an air of patriotism that sends a thrill of joy through every patriot's heart and moves the arm of the soldier to duty and battle. When the storm rages around us, and our brothers are falling by our side, these letters urge us forward to Victory or death, standing by "the glorious Stars and Stripes," the emblem of our nationality.

On behalf of the members of the regiment which I have the honor to command, we tender to you our sincere thanks for those noble sentiments which are worthy to emanate from a *true American mother;* and we would say to you, and to all our mothers, wifes, sisters, and daughters, in our distant homes: you can do much in assisting us to pute down this rebellion, by letting us know you think of us in the greatt work in which we are engaged, and that your eyes are upon us, following us far down here in the battlefields of our country.

It causes cheerfulness to pervade our ranks. And above all, to know that your prayers are daily ascending to God, we cannot but think that Victory will soon perch on our banner.

Your son is gone. But *he is a noble boy,* a good soldier. He stood with his comrades amidst a shower of bullets at the battle of Fredericksburg with the coolness of tried soldiers. On their return from the front line, I said to them through their [company] commander: "You are Veterans!"

I feel with you a deep interest in the spiritual welfare of the regiment, as well as for its "Military form." And if God spares me and gives me grace and strength, I shall endevor to work for its good. . . .

Camp Fitzhugh Farm, Va., March 28th 1863

My dear daughter,

I have just finished a letter to your mother and now have a few minutes to spare you a few lines. Adjt. Schoonover is married. He sent us his cards, one of which I enclose. I did not know a word of it before. . . . Capt. Meeker, whose card you also have in your album, went home on a leave of absence and married. This is the way our young men are doing. Get a leave of absence, go home, get married, and think of their darling wifes in camp and on the march. Well, they will have someone to leave their estate to and to draw their pensions. . . .

         Camp Fitzhugh Farm, Va., March 30th 1863
My dear Ellen & family,
  I am very sorry to inform you that Genl. Carr is about leaving us. The circumstances are these: Col. Carr was nominated by the President last fall for Brigadier General at the request of Genl. Hooker and for meritorious conduct. He having fought well in many of the battles. Having no friends at court to urge his confirmation by the Senate and relying on his own merits and Genl. Hooker's reccomendation, Carr attended strictly to his business and paid no attention to it. He supposed all would be right.
  But he had an enemy that was working against him: Col. Marston of the 2nd New Hampshire Volunteers of this Brigade.[45] Col. Marston was also a member of Congress. While acting as Colonel here, he took offense at Carr because Carr would not let him do as he pleased—i.e., be away from his regiment. And it is said that Marston swore that he could make and brake Generals. So, you see, he has been working with the President and War Department, and has prevented Carr's confirmation. Col. Marston was also nominated for Brigadier General. I cannot say whether he was confirmed or not but I rather think that he was. We all now fear that now he will be placed over us in Carr's place. All the officers in this Brigade are friendly to Genl. Carr and, of course, are very opposed to Col. Marston. Carr is a splendid man, a good General, and his heart is in the work. He is *a grate Union man* (with or without the nigger), and a warm supporter of the administration. He wished to stay in the Army to do or die for his country. A great friend of the Volunteers and opposed to Regulars, he is a very kind and sociable man—ever ready to do an act of kindness to those who needed it.
  When he was nominated for General, Carr was in command of this Brigade. A Colonel was appointed by the Governor of New York to take his place in Carr's regiment. So you see that he was thrown out altogether. Late last evening we got the intelligence that he was to leave today. I received an invitation to go up to the Headquarters of

  45. The rift between Carr and Col. Gilman Marston arose over the latter's pending promotion to brigadier. Marston got his general's stars in April—and with them assignment as commander of the prisoner of war camp at Point Lookout. Otis F. R. Waite, *New Hampshire in the Great Rebellion* (Norwich, Conn., 1873), 119.

the 26th Penna. and take with me all my field, staff and line officers and bid the General farewell. All the Brigade officers were there (a surprise to the General). A fine band seranaded him and bid him farewell. I felt pity for his wife. She is here and a real patriot. Her heart is in the war for our country; she wanted her husband to stay to the last. Like yourself, her love for country overrides personal comforts and pleasures. And as much as she loves her husband, she would rather see him come home a corpse than to disgrace himself.

What *Spartan* ladies we have in our country. Well, I wish we had more of them. We would have less Copperheads and fewer traitors to dissemanate their rank poison through the minds of the ignorant, fewer to brake down our Government and ruin our land. God save our people.

Afternoon—3 p.m. I stoped writing this morning to attend to some business. Very soon I had a call from Genl. Carr and lady and Mrs. Richardson, the wife of the Lt. Colonel of the 16th Mass.[46] She is from Cambridge and a very polite and accomplished lady. The General invited me to ride with them. We called on Genl. Berry,[47] where I met Mrs. Benedict and Mrs. Farnum. I was pleased with Genl. Berry's appearance. Mrs. Farnum, of whom I have heard so much, did not strike me very favourably—rather good looking but has a masculine appearance, making quite a contrast between her, Mrs. Richardson, or Mrs. Benedict. We also rode to an old house in front of our old camp where a court marshall is now holding to give the General a chance to say good by to the officers. We then returned to Genl. Carr's Headquarters. I then saw Mrs. Richardson home to her camp. The ladies are looking daily for an order to leave camp for home prior to our moving.

Four hundred men from our regiment have gon out on picket duty under the command of Lt. Col. [Stephen] Moore. They had to make up a deficiency in the 2nd N.J. Brigade, which is so much smaller than ours. Since our men had to report to a Colonel whose rank is junior to mine, Genl. Carr said that I was not to go.

46. McAllister was referring to the wife of Maj. Samuel W. Richardson, a former deputy sheriff of East Cambridge, Mass. Richardson did not become lieutenant colonel until June, 1864. Mass. Adj. Gen., *Massachusetts Soldiers,* II, 220.

47. Hiram G. Berry, a native of Maine, had served as a carpenter, state legislator, and mayor of Rockland before becoming in 1861 colonel of the 4th Maine. Conspicuous service in the field brought him command in January, 1863, of the 2nd Division, II Corps. "He had rather the appearance of a farmer than that of a brigadier general," de Trobriand recalled, but he was "as faithful to his duty as he was devoted to his soldiers." De Trobriand, *Army of the Potomac,* 328.

On Saturday evening Col. Moore and I rode over to the Christian Commission and got tracts and papers for the Sabbath. I also had the regiment canvassed and found that we wanted nearly *three hundred* testaments to have the men fully supplied. We got all we wanted and distributed them that evening. I also invited one of the Commission to preach to us, as Mr. Knighton is still absent. A Mr. [George E.] Street came and give us a good practical discourse. The regiment turned out well and attention was good. I had all the tracts and papers distributed before brackfast. All the men are anxous to get them. There is a grate improvement in our regiment as to morals.

The inclosed letter is from Mrs. [David] Hatfield. Poor woman, she has a hard time geting along. I think we ought to help her a little. Her husband fought bravely and died fighting for his country. She will get her pension and also his back pay, but it is very slow work. If you can send her anything, do so. . . .

The Paymaster is coming this week. I will send you a nice *big pile* as soon as I get it into my hands. . . .

Camp Fitzhugh Farm, Va., March 31st 1863

My dear Ellen & family,

I have received the box—contents all safe. It will come in first rate, as the old box is nearly all out. It has don us good service, especially the butter and dried fruit. This came right to hand, and on a march the ham, dried beef, and fruit are just the thing. I am very much obliged to you all for the box. . . .

I am happy to inform you that Genl. Carr is reappointed and will stay with us. I am rejoiced, as well as are all the officers & men in the Brigade. We have quite a snow—ground covered, bad roads again. Today Dr. Byington left us for home. I am very, very sorry. But so it goes. We lose a good Surgeon. I sent with him the sketches of my Headquarters. They were sketched by Sgt. [John H.] Smith of Co. I, the man that wrote the letter published in the paper I sent you. He is a smart, intelligent man. He desires to be higher. If I live, he will be. . . .

Camp Fitzhugh Farm, Va., April 7th 1863

My dear Ellen & family,

. . . Yesterday morning we had a grand Cavalry review. We had an invitation from Genl. Stoneman, Chief of Cavalry, for all officers to attend, as President Lincoln and his lady were to be present.[48] I rode over with my field and staff. The long lines of cavalry stretched out right and left as far as the eye could carry. The day was not very favourable—not that it rained but it was chilly and wet under foot. Nothwithstanding all this, there was quite a sprinkling of ladies present, most of whom were on horseback, and some in ambulances. Mrs. Lincoln was in a four-horse carriage. The President and his escort rode around the lines. I did not go with them, as I cared but little about taking them for three or four miles' ride at a pell mell rate—and in the mud at that. Instead, I preferred taking a moderate ride with Col. Moore around the outside, and we reviewed the Cavalry to our satisfaction and with one-fourth of the riding. After this, regiment after regiment, Brigade after Brigade, passed in review. It was a splendid sight. As a general thing the horses looked well, much better than they used to do. Each regiment had its pioneer corps, armed with axes and spades in addition to side arms, the same as the Infantry regiments. A number of the regiments, and all of the Brigades, had full bands, all mounted on horseback. As they passed the reviewing officers, they filed out of the column, faced the officers, and played until the regiment or Brigade to which they belonged passed by. Then they dropped into the rear. The whole thing passed off handsomely. The most novel sight was the long trains of mules with pack sadles on and ropes ready to tie the loads on their backs. This is a new and novel idea and is calculated to help us along in tight marching order—to pass roads that are very bad and when wagons cannot keep up with us or reach us with supplies. I have no doubt but that it is an excellent plan and will work well.

Today we were to have our review. We were ready to march from camp at 9 a.m., and remained so until about 1 p.m., when an order came countermanding the review and inviting the field officers to go up to Genl. Sickles's to receive the President, who was to come there at 2 p.m. After we received him, he was to visit all our camps. According to orders, Lt. Col. Moore and myself road up to Genl. Carr's Headquarters. Soon the General and his lady were ready to go. Mrs. Carr went in an ambulance and we rode with the General. All the field officers of the Brigade, all in our best suits, swords and

48. President and Mrs. Lincoln reached Hooker's headquarters a day ahead of schedule. The arrival of the presidential party, Col. Wainwright noted, "created quite a commotion on Hooker's back stairs, hustling off some of his female acquaintances in a most undignified way." Wainwright, *Diary of Battle,* 177. For details of the great review, see Noah Brooks, *Washington in Lincoln's Time* (New York, 1958), 51–55; Charles E. Davis, Jr., *Three Years in the Army* (Boston, 1894), 198–99; Cudworth, *1st Massachusetts,* 352–53.

sashes, road over to Fitzhugh House. There were about two hundred officers, all waiting to see the President. The ladies were out in their best and in their full strength. But few could get into the house and the day was cold and raw, making it very unpleasant to wait long on the arrival of the President.

Genl. Hooker and *Uncle Abraham* stole a march on us and went around all our camps while we were waiting for them at the Fitzhugh House. It was way after 4 p.m. before the long-looked-for guests arrived. They finally came to the joy of all present, dismounted, and passed through the crowds, the President shaking hands with two or three he seemed to know. Then into the house they went. There Mr. Lincoln was introduced to the ladies. In about ten minutes he came out on the porch and shook hands with all the officers. Genl. Sickles introduced me to him as the Colonel of the 11th New Jersey regiment, "a regiment now known all over the land." The house being crowded, and having no desire to stand in the cold any longer, I mounted my horse and with Col. Moore came home. Tomorrow we have our review. We had a very fine band playing and my horse got loose. But instead of running off, he ran in a circle—keeping time to the music, with his head up as bold and graceful as you could wish.

In my next letter I will tell you something as to how the ladies looked—and also about Mrs. Salm Salm,[49] sometimes called Mrs. Slam Slam. I just learned yesterday who she was. . . .

Outpost picket near the Rappahannock,
April 10th 1863

My dear Ellen & family,

Here I am seting at my tent door writing to you. I have a nice location with the colors, both state and national, floating to the brease in front. Sgt. Smith, our artist, is to make a drawing to send you. I think it will look well. The Adjutant is now busy making a drawing to send to his lady. We have a fire in the front, a table a little to one side, and pine forest all around. I may not be able to send you the drawing today, as the mail may come along very soon. So I will send you this now and the drawing tomorrow.

49. Prussian Prince Felix Salm-Salm was then attached to Gen. Louis Blenker's division. His wife was in great demand at all army social functions. Commenting on Mrs. Salm-Salm and Mrs. Farnum, Wainwright stated: "Both have been handsome women in their day, and are still good-looking enough to stand very well in the eyes of General Joe [Hooker]." Wainwright, *Diary of Battle,* 175. See also Swanberg, *Sickles the Incredible,* 171.

I was the field officer of the day yesterday and up till 8 o'clock this morning. I road the whole line this morning from the Rappahannock on our left to our extreme right. I started at 5 and finished before 8 a.m. I saw the Rebel fires on the opposite bank of the river. We have at least four miles to picket. The Brigade officer of the Day has to ride over this rought twice a day—hills & hollows, gulleys and swamps. But Charley understands his business and is good on a jump. I was very much amused today while riding along. The Adjutant and I crossed the bridge over a deep gulley. Our mounted orderly thought he would jump it. In doing so, he drew in the rains too soon and prevented the horse's hind feet from touching the opposite bank. Down fell the horse, right on his tail, with his head right up and the orderly fast between the bank and the horse. However, he soon extricated himself and the horse jumped out. Neither were hurt. I wish I had a picture of the horse and the man. You would have thought them to be one and the same anamel. . . .

Outpost Picket on the Rappahannock,
April 11th 1863

My dear Ellen & family,

I received two nice, interesting letters from home last evening—one written by Henrie and the other by Sarah. I ought to answer them separately, but time will not permit. As to the time of Sarah's getting married, I would like it fixed so it would suit me to have a furlough. That depends on circumstances, army movements, etc., over which I have no control. But if I am still living after we march and have a battle or battles, I will try and arrange to suit the parties concerned. I do think that November is a good time, but I will not object to any time if it suits my going home. If you think of having it without me, why go ahead. July is a strong time of year to get married. If I can get a furlough at that time, why let it take place then. . . .

I have just returned from a nice ride down the river, where I saw the Rebels on the opposite bank. They were trying to send us a paper by making a little boat on which they put the paper, then took it upstream, let it loose, and perchance it might reach our side. But the attempts this morning proved failures.[50]

50. For other instances of widespread fraternization at this time, see Illinois Commandery, M.O.L.L.U.S., *Military Essays and Recollections* (Chicago, 1891–1907), II, 51; Ford, *15th Massachusetts,* 242; Joseph K. Newell (ed.), *"Ours": Annals of the 10th Regiment Massachusetts Volunteers* . . . (Springfield, Mass., 1875), 189–90.

This day is quite warm and like spring. There is some cannonading at a distance. But what it is we don't know. . . .

Camp Fitzhugh Farm, Va., April 14th 1863

My dear Ellen & family,

We are all in a bustle geting ready to move forward. We are just now going to march up to the Brigade drill ground to be inspected with five days' rations in our knapsacks and three more in our haversacks. I do not think we will move this evening or tonight but will no doubt very soon. The army is moving from Washington and around us here. . . . Hooker will move rapidly. Fighting will be the order of the day. Where or how I can't tell, but we will move towards Richmond. The troops that have gone has gone up the river. We may go up or very likely will go down. . . .

Camp Fitzhugh Farm, Va., April 15th 1863

My dear Ellen & family,

I wrote you a hasty note yesterday in which I told you of our preparations to move and that from all appearances we would soon be before the enemy. I was sure that today we would bid adieu to our camp and be on the march. Everything seemed to be in readiness and orders flowed in rapidly. But last night it commenced raining and this morning was very wet, causing some orders preparatory to a forward movement to be countermanded. Since then the storm has increased with a terable force. It is raining in torrents with a strong east wind. Step outside the tent and it will take but a very few minutes to get wet to the skin through. We are very fortunent in not having broken our camp. A few hours more and it would have been done. I know not the movements nor position of our army, save that the camps near us have not been broken up. But thousands must be on the march in this raging storm. Oh, how I pity their situation. . . .

The cavalry have gone up the river and, I think, have crossed. We heard firing yesterday and this morning but have learned nothing deffinently. If the movement has commenced and gone a certain distance, we may yet be under the necessity of going forward—storm or no storm. Some think that the cavalry have gone up the river, crossed, and will get in the rear of the Rebels near Kelly's Ford and capture or drive them away so that we can go up and cross. Others think that they have gone in the rear of Fredericksburg to destroy the railroad and cut off communication with Richmond while we attack them in front. I am now satisfied that we are going towards Richmond. . . .

Camp Fitzhugh Farm, Va., April 17th 1863

My dear Ellen,

We are still here but ready to move at the word go. Our Paymaster is due here this afternoon and I will forward to you the amount that I can spare. . . .

We are to move forward with eight days' rations, during which time we will not see our teams. Our Chaplain declines going with us and wants to stay with the teams. To this I object, as all Colonels do. Chaplains ought to be where they can do good. Mr. Knighton is in a bad humor and says he has no horse, &c. I told him he had had time enough to procure everything. He then says he has no money, &c. . . . I only wish he would resign. He is of no earthly use to us here. He has not held a prayer meeting or don anything for the good of the regiment. He stays in his little tent and reads books, magazines, &c. He is disliked by all. Just look at the condition of the regiment. After I supplied them with 300 testaments, what kind of chaplain would let the regiment get in its present condition? Nor has Mr. Knighton helped me with the tract business. I want a man that will work right up in all that is good. He is a perfect drag.

Here comes the long looked for Paymaster, Maj. [Moses F.] Webb, so I must close. . . .

Camp Fitzhugh Farm, Va., April 19th 1863

My dear Ellen & family,

I wrote you a short letter last evening and then went over to the Christian Commission. Capt. Hill accompanied me. We got all the tracts that we wanted and, at their urgent request, staid for their evening prayer meeting. It was very interesting. I suppose that there were four or five hundred men present, among whom were very many recent converts. It reminded me much of our New York Union meeting in 1857. The Christian Commission have established there headquarters about three miles from here, and around it there has been a grate revival. Oh! What a blessed thing it is to have such meetings in the army! And the good that the commission has don extends all through the army. The tracts are circulated, much wanted, and read with grate care. It has also stirred up the chaplains to more active duty. . . . In some cases, the chaplains have taken exceptions to the commission. They think that they have infringed upon their rights. The chaplains think this because they were asleep and need waking up. Mr. Knighton is down on this commission and in favor of Mr. Alvoord.[51] If I had time I could tell you why. But I will not now. Anyone attending these [Christian Commission] meetings, and who has the cause of Christ at heart, will say: "God speed to the good work!" . . .

Tell Dr. [Roderick] Byington it is reported here that Governor Parker objects to appointing Capt. Hill a Major, because Hill with all of us except Capt. [Dorastus] Logan signed the resolution against the State Peace Resolution. Well, I am proud that my name is there. If Governor Parker is going to act in that way, he will be very unpopular. . . .

Camp Fitzhugh Farm, Va., April 20th 1863

My dear Ellen,

. . . Capt. [Thomas J.] Halsey went over to the Christian Commission last evening with the money we had collected. The meeting had commenced. An opportunity offering itself, Halsey rose up and spoke in favor of the support of the Commission and stated that he came over at the request of his Colonel to bring them a small donation. All eyes were turned on him. They finally asked him if it were not from the 11th New Jersey. He said that it was. They received it with thanks and said they would forward it to Mr. [George H.] Stuart immediately. I did not intend that it should become a public matter, but that the Captain should give it quietly to one of the agents. But if it will have the effect of stimulating other regiments to follow our example, and by that means increase the means of doing good, I am satisfied. . . . It may be said that the officers should have subscribed more. You must recollect that only one or two of them— Lt. [Edward D.] Kennedy and perhaps Capt. Halsey—profess any religion.

Mr. [George E.] Street, one of the commissioners, told me that the other day a private soldier entered the Commission tent, give him

---

51. Probably J. W. Alvord, an official in both the American Tract Society and the Freedmen's Bureau. At this time he was a government agent working in the Washington area. Robert W. Lovett, "The Soldier's Free Library," *Civil War History,* VIII (1962), 61–62; Howard, *Autobiography,* II, 271; George Templeton Strong, *Diary of the Civil War, 1860–1865* (New York, 1962), 212.

five dollars, and declined to give his name. He was asked if he was or had been a member of any church. He answered no, but he said that he was satisfied of the good that the Commission was doing and he wished to help them. . . .

Camp Fitzhugh Farm, Va., April 21st 1863

My dear Ellen & family,

. . . We are still here. Something is going on but no one knows what it is. . . . As to the consolidation, it is not to take place now. When it does, it will not effect my regiment, as we have over five hundred men. On that score you need not expect me home.

I am sorry to say we have lost Capt. Hill. You know that there was a contest in this regiment as to who should be Major. The Field & Staff were for Hill, nearly all of the Line against him except Capt. Lloyd, who with the officers went with us. The Governor don't like our Republican regiment too well at best, and no doubt he wishes to get a large sprinkling of Democratic officers here. And as Capt. Hill and his father [52] are warm Republicans and very influential, the Governor no doubt thinks it best to have a change. But Hill is a good officer and has many friends. The Governor has thus appointed him Major in the 12th New Jersey. We are all disappointed and down about it. I expect one of these days that some Copperhead soap-stick will present himself to me with a Major's commission and settle down among us to teach that it is wrong to pass *Union resolutions.* . . .

All the Field, Staff & Line officers signed a petition in favour of Adjt. Schoonover. But I fear that it is too late—that the appointment is already made of some good for nothing Copperhead. Capt. Hill leaves us tomorrow.

I road down to the Lacy House to see Mrs. Harris, but she was not in. I saw a Rebel regiment drilling across the river. All is quiet. . . .

Camp Fitzhugh Farm, Va., April 25th 1863

My dear Ellen & family,

The storm ceased least evening and this day has been very pleasant. We have some wind; but when compared with the last two days,

---

52. John Hill of Boonton became speaker of the New Jersey House of Representatives and later served two terms in the U.S. Congress. *N.J. Biographical Encyclopaedia,* 543.

it was "perfectly splendid," as Sarah would say. The roads have dried out very rapidly today. The day is past and gone and another week has ended, never to return but in remembrance of the past.

Our Governor is in the neighbourhood. We are expecting him on Monday. Our men have been very busy today fixing up our camp so that the Governor will see that the 11th Regiment knows how to have a nice camp as well as pass resolutions. Our evergreens were very much faded and have nearly all been removed, though I don't think the camp looks as well as it did when first fixed up. But still it is ahead of other camps around us.

Governor Parker reviewed one of our state Brigades today and is to review the 1st and 2nd Brigades tomorrow (the Sabbath).[53] On Monday he calls on us and other stragling regiments. He has not appointed a Major for us yet. . . . I expect to have a talk with him on the subject. I am responsible for the Regiment and ought to have the power to say who I will have around me. . . . But I don't think he will give us what we want. He will do with us the same thing that he don with the 12th and 15th Regiments: give us a stranger. . . .

Camp Fitzhugh Farm, Va., April 27th 1863

My dear Ellen & family,

I did not write you yesterday as we were kept very busy. The cause of it was the coming of Governor Parker. Genl. Sickles decided to order out this Division (Berry's). The 2nd New Jersey Brigade is in it, and our Regiment (the 11th) is in the First Brigade. Well, we had a nice review. Governor Parker was highly pleased and showed off to an advantage. After we passed in review, I received an order to stop my regiment opposite Genl. Mott's Headquarters. Mott commands the 2nd New Jersey Brigade. We did as ordered and halted until Genls. Mott, Carr, the Governor, and their *retinues*—including nearly all the field and staff officers of the old 1st Jersey Brigade, who accompanied the Governor over from their Brigade, rode up. We were drawn up in line to receive the Governor, opened ranks, presented arms, and received the Governor handsomely. He made a short, good, patriotic speech, to which I replied in a very short speech to the satisfaction of all. The whole thing came off handsomely. Our regi-

---

53. For comments by New Jersey soldiers of Parker's review, see Rusling, *Civil War Days*, 301; Marbaker, *11th New Jersey*, 53; Reeves, *24th New Jersey*, 32.

ment was very creditable, all complimenting it very highly for its appearance and efficentcy in drill. Our fine health astonished the Governor, Genl. [Robert F.] Stockton, and Genl. [Lewis] Perrine, who accompanied him. They had heard that we were all sickly and dying. The 11th stands second to none in the army and is known all around.

The regiment then went home. I was invited to accompany Governor Parker to Beam's battery [54] and then here to see our camp. When we arrived here, our boys were drawn up and received the Governor with three harty cheers. He was highly pleased and praised our camp as splendid. Our camp threw in the shade all the camps in the army.

I have just learned that Governor Parker has since spoken in the highest terms of our regiment. In the review Genl. Sickles pointed us out to the Governor and complimented me very highly last evening.[55] Sickles thinks well of the 11th.

The Governor is aware now that we can march well, drill well, show off well, and pass resolutions. The Governor will be all right on the war question.

The New York boys call us the fancy-stepping regiment, owing to the neatness of our camp.

After the Governor left, we had Divine Service. Mr. Fay [56] and Miss Gilson [57] were here to tea and staid for our meeting. Miss Gilson is a beutiful singer. She was waiting to see me, as an order had just then been sent around ordering all citizens away from camp. She and Mr. Fay thought that they had to leave. I told them that as their mission was intirely benevolent, it could not be possible that the order

54. McAllister was referring to Battery B of the 1st New Jersey Artillery. Its first commander, Capt. John E. Beam, had been killed at Malvern Hill. Capt. A. Judson Clark was then in command. *N.J. Record,* II, 1380.

55. Praise of the appearance of Sickles' III Corps was by no means unanimous. Provost Marshal Marsena Patrick observed: "Sickles & most of his crew are poor—very poor concerns, in my opinion." Patrick, *Inside Lincoln's Army,* 238.

56. Mayor Frank B. Fay of Chelsea, Mass., was one of the first civilian volunteers to enter the field and minister to the individual needs of the soldiers. See his *War Papers of Frank B. Fay* (Boston, 1911), 25, 48–49, 62–71, 132–33.

57. Helen Louise Gilson, mentioned prominently throughout McAllister's letters, was Fay's teen-age niece. Her many services on behalf of soldiers' morale led a member of the 5th New Jersey to state: "There isn't a man in our regiment who wouldn't lay down his life for Miss Gilson." Sgt. Marbaker summarized the work of Fay and his niece with the comment: "Only those who were recipients of their care can make a just estimate of their services." Brockett, *Woman's Work in the Civil War,* 133–48; Marbaker, *11th New Jersey,* 79. See also Fuller, *Chaplain Fuller,* 290; Adelaide W. Smith, *Reminiscences of an Army Nurse during the Civil War* (New York, 1911), 107–9.

applied to them. It did not apply to Mrs. Harris and the ladies of the hospital and should not apply to them. While we were discussing the matter, in came an order from Genl. Sickles, saying it did not apply to them at all, which grately relieved their minds. Miss Gilson wanted to arrange with me for accompanying us on the forward march. She said she had been in the war from the beginning and wished to remain to the end. Sickles's order came in time, and she remains in our Corps Hospital. They live at their own expense, and Mr. Fay lays out large sums for the sick. They are very wealthy, very polite and refined people.

Another review took place today in our Corps. Mr. Seward [Secretary of State] came and all was turned out to receive him. I don't know who was with him, but there were two four-horse carriage loads of ladies. The review came off very well. It took place this forenoon. This no doubt finishes the reviews, as this evening we have marching orders and we move tomorrow. The hour is not fixed, but I think it will be before tomorrow night. . . .

Camp Fitzhugh Farm, Va., April 28th 1863

My dear Ellen,

I wrote you a long letter last night, telling you about our review and also that we had orders to be in readiness to move at short notice. It is now 9 a.m. The moving order has not yet come, but we are expecting it every hour. It is said that some of the troops have moved. Our Corps and more, I know, have not moved. But before I close this letter, we may all be on the march. It has clouded up for a storm again; I dread these storms on a move.

Mr. Knighton has tendered his resignation and I have approved it and sent it on. No doubt it will go through. I cannot see how any patriot can resign on the eve of a move, but some people can do anything. . . . I am very anxous to get a good hard-working chaplain. I have been so disappointed in the person of my choice that I feel a delicacy in nominating someone and think of leaving it up to Col. Moore. Mr. Bacon,[58] one of the Christian Commissioners who preached to us, would like to have it, and I think that he would suit us. He is from Connecticut. You know that Jersey likes to have her

---

58. Joseph R. Bacon, then residing in Philadelphia, joined the Christian Commission in 1863 for a one-year tour of duty. Moss, *Annals of the U.S. Christian Commission,* 604.

own sons in these posts of honor. However, let us all do what we can towards having the place filled. . . . Greate good can be don here if we have the right kind of a man. . . .

3 p.m. We have received orders to be ready to move in an hour. . . .

7

Chancellorsville and Gettysburg

THE POWERFUL ARMY OF THE POTOMAC, still staggering and unsure of footing, moved forward again toward the forces of Robert E. Lee. The army possessed the courage of patriots and the muscles of a giant; all it needed was someone to lead it to triumph. That person was not to be General Joseph Hooker.

"Fighting Joe" Hooker had every reason to feel confident late in April, 1863, as he moved into the Wilderness. Around him clustered an army of 134,000 men—more than twice the number that Lee could bring to bear against him. His strategy seemed unbeatable. Seven corps would turn both Confederate flanks, overwhelm Lee's forces, and then march victoriously to Richmond. The second largest of the army corps was Sickles's III—"proved fighters who felt with some reason that they could lick anybody if the terms were anywhere near equal." [1]

Such terms did not prevail at Chancellorsville. At a critical moment in the Federal advance, Hooker later confessed, he lost confidence in himself. He halted his troops and, consequently, left himself open to a slashing flank attack on May 2 by Stonewall Jackson's veteran brigades. McAllister's regiment reached Chancellorsville just as the XI Corps on the extreme right bolted to the rear in panic. Any offen-

1. Swanberg, *Sickles the Incredible*, 178.

sive the 11th New Jersey may have envisioned never materialized. Events compelled the men to rush "into the breach," McAllister wrote. Only after hard fighting and heavy casualties was the Federal line maintained. During this action was one of the few times in the war McAllister lost his temper. He encountered a fleeing soldier and literally beat the fugitive into joining the ranks of the 11th New Jersey.

McAllister penned a long narrative (herein printed in full for the first time) of his role at Chancellorsville. In it he described such events as the severe fighting extending over several days, his going alone into the woods to pray, and why after the battle he was reported as missing in action.

A month of inactivity followed the defeat. McAllister spent a good portion of this period in speculating on the army's future movements and in refuting charges levied by Belvidere Copperheads that he had been derelict in his duties at the recent engagement. The Colonel was still smarting from the accusations when the Army of the Potomac left northern Virginia and moved rapidly into Pennsylvania to combat Lee's invasion. On June 28 General George G. Meade succeeded Hooker as commander of the army. "We didn't know much about Meade," one soldier stated, "and [we] didn't spend any time in looking up his history. All we wanted was a fair chance at Lee's army." [2]

The chance came July 1–3 at Gettysburg, and with that opportunity the Army of the Potomac came of age. Sickles' corps reached the town on the night after the first day's fighting. The following morning, in an action still debated by military historians, Sickles advanced his corps so well forward of the main Federal lines that it stood alone, with both flanks open. McAllister's 11th New Jersey hastily took up a position in a peach orchard alongside the Emmitsburg Pike. Here the principal Confederate attack came on the afternoon of July 2; and in apparently the first exchange of musketry, Colonel McAllister fell seriously wounded.

♣

2. J. D. Bloodgood, *Personal Reminiscences of the War* (New York, 1893), 128.

On the bank of the Rappahannock, April 29th 1863
My dear Ellen,

I wrote you last evening that we were just starting. A few minutes after doing my letter, Mr. Gridley, the sutler,[3] returned and handed me the receipt for $46 from the express company. I was just mounting my horse to leave and handed it to the Postmaster, with directions for him to enclose it in my letter to you.

We marched till 10 o'clock last night and encamped within 500 yards of the river and about two miles from Fredericksburg. This morning we marched up the river a very short distance and stoped. It is now sundown and we are still here. The 1st Corps has crossed here without opposition and is, I believe, in the neighbourhood. Our Corps, the 3rd, are all here. The 4th Corps has gone upriver above Fredericksburg. I have not heard whether they have crossed. I think they are crossing, though there has not been much firing. What is to be don we don't know. It is said that Hooker keeps his plans to himself. I think that we will be thrown across tonight; but whether it will be here, lower down, or higher up, is yet to be seen.[4] God grant us success. I have no doubt but that we are on the eve of hard battles. Time will determine. My health is good. The spirit of the army is good. . . .

Battlefield Reserve, May 2nd 1863
My dear Ellen & family,

I will write but there is no certainty that you will get it for a long time, as all our mails are stoped. We are now to the right and rear of Fredericksburg, at present on the reserve. But we expect to engage the enemy at any moment. The firing has been quite brisk, though it has now (9 a.m.) ceased. The enemy are trying to break our lines. They were at it all afternoon yesterday, and we marched up here to assist our troops. Our position is a strong one and we can keep

3. Sutlers, a necessary evil to every regiment, sold food and supplies to soldiers, sometimes at astronomical prices. The historian of McAllister's regiment once observed: "The sutler, as usual, profited immensely by the coming of pay-day." Marbaker, *11th New Jersey*, 36. See also Henry Morford, *Red Tape and Pigeon-Hole Generals* (New York, 1864), 247–63.

4. Hooker's basic strategy was as brilliant as any conceived in the war. Three Federal corps would remain at Fredericksburg to keep Lee immobilized; four other corps would move up the Rappahannock, cross the river, and assail Lee's left. The Confederates would then be caught between a massive pincer, each jaw of which was larger than the Southern army. It was an excellent plan, but one whose success depended on Lee's remaining stationary. As events proved, Lee did the exact opposite.

them at bay. I presume that we will advance on them very soon. . . . You ought to have seen our boys coming here last evening on the double quick after hearing the firing—high spirits, ready and willing for the fight.

We have had hard marching for two days. Yesterday about noon we came up from our left and crossed the river at Banks's Ford. The report says that the Rebels are evacuating Fredericksburg and that Genl. Stoneman has cut their communication to Richmond.[5] . . .

I have a chance to send this over the river and will mail it. Firing has ceased. Genl. Sickles says that we will be engaged this afternoon. Another report says that the Rebels have been reinforced, and it is also said that they are falling back some ¾ of a mile. Genl. Hooker is in fine spirits and says our success is assured. I hope it is so.

I am seting at Charley's head. He lays his head on my shoulder as much as to say, "My regards to you all." He is very fond of this kind of life, though he sometimes has to go without rations. . . .

The Adjutant's horse just backed into me and caused me to tear this letter. He is a nasty animal. He has not hurt me. He is not Charley by a long piece. . . .

Camp near Falmouth, Va., May 6th 1863

My dear Ellen & family,

I have only time now to say that God has spared me through those terable scenes and hard fighting for several days, and that I came out unscathed—not hurt in the least. Our regiment was all through the hard fight and have don nobly. We have lost more heavily than any other regiment: about 25 killed and 130 wounded.[6] The figures are not correct but in that neighbourhood. Then we may add the missing, which will swell the killed list. Lt. Kennedy is, like myself, all right. There is but one person from Belvidere killed. I will write you the particulars. . . .

Camp Fitzhugh Farm, Va., May 7th 1863

My dear Ellen & family,

I wrote you a few lines this morning in a greate hurry. Mr. Fay called this morning and congratulated me on my safe return. He said

5. The report was false.
6. At Chancellorsville the 11th New Jersey suffered 18 killed, 146 wounded and 5 missing. Its losses were by far the largest of any of the five regiments in Carr's brigade. *OR,* Vol. XXV, Pt. 1, p. 178.

that news of my death had gone home and that he had tried to telegraph you to the contrary. But no messages were allowed to be sent. He said that if I would write you, he would wait a few minutes and take the letter to Washington and mail it. Mr. Fay is the rich and benevolent Massachusetts gentleman of whom I have spoken before. He accompanied Miss Gilson in her mission of benevolence and attention to the sick soldiers.

The report of my having been killed arose from the fact that my regiment was the last on the battlefield—or that part of it that fell into enemy hands—and stood alone, unsupported, and amidst an unprecedented shower of musketry, grape and cannonballs. This Sunday's fight is said to be the hardest battle of the war.[7] And there in the very hotest part of it I stood with the gallant 11th—with the enemy on my front and right flank pouring into my ranks the balls, large and small, of death and distruction.[8] Amidst it all there could be seen the Star-Spangled Banner and our State Colors, standing erect though riddled to pieces. Both flag staffs were broken by the shots of the enemy. Undaunted, our brave and gallant colorbearer, Puget[9] and his guard, bore them along in towards the enemy's lines. Then their forces would drive us back, a short distance only. As soon as we could get to the left and rear of the enemy's flank, we would pour into them our grape and ball, rally again around our standards, and on, on to the charge. All the line on the right of me had now given way. I still continued, depending on a battery on the plank road on my left and the line in my rear, as well as the 2nd New Jersey Brigade on the left of this battery—all of which stood firm.

Yet I was not connected with either. I threw forward my left so as to form an apparent connecting link. In this position we kept the enemy at bay for a considerable time. The horses of the battery on the road were now all shot down. The gunners hauled the artillery by hand and retreated. The line in my rear give way, and then the 2nd New Jersey Brigade retreated. I saw that part of the field was now lost and ordered a retreat—but firing all the time until we crossed the road. Then we united with the scattered troops and charged on the

---

7. Years later a Maine soldier remarked: "No bloodier struggle ever raged on the American continent than where Sickles on that Sabbath morning [May 3] stayed the tide of the rebel advance." Theodore Gerrish, *Army Life: A Private's Reminiscences of the Civil War* (Portland, Me., 1882), 91.

8. As McAllister pointed out in the battle narrative that follows, the 11th New Jersey was in the second line of battle. About 150 yards in front of it were the Excelsior Brigade and 1st Massachusetts. The task of all these units was to try to stunt Stonewall Jackson's onslaught down the Plank Road.

9. This was Sgt. Albert Du Puget, whom McAllister cited for bravery in his official report. *OR*, Vol. XXV, Pt. 1, p. 458.

cannon pits—small works thrown up for the protection of our guns but now in the hands of the enemy. We drove the Rebels out and took possession. But it was impossible to hold them. We had to retire towards a line of artillery near Genl. Hooker's headquarters. Here we supported a battery. Capt. [William H.] Lloyd had three men killed in his company with one shell.

The artillery was most terrific. Our cannoneers worked hard. Many of the guns and horses fell before the enemy fire. Some could scarcely be worked at all. Shots and shells were falling in every direction, ploughing up the ground beneath our feet.

Here I will relate a little incident. A lot of men from diffirent regiments, not liking to stand out in the open ground, huddled up behind a small outhouse. An officer rode up to me and asked me to make a detail of men to go for more ammunition. I was doing so when he returned and said, "Don't take your men; they are in line. Send some of these men who are doing nothing."

I went to the end of this building and ordered these idlers to go. Two of them started at my command; the rest hesitated and did not move. I told them that they must go. At this moment a cannon ball passed through the house and killed two or three of them. The rest moved without my having to say anything more.

This battle is what is called Chansollisville. Genl. Hooker rode through our lines, rallying the men. Genl. Sickles acted the part of a noble and brave man. He is a good officer, no mistake about it. This line of batteries had now to give way a little further. I told Genl. Sickles that here I was with the remaining part of my regiment. "What shall I do?" I asked.

"Fall in here," he said, "with no reference to regiments, brigades, or divisions. You are all my men! We must hold this line if every man of us should fall!"

We did so, and the day was ours. The enemy's onward progress was stoped, and they could push us no more.

I will continue in my next letter. This is only a discription of Sunday's fight. Saturday and Monday I will give you later. Oh! Let us as a family thank God for His kind protection over me in these terable battles! . . . Capt. Lloyd acted bravely. He is a good, brave officer. I am proud of my regiment. . . . It is said that we move across the river again in a few days. Don't be discouraged; the day will yet be ours. . . .

Camp Fitzhugh Farm, Va., May 9th 1863

My dear Ellen,

... Everything hear looks like moving forward. We are going to advance somewhere, but I don't know in what direction. My regiment is now very small. One other such a battle and we are used up. Our Division saved the army. We have suffered terably and our regiment more than any others.[10] ...

You recollect Sgt. Lindley of my Regiment. He had his wife at Mrs. Roberts's when you were there. He was killed and his body left on the battlefield.[11] Lt. [Lott] Bloomfield and Lt. [Edward] Kelly were both killed and their bodies fell into the hands of the enemy. Poor Mrs. Lindley, I pity her. She gave me many instructions as to her husband if he should fall, but I cannot fulfill my promise to send the body home, as the enemy got the ground. ...

Camp Fitzhugh Farm, Va., May 10th 1863

My dear Ellen,

It is my intention to write you a correct history of all the scenes through which I have just passed. I will send you by tomorrow's mail my official report of my regiment, which is in itself a correct history. I wish you to file it away. I do not wish it to get into the hands of anyone who might in any way have it published. This must be avoided.

... I wrote you yesterday a hurried account of Sunday's battle. When I have time I will write you about the Saturday and Monday battles. The reason I wrote about Sunday first was that it was the greate battle of the war.

The prospect is that we move across the river again very soon. Stoneman has turned up down at Fortress Monroe, having played smash with the railroad leading to Richmond.[12] Had Hooker known this sooner, or had it been done sooner, our campaign would have

---

10. McAllister exaggerated slightly. Of forty-two regiments in Sickles's corps, six had higher casualties than the 11th New Jersey. *Ibid.*, pp. 177–80.

11. This is an error. Sgt. George Lindley of Co. K was not killed in the battle. *N.J. Record,* I, 580.

12. Gen. George Stoneman's cavalry corps did stage a raid in the direction of Richmond. Yet "our only accomplishments," one trooper sneered, "were the burning of a few canal boats on the upper James River, some bridges, hen roosts, and tobacco houses." A portion of the raiding force managed to reach the safety of the Federal lines at Yorktown; the remainder galloped back to Hooker's army. Shortly thereafter a disgusted Hooker removed Stoneman from command. Shelby Foote, *The Civil War* (New York, 1958–63), II, 314; *OR,* Vol. XXV, Pt. 1, pp. 1057–65.

been a complete success. It seems now that we have punished the enemy more severely than they have us. Their killed lay in thousands. Their loss is much heavier than ours.[13] . . .

McALLISTER'S REPORT TO ELLEN OF THE BATTLE OF CHANCELLORSVILLE [14]

On Saturday afternoon [May 2], as we lay in mass column on this side of the river near Chancellorsville, a solid shot came amongst us and took the leg off of Capt. Meeker's servant, a colored boy, as he was making a love ring. His other leg was badly wounded. Though our men lay thick and close around him, no one else was hurt. This opperated badly on our servants. We could not keep them up with us afterward on account of fear. Our Corps was laying as a reserve, though we had been now almost twenty-four hours in that position. But we were not to remain much longer.

The enemy made an attack on our right and left and forced our first lines hard. The firing became hard and harder, and the enemy seemed to approach. Our left stood firm, but the right fell back. In a moment we were to arms and moved forward rapidly to the Plank Road past Genl. Hooker's Headquarters. As I looked up the road, I beheld the 11th Corps coming down it—wagons, ambulances, horses, soldiers armed and unarmed—pell mell, real Bull Run style.[15] We now had to throw ourselves into the breach, or all was lost.

It was a trying moment. Good Generals and brave hearts were only equel to the task. It was do or die with us. A few minutes lost and all would be gone. The gallant Hooker, the brave Sickles, the noble Birney, to say nothing of Genl. Carr and other brave officers,

13. Confederate losses at Chancellorsville totaled 10,281 men. The Federals suffered 17,287 casualties. Sickles' corps, with 4,119 killed, wounded or missing, had the highest percentage of loss in any corps. *OR,* Vol. XXV, Pt. 1, pp. 192, 809.
14. McAllister's official and diary-like report of the battle is in *OR,* Vol. XXV, Pt. 1, pp. 456–59. It lacks the detail of this private narrative, and it bears but little resemblance to this account. For other commentaries on the 11th New Jersey at Chancellorsville, see *Historical Magazine,* Ser. 2, Vol. VII (1870), pp. 190–94; Marbaker, *11th New Jersey,* 57–76.
15. Sickles reported: "The fugitives of the Eleventh Corps swarmed from the woods and swept frantically over the cleared fields, in which my artillery was parked. The exulting enemy at their heels mingled yells with their volleys, and in the confusion which followed it seemed as if cannon and caissons, dragoons, cannoneers, and infantry could never be disentangled from the mass in which they were suddenly thrown." *OR,* Vol. XXV, Pt. 1, pp. 387–88.

road at the head of our gallant Division. The order came down the line: "Double quick!" Three times three cheers resounded in the air. Our boys were ready and willing for the fight. The flying soldiers of the 11th Corps would not heed our orders to fall in with us. They were panic-stricken and perfectly worthless. But our brave boys heeded them not and treated them with *perfect contempt.*

On and on we went. Regiment after regiment filed into line of battle to the right and left of the road. "Charge! Charge!" resounded through the woods. The roar of musketry and the booming of cannon was terrific. The tide of battle was turned. The Rebels stoped their onward progress, checked, and the day was ours. The Army of the Potomac was saved from distruction. I am told that Genl. Sickles was in advance of our lines among the enemy for fifteen minutes or more, and the wonder is how he got out. Several Rebel officers, or aides, road out with our officers, thinking that they were theirs. Greate credit is due to both Genl. Sickles and Genl. Berry.[16] As I filed my regiment into line, Berry rode up to me and said, "Now, Colonel, do your very best."

"Yes, General, I shall," was my reply.

I knew that I had the boys that would fight and felt confident that we would make a good one. That noble and brave man [General Berry] rode along the lines of battle that night. Wherever there were points of danger, words of comfort and encouragement fell from his lips. He knew well the responsibility that rested on him; and like Leonidas and his brave band, he was ready to do or die.

This night was one of toil, trouble, danger, and watchfulness for our army & our Country. These scenes I shall never forget. The night was beautiful and clear; the moon shone brightly. But the heavy forest above our heads cast a gloom around us. All would be still and calm one moment; then "Crack!" would go a gun, followed by many others. This told us that we were again attacked and that our pickets were engaged. This was soon followed by a tremendous roar of musketry.[17] The enemy massed in front of us and determined to brake our lines. Now hark! Our batteries belch forth their storm of iron. The very earth trembles beneath our feet. The Rebel columns slow down, then retire. Our army cheers. The day is yet ours.

Now all is calm and beautiful once more, but the calm is short. The Rebels cheer and cheer. The report is that reinforcements have

---

16. This first portion of McAllister's narrative, in slightly edited fashion, appears in Gould, *Hiram G. Berry,* 270.
17. The section beginning with the sentence "As I filed . . ." and ending with the sentence "This was soon followed . . ." is also in Gould, 262.

come to their aid. Soon the pickets are again engaged. They fall back. The clash of small arms resounds long and loud. A desperate hand-to-hand engagement is upon us. The Rebels press us hard. But behold the flash of our frowning batteries. Now the iron hail drives through the forest over the heads of our men in line of battle and falls into the massed columns of the enemy, carrying death and distruction into their ranks. Trees fall before this terable storm.

The lightning flash of batteries, the roaring of artillery, the crashing of timber, and the bending and whirling of the forest, was a spectacle to be seen and heard that night—more easily imagined than described. Again the enemy retire, and our brave heroic band sends out on the still midnight air cheer after cheer. The day is yet ours.

"What is that?" asked an officer at my side.

The Rebels cheer and cheer, and continue to cheer, drownding out the groans of the wounded and dying. It is that Jackson and his forces have arrived to their aid. All is now still. Our men slumber on their arms. A calm of two hours pervaded the two contending armies. But it was only the calm that procedes the terable storm. I walked the woods and thought of loved ones at home, knowing well that tomorrow would send mourning and grief to many of our homes and families.

Our men, exhausted by the excitement and fatigue of the day, and worn out by the terable strugle through which they had just passed, fell asleep on their arms. I bowed down by the root of a tree and thanked God for His protecting care over me and my regiment that day and asked continuance of it through the day that was about to dawn upon us. . . .

It was but a short time until I heard a horse approach. An aide rode up to me and said in a low and surprised tone: "General Carr's compliments, sir. He wishes you to move your regiment out to the road."

In a minute we were all up, and we moved towards the road. Genl. Carr met me and directed me to form a line of battle with my left resting on the Plank Road and the line at right angles with it. This was soon accomplished and our men lay down once more, waiting for the impending strugle. The 11th Massachusetts, Col. Blaisdell commanding, came up from the left of the line and filed into place on my right. I do not know what regiment was on his right,[18] but the line was a very long one. We were now on the second line of battle. The 1st Massachusetts, Col. [Napoleon B.] McLaughlin commanding, was on

18. The 26th Pennsylvania was in position on the right of the 11th Massachusetts. *OR,* Vol. XXV, Pt. 1, p. 452.

the first line. His left rested on the road in front of me. [Capt. Thomas W.] Osborn's battery was in the road on our left, and another line of battle was in my rear. The 2nd New Jersey Brigade, commanded by Genl. Mott, was on the left of the road, corresponding with our two first lines. To the rear of this Brigade were a number of batteries on an elevation, so they could fire over our heads. These, together with Osborn's battery in the road, made a fearful havoc among the Rebels that night and were now ready to do the same again.

The dawn [of May 3] approached; and we well knew that with it the stillness of that beautiful Sabbath morning would be broken. In a few minutes the pickets were engaged. Soon came a continuous roar of musketry and the Rebel hosts were upon us. The battle was begun, with no stoping, no breathing space, but a long, fierce, and desperate contest. The Rebels were massed in our front; and regardless of their own lifes, they were determined to break through our lines. Our artillery opened with a terable force and poured out death and distruction. The Rebels responded with theirs. Thus for two long hours this terable contest raged, with nothing diffirent on either side, each holding its own. The musketry & cannonading combined was the most terrific I have ever witnessed.

At last I saw the line before me fall back. Col. McLaughlin approached me. I asked, "What is the matter?"

He said, "My left wing has given way, but my right wing is still standing. I am going to rally my left."

I looked back to see if Genl. Carr would order me forward. He did not do it. Then I sent my adjutant to him to find out if I should advance or remain in my line. Genl. Carr replied to remain as I was but to wheel my left wing a little around so that my men would not fire into the right wing of the 1st Massachusetts. I did so and ordered them to commence firing. I also told the right wing to remain as it was and not to fire until I gave the order.[19] The left wing commenced firing. I soon found that the Rebels were firing at my right wing. I then ordered that wing to fire, which was done with effect. Very soon I discovered the Rebels flanking us. I then alined my battallions and made a right wheel and poured a few volleys into them that caused

19. Some controversy involving McAllister occurred at or near this point in the battle. Sickles, seeing that the flank of the 1st Massachusetts was in danger, dispatched his chief of staff, Capt. John S. Poland, to order the 11th New Jersey to advance and drive back the Confederates. "Unfortunately," Poland reported, "my authority was questioned at an untimely moment." Sickles also alluded to McAllister's hesitation; however, McAllister made no mention of the incident in his report. *Ibid.*, 393, 450, 457.

them to fall back. My own line to the right had given way. The line in my rear was still holding, as well as the battery in the road and the 2nd New Jersey Brigade. In its position my regiment made a connecting link from the line in my rear, the battery in the road, and the Jersey Brigade.

The progress of the Rebels was now checked at these points, though they advanced and readvanced upon us. We charged and recharged on them, all in front of our old line. But finally all of our right had given way to other lines in the rear of us, and the line in my rear had retreated. The horses in the battery were shot down and the battery was hawled off by hand. The Jersey Brigade were falling back, Genl. Berry was killed,[20] and our brave boys were surrounded on three sides by Rebels. There was nothing left for us to do but to retreat, which we did, still keeping up a fire until we crossed the road and united with other troops. Then we drove the Rebels out of the cannon pits which they had just taken from us. We could not hold the pits long, but had to retreat slowly towards the Headquarters house.

We reached a battery and acted as a protection for it. Here we lost some men. This battery too had to fall back. Then we fell into another line of defense at the Headquarters house and protected our artillery. Here Capt. Lloyd had three men in his company killed with one shot. Here Genl. Sickles could be seen in the hottest of the fight, rallying the scattered forces. . . .

During all this time the artillery was hard at work. While our guns were sweeping the enemy's ranks, their shells were falling and bursting amongst us very rapidly. It was a fearful time. Many of our troops, exhausted from six long hours of fighting, lay prostrated on the ground amidst bursting shells. Officers like myself moved among them, back and forth along the line, and encouraged the men in the midst of that iron storm.

Some scattered troops from diffirent regiments, seeking a place of comparative safety, huddled up against the ends of buildings, fancying that they were safe. This was the time when an officer road up to me and asked me to detail ten of my men to go for ammunition. I was making the detail when he returned and told me not to take my men, as they were in line and doing duty, but to take the men that were doing nothing. He pointed to the men by an old outbuilding nearby. I walked up to them and gave the order to go for the ammunition. Three of them obeyed; the others resisted. I told them they must

20. Berry was shot at 7 A.M. on May 3 and "died heroically" twenty-six minutes later. *Ibid.,* 447; Gould, *Hiram G. Berry,* 266–67.

obey the order. They still held back. At this moment a shell passed clear through the building, busted in the midst of the squad, killed several and wounded others. Those that escaped had not to be told another time. This line could not now be held. But fresh troops came up and formed a little in our rear, and the onward progress of the enemy was stayed.

We now joined our own Brigade and lay in line of battle in our old column. We lay under a gauling fire of shells for a little while. The Rebels now give it up, and we fought no more that day. There was considerable artillery firing and some skirmishing, but no regular battle. Having several lines in our front, we were moved back. We were tired out and needed rest. Our men lay on the ground and were soon fast asleep, worn down by six hours of hard and continual fighting, and with a terable loss of men. But we rested with satisfaction that, with the help of God, our Corps saved the army.

In that long and desperate battle, deeds of heroism were displayed worthy of brave men with brave hearts—deeds of which we and our children may well be proud. It was the hardest battle of the war, made so by the giving way of the 11th Army Corps (or "Flying Dutchmen," as we call them). A braver or truer man than Genl. [Oliver O.] Howard never drew a sword; but neither his bravery, nor his skill as a General, could stop the panick when once it had commenced. We tried in vain to stop them, but to no avail. We had no time to parley, but had to rush in and fill up the breach to save the day. A few of them were turned into our ranks and had to fight. One Dutchman came to me as we formed in line and inquired for his regiment. I told him that it had gone back, that he could not find it now, and that he must fall in with my regiment and fight. To this he objected. I rode up to him and, between the use of my sword and my right foot, which I disentangled from the stirrup, he was glad to take refuge in my ranks. He fought all through the battle with us until we charged the cannon pits, when, I am told, he was wounded and fell into the hands of the enemy.

Capt. Gammell [21] of the 11th Massachusetts came to me and said, "I am here with eight men and would like to fight with you."

I cheerfully accepted their services. They don splendidly, for which I give them credit in my official report.

The cause of the report of my being killed, wounded, &c., as well as Adjt. Schoonover and Col. Moore, arose from the fact that we

21. A Charlestown, Mass., wheelright before the war, Albert M. Gammell was captain of Co. D, 11th Massachusetts. He was accidentally killed Dec. 16, 1863, while on duty in Boston. Mass Adj. Gen., *Massachusetts Soldiers,* I, 804.

were with our regiment and were last seen fighting by some who were retreating. We were fighting alone, almost surrounded by Rebels. They no doubt thought that we were taken prisoners. When the regiments of our Brigade were forming away back in the rear of us, some officer asked for the 11th New Jersey. Another officer replied, "They are fighting on their own hook and still at it among the Rebels."

Had it not been for us, the 2nd New Jersey Brigade would have been flanked. Col. Sewell of the 5th New Jersey came to me the other day and thanked me on behalf of himself and his regiment for the noble and brave manner in which we stood by them.[22] It was owing to our fighting and holding our position that they were able to take the Rebel colors which give them so much honor. All unite in praise of our gallantry. Genl. Carr says that we have don nobly and fought splendidly.[23] I hope that they will do us justice in their official reports. There is no question of one thing: the New Jersey troops are among the best troops in the field, and have shown themselves to be so.

After Genl. Berry fell, Genl. [Joseph] Revere assumed command of our Division. Strange to say, he started off towards the river with a portion of the Division and with no orders to do so. He had with him a few of my officers and men that were not with me after we crossed the road and charged on the cannon pits. Some two or three of my officers were with him. One or two of them had been wounded and had been sent back. When they asked Genl. Revere where I was, he told them I had been killed and that my regiment was prisoners. He no doubt thought so. This was a bad move for the General, as he went without orders and is still under arrest for it.[24] It is a most unaccountable thing, for we consider him a good and brave officer.

The command then devolved on Genl. Carr. The last of the fighting of my regiment was not seen by him. I am sorry for this. After we went back and other troops took our place at the lines near the

22. Sewell temporarily commanded the 3rd Brigade of Berry's division. Two of his regiments, the 5th and 7th New Jersey, together captured eight stands of Confederate colors. Sewell stated in his official report that McAllister "very gallantly responded" to his call for added protection of his flank. *OR,* Vol. XXV, Pt. 1, pp. 473–74.
23. Carr officially termed the regiment's conduct "highly creditable." *Ibid.,* 445.
24. Following the death of Berry and the wounding of Mott, Gen. Joseph Revere assumed command of what was left of Hooker's old division. Sickles alleged that Revere, heedless of the murmurs within the ranks, "shamefully led to the rear the whole of the Second Brigade and portions of two others, thus subjecting these proud soldiers for the first time to the humiliation of being marched to the rear while their comrades were under fire." Revere was speedily placed under arrest, court-martialed, and dismissed from service. *Ibid.,* 392, 445, 460–62.

Headquarters house, the building took fire from the enemy's shells. This was not only Hooker's headquarters but was also used as a hospital. I fear that some of the wounded were burnt with the building. The woods where our wounded lay also took fire, and no doubt many shared the same sad fate. It is horrible to think of it, yet some will no doubt survive to tell the particulars of these sad and painful stories.

When we lay in the last line of battle, in the Massachusetts camping ground, the enemy's shells were bursting by hundreds around us. This was the hottest artillery fire I have ever been under. Our men were so exhausted that a large portion of them fell asleep. Fighting such battles is the hardest work I ever undertook. We became perfectly exhausted. Remember that this was all done without any brackfast, the battle commencing very early in the morning. Some of the men may have had some hard crackers in their haversacks. But a large portion of haversacks and knapsacks containing provisions were left at the camp. We left the evening before in a hurry and run up to the road at double quick to stop the progress of the enemy, who were driving the 11th Corps. It was fight all night and all day, with no time to eat and no chance to get provisions to us.

Our colored servants were scared almost to death and were far in the rear. I did not see mine for two days. He got down as far as the river, and I did not see him until I was coming home to camp. I don't think that they will go with us again. I wish I had a servant with nerve that would stick with me all the time.

The enemy was now repulsed, and our army was busy throwing up entrenchments. The news arrived of our being in possession of Fredericksburg and the hights. We were all confident of success, and confident also that the 6th Corps would soon be with us. Then we would move forward in triumph. But here we were doomed to disappointment. The enemy reoccupied Fredericksburg and its hights, and the 6th Corps had to cross and recross the river.[25] It was then and not until then that Genl. Hooker had to plan a retreat. Our prospects before this were bright. But we can trace it all to the giving way of the 11th Corps.

The pioneers were all very busy in throwing up breastworks on three sides of our camp—from the river up to and near Chancellorsville, a distance of five miles. We rested that evening and night. The

25. Gen. John Sedgwick's VI Corps fought its way through Fredericksburg and, after a severe contest, occupied the city's heights. Then it moved westward to attack Lee's exposed right flank. Yet owing to Hooker's inactivity after two days of fighting, Lee shifted his lines and furiously assailed Sedgwick's corps at Salem Church. Sedgwick barely managed to extricate his men under cover of darkness.

pickets were attacked very frequently. About the middle of the day on Monday [May 4],[26] I was ordered with my regiment as a support for the Berdan Sharpshooters. We were conducted to an elevation in front of our camp and breastwork and in range of our guns. Our instructions were that if the Sharpshooters were driven in, we should resist the enemy's advance. Up to this time the enemy had not brought artillery to bear on our picket support. These pickets had fallen back a little and permitted the enemy to plant a battery on the crest of the hill. It had got our range and was ready to sweep us with canister.

Very soon the pickets were engaged; a portion of them ran out. I went to the left to ask the Major in command of the sharpshooters [Homer R. Stoughton] if his men were all out. He did not seem to hear me. Just at this time an order was given to fall back. I thought at first that it came from this Major [Stoughton]; but it turned out to have come from an officer in command of the pickets on our right. This officer told me afterwards that he had orders to fall back so as to let our batteries open on the enemy.

My officers and men took the order for mine and started back just at this time. The enemy's batteries opened on us with grape and canister. At the same moment, our batteries opened on them with a very low range. The Rebels then fired a volley of musketry on us. I ran in front of my regiment, threw up my sword, and ordered: "Halt!" The Adjutant and Col. Moore assisted me. We tried in vain to reform the regiment. Had we succeeded between the two fires, it would have been don at a greate loss of life. Our right wing went back to a reserve and halted. Our left filed into rifle pits that were towards the fortifications. I intended for us to stop here, but the enemy had the range and we could not stop. So we passed into our own works until the firing ceased. Then we reformed and went back to our original position. The range of the enemy's guns was such as to sweep our regiment. Our own guns cut the ground where we were. It thus was impossible for us to stay with any safety between the two artillery fires. We lost in this affray 20 men wounded.[27]

We now returned with different orders. Still it was a most dangerous position. We had to lay flat on the ground; the moment one of us would lift his head, we were shot at. A number of bullets were

26. In his official report McAllister put the time at 2 P.M. *Ibid.,* 458.
27. McAllister's regiment suffered embarrassment as well as losses. Col. Hiram Berdan, temporarily commanding a brigade during the battle, reported: "On Monday evening, the Eleventh New Jersey, which was acting as our support, was alarmed by firing on our right, and it opened fire upon my Second [U.S. Sharpshooters] Regiment, which was deployed in its front, wounding 5 of my men." *Ibid.,* 503.

fired at us by Rebel sharpshooters. They came closer than was pleasant. An attack was made on us that night, but the enemy were driven back by my pickets and a piece of artillery in the field to my right.

In the morning [May 5] we were attacked. Before the sharpshooters were out of the woods, our own artillery opened on the Rebels, ploughing the ground where we lay. One of our men was wounded by our own shells. I don't know who planned the placing of a regiment there, but I do say to put us there was a *perfect outrage*. The officer that did it ought to resign and study military science before he got a commission again—or be placed for twenty-four hours where we were.

There we were for twenty-four hours, burning in the hot sun, no shelter whatever, shivering in the cold through the night, and with orders not to fire a gun but to lay there as marks for the enemy's sharpshooters. The pretended pickets that were to watch the Rebels would only go a little in advance of us so that they could conceal themselves in a ravine in front of us and be sheltered by the trees. This was the hardest service that I ever done in my life. In it we lost 23 men wounded, and many of our men are sick from that exposure.

On Tuesday the 5th we were relieved by the same regiment that we relieved the day before. We came into the fortified camp, well near done out, and rested until evening. We had a heavy shower of rain and got soaking wet. Darkness came on and we received orders to be ready to move in, fall in, &c. We stood there in the rain till about 11 o'clock. Then came an order to go into camp. We unpacked and fixed ourselves as comfortable as we could—without clothes and either wet blankets or no blankets, as the case might be. I had just got to sleep when we were again called up to move, which we did, and daylight found us near the river. We crossed and came directly here to camp, having ended the campaign.

You now have a correct history of the movements of the 11th New Jersey Regiment in connection with this important campaign, and you know the part we took in it.

Capt. Kearny and Adjt. Schoonover are among the bravest officers I have ever seen. Their chance of promotion is very good. I owe them much for their daring and gallantry. Capt. Lloyd behaved with grate coolness and is deserving of greate praise. A large number of my officers done well. Some few of them went back very soon with very slight wounds when they should have held on longer. But of them I don't complain. One good officer in battle is worth a dozen poor ones. We have many brave men in this regiment. I only wish our thinned ranks were filled up.

[310] ✗ THE McALLISTER LETTERS

Camp Fitzhugh Farm, Va., May 11th 1863

My dear Ellen & family,

. . . I have some pieces of shell here . . . that was throwed and busted in our regiment, wounding some of our men. I will try and send them by express. Photographs of Capt. Kearny & Lieut. [Sidney M.] Layton you will find inclosed. Kearny is a brave man. You must send me a lot of my photographs. All the officers want them. The loss of Bloomfield & Kelly is a grate loss to us. The inclosed circular is a Rebel one that I picked up in one of their camps. The story of Col. Moore and myself being lost is going the rounds of all the papers. I saw the *Tribune* corrispondent who said that he would correct it.

I have so much to do. We are under marching orders with cooked rations on hand. . . . I had thought if we were to rest here for a few days that I would get a leave of absence and go home. But I can't get it now. It is too soon to ask. . . .

Camp Fitzhugh Farm, Va., May 13th 1863

My dear Ellen & family,

. . . The news has just reached us here that Stonewall Jackson is dead.[28]

Col. Moore is not well and is very tired of the service. We have no Major yet. The Governor has acted badly in this matter. Maj. [John T.] Hill is now in command of the 12th New Jersey. His Colonel is wounded and his Lt. Colonel is sick.[29] He will soon be a Colonel.

Mr. Knighton's resignation has not been accepted. I don't know much news. We [still] get the credit of saving the 2nd New Jersey Brigade from being flanked. No troops in the field are equel to the Jersey troops. . . .

Camp Fitzhugh Farm, Va., May 14th 1863

My dear Ellen & family,

I have just finished my long account of the last campaign & battles, &c. I wish Henrietta to make copies for Brother Nelson, L.

28. Confederate Gen. Thomas J. Jackson was accidentally shot by his own men on the evening of May 3. The amputation of his shattered left arm led to pneumonia, and on May 10 he died at Guiney's Station, Va.

29. Col. J. Howard Willetts and Lt. Col. Thomas H. Davis commanded the 12th New Jersey. Owing to battle wounds, Maj. Hill never rose above that rank.

Wilson, and any of our friends. You need not send the description of the last day on picket duty. That is for yourselves. It casts some reflection on somebody, and it may not be best to send it around.

A large number of ambulances have passed here today with our wounded. They came across the river. Sgt. Lindley, who I wrote you was dead, was among them. He is still living but badly wounded. Another private first reported dead is wounded and among them. I suppose that some of our missing are also dead. Our whole loss in killed, wounded, and missing is 169, a big loss for a small regiment. A greate many of them are but slightly wounded, while some that were wounded are since dead. . . .

I think Genl. Hooker is a good general and has don the best he could. The Rebellion will be put down, but it is the work of time. Let us have patience and all will be right. . . .

Camp Fitzhugh Farm, Va., May 15th 1863

My dear Ellen & family,

. . . I had to laugh at my orderly [30] this evening. He said that he got a letter from home, and his father said it was reported that our regiment acted badly, that I was not with it, &c. If I was not, I don't know who was. And if the regiment did not act nobly, I don't know what regiment did. The bravery of the 11th New Jersey is the theme of conversation through all our camps. Col. Sewell has made very favorable mention of it in his report and has spoken to myself and others in glowing terms of praise. Genl. Carr has also spoken in the highest terms of both officers & men of my regiment—as strong as language can make it.

What is this report in Belvidere which Sellers speaks of? Let anyone come and see our thinned ranks and go down to the hospital as I did today and see 95 of our wounded—besides those that have gone to Washington. Then they can take into consideration the dead on the field and say that we don badly. . . .

I think it possible that we may remain here or near here for some time. I asked Genl. Carr as to my geting a leave of absence. He shook his head as much as to say no. I then told him my reason for it was to attend the wedding of my daughter. He told me to call on Genl. Sickles and state the case to him, and that most likely he would grant it. I will do so and let you know. Let Sarah get ready and I will tele-

---

30. Then serving as McAllister's orderly was Private (later Corporal) Cornelius G. Sellers of Co. I. *N.J. Record,* I, 576.

graph you as to the time of my coming. . . . I had thought how nice it would be to have it the 1st day of June, my birthday. But that is not a marrying day, being Monday. . . .

Camp Fitzhugh Farm, Va., May 16th 1863

My dear Ellen,

. . . I have not yet called on Genl. Sickles but will very soon —perhaps Monday. He and Genl. Hooker have been at Washington. No doubt they know what they are going to do by this time. If we remain here, I think my chance for a leave of absence is good. If we are to move, I can not get it at all. But I will make the attempt; they can do no more than refuse it to me. One thing will opperate against me: I have no Major yet, and Lt. Col. Moore is sick and in the hospital.

I fear that he will not soon return. He is very sick of the service and has no inclination to go into battle again. I think he will work himself out of the service, if it is possible. His family is very patriotic when there is no fighting to do—but not so much so in times like these. He don very well, but the force of example was the cause of it. Remember that this is between ourselves. He makes a good officer and a pleasant companion, and I would not say anything [in public] that would hurt him.

After they have fought one battle, a greate many men and officers think they have don enough and ought to go home. The Colonel is of that opinion. I differ with him on this subject. He talks of his family, &c. I tell him that I have a family that is as dear to me as anyone's family can possibly be. He replies that his children are not all grown up and are dependent on him for a living. I reply that my family are all very patriotic; and while they love their husband and father, they love their country none the less. . . .

Camp Fitzhugh Farm, Va., May 17th 1863

My dear Ellen & family,

Before retiring to rest for the night, I thought I would write you my usual daily letter. I have just come in from Divine Service. Mr. Knighton officiated in his usual style—not particularly interesting. It was cool and pleasant to hold the meeting out in the open air.

I received your nice and interesting letter of the 14th this evening. I like very much the suggestion that Henrietta write one of her real patriotic letters. It should have a word of incouragement for our soldiers and praise for the gallantry they have displayed on the battlefields of Chancellorsville. Speak of the brave manner in which the Division rushed into the breach made by the unexpected retreating of the 11th Corps. Speak of our gallant officers—Genls. Berry and Carr —rushing at the head of the column to fill up the gap. Tell what our noble regiment don in that trying hour to save our army—how nobly they withstood the raging storm of battle that night and the next day. If you can, say a word in favour of the gallantry of Genl. Sickles. You have all the facts before you. . . . It is just such letters that I want in the army. The ladies of our land could do much for our cause & country in this way, and they ought to do it. Hold not back your words of incouragement. The soldiers of your country need it. Let them know that you care for them and they will fight all the better. . . .

Did I tell you that Col. Beaver of the 148th Pennsylvania Regt. was wounded in the late battle? His wounds, I do not believe, are dangerous. I called to see him the other day on my way out to the pickets.

Sarah's big man was not in the fight on Sunday. He was in the artillery fire on Monday. The reason he was not in the action on Saturday evening and Sunday was that he was left to guard knapsacks in our camp. He was not with us until we fell back to there. Our knapsacks then fell into the hands of the enemy.

Tell Amy [31] that I am much obliged to her for remembering me in her prayers. I believe in prayer, and I thank God that I have so many praying friends. . . .

Camp Fitzhugh Farm, Va., May 19th 1863

My dear family,

I have just got up out of bed and now have only time to write you a line. We move our camp today about ½ mile from here in a beutiful spot. We are all moving from the damp brush huts on account of health.

I received a long, kind letter from our friend, Charles Scranton, in which he complimented myself and regiment for our bravery, gallantry, &c. At the same time he told me that he and Mrs. Scranton met someone (a Copperhead, of course) on the [railroad] cars who was busy circulating a report that I acted cowardly in the battles. Col. and Mrs. Scranton pitched right into him and he sulked off, &c.

31. Amy was one of a succession of house servants employed by Mrs. McAllister.

Well, I feel quite easy about such reports. They are not known here in the army, and the man that would say such things here would soon get his apple cart upset. All officers and men speak of me in the highest terms. . . . I am much obliged to Col. Scranton for his kindness and the interest he has taken in the matter. . . . I wish I had those base, lying Copperheads here. I would lead them to places that they would be glad to get out of. You know that these reports are got up and circulated because I am the Colonel of a regiment that passed the first resolution in the Army of the Potomac against the Copperheads. Well, they will not make much out of it. . . .

Camp Fitzhugh Farm, Va., May 21st 1863

My dear Ellen & family,

I wrote you a long letter last evening relative to those base charges, which, by the way, don't give me as much trouble as you would suppose. I am conscious of having don my duty in every case nobly and faithfully and have fought in five regular battles, always right up with my regiment and never away from it. I have received the credit and approbation of all my commanders. No man in the army has ever charged me with cowardice; but on the other hand, I have thought I was too rash. These base scoundrels that make these charges are the kind of men that . . . would not go within five miles of a battle.

We have a beautiful new camp in a lovely spot. We are geting it fixed up nicely. The order for cooked rations on hand has been revoked, so I think we will remain here for a time. I have been informed that Mrs. Carr and the other ladies that were here last winter are coming back. How would you like to run down and see me? If so, I will get an additional tent. There are no houses for miles around. . . .

We have no Major yet. Lt. Col. Moore is geting his leave of absence through, so I am alone. I think it very doubtful of my geting a leave for some time. It may by the last of June or the first of July. . . .

New Camp Fitzhugh Farm, Va., May 22nd 1863

My dear Ellen & family,

. . . I wrote you a long letter for yesterday's mail in regard to the slanders cooked up in Belvidere or Warren County against me.

I say your town and county, because they have not been heard of in any other part of the state. My regiment is from all parts of the state, from which we hear daily, and not a word about it. But on the other hand, we receive letters saying the 11th New Jersey has made an honorable name. Warren County is left to do the *dirty, mean* work of slandering true and brave soldiers.

I visited our Corps Hospital, where some of our wounded are. You ought to have seen them as I entered their several tents. Joy beamed on their countenances as I approached them; and when they were not too much disabled by extending their hands for a harty shake, these wounded men showed a devotion to me that only wounded soldiers can show. Let those Copperheads talk to these men about me, and they will soon learn where I was in the battle. . . .

Genl. Hooker passed through our Corps Hospital the other day and shook hands with all the wounded soldiers. They are all highly delighted with him. He is the essence of kindness. He took dinner with Dr. [Edward F.] Welling, who has charge of the hospital. He asked the Doctor what regiment he belonged to. Dr. Welling replied, "I am proud to say that I belong to the 11th New Jersey."

The General said, "Yes, and you should be. It is a gallant regiment. It fought splendidly, and all officers and men deserve credit."

Capt. [William B.] Dunning, a splendid officer and one that done his duty, has been assailed by the Copperheads of Elizabeth, his home town. He is accused of cowardice in a piece published in a Copperhead paper. I have just refuted the charges as a base lie. All our officers will be assailed on account of those famous resolutions. Well, let them go ahead. We will manage them. We are a unit among ourselves; and with the assistance of our friends at home, these enemies will soon find themselves nowhere. . . .

Camp Fitzhugh Farm, Va., May 23rd 1863

My dear Ellen & family,

. . . We have one of the nicest camps in the Army of the Potomac. It is a real cozy place, handsomely fixed. The men have their shelter tents all up from the ground so that the air rushes in below their beds. They can also be kept clean. The streets are all lined with pine bushes planted for the purpose. The line officers have fixed up very nicely. We are building arbors and rustic arches under which we have rustic lounges, plaited in with cedar bushes. Capt. Lloyd has two of these and lies back in fine style. Others are following his example. My Headquarters is right here in the woods, between two dogwood trees that form a complete archway. In front of my tent I have a nice platform made out of round logs and covered with cedar bushes as a carpet. At the sides I have two lounges . . . which is equel to anything I have ever seen in your fine county seats. The avenue leading up here is lined on either side by hedges made of pine. Dr. [George T.] Ribble is fixing up as handsome as I am, and Adjutant Schoonover is not far behind. Nature has done a grate deal for us, and we add a little to it. It is decidedly the most butiful camp I have ever seen.

Genl. Carr road up here the other day. "Well, Colonel," he said, "I envy you."

"Why, General," I answered, "your own beautiful location is splendid."

He said, "I am glad that you got such a pleasant place."

"Thank you," was my reply.

This was before he began to butify his own camp.

We have little streams on three sides of us. We have built dams and made nice bathing places. It is so pleasant here that I dislike to go out. We get burnt by the scorching sun and suffer from the dust of burnt up places. Nothing is before us except the forelorn, desolate, and forsaken old camp that we have left to the moles and beetles.

I have given you but a faint discription of our camp. Send me some drawing paper and I will get Sgt. [John H.] Smith to make you a drawing of it. You can send the paper in a little roll. It will make a picture worth having.

It will be nearly a month before I can go home. Col. Moore started yesterday on a 30-day leave—10 days more than he asked for. He says that he will be back before that time. If so I can get home sooner. But it is not safe to calculate on my being home before a month. Col. Moore is going to bring his wife and family back with him. . . . I am told that nearly all the ladies that were here last winter are now coming back. Would it not be a nice trip for you to come and see me?

Miss Gilson called on me last evening with Dr. Welling. She was perfectly delighted with our camp. She and Mr. Fay will be here this evening to take tea. Mr. Fay is the Massachusetts gentleman who furnishes so many of the comforts for the soldiers. Miss Gilson administers to their wants and makes herself generally useful. She is pretty and highly accomplished. Her whole time and thoughts are devoted to the sick and wounded soldiers. Notwithstanding her youth, she attends them like an old maid or married woman. She is a butiful singer and often stops as she goes along the isles of the tents and sings for them, geting the soldiers to join in with her. She is truly a benevolent lady.

Dr. Welling is terably down on the person or persons in Warren County who have circulated the report against me. The report does not seem to be anywhere but in your county. Loyal people at home should put down such base slanders and show no mercy on the authors of these lies. . . .

Camp Fitzhugh Farm, Va., May 25th 1863

My dear Ellen,

I did not write you yesterday, the first day I have missed for some time. . . . Genl. Carr has been in command of the Division since the death of Genl. Berry. But yesterday Genl. Humphreys [32] came and relieved him. Humphreys outranks Carr, who is now with our Brigade. . . .

If I get home at all on furlough, it will not be before the latter part of June; and it may be doubtful then. But if I fail to get a leave, I will see Genl. Hooker himself. I am pretty sure he will grant a leave of absence on such an ocasion. You know that there is an order against Colonels or commandants of regiments geting leaves of absence. All officers below them can get this privilege. Brigadiers are like us Colonels: they have to attend to their commands. . . .

Camp Fitzhugh Farm, Va., May 26th 1863

My dear Ellen & family,

Last night I received a letter from Sarah dated the 22nd. I could not comply with the request to send the reports of Genls. Carr and Sickles. In the first place, I have not got them. Genl. Carr told me what he said—that he had given myself and regiment grate credit for gallantry. I don't think Genl. Sickles has finished his yet. He had not the other day when I called on him. I could not see him, for he was engaged in writing it. Besides, if I had their reports and published them, I would loose my commission. They go on up, and the whole are examined by Genl. Hooker. He then reports to the War Department.

32. Andrew A. Humphreys, McAllister's corps commander through most of the remainder of the war, was a distinguished engineer whose slim build could not conceal his aristocratic mien. Promotion in the Civil War came slowly to Humphreys because of his close prewar friendship with Jefferson Davis. However, he proved a thoroughly devoted soldier—one noted for clear perception, coolness under fire, and a narrow red necktie that became his trademark.

Then they may or may not be published. It may not be expedient to publish mine at present. But the time is coming when it will. History will record the reports and do justice to all.

Inclosed you will please find an extract of a letter from Genl. Carr to Governor Parker, in which he speaks in language that can not be misunderstood as to myself and regiment. This letter has gone to Governor Parker and Genl. [Robert F.] Stockton. You know that they were dissatisfied with our resolutions against the Copperheads. This letter has certainly convinced them that we fight as well as pass resolutions.

Capt. Kearny has been commissioned Major of this regiment. He will send Col. Scranton this extract. . . .

Camp Fitzhugh Farm, Va., May 31st 1863

My dear Ellen & family,

Your letter of the 26th came to hand last night. I hope that the package of clothing may arrive safely and before we leave here. . . . For we will no doubt have to move. The 1st Corps has moved up the river, it is said. The Rebels are making some demonstrations; but we don't know what it is and may have to move according to circumstances.

I cannot advise as to how to get Sarah's wedding things. When Col. Moore comes back the last of the month, and if we are still here, I will make every effort to get home. But if the Rebels are annoying us, I can't. You know that our force is small, and troops are leaving every day. But Sarah can get ready and I will be there if possible. . . . Have plenty of cake, as I must bring some of our friends here who stood by me in the dark hours at Chancellorsville. While I should like to give all a piece of cake, that would be out of the question. But I can so far as the officers are concerned, and including Sarah's big man and a few meritorious soldiers.

Tomorrow is the 1st day of June and my birthday. I am fifty years old and have lived half a century. . . .

Camp Fitzhugh Farm, Va., June 4, 1863

My dear Ellen,

We received an order in the night to be under arms by daylight. What is going on I don't know. However, I suppose a rumor of a cavalry raid or something of the kind. It is hard to tell what the Rebels are going to do. I hear no firing, and all seems to be very quiet. I suppose it is a false rumor. We will know by and by what it means.

I attended a very solom funeral yesterday in the 1st Massachusetts Regt. of our Brigade—a young surgeon who had been with the regiment but a short time. He had graduated from one of our medical institutions and came to the army. He was at the battle of Chancellorsville. He died of typhoid fever. A Sargeant that was wounded in the late battle also died and was buried at the same time.[33] The funeral ceremony at the camp was very solom. The coffins were then laid on two caissons, each drawn by eight horses. The coffins were covered by the national colors. An escort of about fifty men, armed, led the column with a fine band of music playing the slow and solom "Dead March." We followed the corpses; then came the Surgeons—seventeen in number, then the officers, followed by the privates. The whole thing was very sad and solom. We moved along at the dead march until we arrived at the Division burying ground. A hymn was sung, the caskets lowered, muskets fired, and we bid adieu to the remains of these brave men.

The young Surgeon was a very promising youth, a native of Scotland, and with few friends in this country. Here he lays far from home and kindred. But this is war, sad war.

One of my Sargeants in Co. D who was wounded severely in the late battle fell into the hands of the Rebels. But he was paroled and sent over with the wounded. He will live but a day or two.[34] I called to see the wounded yesterday and found most of them improving except Sgt. Allen. He has very respectable relatives in the State of New York who are always inquiring of him through Genl. Carr. Poor fellow, brave man, he will soon be gone. We have lost a number by death from their wounds. . . .

Camp Fitzhugh Farm, Va., June 4th 1863

My dear Ellen & family,

Yours of the 1st is at hand. . . . I cannot say positively as to the time when I will be home. There is no use in asking Genl. Hooker

33. Asst. Surgeon Neil K. Gunn died after a two-week siege of typhoid fever. He had been in the army a total of twenty-six days. Buried alongside him was Sgt. Thomas H. Bigelow of Co. H, 1st Massachusetts. Bigelow succumbed to wounds received at Chancellorsville. Cudworth, *1st Massachusetts,* 379.

34. Sgt. Emory D. Allen died June 11, 1863, at the division hospital near Falmouth. *N.J. Record,* I, 557.

until Col. Moore returns or writes when he will return. But I think I will be at home at the time spoken of—the 1st of July. . . . To know certainly, I would not only have to ask Genl. Hooker but also Genl. Lee, to know when or where he is going to attack us. This, you see, is the grate difficulty. . . . It is thought by some that we are going to move from here. Some apprehension is present of an attack. But I can't think so. . . .

Camp Fitzhugh Farm, Va., June 5th 1863

My dear Ellen & family,

We came out on picket this morning. All sorts of rumors as to our intended movements are going around. Rations are ordered to be cooked so as to be ready to move at a moment's notice. This afternoon we heard heavy firing down the river. I would not be at all surprised if we should have some hard fighting to do very soon. . . .

June 6th. The firing last evening was caused by the crossing of the 11th Corps at Fredericksburg. The Rebels in the rifle pits fired on our gunners. Our artillery opened on them, drove them back, and then crossed.[35] I have not yet heard the particulars. . . .

Camp Fitzhugh Farm, Va., June 9th 1863

My dear Ellen & family,

I received two letters from you yesterday, both of the same date. There is no doubt but these vile reports have don me more good than harm. The citizens of Belvidere who were so ready to believe them now see how I have acted, which perhaps they would never otherwise have known had not my friends taken the course they did and published those letters. Many would have believed that I had acted badly. Of course, I would rather nothing had ever been said. The only way to stop it, however, was to do as was done by my friends. You will find that there will be no danger hereafter on that score. . . .

We came in from picket duty yesterday. Things are quieting down and we may not move at all. I may get my leave in a few weeks. . . .

35. Only a brigade of Vermonters crossed the river, and they failed to drive the Confederates from their rifle pits. *OR,* Vol. XXVII, Pt. 1, pp. 676–78; Pt. 2, p. 347.

I wish you would send me more drawing paper, so Sgt. Smith off duty can draw some more pictures of the camp. He will soon be a commissioned officer, as I have nominated him to the Governor for a lieutenancy and am looking for his commission every day.[36] He fought splendidly. I give the commission to him as a reward of merit. You will be pleased to hear this. The Copperheads had better not raise their heads to bite me while Sgt. Smith is on hand.

I will send you by express some petrified wood that I got while on picket. It is hickory wood, the best I have seen. Keep the large piece and give the small one to Rev. [Henry S.] Osborn with my compliments. He will consider it a greate treat. . . .

Camp Fitzhugh Farm, Va., June 10th 1863

My dear Ellen & family,

. . . All seems quiet here now. I think that Genl. Hooker is keeping the enemy from reinforcing down south until Vicksburg falls. He is wide awake and is not, or will not be, idle. Some considerable firing occurred up the river yesterday, but we have not heard what it was. Our forces are very much scattered at present—all, no doubt, for some good purpose.

I am sorry to say that my orderly, Cornelius Sellers, is down with the typhoid fever. The doctor will visit him today. He is at the Corps Hospital. I fear that he is bad. He was attacked just like the young doctor whos funeral I attended in the 1st Massachusetts on Saturday last. The head was attacked first. I don't like his symptons and have been very anxous to get him home, but I can't unless he gets better. For some days I have been doing all I can. If I had not been called out on picket last Friday, I would have got his furlough for him and he might have been home [when the fever struck].

The doctor will write for his father to come on. Let him come to Washington, recommended by one or more of our prominent men, and he will have no difficulty in geting a pass. The boy does not know anyone, though he is not very weak.[37] We are geting a good deal of typhoid in our Corps Hospital—and bad cases at that. Col. McLaughlin of the 1st Massachusetts has been down with it. I called to see him last night. He is some better and at his own tent. . . .

36. John H. Smith's promotion to lieutenant was made retroactive to June 2, 1863. *N.J. Record*, I, 567, 575.

37. Pvt. Sellers survived this attack of typhoid fever and served with the 11th New Jersey to the end of the war.

Camp Fitzhugh Farm, Va., June 11th 1863

My dear daughter Hennie,

... Tell Sarah that in sending the drawing paper to roll it around a stick or something that will keep it from being all messed up. Our mails are handled very roughly.

Sgt. Smith is busy at work in drawing our camp. He is not Sgt. Smith anymore but Lieut. Smith. I presented him with a commission last evening, much to his satisfaction. He fought bravely in the battles and merited it. He can do more than write; he can fight.

You asked me if we have many nice little birds here. I think you have more birds in Belvidere than you would see here for months. Why, I can't say, but this country is scarce of them as well as everything else—except for the Whippoorwills, which are hollering around us all night long. I shall never forget the screams of the poor Whippoorwills at the battle of Chancellorsville on Saturday night, May 2. Amidst the lightning flash and roar of our artillery and musketry, and the storm of lead and iron, the screams of the poor bird could be heard mingled in distress with the groans of dying and wounded. But far above them I could hear one poor soldier—a Rebel, I think—suffering excruciating pain. This was the time that Jackson was mortally wounded. ...

Camp Fitzhugh Farm, Va., June 11th 1863

My dear family,

We have just got orders to move. Here comes an order to form the line and brake up this butiful camp.

Rappahannock Station, Saturday morning, June 13th. We have by hard marching and forced marches arrived here. Last night we were worn out completely.[38] Our regiment stands it better than any other. I am very well and never enjoyed better health in my life. I don't know what we are at but guess it is to watch Genl. Lee and

---

38. On June 12, McAllister officially reported, his men were on the move for fifteen consecutive hours. "A very hard march, the heat and dust being almost intolerable and water scarce; yet the men kept up well." *OR,* Vol. XXVII, Pt. 1, p. 552. An officer in a sister regiment was caustic in his comments on the march. "Caligula and other monsters of antiquity never displayed a more diabolical spirit than certain generals in the corps, who murdered the unfortunate soldiers that were compelled to obey their orders, by exhausting their strength, and needlessly exposing them to the rays of the sun, which, through their cruelty, became as deadly as Minie balls." Blake, *Three Years in the Army of the Potomac,* 191.

prevent him from making a rade into Maryland and Pennsylvania. Our whole Corps came but we are now very much scattered. The advance guard of our Army was driven in yesterday, but I have heard nothing of it since. One of our divisions is not up yet. One is up to our right. We are about two miles from the station towards the run. You will hear from us soon. . . .

Beverly Ford, Va., June 14th 1863

My dear Ellen & family,

I wrote you yesterday. We have thrown up some breastworks to protect our gunners and rifle pits close to the ford to protect our pickets. We are constantly on the alert and would not be disappointed if we got into a fight any hour.

Our troops are all along this river and, of course, have but small forces at any one place. From the clouds of dust seen yesterday on the Rebel side of the river, we have reason to believe that they have been moving to our right. It is possible that they are trying to flank us, or it may be to move northward. But I can't think that they will do the latter and leave their army here. We look for hard fighting and a good deal of it. I have been informed that the 1st Corps has come up, but I have not seen it and can't vouch for it. I am satisfied that Hooker is wide awake and will not be caught asleep. We will be ready to meet the enemy at any point that he may attack us. You will know more about our movements from the papers than I can tell you.

This country is much better than any I have seen in Virginia. There are some fine farms, but war will soon destroy them all. We are now twenty miles nearer Washington than at the old camp. We are about 1½ miles from the Orange & Alexandria R.R. and Rappahannock Station. Look on the map and you will see our position exactly. We had a hard march to get here. We marched 24 miles through heat and dust. I am happy to say that my regiment stood the march first rate. It came up solid, with hardly any stragling. I brought more men into camp than any two of the other regiments, for which we get a grate deal of credit. *I tell you that it is an honor to belong to the 11th New Jersey.*

My health is first rate, for which I am thankful. Let us pray God that I may be ready and willing to meet any immergency that may occur, and do my duty to my God and my country. These are trying times and we must make sacrifices. . . .

[324] ✗ THE McALLISTER LETTERS

Bivouac, Manassas Plains, Va., June 17th 1863
My dear Ellen & family,

I wrote you when we were at Beverly Ford on the Rappahannock. We had a quiet Sabbath and time for Divine Service. We all felt much better from the fatigues of the hard march. On Sunday, just at dark, we were ordered under arms and soon moved off in this direction. We marched all night and arrived at Cedar Run about 7 a.m. Our men were very much fatigued. The dust was terrible. We now took breakfast (hardtack, pork and coffee) and laid down to sleep.

About 1 p.m. came an order to move and information that the enemy had arrived in force at Beverly Ford, the place we had left. Whether they had crossed or not I can't tell. Our rear was not attacked. We started our march. The day was exceedingly hot, roads more dusty than I had ever before witnessed. But on and on we went. Many were the men that fell out and lay stretched all along the road, overcome by heat, choked with dust and panting for water.[39] It was easy for us to tell that this was a forced march. An immergency required that we should go forward. In fact, all our marches thus far are forced marches. Many of us fell asleep on the roadside when we stoped, having marched all Sunday night and being completely worn out. About 11:30 at night we arrived at Manassas Junction and halted. We laid down on the ground, without supper, and in a few minutes all in the Division were in the arms of sleep. Thus passed Sunday night, Monday, and Monday night.

Tuesday morning we received rations and soon had orders to move. We fell in and went about 1½ miles, halted and pitched shelter tents. We had a delightful rest in the afternoon and slept well during the night. After breakfast we had orders to fall in and marched but a mile, when we reached the famous Bull Run. We halted and received orders to go in and take a good bath. We stacked arms and the whole Division were soon stripped and enjoying the bath to our satisfaction. You would have laughed if you had seen a few of us officers who went far up the stream bathing and washing our underclothing. Recollect that we have no change of clothing with us. We

---

39. Gen. Carr stated that this march was "one of the most severe in my experience, the air being almost suffocating, the dust blinding, and the heat intolerable. Many men suffered from *coup de soleil,* and a large number sank by the wayside, utterly helpless and exhausted." Straggling reached such proportions that only 25 of 250 members of the veteran 7th New Jersey stumbled into camp at day's end. *OR,* Vol. XXVII, Pt. 1, pp. 530, 542; Samuel Toombs, *New Jersey Troops in the Gettysburg Campaign* (cited as Toombs, *New Jersey Troops*) (Orange, N.J., 1888), 105–6.

are all like terrapins—all we have is on our backs. You know I never washed anything before, and I don't think I did it very nicely. But as it is the first time I ever washed my clothes, you will have to excuse the color and bad appearance.

After this delightful wash we took dinner of the standing dishes: *hardtack,* fat pork and coffee. This we have morning, noon, and night. I tell you it is good when we are hungry. At 3 p.m. we fell in and continued our march. We halted on the road leading towards Leesburg, about half a mile from Centreville, stacked arms, and I am now writing under a delightful shade. We will probably stay all night and resume our march in the morning. Rumours are afloat of Lee's advance being at Chambersburg. Let it be so. It will waken up some of the Copperheads and bring them out for or against the war. If the latter, let them join Lee, take sides with the Rebels, and we will talk to them at the cannon's mouth in a way they will understand. Any young able-bodied man who can possibly leave home and don't join the army now has no love for his country and does not deserve to be protected by our Government. Let Pennsylvania attend to Lee in the front, and Genl. Hooker will attend to him in the rear. . . .

Here comes Miss Gilson and Mr. Fay to be with us on the march. She is a grate help to the sick and wounded. She rides on horseback and also has an ambulance. She is a grate favorite with us all.

The mail man is waiting and I must close. . . .

Camp near Centreville, Va., June 18th 1863

My dear Ellen & family,

Last evening I finished a letter and had it mailed. I understand that our letters are going through, though we receive none. I have not received a single letter since we left Fitzhugh Farm. I long to hear from you.

We are now preparing to leave the line of the Railroad and are reducing our baggage. Well, I can't reduce any more. I have not had a change of clothing, but I have a small trunk in the wagon in the rear. Perhaps I will see it some time, if I live. My mattress, bed, pillow, two blankets, and some underclothing I rolled up and sent from our camp with the surplus baggage to Aquia Creek. This I may get, but it stands a good chance to be lost. My overcoat and cape, blanket, shawl, and air pillow is all I have with me, together with a gum blanket. I find it ample, and as much as it is convenient to carry. At night I lay down the gum blanket, on top of which I place my shawl. I then lie down with my head on the air pillow and cover myself with my coat and cape. In this way I sleep soundly with or without a tent. We are so tired that we can sleep any place—and soundly at that. The ground is very dry here—no rain for a long time. We have greate trouble geting water and often suffer from the want of it.

Every hour we are expecting orders to move, though we remain here all day and night. The cavalry and other forces are after Lee. We will move as circumstances require. It is hard to tell what Lee's movements are. But you can rest assured that Hooker is watching him, and that all will be right. In a skirmish this morning, our advance force captured 80 Rebels and five pieces of artillery.[40] They were well on their way to Alexandria.

4 p.m. Cannonading can now be heard. Our forces are advancing and we must have fighting. It is the opinion of some of our military men that we will have a heavy battle in this neighbourhood of the old Bull Run ground. I think it possible. These are exciting times! . . .

Camp at Gum Springs, Va., June 20th 1863

My dear Ellen & family,

. . . Thursday evening [June 18] we moved from the camp we were in the last time I wrote you and pitched our tents here nearer Centreville. Yesterday we had orders to lay out a nice camp, which looked very much as if we were stoping for awhile. But we had just got the stakes in when an order came to be ready to move, and in an hour we took up our line of march. We arrived here at dark last evening and pitched camp. We expect to move any hour. I don't know where we are going but think to Leesburg, about fifteen miles from this place. Since yesterday there has been considerable cannonading in that direction.[41] We suppose we will get into a battle very soon. God grant that it may be successful in our undertaking, and that our arms may triumph. Whether we are going on the defensive or the offensive I cannot tell. Time will tell what our now-mysterious movements are for.

---

40. McAllister slightly confused his facts. The action to which he referred was a June 17 cavalry battle at Aldie between the forces of Alfred Pleasanton and Fitzhugh Lee. Pleasanton reported capturing 63 Confederates and spiking 4 guns; his own losses exceeded 130 men. *OR,* Vol. XXVII, Pt. 1, pp. 688, 906–7; Pt. 2, pp. 739–40.

41. What McAllister heard was a June 19 clash at Middleburg between opposing cavalry. See *OR,* Vol. XXVII, Pt. 1, pp. 909–11, 953–54; Pt. 2, pp. 689–90, 759.

We have had some rain and the dust is well laid, making it much more pleasant to march. The health of our troops is good. My health was never better.

At Centreville there is quite a number of regiments that have been there for a long time and have not yet been in battle. They have a large number of ladies with them—officers' wives. They all dress well, have nice dress parades, and do things up in good style. But they have not done the work we have. You know that we are the fighting Brigade, Division & Corps. If there is anything to be done, we are sure to be in it. We have now seven regiments in our Brigade. The 12th New Hampshire and the 88th Pennsylvania Regiments have been added to us within the last few days. Whipple's Division was broken up and divided around.[42] . . .

Gum Springs, Va., June 21st 1863

My dear Ellen & family,

I wrote you yesterday, telling you where we are and how we got here. Since then we have not had any orders to move. I told you of some fighting to our left and front. I have not learned much relative to it, only that we drove the enemy back and now hold the gap at Aldie. I think we have lost considerable, as I understand that a number of ambulances have passed down the road with our wounded. Before this we lost the Rhode Island Cavalry—some 300 in all. They advanced too far beyond the mountain and were surrounded when they attempted to cut their way through. Only 27 reached our lines.[43] We have taken a considerable number of prisoners, at least even with them. Our men are forbidden to go outside the camps, as gurillas are prowling all around the country and capture our men and officers. We lost a captain belonging to our Corps Staff night before last while on picket. A report says that we have lost a number of officers and men, some from our Brigade. Yet we are on the lookout. There is little

42. At Chancellorsville Brig. Gen. Amiel W. Whipple had commanded the 3rd Division in Sickles' corps. His two brigades suffered frightfully high losses, and Whipple himself was mortally wounded. Nothing remained after the battle but to amalgamate the fragments of his units with others in the III Corps.

43. Col. A. N. Duffie's 1st Rhode Island Cavalry rode into the June 19 action at Middleburg with a total of 275 men. On the following afternoon the unit returned to its Leesburg camp with 4 officers and 27 troopers—"the gallant debris of my much-loved regiment," Duffie wrote. *OR*, Vol. XXVII, Pt. 1, pp. 963–64. See also George N. Bliss, *The First Rhode Island Cavalry at Middleburg, Va.* . . . (Providence, 1889).

doubt but that we will have a heavy battle to fight somewhere in this region soon. It may be here or it may be a third Bull Run battle.

We have not as yet received any letters. . . . Newsboys can't get here. We know nothing as to the outside world. I suppose the Rebel cavalry have not yet reached Belvidere. This is Loudoun County, a much better country than any I have seen [elsewhere] in Virginia. . . .

Gum Springs, Va., June 22nd 1863

My dear Ellen & family,

I had the pleasure of receiving six letters from you last evening . . . for which I am much obliged.

We have had considerable fighting above us. Yesterday cannonading was heard all day long up towards Aldie, not far from here. . . . We were under arms and ready to move at a moment's warning. We are now in line of battle here, and I rather think we are expecting an attack. Things look that way. One thing is certain: we are in the enemy's country. But if we are attacked, we will be able to withstand them, God willing. Our movements depend on the movements of our other Corps. We may remain here and have a fight, or we may move up or down as circumstances require. There is no telling. . . .

Gum Springs, Va., June 23rd 1863

My dear Ellen & family,

. . . My letters may not have gone further than Washington and may be kept there until our whereabouts can with safety be known. This, you know, is always done. . . . Our mail and supply teams all have to be guarded in passing out and into this place on account of the gurillas that are moving all around us.

All was quiet yesterday and last night. Only a few guns were fired yesterday above Aldie. We have not heard further from the battle of Sunday [June 21], except that we drove the enemy back about four miles to Middleburg. I think it was principally a cavalry fight with considerable artillery. . . .

Col. Moore's time is up, but I suppose it is hard for him to find us and get to us. When he does come, neither Capt. Lloyd or I can leave until we settle down again, which may be some time yet. We hope it will not be long, but it is hard to tell what changes may take place. If I am living, I will get a leave as soon as possible. You understand this as well as I can explain it to you. . . .

Gum Springs, Va., June 24th 1863

My dear Ellen & family,

It is now noon and nothing new since I wrote you last. All is very quiet, and not a gun has been fired since. What is doing, or where the Rebel army is, I can not tell. We know comparatively nothing. We are in line of battle, or camped in that way, so that if we are attacked we can spring to arms in a moment. We picket all around. You see, we expect to be attacked on all sides. But this remains to be seen.

This is Loudoun County, and we are in what is called Loudoun Valley. It is very fine country. The farm we are encamped on belongs to a Massachusetts man and is in a good state of cultivation. He had just finished making hay, and it came in good for our horses. He has some five or six hundred acres; we pasture over it all. Our Quartermaster give a government receipt for the hay. We send out foraging parties every day and take all we can get—live on the country as much as we can. Yet we still have to haul daily from Fairfax Station. It is a big job to keep up our supplies; and the farther we advance, the harder it is to get supplies. . . .

Col. Moore has not returned here yet, but I understand he is on his way. I suppose it is difficult for him to get here.

The health of our troops is good. My health was never better. Sleeping in the open air agrees with me first rate.

I bought a mule the other day to carry my baggage, but I have to use him to carry our mess matter and provisions. I hope the mess will get another mule. Then I can carry enough to make me comfortable. If I should be killed, recollect I have my horse and mule. Charley is to be taken home for the children to ride. He is a noble old fellow and belongs to the family. . . .

We have prayer meeting every evening in one or another of the regiments in this Brigade. The 12th New Hampshire has a splendid chaplain.[44] He takes his singers out and commences singing a hymn. Soon he has a large congregation around him. Then he reads a chapter [from the Bible], explains it, preaches and prays. . . .

---

44. Chaplain Thomas L. Ambrose of the 12th New Hampshire died July 24, 1864, from a Confederate sharpshooter's bullet. Bartlett, *12th New Hampshire*, 94, 479–80.

Bivouac at Taneytown, Md., June 30th 1863

My dear Ellen & family,

After long, hard and fatiguing marches,[45] we arrived at this place last evening. We are now within five miles of the Pennsylvania line, heading towards York or Gettysburg. I moved to Burkitsville at Crampton's Pass. From there we marched to Middletown, thence to Frederick City, and from there to this place, passing through a greate many little towns and a most magnificent country under a high state of cultivation. I must reserve the discriptions for another time. But one thing is certain: the inhabitants are *very loyal*. They receive us with flags waving and show every demonstration of joy at our approach. At the forks of the roads, along the roadsides, and in the villages, they are collected to see the army. They seemed more loyal than the people in some parts of the North. . . .

I don't know what is before us. But we suppose we will have some fighting to do. If we get a little rest, we will be ready for it. We have now travelled about 150 miles or more, and have performed the longest and hardest marches of the war. As a general thing, the troops are in good spirits and in good health. This country is healthy—good water, pure air, very different from Virginia.[46] We seem to breathe another atmosphere, and the men seem to be perfectly delighted. . . .

NOTES ON THE CAMPAIGN OF GETTYSBURG [47]

The latter part of our journey to Gettysburg was very hard. It might be termed forced marches, especially since we knew where the enemy was going. After we crossed the Potomac and got fairly into Maryland, the spirits of our men were so much better. They were ready to endure more hardships, if necessary. I will tell you why.

The contrast between this country and its people with Virginia and her inhabitants was remarkable. We were coming out of a poor,

---

45. For details of the 11th New Jersey's march to Taneytown, see *OR*, Vol. XXVII, Pt. 1, p. 552.

46. See Capt. P. J. Kearny's descriptions in *Historical Magazine*, Ser. 2, Vol. VII (1870), p. 195.

47. McAllister probably wrote his notes on Gettysburg while recuperating in Belvidere from his battle wounds. In any event, he was not himself when writing this account. His eloquence is lacking, the organization is poor, and the grammar is the worst of his many writings. His official report of the Gettysburg battle, submitted Aug. 3, 1863, is a marked improvement to this narrative. See *OR*, Vol. XXVII, Pt. 1, pp. 551–53.

miserable, forelorn country—whose people looked as if they had lost all their friends and were themselves enemys to all the world around them—to a country well cultivated, yielding a rich return for the labour bestowed, and with a prosperous and patriotic people. As we marched through Maryland, everything from the beautiful green forests which crowned the hills to the waving grain ready for harvest in the valley seemed to rejoice in the sunlight. The country was, to us who had been shut up for so long in old Virginia, perfectly magnificent. Add to this what means far more to a soldier: a warm welcome.

The people were assembled all along the route to meet us. At every crossroads they brought us water and provisions. In the country and in towns, from the windows and from the balconies, they greeted us, with our own dear old flag; and making to us one grand ovation. I believe that this warm welcome from our Union friends in Maryland had much to do with preparing our men to meet the storm of battle just beyond the border of that state.

In passing through Frederick, we could easily see who were our friends and who were our foes. All our friends were demonstrating for us. One old gentleman stood at a third story window, threw out a large flag on a long pole, and kept crying continually in a loud voice: "Oh, long may it wave, o'er the land of the free and the home of the brave!"

As each regiment passed under that flag, its members took off their hats and gave three cheers. After passing through Frederick, we halted in some woods alongside the road and received the announcement: "Forty minutes for coffee." This was not welcome news to our worn-out soldiers. That day they had marched 31 miles and they had expected to rest here for the night. But this order blasted all hopes of the rest to which they had looked forward that wearisome day. It meant onward, onward.

Few fires were built and little coffee was made. Most of the officers and men threw themselves on the ground, too tired to make any effort. As I looked around and saw the troops so completely exhausted, I said to an officer beside me, "I fear we can never move at the given time."

At the end of forty minutes, all the bands struck up a lively tune. Our men sprang to their feet, and on we went. It was wonderful, and the music accounted for it. It had the power to inspire even these men who had endured a long, hard march under the burning sun— and to renew that spirit in the evening perhaps even for a night march.

While in bivouac on the road from Taneytown to Gettysburg, an order came from Genl. Meade, who had just assumed command of the army. It was read separately to each regiment. This order from their new commander urged the men to be true to themselves and their country in the grate battle so soon to be fought in Pennsylvania. After reading the order, each regimental commander was to address his men and urge them to stand firm, &c.[48]

July 1st. We now passed on very rapidly. About noon we halted to make coffee. News was received that the 1st Corps was already engaged with the Rebels at Gettysburg. We soon renewed the march. The sun poured down a torrid heat, but on, on, we pushed. Scores of our men, overcome by heat and exhaustion, fell out by the wayside; but we did not slacken our pace. Soon we heard the roar of artillery far away on the soil of Pennsylvania. Yet the distance to the battlefield was so greate that it would be some time before we could render any assistance to our friends. Our column pressed forward, the spirits of the men buoyed up by the roar of artillery. After awhile the sound died away. The twilight of evening closed around us. All was quiet save for the tramp, tramp, tramp of our brave boys marching to victory. For many of them, that victory was death.

About the middle of the night, we reached what the next day was to become the memorable battlefield of Gettysburg. We lay down and were soon asleep. We had no supper. Morning dawned, with little or no breakfast, as our provision trains were not yet up. A heavy fog hung over the town. We could see but little. Soon we were taking our several positions for the greate struggle. Some firing was heard at diffirent points, but nothing general. The day wore away; we changed our positions several times. Then, after deploying in line of battle, we moved forward to the crest of a hill. The right of my regiment rested in the corner of the apple orchard.[49] Here we lay down, ready for action as soon as the artillery fight was over, and ready to receive the Rebels when they charged us.

Here allow me to say that this artillery was no ordinary kind. It was very brisk and extremely fierce. Could I have divested myself of the thought that great numbers were being hurried into eternity, and

---

48. In Meade's announcement to the army he called on all officers to explain to the men "the immense issues involved in the struggle" and to impress upon them that "the whole country now looks anxiously to the army to deliver it from the presence of the foe." Meade closed his directive with the statement: "Corps and other commanders are authorized to order the instant death of any soldier who fails in his duty at this hour." Marbaker, *11th New Jersey,* 91; Andrew J. Boies, *Record of the Thirty-third Massachusetts Volunteer Infantry* . . . (Fitchburg, Mass., 1880), 32.

49. McAllister, of course, was referring to the peach orchard just to the west of Little Round Top.

great numbers more were being wounded and maimed, I should have exclaimed: "Perfectly magnificent!" [50]

The enemy let loose on us, not only with the artillery in our front but their reserve artillery as well. The roaring cannon, the swift flying solid shot, and the bursting shells carried off the branches of the [peach trees] like chaff in the air. Our brave artillerymen, mounted on their horses, galloped up to the crest of the hill, unlimbered, ranged their guns, and fired till the enemy got their range. Then they limbered up, mounted, rode off in a circle, came back to the crest of the hill, got another range, and gave another effective fire. Men were shot down; horses were cut down and replaced. Yet off they went into action again to send the fiery messengers of death into the enemy's ranks. All this I heard and saw. But so fierce, so exciting, was the scene that no pen can give a discription of it.

The artillery slackened off. Then came our time of battle. The enemy charged; our pickets were driven in. I ordered: "Attention! Fire!" [51]

At that moment a Minie ball pierced through my left thigh and a piece of spent shell hit my right foot. I was carried to the rear,[52] supposedly mortally wounded. About the time I fell and was carried back, Maj. [Philip J.] Kearny, on whom the command of the regiment would have devolved (Lt. Col. Moore being absent through sickness), fell mortally wounded and was taken back. For five days we lay side by side in my tent on the field. We were then carried on stretchers to Philadelphia, where we parted, never to meet again on earth. He was taken to New York and I to my home in New Jersey. Maj. Kearny was a brave young officer. He loved the service. He would push into the thickest of the fight, his brave example stimulating the men to follow him. No duty was too arduous for him, no danger too great.

Capts. [Luther] Martin, [Dorastus] Logan, and [Andrew H.] Ackerman died in this bloody field a few minutes after I fell. They were all officers who had good military records, and who were ever ready and willing to do their duty. Had they lived, each of them would

50. "So exciting was it all," McAllister recalled years later, "that I could not keep lying down but had to jump up and watch the grand duel." McAllister to Samuel Toombs, Jan. 10, 1888, McAllister Papers.

51. The better descriptions of the fighting of which the 11th New Jersey was a part are in Marbaker, *11th New Jersey,* 96–109; Hanifen, *1st New Jersey Artillery,* 67–78; Bartlett, *12th New Hampshire,* 120–29; Haynes, *2nd New Hampshire,* 137–44; Toombs, *New Jersey Troops,* 193–214, 237–44.

52. The men who assisted McAllister to the rear were Capt. W. B. Dunning of Co. K and Martin Litsworth of the pioneer corps. William B. Dunning to McAllister, Aug. 4, 1863, McAllister Papers.

have made his mark. With one half of the officers and men killed and wounded, with a heavy flank and front fire, the wonder is how the regiment held together even as long as it did. Greate credit is due the remaining officers and men for the gallantry they displayed on that hard-fought field. Capt. Lloyd and Adjt. Schoonover are deserving of greate credit. Both were wounded, and their comrades fell thick and fast around them. They filled all the field posts from Colonel to Adjutant, encouraged the men to stand firm, changed front as directed, and fought on until the heavily reinforced columns of the enemy rolled them back. But with our reinforcements they came again to the front.

(Since McAllister fell wounded just as the 11th New Jersey moved into battle, it seems fitting to add here the official report of the regiment's subsequent action at Gettysburg. Lt. John Schoonover wrote the report, and it is published in OR, *Vol. XXVII, Pt. 1, pp. 553–55.)*

Camp near Beverly Ford, Va., August 7, 1863

Captain [LeGrand Benedict]:

In continuation of the inclosed report of Col. R. McAllister, I have the honor to submit the following:

A few minutes previous to the command "Fire!" spoken of in [Col. McAllister's official] report, Major Kearny, then standing near me on the left of the line, was struck by a Minie ball in the knee, and immediately carried to the rear.

At this moment, Battery K, Fourth U.S. Artillery, then stationed a short distance to the left and front of the regiment, limbered their pieces and passed by our left to the rear, closely followed by a line of the enemy's infantry, upon which our regiment opened a rapid fire. I then passed rapidly to the right of the regiment, in order to inform the colonel of the absence of the major, and learned that he, too, had been wounded and taken to the rear. I immediately notified Captain Martin, the senior officer present, that he was in command of the regiment, and again passed to the left of the line, when an order was received from Brigadier-General Carr to slightly change the front by bringing the left to the rear. This being executed, the entire regiment opened an effective fire upon the advancing line of the enemy.

At this point, word was conveyed to me that both Captains Martin and Logan were wounded and being carried to the rear. A moment later, and Captain Ackerman fell dead at my side. The two former were killed before they reached a place of safety; and in justice to the memory of these three officers, permit me to bear witness to their unexceptional good conduct—ever to the front, distinguished for personal bravery, they leave behind them a spotless record.

By this time Captain Lloyd had been wounded, and Captain Dunning being absent in assisting the Colonel to the rear, I assumed command of the regiment. The fire of the enemy was at this time perfectly terrific; men were falling on every side. It seemed as if but a few minutes could elapse before the entire line would be shot down, yet the galling fire was returned with equal vigor. Slowly and stubbornly the regiment fell back, keeping up a continual fire upon the line of the enemy, which was still advancing, until more than half its numbers had been killed or wounded.

Up until this time both men and officers nobly did their duty, but the ranks becoming so decimated and mingled with wounded men and the line in the rear, and having a short time previous been struck with a piece of shell in the breast, I found it impossible, under those circumstances, to longer keep the line together.[53] At this time we neared the caissons, which were in line across the field to the left, when I was struck the second time with a buck-shot, and being nearly exhausted in my effort to rally the men, and from the wound in my breast, I was counseled to go to the rear.

A portion of the regiment was rallied some distance to the rear by Captain Lloyd, and charged in line with the remainder of the brigade to a point near that occupied durring the hottest of the action. Remaining there a short time, it marched some distance to the rear, and bivouacked.

Being able to ride, I joined the regiment on the morning of [July] 3d, and again took command, by request of Captain [Samuel T.] Sleeper, the senior officer present for duty. A number of officers and men also joined the regiment, having been collected near the stream farther to the rear.

Moving a short distance to the front, the regiment was halted until 3 p.m., when it was ordered out double-quick with the remainder of the brigade on the road to Gettysburg. Proceeding nearly a mile, it was halted and formed in line of battle in rear of the batteries occupying the crest of the hill in front, the brigade being in column of regiments. The regiment remained in this position for nearly two hours, under a heavy fire of shot and shell, yet but one man was

---

53. Although several members of the 11th New Jersey bolted to the rear in panic during the later stages of the day's action, McAllister stated positively: "I did not see a man of my Regiment . . . flinch or show the least cowardice under that terrific cannonading or the fierce charge which we met." McAllister to Samuel Toombs, Jan. 10, 1888, McAllister Papers.

slightly wounded. During the time my horse was struck by a spherical case shot, from the effects of which he died the next day.

About 5 p.m. the regiment returned to its former position, where it remained for the night.

In conclusion, permit me to mention the general good conduct of both officers and men both upon the 2d and 3d. To mention some might do gross injustice to others, but I cannot pass by the untiring efforts of Lieutenant [John T.] Buckley to rally the men. Captain Lloyd and Lieutenant [Ira W.] Corey also deserve special mention for their coolness and bravery.

As an individual act of bravery, I desire to mention Corpl. Thomas Johnson, of Company I, whom, when two color-bearers had been shot down, I ordered to take the colors and advance 20 yards to the front, as the regiment was then wavering. He did so, and did not leave his position until ordered to the rear.

The services of Lieut. James Baldwin on the 3d, as acting adjutant, were invaluable.

In the action of the 2d, the regiment sustained a very heavy loss. Out of 275 officers and men taken into the fight, 18 were killed, 130 wounded, and 6 missing, making a total of 154.[54] . . .

54. The revised medical report for the battle of Gettysburg listed the 11th New Jersey's casualties as 17 killed, 124 wounded, and 12 missing. *OR,* Vol. XXVII, Pt. 1, p. 555.

8

"The Races Campaign"

THE 11TH NEW JERSEY lost one third of its complement in the fighting at Gettysburg. After the battle a Jersey soldier in another unit observed that the 11th "numbered but two hundred men; sickness and death on the battlefield had thinned their ranks, but still they were ready for the contest and as eager as ever to be led forward."[1]

Early in October a weakened McAllister rejoined the regiment at Culpeper, and for a month he served as temporary commander of the 1st Brigade, Prince's Division, III Corps. Generals Humphreys, Carr, and others made efforts to secure him a brigadier's promotion. Yet the stars of a general were not to come to McAllister for another year. Moreover, he soon had to relinquish brigade command to a fellow colonel who ostensibly manipulated seniority of rank in order to gain the post.

Military operations in Virginia during October-December, 1863, consisted of maneuvering and countermaneuvering by the two opposing armies. In October Lee made a threatening move on Washington; Meade promptly retreated with his army to Centreville. The following month Meade dispatched five corps across the Rapidan and toward the Rappahannock in an attempt to flank the strong Confederate

---

1. J. Newton Terrill, *Campaign of the Fourteenth Regiment, New Jersey Volunteers* (New Brunswick, 1884), 21.

positions near Mine Run. Lee adjusted his lines and easily checked the Federal thrusts. A planned Confederate counterattack failed when Meade retreated under cover of darkness. "I am too old to command this army," Lee stated disgustedly. "We should never have permitted those people to get away." [2]

McAllister termed this two-month series of advances and withdrawals "The Races Campaign." His lengthy account of the Mine Run Campaign is an exceptional document—not only for its descriptions of operations but more so for the moving manner in which he captured the deep emotion of the men prior to an assault few of them thought would be successful.

As the 11th New Jersey filed into its winter quarters at Brandy Station, a member of the II Corps wrote of the autumn's operations: "The fall campaign in Virginia may now be considered as closed, I should think, and as a pretty even thing, on the whole. They have made us a visit, and we have made them a visit. There has been a see-saw game across the Rappahannock, in which each side has gone up and gone down; and nobody can say which has kept the longest end of the plank." [3]

♣

Washington, D.C., October 2nd 1863

My dear Ellen,

I arrived here safely. Major [Charles M.] Herbert is with me. I did not get my pay, as there is an order preventing us from geting it until those that have Surgeons' certificates report to their regiments. The paymaster was very polite but would not violate the rules. He told me that if I go and join the regiment, I could get a leave for a day and run down here. He would then pay me the amount I have in arrears, $727. Another month and it will be six months without pay. I will try and get the leave, but it may be some time before I can get it. . . .

2. Freeman, *R. E. Lee,* III, 202.
3. [Samuel W. Fiske] *Mr. Dunn Browne's Experience in the Army* (Boston, 1866), 326–27.

I start for the regiment very soon. . . . The 11th and 12th Corps have gone west. . . .

     Camp near Culpeper Court House, Va., October 4th 1863
My dear Ellen & family,
 . . . Genl. Carr has been assigned to the command of the 3rd Division of this Corps. He has just handed over the command of this Brigade to me.[4] So I am a Brigadier General for the time being. Genl. Carr says that it will be a permanent thing for me, as Col. Blaisdell, the only senior I have in the Brigade, is not at all likely to return. But I heard one of his officers say that he will be here in a few days. If so, I will loose my Brigade command. But I am all right for a Brigadiership. Genl. Carr has already sent in my name for a brevet without my asking for it. In a day or two he will write me a strong letter for promotion which I will try and get backed up by Genl. [Andrew A.] Humphreys and Genl. Sickles. I will place this in Ex-Governor Newell's hands. I have written Brother Nelson to send on his letters. So you see that I am at work. I shall not be disappointed either way.
 Our regimental officers procured the 11th Massachusetts band and gave me a serenade & welcome home last evening. We had some speaking and considerable cheering, and everything passed off well. All seem glad to see me. They did not expect me so soon. I am among the first of the badly wounded officers or men from the Gettysburg fight to return. So you see that I will not be court-martialed.
 Genl. Carr has signed a leave of absence for me for 36 hours to go and get my money at Washington. . . .
 Inclosed you will find photographs of Genl. Carr, his wife and daughter. Genl. Carr very kindly gave them to me and desired to have Sarah's photograph. I give it to him and wish Sarah to have these. She must send me another one without delay. Mrs. Benedict's card is also inclosed. This I will give to Hennie. Capt. Benedict give it to me for remembrance. Take care of it. Capt. Benedict is going with Genl. Carr. I am sorry to loose him. I will have to get another Adjutant General [for the brigade]. . . .

 4. McAllister was temporarily in command of the 1st Brigade, 2nd Division, III Corps, which consisted of the 11th and 16th Massachusetts, 11th New Jersey, 26th and 84th Pennsylvania. *OR,* Vol. XXIX, Pt. 1, p. 220.

Headquarters, 1st Brigade, 2nd Division, 3rd Corps
October 5th 1863

My dear Ellen,

You see by the heading that I am now in command of the Brigade—this old veteran Brigade, and I am received very cordially. I have moved the Headquarters up on a butiful knoll. Our tents are placed in a semi-circle and fenced in with a line of poles all around. We have the Stars and Stripes floating to the brees from the top of a beautiful flag staff. Right in front of my tent we have a large fire burning very brightly, throwing its rays and heat around, and making it quite comfortable. All say that I have nice Headquarters.

Genl. Carr left at 8:30 this morning. Previous to his leaving, all the commissioned officers of the Brigade, plus the band, came down to pay our respects and bid him goodby. The band struck up; after it played for a time, I addressed him on behalf of the officers and men of our Brigade. I spoke to him very feelingly in regard to our connection—the pleasant hours spent together, the toils, fatigues and dangers through which we passed, and the noble manner in which he stood amidst the storm of battle. Tears came into the General's eyes, and it was with greate difficulty that he replied. The scene was truely a sad one. After he closed his remarks, we all passed around and give him a harty goodby and a good shake by the hand. Then he and his staff mounted and turned away from this veteran Brigade with sad, sad hearts. Capt. Benedict came back this afternoon and complimented me for the manner in which I spoke and conducted the whole affair. He said the General was so sad that he did not utter a word until he got to the new headquarters. But, said the Captain, Genl. Carr was highly gratified with the whole proceeding. This event would have taken place last evening, had it not been the Sabbath.

And now the responsibility is on me, for the time being at least. I have to control and conduct this noble old Brigade. I trust that by the help of God I may be permited to do so with ability, and that it may not, while in my hands, loose any of its former renown but rather continue to add new honors to the many already won. . . .

October 6th 1863, 11 p.m.

My dear family,

I had just laid down to sleep when an order came to be ready to move at precisely 4 o'clock in the morning. Our Division only is to make a reconacence. It is said that the enemy are trying to turn our right flank. Our cavalry are going out and we go to support them. It is most likely we will get into a brush before we get back. It is raining and we will have a hard time of it. . . .

Culpeper Court House, Va., October 7th 1863
My dear Ellen,
. . . I wrote you last night that we had orders to move and expected to be off before morning. We had everything packed, and I could have been in the saddle in about ten minutes. I lay down with my pants on. I did not sleep very sound, as I had a greate responsibility resting on me. Well, we were not disturbed and have not moved yet. But the prospects are that we will move somewhere very soon. One report today is that the Rebel cavalry—all of Genl. [J. E. B.] Stuart's force—have left our rear. Another report is that they were not there at all. But I think this last is not the case. They must have been there or we would not have had the orders.[5]

I am still in command of the Brigade. I get along very well and like it very much. This is one of the finest Brigades in the army. It is called the *Veteran Brigade.* It is an honor to belong to it. It has lately received a large number of recruits. I have two Pennsylvania regiments, two Massachusetts regiments, and the 11th New Jersey—in all, five regiments. The 1st Massachusetts left and are at New York. The 12th New Hampshire has also left. But the Brigade is larger now than it was before, as the 84th Pennsylvania joined us, as well as the returned paroled prisoners. New recruits swell us up to nearly 2,000 men. All the old regiments are filling up except New Jersey. A grate deal is said against her for forming new regiments and not filling up the old ones. Genl. Mott's brigade are all New Jersey regiments, and his brigade is not one half as large as mine. One thousand paroled prisoners came up today. We only got about 20 of them. Genl. Carr got a whole regiment of them captured from Milroy at Winchester.[6]

The 3rd Corps Union is going to be a nice thing. I have joined. We are to have a splendid badge, which we are always to wear. I represent this Brigade in their meetings. If a member of this Union dies or gets wounded, he is to be sent home and, if in need, supported.

5. On Oct. 1, a portion of Stuart's cavalry attacked Federal pickets along Robertson's River. Stuart followed this up with an Oct. 7 foray against Federal outposts near Utz's Ford. *Ibid.,* 204, 211.
6. Moving northward toward Pennsylvania, Lee on June 15 had trapped Gen. Robert H. Milroy's small force at Stephenson's Depot, near Winchester. Milroy managed to escape, but 4,000 of his men were forced to surrender.

Each member pays ten dollars initiation fee and six dollars a year thereafter. The money is laid out in New Jersey stock. It is a bond of union to bind the officers together for life. A history of the Corps and the officers will be written.[7] The 3rd Division (Genl. Carr's), is not included, as it came in after the battle of Gettysburg. All the corps are jealous of us. We are considered *the fighting Corps,* and it is esteemed a grate honor to belong to it. Our history will be splendid and will fill many bright pages in our country's history. The 6th Corps are down on us because we have fought more than they did and are more honored. . . .

If we get settled in camp this fall, Genl. Carr is going to have Mrs. Carr here. I will invite some of my family and we will have a nice time of it, won't we? . . .

Culpeper, Va., October 11th 1863

My dear Ellen,

I wrote you last in camp in this place, just as I was starting with my Brigade to the front at James City to support [General Judson] Kilpatrick's cavalry. Though my Brigade was not actively engaged, we had a lively time of it. The enemy came in large force. . . . The cavalry done the fighting.[8] We lost some ground about the middle of the afternoon yesterday, but we held them in check. Towards evening we drove them back. As the fight was entirely a cavalry one, we were ordered to come here. We are all ready to move but know not the destination. I think we may cross the Rappahannock, but I don't think we will go far. The weather is beautiful, my health is good, and the men are in fine spirits. . . .

October 12th 1863. We fell back to this side of the river yesterday. We crossed at Freeman's Ford and I am picketing to this place, Beverly Ford. We have had but little fighting as yet, and orders have just come that we are to advance across the river again. Two divisions of the 5th Corps are now crossing and moving towards Brandy Station.

7. Such a history never appeared. Gen. J. Watts de Peyster allegedly compiled a lengthy history of the III Corps. It went unpublished for want of financial assistance. The literary work closest to what McAllister envisioned is William P. Shreve's short summary, *The Story of the Third Army Corps Union* (Boston, 1910).

8. On Oct. 10 Confederate cavalry crossed Robertson's River and attacked the picketing 5th New York Cavalry. The New Yorkers fell back to James City, where Federal reinforcements repulsed the Confederate thrust. McAllister's men took no part in the engagement. *OR,* Vol. XXIX, Pt. 1, pp. 374, 389–90, 439–40.

We may soon hear firing, and a general engagement may be thus brought on. I don't understand the movements.[9] . . .

Union Mills, Va., 4 miles from Fairfax Station
October 15th 1863

My dear Ellen,

I wrote you a short letter from the pickets on the Rappahannock. The next morning we continued the retreat and reached Greenwich in the morning. We stoped and rested two hours, then started, reached Centreville last evening, and came here today. The Rebels are all around us. We have fighting among my pickets now. I don't know how soon we will be engaged. I have not been under fire yet. The 2nd Corps did good work yesterday—took 11 pieces of artillery and some 800 prisoners.[10] We will have a grate battle before long. Our army is in good spirits and will whip them. This is the impression in the army, and, by the help of God, we will. . . .

I am hurried for time; my Brigade is in line of battle. Send this on to Sarah, as I have not time to write her. . . .

Union Mills, Va., October 16th 1863

My dear darling daughters,

Last evening I received three letters from home, dated the 10th, 11th and 12th, from you all. I need not tell you that they were welcome visitors. I learned from your mother that you are both in Elizabeth. I can't, for the want of time, give you a discription of all our movements.

I am sitting here on the ground without a tent. It is a very damp, rainy morning. We have been on the march forward and backward ever since the 8th, living on hardtack and lying on the ground without

---

9. Owing to Meade's inactivity, Lee seized the initiative and sought by maneuver to force the Federal army back to Washington. Confederates successfully flanked Meade's army from the Culpeper line; the Federals "entered upon the race for Centreville, the enemy following closely." However, Lee's advance elements collided at Bristoe Station with part of the Federal army and suffered a stunning reverse. *Ibid.*, 406; Marbaker, *11th New Jersey*, 123.

10. Confederate Gen. A. P. Hill's corps was assigned the task of flanking Meade's army. Hill's troops arrived at Bristoe Station on Oct. 14 to find thousands of Federals massed in confusion at the river crossing. Hill promptly hurled his brigades against the III Corps—only to realize too late that he himself had been flanked by the concealed II Corps. Hill's losses included 5 cannon and 450 men captured. *OR*, Vol. XXIX, Pt. 1, pp. 237–43, 426–28; Francis A. Walker, *History of the Second Army Corps* (cited hereafter as Walker, *Second Army Corps*) (New York, 1887), 321–64.

any covering. My health is good and I stand it first rate. At first, my wound hurt me some in riding, but now I can stand it first rate. The Rebels are firing on us from the rear and flanks. As yet I have not been engaged with my whole Brigade, but my pickets have to some extent. We are all expecting a general engagement. Lee is following us with a large army of 80,000 men.[11] We have been moving back towards Washington. A battle must take place very soon. We know not the hour. The enemy is working on our flanks. What our program is I don't know. We hope all is for the best. We have got the best of the fight in all, or nearly all, of the skirmishes. We have taken a large number of prisoners and eleven pieces of artillery. The 120th New York lost 40 men taken prisoners at James City when we went out on a reconnaisance at that place.[12]

My Brigade are now under arms, with horses saddled, ready to move at a moment's notice. These are stiring times, and all is in doubt and uncertainty. What Genl. Lee is up to we will soon know, and you may look for a hard-fought battle.

I am still in command of the Brigade and get along very well. I got back well and in good time. I am among the first badly wounded men from the Gettysburg fight that have returned, and I get a great deal of credit for it. Nothing would have been said or done if I had staid [at home] a week longer.

Charley is very well but rather poor. He is not geting any fatter, as for days we are without food of any kind. The provisions you and your kind mother put up for me came in good—make no mistake about it. I only wish I had such good living now. But we get along pretty well, all things considered. . . .

Here comes an order to reinforce Genl. Mott's Brigade, as the enemy are in his front. . . .

4:30 p.m. All quiet. We did not have to go to Genl. Mott's relief. The Rebels are not pushing us today. It is raining and now disagreeable.

The 1st Massachusetts Regiment just reported to me. They just came from New York.[13] I have command now of six regiments in the old veteran Brigade.

11. The Oct. 20, 1863, returns for the Army of Northern Virginia showed 53,031 men present for duty. *OR,* Vol. XXIX, Pt. 1, p. 405.
12. The 120th New York caught the full force of the Confederate attack at James City. Its casualties were 1 known dead and 113 missing out of 211 engaged. *Ibid.,* 319, 328–29.
13. Late in July the 1st Massachusetts went to New York City to assist authorities in quelling draft riots and associated disorders. Not until mid-October was the atmosphere of the city such as to permit the regiment to return to the field. Cudworth, *1st Massachusetts,* 420–33.

"THE RACES CAMPAIGN" ♣ [345]

I have just received Sarah's nice letter. I am rejoiced that she is so much better—and I rejoice with you in the elections. Capt. Lloyd is well and geting along well. . . .

Union Mills, Va., October 18th 1863

My dear Ellen & family,

. . . The enemy have taken the back track and have gon from our immediate front. We have been under arms almost constantly up till this time; and unless we move after them, we will have some rest. Some of the other Corps and the cavalry are now following them. We may go, but I think not.

Genl. Sickles arrived here yesterday. I called with the Generals and Brigade commanders at Corps Headquarters to receive him. Genl. [William H.] French sent his carriage & four to the railroad to bring him up. After taking some refreshments, he mounted a horse and road through our lines—to the greate satisfaction of our boys, who gave him the heartiest cheering I ever heard.[14] The reception was the warmest I have ever seen. There is no mistaking the fact that Genl. Sickles is very popular in this Corps, and that all officers and men like him very much. He has not been very social with them, but still they like him for his bravery & gallantry. He loves his country and is willing to fight for it. He lost a leg [at Gettysburg] and is now willing to try the dangers of the battlefield again—willing to go into the thickest of the fight when a battle is raging. We have all seen this and cannot but respect the man.

French [15] is not very well liked and is somewhat displeased with the grate attentions paid to Genl. Sickles. Genl. French is an Army

14. Sgt. Marbaker commented: "So great was the enthusiasm, and so eager were the men to get near [Sickles], that it was with the greatest difficulty that he could make his way through the crowds that collected about him." *11th New Jersey*, 125. See also John D. Billings, *History of the Tenth Massachusetts Battery of Light Artillery* . . . (cited hereafter as Billings, *10th Massachusetts*) (Boston, 1909), 144–45; Floyd, *40th New York*, 208–9; Craft, *141st Pennsylvania*, 155.

15. Baltimore-born William H. French was a Regular Army man whose military star never shone brightly. An overfondness for liquor proved his ruin a month later at Mine Run. The men in the ranks were almost unanimous in their contempt of French. As one Massachusetts soldier described him: "Habitual drunkenness had covered his face wtih frightful blotches, and destroyed his control over some of his muscles; the cheeks twitched convulsively, while the eyes and mouth opened and closed in a comical manner which would have insured the fortunes of a clown." Blake, *Three Years in the Army of the Potomac*, 517, 530–31, 547–48; Goss, *Recollections of a Private*, 235; Theodore Lyman, *Meade's Headquarters, 1863–1865* (Boston, 1922), 10.

officer and Genl. Sickles is from the Volunteers. All these army officers are affraid of Sickles and look on him with more or less jealousy. There has always been too much of this in our army for the good of our country.

Owing to hard marching and bivouacking, and all being constantly on the alert, I have don nothing in the way of promotion. As soon as we are settled down again, I will attend to it. Genl. Carr told me last evening that he would write his letter in my favour and get Genl. Sickles's endorsement on it before the General leaves. The General is not going to stay and take command at this time. His leg is not yet entirely healed. I think I will have time to get all things fixed right. . . .

I am still rejoicing over the election returns. I have not heard any expression but that of joy over the result by anyone in the army. . . . One is either for our country or against it—only two parties. We understand it fully here and have but one party. Like the rest of us, Genl. Sickles has throwed all his politics aside. He goes rejoicing with us. . . .

Bristoe Station, Va., October 20th 1863

My dear Ellen,

Yesterday we moved up the railroad to this place. We have not seen the enemy yet. The cavalry have driven them back. Only a few shots have been fired in our front. We move this morning at 6 a.m. to Buckland Mills.[16] I don't know exactly where it is, but I think it is towards Warrenton. It is expected that we will have a fight. . . .

Our movements prevent me from geting my pay. You will have to use your interest money for your debts. You will get a big pile from me after a while. At the end of this month the Government will owe me over one thousand dollars. . . .

Catlett's Station, Va., October 21st 1863

My dear Ellen & family,

I did not write you yesterday for the want of time. Yesterday morning we left Bristoe Station and struck off to the right towards

16. Buckland Mills, more a name than a community, lay almost midway between Warrenton and Gainesville near the Warrenton Turnpike. See *Official Atlas,* Plate XLV, Map 6.

Warrenton. We arrived at Greenwich, the small English village, where we bivouacked on our retreat when we were pressed by the Rebels.[17] We staid there last night and this morning started for this place, where we arrived about the middle of the day. We are now going into camp this side of Cedar Run and right by the [Orange & Alexandria] Railroad.

We are now by the Cedar Run railroad bridge, distroyed by the Rebels, and quite near the old ground on which we camped in March, 1862, when I was under Genl. Kearny. And if you recall, it snowed so hard and we had such a terable hard time of it. Well, the Rebels have destroyed the railroad completely from Bristoe Station to the Rappahannock. There is no destruction below Bristoe; the cars are running to that place. It is five miles below here. The Rebs have torn up all the track, burnt and bent all the ties and rails by laying the rails on piles of ties set afire. When the rails were heated, the Rebels would bend them with their own might. Not a rail along here will do to lay again. Not a tie is left. All are burnt and the bridges are all destroyed.

The enemy evidently want to be left alone. I understand that we are repairing the railroad and are to remain here for awhile. But there is nothing positive. The Rebel drums are in our hearing. Whether they will fight us, or we fight them, remains to be seen. They have thus far retreated before us, after we hurried on them at Centreville. They have don their work of distruction and, I think, will go [back] across the Rappahannock.

I have laid out a nice camp for my Brigade, whether we stay or not. I am very tired—was General Officer of the Day last night and am in want of sleep. I hope to get a comfortable night's rest tonight.

You ask me to send you money. I would do so cheerfully, but I can't get to Washington or get a leave to enable me to get the money at the present time. But it will be all right soon. . . . On the last day of this month, we shall have muster. I shall have owing me about $1100, most of which you will get when I get my pay. . . .

Wednesday morning, October 22nd. The mail did not come last evening, so my letter was not sent. I had a good night's rest and feel comfortable this morning. All is quiet, nothing new. All of us wonder what we are going to do. Some say that we are going down [to Tennessee] to assist [the army under Gen. William S.] Rosecrans. There are numerous other rumours.

17. For an incident involving McAllister's regiment and a resident of Greenwich, see Marbaker, *11th New Jersey*, 126.

Our boy John [18] has become tired of army life and talks sometimes that he would like to quit and go home. I told him that he would not leave me now. I again told him that I would let him go home as soon as I could procure another servant. He then came to me and said for me not to procure one for a month or so. He is full of notions, and there is no stability about him. I wish you would see that colored man, Henry Steuart, that I told you about. He lives with the hotel keeper up near James Robeson's office. He wants to come. If Henry will come, I will send him a pass. John can't get away without my consent and a pass. But if he is not satisfied, he will do me no good. I have borne his expenses thus far; if he goes home, he will find that he will have to bear his own. It is poor encouragement for me to get him comfortably clothed when I don't know what he will do. I think he is affraid. However, he has had very easy times. He does not even have to attend to my horse. . . .

Catlett's Station, Va., October 23rd 1863

My dear Ellen & family,

Your very kind letter of the 21st just came to hand. There is nothing new here. Heavy work details are rebuilding the railroad. We will be here for some time.

I have this evening received Genl. Carr's letter to the President for my promotion.[19] It is a strong letter. Now I wish to get Major Genl. Humphrey's indorsement on it and also Genl. Sickles's. Humphreys is away at Warrenton, the Headquarters of the army. Genl. Carr says for me to go up there in person. I will try and get leave tomorrow. It is a long ride. I will then have to send the letter to Genl. Sickles. Some days may pass before I can get all this done. But I will hurry it up as soon as possible.

I have received a letter from Brother Nelson, who says that Governor Curtin was about to write a strong letter in my favour. No doubt it is now in the hands of Ex-Governor Newell. I wrote Newell tonight, and hope all will be right.

As I have been very busy today and am tired, and as it is now late, you will excuse me for not writing more tonight.

Love to all my family and a whole bushel to yourself. . . .

18. John Nixon was McAllister's camp servant.
19. Carr's letter to Lincoln, dated Oct. 23, 1863, described McAllister as "a cool, intrepid and skillful commander." Baldwin MS., 59.

Catlett's Station, Va., October 25th 1863

My dear Ellen,

I wrote you last evening and said that we had marching orders and that I did not expect to sleep any last night. We did not march, but the moving around of orderlies and orders kept me from the pleasure of good sound sleep. The Brigade that was to have gone out on a reconnaissance [to Bealeton] did not leave untill this morning. We are not called on to go out and support it. But a telegram from Army Headquarters this evening says that the enemy are now moving around on our right in order to flank us, and that our Division, the only troops on this side of Cedar Run, must fall back on the Catlett's Station side, take a strong position, and prepare to defend ourselves. We are now on the south bank of the creek, and our orders are to go across to the other side, about half a mile from our present position. We were to brake camp and move over tonight, but the order was countermanded and we wait till morning. Genl. Prince [20] told me this evening that everything tended towards a battle at or near this place. . . .

The weather is quite cold. Yesterday I had a chimney built to my tent and I am very comfortable. I am now sitting beside a nice cozy fire; and if I had you and my family here, I would be real happy. . . . My Headquarters are nicely situated in what was once a fine yard of trees and shrubery—in front of what was then a very fine house but is now a mass of ruins. The property belonged to a Dr. Shoemaker.[21] The house cost nine or ten thousand dollars to build. Several thousand dollars worth of furniture was in it at the time of its distruction. The 11th Corps camped near this place last summer, and it is said that some of them fired the building. It is just like them. It was a very beautiful place but a desolation now. The railroad crosses the creek quite near here. The bridge as well as the railroad is completely destroyed.

20. Brig. Gen. Henry Prince then commanded the 2nd Division, III Corps. A Maine-born professional soldier who had fought with some distinction in the Mexican and Seminole wars, he entered the Civil War from a desk job. "His long service in the pay[master's] division seems to have unfitted him for fighting," one soldier believed. Prince was never a conspicuous figure on or off Civil War battlefields. He retired from the army in 1879 and committed suicide at the age of seventy-one. Alfred S. Roe, *The Fifth Regiment, Massachusetts Volunteer Infantry* . . . (Boston, 1911), 216; *The Union Army* (Madison, Wis., 1908), VIII, 205.

21. McAllister was obviously referring to a Dr. Shumate, whose estate lay a mile south of Catlett's Station in the apex formed by Cedar Run and the Orange & Alexandria Railroad. *Official Atlas,* Plate XLV, Map 6. "The surrounding inhabitants," Sgt. Marbaker noted, "professed to be pure and unadulterated Unionists. . . . However, I think their Unionism lasted only so long as the boys in blue remained with them." *11th New Jersey,* 127–28.

The desolation of war is on every hand. *The whole country is a barren waste.* There are but few inhabitants remaining, and they are in an almost starving condition. How the Rebels can carry on the war longer is a mystery to me. . . .

Catlett's Station, Va., October 27th 1863

My dear Ellen,

After the close of a hard day's work as General Corps Officer of the Day—altering, fixing and establishing picket lines—I came into camp very tired. But before I retire for rest, I will write you a few lines. For it is pleasant for me to communicate with you, notwithstanding the fact that I have not had a good night's sleep for several nights. Rumours of the enemy's approach caused us to be continually on the alert and very often under arms. Last night we expected to fight a battle this morning and prepared for it. But the enemy stoped their advance, took the back track, and have gone further from our flanks to try the flanking system again. Yesterday their cavalry, with artillery and two brigades of [General Richard S.] Ewell's Corps, advanced on Bealeton and drove back our pickets and cavalry.[22] We expected them to reach here by morning. But their progress was stoped by our troops before they reached here. We could have given them a warm reception, had they come down on us. . . .

Well, I get along finely with my Brigade. I can handle it first rate. It is larger than either of the other two brigades. We have three brigades in the Division. Genl. Mott commands the Jersey Brigade,[23] Col. Brewster the Excelsior Brigade,[24] and your Husband the 1st Brigade. This makes up the 2nd Division, which is commanded by Genl. Prince. I like Genl. Prince very much. He is a very pleasant officer and seems very well disposed and kindly towards me. . . .

Catlett's Station, Va., October 29th 1863

My dear Ellen,

The storm cloud of battle has for the present passed away. The enemy have retreated across the Rappahannock, and all is quiet in our

22. At this time the Confederate army was playing a game of watching and waiting. Ewell's men were then engaged in nothing more exciting than the construction of winter quarters.

23. Mott's brigade then consisted of the 5th, 6th, 7th, and 8th New Jersey, plus the 115th Pennsylvania. *OR*, Vol. XXIX, Pt. 1, p. 220.

24. Col. William R. Brewster's Excelsior Brigade contained the 70th, 71st, 72nd, 73rd, 74th, and 120th New York. *Ibid.*

immediate front. Whether we are to follow or remain is a question for time to tell. We are hard at work on the railroad and will soon have it completed to this place. It is then most likely that we will move forward, but I don't know.

Inclosed you will find Maj. Herbert's letter.[25] Now we will see what Ex-Governor Newell says. Yesterday I called on Genl. Humphreys. He informed me that he had already recommended me [for promotion] in the regular way. In his official report he mentions me for promotion with others. He said it would not be doing justice to them to doubly recommend me in this way, as he has not don so with them. After talking over the matter, he asked me to leave the papers. He said he would think about it. I can well see his position. But I hope that he will depart from the rule in this case and indorse my papers. If he don't, the recommendation he has already given me will do admirably. . . .

I have not had time to write to the children, and they don't seem to have much time to write to me. . . .

Warrenton, Va., October 31st 1863

My dear Ellen,

I have but this half-sheet left of my home paper, and it is pretty well bloted. I wrote you yesterday morning that we were about to move. We came here and encamped in line of battle. The country is full of gurillas; our object is to protect the railroad builders and make [Warrenton] Junction a place to receive supplies. The branch line is not disturbed up to Warrenton. We will soon have the main line completed to the Junction. I do not know what they intend to do further.

Last evening I received your letter of the 28th. I will not pay Henry Steuart $20 a month plus expenses. Let him go about his business. James Pitzer, the Doctor's man, says that he will come. He lives in your town and wants a place here. . . . It is very hard to get servants in the army. They are afraid of geting hurt, and yet I only know of one that was hurt or wounded. That was at Chancellorsville. . . .

25. Herbert's letter of Oct. 23, 1863, is in the McAllister Papers.

Warrenton, Va., November 1st 1863

My dear Ellen,

Last evening I received your nice letter of the 29th. I find that your letters come through in two days, not over three. How soon do you get mine?

We are still here, encamped in line of battle. But as yet all is quiet. The guerillas are prowling around us.

I was very much amused last evening. I rode over to Division Headquarters. While talking to Genl. Prince, a prisoner was brought in. His story was amusing. The evening of the day we left Catlett's Station, our pickets were in part drawn around Weaversville. Three ambulance drivers went out to hunt for persimmons. While they were thus engaged, a party of Guerillas came on them and captured them. One of their number, a Dutchman by the way, was ordered to take these Yankees over to the Rebel lines. He started with his precious charges—he on horseback and they, of course, on foot. It was night. After travelling awhile, our boys complained that they were very tired. They insisted on resting all night. The Reb, wishing to be very kind to our boys, agreed to it and ordered supper at a farm house for all. He said this cost him seven dollars. They slept together in a barn.

The next morning, they started again on their journey. The Reb had a very poor horse. On coming to a fence, he ordered the Yankees to take down the fence. They obeyed; but each one took a rail, surrounded horse and rider, took his pistol, and ordered him to surrender. His horse was so poor that he could not ride fast, and the Yankees had his pistol.

He was just brought into our lines, and I heard him telling this story, to the amusement of all present. It was laughable to hear him tell all about it. He said it was a daring thing for them to do—a heroic act. He seemed to take it well and was in fine humor.

He told us that at Dumfries he had bought a lady's hoop skirt and some calico for his lady love. He had tied them to his horse. The Yankee boys took these and dressed his old horse all up to nature. The fellow really liked the girl, for he felt disappointed that she would not get the longed-for articles. Major Hamlin (son of Vice-President Hamlin),[26] being present, said, "Never mind, sir, I will send these articles under a flag of truce and she will get them yet."

But the man said he preferred not to tell her name.

The whole thing was truly a rich one. You may well imagine how we all enjoyed it. . . .

26. Maj. Charles Hamlin was Gen. Prince's assistant adjutant general.

Warrenton, Va., November 2nd 1863

My dear Ellen & family,

I was Corps Officer of the Day today and had a hard ride along a long line of pickets. I feel very tired. But before retiring I will write you a few lines.

Though we have no orders yet, everything indicates a move on our part forward towards the enemy. The Pontoons came up today, which indicates crossing the river. The enemy holds all the fords on the Rappahannock River, and we will have to drive them away before we cross. Of course, I don't know the plan of campaign; but I have no doubt of our moving. We may move any day, perhaps tomorrow. You will hear of it soon, if it takes place.

I have nothing new to tell you about. The cause of seniority between Col. Blaisdell and myself will no doubt be decided soon. He may gain it; but, according to orders, I don't see how he can. Rank takes place by muster and not by date of commission. I was mustered in four months before he was, and his commission is about four months older than mine. Well, I will be satisfied, no matter how it turns. It will have no bearing on my appointment. . . .

Warrenton, Va., November 3rd 1863

My dear Ellen & family,

I wrote you last night that I thought we would move forward soon, perhaps today or tomorrow. We have not started yet, but still think we will cross the Rappahannock again and give battle to the enemy, if they can be found. They are guarding the fords, but what force they have I am unable to say.

I am still in command of the Brigade. It is thought that I will remain in command, unless Col. Blaisdell can get an order to be mustered back. This is very doubtful; and even if he does, it will take a considerable time for him to do it, as it must go back to the War Department. He never dreamed of my claiming the right of seniority, and he thinks it strange that I have been so short a time in this Brigade and yet rank him. But this is law and he can't get out of it. If he gets a decision in his favour, I will submit cheerfully. I have not seen him, nor have I had any conversation with him on the subject. It is a matter for the higher courts to decide and not for us. So there will be no hard feeling on the subject.

[354] ⚔ THE McALLISTER LETTERS

Warrenton, Va., November 6th 1863

My dear Ellen,

... I have had a good night's sleep and feel rested. I am Corps Officer of the Day again. One of our Brigades has been detached to the railroad below to guard it, so Genl. Mott and I have to be Corps Field Officer of the Day every other day for the whole Division, including Col. Brewster's brigade, which makes it hard for us. Genl. Mott was on yesterday. I was in the day before and now go on today. Then Carr's Division have it for the next three days, &c.

I spent the evening with Genl. Carr. He is close to me and was very pleasant. He desired to be remembered to you.

Today I hope to hear good, cheering news of the election in your state and New York. If the ladies of New Jersey had been permited to vote, I would have been assured that all would be right. The Copperheads would hide their heads. ...

Warrenton, Va., November 6th 1863

My dear Ellen,

I have just returned from prayer meeting. We have a prayer meeting every night when we are not on the march. I attend as often as I can. We had a very nice little meeting tonight. ...

We are expecting to move forward any hour; we may get orders to move before morning. I don't know what the plan is, but time will develop it.

Our army was never more healthy than it is now. I have seen but one funeral since I came out this last time, and that death was caused by the accidental discharge of a gun.

All the Elections went right but in our state.[27] It stands alone against her sons in camp and on the battlefields—ninety-nine out of a hundred of whom are directly against them in what they call politicks. But we say to those against the interests of their country and ours: let them come here and help to put down this rebellion. Then they will be right on this question. ...

27. In the state elections of that year Democrats managed to retain their majority in New Jersey. Yet, one political observer noted, "even in that benighted region Copperheadism loses ground." Strong, *Diary of the Civil War*, 368.

Brandy Station, Va., November 9th 1863

My dear Ellen,

It is now 8 p.m. I wrote you a few lines this morning in a hurry, supposing that we would move forward. But we had no orders to move until late this afternoon, when we got under arms. But it was countermanded. We formed line of battle on this ground, pitched our tents in rear of the line of muskets, and are once more in camp ready to defend ourselves if attacked. Our cavalry have been up near Culpeper, five miles from here. . . .

We have taken in all about 2,000 prisoners and sent them to the rear.[28] Our Corps crossed at Kelly's Ford and the 6th Corps crossed up at Rappahannock Station, three miles above us. They had a harder fight than we had, lost more men and took more prisoners than our Corps. We lost but one dozen men and took 300 prisoners. My Division was not engaged at all. It only acted as a support to the 1st Division. The old Jersey 1st Brigade, commanded by Genl. Torbert, was not engaged with the 6th Corps. I saw some members of it the next day. It was expected that we would all be engaged the next morning. The 3rd Division, Genl. Carr's, was thrown in line of battle to commence the attack. My Brigade was in the second line to support him. But the enemy left. Carr moved over here and we followed up, together with the 6th Corps in our rear. Genl. Carr, I understand, lost a few men but not many. This afternoon our Division was to advance and support the cavalry. But as I said before, the order was countermanded and we are here yet. How long we shall remain I can't tell.

The Rebels made grate preparations for winter quarters for miles along the road. They have been puting up log huts, large and small. There must have been quite a force of them. They left in a grate hurry, leaving some trunks behind as well as bread baking on their fires in some places. . . .

Dear Ellen, this, the 9th day of November, is the aniversary of our marriage. What a pleasant time we have had during our married life. It is pleasant to look back on it and to live again in immagination many of the scenes through which we have passed. May God continue to protect and prosper us in times to come as he has don in the past. . . .

28. On the afternoon of Nov. 7 at Kelly's Ford, two Federal brigades assaulted the lines of Confederate Gen. Jubal Early. The charge caught the Confederates by surprise. Over 1,700 of their number were captured. The Federals suffered 461 losses, 12 of which were from McAllister's brigade. *OR,* Vol. XXIX, Pt. 1, pp. 558–61, 575; Wainwright, *Diary of Battle,* 298–301.

Brandy Station, Va., November 10th 1863

My dear Ellen & family,

... I told you that if the [servants] had not started yet to keep them back until I wrote you for them to come on. They can now come on without any danger. The railroad is buisey, and they can come on as far as the cars run and then follow the road up to this place. There are always wagons coming up; they can follow one of the wagon trains. I don't know but think we will remain here for some days at least. So the sooner they come, the better. The railroad will soon be finished to the Rappahannock River. On this side it has not been distroyed, so we will soon have the cars runing up here. It is five miles to the river at Rappahannock Station, where the battle was fought on Saturday last by the 6th Corps. Our Corps fought at Kelly's Ford, several miles below, at the same time. I wrote you the facts concerning the action at both fords.

The weather is now quite cold. This morning the Blue Ridge [Mountains] were covered with snow. The cold winds of the north chill us all very much. Our men have shelter tents and large camp fires and are more comfortable than one who has not been in the army would suppose. However, on our marches we often lay down on the cold ground without any tents. If we have a blanket, we are very fortunent. Yet we sleep soundly and raise up in the morning and continue our march. The wagons are often in the rear. Officers' tents and blankets are with them. I have a wall tent and a nice new stove in it and am now very comfortable. But on a march we cannot have these all the time. Plenty of men wait on me. When we stop for a day or two, we are very comfortable. The men build sword chimneys and are much more comfortable than you would imagine. Tell them to fix up comfortable and they will soon do it. ...

Brandy Station, Va., November 11th 1863

My dear Ellen & family,

... Today we changed camp and are now about three fourths of a mile from the Station. All are in line of battle and are camping this way—ready at a moment's warning to receive the Rebels. Our campaign ground is much better than the one we left; it is on higher and somewhat drier ground. Our line runs right through the new and unfinished Rebel camp that was prepared and preparing for the winter. It has nice log huts, clapboard roofs, and good chimneys. One half of them were unfinished and, of course, cleaner than they would otherwise be. I learn that there were two divisions camping here. These preparations for the winter were very extensive. They never dreamed that Yankees could build railroads so rapidly and dusturb their quiet repose before they got comfortably fixed in their new quarters. Our rapid advance must have been a greate surprise to them, from the manner in which they have left everything.

We now hold Culpeper and Pony Mountain that we were under arms to go out and take last Monday evening. But as I told you before, the order was countermanded. The next day the cavalry advanced and drove the enemy out of Culpeper and then found that they had left Pony Mountain. I learned today the reason we did not go. If there were infantry on that mountain, they could repel a large force and beat us back with greate loss. The mountain is so steep that men could hardly get up in daylight, let alone after nightfall. This mountain is about a mile beyond Culpeper and a little to the left. . . . But we have it now without fighting for it.

John Minor Botts [29] lives close by. A part of our camp is on his land. I will most likely be there tomorrow, as I am Corps Officer of the Day. The Rebels destroyed his property at a terable rate. Last evening we received orders from Genl. French that we must not destroy any of his fences, &c. You know that he was again taken prisoner after our army retreated and was put in prison. His daughter went with him. He is now paroled and at home. You cannot immagine the distress of the inhabitants in this part of Virginia. *Starvation stares them in the face.* Mr. Botts says that you cannot get a barrel of flour in Richmond for love or money. People here are actually lean and poor for the want of something to eat. A man told one of our officers yesterday that two of his children died of starvation. But why don't the Rebel masses rise up and outlaw the Rebel Government, hang the leaders, and put an end to this terable strugle? If we can hold our lines east and west, the whole so-called Southern Confederacy must cave in before the next harvest. The want of bread will do more towards puting down the rebellion than the bayonet.

29. The "tough and terrified" John Minor Botts, who proved to be "a hot potato" for Confederate officials, had been a distinguished Whig legislator and congressman from Virginia. In the 1860–61 secession crisis Botts was an outspoken Unionist. This led to his brief imprisonment shortly after Virginia left the Union. Upon his release Botts returned to his farm, five miles north of Culpeper, and for the remainder of the war openly defied all Confederate authority. Lyman, *Meade's Headquarters,* 46; Billings, *10th Massachusetts Battery,* 189–90; Jesse B. Young, *What a Boy Saw in the Army* (New York, 1894), 376–79; Miller, *Photographic History,* VII, 195, 197.

[358] ✗ THE McALLISTER LETTERS

When we crossed Kelly's Ford, the Rebel soldiers came down towards the ford, not knowing what was going on. They came to see about geting their rations and fell into our hands. They said they had had nothing to eat for two days. I never saw prisoners so pleased with their situation as those that we took—three squads, hundreds together, all grinning from ear to ear, aparently with joy in their new situation. (Only the officers looked sullen.) One new conscripted officer expressed satisfaction. On our rought this way, I was told of a colored woman who had her arm taken off by a cannon ball passing through the house. She was sitting on a wood pile, laughing and rejoicing at our approach. I was called on by a doctor to go into a house and see a Rebel who had been wounded in this battle. But it was too late; he soon died. On the march at the head of my Brigade, I saw a dead Rebel. The ball had passed through his head. He lay unburied, with no one to care for him. I thought of his friends—mother, sister, wife. But alas, such is the fate of war.

At the crossing one of our wounded men was strugling in the water. A Rebel surgeon jumped in and saved him. An officer of our army, looking at the cold and wet Rebel prisoners passing by, steped forward and gave one of them a drink of liquor from his canteen. While this officer was performing this very act, a rifle ball passed through his abdomen and gave him his death wound. One of our gunners pulled his finger off the touch hole too soon. The explosion took place before the rammer was pulled out, took off the arms of the man that was working the rammer, and blew his eyes out. These are a few incidents of this campaign that I thought might interest you. There are many more, but I cannot think of them now. . . .

I learn that the paymasters are coming. This is good news, of course. . . .

Brandy Station, Va., November 12th 1863

My dear Ellen,

. . . I called on John Minor Botts today. He lives in good style. He very pleasantly introduced me to his two daughters, one of whom has just got out of a sick bed. She had typhoid fever and looks miserable. In fact, both of them look badly. No wonder, with cannon balls whizing around them at diffirent times. This land has been the scene of some three or four battles while they have been living here. We are now protecting the family and their property. They are strong for the Union and have been treated so badly by the Rebels. Mr. Botts read us a strong letter that he wrote and sent to the Richmond *Examiner* [30] for publication. But I do not think that he will get it published. They will not dare do it. More on the subject again. . . .

Brandy Station, Va., November 13th 1863

My dear Ellen,

The Paymaster [Major Moses F. Webb] is here and paying. Col. Schoonover has just got a leave for six days. He will leave here on Sabbath morning and will arive in Belvidere by the Monday noon train. . . .

I have just got a check, payable to you, on the United States Treasury for $800. Col. Schoonover will hand it to you. You can get it cashed at the Belvidere bank, or use it to buy United States Stock. . . . I will also send you my watch, which I wish you to keep wound up. Not under any condition let it run down or stop, as it spoils a watch to have it in this way. I expect my new one any day.

It is now rumoured that we will move in a few days. It is thought we will on Tuesday move forward to the Rapidan, or further. Things look like it now. There will be no winter quarters for us this winter. The weather is very fine; the cold has passed away for the present. But we must soon look for a change for both wet and cold. . . .

Brandy Station, Va., November 15th 1863

My dear Ellen,

I wrote you on Friday night that Col. Schoonover had a leave and would bring your money to you. He started yesterday morning, and I telegraphed you that he would be at your place on Monday noon and for you to meet him. . . .

This morning heavy cannonading was heard towards the Rapidan. I do not know the cause of it. Immediately afterwards, an order came from Corps Headquarters to be ready to march at a moment's notice. We have made all the preparation we can and we may start very soon. I am now satisfied that we will move forward. In any event, our stay here will be but short. . . .

30. Under the editorship of the caustic and anti-Davis journalist, Edward A. Pollard, the Richmond *Examiner* became to one contemporary "the Ishmael of the Southern press, so far as it is against everybody." Clement A. Eaton, *A History of the Southern Confederacy* (New York, 1954), 229.

Sunday night [November 15]. Before retiring, I thought I would inform you that we have not moved today. The cannonading ceased, and all day has been very quiet. I do not know the cause of it. We have just received orders to appear on review tomorrow. Some Britchish officers are going to look at us. So I suppose that we will not move tomorrow. But everything indicates a move very soon. We have had a good deal of rain and the roads are bad. . . .

Brandy Station, Va., November 16th 1863

My dear Ellen,

It is now very late; but before I retire to rest, I must write you a few lines. . . .

We are still here and talk of moving tomorrow. But we have no orders to that effect yet. Cars came up today to this place and can run clear up to Culpeper. The Yankees have rebuilt the road much sooner than the Rebels thought we could.

We had a review today of our Corps in honor of four Englishmen.[31] There was a Colonel, two Captains, and a Lord. The Lord is a very small man, boyish in appearance. They seemed highly pleased with our troops and said we look much better than their troops did during the Crimean War. My Brigade looked very well. Genl. Carr complimented me highly and said that he had never seen it look better than it did today. This was quite a compliment, was it not?

You ask me about Col. Blaisdell and if I have got ahead of him. He was and is very much disappointed. He sent a paper up through all these headquarters, which I suppose has gone to the War Department, asking to be mustered back. I have not heard the result yet. It may be that he will be successful. If so, I am satisfied. But if the War Department does muster him back, they will be breaking their own orders and opening the door for hundreds of others doing the same thing. It will be a dangerous precedent for them. I make no efforts, let them do as they please, and will abide by the decission.

31. The "four gents, much braided and striped," were Capts. Peele and Stephenson, Lt. Col. Earle, and Lord Castle Cuff. "The noble Lord," one of Meade's staff observed, "is, I say, about sixteen, and, with his cap off, is as perfect a specimen of a Pat as you ever saw; but he is manly, and not so green as many I have seen double his age." All four visitors were members of the English Guardsmen. Lyman, *Meade's Headquarters,* 49; Meade, *Letters of George G. Meade,* II, 156. See also George A. Hussey and William Todd, *History of the Ninth Regiment, N.Y.S.M.* . . . (cited hereafter as Hussey and Todd, *9th N.Y.S.M.*) (New York, 1889), 305; Frank Rauscher, *Music on the March, 1862–1865* (Philadelphia, 1892), 135.

I sent Genl. Carr's letter of recommendation to Genl. Sickles to get his endorsement on it, but as yet I have not received it back. I am looking for it daily. I will forward it and the other papers to Ex-Governor Newell, who will take them in person to the President. . . .

I will have to buy another horse, which will take some money. But I have been very fortunate in keeping my horse so long. Charley is still a good horse. Few horses have stood so much as he has. . . .

Headquarters, 11th Regt., N.J.V.
Brandy Station, Va., November 17th 1863

My dear Ellen,

You can see by this letter that I am no longer commanding the Brigade. Col. Blaisdell got an order from the War Department to muster him back to the date of his commission—prior to February, 1862. So he has got it at last and ranks me. Well, I am satisfied. I will not have quite so much responsibility and, as I said before, it will not effect my appointment in the least. So it goes. I had a very pleasant time while in command. I have don more marching in this time than the Brigade has ever don before in the same time. This morning Genl. Prince complimented me very highly for the manner in which I have handled the Brigade. He expressed sorrow for the necessity of my leaving it. But such is rank. No matter what a man's character is; if he outranks me, I must obey him.

There is nothing new here. We are still expecting every day to move. . . .

Brandy Station, Va., November 20th 1863

My dear family,

I thought it best to let John [Nixon] go before we moved from the railway. If he were to go with us, he might have a long way to travel and would stand a good chance of being picked up by Guerillas. John has been doing very nicely lately. He has kept my clothes nicely washed and everything in good order. If he tries, he can do well. You had better get him in at Miss Bacon's. He promises me that he will stay nights at the next good place. I think he will suit her very well and would not be a high priced servant. His coming here has don him good.

Preparations are all made for a move. Last evening the old Pontoons arrived. This looks like crossing the Rapidan. If so, we will have hard fighting. There are natural defenses, independent of the earthworks, and they are very strong.

I hope Col. Schoonover and my boys will arrive in time before we move. . . .

Brandy Station, Va., November 22nd 1863

My dear Ellen,

Col. Schoonover and the three servants arrived here safely last evening amid a storm of rain. It rained all day yesterday. It is now clear on this Sabbath morning.

As I have yet but one horse, I think I will arrange it for Morris White to go to Capt. Lloyd until I may want him. At present I can do very well with one servant.

The provisions have all arrived safely, and I tell you that they will come in good. Today we will have the chickens for dinner. I tell you that is something real nice for us to have out here. The bread and cakes will be fine; the dried fruit will be the best of all, for we can keep it for a longer time. I am very much obliged for all the provisions. . . .

We are still here and I can't see how we can move now until the roads get much better. We are liable to stick fast in the mud as we did last winter.

Inclosed you will find a letter from John Nixon. It came here by mail last night. I don't suppose that it is of any account. I also received one from his father, in which he expressed himself uneasy about his son's health. John never looked half so well in his life and never had better health. His father is a poor old drunken fool, and John is nothing but a baby. However, I think he may now do better. If Miss Bacon takes him and is real strict with him, he may do very well. I hope so, at least. John left here with more than thirty dollars in his pocket—more money than he ever had in his life, and more than he will have again. He fell out with the bread and butter when he left here. He made twelve or more dollars by washing clothes here. . . .

Brandy Station, Va., November 23rd 1863

My dear Ellen,

We move in the morning, though we have not yet the written orders. Genl. Prince told me that we would and I have no doubt but that we will. It is now near 8 p.m. and I have returned from our usual prayer meeting. Orders generally come in very late—from 10 to 12 and 1 o'clock at night—so we will get the order yet. No one appears to know when or in what direction we will move.

Inclosed you will find a letter from Capt. Stagg.[32] I have sent him a letter of recommendation. You will mearly file the letter.

Tell Sarah that I will write her as soon as I have time—on the march, if possible. It may be some time before you receive any letters from me. . . .

Brandy Station, Va., November 26th 1863
5 a.m., Thanksgiving morning

My dear daughter & niece,

I wrote to Sarah last night and suppose that your mother and aunt is there. . . . We have orders to move in an hour (at 6 a.m.). We are going to cross the Rapidan River, and we expect to have a battle in crossing. Our Brigade is in the advance and will be in the fight first. I hope we will be successful and cross without much loss of life; but the natural defenses there are said to be strong and independent of the earthworks. I can't write you a [long] letter. I must get ready to go. God bless you all. . . .

Brandy Station, Va., December 3rd 1863

My Dear Ellen,

We have just returned from a hard campaign and battle.[33] As you are aware, we broke camp on Thanksgiving Day and started for Jacob's Ford on the Rapidan. On arriving there, my Regiment was selected to cross in the first boats, into which our men jumped with a will. I was among the first to land on the opposite shore. We soon formed, deployed as a skirmish line, and up the steep bank we went. The Rebel cavalry fired a few shots and disappeared. Soon our Corps was all over, and on we went. Again the Rebels fired;[34] again they

---

32. Theodore Stagg resigned Dec. 28, 1862, as captain of Co. G. *N.J. Record,* I, 567.

33. McAllister's report of the Mine Run Campaign is in *OR,* Vol. XXIX, Pt. 1, pp. 768–69.

34. Pvt. A. B. Searing of the 11th New Jersey claimed to have been witness to an unusual scene at this time. "We had advanced about four miles when, from a mill in front, our column was again fired upon. The firing resulted in the wounding of a dog. As it came yelping to the rear, it was followed by the doctors and other non-combatants, who no doubt—like the dog—thought the rear the safest place." Marbaker, *11th New Jersey,* 132.

fled. Night coming on, we lost our way. Coming to a creek and a mill, we halted and found ourselves near the Rebel works. So we turned back for about a mile and bivouacked for the night.

Early the next morning, Friday the 27th, we started early and again met the enemy in strong force. Skirmishers were thrown out. I was ordered to support them, which I did. Then I was again ordered to relieve Col. [Napoleon] McLaughlin, he being out of ammunition. I did so and kept up a brisk fire for one and a half hours, driving the Rebel picket line back. The enemy tried to turn our flanks, but regiments were sent in to the right and left of me. The 26th Pennsylvania was on my left and the 5th Excelsior [74th New York] on my right. The Rebels advanced towards our lines. The 26th Pennsylvania gave way, carrying with it a few of our men. We soon brought the latter back into their place and helped to rally the Pennsylvanians, who came up to the work in good earnest.

The battle now raged furiously all along the line. Only a part of our Corps was engaged.[35] My men fought bravely. I was in fine spirits, hoping that success would crown our efforts.

The enemy advanced rapidly. The 26th Pennsylvania on my left and the 5th Excelsior Regiment on my right gave way. I beheld their flight with astonishment and saw the danger I was in with my Regiment. New York on one side of me and Pennsylvania on the other, both giving away at the same time, left me standing there with my little band of heroes, undaunted and unmoved by the advancing foe. Yes, there stood the 11th New Jersey in the midst of this storm of battle, ready and willing, by the help of God, to do their duty even to the death.[36]

We held the enemy in check in our front, but it was impossible for us to prevent them from flanking us. All the line had now given way, but still our men were standing firm and fighting splendidly. The Rebels advanced on my flanks; three minutes more and my regiment and I would have been prisoners. I then ordered a retreat. We fell

---

35. Gen. French's tardiness in getting the whole of the III Corps into position was the critical factor in the battle. That he was intoxicated during the engagement is rather conclusive; and when he finally rode into the hard-pressed lines, he was greeted with such loud catcalls as "Tap old whiskey barrel with a bullet!" Goss, *Recollections of a Private,* 247.

36. During the fighting two members of the 11th New Jersey started to the rear with a comrade on a stretcher. Suddenly a cannon ball whizzed overhead and exploded in the ground nearby. The stretcher-bearers promptly dropped their load and scurried for safety. "Imagine their surprise," the regimental historian wrote, "when the wounded man, who previously could not walk, hastily jumped up and outstripped them in the race." Marbaker. *11th New Jersey,* 137.

back to the battery, which opened upon them and drove them back.[37] [David B.] Birney's Division, with a part of the 6th Corps, were now ordered in. We soon regained the lost ground. Night ended the contest in our favour. Before morning the enemy were gone.

In this battle we lost 6 men killed on the spot, 20 wounded, and some 3–4 missing, out of 150 who went into the action. The enemy were so close on us before we retreated that they caught hold of one or two of our men and took them prisoners.

I forgot to tell you that we have had new colors presented to us by the State. This is the first battle that they were in. Johnson,[38] who carries the American flag, was determined to show the Star-Spangled Banner to the best advantage before the enemy. When retreating, and on reaching the open space at the crossroads, he unfurled the flag to the breeze and waved it right and left in the very face of the enemy. He is one of the bravest men I have ever seen. John Barry[39] has just come in to see me. He says that he was the first to jump from the boat to the shore and that he held the boat till we all got out. He wants me to mention him. He is a brave boy. My Regiment has fully sustained its reputation for gallantry and is favorably known all through the Army of the Potomac as a fighting regiment.

The morning of [Saturday] the 28th dawned with our Regiment on the picket lines. We had to relieve the 6th Corps. The night had just passed away in silence and sadness—silence because the roar of musketry had ceased, and sadness at the thought of our brave men who had fallen in battle and were now no more. The night was bitter cold. The north wind and cold frost made us suffer. Those who had no blankets suffered terably. I tried to sleep with only my overcoat, not having any blanket, but soon awoke almost frozen. After we moved into the woods, it was somewhat warmer. Those who were not on duty soon fell asleep.

I sent out a party to hunt for our dead and wounded. They brought in some poor fellows almost frozen. One of them soon died. Another had a leg amputated but is still living and will recover. In the morning the brigade pioneer corps went out and buried the dead.

---

37. At this point French "was watching with anxiety the progress of the strife. His eyes snapping fiercely (for which he was particularly noted), he would occasionally ejaculate to [an] artillery officer: 'Now then, double shot 'em! Double shot 'em!'" Osceola Lewis, *History of the One Hundred and Thirty-eighth Regiment, Pennsylvania Volunteer Infantry* (Norristown, Pa., 1866), 56.

38. Probably Cpl. George H. Johnson of Co. A, who was promoted to sergeant shortly after the campaign. *N.J. Record,* I, 543.

39. McAllister did not mention in his report Pvt. John Barry of Co. C, who was later killed in action during the siege of Petersburg.

Arms and accoutrements were gathered up and some destroyed, after which we resumed our march by another road and turned our backs on this sacred spot—a place long to be remembered by our Regiment, Brigade, Division, and Corps. For there was a scene of deadly strife, and there rolled the tide of battle for one whole day, with doubts and fears as to who would be successful. The battle continued long after dark. Finally the enemy were repulsed and we were masters of the field.

The enemy tried to prevent us from forming a junction with Genl. [Gouverneur K.] Warren. Had we not missed the road we could have formed the junction that morning, instead of fighting all day. Where the fault lies I know not. It is one more battle for the 11th New Jersey, one more record for these brave men. New honors cluster round her standard. A few of our men still survive the shock of battle to tell the stories of the brave who have given their lives as a sacrifice on the altar of their country—who have so often with them in the dark hour of battle rallied around the flag, in obedience to orders, and pressed once more the enemy's advancing columns, to do or die for their country.

Our Regiment, in the year going out, has fought five battles. Some of them are the hardest of the war. We have here for duty only about 80 men to carry muskets. Many have fallen in battle, many have been wounded, others have died, and some have been discharged.

We moved towards Robertson's Tavern. On reaching it we found that we had made a junction with Genl. Warren. He was pushing the enemy. We marched on up the turnpike and stoped till evening. We resumed the march, continued for some two miles more, then stoped and bivouacked for the night.

November 29 [Sunday]. We were up early and continued our march towards the plank road in the direction of Orange Court House. Our Division alone was to support Genl. Warren, who was to advance on the plank road. We were to prevent him from being flanked. The Brigade was now under my command, as Col. Blaisdell was Corps Officer of the Day. Warren advanced up to the enemy's works, and we all halted for the night. In the middle of the night we were awakened and I was ordered to report to Genl. Warren on the plank road at 4 a.m. The Division was delayed some on account of distributing rations and ammunition. But before day we were on the move and soon found ourselves in line of battle, right in front of the enemy's fortifications.

I was officially told to prepare for a charge, that we were about to make a grand charge with 30,000 men on a line three miles in length. The ball would open on the right and continue to the left. The artillery on the right would open at 7 a.m. and we would make the charge at 8 a.m. The morning was bitter cold. No fires were alowed. We had to walk about to keep ourselves warm.

Our line was along a ravine, out of sight of the enemy's works. But officers and men, at the risk of being fired at, would go up to the crest of the hill to take a look at the fortifications. Our pickets occupied this hill and often had brisk firing. To make the charge, we had to pass over this hill, down into a ravine, over a fence, through a marsh, up another hill, and then over their works. The more we looked at it, the more difficult the task seemed to be—and the more doubtful the result. We had no artillery to bear on this part of the line, while the enemy had their batteries placed to enfilade, or crossfire, and rake us in all directions. If we once started, we could not stop; for it would be our distruction. To fail would be our ruin. What we saw were only the outer works. Timber was felled in every direction in the rear. If we drove them from the first, we would still have to fight them in the last.

We had three lines of battle. My Brigade as usual was on the first line and would have to bear the heavy brunt and receive the terable fire prepared for us. Brig. Genl. [Alexander S.] Webb of the 2nd Corps was on my left. Genl. Carr with his division was on my right. The Excelsior Brigade, as well as Genl. Mott's Jersey Brigade, were in my rear. There we stood, with anxiety, waiting for the signal to move forward to the charge.

Notwithstanding the order for the men not to go over the hill and be seen by the enemy, many went to take a peep at the works that they were about to storm. Of course they debated in their own minds and with their comrades the chances pro and con relative to our taking the works. The officers nearly all took a view of them. For some time I lingered on the crest of the hill with a glass, looking right and left, discovering here a battery, there a redoubt, yonder an abattis, here a railroad cut, there an embankment—all making a strong line of defence. The road would be a hard one to travel.

I made up my mind that we could take it, but that it would be at a fearful loss of life. One half or more of our number would fall in the attempt; and if we should fail, it would distroy our army. Our wounded would perish from cold if they could not be gotten off the battlefield. Even if they could be taken off, the field hospitals were without any shelter—just in the woods—and the patriots would freeze even with all the attention that could be given them there. The day was so cold that the breath was freezing on the bridle bits of the horses. A wounded man falling midway between the lines could not get away; for in attempting it, he would most certainly be shot, and no assistance could reach him unless we were altogether successful.

I am not certain whether I told you that I called together the commanders of the regiments. I explained to them what had to be done and told them that they in turn should tell their company officers and they their men. This was all done. All now seemed to feel the magnitude of the task before them—the responsibility resting on each one, the grandeur of the charge if successful, the slaughter of our Army if defeated. Stillness mingled with sadness pervaded our ranks. Many, no doubt, were the secret prayers that went up to God that day. Thousands and tens of thousands of thoughts winged their way to loved ones at home—loved ones who little knew of the dangers that hovered around their husbands, sons, and brothers far away in the fields of strife. Is it to be wondered that visions of widows and orphans were before us? Or that large numbers of pocketbooks and little keepsakes were handed over to the Chaplains to be sent to those dear ones at home to whom they could not give a last farewell kiss or lingering look before the charge was made.[40]

Officers and men, though sad, were resolute and seemed ready and willing to gather up their all in a bundle and lay it upon the altar of their country. Genl. Warren, who had command of these 30,000 chosen troops, passed along the lines several times, giving orders preparatory to the grand charge. Orderlies were riding to and fro, here and there, carrying orders.

Hark! That rolling thunder! It is the cannon! The ball is opened! The charge will soon be made!

The men sprang to their arms and dressed their lines. But no word came yet to move forward. What is the matter? asked one to another. Why do we linger so long? Why not do what we have to do and be done with it? These questions were heard many times that day.

The artillery ceased to roar. Men left the stacks and walked around to keep warm. Hour after hour rolled away. Doubts as to whether the charge would be made at all were expressed. Then followed the whisper that the charge was postponed. The works were found to be much stronger than expected—the sacrifice too much to

---

40. "Perhaps there never was an hour in the regiment's history when both officers and men so thoroughly realized the great danger of an undertaking as they did upon this occasion. . . . I doubt if on any similar occasion in the experience of the regiment so many valuable addresses and messages to friends were given to the chaplain as there were on that cold winter morning at Mine Run." Marbaker, *11th New Jersey,* 143.

gain a worthless prize, which we would not hold if we had possession It would be a barren victory.

The countenances of our men now began to brighten and the apparent sadness wore away with the passing day.[41] The twilight of the evening began to spread its mantle over the ravines and hills around us. The north wind with its chilling blast made us all feel that we would love to be home by our firesides.

At length the order came to fall in, make no noise, and pass off quietly. A march of two or three miles followed. We bivouacked in the woods, made large fires, and were soon asleep. Thus ended the exciting scenes of that day, a day that will not soon be forgotten.

Having lost so much sleep the previous night, the men slept soundly rolled up in their blankets. They awoke from their slumber at daylight on the 1st of December to be greeted by the piercing cold wind, which howled through the forest and rattled the dry leaves above our heads. Soon the camp fires were burning brightly all around us as the men busily prepared their breakfast. The fore part of the day wore away; then came an order for our Brigade to report to Genl. [David M.] Gregg down the plank road, about five miles toward Chancellorsville.[42] I learned afterwards that the cavalry had been attacked by the Rebels two days in succession. We had to support them. Col. Blaisdell was in command of the Brigade. We soon marched away from our pleasant fires, again into the cold wind, not knowing where we were going or what was before us. But we had good reason to suppose that a march and battle would be our lot. Down the road we went.

About 3 p.m. we arrived at Parker's Store, the headquarters of Genl. Gregg. His command lay all around. We formed a line of battle and built fires. The broad dark mantle of night now spread over us After placing the proper pickets and guards, as well as sentinels over our headquarters—with the usual instructions to be on the alert and give me due notice of the first approach of the enemy or firing of a gun, we all laid down. We rolled up in blankets on the frozen ground, put our feet towards a nice warm fire, and was soon fast asleep.

At 11 p.m. I was awakened by the rolling noise of moving troops. On inquiry I found that our army was all in motion. I supposed that

41. When the order came canceling the assault, "officers and men breathed freely once more, and many were the expressions of admiration for General Warren and his wise decision." *Ibid.*, 144. Cf. Blake, *Three Years in the Army of the Potomac*, 262–65.
42. Gregg, then at the head of the 2nd Cavalry Division, reported "two brigades of infantry from the Third Corps" under his command during the Nov. 30-Dec. 1 operations. *OR,* Vol. XXIX, Pt. 1, p. 807.

we were going to Chancellorsville, 15 miles right down this road. Cavalry, artillery and infantry—all arms of service—passed on, but no orders came for us to move. I now seen plainly that our Brigade had the honor, toil, difficulty, and danger of protecting the extreme right and rear of our army on their retreat. We were to support the cavalry. We all felt our position without saying anything. About 2 o'clock I had orders to fall in and be ready to move. We left our pleasant fires and halted for further orders.

The morning of [December] 2nd was exceeding cold. Men were shivering from the cold and could not keep warm. But we had to stand there and *wait, wait,* until our patriots were almost exhausted and before the long lines of troops had passed. Finally, along came thousands of infantry, representing several corps, and with comparative few officers. These turned out to be the front line pickets, the last to leave the front. Their places would be filled, if filled at all, by the enemy.

I now saw that we were to have great difficulty keeping up the straglers that would fall out from this conglomerate mass which was already tired from the march. Daylight dawned upon us, and the rear had not yet passed us. Finally it came. We moved out with nothing but one cavalry regiment in our rear. We had gon but a short distance before several men began to fall out—stop and make coffee, &c. I was in the rear of our Brigade. I would encourage, plead and expostulate with them to fall in and move with us. I told them that this was the rear of the column, that if they stoped long the Rebels would come along and carry them back as prisoners. For a time I succeeded in geting all to move along. The cavalry behind us was hard at work in the same way. It was assisted by a mounted provost guard. As I passed on, I found many that would not heed the warnings given them. I became exhausted from talking, pleading, urging and ordering.

After passing down the plank road for about five miles, we turned off towards the Culpeper ford. The straglers now became a heavy sight upon us. Worn out with fatigue, I give it up and left the work for the Provost and the cavalry. On reaching the river, we crossed on the Pontoons. While others turned up the river, we turned down towards Ely's Ford, to support the cavalry in case the enemy attacked them. The straglers were coming up and some of them came across the river. But before we got out of sight, the Pontoons were taken up. Those that came up afterwards had to wade the river—so much for being indiffirent and disobeying orders.

Just as we were leaving Ely's Ford, the enemy made their appearance on the opposite side of the river. I have no doubt but that they picked up many of the straglers. It is said that they did not, but I have good reason to believe that many were taken prisoner. However, they are a class of men that we don't regard as worth much in the army.

We marched some two or three miles in this direction that evening and bivouacked for the night. The next morning we started for this camp and arrived here early in the evening of the 3rd. Here we found ourselves at the end of this campaign.

I have now given you a pretty full account of our movements—marching, fighting, &c. You can see that my Regiment was in the advance of our Corps when we moved forward, and was in the rear of the whole army in coming back. It is always honored with the posts of danger. God has watched over and protected us. Except for those who gallantly fell in battle, He has brought us back to camp in safety—for which, as a Regiment, we have greate reason for thankfulness. . . .

Brandy Station, Va., December 6th 1863

My dear Ellen & family,

. . . I have no assurance that I can get home for Christmas. You can now send me a box at any time. But send it to Genl. [Lewis] Perrine, State Quartermaster at Trenton, who takes charge of it and sends it to our state agency in Washington. [Lieutenant] Colonel [John C.] Rafferty, the State Agent, will see that we get it. The State pays all the expenses after it gets to Trenton, and we are certain to get it. . . . Send me a turkey for Christmas. If I don't get home, it will be all right; and if I do get home, the others less fortunent than myself will have the benefit of it.

I don't think we will stay here long. Every day we have had orders to move which have then been countermanded. Yesterday we thought we were certainly going, but it was countermanded. . . .

I am now very well but had a bad cold on the march and was quite sick. I improved before we returned to camp. I was so hoarse that I could not give an order, and yet I had command of the Brigade the day of the intended charge. . . .

Brandy Station, Va., December 8th 1863

My dear Ellen,

Inclosed you will please find the last sheets of my detailed account of our last advance over the Rapidan—where we were lost and wandering in the Wilderness. It may well be called the Wilderness, for there is not one acre of land in a hundred that is cleared. A good deal of amusement arose from the fact that Genl. Prince became lost.[43] Some say that "Prince of the House of David was lost with his children and wandered about in the Wilderness." It was a hard, sorry time for us, a terable place to fight a battle. We could not tell where we were going and could not see the enemy until they were upon us. I hope that my account will prove interesting to you. I fear that it will not, as I have not taken the pains that I should have taken with such a paper. I was interrupted so many times while writing it. . . .

43. In advancing his division to the front, Gen. Prince came to a fork in the road. He spent two hours deliberating which road to take, ended up choosing the wrong one, and marched into "the bowels of the enemy." His men had literally to fight their way back to safety. Blake, *Three Years in the Army of the Potomac,* 255; *OR,* Vol. XXIX, Pt. 1, pp. 15, 237, 736, 739, 762–63.

9

Brandy Station Hibernation

THE INDECISIVE Mine Run Campaign concluded the third autumn of fighting in Virginia. The mighty hosts of Meade and Lee encamped in proximity to each other for a winter of watching and waiting. "A narrow ribbon of water, called the Rapidan," wrote one Federal soldier, "was for a whole season the Rubicon dividing two provinces, the passing of which by either army would be the signal for battle." [1]

McAllister's regiment pitched its tents and constructed winter quarters in the vicinity of Brandy Station on the Orange & Alexandria Railroad. Save for ten-day furloughs in December and March, the senior Colonel remained in camp with his troops. No military activity of consequence broke the hibernation of the III Corps. A repetitive sentiment expressed throughout McAllister's letters for this four-month period was: "Nothing is new; all is yet quiet."

That winter several camp matters occupied McAllister's thoughts. He finally obtained an industrious chaplain for the 11th New Jersey. His initial delight at the construction of a brigade chapel turned to disgust when rowdy elements from a sister regiment commandeered the building for their own inappropriate functions. One of the camp servants died of

---

1. George A. Bruce, *The Twentieth Regiment of Massachusetts Volunteer Infantry, 1861–1865* (cited hereafter as Bruce, *20th Massachusetts*) (Boston, 1906), 325.

typhoid fever; the usefulness of another became suspect. McAllister expressed mixed feelings both when a deserter from his regiment was condemned to the firing squad and when the man gained a reprieve on the eve of his scheduled execution. The growing antithesis between McAllister and Colonel William Blaisdell of the 11th Massachusetts culminated in an unusual breach of military discipline.

The approach of spring brought U. S. Grant and army reorganization. Like many of his fellow officers, McAllister was not impressed by the "Hero of the West." Nor was the Colonel happy over the consolidation of the battle-riddled divisions of the army into three corps. This meant the end of the old III Corps, most of which became a part of Winfield Hancock's II Corps. Those who had served proudly under Stoneman and Sickles displayed their resentment by continuing to wear the diamond-shaped badges of the defunct III Corps.

♣

Brandy Station, Va., December 9th 1863

My dear Ellen,

Before the mail leaves I shall write you a few lines, though I have nothing particular to communicate. According to an order esued long since, there are no leaves of absence granted unless from disability. Quartermaster [Garret] Schenck had important business but was refused. And unless an order granting them comes, my chances for geting one is very slim. Though I will try for one, don't calculate too much on my being at home. At any rate, send me the box—turkey and all. . . . Col. Schoonover and Dr. Welling each have got a box, and we are living right well. Schoonover has butter, chestnuts, hicory nuts, honey, and lots of nice things. There is just three of us in the mess: Schoonover, Welling and I, together with our servants.

Genl. Torbert has written a strong letter in favour of my promotion. The letter has gon on and by this time is in the hands of Governor Newell. . . .

Brandy Station, Va., December 9th 1863

My dear Ellen,

I had concluded not to write this evening, as I wrote this morning and have realy nothing new to communicate. But I decided to write you a few lines before I retired. . . .

The appearances are now that we may remain here for a time. Though we have had reason to think we may move every day, until now it looks more like staying. But it is hard to tell what is before us. We can't campaign here in the winter. It has been tried and proved a failure, and so it will every time it is tried. Some thought that we might now move back over the Rappahannock, but I think not. . . .

I went up to the 6th Corps today in company with Dr. Welling and Col. Schoonover. We visited our old friends in the 1st [New Jersey] Regiment and Brigade. I saw Col. [William] Henry. He was very well, and so were all the rest. I did not see Genl. Torbert. He had road out. Dr. [Lewis] Oakley and Lieut. [Charles R.] Paul are both well. I saw Dr. Osburn,[2] who inquired particularly for you and said that his wife often speaks of you. It was like home to see all the old friends. Mr. [Robert B.] Yard is as kind as ever. He has lately lost his mother and could not get home to see her.

Every evening we have a nice little prayer meeting. Our Chaplain is a most faithful and hard working man.[3] His heart and soul is in the work. He is well liked by all. He is a very excellent man, and we are fortunent in geting him. He is doing good among us. . . .

Brandy Station, Va., December 11th 1863

My dear Ellen,

Yours of the 9th just came to hand. Yesterday I sent in my application for leave of absence and have a fair prospect of geting it.[4] Today an order came down granting leaves as was the case last year under Hooker. So there will be no difficulty in geting mine. I want to leave so as to be home on Christmas Day. Christmas will be the last

2. Dr. Joseph D. Osborne was surgeon of the 4th New Jersey.
3. Chaplain E. Clark Cline, the field minister McAllister most preferred, was a native of Warren County and a graduate of Princeton Theological Seminary. In September, 1863, Cline left his post with the Christian Commission to become chaplain of the 11th New Jersey. Sgt. Marbaker wrote of him: "In all the varied and self-denying duties which the earnest and devoted Chaplain performed, no one in all the service was better fitted, or served more faithfully, than Chaplain Cline." *11th New Jersey*, 52, 122, 347, 352–53.
4. See McAllister to Maj. O. H. Hart, Dec. 10, 1863, McAllister Papers.

day that I will be at home. I will, if I get started for home on Wednesday morning [December 16]. Dr. Welling will be with me and will visit Belvidere. Alice ought to be at home. I want Sarah to come home at that time. I will only be there one week, and I want us all to be together. I would like to have a nice party before Christmas so that Dr. Welling can attend. The Doctor wants to spend Christmas at his home. I will write or telegraph you the day I will be at home and all about it.

I wrote you that Sarah's big man was wounded at Gettysburg and is now in the hospital and not with us at all. . . .

Brandy Station, Va., December 14th 1863

My dear Ellen,

Yours of the 11th came to hand today. My leave has not come down yet, but I think that there is no doubt but that it will in a day or two. So I will be home by Saturday night at least. . . . You may calculate with considerable certainty on my being at home soon. . . .

I wish you to remember the families in Belvidere who have lost their husbands in battle and give them something on Christmas. Remember the old lady, Mrs. Grear, we called on who had a son in my regiment who was killed.[5] Sarah writes me that she is going to attend to the Hatfield children at Christmas. Two members of my regiment who were killed in the late battle have families in Newark. When I get home, I will tell Sarah about them and get her to call and see them. The dying message of Joseph H. Frazier [6] of Newark to his mother was: "I die for my country." A noble and brave man was Corporal Frazee. His mother's address is 18 James Street, Newark. Sargeant [Alfred] Smith's wife is Mrs. [E. A.] Elizabeth Smith, 94 Madison Street, Newark. Sgt. Smith was a noble and brave man and, what was better than all, a religious man. He died on the field, shot through the head. His bosom companion, Corporal [Thomas] Blackwood, one of our praying members, was only saved by a testament in his pocket. The ball lodged in it.[7]

These are the widows and orphans for whom I feel a deep interest. The 11th New Jersey have many such, scattered all over the state. I hope that a patriotic people will not let them suffer. They are our country's defenders, and deserve to be taken care of. . . .

5. Pvt. Valentine Grear of Co. B was killed in action Nov. 27, 1863, at Mine Run. *N.J. Record,* I, 550; Marbaker, *11th New Jersey,* 134, 141.
6. For details of Cpl. Joseph H. Frazee, see Marbaker, *11th New Jersey,* 68, 135, 137.
7. More facts on this incident are in *ibid.,* 138.

Brandy Station, Va., December 16th 1863

My dear Ellen,

I expect to leave this place on Friday morning [December 18], spend a few hours on business in Washington, then go right on to Trenton, stop and see the Governor, run out and see Dr. Welling's father and Governor Newell. Then I will be back in time for the Belvidere train and will reach home Saturday evening. I have the leave and am only waiting for Dr. Welling to get his. . . .

(McAllister was at home from December 19 to 29.)

Brandy Station, Va., December 30th 1863

My dear Ellen & family,

After leaving you at Philadelphia, I took my seat in an as-usual crowded car. We travelled a mile or more, then got out and ran a short distance, as all wanted to procure seats. I got into another crowded car, where I could not sleep or rest with any satisfaction. The train was behind time and went along very slow. We did not arrive at Washington until 9 a.m. I hired a carriage and reached the military train in time. There was one passenger car for Genl. Engle's [8] party; us smaller fry had to go in box cars. Yet these box cars were nicely fixed up with both seats and windows—a grate improvement on them since we went down. The train arrived here on time—the first train to arrive on time at any point since I left.

I had considerable diarrhea but got along pretty well. I had a good sleep last night and feel first rate this morning.

I hope you, dear Ellen, got home safely and are now, like myself, over the fatigue. *Mud, mud,* is the order of the day here. Splash, splash, we go all day. . . .

Brandy Station, Va., January 1st 1864

My dear Ellen,

I wrote you a short letter day before yesterday but I did not write you yesterday, as I was Division Officer of the Day and was not at home until this morning. All day yesterday it poured rain and I was

---

8. McAllister was referring phonetically to Brig. Gen. Rufus Ingalls, quartermaster general of the Army of the Potomac.

out nearly the whole time. However, I established my Headquarters at a house in the rear and center of the line. A widow lady and daughter were the ocquipents. Massey was the name.[9] They were very pleasant and kind. They had a good fire to dry myself by, a passable supper (good for this country), and a good bed to sleep in. All added very much to my comfort, and I don't now feel any worse for being thus exposed. However, I was up at 4 a.m. and before daylight went along a line that is five miles in length. After I get sleep, I shall feel first rate.

This afternoon has blowed up cold and is freezing very hard. The ground will carry a man now and, by morning, horses and wagons. The weather here, I think, is as cold as with you. The mountains in the distance are covered with snow, but here it all fell out in rain. Oh! The mud and the roads! You can't immagine their condition. . . .

I wish you would send me a couple of tablecloths. It would add very much to the appearance and comfort of our table. You can send them by express. They need not be expensive or large. . . . I must close, as I am very tired and it is geting colder every hour. . . .

Headquarters, 11th Regt., N.J.V.[10]
Camp Brandy Station, January 1st 1864

O. H. Hart, Adjt. Genl., 3rd Corps
Sir:

I have the honor to report as Division officer of the day as follows:

December 31st. I visited the picket line from Corps to Corps and established my Headquarters in a house on the left and rear of the 3rd Division pickets. In the afternoon I went along a portion of the lines. This morning at 4 a.m. I commenced on the right and visited all the posts. I am happy to say that I found the officers and men doing their duty faithfully.

Our men suffered much from the severe storm, having almost no shelter. Their tents being fastened on their huts, they could not well bring them along. I have been thinking that a small outlay by the Government could be used for covering the huts and could be built by the users. The picket line could be relieved from these comfortable

---

9. The most detailed map of the Brandy Station area during this period shows no residence owned by a Massey family. See *Official Atlas,* Plate LXXXVII, Map 3.

10. This report, not published in the *Official Records,* is added here to McAllister's home correspondence.

quarters every one or two hours as circumstances required and add much to the comfort and health of the men.

The left wing of our pickets experience much difficulty and delay in crossing the mountain run stream for the want of a bridge.

The distance of the picket line from camp, and the length of the line itself, makes it a matter of necessity for the officer of the day to have an orderly. . . .

Brandy Station, Va., January 2nd 1864

My dear Ellen & family,

Your kind letter of the 30th was received the next day after date. The letter came through unusualy quick. I would like to have more of the same sort. . . .

There is some talk here of our moving. The sick are ordered to the rear, which is one of the signs of a speedy move. Where, I know not. It may be a reconnicence. Some say that we are going to Tenesee to join the southwestern army. But there is nothing known yet as to what we will do. . . .

The apple is a fine one. I have eaten half of it. The other half I will enjoy today. Apples are hard to get here and are very expensive to buy. This was quite a treat—worth about ten cents here. It was so large and fine. . . .

I am rejoiced that there is a religious interest in your town. I hope it will continue. Our meetings are crowded every night. I hope to see good results from them. . . .

Brandy Station, Va., January 3rd 1864

My dear Ellen,

. . . The weather is severely cold after the rain storm. It cleared up cold. Yesterday (Saturday) was one of the coldest days I have experienced in camp. It was as much as we could do to keep warm. The ground is very hard froze, but this morning (Sunday) is not quite so cold. I feel very well now, have very little diarrhea, and am in hopes I will soon be entirely clear of it. It is so unpleasant to have.

Morris White [11] has been very ill but is now better and will soon

---

11. Both Morris White and Jerry Steele (the latter mentioned a few lines farther) were Negro servants at McAllister's headquarters.

be about again. He took ill very sudenly. Captain Lloyd says that as soon as he is able to travel he will send him home—perhaps go with him. Jerry Steel is doing very well, attends to things nicely, and is hearty as a buck.

We have no news here. All is quiet, nothing stiring. Even Mosby [12] is keeping his distance from us. We are not receiving papers regularly. I don't know what is going on. . . .

Brandy Station, Va., January 4th 1864

My dear Ellen,

I have been very much disappointed in not receiving any letters from you since I came back.[13] Why don't you write? I have written almost every day.

I wrote you that Morris White was better and thought he would get well. He is now worse and the doctors has doubts about his recovering. Every attention is paid to him that can be. He is in the Hospital with the soldiers and has all the attention that they get. I fear the worst. The other boys are very well.

No news of any importance here. All is quiet. Cold weather—this morning looks like snow. This is world prayer meeting week, and we are observing it with our little band of praying men. What a splendid chaplain we have. . . .

Brandy Station, Va., January 5th 1864

My dear Ellen,

Morris White died last night. He was buried today. Jerry wrote this morning and the Chaplain will write. Every attention was paid to him that possibly could be. The doctors were on hand and don all they could. He commenced bleeding from the lungs. They got that stoped and he was decidedly better. But it ran into typhoid and he sunk under it. He was decently buried, the Chaplain performing his part.

12. John S. Mosby, dubbed "The Gray Ghost" by friend and foe alike, commanded a group of Confederate partisan rangers whose forays through northern Virginia kept Federal officials in constant anxiety. On the date of McAllister's letter, Mosby surprised and routed a Federal detachment at Rectortown, Va. *OR,* XXXIII, 9.

13. McAllister clearly had forgotten receiving Ellen's letter of Dec. 30, which he had acknowledged on Jan. 2.

He had a much better coffin than most of our soldiers have. He wanted to go home so badly, but he was not able to travel after he took sick. He has gon to his long and last home. Tell his friends that they have my sympathy.

Tonight I received your first letter, written on the 1st, and also one from Sarah of the same date. They were both welcom visitors. I hope I will get more of them. . . .

I send you the constitution of our 3rd Corps Union. We had a meeting today and appropriated $400 to the widows of two officers killed in the last battle in the Wilderness—called the battle of Payne's Farm. That is $200 each. If they are in want of more, they will get it from time to time. If Mrs. Hatfield's husband had belonged to this society, how nicely she would get along. We pay the expense of embalming the bodies and send them home. We bear all the funeral expenses and then see that their families don't want for anything. It is entirely a benevolent institution. We have not yet received our badges but will in a few days. Tiffany & Co. had one in their show window on New Year's, and it is said to be perfectly beautiful. They are manufacturing them for us at cost. We are to pay $25 each. . . .

Brandy Station, Va., January 11th 1864

My dear Ellen,

I have received the box. As yet I have only opened it on the top. Things are somewhat jumbled up but nothing as I can see is injured. I will examine it today and have the turkey for dinner. This will be quite a treat. . . .

We have finished our little church. It will hold about 75 persons. We have a fireplace in it; if it is not warm enough, we will pute a stove in it. We hold prayer meeting every evening. Now that we have a larger building and more room, the meetings will be much better attended. Last evening we had a large attendance, it being the first evening in the church. There is a very good religious feeling in the regiment, and I hope your prayers will be for the outpouring of God's Holy Spirit on our little regiment.

You may ask what kind of church we have. Well, it is 13 feet in width, 24 feet in length, has a fireplace in one end and a door in the other. It is built of logs, plastered in the cracks, and covered with shelter tents. We intend covering the ground with pine bushes. We have log seats. We find that it is quite an improvement on the outdoor worship—around an open fire and without any seats. . . .

Brandy Station, Va., January 13th 1864

My dear Ellen,

. . . The box came all right and its contents are good. We have eat the turkey and one chicken. The other chicken we will have for today's dinner. The fruit is fine—in fact, everything is good, first rate. Such boxes are worth geting. I hope to have another one after awhile.

Ira Smith [of Company I], a deserter from our regiment, is now under sentence of death and is to be shot on the 29th with two others —one from each brigade in our Division. Smith is from New Brunswick. He has no father or mother living but has one sister. He was a bricklayer by trade. He has always been adicted to intemperance. He says that he was drunk when he deserted and drunk when he reinlisted in the 26th Pennsylvania Regt. He deserted at or after the battle of Gettysburg. He was on cattle guard at the time. He has never been in any battle because he was always guarding cattle. I feel deeply for the poor man. But his case is a clear one of desertion, and then his reinlisting and receiving the bounties in another regiment makes it still worse. He says now he was always a wild, wicked youth. His sister was a member of the German Reformed Church. He never professed anything.

His comrade was in last night, pleading with me in his behalf. But I can do nothing in his case. There are no paliating circumstances on which we can rest a plea. And besides, we have had so many desertions that there must be an example made.[14] True, "the ways of the transgressor is hard." Our ever-faithful chaplain is with him every day, and our prayers go up for his conversion and redemption. You join with us in our supplications to the Throne of Mercy. . . .

Brandy Station, Va., January 20th 1864

My dear Ellen,

. . . I had another terable wet day to be on picket, though I was more comfortable than the day I was on before—the last day of the year and New Year's morning. I stoped at the same house, Mrs. Massey's, that I staid at before. They had good warm fires and I got completely warmed up. I had a good sleep and feel none the worse.

---

14. As of Jan. 1, 1864, a total of 122 men had deserted from the 11th New Jersey. Of that number, 82 deserted while the regiment was training at Trenton, 19 deserted prior to the battle of Fredericksburg, and the other 21 "went over the hill" during 1863. Marbaker, *11th New Jersey,* 146.

A gentleman, the Rev. Mr. Rinker,[15] a Presbyterian clergyman, has been with us for a week or more and was anxous to visit with me on the picket line. Though storming as it was, he went with me and staid all the time. He enjoyed it very much. I laughed at such a trip for pleasure. He was good company and added much to my pleasure. He lives in Morristown, N.J. He has preached several times to us here and we have had a full house. Every night is a prayer meeting, and the house is full. There is a very good feeling in our regiment now. Our Temperance Society numbers 45 members and is increasing. Mr. Rinker give a fine temperance address. He thinks I have a modle regiment in morals, religion, discipline, &c. He leaves for home this morning. . . .

He knows Mr. Knighton and saw him before coming here. I inferred from what he said that Mr. Knighton give him a wrong impression of everybody and everything, our regiment in particular. He says that he has found everything so diffirent from the way it was represented. He is astonished to see the state of morals and religion in the regiment and army so much better than he had it represented to him. Mr. Knighton ought to be ashamed of himself and forever hold his tongue. . . .

Brandy Station, Va., January 20th 1864

My dear Ellen,

I wrote you a hasty letter this morning. I have just returned from prayer meeting and thought that I would write you again before I retired for rest. . . .

I took dinner today with Genl. and Mrs. Carr. Both inquired very kindly for you and desired to be remembered. Genl. Birney [16] arrived while we were at dinner. He is very pleasant and kind to me—always askes me to call and see him. There is to be a large party on Monday night at Genl. Carr's Headquarters. *It is to cost $2,000.* Tickets are sold at $10 each. This will take a lady. A building has to be pute up to hold it. The Botts family are all to be there, as well as

---

15. Probably the Rev. Henry Rinker, who graduated from Princeton Theological Seminary in 1851 and later became an army chaplain. Edward H. Roberts, *Biographical Catalogue of the Princeton Theological Seminary, 1815–1932* (Princeton, 1933), 166.

16. Born in Huntsville, Ala., David B. Birney was the son of a prominent abolitionist. He was a highly successful prewar attorney. In spite of no military experience, and largely at his own expense, Birney recruited and became colonel of the 23rd Pennsylvania. Valiant service in battle soon brought him promotion to major general. At this time, however, he had less than ten months to live.

some twenty ladies from Washington. I understand that at first it was only to be a small select party projected by Genls. Birney and Carr. But the program is now changed; other hands have got hold of it and it will not be quite so select. Two tickets are sold to a regiment. I have not embarked in the business, and none of my officers as yet have expressed a desire to go. In fact, only four in our Brigade are going. There is to be dancing—and no doubt plenty of liquor afloat. Mrs. Richardson, Maj. [Samuel] Richardson's wife who is now here and very intimate with Mrs. Carr, told me today that she was not going. She asigned as a reason that those ladies from Washington would be dressed to attend a ball; and she, as well as other ladies in camp, have only clothes calculated for camp and not the ballroom. But if it had been what first was contemplated—a social party—their clothes would have answered and they would have gone.

There are quite a number of ladies now in camp, notwithstanding the trouble in there geting passes, and then only for twenty days at a time. They have to go to Army Headquarters to get them. We have none in our regiment as yet, but expect Miss Gilson soon. It is a miserable place for ladies to come. Our camp is so poor, low, and mudy. Genl. Carr has a nice large house, and his wife is comfortable.

The Rebels are deserting in considerable numbers and coming into our lines.[17] Some of them say that in front of us, on the other side of the Rapidan, they have five lines of pickets—not to keep us from going over, but to keep their men from deserting to us. However, I still look for hard fighting this coming summer, unless the Rebel army is completely demoralized. It will be their last hope. With them it is do or die. One more year and the Rebellion must come to an end. But it is hard to tell what is before us. This year will be one of greate events, and God grant that it may bring success to our cause. . . .

Brandy Station, Va., January 22nd 1864

My dear Ellen,

I have just received a letter from you dated the 19th. It is always pleasant for me to receive these home letters.

Dr. [George T.] Ribble came back this evening. He told me that he has a few things for me. I see by your letter they are those things for the two men that helped me off the battlefield. I am very glad that you sent them. I will give them to the men as soon as I get them. . . .

17. Verifications of large numbers of Confederate desertions are in Hussey and Todd, *9th N.Y.S.M.*, 311–12, 316; Wainwright, *Diary of Battle*, 313.

We have delightful prayer meeting. Our little church is full every night. We have a grate deal of interest in religion in the regiment. Several have come out and taken a decided stand for Christ. Tonight two rose for prayer and asked for our prayers. I do think that we are in the era of a greate revival among us. I pray God that it may be so. . . .

Brandy Station, Va., January 24th 1864

My dear Ellen & Henrietta,

. . . Inclosed you will please find the quarterly report of our chaplain ending the last of December. I thought it would interest you and some of our good people in Belvidere. Miss [Sarah] Gill no doubt would like to see it. . . . You know it is the duty of chaplains to make these quarterly reports. The next quarterly report will show much better. . . . Our Temperance Society now numbers 56 members and is still increasing. . . .

Good morning, my dear family. I had a comfortable night's rest.

I have nothing new to communicate this morning. The weather is quite mild. . . .

It is reported that Col. Blaisdell will be made a Brigadier. I don't know what foundation the rumor has, and I don't understand how a man of his caliber in tactics and morals could get such an appointment. I think him totaly unfit for the position, though I am not at liberty to say so. I have been recommended for a Brevet for gallantry by Genl. Carr and Genl. Humphreys; but that is the last I have heard of it. This is poor incouragement for an officer who has everything in the way of danger. Blaisdell was not at Gettysburg. He was absent five months on some frivolous pretense.[18] His appointment may not prevent mine; but it lessens my chance, as but few will be appointed—to fill existing vacancies which, I believe, is not numerous. Well, I shall discharge my duty to my country. I would rather be right than do wrong to get promoted. . . .

Brandy Station, Va., January 27th 1864

My dear Ellen,

. . . The weather is quite mild here and the mud is drying a little. I am busy in ditching and draining our camp. We think we can

---

18. Following a sick leave in June, 1863, Blaisdell spent the next four months on recruiting duty in Boston, Mass. Blaisdell's compiled service file, National Archives.

dry it to some extent. Some regiments have moved onto other ground to better their condition. We will try and make the best of what we have. Our buildings are all up, and it takes a grate deal of labor to move and fix up a new camp. We have a good stable and all other necessary buildings, including a church. . . .

Friday is the day that our man Ira Smith is to be shot. The others that were to be shot at the same time have been reprieved. We feel that inasmuch as others have been reprieved, he ought to be. Governor Parker and others are working for him. But I think his case is hopeless. I feel for him. The Chaplain calls on him every day. Smith seems to think that he is a sinner, but the Chaplain thinks he does not show true repentance. I called to see him and talked some with him on the subject of his soul's Eternal welfare. It was a sad spectacle to me. All three were in rows, greate, hearty, stout men. To think that they would run off and desert our cause and country while other, puny, delicate boys remain to fight our battles. I have but little sympathy for the traitor in any shape. I saw a letter written by Miss Smith, his sister. . . . Poor girl, I pity her.

The ball passed off and is now among the balls that have been.[19] Captain Lloyd was there. There were about thirty ladies in all, and three hundred officers. The ladies, I am told, did not look well, as they had not time to get their ball dresses. The fixings on that ocasion were much wanted. The supper, it is said, was good. Dr. Ribble was also there. So your Belvidere was represented. Most of our Generals were there except Genl. Prince. He did not go on account of the death of his mother.

I am rather inclined to think that it was not the brilliant affair that was expected. I would not leave my daughter go to such a mixed gathering, and I think that many parents in Washington thought the same. All did not come that was expected. John Botts and daughter were present. . . .

19. This was the ball given by Gen. Carr and mentioned earlier by McAllister. Among those in attendance, Gen. Humphreys wrote, "were some interesting ladies, fragile looking creatures who at three o'clock in the morning wished the ball would continue until ten." Henry H. Humphreys, *Andrew Atkinson Humphreys: A Biography* (cited hereafter as Humphreys, *A. A. Humphreys*) (Philadelphia, 1924), 215. A New Jersey officer observed that most of the generals at this affair "were better at fighting than at dancing." Terrill, *24th New Jersey,* 50–51. See also E. M. Haynes, *A History of the Tenth Regiment, Vermont Volunteers* . . . (Lewiston, Me., 1870), 59; Charles H. Banes, *History of the Philadelphia Brigade* (Philadelphia, 1876), 213.

Brandy Station, Va., January 29th 1864

My dear Ellen,

. . . Ira Smith has been reprieved, so we have not the unpleasant duty of seeing him executed today. All three men have been reprieved by the President.[20] While I am glad that Smith has been, I fear that it will incourage desertion. His poor religious sister will be overjoyed on hearing it. We made Smith the subject of our earnest prayers for days. I only hope that he will continue as he has resolved to do. If he was here with us in the regiment, I would have greate hope. But being in the guard house at Division Headquarters, I fear he will go back to his old habits. It is not a full pardon, only a reprieve. He may be executed yet, but it is not likely.

Col. Blaisdell has not, and I do not think he will, get his promotion. Genl. Carr says that he will not. Those pieces that appeared in the Boston papers are written by a tool of his in his regiment and don't amount to anything. I have at long last heard from Genl. Sickles through Genl. Carr. He says that he will fully and heartily endorse Genl. Carr's and Humphreys's recommendations for my promotion and will enquire for and hunt up the papers that have never reached him and endorse them with a good will. There will be but few appointments made. Only one has yet been made in the army. I may not get it, but I surely will later if I remain in the army. . . .

Brandy Station, Va., January 30th 1864

My dear family,

. . . Col. Schoonover has arrived. He is looking badly. He informed me that he staid with you one night. No doubt he told you all. I have had but little conversation with him yet, as it was night before he arrived here. The train ran off the track. Nobody was hurt. The road seems to be very unsafe for some time past.

Mr. & Mrs. [Frank B.] Fay have arrived with Miss Gilson. Dr. Welling is now in charge of our Division Hospital, a short distance from here. All are going there to do good. This arrangement will brake up our mess, as the Doctor will hold on to the cook. He is the doctor's servant. The doctor, Col. Schoonover, and I messed together. The two Asst. Surgeons, the Adjutant, and the Chaplain were in another mess. I don't know how we shall arrange it now. We will see.

---

20. On Jan. 26 Lincoln issued a presidential proclamation to "suspend execution of sentence in all the capital cases." Smith subsequently transferred to Co. K, 12th New Jersey, and served out his three-year enlistment. Roy P. Basler (ed.), *The Collected Works of Abraham Lincoln* (New Brunswick, 1953–55), VII, 152; *N.J. Record,* I, 577, 624.

We have had fine weather, almost like summer. This morning looks like rain.

At this time a large number of strangers are visiting the camp.[21] I do not see much prospect of filling up my regiment. Of the recruits that are raised in New Jersey, a large portion of them go into the Cavalry and Artillery. But few go into the Infantry.[22] There are not near the number raised that is stated in the papers. Genl. Mott is very much discouraged, as well as myself. Our skeleton regiments will be used up in one more good fight. The people of New Jersey are more anxous to fill their quota than they are to fill up the old regiments, which is a greate mistake. The blacks they raise all go to new regiments, of course, and do not help to fill the old. . . .

Brandy Station, Va., January 31st 1864

My dear Ellen & family,

We had an excellent temperance meeting last night and added many to our pledge. We were addressed by the Chaplain of the 1st Massachusetts [Warren H. Cudworth]. He interested the audience very much. We will soon have a large portion of my regiment enrolled in the Temperance Society, line officers excepted. Captain [Samuel T.] Sleeper is the only one who has signed up.

I wish you to send me a little money, as I am short. Say ten dollars, and send it in a letter. I have to pay for a badge in the 3rd Corps Union, or I could do without it. Yet for a very important reason I wish to get it at once. I know that you are short; but as I said before, you can overdraw at the bank. I do not like to borrow from anyone here, as I myself don't lend money.[23] . . .

The weather has set in damp and rainy. We had most delightful weather for some time past. It was like summer. . . .

21. Sgt. Marbaker considered the five months spent at Brandy Station "the most pleasant period in our army experience." Much leisure time prevailed; every mail delivery brought letters and packages; few threats emanated from Confederate lines; and a host of wives, sweethearts, and loved ones visited the Federal camps. "If a strange lady was seen issuing from headquarters, a review of some kind was sure to follow in a few days." Marbaker, *11th New Jersey*, 150.

22. McAllister was correct about men flocking to join artillery and cavalry units rather than taking their chances with the infantry. The normal regiment consisted of no more than 1,000 men; yet soon to rendezvous at Washington were such newly formed units as the 7th New York Heavy Artillery (1,835 men), 1st Massachusetts and 2nd Connecticut Heavy Artillery (1,700 gunners each), and the 2nd New York Heavy Artillery (1,679 men). *OR*, Vol. XXXVI, Pt. 3, p. 665.

23. This was in marked contrast to McAllister's lenient policy in the first months of the war.

Brandy Station, Va., February 4th 1864

My dear Ellen,

I have not received any letters from you for two or three days. I did not write yesterday. I feel very well except for a bad cold—the first that I have had this winter. I hope it will soon be better.

There is nothing new or strange here in camp. All is very quiet, although all the sick have been removed back to Washington. There is nothing to indicate a move. The Corps is under the command of Genl. Birney. Genl. French is home on a leave of absence. I am told that Genl. Sickles has command of the defences of Washington.[24] I wish he could get his request complied with to get this Division, or the whole Corps, with him. It would be nothing more than right to bring those large regiments and brigades that have been so long around Washington to the front and let us go back there. We could then recruit and fill up our thinned ranks. But it is said that the War Department will not agree to it. So we must keep on and fight all the battles while we have a man left. As I have often said, a few troops do all the fighting.

Our Temperance Society still increases. The Rev. Dr. Smith [25] from Philadelphia addressed us last night. He is a Baptist minister and a very excellent speaker—a most splendid preacher. The 11th Massachusetts have formed a temperance society. [Lt.] Col. [Porter D.] Tripp, commanding the regiment, was the first man to join. They have about 70 members. The 26th Pennsylvania had a meeting last night to form a society. I have not heard from them. You see that the good work is going on among us. Our religious meetings are well attended, and many are coming out on the side of the Lord. . . .

Brandy Station, Va., February 5th 1864

My dear Ellen,

I have just received your kind letter of the 2nd, inclosing ten dollars, for which I am much obliged.

In my last I told you that I was not well. I am now having one of my usual billious attacks, only lighter than usual. I will soon be well again. The fact is that for the last several weeks we have been

---

24. The report was untrue. Lincoln had just asked Sickles to make a tour of Federal-held Southern ports in order to ascertain the effects on the populace of the Emancipation and Amnesty proclamations. On his return to Washington in May, 1864, Sickles was appointed inspector general in Sherman's army.

25. The Rev. J. Hyatt Smith was pastor of the Eleventh Baptist Church in Philadelphia.

living on salt fish—salmon and mackeral. You know that salt fish always destroyed that regularity which is so esential to my health. When I have fresh meat, I am always healthy. Yesterday I took some medicine and staid indoors. Last night I had to take pills. They did not opperate until about the middle of the day, after which I felt better. I will return to duty soon. I am satisfied that if I had not taken care of myself and taken the medicine, I would have been quite sick.

Mr. & Mrs. Fay left for home today. Miss Gilson remains to assist at the Division Hospital. She is a most amiable and excellent lady and a good nurse. This morning she left here and went over to the hospital. But she said if I got worse she would come and attend to me. Mr. Fay is one of the most distinguished and benevolent gentlemen I ever met—so kind, so benevolent. He has left all the comforts of home, and resigned the office of Mayor, to come out here to the front to spend his time and money for the good of the soldiers. But few men in his situation would do it.

Captain [William H.] Lloyd will most likely leave us for awhile and go up to Genl. Birney's Headquarters. Birney is having him detailed as one of his aides. As Lloyd has don so well here in all the battles, and as he desired to go, I will consent to it. Without my consent he could not go. He has shown some anxiety to get out of the service. But the prospect of geting on a horse will cure him of this idea. . . .

The 26th Pennsylvania have also formed a temperance organization, with 26 members at the first meeting. The Lt. Colonel commanding the regiment [Robert L. Bodine] is the president. Several officers have signed their names. So goes the good work in the army. . . .

Brandy Station, Va., February 6th 1864

My dear Ellen,

. . . I have felt quite sick today, but the doctor says I am realy better. This morning at 5 o'clock we were all wakened by orders to move at 7 a.m. All was in readiness at the hour appointed. Firing commenced along the Rapidan quite early and continued at intervals all day.[26] It was quite brisk until late this evening. Our Corps left this

26. On Feb. 6 elements of Gouverneur K. Warren's corps crossed the Rapidan at Morton's Ford, drove back the Confederate advance guard, and continued their thrust until checked by Southern forces in strength. Federal casualties in this curious affair were 270 men. *OR*, XXXIII, 114–20, 140; Cudworth, *1st Massachusetts*, 447–48.

evening about 4:30. It is said that it is a reconnaicence in force—that the 1st and 2nd Corps were crossing this evening, and that the 3rd and 6th Corps were to act as the reserve. Be this as it may, a few more hours will develop the whole movement. I feel that I ought to be along, but the doctor foiled my going, as I am sick and taking medicine.

It has been raining. Exposure tonight would no doubt lay me up for some time to come. So it is better as it is. If, however, our army should hapen to get into a general battle, I may go out. . . .

Good Morning. It is 8 a.m. Nothing is new; all is yet quiet. The night passed quietly in camp with no firing on the front. I have not heard from there yet.

I might say that I am a little better this morning. I have some fever yet, but I will be well soon. Don't be at all uneasy about me. . . .

Brandy Station, Va., February 7th 1864

My dear Ellen,

I feel a little better this evening but have to pass much more bile before I am intirely well. Our Division have returned. They had a hard march without doing much. They only went a mile or so beyound Stevensburg, a little beyound our picket lines. They did not go near the river. They had no fighting and did not see the enemy. One division of the 2nd Corps crossed the river, had some considerable fighting, and took, I believe, a few prisoners. Our officers who have just returned know but little of these operations. It was mearly a reconnaicence, and no doubt its object was accomplished. Perhaps they wanted to see if the enemy was there. I am glad I did not go, for it would have laid me up. . . .

Brandy Station, Va., February 9th 1864

My dear Ellen,

I rested well last night and feel much better this morning. I will soon be able for duty again. Miss Gilson calls to see me every day. She is very kind. I will soon be able to ride out.

Nothing is new here. The papers give the 3rd Corps credit for crossing the Rapidan. This is a mistake. Only one division of the 2nd Corps crossed. Our Corps was not in sight of the enemy.

Your kind favour of the 5th came to hand last evening. I have been receiving your letters regularly. Since the children have all gone, you write daily. This is right, for I am always anxous to hear from home.

I will receive your box with pleasure. By the time it gets here, I will be alowed to eat everything that it contains. It will come in first rate. . . .

Brandy Station, Va., February 10th 1864

My dear Ellen,

I wrote you yesterday morning, in fact every morning. I did not receive a letter from you last evening. But on Tuesday evenings we always have little mail, owing to the fact that few mail trains run on Sunday.

I feel better this morning and will soon be on duty again.

Some of the paymasters are here; yet Maj. Webb, our paymaster, has not arrived. He has got the money, but it is in large bills and he is having difficulty in geting it changed into small ones. As soon as he gets the small ones, he will come on. I hope he will soon come. On the last day of this month, two more months' pay will be due us. If he waits a little longer, he can pay us for four months instead of two.

Last night was cold. The ground froze hard, and there is ice in my tent. It will be beautiful today and then most likely will become mudy. . . .

Brandy Station, Va., February 13th 1864

My dear Ellen,

I am geting along very well and will soon be on duty again. Nothing is new in camp except a little excitement in regard to the lovers of pleasure using our Brigade chapel last night for a dance.

In the begining of the winter, a detail of men was made from day to day to build a Brigade chapel for all the regiments. The Christian Commission furnished a fly to cover it. It was unfortunately located, no one knows why or by whose authority, in the 11th Massachusetts Regt. Doubts were then entertained by some of our good people that it might be turned to a bad use. However, it was built and the Rev. Mr. Smith from Philadelphia helped to dedicate it.

To our greate surprise, we found that it was turned into a dancing room. Last night, though preaching had been appointed in it, a large party assembled there for a ball. On learning yesterday what was going on, some of our Chaplains called on Genl. Prince, stated the facts to him, and desired that it should be stoped. But Genl. Prince decided against the wishes of our Chaplains, saying at the same time that he had often attended balls in churches. (It happens that he is a Unitarian.) The ball opened last night and continued until this morning. When the lovers of pleasure found an opposition to their use of the church, they took off the Christian Commission flag and pute on another one.[27]

I have never been in the Brigade Chapel, as we have our own regimental one and meet in it every night. I was invited to attend the ball, but you need not ask me if I went. I don't invest in such securities. The Chaplain of the 11th Massachusetts is a *poor, miserable nobody,* or he might have prevented it.[28]

Chaplain [Charles A.] Beck of the 26th Pennsylvania was asked, "Who had charge of the Brigade Chapel?"

He answered, "The Devil!"

He too had his own chapel and had not paid any attention to the Brigade church. . . .

Brandy Station, Va., February 15th 1864

My dear Ellen,

Yesterday was the Holy Sabbath and we had some delightful exercises. In the evening we had a pleasant prayer meeting. Sgt. [George C.] Boice, our Quartermaster Sargeant, came out and asked for our prayers. He made a few remarks and then led in prayer. On dismissing us, our Chaplain asked those who wished to stay and have a little conversation and prayer to remain. About 30 stayed. Two or three more came out and declared themselves on the side of the Lord. . . .

27. For varying opinions on the use of the brigade chapel as a dance pavilion, see Marbaker, *11th New Jersey,* 154–55; Blake, *Three Years in the Army of the Potomac,* 271; Gustavus B. Hutchinson, *A Narrative of the Formation and Services of the Eleventh Massachusetts Volunteers* . . . (cited as Hutchinson, *11th Massachusetts*) (Boston, 1893), 55.

28. The Rev. Elisha F. Watson, a native of Boston, was dismissed Feb. 23, 1864, as chaplain of the 11th Massachusetts. Mass. Adj. Gen., *Massachusetts Soldiers,* I, 737.

Brandy Station, Va., February 17th 1864

My dear Ellen,

. . . Today it blew up very cold. Last night was terably cold, and it still continues. . . .

No paymaster yet. On the last day of this month there will be four months' pay due us. I will have over $700 coming. It takes all their money to pay the veteran troops; and as we have more than one year to serve, we can't reinlist now. Our men are deprived of furloughs and also of their pay at present. . . .

Brandy Station, Va., February 20th 1864

My dear daughter Hennie,

You don't write me very often. But I know you have to keep close to your studies and have not the time, so on that ground I will excuse you. I miss your nice interesting letters very much. My family is so much scattered now that it is almost impossible for me to keep them all posted. I wish your mother to send you and Sarah any letters of mine that might be interesting to you.

The weather here is intensely cold. Though we have no snow, I see the Blue Ridge Mountains are covered with it.

I have got quite well again. I am on duty and can ride out. Our religious interest still continues. Though we have no excitement, all moves on slowly and silently. Our temperance society is increasing and doing good amongst us. We now have about 70 members—one half of the regiment present for duty. Similar organizations have been formed in this Brigade and have met with success. . . .

Brandy Station, Va., February 23rd 1864

My dear Ellen,

Dr. Welling went home on a sick leave. His colored servant is our cook. He went home on a visit, so Jerry thought that he would have to visit his wife. Nothing would do but he must go home. He says he is coming back in about two weeks, but it is hard to tell. He has been with me three months. With what you gave him, he was paid in full for two months. When he left yesterday morning, I gave him eight dollars on the present month, leaving but six coming to him—even if I do not charge him for his clothes. If I do charge him with his clothes, he is in debt to me. . . . It will take one full month's wages for his train fare going and coming. It is rather expensive for him.

I am now without anyone to wait on me except my orderly. Dr. Ribble's man is attending to my tent. Jerry is very slow and very dumb; but when he once learns a thing, he attends to it ever afterwards and on the whole makes a pretty good servant. . . . They will be after him to enlist—offering bounty, &c. But Jerry knows and says that he has never had such fine, easy times in his life.

The Paymaster is here, and in a day or two I will get my pay for two months only. Nearly four are due. I can't send you at home as big a pile as usual, as I have four months' board to pay which is very heavy. I can't let you have $110 this time; but if they pay in March, I will be able to send $200 or $250. . . .

Inclosed you will find [a picture of] Captain Cory, a gallant officer. He was the officer—then a Lieutenant—who at the battle of Gettysburg ordered his men to shoot Genl. Barksdale.[29] . . .

Brandy Station, Va., February 26th 1864

My dear Ellen,

I wrote you yesterday morning, inclosing a check to your order for $110. I hope it will arrive safely.

The weather is fine here now. How long it will continue is hard to tell. I wish the Rev. Mr. [Henry S.] Osborn would come out to the army now. The weather is so pleasant and I know that he would enjoy it so much. I would do all I could to make it pleasant for him. Give him my compliments and tell him what I said. He will have no difficulty in geting a pass at Washington. Citizens are coming daily. Our state agent, Col. Rafferty, will procure him one. I would like him to come now, before our Chaplain goes home on leave of absence. Our religious interest still continues. I am glad that you have such pleasant meetings at your church. I hope that good work will continue and many souls be saved.

We have now one review after another, division after division. Carr's Division was reviewed yesterday, ours is to be reviewed today, and the 3rd Corps tomorrow. There is much talk about changes, consolidation, &c. What form it will asume we know not. If it comes, some Generals will be thrown out of commands. However, it may not come to anything. No Brigadier Generals are made now—caused, I

---

29. During the July 2 fighting at Gettysburg, Capt. Ira W. Cory ordered his Company H to concentrate its fire on a Confederate officer astride a white horse. The men did so, and the volley knocked Gen. William Barksdale to the ground. At least five bullets pierced the Confederate brigadier. *OR,* Vol. XXVII, Pt. 1, p. 555; Marbaker, *11th New Jersey,* 60, 98, 353–54.

think, by the intended change. Well, only so long as the Rebellion is pute down. I don't care about personal interests. I have don my part and hope to continue to do so as long as I am in the army.

Your kind letter of the 23rd came to hand last night. You aske me if it is right for you to give support to the Freedmen and to the preacher for their assistance. *Why, of course it is.* I have just given ten dollars to the Christian Commission [for that purpose]. We have raised among the officers about sixty dollars for this noble purpose. We are the only regiment that I have heard of doing anything in that way. God has given us the means and we must not be stingy and withhold from Him. . . .

Brandy Station, Va., February 27th 1864

My dear Ellen,

I have but time to write you a line, as the mail will soon close.

I informed you that the box had arrived, but at that time I had not examined it fully. I have since took out all the contents and am happy to say that they are all in a good condition. The chickens had a little mould on them, but not enough to hurt them. It is a nice present —one that we enjoy very much. We are much obliged to you for such nice gifts and eatables. Butter is fifty cents a pound here. I know it is high with you, but not near so high as we have to pay for a poor artical here. It is very expensive to live any place now. But we have reason to thank God that we have the means to pay for what we want.

I have half a notion to apply for a ten-day leave of absence and run home. I have not decided whether I shall do so or not. If so, it is to see my family.

Yesterday was very cold and blustery. Today is nice and warm. We have a review of our Corps today, so I must get ready for it. . . .

Brandy Station, Va., February 28th 1864

My dear Ellen,

Yesterday the 6th Corps, one division from ours and, it is said, one division from each except the 5th Corps, have gon to the front. A reconnaicence, we suppose. What the object is we don't know. For once our Division is left in camp. But we may have to follow soon. I suppose it has something to do with the movements down southwest.

We have had very fine, dry weather for some time. It now looks like rain. If so it will be bad for moving, marching, &c. . . .

I just received an order to be ready to move at a moment's notice. . . .

Brandy Station, Va., March 1st 1864

My dear Ellen,
. . . Though we are under marching orders, we have not yet moved. The 6th Corps and the 1st Division of our Corps have gon to the front to hold the enemy, while a large force of our cavalry have got around in the enemy's rear and are on their way to Richmond.[30] You will hear of stiring news in a few days, if all goes right. It looks now as if it might prove a success. God grant that it may and that our prisoners may be released from their terable suffering. Let us hope and pray.

Brandy Station, Va., March 2nd 1864

My dear Ellen,
We have had nothing reliable from the front yet and know but little as to what is doing. We heard a few guns yesterday but not many. I think today will bring us some news. We are still here. . . . It is a cavalry raid on our part; the Infantry is mearly holding the Rebels here while our cavalry push on in their rear. It is a bold undertaking. God grant that it may prove a success.

It rained and snowed and froze last night. This morning is clear, and the day will be milder after the sun gets up. . . .

Later. The raid is over. Our troops have come back—all except a party of Cavalry that hurry on towards Richmond. . . .

Don't give Jerry Steele anything, unless he is ready to come back. It was a foolish thing for him to go home—spending his money for nothing. He can't expect to give all his money to his wife and then have lots of money for himself. When he is ready to come back, give

---

30. A cavalry raid on Richmond by troops under Gen. Judson Kilpatrick and Col. Ulric Dahlgren began with great expectations and ended as a fiasco. Home guard and convalescents manning Richmond's defenses repulsed the attack, killed Dahlgren, and sent Kilpatrick and the survivors of his force fleeing to the safety of Yorktown. Meade's aide, Col. Theodore Lyman, who regarded Kilpatrick as a "frothy braggart without brains," wrote of the troopers huddled at Yorktown: "Now all that cavalry must be carried back in steamers, like a parcel of old women going to market. Bah!" Lyman, *Meade's Headquarters,* 79.

him enough to bring him here. If he is not coming back, let him go—to grass, if he chooses. I can get along without him. He has cost me a considerable sum. Six dollars is all that is coming to him. Then he is not charged with the $5 you give him to come here, nor a cent for clothing, blankets, or shelter tent. Taken all together, he has cost me a nice penny. But I would not care if he had only staid a reasonable time. He would then be worth something to me. . . .

Brandy Station, Va., March 8th 1864

My dear daughter Henrietta,

Your very kind letter of the 4th came to hand last evening. Your requisition for brass buttons will be filled as soon as circumstances will admit. I have eight on one vest that I will send you. I wore them in the last battle (Locust Grove). I think I have a vest at home with that number. I wore it in the battles of Chancellorsville and Gettysburg. You can have it if your mother has not given it away. . . . You must have them nicely cleaned up before you give them to anyone. The buttons have an egle on them and a letter "I" in the center. The "I" stands for Infantry. The little stars you speak of belong to Staff members and none other. Some members of the Staff are never in a battle, but some are. The Asst. Adjt. Generals and personal aides are carrying orders during battles. Quartermasters and Surgeons are not often under fire. So these kind of buttons are not what you want. . . .

Tell the young ladies that they are perfectly welcom to the brass buttons. I consider it quite a compliment to have them wear them. But by the time they wear them as long as I have, they will get tired of them. . . .

Brandy Station, Va., March 12th 1864

My dear daughter Henrietta,

I have not succeeded in geting my leave of absence. It was rejected because we had one field officer away—Maj. [Thomas J.] Halsey on recruiting service. However, I will try it again and may get it through. If so, I will let you know.

I am in command of the Brigade. Col. Blaisdell is away for a few days. Your mother may be in your city [Philadelphia] by the time this letter reaches you. . . .

Brandy Station, Va., March 13th 1864

My dear niece [Alice],[31]

I wrote you yesterday that I was disappointed in not geting my leave. I have sent up another request and have arranged for its passage, if no sudden amount of movement takes place. So you will likely see me in Belvidere before the week is out. I would like to meet Dr. Welling there. Hope I will.[32] . .

Brandy Station, Va., March 29th 1864

My dear Ellen,

I stoped off at Trenton, made arrangements for filling up Co. C of my Regiment, and came on to Philadelphia that night. The next day I took the noon train for Washington and arrived there at dusk. I called on Genl. Sickles. He was out. I called on Capt. Benedict, but he was also out. I met Maj. [Charles] Hamlin at Willard's. He told me some news and was very kind.

I took the morning train and arrived here at 3 p.m. I found that not only our Corps but also our Brigade had been broken up.[33] The 1st and 2nd Divisions of the old 3rd Corps are now attached to the 2nd Corps. The 3rd Division of the 3rd Corps is now attached to the 6th Corps. The 11th New Jersey, 1st Massachusetts, 16th Massachusetts, and 26th Pennsylvania of our old 1st Brigade are now united with the old 3rd Brigade (called the "2nd New Jersey Brigade") and commanded by Genl. Mott. The 11th Massachusetts and 84th Pennsylvania are now in the Excelsior Brigade. All are in the same division.

So far as it regards the braking up of the Brigade, and the placing of my regiment in the old Jersey Brigade, I am not only satisfied but pleased. Genl. Mott is a good brigade commander and a gentleman,

---

31. McAllister's first efforts to obtain a furlough met with failure. Since Mrs. McAllister was then visiting friends in Shippensburg, Pa., the Colonel addressed his letter to Alice R. Dick. She was the only one then at the McAllister home in Belvidere. See McAllister to J. M. Norwell, Mar. 12, 1864, McAllister Papers.

32. Starting Mar. 19, McAllister was on a ten-day furlough. His orderly, Pvt. John Labort, accompanied him to Belvidere. McAllister's service file.

33. Because battle losses had so depleted the army's ranks, Meade recommended that the five corps be consolidated into three. The War Department approved the suggestion on Mar. 23. The II, V, and VI Corps retained their identities. The thinned ranks of the III Corps were reorganized into divisions and assigned to either the II or the VI Corps. The I Corps likewise ceased to exist. While the consolidation no doubt improved efficiency, it had a harmful effect on the *esprit de corps* of units from the proud I and III Corps. *OR*, XXXIII, 638–39, 722–23, 735–37; Walker, *Second Army Corps*, 397–403.

and it relieves me from that poor miserable creature, Col. Blaisdell.[34] He has had to return to his regiment and is hopping mad. I am rejoiced and so are all my friends. I have laughed more than I have for a month at this turn of events, braking up that abominable clique and returning them to their regiment and companies. It is said that Col. Blaisdell and his friends are all under arrest.[35] I am glad of it. My friend, Genl. Carr, commands our Division. I am right among my friends and am happy. . . .

Brandy Station, Va., March 30th 1864

My dear Ellen,

. . . I am very well and quite happy over the manner in which Col. Blaisdell has been thwarted in his schemes and plans and put back in his regiment. A lot of his friends are under arrest for holding an indignation meeting and blackguarding Genl. Carr. No doubt they will be dismissed from the service. I hope that Blaisdell will be caught in the same trap.

There was to have been a review of the 2nd Corps yesterday, but it rained and the orders were countermanded. If it had taken place, I would have been in command of the Brigade—9 regiments. Genl. Mott being sick, I was the ranking officer. Would not that have made Blaisdell mad, hopping mad? . . .

The interest in our religious meetings is decidedly on the increase. I never saw the like of it. We have not told the half of it. God grant that it may continue. It is delightful to be at these meetings. We have them every night. What a change in our regiment, and it is for the better. Pray, oh pray, for us, and we shall remember you in our prayers. . . .

---

34. One source attributed the ill will between McAllister and Blaisdell to the latter's penchant for whiskey. According to camp rumor, Blaisdell once swore that if he obtained command of the regiments by Christmas "he would have the entire brigade drunk." In any event, the lax discipline present when Blaisdell was in command contributed highly to his failure to receive a brigadier's promotion. For example, see *OR,* Vol. LI, Pt. 1, pp. 1040–41; Marbaker, *11th New Jersey,* 152–53.

35. Blaisdell was not arrested, but several of his subordinates spent up to three weeks in the stockade awaiting trial for the misconduct which McAllister subsequently describes. For a version of the controversy by one of the officers arrested, see Blake, *Three Years in the Army of the Potomac,* 272–73. Cf. Marbaker, *11th New Jersey,* 133.

Brandy Station, Va., March 31st 1864

My dear Ellen & daughter Sarah,

... The exciting scene of yesterday was when an order came down from Genl. Hancock [36] to arrest and take under guard the officers under Col. Blaisdell who, at his insistence, held the indignation meeting. The guards took them, horses, servants, baggage and all. I am only sorry that the old chief of trouble and contention was not among the number taken. He is the man that ought to be caught. He has tried to do more to injure me this winter than any officer ever did. Yes, I wish old Blaisdell was among them. They have only caught his tools.

This is the party that was prominent and conspicuous in taking the church for a dance hall. You see how things work. . . .

Brandy Station, Va., March 31st 1864

My dear Ellen,

I have only written you hasty letters since my return to camp. In these I have touched on matters and things. I wrote you this morning; and having just returned from prayer meeting, and having a little time before retiring, I will write again.

While I have mentioned prayer meetings, I would say that the interest still continues and, I think, greater than before I went home. Tonight the house was full, and quite a number have remained behind to have a social meeting by themselves. Captain Sleeper [37] has become an earnest and very hard-working Christian. He makes a most exceldent prayer. Almost all take part. We had a very solom meeting this evening, although our chaplain has not yet returned and no member of the Christian Commission was with us. I have never seen a better state of feeling in religious matters than is to be seen in this regiment at the present time. I hope it may continue and we may be drawn from the ways of sin and death.

---

36. The very able Winfield Scott Hancock commanded the II Corps. During the Peninsular Campaign McClellan referred to him as "Hancock the Superb," and the title stuck. An Assistant Secretary of War summarized Hancock by writing: "He was a splendid fellow, a brilliant man, as brave as Julius Caesar, and always ready to obey orders, especially if they were fighting orders. He had more of the aggressive spirit than almost anybody else in the army." Charles A. Dana, *Recollections of the Civil War* (New York, 1902), 190.

37. Samuel T. Sleeper, "a brave, conscientious and upright soldier," entered service as a lieutenant in Co. I. His promotion to captain came in June, 1863. He was killed in the May, 1864, battle of Spotsylvania. Marbaker, *11th New Jersey*, 76, 362–63.

Tomorrow Capt. Bigelow,[38] one of the officers who was conspicuous in holding the meeting to express disgust at the braking up and consolidation, as well as abuse of Genl. Carr, has his trial. He no doubt acted under directions of Col. Blaisdell. He was the mouthpiece. Lieut. Blake,[39] Quartermaster Forrest,[40] Capt. Smith [41]—all of the 11th Massachusetts (Blaisdell's regiment) will have their trials. Captain Thomas [42] of the 26th Pennsylvania is also under arrest for acting as president of the same meeting. But he was unfortunately drawn into it. Our officers very fortunately kept out of it. Those that were there opposed the meeting and are the principal ones against them. I am only sorry that Col. Blaisdell was not there instead of behind the screen. He would then have faced the fate of his friends. But I think he will be caught yet. I hope that he will. He has tyrannized over me for several months, and abused me as he has abused Genl. Carr. Now he has got to the end of his string. The tables are turned. He is under and I don't believe he will ever rise again.

When I commanded the old Brigade, I got Captain Bigelow his position as Inspector General. After Blaisdell came into power, Bigelow was ready and willing to do his dirty work. He has thus been caught in his own trap. A common saying here is that Capt. Bigelow has as many faces as a State House clock, which I know to be very true. Lt. Blake is a lawyer and has some smartness about him. But having a dislike for Genl. Carr because the General had him court-marshalled, he has never forgive him and has been doing all he could against him and against Carr's confirmation at Washington. Lt. Forrest is considered quite smart and was Blaisdell's trumpeter, blowing his horn through the papers. Several pieces that appeared in the Boston papers, as well as pieces in the Harrisburg *Telegraph,* were written by him. (He had a brother in the latter office.) These pieces were blowing up the brave and gallant Col. Blaisdell for a star on his shoulder, which has not come nor never will. Forrest is a greate drunkard

---

38. James R. Bigelow was a former bookseller in Boston. He was court-martialed and dismissed from service Apr. 25, 1864. Mass. Adj. Gen., *Massachusetts Soldiers,* I, 770.

39. Henry N. Blake was a Dorchester attorney before the outbreak of the war. He apparently was the one least affected by this incident, for on Apr. 26, 1864, he received promotion to captain. *Ibid.,* 808.

40. Regimental quartermaster George Forrest, a Boston publisher before the war, was dismissed from service Apr. 30, 1864. *Ibid.,* 764.

41. Probably Lowell machinist Walter N. Smith, who shortly became captain of Co. B, 11th Massachusetts. *Ibid.,* 752.

42. Edward C. Thomas was captain of Co. C, 26th Pennsylvania. He escaped any disciplinary action from this episode and was mustered out of service with his company in June, 1864. Records of the Adjutant General's Office, Commonwealth of Pennsylvania.

This photograph of Robert McAllister was made while the Colonel was recuperating in Belvidere from wounds received at Gettysburg.

McAllister astride Charley, his favorite horse, in January, 1862

Col. William Blaisdell

Brig. Gen. Joseph B. Carr

Maj. Gen. Andrew A. Humphreys

*Mathew Brady photograph of
Brig. Gen. Régis de Trobriand*

and is mean enough for anything. After the Christian Commission took away the flag for the Brigade Chapel on account of the fuss about the dance, Forrest wrote a miserable, low, blackguard piece against the Commission and religious people in general. It was the most wicked and blasphemous thing I ever heard of. It was sent in for publication, but I suppose the editor would not publish it. Had it been published, it would have ruined Blaisdell. It was written for him.

As we look up the little knoll on which Blaisdell had his headquarters—now a ruin and desolation, we say: "How have the mighty fallen!" They were the most uncouthed, wicked, medlesom, and abominable pack I ever knew at any decent headquarters. They were disliked and detested by all, and we are glad that they are broken up and laid aside.

While I was at home, there was eight inches of snow here. The mountains are still covered with it. We had a heavy rain day before yesterday. It rained all day and night. . . .

Brandy Station, Va., April 9th 1864

My dear Ellen,

. . . You ask how it comes that I am still in the 1st Brigade. In answer I would say that it is not the same first of the old Brigade. Every division has its 1st brigade. Our Division is altered from the 2nd to the 4th. But still we are the 1st Brigade of the 4th Division. Our old Brigade was divided—a part pute in the New Jersey Brigade, commanded by Genl. Mott, and the other part pute into the Excelsior Brigade, commanded by Col. Brewster. . . . But our transfer is only temporary. We still retain our [3rd Corps] badges.

Now you see that Col. Blaisdell and I are in the same division but in different brigades. Of course, I have nothing to do with him. I am the ranking Colonel in my Brigade. When Genl. Mott is sick or absent, I am in command. Today Genl. Mott was Corps Officer of the Day. This Corps was to have been reviewed by Genl. Grant,[43] and I was in

---

43. The victorious siege of Vicksburg, Miss., and a smashing triumph over Braxton Bragg's Confederate army at Chattanooga, Tenn., led Lincoln on Mar. 10, 1864, to name Gen. Ulysses S. Grant supreme commander of "all Armies of the United States." Grant came east and made his headquarters with the Army of the Potomac. His arrival at Brandy Station "produced no unusual enthusiasm" among the men. A Maine officer felt that "after the debonair McClellan, the cocky Burnside, rosy Joe Hooker, and the dyspeptic Meade, the calm and unpretentious Grant was not exciting" in either appearance or conduct. *OR*, XXXIII, 633; Rauscher, *Music on the March,* 152; Abner R. Small, *The Road to Richmond* (Berkeley, Calif., 1939), 130.

command of this Brigade. But it rained and the review did not take place.

I am still in command of the Brigade, and likely will be very frequently. Blaisdell is the ranking officer in the Excelsior Brigade, after Col. Brewster, and will likely be in command of that brigade as I may be of this. Still, he will not interfere with me. His regiment goes out of service in a short time. And I think if Blaisdell does not get command of a Brigade, he will go out with it. But his chances of being made a Brigadier are very poor. He will never raise the star. He has lowered himself very much in the estimation of all good officers. In fact, he has now no standing. He undertook to kill Genl. Carr and myself. But instead of accomplishing that, he killed himself. Very few Brigadiers are made now. There are few brigades—and many Brigadiers back in the rear that have to be provided for. But these take good care not to get into battle. They leave command at that time to the ranking Colonels. Yet they are always on hand about pay time. In this Corps several Colonels who have commanded brigades for a year or more are now back commanding regiments.

You ask what claims has Genl. Torbert. I answer *West Point.* That influence is still heavy and is at war with those of us who have not been through that mill. The greate opposition to Genl. Sickles comes from that source, and I would not be surprised if it will even pute Genl. Birney down. Genl. Meade don't like him, nor does he like the 3rd Corps. Genl. Birney's testimony before the board of inquiry at Washington was rather favourable to Sickles and against Meade to some extent.[44] This has added to the dislike.

Genl. Torbert, I understand, has been asigned to a cavalry division.[45] I don't know who will take command of Torbert's Brigade. Col. [Henry W.] Brown of the 3rd New Jersey is the ranking Colonel, and the only New Jersey Colonel that ranks me. He has long been pushing for a Brigadiership. But whether he will get it I can't tell. I know very little in regard to myself. Finding that there are but few

---

44. Gens. Sickles and Abner Doubleday testified before the Committee on the Conduct of the War that Meade twice ordered the army to withdraw during the first stages of the battle of Gettysburg. In addition, they felt that Meade had possessed no battle plan and, once victorious, made little or no effort to pursue the defeated Confederate army. Meade vigorously denied the charges and in the end was exonerated. An artillery officer writing of the hearings singled out Sickles and Doubleday for strong censure. "A pretty team!—Rascality and Stupidity. I wonder which hatches the most monstrous chicken." Wainwright, *Diary of Battle,* 325.

45. Torbert had been in command of the 1st Brigade, 1st Division, VI Corps. On the date of McAllister's letter, he assumed command of the 1st Cavalry Division. *OR,* XXXIII, 786, 830, 1033.

appointments, I have given myself no trouble about it, nor will I at this time.

I see Genl. [William R.] Montgomery has been dismissed.[46] Why, I can't tell. I am sorry for him. Genl. Birney says he is not dismissed but only droped from the rolls, having no command. Why don't they drop more that have don less for their country? . . .

Tremendous rain storm. It has been pouring down in torrents all day and no slacking yet. . . .

Brandy Station, Va., April 11th 1864

My dear Ellen,

The storm seems to be over, and it has cleared up. But the roads are in a terable state. If it does not rain soon again, they will dry up in a reasonable time.

All the ladies, including Miss Gilson, and also the sutlers, are ordered to leave. This looks like a move. We are expecting a hard campaign, in which we will have to do a greate deal of fighting.

Yesterday we had the Lord's Supper administered at the Brigade Chapel—not the old brigade chapel where the dance was, but the 2nd New Jersey Brigade (now ours). All the chaplains were present, representing 4 denominations—Presbyterian, Methodist, Baptist and Congregationalist. It was a strange sight, and a pleasant one, to think of the harmony that exists among the different sects. . . .

The religious influence in this regiment still continues. . . . I have never witnessed anything like it. When our regiment is not on picket, our church is crowded for preaching and for prayer every night. After the regular meeting is over, a large number still remains for conversation and more prayer. And after these are dismissed and the Chaplain comes away, a number still remains for prayer. During the day many resort to the chapel for prayer, as well as to secret places far from camp. One day I was riding out to hunt a safe place to fire at a target. I rode up on a little bluff; and as I reached the summit, I heard a voice. On looking down into a stone quarry I saw two of our boys earnestly engaged in prayer. I turned away as quietly as possible, thinking how delightful it was to find such deep religious feeling in my regiment. . . .

46. Montgomery officially resigned from service Apr. 4, 1864, "on account of failing health." However, Lincoln mustered him out of service before Montgomery's resignation was submitted, and the "ailing" general lived until 1871. Montgomery's service file; *The Union Army*, VIII, 179.

Brandy Station, Va., April 11th 1864

My dear Ellen,

I wrote you this morning. I have just returned from prayer meeting. It is now late, but I will write you some before retiring.

. . . This afternoon a number of officers of this Division (the old 2nd but now called the 4th) had a very pleasant meeting at the Division Hospital to present Miss Gilson with a diamond ring and breastpin.[47] During last summer the officers of this Division thought it proper to make her a present and acknowledge to her the many obligations we were under for the kindness and attention shown by her to our sick and wounded. The money was raised to buy a ring and a pin, but the purchase was only made a short time ago. The money was placed in Mr. Fay's hands. When in Boston he purchased the diamond ring for $110 and a pin for the same amount.

Today we met to present them. Miss Gilson was very busy packing up to leave and was hard at work when Dr. Welling told her to dress herself, that some friends were gathering to tell her goodby. She knew nothing about what was going on. We were all seated in a large Hospital tent when she came in. After a few words of conversation, Dr. Welling rose and made a very excellent speech. He spoke of the sacrifices she had made to come out and see to the wants of the soldiers, the dangers to which she had exposed herself—having been under the enemy's fire, and the greate advantages she had been to the sick and dying. After this Dr. [James T.] Calhoun followed with another speech and presented the two articals, placing the ring on her finger and puting on the breastpin.

Miss Gilson rose and made a very handsome reply. Though intirely unprepared, she came off splendidly. All were delighted. After she sat down, Chaplain [Joseph] Twichell, who spoke so eloquently at the Commission, made a very handsome address. Chaplain Cudworth of the 1st Massachusetts made the closing speech, and the presentation was over. Mrs. Carr and Mrs. [Orson H.] Hart were the only ladies present except Miss Gilson. The whole affair passed off very pleasantly. We also had a reporter from the [New York] *Tribune* and one from the [New York] *Herald* present. . . . We are sorry that Miss Gilson has to leave. She is esteemed by all.

There has been no trains up for two days, owing to the high water destroying the bridges. But we hope to have a mail in the morning. The preparatory steps for moving still goes on. No doubt but

---

47. Mr. Fay and Miss Gilson spent a good deal of their time in visits to the 11th New Jersey because of their close friendship with Surgeon Edward Welling. Fay, *War Papers,* 92.

when the roads dry up we will all pull up stakes and march forth to battle. . . .

Brandy Station, Va., April 16th 1864

My dear daughter Henrietta,

I have not been receiving many letters from you, nor from Sarah, and your mother's letters are few and far between. This should not be, for the time is close at hand when we cannot send letters to each other. Rumor in camp this morning is that our outgoing mails will be stoped. I cannot vouch for the truth of it; but it is probable, as the commanders don't wish the Rebels to know the strength of our army. At any rate, when we march we cannot send out and receive letters. But up to that time I can receive yours, even if you do not receive mine. Write all you can and I will do the same until I find they won't be sent.

I am temporarily in command of the Brigade. Genl. Carr is absent on a short leave for a few days and Genl. Mott is in command of the Division. Being the senior officer, I am in command of the Brigade. We had a review day before yesterday of our Division. It looked splendid.[48] This Division and Birney's is all that is left of the old 3rd Corps. Birney's is now called the 3rd Division, and ours the 4th, of the 2nd Corps. . . . You will find that this Corps will take an active part in the coming battles. I have been particular in telling you all about our numbers, so that when the corrispondents of papers talk about divisions, you will know all about them. It is important that they should. You remember the trouble your Uncle Nelson had in finding me when I was wounded, because the reporters placed me in the 6th Corps hospital instead of the 3rd. This mistake was caused because the 6th Corps lay near our Hospital that night. In the morning we moved to another place to get out of range of the enemy's guns. . . .

I have got my new horse and he performs well. He is a splendid riding horse. He goes along at any gate that I want and very easy; he stands the music well. He is quiet and yet spirited. I like him very much. . . .

48. Gen. Meade noted: "These troops all looked splendidly, and seemed, officers and men, in fine spirits." Meade, *Letters of George G. Meade*, II, 190.

Brandy Station, Va., April 22nd 1864

My dear Ellen,

. . . This morning is beautiful and mild. I am delighted with my horse. He is all that I desire. You could ride him, he is so easy. If anything happens to me, you ought to have him to ride as a family horse.

You may think it strange when I tell you that the top of the Blue Ridge Mountains has been covered with snow for at least four weeks past. The like never was known here so late as this. It has now about disappeared.

The paper says that our Corps was reviewed. This is a mistake; it has not come off yet. But we are expecting it every day. The Divisions have been reviewed. It is a splendid Corps. You will hear from it, for it is destined to perform an important part in the coming battles.

The greate battles of the war are coming off soon and they too will be in Virginia. . . .

Brandy Station, Va., April 24th 1864

My dear daughter Henrietta,

. . . We are expecting to march any day. All are ready for a move, and we may leave here at any hour. We know not where we are going. Genl. Grant has the secret of keeping his own secrets, which, by the way, is a good thing for the success of our cause.

Our Corps, the 2nd, was reviewed last week, and it looked splendid. The 3rd and 4th Divisions (the old 3rd Corps) looked well and marched a little better than the 1st and 2nd Divisions (the old 2nd Corps). We still have our diamond badges on our caps, and we are still proud of the old 3rd. So you see in our Corps we have two sets of badges distinguishing the old 3rd Corps from the 2nd, but now all called the 2nd under the new arrangement. . . .

Genl. Grant reviewed us, and he expressed himself highly pleased with the troops. He has now reviewed the fighting portion of the Army of the Potomac, and it is said that he has never reviewed a finer army. The world has never seen better troops. The Western army does not compare with our army in appearance and discipline.

Genl. Grant is not a very fine-looking General, but he has the appearance of a man of determination. He seemed to be thinking of something else than reviews, for he often forgot to return the salute of officers in passing. No doubt he was thinking of the greate work before him and forgot that he was the reviewing officer of the day. . . .

Brandy Station, Va., April 24, 1864

My dear Ellen,

. . . I am sorry to tell you that we are likely to loose Genl. Carr.[49] You know that last year he was not confirmed; and the President, at the request of Genl. Hooker, reappointed him to date back to his first appointment. This winter Congress passed a law that no commissions can be dated back. He can get his confirmation through, but he will be junior to everybody of the rank of Brigadier General and would have to take a Brigade and serve under those who have heretofore served under him. (In this case Genl. Mott would take the Division and Genl. Carr the Brigade.) This Genl. Carr will not do under the circumstances; he has been a division commander for a long time, although he had but a brigadier's commission—and not confirmed at that. By accepting the commission now, and not dated back, would keep him with the Brigade for a long time, while those who have served under him would be commanding divisions. You understand his position. He will not accept; and like two others just confirmed under the same circumstances, he will resign.

This I am very sorry for, for he has always been a warm friend of mine and I consider him an excellent officer. I would much rather he would stay—yes, ten times rather he would. If he leaves . . . I fear that they may send some Brigadier General here which I do not want. . . .

Brandy Station, Va., April 27th 1864

My dear Ellen & family,

. . . We are still in our old camp, though Birney's Division have moved out into the open field. No doubt we will do the same, if we do not start off on the coming campaign. We are all ready to move and awaiting orders. I suppose some other portion of the army is not yet ready and we are waiting on it. No doubt but that we will soon have stiring times, accomplish a grate deal or loose a grate deal. I am very well. . . .

---

49. On Apr. 30 Meade informed Sec. Stanton that the uncertainty of Carr's promotion had "greatly impaired" the efficiency of the II Corps. Although Carr was then in command of a division, Meade stated, "it is well understood that the Senate have refused to confirm him with the date of his appointment, and it is expected he will be junior to General Mott, now commanding a brigade in his division. This is producing disquiet and bad feeling, and I desire, if possible, to have the matter definitely settled one way or the other before the army moves." *OR,* XXXIII, 1025.

Brandy Station, Va., April 28th 1864

My dear Ellen,

Inclosed you will please find a certificate of membership for the 3rd Corps Union, which I wish you to keep. . . . You will also find a new constitution and by laws which have just been passed by the Union. It is well enough to preserve these things. They may all be of use to you if I should die.

This morning is somewhat cold, but it is dry. We have not moved yet. We learned with surprise yesterday that [Ambrose] Burnside with his [9th] Corps is coming here.[50] Everything seems to be a mystery to us.

I have been amazed at the papers announcing my being temporarily in command of the 2nd New Jersey Brigade. I only had the command one week while Genl. Carr was at home.

I understand that as soon as he got here with his famous 10th [New Jersey] Regiment and found there was a vacancy in the 1st New Jersey Brigade, Col. [Henry] Ryerson got a furlough and went to Washington to push his claims for the Brigadiership—I suppose for gallantry displayed in the coal regions. I have not learned his success.[51] If he should get appointed, there will be much dissatisfaction. There are New Jersey Colonels here who have fought many, many battles. I do not think he will get it. Col. [Henry] Brown of the 3rd New Jersey ranks us all. Then I stand next. I understand that Ryerson is working against Brown. Col. Brown is now in command of that brigade, but *unfortunately* he was born in Pennsylvania. This greate crime, no doubt, is used against him. He hails from Philadelphia, has never been a resident of our state, but has fought not only for New Jersey but for the whole Union. . . .

Brandy Station, Va., May 1st 1864

My dear Ellen & family,

It is now 9 p.m. and I have just returned from prayer meeting. This evening was set apart for special prayers for our country and our cause in the approaching campaign. . . . Henrietta writes me that

---

50. Burnside and his corps, on duty in Tennessee, were ordered in mid-March to rejoin the Army of the Potomac. The men of the IX Corps were filing through Manassas as McAllister wrote his letter. Like McAllister, Burnside was completely ignorant of Grant's plans. *Ibid.*, 678, 954, 1004.

51. Col. Henry O. Ryerson never succeeded in his attempts to gain a brigadiership. He was killed in the May 6 fighting in the Wilderness.

in Philadelphia they are holding daily prayer meetings for the same purpose. . . .

Just as we were coming out of church, we heard some cheering and saw a greate light. We soon found it to be the grate dance hall on fire. This is the building that the lovers of pleasure pute up after the fuss about the use of the chapel. It has been used for shows, nigger dances, &c. These people got to fighting among themselves, and some of the dissatisfied has fired the building.[52]

Inclosed you will please find a few little wild flowers for you, dear Ellen. I kissed them. I would send you more and better ones, but this is a very poor country for flowers. Accept them as a love offering from your soldier boy.

A report here is that not only Genl. Burnside is here with his Corps, but that Genl. Hooker is also here, or rather at Harper's Ferry.[53] It seems now that we are going to have our forces concentrated. The Rebels are also concentrating their forces. So we are likely to have a Waterloo battle.

Good Morning. I had a sweete night's repose. This is a butiful May morning. This day one year ago we fought the Chancellorsville battle, and also fought the next day. . . . What a change another year will bring time alone will tell. . . .

Brandy Station, Va., May 3rd 1864

My dear Ellen,

. . . I feel sad this morning. My friend, Genl. Carr, leaves us today. He is ordered to report to Genl. [Benjamin F.] Butler. I told you of the difficulty about his rank. He cannot date back to his first appointment; so, you see that he is outranked by nearly all the Brigadier Generals in this Corps. To relieve him of this difficulty, his friend Genl. Meade got Genl. Grant to order him to report to Genl. Butler, where he will outrank other Brigadiers and will have command of a division. Genl. Mott, I suppose, will take command of our division today—whether permanently or not I can't tell. If so, and no other Brigadier comes here, I will be in command of the Brigade. But I

---

52. "The [winter] season closed with a grand conflagration," noted Sgt. Marbaker. "Some incendiary fired the building, and in spite of the heroic efforts of the New York firemen from the Excelsior Brigade . . . the building was entirely consumed. No insurance." *11th New Jersey*, 155.

53. The report was untrue. Hooker was then at Chattanooga, having just assumed command of the newly formed XX Corps. *OR*, Vol. XXXII, Pt. 3, pp. 221, 270.

don't know what the arrangements are. As soon as I get my brackfast, I will go over and call on Genl. Carr and have a leave-taking. . . .

Brandy Station, Va., May 3rd 1864

My dear Ellen & family,

It is now quite late, and we are all ready to move tonight at midnight. In four hours we will be on the move and no doubt engage the enemy soon. I think that it is a general move. You will hear of battles, perhaps before this reaches you. God grant that we may be successful.

Genl. Carr has left. Genl. Mott commands the Division and I am in command of the Brigade. I hope and pray that God will give me mind and judgement to manage the Brigade and enable me to do my whole duty to my country. . . .

10

Bloody Route to Petersburg

ONLY A REGION of such confused geography as the Wilderness could have concealed the vast army that Grant on May 4, 1864, led southward across the Rapidan. The Army of the Potomac numbered 118,769 men. Its battle position—two ranks in front and a third in reserve—could assault or defend a normal area twenty-one miles wide. In open battle this gigantic host would indeed be formidable, if not impregnable.

No one knew this better than Robert E. Lee. The Confederate commander's counterstrategy was a shrewdness born of necessity. Lee concealed his smaller army in the dark, tangled undergrowth of the Wilderness, waited until the Federal divisions were jammed and confused on the narrow lanes winding through the forest, and then struck with full force. The battle of Wilderness (May 5–6) was a stand-up, personal contest on both sides. Some officers literally lost their commands in the snarled woods and rough terrain. "Maneuvering here was necessarily out of the question," an artilleryman wrote home, "and only Indian tactics told." [1]

Gershom Mott's division (to which McAllister belonged) saw bitter fighting on both days of the battle. Twice the division fell back before Confederate attacks. Although the unit's

---

1. Kitching, *Memorials*, 124.

behavior was questionable, no onus could be placed on McAllister. Both of his horses were killed in the battle, and he himself suffered a slight flesh wound. On May 10, after Grant had fought his way to the vicinity of Spotsylvania, McAllister's troops failed in an assigned assault and thus added to the doubts of some regarding the division's fighting qualities.

Such doubts were dispelled two days later. McAllister's brigade led the II Corps in a massed attack on a salient of the Confederate line known thereafter as the "Bloody Angle." The 11th New Jersey lost one third of its complement in the fourteen-hour engagement. With Lee's army still intact, Grant continued his eastward "sidling" in an effort to get between Lee and Richmond. McAllister was involved in the fighting at Bowling Green, the North Anna River, and, to a lesser degree, Cold Harbor. "It is the hardest campaigning I have ever seen," he wrote of Grant's advance. "I would not have believed that I could have gone through it."

In mid-June the Federal army crossed the James River and struck at Petersburg, twenty-five miles south of Richmond. Two quick assaults failed to effect the city's capture. Lee's main army then arrived, and each of the opposing forces began preparations for a siege. The failure to take Petersburg was a painful blow to morale in Grant's army. "The men no longer possessed the spirit shown at the beginning of the campaign," a Federal infantryman commented. The "character and frequency of the battles in which they had been engaged had reduced the physical and moral strength of the army" almost to the breaking point. "Rest and recuperation were necessary to restore the physical and moral energies, but there was much gone that could not be restored." [2]

♣

2. Bruce, *20th Massachusetts,* 406. See also Lyman, *Meade's Headquarters,* 168–70; Frank Wilkeson, *Recollections of a Private Soldier in the Army of the Potomac* (New York, 1887), 173–74, 185–87. A contrary view is in Dana, *Recollections of the Civil War,* 221–22.

Chancellorsville, Va., May 4th 1864

My dear Ellen,

Here I am, writing this letter on my lap on the battlefield of Chancellorsville. We have reached this far without fighting—an unexpected matter for us.[3]

I have been over the battlefield this evening and found the bones of our dead laying and bleaching on top of the ground.[4] Some sight where my regiment fought so gallantly! They had had a light covering of earth, but the bones were washed out. The trees and timber was cut to pieces. I did not sleep any last night and but little the night before. I must lay down and get some rest. You will excuse me from writing no particulars at this time.

Inclosed you will find two or three pretty violets and flowers that I picked up on the very ground where my regiment stood and fought so splendidly. The ground was made rich by the blood of our brave soldiers. I thought the flowers would be a relick prised by you.

We will not be here long; we will be kept moving. . . .

Battlefield of the Wilderness, May 6th 1864 [5]

My dear family,

Saturday morning, May 7th. Yesterday at 4 p.m. I had just written the above when the enemy opened on us with one of the most

---

3. Because it was assigned the duty of escorting wagon trains, the 11th New Jersey did not begin its march into the Wilderness until the morning of May 4—six hours after the lead elements of the Federal army had crossed the Rapidan. McAllister's men reached Chancellorsville at 5 P.M. "We had marched about twenty-five miles, the day had been unusually warm and many officers and men were overcome with the heat, those showing the least endurance who had indulged the most freely in commissary whiskey during the winter." Marbaker, *11th New Jersey*, 160–61.

4. "Among many ghastly relics picked up was a skull, the cap still upon it, and upon the visor was stamped 'D. Bender, Co. H, 11th N.J. Vols.'" Sgt. Daniel Bender had been killed May 3 at Chancellorsville. *Ibid.*, 70; *N.J. Record*, I, 573. See also Goss, *Recollections of a Private*, 267; Wilkeson, *Recollections of a Private Soldier*, 49–50.

5. McAllister never had the opportunity to compile a detailed narrative of the Wilderness fighting. In brief, the V and VI Corps on May 5 attacked Lee's semiconcealed army. When Confederates broke through the lines of the VI Corps, Winfield Hancock rushed his II Corps into action along the Orange Plank Road and managed to stem the Southern advance. On the following day Hancock renewed his attack on A. P. Hill's brigades. Suddenly Confederate Gen. James Longstreet unleashed four brigades on Hancock's flanks. Portions of Francis C. Barlow and Mott's brigades gave way, occasioning a withdrawal by Hancock's entire corps. Mott's command, to which McAllister belonged,

terrific fires I have ever been under. They hurled their columns, massed in close formation, right in our front with a terable onset. My Brigade was in the second line. The first line fought splendidly until their fifty rounds of cartridges was exhausted. Then our line took the brunt of the battle and done well—yes, fought splendidly and made a terible slaughter amongst the Rebels. I can't now give you the particulars.

We fought all day yesterday and I have lost both of my horses. Both were shot while I was on them. The Black was killed in the forenoon and Charley in the afternoon. I have a slight wound—just a bruise by a minie ball, close to my old wound. I came off the field to the 2nd Corps Hospital. But I feel so much better this morning that I am about to start for the front and resume command of the Brigade, as we expect to have another battle today.[6] We fought yesterday from daylight until 5 p.m. In the morning we were very successful. Towards noon the tide ran against us. In the evening we rolled it against the enemy. Things are looking well now.

We also had a battle day before yesterday. Our Division did not do well; but yesterday we done so well that we have gained all and more than we lost then. I am very much used up but, by the help of God, will keep on. I have not lost anything personally on the score of bravery. My noble war horses were both killed on one day, within a few hours of each other, but I have been mercifully spared thus far.[7] . . .

---

came in for strong censure from those who were unaware of the untenable position Mott's troops held following Longstreet's assault. McAllister's official and extensive report of the Wilderness is in *OR*, Vol. XXXVI, Pt. 1, pp. 487–90. See also *ibid.*, p. 682; Marbaker, *11th New Jersey*, 161–65; Lyman, *Meade's Headquarters*, 93; Humphreys, *Virginia Campaign*, 33n., 43–44.

6. McAllister rejoined his command at noon on Saturday, May 7. *OR*, Vol. XXXVI, Pt. 1, p. 490.

7. On the night of May 7 McAllister's brigade began marching eastward toward Spotsylvania. It was the last unit to leave the field of the Wilderness. "The boys made up their minds," stated Sgt. Marbaker, "that 'Meade's and Lee's express route,' as they called it, was to be abandoned, and that Grant proposed to establish an office nearer Richmond." But the night movement of May 7 made a lasting impression upon many of the men. "The stillness of the night, the gloom of the forest, so deep as to be almost shadowless, making the forms of comrades only a pace or two distant look like dim silhouettes against a darker background; clumps of bushes, stumps and fallen limbs took weird and threatening shapes; imagination played fantastic tricks, and fallen logs became lurking foes and the harmless murmur of each gentle breeze the voice of waiting enemies, and as we moved slowly forward through the gloom our feet would come in contact with some yielding substance, and, reaching down, our hands perhaps would fall upon the clammy face of a corpse, for the woods was filled with death's ghastly trophies." Marbaker, *11th New Jersey*, 166–68.

Battlefield near Spotsylvania Court House, Va.
May 11th 1864

My dear Ellen & family,

I have just learned that a letter could be sent out. We are still fighting—every day since the 5th. God has spared my life thus far, for which we ought to be thankful. Yesterday morning we came down here from Todd's Tavern. The battle has been going on ever since. We have drove the enemy some, but their position is a strong one and our loss is very heavy. The troops whose term of service is just coming to a close do not fight well. I am sorry to say that in our Division we have too many of this kind.

In a charge I made yesterday, we were repulsed when we ought to have been successful.[8] The general charge all along the line was somewhat of a failure. But we are still fighting them and hope to gain the victory.

This campaign beats all the rest in desperation and determination. God only knows the result. I expect soon to go forward again into the raging storm of lead and iron. I wrote you yesterday that I lost both my horses in battle. I had to charge through a thick woods and went on foot. We have already fought many battles; and from present appearances will have to fight many more before we get through. We are not now with the 2nd Corps. Since yesterday morning we have been fighting with the 6th.[9] . . .

Belvidere, N.J., January 24th 1882

Major General Mott
My Dear General,

As promised in my last letter to you, I have been looking through my military papers to revise my memory of the Spotsylvania bloody

---

8. On May 10 Mott's division was both tardy and inefficient in making a probe of the Confederate defenses at Spotsylvania. The Federals drove in Confederate pickets, only to walk into an enfilading fire from concealed Southern batteries. Mott's men fell back "in some confusion." One of Meade's staff officers wrote contemptuously that "the whole army would have been stronger without Mott's division." Assistant Secretary of War Charles Dana added: "We were disgraced by a retreat of that division, without loss, and apparently without any considerable force to oppose them. They advanced into the woods with orders to attack, but came out again at once, like cowards." *OR*, Vol. XXXVI, Pt. 1, p. 490; Marbaker, *11th New Jersey,* 168–69; Lyman, *Meade's Headquarters,* 208; Dana, *Recollections of the Civil War,* 67.

9. Following the action of May 10, McAllister's regiments fell back behind the VI Corps and, for the next several days, acted as a bridge between that wing of the army and the IX Corps. *OR*, Vol. XXXVI, Pt. 1, pp. 65, 330, 490–91.

field. I will only give you an account of my own Brigade and what I saw around us.[10]

As you are aware, my Brigade at that time was the 1st Brigade, 4th Division, 2nd Corps. If I am not mistaken, it was composed of the following regiments: 5th, 6th, 7th, 8th and 11th New Jersey, 1st and 16th Massachusetts, and the 26th Pennsylvania. I do not know where the 120th New York was at that time. You know it was one of my regiments during the remainder of the war. You were commanding the Division.

After several ineffectual attempts to take these works at Spotsylvania, we were, on the morning of May 12th 1864, in two lines of battle as you have stated. My position was on the right of your Division.[11] I know not, nor ever heard, of any circular of instructions such as you speak of.

At early dawn the order forward was given.[12] At first we moved slowly up through the woods. When the first line reached the open field at the top of the hill, in sight of the Rebel works, we rolled out a tremendous cheer. It was taken up by the second line, and our boys started forward at a run. The first line parted in the front, leaving a long open space. Up to and partly into this space my Brigade went and struck the enemy works at the Salient. At this place the enemy had a field battery of 8 to 10 guns. I ordered some of my men to drag back the guns to our side of the works. The balance of the Brigade I ordered to push on towards the enemy.

But we soon discovered another line of Rebel works with large reinforcements coming to their aid. I ordered an about-face, retreated to the first line, and completed the hauling off of 8 guns. I found enough men in my command to man two of them. By the time the men had the guns on our side of the works and my line formed, the

10. McAllister's report of the Spotsylvania action is in *ibid.*, 490–92. Years after the war he wrote another summary of the brigade's action that is printed in Johnson and Buel, *Battles and Leaders,* IV, 176.

11. Initially, McAllister's brigade was part of the second line of attack against "The Salient" (or "Bloody Angle"). But shortly after the assault began, the brigade moved into the first line to fill a gap between the divisions of Birney and Barlow. In so doing McAllister's was the first Federal unit to strike the Salient. Its point of attack was the western face of the apex, which was then defended by the celebrated Stonewall Brigade. Marbaker, *11th New Jersey,* 171–76; McHenry Howard, *Recollections of a Maryland Confederate Soldier . . .* (Baltimore, 1913), 296–98; Robertson, *The Stonewall Brigade,* 221–26.

12. It should be remembered that the battle of Spotsylvania occurred amid heavy rain. McAllister stated in his official report: "Guns would become foul, when we would order the men back to wash them out and return to fight on. The rain poured down, the mud became almost impassable, men became exhausted . . ." *OR*, Vol. XXXVI, Pt. 1, p. 491.

enemy came in force determined to dislodge us. They succeeded in carrying the works to my right up to the Salient. Encouraged by their success so far, and with traverses in their recaptured works behind which their sharpshooters could take deadly aim and be protected, our position was critical.

Many officers without men, and many men without officers—all of whom had been driven from our line to the right—came to our assistance here and fought nobly. Here we had representatives from many regiments. Brigades and Divisions were all inspired with one serious thought: we must hold this point or lose all we had gained in the morning. The contest was life or death.

These massed columns pressed forward to the Salient. The Stars and Stripes and the Stars and Bars nearly touched each other across these works. Here, on both sides of these breastworks, were displayed more individual acts of bravery and heroism than I had yet seen in the war.[13] The graycoats and bluecoats would spring with rifles in hand on top of the breastworks, take deadly aim, fire, and then fall across into the trenches below. This I saw repeated again and again. More troops came to our aid and took a hand in the fight. A new line of troops was formed at an obtuse angle from this fighting line to stay the progress of the enemy on the right. But they no sooner formed than they were swept away by the enemy's deadly fire. This was where the 16th Massachusetts lost so heavily. Its brave commander, Waldo Merriam, was killed.[14] This was also where your Asst. Adjt. Genl., [Captain] T[homas] W. Eayre, was killed. The Colonel and his regiment were all fighting so splendidly.

The fighting lasted all day, and the rain poured down. Many of our men sunk down exhausted in the mud. Ammunition would give out, and more would be brought up. The rifles would become foul. We sent men back by companies to wash them out, after which they would return and renew the fight. It was before our line that the big tree was cut down by rifle balls.[15] The stump of it was exhibited at the Centennial in Philadelphia.

13. See similar statements by McAllister in *ibid.*, p. 492; Johnson and Buel, *Battles and Leaders*, IV, 176. To one Federal soldier in the ranks, however, the army seemed to be "suffering ruinous waste. With all its losses no appreciable advantage had been gained." Alanson A. Haines, *History of the Fifteenth Regiment, New Jersey Volunteers* (New York, 1883), 181.
14. Merriam fell dead while leading his regiment in the assault. *OR*, Vol. XXXVI, Pt. 1, p. 339.
15. Confederate Gen. Samuel McGowan wrote: "To give some idea of the intensity of the [rifle] fire, an oak tree 22 inches in diameter, which stood just in rear of the right of [my] brigade, was cut down by the constant scaling of musket-balls, and fell about 12 o'clock Thursday night, injuring by its fall several soldiers in the First South Carolina Regiment." *Ibid.*, 1034.

[420] ✗ THE McALLISTER LETTERS

Night closed in upon us. The minute we could slack fire, the enemy, determined to gain this point, would close in on us. Had they succeeded in driving us from there, all we had gained would have been lost. But at 3 a.m. the battle was over and our victory complete. I need not describe to you the scenes of battle, the horrible sight the next morning of the dead and dying mass of humanity that lay in the trenches on the Rebel side of the works, and the dead that covered the ground on our side.[16] . . .

Spotsylvania Court House, Va., May 15th 1864

My dear Ellen & family,

Just as I was leaving the battlefield this morning, I wrote a line or two. But as we have stoped here for a short time, and as I find that the mail has not yet gone, I will write you a little more.

After the battle of Spotsylvania we remained the masters of the field, strengthened our works, and buried the dead of both armies. We now seem to be moving onward. We lost very heavily; the North will be in mourning. But the Rebels have suffered beyond description. I have never witnessed such scenes. At a point where I stood for at least 14 hours, urging the men forward and to stand firm, the slaughter was terable. It was the assailant point when the enemy retook the earthworks, and to give that up would be destruction for our army. There we stood and there we fought one whole day and till 3 o'clock in the morning, when the enemy finally withdrew. The Rebel dead were piled up on their side of the works, presenting a horrible spectacle. Many wounded were among the dead, with the dead lying on them. We finished burying them yesterday.

Such a sheet of fire and storm of leaden hail the historian has never yet recorded. I saw it all and, if I am spared, will give you a description of it. We have this morning destroyed waggon loads of muskets, as we cannot bring them with us. We captured 20 pieces of artillery; 18 pieces we got day before yesterday, and yesterday we got

16. Figures on the casualties at Spotsylvania are variable and contradictory. At least 3,560 Federals were wounded in the one day's fighting, and one source placed total Union losses at 6,820 men. Estimates of Confederate casualties range from 5,000 to 9,000 soldiers. The 11th New Jersey lost 70 out of less than 200 men engaged. *Ibid.,* 149, 231; Marbaker, *11th New Jersey,* 181; Thomas L. Livermore, *Numbers and Losses in the Civil War in America, 1861–65* (cited hereafter as Livermore, *Numbers and Losses*) (Boston, 1900), 112–13; Freeman, *Lee's Lieutenants,* III, 409.

the other two. The Rebels had hauled them back in the woods, and they lay between our line of pickets. But yesterday we opened heavy artillery fire and drove the Rebels back and hauled off the two pieces, making 20 in all captured by our Corps alone. My Brigade took eight pieces. We manned two of them (we had not gunners to man them all) and turned them on the enemy. So much for Jersey in this great fight. On the right, where my right was turned, all regiments, brigades, divisions, and corps had a hand in this fight. No one can claim all the honors; our troops were all mixed up.

Captain Sleeper, a gallant officer in the 11th New Jersey, was killed; Lt. Eagen also.[17] As usual, the 11th New Jersey has suffered a good deal. Our loss in killed and wounded in the Brigade is 700 up to this time,[18] not including straglers and those that may have been taken prisoners. In this great fight—in fact, in the two great fights, my Brigade has fought splendidly. . . .

Spotsylvania Court House, Va., May 16th 1864
My dear Ellen & family,

I wrote you two letters yesterday; and just as I was finishing the last one, an order came to fall in. We soon found ourselves double-quicking it towards the enemy.[19] The picket line had given way, and we rushed in to stop the progress of the enemy. We had considerable firing when the enemy opened an enfilading fire upon us in our rifle pits. One ball—a shell that did not burst—passed through one of the traverses against which Lt. Baldwin, Col. Schoonover, and myself were standing. It instantly killed Lt. Baldwin—hit him fair on the head.[20] He never spoke. Fortunately, the shell did not burst and fell

17. Lt. William H. Egan of Co. C was the second man to be killed by one bullet. The ball first passed through and killed Pvt. Nathaniel Cole of Co. I, then inflicted a mortal wound on Lt. Egan. Marbaker, *11th New Jersey,* 176–77, 298, 362.
18. In the period May 5–21 McAllister's brigade suffered a total of 645 casualties. Fifty-three of these were in the 11th New Jersey. *OR,* Vol. XXXVI, Pt. 1, pp. 122, 140.
19. The 11th New Jersey moved forward at dawn to occupy some partially abandoned earthworks. Confederate sharpshooters picked off several Federals during the advance. That afternoon, after the regiment obtained control of the works, an enemy battery opened fire on that sector. Yet the New Jersey troops maintained their position until ordered on May 17 to retire. *Ibid.,* 494.
20. Lt. Col. Schoonover reported that Lt. Joseph C. Baldwin of Co. E was killed when "struck on the head by an unexploded shell." *Ibid.* See also Marbaker, *11th New Jersey,* 178–79, 344, 354.

at our feet. If it had bursted, it would likely have killed several more of us.

We lost about 20 in my Brigade in this affair. We seem to have the luck to be engaged in all the battles from day to day. When this fighting will end God only knows.

Lt. Baldwin was a splendid officer and a warm friend of mine. I had him on my staff; but as Genl. Mott was in part commanding the Brigade yesterday, Baldwin had just returned to his company a few hours before his death. Lt. [Edward D.] Kennedy, as you are aware, was wounded at the battle of Brock Road [on May 6]. I suppose he is now at home. [Jonathan] Fitzer of your town was also wounded. As yet these are the only two wounded from Belvidere. Edward Nelson [of Company D] is at the Hospital with a sore foot. The other one is here and is well. He was in all the battles.

Yesterday morning we moved from the old battlefield, and it looked like leaving. But we have worked around to very nearly the same place. It is all one great battlefield for miles & miles. We know very little as to what we have done or what we have gained, further than that we have fought them from day to day with the advantage on our side. What the movements elsewhere are we don't know. You are better posted than we are. I hope all is working right.

Many are the brave and gallant officers and men that have laid down their lives for their country in this campaign. The loss in our little regiment numbers 57. Six were killed, three of whom were officers—and good ones at that. . . . I have lost so many of my warmest and best friends. It makes me feel so badly. . . .

Spotsylvania Court House, Va., May 17th 1864

My dear Ellen,

We are still here, fighting a battle every day. We expect to fight another big battle soon, perhaps today. The enemy shell us occasionly and may make an attack on us any hour. My health is pretty good, considering the exposure. We did not move back but merely changed front so that our lines runs a different direction. We expect to shell them this morning and try and drive them out of their works if possible. The object is to know if they have a large or small force here. We think that they must give away, as Richmond is menaced from other quarters. But you know more than I do. . . .

If anything happens to me, I want you to remember that I have lost both my horses and that you are entitled to full pay for them.

Black horse	$300
Charley	200
navy revolvers	75
equipments	25
	$600

They may not pay more than $200 each for horse and equipments. But the above is less than I would have taken for them. The bill, with the evidence of these horses being shot, must go up to the 2nd Corps auditor at the War Department. In the course of time you will get it. If I live, I will get it. If I don't, you must attend to it. . . .

We have but one line officer on duty, owing to our recent losses. The rest are killed, wounded, and disabled by sickness. . . .

Spotsylvania Court House, Va., May 18th 1864
My dear Ellen & family,

I have written you almost every day. We are now on our old line that we took from the Rebels. We have had another battle today but not a general one.[21] The object, I think, was to charge the enemy's works in front of us. But it did not progress long and we fell back to our works. We are now on our old line that we took from the Rebels. The enemy are strongly intrenched in our front. Our Division did not advance but was on the reserve. Yet we had some loss from the enemy's shells. My little Brigade has lost over 800 men in all the battles.

The Division has been consolidated.[22] Genl. Mott has no division and is now commanding the Brigade. I have today come back to the Regiment. Our old 3rd Corps will soon be extinct—or not more than 2 brigades. It is now reduced to one division. The term of service of many expires soon, and they are going home.

I have been very tired and worn down by fatigue and exhaustion, but I now feel much better and my health is good. I expect a battle tomorrow. It may be a hard one. It is fight, fight, every day. . . .

21. On May 18 McAllister's men came "under a heavy shell fire" while making an inconsequential probe of the Confederate left. *OR,* Vol. XXXVI, Pt. 1, p. 494.

22. Heavy battle losses, and the expiration of the terms of service of many regiments in Mott's division, had reduced that unit to little more than a brigade. On May 13 it was consolidated with Gen. David Birney's 3rd Division of the II Corps. Mott himself narrowly avoided being mustered out of service. *Ibid.,* 72, 156, 361, 502; Lyman, *Meade's Headquarters,* 114.

Spotsylvania Court House, Va., May 20th 1864

My dear Ellen & family,

I was just agoing to write you last evening when we had to fall in and march off at a double-quick on account of the Rebels attacking one of our supply trains. We left our trenches yesterday morning, came here to the Anderson Farm,[23] and was resting when the attack was made. A new artillery brigade, though without their pieces but armed as we were with muskets, were on duty at this point near the road leading to Fredericksburg. The Rebels came down upon them with some force, drove them back, and would have captured the train had it not been for the old troops who rushed up to the rescue. These new troops had never been in battle before. They had been around Washington up till this campaign and had not participated in any of the engagements. Some of them fought well; but having several lines of battle and becoming somewhat panick stricken, they *fired into each other* and lost fearfully. It is said 500 were killed and wounded.[24]

When our veterans went up, the Rebs fell back. We lay on our arms all night without our blankets, and I felt very chilly and cold this morning. But I am all right now. We went out on a reconnaicence this morning and found no enemy. We are now back resting, but may move any hour. One hundred Rebels came in and give themselves up this morning. I do not know what stories they tell. I rather think Lee is retreating and that we will soon be after him. This is a hard campaign, puting in the shade all others. We are completely worn out; and if we do not rest, we cannot do much. A little repose and we can continue to march and do battle.

Our Division has, as I said before, been consolidated with Genl. Birney's. Genl. Mott is in command of the Brigade, and I am with my Regiment. This is entirely satisfactory to me. I have lead the Brigade into all the battles thus far. Permit me to say I trust that I have fully sustained my former reputation for bravery and gallantry. They all say that I fear no danger and make everybody fight. I have never be-

---

23. The Edmund Anderson farm was located one and a half miles northeast of Spotsylvania near the north bank of the Ny River. *Official Atlas*, Plate LV, Map 2; *OR*, Vol. XXXVI, Pt. 3, pp. 191–92.

24. McAllister was describing the May 19 engagement known as the battle of Harris' Farm. Some 500 Confederates were captured in the action. Yet the 1st Maine Heavy Artillery, in its initial battle, lost 466 men. An artillery quartermaster described the mismanaged affair by writing: "First there was Kitching's brigade firing at the enemy; then Tyler's men fired into his; up came Birney's division and fired into Tyler's; while the artillery fired at the whole d——d lot." Wainwright, *Diary of Battle*, 379; *OR*, Vol. XXXVI, Pt. 1, pp. 478, 600–1; Horace H. Shaw, *The First Maine Heavy Artillery, 1862–1865* (cited hereafter as Shaw, *1st Maine Heavy Artillery*) (Portland, 1903), 109–11.

fore exposed myself so much, and I rest easy from the knowledge that I have faithfully done my duty. Whether I will get credit for it from Genl. Mott is yet to be seen. I am not a favorite of his. He has his favorites, however, in Col. [John] Ramsey and Col. [William J.] Sewell—both aspiring for promotion. My ranking them was a bitter pill for them. But with both officers and men I have raised myself and stand first rate. They can not and dare not say anything against me. I went, by the help of God, where the bullets were the thickest and where the danger was the greatest. I will tell you confidentially that Genl. Mott has killed himself—and has himself to blame. This is in confidence. If I live to see you, I will tell you all.

Permit me to say that I am all right and feel happy. Our loss in the Brigade [is such that] we have not been able to get our dead officers' bodies sent home. It was as much as we could do to get the wounded back. . . .

Trenches near Bowlinggreen, Va., May 23rd 1864

My dear Ellen & family,

Our communication was cut for a day or two until last evening. All is right again now. You know that we had been fighting Lee daily in his new trenches. So Grant began his strategy, and our Corps was moved off quietly Friday night [May 20] on Lee's [right] flank towards Bowling Green. It is a splendid point for defence. We were not too soon, for a body of Rebels came from Richmond to occupy this place. But we were a little ahead of their main body. After driving them away and capturing about 60 Rebels, we had the place and lost no time in defence.[25] We built fortifications.

Here is an order to move. I must close. . . .

---

25. On the morning of May 21 elements of the II Corps occupied Bowling Green. Facilitating the capture of the town was McAllister's former commander, Alfred T. A. Torbert, whose horsemen routed the defenders and captured 66 Confederates in the process. "Before the war," Marbaker observed, Bowling Green "contained a free population of about 250; now not an ablebodied man remained, and the women, many of whom were clothed in mourning, took care to let us know that they were bitterly disloyal, and many were the prophecies of evil bestowed upon us." *OR*, Vol. XXXVI, Pt. 1, pp. 362, 812–13; Marbaker, *11th New Jersey*, 183. See also Wilkeson, *Recollections of a Private Soldier*, 104.

In the trenches, south side of the
North Anna River, May 25th 1864

My dear Ellen & family,

As usual I have but a few minutes to write. Work, work, fight, fight, takes all our time. We sleep but from two to four hours per day. It is the hardest campaigning I have ever seen. Before it commenced, I would not have believed that I could have gone through it. . . .

The last hasty note I wrote you was from the trenches at Milford Station near Bowling Green. The enemy had left their works at Spotsylvania and were on the retreat. You know that our gallant Corps flanked them. So up, out of our fine works we went after Genl. Lee. When we came to the river, the enemy were ready to dispute our passage. At them we went and drove them from a redoubt on the north side. This gave us an advantage. We threw up breastworks and, at daylight yesterday, we stood face to face with the enemy. Our sharpshooters opened on them so they dare not show their heads. During the night they fired the railroad bridge and burned it down. They also set fire to the road bridge. But we fired at them, drove them back, and saved the road bridge.

About 10 a.m. we crossed the river with 100 men, 50 from my Brigade and 50 from Col. Egan's,[26] and stormed the redoubt on this side. I followed with my Brigade under a severe shell fire. Soon the Stars and Stripes were flying over the redoubt, and the line of works on this side was ours.[27]

Mott is in command of the Brigade, but thus far I have had command in all the battles. This is strange but true.

The enemy now began to push us back into the river. We drove them back and, at this writing, have several lines of works. We calculate that we can hold them. It is expected we will have hard fighting today. . . . The enemy are pressing us a little now. I must go to my Brigade. I can't tell you one-hundredth part of the scenes and facts of

26. Col. Thomas W. Egan of the 40th New York temporarily commanded the 1st Brigade of Birney's division.

27. This action was an attempt by Grant to get a bridgehead on the south bank of the North Anna River and thereby force Lee from his strong works. Mott's brigade captured the redoubt overlooking the railroad bridge after "a fearful fire from the enemy's batteries." Yet Lee adroitly interposed his forces between the corps of Warren and Hancock, thus isolating both. Outmaneuvered, Grant withdrew his troops to the north bank of the river and undertook another flanking movement. *OR,* Vol. XXXVI, Pt. 1, pp. 363, 495; Mrs. Arabella M. Willson, *Disaster, Struggle, Triumph: The Adventures of 1000 "Boys in Blue"* . . . (Albany, N.Y., 1870), 252; Miller, *Photographic History,* III, 76.

interest. For this you must wait. If I am spared, it will be an interesting history [to tell].
. . . The cannon is roaring. I must close. . . .

                        Line of battle, North Anna River, May 26th 1864
My dear Ellen & family,
    I wrote you yesterday morning from the trenches on this side of the river, but a little in the rear of this, as we have moved to a new line of breastworks in front. Our Brigade is always in the extreme front. The enemy is facing us and making a strong resistance. We have effected a crossing with nearly our whole force. Our Corps is the only one that succeeded in driving in the enemy's lines and crossing. The others had to cross at our point. We are now very near Hanover Junction. This is the point for which we are now contending. Whether we will advance directly against their works, or practice strategy as we did at Bowling Green, I do not know. We can't do too much of the former, as we lose too many men. Our ranks melt away like snow under an April sun. With our army thus depleted, as it has been in the first eight days' fighting, it is time to adopt other measures. We have fought almost every day since that time. But having breastworks and continually erecting new ones, we have saved our men and our army is in a good fighting condition.
    Yesterday morning I closed my letter in great haste amidst the firing of pickets and the booming of the cannon. I said we were going into battle. I closed and rushed out. But it soon subsided and nothing more occured during the day except skirmishing. In the evening we moved forward to this new line, and I had more sleep than I have had for a week—though we are right under the enemy's guns. What the program for today is I can't tell. Though Genl. Mott is in command of the Brigade, I am always on the front line and in command. They all say that I am the "fighting commander" of the Brigade. The General is in command when all is quiet. His Headquarters are well to the rear, and he don't seem to be anxous to get to the front. However, this is confidential. It seems to be a strange way to do business, but it is.
    When I was bruised on the old wound, Col. Ramsey [of the 8th New Jersey], who was not in the battle of the Brock Road (but who went down to the hospital on a slight pretext of indesposition), came back on hearing that I was wounded and took command for a few hours. I now see it reported in all the Jersey papers that he is in com-

mand. This is not true. I resumed the command the next day at noon and continued in command up till Genl. Mott was relieved of command of the Division and came back to the Brigade. . . .

I have not time to write to Hennie or Alice. You will have to keep them posted as to my movements. . . . Captain Lloyd is well and looks healthy. He has come through thus far unharmed. He is a good soldier and officer, always at his post.

This campaign may last a long time—with just such fighting as we have had—for twenty days or more. Our men are confident of success, and that the day will be ours. . . .

North Anna River, May 26th 1864

My dear daughter Hennie,

I have not had time to write many letters, so I wrote them to my family and directed them to your mother. . . .

We have had terrible hard fighting. Nothing can exceed it. I have been in almost every battle, sometimes commanding my Regiment and sometimes commanding my Brigade. . . . It was in the battle of the Wilderness that I lost my horses. I was in command of the Brigade. In the morning [of May 6] we advanced some two miles through a thick woods and underbrush and drove the enemy back. But about noon the enemy turned our left flank. [General James] Longstreet came pouncing upon us with a heavy force, and we were compelled to change front to the rear. In doing this and in forming different lines, my black horse was shot but not killed. He trembled, but I still remained on him until I arrived at the Plank Road. There we went into the breastworks. We rallied our men and got the lines ready for action, expecting Genl. Lee. I sent my fine black horse back to the rear, where he died that evening. I then mounted Charley. The enemy soon made an attack. It was a furious one. It was massed troops trying to make the attack so as to break our center. Charley never seemed to be more in his element than he was in this battle. I rode the lines back and forward. He carried his head amidst the roar of cannon and musketry and entered into the very spirit of the contest. Near the close a ball passed through his neck through the large arteries. The blood passed out on both sides of his neck in large streams. I dismounted; and just as I reached the ground, another ball hit him in the shoulder. He jumped back, pulled the reins out of my hand, and went off at a gallop with the blood streaming from him. I never saw him again, but heard of him lying dead a short distance from the scene of action.

I started on foot along the line. Then I was hit close to my old wound by a spent ball which caused me great pain and almost the loss of the use of my leg. For a few minutes I could not walk, but near evening I managed to hobble back towards the rear. By this time my aides and orderlys had all disappeared. I got within hailing distance of a division aide and told him that I could not continue in command. I went back a short distance and then lay down. After awhile an ambulance came along. I got into it and was soon at the hospital. They bathed my wound. The next day, though quite lame, I returned, took command, and have been in every engagement since. I can't tell you how many, but we have fought from day to day and from place to place.

We had hard fighting in the battles near Spotsylvania Court House. There my Brigade did splendidly. To give you a description of this charge and battle would take pages and more time than I have at present. Then we came on with our gallant Corps to Bowling Green, beat the enemy, and put up strong works there which caused Lee to retreat from his stronghold. We then came on to the North Anna River and found the enemy ready to dispute our passage. Our Corps soon took possession of a redoubt and rifle pits on the north side of the river. Then under the darkness of night we threw up a line of works and at daybreak were ready to open on the enemy. No general attack was made. But the pickets and artillery were at work.

About 10 a.m. we advanced 100 men to storm a redoubt and succeeded in taking it. Then Genl. Mott ordered me to advance my Brigade. This was no sooner said than I was moving off at the head of the column amidst a storm of shells. On we went and took the enemy's line of works on this side of the river. The enemy have tried and retried to retake them but have not yet done so. We are in possession; and by the help of God, we will keep them unless Genl. Grant thinks best to go round their flank. We have skirmishes and cannonading all along, from hour to hour, from day to day, with hard-fought battles occasionly. I have been mercifully spared thus far, for which we ought to be thankful. . . .

Trenches across the Pamunkey River
15 miles from Richmond
May 29th 1864

My dear Ellen,

We left our position on the North Anna day before yesterday and again moved to the left on Genl. Lee's [right] flank. We crossed the Pamunkey River last evening and came to this place, about two miles from the river and 15 miles from Richmond. Our cavalry are now opening communication in our rear to the White House. "Baldy" Smith's forces [28] are said to be there. If so, he will no doubt join us and our armies will be united for the advance on Richmond.

We have not had much fighting for the last day or two. We have been out on this campaign for twenty-six days, have done some very hard marching, and have fought some hard battles. It is said, and I believe it, that we have been under fire over 20 days. The time of some of our troops is expiring. In our own Brigade the 1st Massachusetts has gone home and the 26th Pennsylvania goes today—that is, the portion that has not reinlisted. The reinlistments have been less in our Division than in most others, and every month some of them will be going out. However, and owing to new accessions, our army is larger than it was when we started.[29]

We are geting a large army here. We have many regiments that have been over two years in the service and, until this campaign, had never been in battle. They have heretofore been in the defences of Washington. We have a regiment of this kind just put in our Brigade. It numbers 900 strong. They are called "the heavies," having enlisted as heavy artillery.[30] They were brought out of the Washington area well drilled, but, I fear, for poor fighting and campaigning.

We threw up breastworks last night, expecting Lee to attack us. Just now Burnside's Corps is marching past towards the front. What is to be the next move on the chess board by Genl. Grant I don't know. They can't go far to the front until they encounter the enemy. Our cavalry had a fight yesterday in our front before we came up, and I understand it was a pretty severe one. But we were successful.

7 a.m. [May 30]. All quiet yet. The 5th Corps are now passing on towards Richmond, or, I suppose, only in front of us to put up a line of works a little more in advance.

---

28. On May 31 Maj. Gen William F. Smith arrived at White House from Butler's army with his XVIII Corps of 16,000 troops. Smith had served as Hancock's superior during the Peninsular Campaign and as an engineer to Grant in the Western campaigns. However, a carping, cantankerous nature, plus the look and bearing of a Prussian field marshal, held back numerous promotions for Smith.

29. Some 28,000 recruits and reinforcements joined Grant's army in the May 4-June 12 period. At the same time, however, 19 regiments were mustered out of service and 52,700 men were casualties of the fighting from the Wilderness to Cold Harbor. *OR,* Vol. XXXVI, Pt. 1, pp. 133, 149, 164, 180; Vol. XL, Pt. 1, p. 623.

30. The 1st Maine Heavy Artillery at the outset of the campaign had numbered 1,789 men. *Ibid.,* Vol. XXXVI, Pt. 1, p. 665.

I am trying to buy a horse from Major [Samuel G.] Moffett [of the 26th Pennsylvania], who is about to leave with his regiment. He is asking $140. I will not give him so much. I have offered him $125. . . . I have been riding one of the U.S. old plugs and am very tired of riding such a poor horse. This horse of Major Moffett's is a good riding horse and will carry me along nicely—but not like poor Charley or the black charger by a long slice. They were hard to beat. I will not buy such expensive horses until I am through this campaign, if I get through. . . .

In the field, June 1st 1864

My dear Family,

. . . I have but time to say that I am very well and thus far safe. We are about 7 miles from Mechanicsville. We have been in this neighbourhood since Sabbath evening [May 29]. We have thrown up works, had constant fighting, and stormed and took the enemy's outer works yesterday with our Division.[31] This morning we have left them for some movements. I know not why. . . .

Trenches near Cold Harbor, Va., June 3rd 1864

My dear Family,

No mail for several days, but we are promised one tomorrow. I have but a few moments to write you a line or two. It is now dark and the mail goes right out.

We have had hard fighting today along several parts of our lines.[32] This morning our Corps stormed the enemy's works, succeeded in

31. McAllister's official report of the May 31 activities is neither elaborate nor dramatic: "The regiment, with a portion of the brigade, moved to the front in the forenoon, crossed the valley and took position on the opposite height, and during the day threw up three lines of works." McAllister's minimization notwithstanding, the fighting on that date was more than a skirmish. *Ibid.,* 467, 496; Pt. 3, p. 335; Kitching, *Memorials,* 137–38; Charles A. Page, *Letters of a War Correspondent* (Boston, 1899), 78.

32. Cold Harbor was a costly, senseless battle for which Grant alone must bear the awful responsibility. Irritated at the continual failure of his flank movements to trap Lee, he ordered three corps to make a June 3 frontal assault against the entrenched Confederate army. Over 7,000 Federals fell in less than half an hour's fighting. Years later Grant confessed: "I have always regretted that the . . . assault at Cold Harbor was ever made." *Personal Memoirs of U. S. Grant* (cited hereafter as Grant, *Personal Memoirs*) (New York, 1885–86), II, 276.

taking the first line but could not hold it. My Division (Birney's) was the reserve. We lost in our little regiment only six men wounded. We left our position and came from the right of our Division to the left of the 5th Corps. We have thrown up breastworks under shell fire but got along safely, have them finished, and are ready for the Rebs to attack us. Since dark they have been attacking us on our left; and from the firing I have no doubt we have whipped them. All is quiet now. Our loss today is considerable.

I am well, and so is Captain Lloyd. I saw him a few hours ago. The 6th Corps suffered heavy loss yesterday. My old regiment, the 1st [New Jersey], lost heavily.[33] Col. [William] Henry was wounded. I hope it was not mortally. Terable fighting, the likes of which was never known. The Jersey troops all fight well. The Rebel prisoners say that they are tired of it and hope it will be stoped soon. We took a large number of prisoners today. . . .

We know not what a day may bring forth. Let us all put our trust in God, and He will guide us safely through. . . .

Trenches near Cold Harbor, Va., June 4th 1864

My dear Ellen & family,

. . . While I was writing you last evening and afterwards, a battle was going on in a part of our Corps—Barlow's Division, away to our left (we having been detached a few hours before to this place).[34] The Rebels met with a repulse and a heavy loss. I wrote you that this same Division charged in the morning on the Rebel works, took the first line but could not hold it, and had to give it up. We were supporting him. In the evening after dark the Rebels massed their troops. Barlow got this knowledge and prepared for them. He got his artillery in position, then instructed his pickets to fall back gradually, which they did. The Rebel horde moved up towards our works. Then our lines—infantry and artillery—poured into them and repulsed them with great slaughter. . . .

Except for some shelling since, we have been quiet here. Since coming to this point last evening, we have built a few lines of breast-

---

33. The 1st New Jersey lost 5 killed, 25 wounded and 3 missing in the battle of Cold Harbor. *OR*, Vol. XXXVI, Pt. 1, p. 172.

34. A former newspaperman and lawyer, Francis C. Barlow joined the Federal army as a private and earned his major general's stars at Spotsylvania. On the night of June 3 the twenty-nine-year-old "Boy General" reported, he repulsed a Confederate counterattack made against his lines. *Ibid.*, 369.

works and can repel any attack that the enemy may make on us. I only hope that they may come ahead. There is some firing now, but it will not amount to anything. It is now 12:15 p.m. These are very long days to fight when we begin as early as we did yesterday morning and hold on as late as we did last night. . . .

I have not heard again from Col. Henry. I fondly hope that he may live. Col. [James A.] Beaver [35] commands a regiment, the 148th Pennsylvania. He is under Genl. Barlow and must have been in the charge yesterday. I hope he is safe. Captain Lloyd was here an hour ago and is well. He met with a narrow escape yesterday from a bursting shell but was not touched.

Many are the gallant officers and men that have fallen in this campaign, and many more will have to give their lives up as a sacrifice for the good of their country. There is a great deal of suffering here among the native women and children. No men are to be seen; all are in the Rebel army. There are no crops worth speaking of. What we see is very poor. . . .

Barker's Mill, near the Chickahominy River
June 6th 1864

My dear Ellen & family,

I wrote you on Saturday [June 4], and the mail left yesterday.

Since then we moved to the left and joined our own Corps. We went on Saturday evening to the rear and had a nice rest, remained there until about 4 p.m. [Sunday], when we moved to the front and had a heavy cannonading over us for about half an hour. It was dark and the scene was most terrific—though, strange to say, we had but one man wounded. We came out to get in position and waited till dark covered us. The pickets became alarmed and fired; then the artillery on both sides took it up, and the stillness of the Sabbath evening was broken by an artillery duel. The fiery balls flew over us and through the pines, bursting around us to an extent that one unaccustomed to these scenes would naturally suppose that one half of our army would be destroyed. After it was over, we marched on to our place and, before day, had constructed breastworks. We are now finishing them and will soon be ready to receive the enemy.

35. Beaver was a law partner in Bellefonte, Pa., of McAllister's oldest brother, Nelson. After the war Beaver married Nelson's daughter, served a term as governor of Pennsylvania, and was for many years a member of the state's supreme court. See Muffly, *148th Pennsylvania*, 235, 238, 756–57, 921.

This ground was occupied by a portion of Genl. McClellan's forces in 1862. Our cavalry occupied this as their picket line up till this morning.[36]

A few feet from here lies the remains of a chaplain.[37] A grave with a considerable quantity of earth above the surface shows the spot where he lies. His name was Bartlett of the 1st Maine Cavalry. He was killed day before yesterday while on the picket line. This country is one vast graveyard—graves everywhere, marking the track of the army on the march and in battles. Scarcely any have died from disease; indeed, I know of none. Our army is very healthy. But war in all its destruction has cut down our brave soldiers. There have been many of our officers and men lost by so many charges. I believe the policy is now to dig parallel lines and work by sieging. Notwithstanding this, we will have to charge sometimes.

I am well satisfied that Genl. Grant understands his business and will eventually succeed. Everyone has confidence in him.

Noon. The Rebs have opened up with shell on us in our new position. No one is hurt yet. They have now stopped. I do not know how long we may remain in this place. The boys call us the "flying division," as we have fought with all corps & divisions, constantly moving around.

We have a nice mill pond here and our boys are enjoying it. Notwithstanding the shells, they continue their bathing.[38] We have just been enjoying some ice found in an icehouse, and we have just got the first lemons I have seen since we started on this campaign—a purveyor having come up with a wagon load to supply Division Headquarters.[39]

36. The 11th New Jersey was making a night movement to its left when Confederate batteries opened fire. Many men immediately scattered for cover. "No doubt some will remember this incident," Marbaker stated, "for the malodorous pits into which some of them tumbled when seeking shelter in the darkness from the enemy's flying missiles." *11th New Jersey*, 189.

37. On June 2, in an engagement at Barker's Mill, Chaplain George W. Bartlett "was struck in the breast by an unexploded shell from the enemy and literally blown to pieces." William E. S. Whitman and Charles H. True, *Maine in the War for the Union* (Lewiston, Me., 1865), 375.

38. "But," wrote Sgt. Marbaker, "our pleasure was not entirely unalloyed, for our friends on the other side, fearful that we would forget them, occasionally kept sending us their iron compliments." *11th New Jersey*, 189-90.

39. Securing adequate rations for the army was a constant problem. So was digesting much of the food meted out to the soldiers. When supply wagons arrived for the 11th New Jersey, a detail of men was sent to bring up several boxes of hardtack. "I think the labor of carrying them was entirely superfluous," Marbaker commented, "for, had they been unboxed, they were sufficiently animated to have been driven up." *11th New Jersey*, 188. See also *OR*, Vol. XXXVI, Pt. 1, pp. 276-79; Wainwright, *Diary of Battle*, 408.

I will close this letter and give it to our Chaplain for fear that something may happen to me or I may fall into the hands of the enemy.

We have no regular mail, only one in two or three days. . . .

Barker's Mill, Va., June 7th 1864

My dear Family,

. . . It is now 5 p.m., and up to this time of day all has been quiet except a little cannonading. Just now a shell came and bursted near us. But it did no damage. We are so much accustomed to these visitors that our boys pay but little attention to them. I have had some rest today and have just been in the millpond to bathe. I feel very comfortable now. I stand the campaign first rate and have excellent health, for which I feel thankful. (Another whizzing shell passed over and far beyound us.)

Today the 5th Corps placed themselves on our left. They reach down to and along the river. The 6th Corps and Burnside's forces are on our right.

You have asked me some questions as to divisions, &c. You know that we belong to the 2nd Corps. This Corps has three divisions. Genl. Barlow commands the 1st. (Col. Beaver is in this division.) Genl. [John] Gibbon commands the 2nd, and Genl. Birney the 3rd. This last is my Division. It is composed of all that is left of the old 3rd Corps, and increased in size by the heavy artillery who have been in the [Washington] fortifications until this campaign. They are armed with rifles just as we are, and they perform the same duty. Gen. Tyler commands a brigade of these heavies. But as they were unaccustomed to battle, they were distributed amongst the old veterans.[40] We got 1,000 in our Brigade. Genl. Tyler had one regiment of them and went into the Irish Brigade, Barlow's Division, and lost a leg. Barlow's Division has suffered terably. Nearly all his Colonels were either killed or wounded. I understand that Col. Beaver is safe, but I have not seen him.

Col. Ramsey, Genl. Mott's pet, was temporarily placed in command of a brigade. Even though Col. Beaver was not in the same divi-

---

40. At the outset of the campaign Brig. Gen. Robert O. Tyler had commanded a heavy artillery division consisting of the 1st Maine, 1st Massachusetts, and 2nd, 7th and 8th New York. The division was broken up on May 29, with the 1st Maine and 1st Massachusetts Heavy batteries assigned to McAllister's division. *OR,* Vol. XXXVI, Pt. 1, p. 140; Pt. 3, pp. 298, 300.

sion, he ought to have had it. When I was in command of the Brigade, I could have had Col. Ramsey dismissed from the service for absence without leave. But I did not proceed against him, and now he commands a brigade. Though commanding a New Jersey regiment, Col. Ramsey is a New Yorker, a good soldier and has made a good officer. When in New York, he is said to have followed gambling for a living. He had no standing socially. But as to this I can't realy say.

As for Genl. Mott, his friends say that his conduct is very strange. He has always been considered as a brave officer. But in this campaign he has certainly taken good care of himself. It is well known throughout the Brigade that I have don the fighting. I am regarded by all as the "fighting Colonel." Mott treats me very well now. He dare not do otherwise. His best plan is to act the gentleman with me. I have no fears on that score. . . .

Barker's Mill, Va., June 8th 1864

My dear daughter Henrietta,

. . . We are still here and have had more rest for the last twenty-four hours than has been our good fortune for some time. We have not had any general engagement for a few days. Quiet reigns along our extended lines, except now and then a whizzing or bursting shell comes along, paying its respects to us.

My Headquarters is close on a mill pond. The boys are bathing in the pond. About one hour ago the enemy's batteries opened in this direction. Several shells passed over us. One fell in the water quite close to some of our boys—indeed, amongst them. They merely looked at the exploding shell and continued their bathing and shirt-washing. At this time of day (1:30 p.m.) the dam is full of our boys. Perhaps before I finish this letter, the Rebels may send more of their unwelcome messangers. You would be surprised to learn how little these tried veterans care about shells. If they are making coffee and one bursts close by, they will continue to make their coffee and have their meal—provided the coffee boiler is not upset by a piece of the bursting shell. But if the same thing occurs amongst green troops, you will see great scadaddling, much to the amusement of the old and tried soldiers. . . .

We are now on a part of Genl. McClellan's old camping ground, one mile or less from the Chickahominy. You may ask what we are doing. I can hardly answer that question, as our lines are all very long and I know but little as to what is going on—only where I am. Some say we are manuvering. One thing is certain: we have not been storming for some days. But whether we will soon is to be seen. . . .

Barker's Mill, Va., June 8th 1864

My dear Ellen,
   . . . I wrote you last evening and cannot now add much that is interesting. All has been quiet thus far for the last twenty-four hours, except for some cannonading. Shells continue to pass over us and burst around us; but no one has been hurt since the Sabbath evening [June 5], when one man was wounded. The enemy have our range and may drop a shell that will do some damage. One fell in the mill dam today—right among the men bathing and washing their shirts. No damage was don. The boys just looked around and then continued to bathe and wash as though nothing had happened. Such is war. So accustomed do we becom to such scenes that we can brave danger to an extent almost incredable.

   Night before last I was up nearly all night directing the building of breastworks. Last night I was so tired that I concluded to have some sleep. Our batteries opened on the enemy and they on us. The whizzing balls passed over and bursted around us. I awakened but found that there was no musketry and that the enemy were not approaching. So I turned over and soon was sound asleep again. The roaring of the cannon and the bursting of the shells did not disturb me.

   Supper is now ready, so I will stop writing for a few minutes.

   6 p.m. Genl. Mott and staff have just called, as well as a number of surgeons—all in conversation. The enemy's batteries opened a terrific fire. Our batteries are replying. One man from the 6th New Jersey was hit by a piece of shell. It is a flesh wound; he will get well. Shells are bursting all around us. The boys have left off their bathing, as shells are bursting right in the water. Our men are now close up to the breastworks. On rolls the roaring artillery and vibrating in the distance far beyound Richmond.

   It is now 7 p.m. Col. Schoonover was struck by a large piece of broken shell right in our midst. It had hit the ground up on the hill, ricochayed, came bounding along, and hit him right in the small of the back. He was sitting down on the ground. After being struck he jumped up. It might have killed him; but, fortunately, it only made a bruise and I think he is not much injured by it. It may keep him off duty for a few days.

5 a.m. I might add that he is now sleeping. I don't know how he feels this morning. I hope he will soon be all right.

Captain [William] Lloyd called here yesterday. He is well, very tired of the service, and anxous to go home.

It is about 8 to 10 miles from here to Richmond. We got a Richmond paper yesterday. They acknowledge a defeat near Staunton by our forces under Hunter.[41] . . .

Barker's Mill, Va., June 9th 1864

My dear Ellen & family,

. . . Thus far this has been a very quiet day—but little if any cannonading and but few musket shots. Yet the Rebel time to open on us has not yet arrived. They generally attack us about 5 or 6 o'clock in the evening. We may yet have a brush with them before dark sets in.

We are receiving some new men: recruits, wounded and convalescents returning to the army. I understand that, notwithstanding the killed and wounded in this campaign, our army is larger than before.

Inclosed you will find a mess receipt, also one for the *Army & Navy Journal*. It is a good paper for facts connected with the army. Their accounts of our movements are considered correct. In the copy I send, you will find marked by my pen a piece styled "Claims of Widows and Orphans." You can see how to get your pension, if I am killed or die, without your being fleeced out of half of it. Save this piece for your benefit or the benefit of others. There are a set of men making money off of the widows and orphans. So take care of these sharks. Attend to it yourself, or get your friends to do it for you, according to these instructions, and you will have no trouble.

I have seen Captain Lloyd today. He is well and all right, though he was, like ourselves, under the heavy shell fire last night. The boys still continue to wash clothes & bathe, swim, &c. We have had more rest this time than we have had for some time, and all are feeling much better. Col. Schoonover is attending to his duties, though his back hurts him. If anything happens to me, he will give a certificate of my horses being killed for your benefit. The Government will owe

---

41. Maj. Gen. David Hunter and an army of 8,500 men were sweeping southward up the agriculturally rich Shenandoah Valley. Three days after McAllister's letter, Hunter left Lexington and the smoking ruins of the Virginia Military Institute.

me quite a sum at the end of this month. Four months' tally will be due: $758. . . .

Barker's Mill, Va., June 11th 1864

My dear Family,

A very sad death occured here today which has made a very deep impression on me.

I was ordered to call on Genl. Smythe [42] and arrange with him for a company of sharpshooters to assist me in driving back the enemy at a point left of here. I took with me orderly Wilson Snooks, rode up to Genl. Smyth's Headquarters, and made the necessary arrangements with him. When I mounted to leave, the General remarked, "Hold on, I will go with you. I want you to look at my lines. I am very close to the enemy."

We came to the forks of the road and turned up to our works. My orderly was quite a distance behind me. As we approached the works, a Rebel sharpshooter fired at us. The ball passed between us and hit my orderly, who fell from his horse and died in a few minutes. He was a very fine young man and lived in Trenton. We buried him under the large walnut tree beside the chaplain of the Maine Cavalry, who was also killed before this. The ball was intended for either Genl. Smyth or me but killed the orderly.[43] . . .

Barker's Mill, Va., June 12th 1864

My dear Ellen & family,

When I wrote you last evening from this place, I did not expect to write you again from here. I have not received any mail today and don't think we will today or for several days. We may move, but I don't know yet.

We have had a very quiet day up to this time, 5 p.m. I hope it

---

42. Col. Thomas A. Smyth of the 1st Delaware was temporarily commanding the 3rd Brigade of the 2nd Division. The action of which McAllister wrote was but a part of the mild skirmishing of that period. *OR,* Vol. XXXVI, Pt. 1, pp. 452–53.

43. Many years later McAllister stated: "I afterward learned that on that morning there was an agreement made between our pickets and the Rebels that neither party would fire on either men or officers on foot but [that] they would fire on those that were mounted." McAllister to unknown addressee, March 28, 1888, McAllister Papers.

will continue to the end of the Sabbath. We had church service today in front of our breastworks under the large walnut tree where, I told you, the Chaplain is buried and my orderly lies by his side.

We have been here just one week, and we are well rested from the fatigues of marching and fighting. We now hold prayer meeting in the trenches. We could not do so heretofore to any extent. Our men were so tired and, besides, we had to work hard in building breastworks. Now we are rested again, and it is so pleasant to hold these meetings. . . .

I am rejoiced that Wilson [Lloyd] is improving in health and has gone to Philadelphia. It will do him good, and I think he ought to take a trip. . . . His health is more important to himself & family than wealth. If he has the former, he can make the latter.

I am glad that Sarah is so brisk. It is right that she should be so. Sarah has a good deal of her father's disposition about her. She bears up under her trials and is cheerful under trying circumstances. I will be well satisfied with either a girl or a boy—just so all are well. It must have a warm welcome and be well taken care of. We can all love it and caress it. . . .

Windmill Point, James River, Va.
June 15th 1864

My dear Ellen,

I wrote you on Sabbath evening from Barker's Mill and gave the letter to the Chaplain, so that if anything happened to me you would get it. . . .

On Sabbath evening, when darkness covered us, orders came to be ready to move. Before morning our Corps had slipped from under the noses of the enemy and were on our way to this place.[44] We reached the Chickahominy without any trouble—not a gun fired at us. Then, by forced march we reached the James by sundown the same evening, a distance of at least twenty-five miles. We did not meet any enemy. Yesterday morning we came down to the bank of the river and commenced crossing on boats. We had no Pontoons laid. It was a slow operation. It was 5 p.m. before we landed the last of our Division

---

44. On June 5 Grant concluded that, owing to the vulnerability of the Richmond, Fredericksburg & Potomac Railroad, it would be impracticable to try and hold a line northeast of Richmond. He determined to execute another flank movement, cross the James, and thus force Lee into a defensive position along the Richmond-Petersburg sector.

here. The other divisions of our Corps have been crossing all night. We are now crossing the artillery and wagons, &c.

This is Windmill Point,[45] also called "Wilcox's Landing." We are now on the south side of the James River, six miles below Harrison's Landing. A part of Genl. [William F.] Smith's command passed up the river in boats and, it is said, have landed far up the river. I have no doubt that as soon as we are all across and ready we will move up this side of the river. But as to our movements, you will be apprised by the papers before this reaches you. We know nothing of our intended movements. But on looking at the map, we can, like yourselves, make a pretty good guess. Genl. Grant is good at swinging round. The Rebels call it "elbowing" them.

Just before we started from Barker's Mill, one of their pickets asked one of my men, "Where is Grant agoing to elbow us again?"

Little did they think it would be so soon. We are now on the natural route to Richmond. If God wills it, we will get there.

You can now see how handsomely Grant has protected Washington and gradually moved round to this place—losing men, of course, but at the same time weakening Lee's forces and destroying all the railroads in his course. We will soon be in the rear of Richmond. It is not worth while to speculate, but I will add: all is right.

This is beautiful country, the only part of Virginia that I have any fancy for. This is a splendid farm that we are on. There is now fighting up the river. I don't know what it is. There is fighting ahead of us. . . .

Our men are in good health and in fine spirits. My health was never better and I am well rested. It is said that we will get a mail now by the new route. I hope we get one today. . . .

Bivouac in the trenches, June 17th 1864, 5 p.m.
My dear Ellen,

I am now writing this in my bivouac under the picket fire of the enemy. My last letter was written at Windmill Point. Grant performed one of his strategic flank movements and, by hard marches, reached this point in sight of Petersburg. We are in sight of the steeples, about

45. Windmill Point lay southwest of Charles City Court House and at a point where the James River was three-quarters of a mile wide. Situated close to the Point was the Wilcox plantation. *Official Atlas,* Plate XCIII, Map 1; Craft, *141st Pennsylvania,* 213.

1 to 1½ miles away. As you will see by the papers, we arrived here on Wednesday evening [June 15] after dark. Butler had that day driven the enemy for miles; and in the evening his colored troops took the line of fortifications which we strengthened and turned to our account.[46]

Last evening we advanced and charged the enemy.[47] I had command of all the New Jersey regiments and was in the front line of our Brigade. Genl. Mott commanded the last line. We had a hard fight. The Jersey troops suffered considerable loss. My regiment lost 36 killed and wounded. Captain [Sidney] Layton is killed. Several valuable men laid down their lives on that field. I was terably exposed; but thank God, He protected me. I was unharmed. God be praised. Let us thank God for His protective care.

The battle ran until 12 midnight. We could not take these works but held the ground taken from the enemy. We threw up earthworks and have been fighting all day to hold our ground. About 1 o'clock this morning I was called on by order of Genl. Birney to take command of this Brigade. The Colonel commanding, Col. Tanat, was slightly wounded.[48] I suppose I will only be in command for a few days. This 2nd Brigade of the 3rd Division, 2nd Corps, is a fine, large Brigade, with over 2,000 men for duty.

Genl. Birney told me confidentially the other day that he will take care of me. I will, if I live, be all right. But it will be a miracle if I live through these scenes. Providence can protect me, but He alone. These are terrible battles. I am more concerned in putting down the Rebellion and geting home safely than I am about promotion. . . .

---

46. While Grant pushed southward against Lee, Federal strategy called for Benjamin F. Butler's Army of the James to advance westward up the river and destroy all railroads leading from the Confederate capital. However, Butler's forces suffered ignominious defeat at Bermuda Hundred. Additionally, Gen. "Baldy" Smith on June 15 failed to attack the Petersburg defenses as expeditiously and vigorously as ordered. That night the lead elements of Lee's army filed into the half-empty trenches around the city. The opportunity for a prompt seizure of Petersburg was gone. In a few days, so was Smith. An exasperated Grant ordered him to turn over his command to another officer.

47. The 11th New Jersey spent most of June 16 in throwing up breastworks. At 5:30 P.M. it participated in a heavy reconnaissance to ascertain the strength and position of the Confederate lines. The Federals were repulsed. Casualties in the 11th New Jersey numbered 5 killed and 35 wounded. "I never saw men act with more steadiness and coolness than did the regiment on this occasion," McAllister reported. "Its loss was heavy, being nearly one-third of the number engaged." *OR,* Vol. XL, Pt. 1, p. 421; Marbaker, *11th New Jersey,* 194–95; Hutchinson, *11th Massachusetts,* 68.

48. Col. Thomas R. Tannatt, officially in command of the 1st Massachusetts Heavy Artillery, was wounded in the June 16 fighting. *OR,* Vol. XL, Pt. 1, p. 184.

Lieut. Johnston,[49] Mary McAllister's lover, came and spoke to me today. He is a very pleasant and nice young man. He is in this Division—at least, I think he told me he was. I asked him to call on me again. I sent my love to Mary.

I am very tired. I had little or no sleep last night, and but little is in store for tonight. I have a large responsibility on me. My large Brigade is all on the front line. . . .

Trenches near Petersburg, Va.
Sunday morning, June 19th 1864

My dear Ellen & family,

I wrote you day before yesterday from near this place and spoke of a battle I was in with the old Brigade. That night (night before last) we spent in fighting, strengthening works, &c. At 3 a.m. yesterday we received orders to be ready for a charge at early dawn. I was to have my Brigade in two lines and lead the advance. We went over the enemy's breastworks without much opposition and drove them about ¾ of a mile, when we run up against another line of works much more formidable. Here we met with hard opposition and had to halt and fortify in order to protect ourselves.[50]

This second line of works was built to lead us into a death trap. I halted my Brigade; alone and personally I went to reconnoiter this second line of the enemy's works. I found them very strong—in the form of a half moon with guns planted to enfilade our flanks as we advanced. I went back and informed Col. Pierce[51] of the situation and told him that to advance into that death trap would be fatal to the Brigade. I asked him to come and reconnoiter with me and see if I was not correct. He did so and came to the same conclusion. He went back to inform our superior officers of the situation.

I knew nothing more till I was ordered to charge. It was about 11 a.m. when we charged, my Brigade leading the van. The Rebels poured down upon us lead and iron by musketry and cannon that cut

---

49. The only officer in the division whose name was similar to the person then courting McAllister's niece was Lt. Philip Johnson of the 2nd Delaware.

50. On June 16 and 17 Federals made strong probes of the Confederate defenses. Each attack incurred defeat and high casualties. Yet on June 18 Grant ordered still a third reconnaissance. This too met with failure. As late as the 18th Meade still believed that "if we engage them before they are fortified we ought to whip them." *OR,* Vol. XL, Pt. 2, p. 165.

51. Brig. Gen. Byron R. Pierce, formerly of the 3rd Michigan, commanded the 2nd Brigade in Birney's 3rd Division.

our men down like hail cuts the grain and grass. We had to advance a long distance up a cleared plain. Our ranks melted away, and we could not advance further. We dropped down; and those who were not killed or wounded—or who had not fallen back—began digging little pits. We remained there for two or more hours. We were then ordered back and lost many men in retiring. Each regiment planted its Colors in line of battle.

I sent back word to Genl. Mott: "I can go no farther. What shall I do?"

He answered: "Remain where you are until further orders."

After a time he sent the order to us to fall back. I returned under a severe fire and reported to Genl. Mott with my Brigade.

He directed me where to form, saying: "We are going to make a charge. You may be needed."

"Where is my old 3rd Brigade?" I asked.

He replied: "They are going in just where you came out."

"God help them!" I exclaimed.

"Why?" Mott asked.

"It is a death trap," I said. "A brigade can't live in there for five minutes."

Just as I said this, an aide rode up. "Move your troops forward to the charge," he said to Genl. Mott.

The order was given; and thus was made the disastrous charge of the 1st Maine Heavy Artillery.[52]

Two or three other brigades, my old Brigade amongst them, were brought up to help in the charge, but they failed worse than we did. The slaughter was terrible. This Division lost in the battles of yesterday far more than 1,000 men.[53] The loss was mostly in the 2nd and 3rd Brigades. The conduct of both these brigades in these charges was highly creditable. . . .

After the Maine Heavies retired, the ground was strewn with

52. "Determined to try what virtue there might be in the enthusiasm of a new, fresh, strong regiment," and "not yet discouraged by repeated failures," Mott on June 18 placed the 1st Maine Heavy Artillery in the first line of battle. The Maine artillerists advanced gallantly across an open field some 350 yards in length. They fell back only after 632 of their 950 members fell dead or wounded. In this assault the artillery regiment suffered the highest number of men killed of any one unit in a single engagement of the Civil War. Walker, *Second Army Corps,* 541–42; William F. Fox, *Regimental Losses in the American Civil War, 1861–1865* (Albany, N.Y., 1889), 5–6, 36. See also Charles Hamlin to McAllister, Oct. 16, 1886, McAllister Papers; Shaw, *1st Maine Heavy Artillery,* 121–23.

53. No figures exist for the division's losses in this action. In the June 15–30 period Birney's division suffered a total of 2,128 casualties. *OR,* Vol. XL, Pt. 1, pp. 221–22, 318.

wounded and dying crying "Water! Water!" No help or relief could be sent them. I have understood that a flag of truce was requested of Genl. Lee and that he refused it on the ground that he had lost no men.[54] Hundreds of our wounded thus died in our sight. We could hear their cries for help, yet we could not rescue them or give them the relief that might have saved their lives. . . . It was perfectly heartrending.

I expect we will have to charge again today. I hope not. We are charged out. . . .

Trenches before Petersburg, Va.
June 19th 1864, 6:30 p.m.

My dear Ellen & family,

I wrote you a hasty letter this morning but could not tell half of what I wanted to say. This is Sabbath evening. We have not had any general engagement today; and, of course, we have not had another of those fearful charges. We have had, comparatively speaking, a quiet day, though the sharpshooters are busy at work keeping in check the enemy's sharpshooters, who are exceedingly troublesome, picking off our men. Also some artillery and a few mortars are at work. The latter is very effective; and between them all we are able to keep the Rebels in check—so much so that they cannot show their heads above their works.

It has got to be this: the Rebels do not and dare not charge on us, and we are not always successful in charging on their works. I don't know what is our program or what course we will pursue. We can reach Petersburg with our guns, and we may do something by way of our big guns. I have no doubt but we will have the town very soon.

We are now on the farm of O. P. Hare,[55] a great sportsman and a man that had a great many fast horses. He lived in great style, and the grounds around his house were magnificent. His house was good for Virginia—stabling splendid, flowers, trees and shrubbery magnificent, furniture handsome. The family left in great haste and did not take their furniture. Our shot and shell has riddled the house and

---

54. This report, of course, was untrue. Moreover, in the operations of June 15–18 the Confederates lost 2,970 men. Livermore, *Numbers and Losses,* 115–16.

55. The Otway P. Hare home stood on a hill where the Federals shortly erected Fort Stedman. *OR,* Vol. XL, Pt. 1, p. 306; *Official Atlas,* Plate LXVII, Map 9.

blown up the furniture. What was not thus destroyed has shared the same fate. It is now a complete destruction. This morning I laid out a breastwork right through Hare's fine grounds—through flowerbeds of all kinds, some of the handsomest fir trees and boxwood I have ever seen—and I must confess that my improvements do not add to the beauty of the grounds. I would not desire to have these defences built on my grounds.

Night is now closing in on us. I have no candle, so I must close for the time being.

Monday morning, June 20th. My dear, dear family, including my namesake, the new recruit,[56]

I have had a comfortable night's rest and feel somewhat refreshed. My Brigade was hard at work all night, building new works up still closer to the enemy's lines. They have extended them very considerably. I was just out making a reconnaisance of the whole line.

There were many of our dead lying unburied on the field between the lines. No party dare touch them. Our extension last night enabled us to reach some of them; others the Rebels would not let us touch. No doubt we will ask for a flag of truce today. The wounded of my Brigade were gotten off night before last. But I am sorry to say that such was not the case with my old Brigade, who made the charge in the evening. Those are the men who are still suffering on the field.

The heavy loss was not among our Jersey troops but was principally among the 1st Maine Heavy Artillery. That regiment was as large as the balance of the Brigade, and it was their first charge. They went further than any of the other regiments and suffered more than other regiments did. Poor fellows, lying two nights and one day without food and water.

The commander of this old Brigade is Col. [Daniel] Chaplin, Colonel of the 1st Maine Heavy Artillery. I consider him a fair officer, but I do think that he might have made more of an effort to get off these wounded. I called on him this morning, wakened him from his slumbers, and told him: "My men have brought off some of yours, but were fired on. I lost one or two. The Rebels said a flag of truce could be had. This morning I passed over the bodies of ten of your men lying dead. A heavy fog hangs over us now, and they can be gotten off."

My regiment was not in that charge. I am glad of it, for we lost near 40 men in the battle the evening I left to take this command. The battle was over before I left. It is now 5 a.m. and the fog still hangs.

56. Robert McAllister Lloyd, the first child of Wilson and Sarah McAllister Lloyd, was born June 14, 1864, at Elizabeth, N.J.

But notwithstanding this, picket firing has commenced. We will have another hot day.

My Headquarters are in the rear of my lines. I have a little breastworks for protection. But we seem to be in line of the sharpshooters. Their balls come along freely, paying their respects to us. Though thousands have passed close by me yesterday and this morning, thank God I have not been in the least hurt. . . . I know you are praying for me, and it is in answer to these prayers that my life is thus spared. . . .

Now what shall I say about little Robert, darling boy? He must be cared for, and he must have a nice little carriage to haul him along the street as soon as he is able to travel. This is to be paid for by his grandmother out of my funds. As soon as Sarah is able to travel, all of you pack up and go to Belvidere and spend the summer in that delightful town. . . . Kiss the little darling for me, and instill into him the love of country so that patriotism may burn brightly in his breast, and that he may do good in his day and his generation. . . .

Trenches before Petersburg, Va., June 20th 1864

My dear Ellen,

This morning I finished and mailed my letter of yesterday evening. That is a long one and will explain much. I see by the papers that we have taken Petersburg. This is a mistake. It is true that [General] Smith took the outworks with his negro troops before we arrived —and, I may say, before Lee's forces had reached here. It was guarded only by Richmond Militia. We came up and, by hard fighting from day to day, have taken the next line and are now within one mile of the town. We have run against a strong line here and are fighting hard for it. I write this under the enemy's fire.

My Brigade is in the front line, right close to the enemy, and are heroically fighting one continual battle. We are so close we can talk to the enemy. We are protected by works; and though our losses are constantly increasing our list of casualties, we can say it is not heavy except when we make a charge. I advanced my line last night and gained some advantage. I have two regiments of sharpshooters at work to keep them down. From the cellar to the garret of the Hare House they are firing at the enemy. The reason the enemy can't shell the house is because these men keep them from loading their guns. Also we have our guns and mortars to play on them.

I have had my Brigade under fire from the day I took it up to this time. My losses are over 400 men. We have worked every night in advancing our lines. We are to be relieved tonight by the 6th and by Burnside's Corps. I have no doubt but that the town will be in our possession very soon, though they are contesting every inch of the ground.

We have got off all our wounded and a large portion of our dead. But no flag of truce yet. Why I can't tell. Poor fellows were throwing up their arms for help, and we could not go to their relief. This was the case yesterday; but on advancing our lines last night, we relieved them and we think we have all except a part of the dead.

Captain Lloyd's Brigade (the Excelsior) is on my left on the front line. He was here a few hours ago. He has escaped thus far and is well. He is a splendid soldier and officer and does not shrink from his duty.

Well, little Robert is a June bird like his grandfather. We were born nearly the same time of the year. . . . I was born in the midst of the War of 1812, and he in the midst of the great Rebellion. These are stiring times, especially out here.

There is a Mr. Humes from Bellefonte appointed Brigade Quartermaster for this Brigade.[57] He reported to me day before yesterday. He is a gentlemanly man. He thinks it terrible to live as we do under bullets. He took supper with me while the balls were paying their respects to us. Several whizzed over while we were at tea. . . .

Trenches before Petersburg, Va., June 22nd 1864

My dear Family,

In my last I said we would be relieved by Burnside. So we were, moved down here to the left, and are throwing up fortifications. I can only say that I am well. Orders to move . . .

Trenches before Petersburg, Va., June 23rd 1864

My dear Ellen & family,

I wrote you a line yesterday morning. While writing, I was ordered to move forward my lines. In doing so we had a severe fire

---

57. Prior to his appointment as brigade quartermaster, William H. Hume of Bellefonte had served as a corporal in Co. F, 23rd Pennsylvania. Records of the Adjutant General's Office, Commonwealth of Pennsylvania.

and had to build our breastworks under the fire of sharpshooters and canister, as well as shell. We lost several men.

The 3rd Brigade, my old Brigade, was on the left. Genl. Barlow was on their left. The 6th Corps was to have been on his left. About the middle of the day the Rebels attacked Barlow's left and threw it into confusion.[58] They let the Rebels in on the 3rd Brigade and my Brigade flanks. We had to fall back under a terrible fire. I lost over 100 men in killed, wounded and missing. I do not mean stragglers. There is no blame on me. I did all that I could do, or anyone else could do. We fell back to the line of works. The enemy got a large number of intrenching tools, and we lost two or three pieces of artillery belonging to [Gen. John] Gibbon's Division on my right. The Rebs attempted to take these works but were repulsed.

Late in the evening I was ordered to make another charge and drive them back. I did so and drove them up out of their own works that they had built after driving us out of ours. We held them till the middle of the night, when I was relieved.

This morning another advance was made, and it was discovered that the enemy had fallen back to their own works. Our army holds the same position that we did yesterday. While we are resting, others are finishing my unfinished works.

My Brigade was under fire from early morning till the middle of the night. I have again to thank God for His protecting care over me. . . .

Trenches before Petersburg, Va., June 24th 1864
10:30 p.m.

My dear Ellen,

I am out of paper. This is the last I have here. I have some in my trunk and hope to get it soon. The mail is just leaving. I am well;

---

58. When Confederate Gen. William Mahone on June 22 discovered a gap between the lines of the II and VI Corps, he promptly hurled his troops into the breach. His Southerners captured 1,600 prisoners, 4 pieces of artillery, 8 stands of colors, and many small arms in what one Federal termed "the most humiliating episode in the experience of the Second Corps down to this time." Losses in the corps in this brief action exceeded the unit's strength during the Peninsular Campaign. Mott's division appeared to have fled more precipitately to the rear than any other of the Federal units engaged. *OR,* Vol. XL, Pt. 1, pp. 411–12; Humphreys, *Virginia Campaign,* 229; Wainwright, *Diary of Battle,* 427; Walker, *Second Army Corps,* 544, 546; John R. C. Ward, *History of the One Hundred and Sixth Regiment, Pennsylvania Volunteers* . . . (Philadelphia, 1883), 229–33.

so is Captain Lloyd. Skirmishing, cannonading and fighting still continues. We have orders to be ready to move. I don't know what is up or where we are going. Time will determine.

    The weather is hot—a great drought, water scarce, and vegetation burnt up. We are all worn down with our fighting and hard work. The like of it was never known. . . .

11

♣ ♣ ♣

The Siege Begins

AN EXHAUSTED, battle-ravaged Army of the Potomac drew to a halt before Petersburg, began a constantly expanding system of breastworks and forts, and waited for its Confederate adversary to collapse. In the first weeks of what would be a nine-month siege, the elements also seemed to be waging war on the Federal army. One of McAllister's men recalled: "The heat was intense, almost unbearable; the roads and fields were but beds of dust, that rose in clouds before every gentle breeze, and everything was covered with the hue of earth. We would long for a breeze to fan away the stifling heat, and, when the breeze came, for a calm, that eyes, ears and nostrils might be freed from the smothering cloud."[1] A Pennsylvania soldier calculated that "one seventh of all the deaths in the Army during this period were caused by sunstroke," and that "one-half of the remainder of the diseases causing death resulted directly from the hot weather."[2]

On the surface, during those long, hot summer months of 1864, it appeared that Grant's army in front of Petersburg was the only Federal force not making progress against the Confederacy. Yet Northern superiority in numbers was subtly beginning to tell; the war of attrition was slowly but surely

1. Marbaker, *11th New Jersey*, 200.
2. Muffly, *148th Pennsylvania*, 475.

swinging to the North's favor. Confederate morale sagged. "The stimulus of victory," Douglas Freeman observed, "could no longer be applied." After the summer reverses "the Confederates took the offensive only when opportunity seemed large or necessity compelled. There was no great battle any day but a small battle every day." [3]

McAllister's brigade was not involved in the July 30 battle of the Crater. However, the Colonel was in a good position to comment pointedly on this mismanaged affair. His regiments did participate in engagements at Deep Bottom (August 14–16) and Ream's Station (August 25). And, like the entire II Corps, the New Jersey veterans had to withstand an almost daily bombardment of Confederate canister and musketry.

When not fighting, constructing new works, or inspecting picket posts, McAllister passed this period in writing home. He continually speculated on the army's future movements. Daily he voiced optimism that "all will be right," even though he wrote lengthy criticisms of substitute hirers, bounty jumpers, and foreigners in the Union army. Lastly, McAllister matched exhilarations over brigade church services with admonitions to his family on the proper care of his newly born and first grandchild, Robert McAllister Lloyd.

♣

Headquarters, 3rd Brigade, 3rd Division,
2nd Corps, June 25th 1864

My dear Ellen,

You will see by the heading of this letter that I am in command of my old Brigade. Col. Pierce has been made a Brigadier General and assigned the command of his old brigade, the 2nd. I was ordered to take command of this, Genl. Mott's old brigade. Genl. Mott is in command of the Division and Genl. Birney in command of the Corps.

3. Freeman, *Lee's Lieutenants*, III, 615.

THE SIEGE BEGINS ♣ [453]

Hancock is suffering from his old wounds.[4] I don't know how long I will be in command of this. But one thing is pretty certain: if I live, I will not be long without a Brigade.

It is a hard time on officers. We have to expose ourselves so much.[5] The men are so completely worn out that we have to make more than ordinary effort to get all to work well. A few days' rest will help us all very much. We have had a very quiet day. I don't know how long it will continue.

The weather is hot and sultry; heat is excessive with hard campaigning. All is right here. . . .

Col. Blaisdell was killed yesterday by a Rebel sharpshooter. He died before he reached his quarters. . . .

Trenches before Petersburg, Va., June 26th 1864
My dear daughter Hennie,

I have received your letter from Belvidere and am rejoiced that you are again at home, and that you and Alice have opened the house. Now I want your mother and Sarah, and my namesake Robert, all to come to Belvidere and you will have a nice time all together. I only wish I could be one of the number. How happy I would be! . . .

We are now resting a little behind these works, but don't expect to have a long rest. We must battle on and on. I cannot now tell you how many battles I have been in. We have seen hard service. Hard is not a name for it. . . .

It is dry and hot—almost punishment. . . .

Trenches before Petersburg, Va., June 27th 1864
My dear Ellen,

. . . We have been lying rather quiet for two or three days, though we have had some firing through the night and day. At this

---

4. The "fatigue and excitement" of the past forty days' campaigning had aggravated Hancock's Gettysburg wounds. Near June 18 fragments of bone from a leg injury worked themselves to the surface of the skin. "Suffering intense pain," Hancock temporarily relinquished command of the II Corps to Birney; nine days later he returned to command. *OR,* Vol. XL, Pt. 1, pp. 307, 318; Walker, *Second Army Corps,* 532–33, 547.

5. In a postwar note added to this letter, McAllister stated: "Commanders of brigades at this time were unusually exposed. Officers and men close to the breastworks were, of course, surrounded by danger; but they were more or less protected by the works, while brigade commanders—being out from the works —were always exposed to the deadly aim of the sharpshooters in going back and forth to the different portions of their commands." McAllister Papers.

time considerable fighting is going on on our right. I think it is up at O. P. Hare's house, where we erected so many lines of breastworks and had so much hard fighting. Since the fighting here on the 22nd, when the enemy attempted to turn our left flank, we have had rather a quiet time of it. The gallant 11th New Jersey has lost very heavily and our ranks were very thin. But yesterday we received 72 new recruits—first rate men—and more are coming. So we will still be a regiment. Recruits are coming in slowly from New Jersey. Now, as the abominable $300 clause [6] is repealed, the President can call for 300,000 men and he will get 300,000 men. Our depleted ranks will be filled up, and the Rebellion must go down. . . .

Trenches before Petersburg, Va., June 28th 1864

My dear family,

My letter of yesterday did not go last evening, as no mail left here. All is now very quiet. Although I am now writing from the same table on which I wrote last evening, I am at the Headquarters of the 11th New Jersey. Genl. Mott has returned to brigade command, and I am back with the regiment.

Within two days we received 72 recruits, and fine ones they are. Our regiment was below 100 men before they came. Our losses have been heavy. They say more recruits are coming. I hope so. I don't think I will be long without a brigade. We will see.

We are now holding our position and resting our troops. We need rest so much. I have not heard a word from Lieut. Paul.[7] He is on the staff of a brigade in the 6th Corps, and they are hardly ever very close to us. I hope he is well. Give my kind regards to Mrs. Paul and tell her that as soon as I hear from [her son] I will write.

Last night we had a little thunder storm but not much rain. It is now much cooler—a greate relief to us. All is quiet today except some little cannonading up about the O. P. Hare House on our right. That point is nearer to town than this. I think they must be mining there, but I don't know. . . .

Well, now, Sarah, how is my little grandson and namesake? I would like to see him. I hope he is better looking than I am. But you say that he is like your mother. That will do, for you know I always considered her good looking. . . .

6. By 1864 the government bounty for recruits had reached its height of $300, with an additional $100 if the enlistee was a veteran.
7. Lt. Charles R. Paul was on the staff of the 1st Brigade, 1st Division, VI Corps. *OR*, Vol. XL, Pt. 1, p. 492.

Trenches before Petersburg, Va., June 29th 1864

My dear Ellen,

Inclosed you will please find two papers relative to my lost horses. You must have some friend or authorized person to present them to the Third Auditor's Office in Washington. Wilson [Lloyd] will get someone to attend to it. . . . The papers are right, and there can be no difficulty about it. Genl. Carr had no difficulty in geting pay for his horse killed at Gettysburg. . . .

We are still here in our camp along the breastworks, making out our rolls preparatory to mustering tomorrow. Four months' pay will be due us. The weather is somewhat cooler. Water is very scarce here. We have to dig for it, as there are no springs. It is pretty quiet along the lines. Some cannonading occurred on our right and left this forenoon. The enemy may attack us at any time. We are preparing to receive the Rebels if they come.

I have some diarrhea but think that it will not be bad. . . .

Breastworks before Petersburg, Va., July 1st 1864

My dear Ellen & family,

I have been quite disappointed in not receiving any letters from any of you this morning or yesterday, though our mails are coming regularly. I hope to get some tomorrow. If you only knew what a pleasure it is to me to get home letters, you would not let a day pass by without writing.

I did not write you yesterday because I was on picket duty as Officer of the Day. I did not have the time or opportunity to write. As I have already told you, we are encamped in line of battle behind breastworks that run along before Petersburg for miles. We are ready to resist an attack when made—but don't think the enemy will attempt to charge our works until they get rested and more troops. By that time we will be rested and have more troops. Recruits are coming in rapidly—large reinforcements, I understand.

We have not taken Petersburg or Richmond yet; but they must, by the help of God, fall into our hands. Genl. Grant is not the man to give up what he undertakes to do, and he will persevere until he accomplishes his object. Let the North send us men. . . . Every ablebodied man ought now to come out, or send his substitute, and the war would soon be over. Our thinned ranks, and the tens of thousands of newly made graves scattered all over these battlefields, as well as the old ones of our fallen heroes, both officers and men, calls in tones of thunder that ought to arrous a nation from its slumbers and awaken a free people to a sense of their duty to pute forth their energy and make the power of this nation felt. . . .

Sarah, why don't you tell me more about little Robert? Is his father pleased with the little darling? Does it cry much, or is it a quiet child? I don't know much about children, but one thing I have learned is that children often cry for water in hot weather. If it is like its grandfather, it will want plenty of this good wholesom beverage.

Have you dry weather there? We have had no rain here for a long time. It is very dry, vegetation is burnt up, and there is a great scarcity of water. We are, as a general thing, pretty healthy. I hope the army will remain so. . . .

Trenches before Petersburg, Va., July 2nd 1864

My dear Ellen,

I have but a moment to write you, as the mail is closing. I received a letter from you today of a late date. It was a welcom visitor. I am well, also Captain Lloyd. Nothing is new here. We seem to be rather quiet, except for a few big guns below us that ocasionaly belch away on the town of Petersburg. The last skirmishing took place near the same place.

The good news is that Wilson and his cavalry are safe.[8] You will see it in the papers. All is right here so far. We will get Richmond yet. Don't dispair.

This is the anniversary of the battle of Gettysburg and the day I received my wounds. I have seen hard service since that time, and hard fighting too. God only knows if I will get through. I look for a hard time to come. . . .

Trenches before Petersburg, Va., July 3rd 1864

My daughter Hennie,

. . . I have received but one letter from you since your return home. I write almost every day to your mother for you all. . . .

We have had no rain since we came here and the ground is ex-

---

8. Reference here was to the June 22-July 1 raid on the Southside Railroad by 5,000 Federal cavalry under Gen. James H. Wilson. The troopers did extensive damage to the Confederate artery, but they had to fight their way back to the Federal lines. Wilson lost 1,500 men, 12 guns, and his supply trains. *Ibid.*, 620–33, 807–10. Cf. Meade, *Letters of George G. Meade*, II, 209–10.

tremely dry. Dust rules the day. Some newspaper corrispondent says that we have had a fine shower. I have not seen it, only a lite sprinkle here. Weather is sickening hot and dry, water very scarce. We have to sink wells. Our troops are so far healthy and are now pretty well rested.

Burnside's Corps are opposit the town. The 5th Corps is on his left and we, the 2nd Corps, are on the left of the 5th. The 6th Corps is on the left of us. Burnside is no doubt mining and working toward the town by slow approaches.[9] They are firing shells at intervals both day & night. They use mortars. We will have the town by & by and expect to get Richmond with the bargin. You can assure my friends that *all is right here*. Only send on more men to fill up our thinned ranks. Do this and the Rebellion will soon be ended.

Genl. Grant says that he is now further on then he expected to be at this time.[10] Our losses are heavy, but it is a greate work that we are engaged in, and we must have men and time to do it.

We have received 82 troops for our little regiment. . . .

Trenches before Petersburg, Va., July 5th 1864

My dear Ellen & family,

. . . You ask me what is our prospects, &c. Genl. Grant says that everything is working right and that he is now further on then he expected to be at this date. It is true we have lost very many men and officers; and with our victories we have had our reverses. But in a campaign like this it can not be expected that all will go in our favour. This is a big work, a glorious undertaking, and you must not expect us to accomplish it in a week or a month. But look on it as the work of time. . . .

We have not had any firing along here for some days. But on our right, down opposit the town, they keep up a brisk firing night and day. We are enjoying our rest to perfection, although we are right

---

9. At that time Burnside's men were in fact digging a tunnel toward the Confederate lines. Col. Henry Pleasants, whose 48th Pennsylvania consisted for the most part of coal miners, had suggested the scheme to Burnside. He in turn passed it along to Meade and Grant. The two commanders agreed to the undertaking "as a means of keeping the men occupied." Grant, *Personal Memoirs,* II, 307.

10. This statement is untrue. On July 2 Chief Engineer of the Army J. G. Barnard began a memorandum with the observation: "The army . . . is now lying without any definite object. Smith's and Burnside's corps are lying in trenches close up to the enemy, carrying on a quasi siege—not decided enough to accomplish anything, but by heat and sharpshooters losing men every day." *OR,* Vol. XL, Pt. 1, p. 584.

under the enemy's guns. If they open on us, we will open on them. As they know that it is a game both parties can play at, I don't think they are desirous of disturbing us. How long we will remain in this position I am unable to say. But be it long or short, I am satisfied that Grant knows what he is about [to do] and will conduct us to success. We have a very strong position. If the Rebels wish to advance on us, we are willing for them to do so. . . .

Trenches before Petersburg, Va., July 7th 1864

My dear Ellen & family,

I intended writing you a letter yesterday evening, but I had just begun when I was interrupted by the arrival of Dr. E. Welling and Rev. Mr. Davis, a member of the Christian Commission, and a Dr. Smith.[11] They all staid for tea. . . .

We have not received any papers this morning and feel very anxous to hear about a part of Ewell's Corps that has gon North.[12] As yet we know but little about it. We think it can't be a large force and will not amount to much. We think it was gotten up to divert Genl. Grant from following out his great campaign. This they cannot do. But one division of the 6th Corps have gon to the assistance of our forces in that quarter. Perhaps troops we don't know of may have gon. Ewell ought to be captured and never permitted to return. I hope that he will be.

The last two days has been very quiet here. This morning some cannonading occurred on our right. The weather continues very, very dry, and the sun is very hot. The greate want here is water. We dig for it and get it in small quantities by diging a few feet. There has been no rain since we came here. The woods are all burnt over and small bushes and timber are all killed. The sun shines down into the dry bushes with extreme heat. There is nothing pleasant for the eye to rest upon.

Oh, how I would like to look once more on the beautiful green fields of the North! What a Paridice to this poor, miserable, forelorn, God forsaken country! The curse of slavery has marked every acre of

11. The Rev. J. B. Davis and the Rev. J. W. Smith were then performing field service on behalf of the Christian Commission. Moss, *Annals of the U.S. Christian Commission,* 603, 627.

12. Shortly after the battle of Cold Harbor Lee dispatched Gen. Jubal Early and a part of R. S. Ewell's old II Corps to counteract Hunter's marauding activities in the Shenandoah Valley. Early routed the Federals, then swept down the Valley in a raid on Washington. Grant rushed the VI and XIX Corps to the defense of the Northern capital.

land, and the desolation of war has laid it all in a barren wast. The F.F.V.'s have left their homes and fled before us like the murderer when pursued by the officers sent to arrest him. Their conscience cries out: "Guilty! Guilty!"

I must confess I have very little sympathy for these people. The women are by far the worst secessionists, and they have much to answer for in bringing on and sustaining this war. When I look around and take view of the battlefields and think of the hundreds and thousands of our brave comrades that have fallen in defence of our dear old flag—fighting to sustain our Government and civil and religious liberty, and to tell the world that Republican Government can be sustained, I must *look with contempt* on those that have helped to mould Southern sentiment and arouse their demon-like passions to prepare these people to destroy this fair fabrick, our Union. . . .

Trenches near Petersburg, Va., July 8th 1864

My dear Ellen & family,

. . . Last night and today we have had more firing on our right, opposit the town than we have had for some time.[13] I think that Burnside is mining, and no doubt that Petersburg will soon fall into our hands. But as to mining, we know nothing about it. Even the persons that are engaged in it are not to divulge anything.

The weather is still very dry—no rain, everything burnt up. I still think this Northern raid will not amount to much. It is only to draw off our forces—to relieve the enemy of their tight position—only a ruse.

I am appointed on a General Court Marshall and will have additional duties to perform. I will have to act as President of the Court.

We now feel somewhat rested from our fatigue of two months' hard fighting and are feeling in better spirits. We no doubt will soon have another hard campaign to go through.

We now have our evening prayer meetings regularly. Attendance is pretty good, though not as good as I would like to see. Many of those that formerly met with us are now killed, wounded and missing. Sad changes. Captain Sleeper, one of our most earnest workers, was killed in the charge on May 12th. He is a greate loss to our regiment, as well as to our religious meetings.

It is now 5 p.m. and a heavy canonnading from both lines, ter-

13. No action occurred during this period other than the daily artillery barrages. *OR*, Vol. XL, Pt. 1, p. 320.

rible booming [can be heard]. Now there is heavy musketry, now a Rebel cheer. What does it all mean? We will hear. It has now slackened off a little, but it is still going on. It will not amount to much. It has rolled from us towards the right. Firing to some extent continues.

11 p.m. Firing has ceased down to the usual amount of big guns. I have not heard the cause. All is as usual. . . .

Trenches before Petersburg, Va., July 9th 1864
My dear Ellen & family,

In my last evening's letter, I spoke of the heavy cannonading and musketry going on on our right. It was the 5th Corps and the right of our Corps. The Rebels seen that we were building a new work in front of our position, and they made a charge to drive our men out of it. But in this they were sadly disappointed. They got a good drubing and were driven back. Then our artillery opened upon them and must have added to the slaughter. Theirs opened on us and don us some damage. But what I don't know. We got the best of the engagement.

From the course pursued by the enemy, they must think that Grant has been foolish to send a greate part of his force to the north and that they can whip us here. In this they will find themselves very much mistaken. This afternoon's report says that they are massing up in front of our Corps. If so, it is no doubt to feel us out. But we are fully ready for them. Let them come on. The battery right beside me has been firing at them for about an hour—with what effect I don't know. . . .

I am having a well sunk right in front of my headquarters. Our regiment have two or three wells, then take our horses two miles to water.

I was on Court Marshall today and tried three cases. We will meet again on Monday. . . .

Very much against my own will and inclination, I burn all or nearly all my letters from home. I keep them a few days, read them over a few times, and, when I think I am going into a fight, I burn them. . . .

Trenches before Petersburg, Va., July 10th 1864
My dear Ellen & family,

This is Sabbath evening, and we have had thus far a very quiet day. Last night there was considerable moving of troops. It is said that the ballance of the 6th Corps has left for a new position. Whether north or south I don't know, and no doubt it is better that we don't. But we can guess. We have been expecting an attack on our lines here, but up to this hour all is quiet.

We get the Northern papers here about two days old and are posted thus far on the Rebel raid in the North. We think that all will be right in that section very soon. Let all the young and able-bodied men turn out at once and do something for their country. If they don't now, they never will. If they had responded to the draft and had not paid the $300 to get clear, or if they had responded to the hundred-day call, this rebellion would have been crushed by this time. I cannot see what people can expect who will not show their courage in a trying time like this.

We have had one church service today and will have another this evening when it is cool. We have not yet got our bough house built over our seats, so the sun makes it very uncomfortable. This evening is cooler.

Captain Lloyd was just here. He is well and says he would like to see you but can't go just now. . . .

Bivouac near the trenches, July 12th 1864

My dear family,

I merely write to tell you that I am well. Our Corps has moved out of the trenches and we are massed here. I think we are going somewhere tonight on some expedition, but I don't know what it is.

I have been on as Corps Officer of the Day and am very tired. There is nothing but sand here and the dust is terrible. No rain yet. I never experienced the like of it. It is so unpleasant and disagreeable; we feel so dirty. May God spare us all to meet again. . . .

Reserve camp in front of Petersburg, Va.
July 16th 1864

My dear family,

It has been several days since I wrote you. I think I have not written since Sunday [July 10], as I was Corps Officer of the Day on Monday and part of Tuesday. Then we went on a move and left our old camp in the trenches. I remember now: the last letter was a short one written in a bivouack on Tuesday after coming off my duties.

When I wrote you that pencilled note, I was sitting under a flag right in a cloud of dust. We were laying under a scorching sun in a field, with the wind continually rolling a cloud of dust that I can compare to nothing better than what we read about as the burning sand plains of Africa. We have had no rain since and long before we came here. The drought and dust is indescribable. No matter where you are— either in camp, on the roads, either on the march, alone on horseback, or on foot, the same cloud of dust is over and around you. The woods will shelter us from it if we can get far enough into it, which is but seldom, for soon the timber is cut down and along comes the much dreded daily companion. And very soon the tramping of the forest grounds causes a dust that is almost as bad as that on the roads and fields. I have seen droughts and dust, but the equel of this I have never seen. How Virginians are going to live for the want of crops is more than I can tell. There must be not war but famine in this state. The growing crops are burnt up by the drought and the fields laid waste by war.

You have had a visit in the North by the Rebels. They seemed to go just where they pleased until the 6th Corps went up. We looked on the raid with interest and anxiety. The mails being stoped prevented us from receiving the news for a day or two, and we had all kinds of rumours. We did not know but that we would be ordered up there. It is said that it was arranged for our Division to go in place of the 3rd Division of the 6th Corps.[14] But Genl. Hancock protested against it, saying that he could not spare this Division. Then Genl. Meade sent the 3rd Division of the 6th Corps and afterward the ballance of the Corps. Had we been sent, the ballance of our Corps, like the 6th, would have had to follow. I hope Lt. Paul will have time to run up and see all his friends. But it is doubtful if he could get a furlough at present, as all are needed in the coming battles.

We have the news here that the Rebels are retreating from Washington and "My Maryland."[15] I hope it is true. But our earnest hope is that many of them may be captured with all their plunder. They ought not to be alowed to get back without a good sound drubing. Here in the army we look upon this raid as a good thing. The North would not fill our depleted ranks. They would rather pay their $300 and let us do all the fighting here and also defend Washington—when

14. Actually, Grant's initial thought was to send all of the II Corps to the defense of Washington. Martha D. Perry (comp.), *Letters from a Surgeon of the Civil War* (Boston, 1906), 210. Cf. *OR,* Vol. XL, Pt. 3, pp. 35–36, 47.
15. The timely arrival in Washington of troops from Grant's army stopped Early from attacking the city. On the night of July 12 the Confederates withdrew and began their return march to the Shenandoah Valley.

THE SIEGE BEGINS ♣ [463]

everyone knew it was not money but men that the Government wants. The mass of the people turned their attention to making money, regardless of our national safety. These Rebel raids stirs the people up and shows them the necessity of immediate action. Now things will go on right again. Our thinned ranks will be filled up and the Rebellion will be pute down.

Even . . . [Representative] David Smith will have to come out or be represented. Oh, how I would like to have a large number of such Copperheads here!

Now you may ask what I am doing, or what is the 2nd Corps doing. In the last letter I told you that I thought we were going on an expedition. We don nothing but go up to the left of our lines and send out a reconnicence to feel the enemy. Then we went to work and leveled a redoubt and breastworks that had been thrown up by the 6th Corps. Thus we shortened our lines. Then we came down here to the reserve camp and were told to fix up a camp. Very soon we found ourselves working night and day in tearing down all the old Rebel redoubts and lines of breastworks that they had thrown up and which were inside of our lines and of no use to us. Why this was done no one can tell.[16] It is said that no one but Genl. Grant knows the object of it. We have now finished that work and today are resting in our camp. Our works are manned by the 5th Corps and Burnside's [9th Corps]. We hold all the ground and picket nearly as much as we did before the 6th Corps left us. We are well fixed for defence if the enemy make an attack upon us. Let them come. . . .

Before Petersburg, Va., July 18th 1864

My dear Ellen & family,

This is Sabbath and I can say that we have comparatively a quiet day. But few guns have been heard in front. It is now 5 p.m. We have just had a nice church service—a good attendance and a good discussion. We will meet again this evening for prayer. . . .

I have this morning a letter from you and Hennie dated the 9th. It is the first I have had for some time. It is possible that the Rebels got one or more letters of yours to me when they captured the Washington train. . . .

We have but little news here from the North, but we understand that the Rebs have left and that Washington is safe. Nothing new here.

16. The men were merely strengthening the siege lines. The II Corps was then in position behind the VI Corps.

My own impression is that this Corps is to be detached on some important expedition very soon. . . . This rest for the 2nd Corps is not for nothing.

I must go to dress parade and will have to close. . . .

In front of Petersburg, Va., July 19th 1864

My dear Ellen,

Last evening I had the pleasure of receiving and reading three home letters dated the 10th, 13th, and 14th. I hope I will now get my back letters. I am sending you another number of the *Army & Navy Journal.* I am sending them all to you, as they contain the best record that we can get. Having them in our open tents, or no tents at all, as the case may be, they become very much soiled. Still, they are in a pretty good state of preservation. The accounts are more reliable than the newspapers of the day. I had intended to send you the July *Harper's,* as I wished you to read a piece styled "Shoddy." But Dr. Heritage [17] borrowed it before we broke the last camp and it can't be found. I suppose he left it there, as we broke camp at night. If you have not seen the piece, let Alice go out and purchase that number at Cassner's. You ought by all means to take one of these monthlys. If not *Harper's,* then take the *Atlantic Monthly.* . . .

Last night we were awakened from our slumbers by an order calling us to arms—stating that two Rebel deserters had come in and said that the enemy were about to make an attack on our lines, on the left of Genl. Burnside and on the right of the 5th Corps. The 1st Division of our Corps moved out to support the right, the 2nd Division the left, and our Division the centre. However, we were not to get under arms before 3 a.m. unless we heard the firing. But at 3 we were to be ready. The enemy did not advance on our works, and all was as quiet as usual—nothing but the ordinary firing. So passed last night. Today I was on the court marshall. It is now 4:20 p.m., and all is quiet.

We are geting much reliable news in regard to the Rebel raid northward. But we understand that they are on the back track. I hope they are. We fear that they will be alowed to get off with their plunder. If so, the North is to blame, for it is not filling our ranks. The Militia alone will not do much against such troops as we are fighting. But mix them up with old troops and they will fight well. When will the Governors of States understand this and quit the popular idea of raising

17. John D. Heritage was asst. surgeon of the 11th New Jersey.

new regiments or organizations and instead fill up the old ones? By past experience this ought to be the cry of every lover of his or her country, for in this way you mix up the zeal of the new troops with the unflinching bravery of the old and can make a good battle.

I would enjoy your vegetables very much, especially those that growed in our garden. But I fear that I shall not soon have that pleasure. The campaign is not yet over, and it is hard to tell when it will be. The army is very well fed. We get potatoes and sometimes we can get a little cabbage. We buy them from the Commissary. The Government is now giving the men more vegetables than we used to get. The Sanitary Commission is doing a good deal in this way. But the army out here at the front don't get much. It is principaly used up at the Hospitals. The other day some came for our regiment. It did not amount to ⅛ of a pound to a man. I don't allow the officers to keep any, but give it all to the men in the ranks. . . .

Before Petersburg, Va., July 20th 1864

My dear Ellen,

I did not write you yesterday as I was out on fatigue duty. Yesterday morning an order came to turn out the Brigade for this duty. At 5 a.m. we started towards the front and found our whole Division there. The object was to dig a covered way 4 feet deep and 12 feet wide, to convey artillery, ammunition, and troops to the front in safety from shells. This covered way is more than a mile long. In military phrase it is called a "covered way," though it is not covered on top. What is meant by "covered" is covered from the enemy in sight and from their guns. The dirt is all thrown up on the dangerous side—the side the balls are coming from—and makes a bank of earth on that side between cuting and embankment of from six to eight feet high. The 5th & 9th Corps are mining toward Petersburg, and Grant will have a cannonading here one of these days that will shake the ground around this place for miles. This covered way is in preparation for that terable opening of artillery that will level Petersburg to the ground, unless the Rebels evacuate the place. We are full of hope here and have the fullest confidence in General Grant. Richmond, by the help of God, will be ours.

We have had a greate deal of firing both last night and all day today.[18] I have no doubt but that it will increase from day to day as we make further demonstrations towards the town. . . .

18. Other commanders reported no marked increase in the daily bombardment of Petersburg. *OR,* Vol. XL, Pt. 1, p. 180, 183, 195, 203.

We have rain, and had a fine rain yesterday. We were all in it. It rained down rapidly, yet we all enjoyed it. . . .

Camp before Petersburg, Va., July 21st 1864

My dear Ellen,

It is now near mail time and I can write you but a few lines. I have just been reading over my home letters, preparatory to commiting them to the flames. It is not safe to have family letters about, as much exposed as I am. As much as I dislike to destroy them, it is the only way.

The weather is much cooler here since the rain. We have some comfort now that we are rid of the dust.

Give my love to Miss Sidney Paul and Miss Wilson. By all means have them to dinner. They were so kind to me and they are so Patriotic. Tell them all that we in the army are delighted with the President's Proclamation calling for 500,000 more men.[19] That is a move in the right direction. Had it been don months since, the Rebellion would have been pute down.

We are pleased with the news from Sherman.[20] He will succeed in taking Atlanta.

We have just heard that the 6th Corps, under Genl. [Horatio G.] Wright, has made a connection with Genl. [George] Crook, commanding a large body of cavalry, and has attacked the enemy's rear at Snicker's Gap.[21] They have killed and wounded some 600 of the Rebels with a fair prospect of capturing their whole trains of plunder. You will see the particulars before we do, as you get the papers much sooner. Things are looking all right here.

When I was writing you last evening, Dr. Welling came in and we got to talking about geting a leave of absence to go and spend a month in Belvidere, and also to bring Col. Schoonover with us. It resulted in all writing a line or two in my letter.

19. On July 18, 1864, Lincoln issued a call for 500,000 additional volunteers to strengthen the Federal armies. Miers, *Lincoln Day by Day*, III, 273–74.

20. The Federal Army of the West, under Maj. Gen. William T. Sherman, was then besieging the railroad center of Atlanta, Ga. On July 20 and 22 Sherman successfully repulsed attacks made on his lines by the besieged forces of Gen. John B. Hood.

21. On July 20 a Federal cavalry detachment under Gen. William W. Averell attacked Gen. Dodson Ramseur's Confederate division near Winchester. The Southerners bolted to the rear in panic at a critical moment in the engagement. Ramseur lost 470 men and 4 guns. *OR*, Vol. XXXVII, Pt. 1, pp. 327, 347, 353.

We have but little amusement here. In fact, we have been so hard worked that until now we had neither time nor inclination to be funny. . . .

Headquarters, 3rd Brigade, July 23rd 1864

My dear Ellen,

You see by this heading that I am again in command of the Brigade. Genl. Birney has been assigned to command of the 10th Corps. Genl. Mott is in command of the Division and I am at present in command of this Brigade. I have my doubts of Genl. Mott's remaining long in command of the Division. I do not think that he stands well enough with Genl. Hancock for that responsible situation.[22] I may be mistaken, but it is my opinion that he will not. I may remain in command of the Brigade, but it is doubtful. When we are in camp, there are plenty of Stars about; but on the eve of a hard battle or march, they disappear and their place is supplanted by Eagles. So I expect to see someone coming around with a star on that will rank and relieve me.

But no matter if he does, I am all right. Genl. Birney will give me a strong letter of recommendation soon, and I will see Genl. Hancock. Genl. Birney says that if there is a vacancy in his Corps he will, if possible, secure it for me. If I am spared, I will get a star by & by. This is all confidential. . . .

Camp before Petersburg, Va., July 25th 1864

My dear Ellen,

I did not write you yesterday. Notwithstanding it was the Holy Sabbath, we had to go out on fatigue duty, very much against my wishes and inclination. We are working on the covered way and the approaches running from it towards our front lines, so as to haul artillery and ammunition right into our redoubts without being injured by the enemy's shot and shell. In building these, we are sometimes fired on by the enemy. Yesterday we had no one hurt; on Friday we had one officer wounded and one man killed not belonging to our

22. McAllister's opinion might well have been valid. After all, Mott's division had given way in confusion on two occasions during the Wilderness Campaign. Hancock was too much of a fighter to overlook such shortcomings. Moreover, Grant did not have full confidence in the New Jersey division commander. See Grant, *Personal Memoirs*, II, 224, 229.

Brigade. We have thus far got along safely. Tomorrow we go on again. One of our Divisions have been pute on the front line; the other two has to take it on alternate days and do this work. We got out at 4 a.m. and come in at 7 p.m., making a long day for men to work. We divide into two reliefs and work two hours at a time. But still it is a long and hard day. Yet it is all for our country. We are making heavy works and have miles of covered way in which we can walk and even ride with comparative security. In fact, we are fixing it so we can live under the iron hail of the enemy's guns. We are preparing to send over to them a tremendous storm of the same material. It looks to us as though we were going to shell and then storm their works. I hope not the latter; for in storming, the chances are against the storming party—two to one in casualties.

I am still in command of the Brigade, and it is thought that I will remain in command of it. Genl. Mott has been assigned to the command of the Division. There has been no man with a star on his shoulder around this way hunting a job as yet. If we move to fight soon, I don't think that there will be. But if we have no fighting to do, they will be here.

When he left, Genl. Mott took with him all the Brigade Staff except Adjt. Genl. [William J.] Rusling, acting aide Lt. [Charles F.] Bowers, and Brigade Inspector [Capt. Rodney B.] Newkirk, leaving me pretty well stripped of help. But today I have detailed Capt. Morrison of the 6th New Jersey [23] and Capt. [Richard T.] Lombard of the 11th Massachusetts as assistant acting aides. These are good, brave men, and men of experience, so I will get along. They are all gentlemanly and fine looking aides.

It is now 9 p.m. Notwithstanding the darkness of the night, the sound of small arms and the roaring cannon can be heard almost constantly along Burnside's lines. There is some firing on the right of the 5th Corps, but not near so much. It seems like one continuous battle. The 5th Corps are expecting us to relieve them and take their places on the front line. Whether we will be ordered to do so or not I can't know.

For some days the news from Atlanta has been pretty good. Though we have met with some considerable loss, yet we think all is right. Atlanta will soon be ours. Genl. Grant receives the dispatches from Genl. Sherman every day, and they are sent to the Corps, Divisions, Brigades and Regiments. So you see we have the news early. . . .

23. Probably Capt. Louis M. Morris of Co. G, 6th New Jersey. No New Jersey soldier by the name of Morrison attained the rank of captain.

Camp before Petersburg, Va., July 26th 1864

My dear family,

We are just now breaking camp and will very soon (in an hour or two) be on the march. We don't know where we are going, but it is on a raid. If so, you will not have letters from me for some days. . . .

In the field before Petersburg, Va., July 29th 1864

My dear Ellen,

In my last I wrote you that we were about starting on what I supposed was to be a raid. We marched all night, crossed the James River near Deep [Bottom], and attacked the enemy.[24] Our skirmish line alone captured 4 20-pounders and 6 caissons. I was not on the skirmish line. We drove back the enemy a considerable distance and came in sight of another strong line of works. Yesterday the cavalry had a fight and captured 200 prisoners. The enemy have weakened their force here. Last night we marched all night and got here just before day.

I think the object is to make a charge here, and I am expecting to get the word "Forward" any moment. It will cause many of us to lose our lives. If ordered, I will do my best. God grant that we are successful, and that His richest blessings be poured out on you all is my prayer. . . .

Camp before Petersburg, Va., July 31st 1864

My dear family,

My last letter was written to you on the eve of our Corps starting to the James River on that expedition. We lost but one man on that occasion.[25] After remaining there for two days and one night, we were

---

24. Grant reasoned that Lee might take advantage of the transfer of the VI and XIX Corps to Washington and attack the weakened Federal lines at Petersburg. Therefore, and with characteristically good generalship, Grant determined to beat Lee to the punch by launching an offensive of his own. Hancock's II Corps and Sheridan's cavalry were ordered to make a thrust from the Federal right. If Hancock's men could break the Confederate lines and open an avenue, Sheridan would strike at Richmond. On July 27 the II Corps reached Deep Bottom and the Confederate works. Fierce probes confirmed that the Southern lines were too strong to break. Sheridan managed to capture 200 Confederates, but on July 28 the expedition returned to Grant's army.

25. The lone casualty was Pvt. Michael Vill of Co. A, 120th New York. *OR*, Vol. XL, Pt. 1, p. 411; Cornelius Van Santvoord, *The One Hundred and Twentieth Regiment, New York State Volunteers* (cited hereafter as Van Santvoord, *120th New York*) (Rondout, N.Y., 1894), 244.

hurried back to assist in the assault on Petersburg.[26] . . . The assault was not made on the morning intended but went off yesterday morning.

All was to be in readyness by daylight yesterday morning. At daylight the mine was ignited but would not go off. It was then examined and the fuse was found defective. It was refixed, then ignited, and the work was don well. The assaulting party entered without much trouble. The enemy rallied but were driven back by our troops. We were considered victorious, and Grant was certain of the prize. But it is said that the reserves did not rush into the breach to support the attacking party. The enemy did rally and succeeded in driving our men back, so that our victory turned out to be a defeat. I do not know the facts but will write you more in detail again.

You may ask where I was. Our Division was pute into the front line of works on our right. The right of my Brigade was on the river. We relieved the 18th Corps so they could support the charge. We were some three miles from the fort that was blown up. As soon as the fort was blown up, our artillery opened up. The cannonading was terrific and continued all day long.

When the charging party succeeded in the morning, orders were sent along for us all to develop the enemy's lines—as it was thought that we had but a thin line to contend against. But this was a mistake so far as it related to my Brigade. The enemy showed himself in force in my front. . . . My Brigade were behind the breastworks. I give the order to fall in—in two ranks—and told them I would give this order in a loud voice so as to be heard by the enemy: "Fourth Battalion! Battalion of direction! Forward, guide center!"

I instructed them that at the word "March!" the rear rank would throw up their guns, to represent the mens' heads. They would give three cheers, which would cause the Rebels to think that we were charging on them. Then they would raise up and fire. I had men watching to see how full the Rebel ranks were.

It succeeded admirably, for the Rebs rose up in mass and fired on us. It was just what I wanted. In this way they showed their num-

26. Grant regarded the July 30 battle of the Crater as "a stupendous failure." The events of the engagement are basically as McAllister described them, though incompetent leadership was the underlying weakness of the assault. As Grant stated: "It cost us about four thousand men, mostly, however, captured; and all due to inefficiency on the part of the corps commander [Burnside] and the incompetency of the division commander [Gen. James H. Leslie] who was sent to lead the assault." Grant, *Personal Memoirs*, II, 315. See also Lydia M. Post (ed.), *Soldiers' Letters from Camp, Battlefield and Prison* (New York, 1865), 429–34; Elbridge J. Copp, *Reminiscences of the War of the Rebellion, 1861–1865* (Nashua, N.H., 1911), 419–28.

bers and I could report a strong line—without the loss of a man—and at the same time deliver a rank fire into the enemy. Had I not done this, I would have had to send over a line of skirmishers. It would have been a forelorn hope; for manned as their works were, not a man of ours would likely have escaped unhurt.

When the charge was made and was at first successful, Burnside reported that there was but a thin line of the enemy and that the whole line could easily advance and take their works.[27] But it was only a short time after that before they drove his forces back to our old lines. If he could have held the line thus taken, we could have advanced and went into the city. But I am sorry to say that it is not a victory. What we will do next I can't tell, but I have no doubt Genl. Grant has a plan ready to carry out.

So you have another Rebel raid in the North.[28] I hope the able-bodied men will all turn out and help us to pute down this greate rebellion. They ought to be proud that they have a country to save. . . .

Camp before Petersburg, Va., August 1st 1864

My dear Ellen,

It is now after 12 o'clock at night. I have received my pay and I have concluded to send you the money by express. Our Chaplain will go down to City Point tomorrow morning and pute it into the express. This is the best way. Another advantage is we are paid with interest-bearing notes that are compounded every six months. At the end of three years you can get the whole with compound interest. If you can spare some of this and pute it in your bank box, it will be a good investment. Mr. Harris will tell you all about these notes. . . .

27. Burnside's first dispatches of the action were optimistic and failed to reveal the dilemma then facing his troops. See *OR,* Vol. XL, Pt. 3, pp. 644–45; Augustus Woodbury, *Major General Ambrose E. Burnside and the Ninth Army Corps* (Providence, 1867), 437–44.

28. In retaliation for atrocities committed by Federals in the Shenandoah Valley, Confederate Gen. Jubal Early ordered two cavalry brigades to make a foray through Pennsylvania. The Confederates reached Chambersburg on July 30; when townspeople refused to meet demands for ransom, Southern troops burned the city. This deliberate destruction became one of the most controversial incidents of the Civil War.

Camp before Petersburg, Va., August 1st 1864

My dear Ellen,

I wrote you a short letter last evening and told you of our return to this camp and of the blowing up of a fort and the successful charge on the enemy's line and of their regaining all they had lost. I also told you that I was on the right of our lines with my Brigade, our right resting on the Appomattox River. The river here has a change of direction, and the enemy occupy the opposit side. They had batteries so placed that they could enfilade us. For that whole day long we were under a heavy shell fire from that direction, as well as a skirmish fire in our front. But we were so well protected that I lost but 8 men. None were killed; one man lost his leg and two more had their arms shot off.

We are now under marching orders again. I know not where we are going. It is our Corps alone. Perhaps it is a raid, but I thought the same before we went to the James. . . . You will no doubt hear of us in a northern direction. God grant that we may be successful. Our Corps may well be called the "Flying Corps," for we go everywhere.

. . . The enlisted men have got their pay raised from $13 to $16 per month. Officers have no raise in theirs. It is impossible for us to hire servants. We were compelled to take enlisted men for servants, which cost us $25 per month. But this took so many enlisted men that the orders now are: if we employ one servant, we pay all that servant cost the Government and also his commutation, which is $150 for two months. I can't get a darky or anyone else that is worth anything. I have my man John,[29] a soldier, and by far the best man I have ever had. He is splendid with horses. My horses are as round as dollars. I need never see to them at all. My boots are blacked every morning before I am up, and all my wants are attended to: clothes washed, &c. I determined, cost what it would, that I would keep him. So I have made arrangements today with Capt. Lombard, who is a member of my staff, that we keep John between us. John attends four horses. In this way I can get along splendidly, have no change in my domestick arrangements, and be able to send home some money. The price of rations and clothing has raised very much. With the additional increase of pay to the enlisted soldier, and those taking off the commutation that officers are alowed, an officer can't hardly live, let alone send home money. They are nearly all sending their enlisted men-servants back into the ranks. How they are to get along I can't for the life tell. However, I am all right. . . .

29. Pvt. John A. Labort of Co. K had been McAllister's personal orderly since mid-May, 1864.

Camp before Petersburg, Va., August 3rd 1864

My dear Ellen,

Inclosed you will please find an Adams Express receipt for $550. The money started north today and will soon reach you. . . . Keep the receipt and you are safe.

I have just received a letter from Sarah, dated July 22, and miscarried owing to the wrong direction. She had the old address—1st Brigade, 2nd Division, 3rd Corps—which will not do now. My direction is 3rd Brigade, 3rd Division, 2nd Corps. Do not, I beg of you, forget this direction. Write it down in large letters, and paisted it up so you will have it when you write your letters. . . .

Musketry and cannon are roaring on our front at this time. Firing last night continued all night. I suppose that the enemy are trying to build up the old blasted fort again and we are trying to prevent it. However, this is only supposition on my part. It was expected that the enemy would attack us last night or at daylight this morning. We were under arms and ready for them, but they did not come. I have no doubt that they will fall on us before long. Yet I am satisfied that if they do, we will get the best of them; so let them come. . . .

As to the [regimental] quartermaster, [Henry] Ridgway was appointed against my will. I have written the Governor relative to it and I will not have him mustered as Quartermaster.[30] There are no quartermasters now. All are mustered into the line. We take men from the line to act as quartermasters. I could not take one from outside and do justice to our brave and gallant men that have fought a score of battles. . . .

Camp before Petersburg, Va., August 4th 1864

My dear Ellen,

Hennie's kind letter of the 2nd is just to hand. I am pleased to know that Mrs. [John] Harris is not discouraged at our reverse. As you say, we must expect reverses in such an undertaking. We are not discouraged here, for the enemy can't drive us away and the Rebel northern raid is only a faint to get us away from this strong position. It will result in good to us—stir up the people to the necessity of filling up our ranks. We are expecting an attack now. . . . Both officers & soldiers says, "Let them try it. We are ready for them!"

30. Ridgeway was a former private in Co. A. He served as regimental quartermaster until January, 1865, when he became a lieutenant in Co. G. *N.J. Record,* I, 542, 544, 567.

Various rumors are afloat as to what is to be don now. One thing is certain: we are strengthening our fortifications.[31] It is said that the Rebs are mining under two of our fortifications. If this is so, we will lead them into a nice trap. We can countermine and know how to head them off with compound interest. Our Corps is on the reserve now and have nothing to do. We are geting our camps nicely fixed up and are having a fine rest. But I don't suppose that it will last long, for we are the Flying Corps. We appear everywhere, and Genl. Lee is after us. Well, I do hope we will get now a good rest, for we needed it.

This is Thursday evening and fast day. This morning at a very late hour we received orders from Army Headquarters to observe this day in accordance with the President's proclamation—suspend all work that is not a military necessity and have church service by the chaplains. This suited me exactly. I concluded to set a good example and have service right here at my Headquarters. The Pioneers soon sprung an arch, wreathed with green boughs, in front of my tent. Then we unfurled two of our national flags and suspended them on the archway. The long avenue extending out from our Headquarters was a day or two ago recarpeted with green brushes that we gathered from the pine forest. It was nicely and neatly laid. This carpet extended right and left into all the tents along the avenue, presenting a very pretty appearance. On the side of this avenue, near my quarters, we had seats for the officers. In front of my tent and right under the arch we had a small stand covered with the Stars and Stripes, on which we laid a Bible. Camp chairs were set around.

The hour (2 p.m.) now arrived for to commence. The band of the 120th New York came and the congregation assembled—my own staff, all the officers that were disposed to come, my pioneers, and the Provost Guard. Father Saverin,[32] an aged Chaplain of this Brigade, conducted the service. His gray head and remarkable form attracts the attention of all strangers. He is a good Christian whose heart is in our country and cause. He gives us religion and patriotism—well to the point. Other chaplains opened and closed [the service] with prayer.

---

31. Such rumors were widespread throughout the Federal lines. On Aug. 3 a Union private recorded in his diary: "Ordered up at 3 a.m. expecting the 'rebs' would blow up the fort. Nothing talked about but a blowup now and many of the soldiers in the forts actually live in fear." Bartlett, *12th New Hampshire,* 225. See also William B. Lapham, *My Recollections of the War of the Rebellion* (Augusta, Me., 1892), 144.

32. The Rev. Thomas Sovereign, chaplain of the 5th New Jersey, was once cited for his "indefatigable labors and untiring zeal" toward incapacitated soldiers. *OR,* Vol. XI, Pt. 1, p. 490.

All went away satisfied with the first service held at these headquarters. You know the band plays church music, which helps very much.

All the regiments in my Brigade had service in the evening. I attended that in my own regiment. Our good Chaplain, Clark Cline, give a first-rate, well-turned discourse on religion & patriotism. The day has passed away very quietly as well as pleasantly, and, I trust, profitably to some of us.

I have now arranged to have Division service by the different chaplains every Sabbath morning at 11 a.m. while we remain in this camp. If my military friends come to see me at that hour, they will have the benefit of a sermon that they did not expect. . . .

Col. [George B.] Wiestling will not make a fortune out of those iron works very soon. Labour is so very high. And if the Rebels come along every few months, they can not opperate. He had better come out with a regiment. War is our business now. Attend to candy shops and other business afterwards. The rebellion must be pute down first. . . .

Camp before Petersburg, Va., August 5th 1864

My dear Ellen & family,

It is now 10 o'clock at night. Before I retire I thought I would write you a line or two, as the mail leaves here before daylight.

This evening I had just returned from Genl. Mott's Headquarters from a 3rd Corps Union meeting. The General had given me several maps of the battle of Gettysburg. I was just cuting a stick to roll two or three of them on, to send to you, when one of Genl. Mott's aides road up in greate haste and said, "Colonel, General Mott's compliments, and have your Brigade formed at once."

"All right," I answered.

I called for my aides to notify the regiments at once. I knew something was up, that the Rebels were attacking our lines. In ten minutes my Brigade was moving out. We marched towards the 18th Corps, the firing being in that direction. The firing now ceased. Soon came along the orders to about-face and return to camp, which we did. I have not heard the particulars yet—only that the enemy attacked us. Some say they blowed up one of our forts. Let it be what it may; they have been driven back. You will see it in the papers and learn the particulars.

I will, if spared and all is right, fix up these maps and send them tomorrow by mail. I want you to have one framed and hung up in the parlour. They are handsom. I will mark the place where I was wounded.

They are knocking away at the front now and no doubt will continue all night.

Yours of the 3rd, and Sarah's of the 1st, was received this evening. Two things I want you and Sarah to quit: Ellen, you quit hoeing in the garden; Sarah, quit calling my namesake "Baby." Robert is its name. . . .

Camp before Petersburg, Va., August 6th 1864

My dear Ellen,

Another quiet day has passed. There was but little firing, but a good deal more now. There always is at night, caused by us preventing the Rebels from building up their demolished fort again. We won't let them work on it during daylight; when they slip in at night, we keep banging away to prevent them from working.

I told you in last night's letter of our sudden call to arms. It was caused by the Rebels attempting to blow up one of our forts. But it was a complete failure on their part. Their ingineering was bad, and they missed the fort by 40 feet. The explosion did not hurt us at all.[33] So we about-faced and came back to camp. We were expecting this, had taken all of our guns out of the fort, and built in the rear a breastwork filled with cannon. So if the fort had been blown up, we could have cut them down by thousands and all would have been well with us still. You see we are on the lookout.

I send you some nice large maps of the battle of Gettysburg— one for our family, one for Sarah, one for my friend Mr. [Israel] Harris, and one for [my attorney] Mr. David Dupuy. Have ours nicely framed and hung up in the parlour. I value this map and no doubt you do. If you want to know where I was, look for Genl. Humphreys' Division and Genl. Carr's Brigade. Look at the regiment next to and on the right of [Lieutenant Francis W.] Seeley's Battery [K, 4th U.S. Artillery] in the orchard, the right resting close to a house on the right of this regiment. I was wounded by sharpshooters firing from this house. . . .

33. In spite of the "sorry piece of engineering" on the part of Confederate miners, the explosion killed seven men in the XVIII Corps. One of the dead was Col. G. A. Stedman, then in command of a brigade. *Ibid.,* Vol. XLII, Pt. 1, pp. 792–93, 807; S. Millett Thompson, *Thirteenth Regiment of New Hampshire Volunteer Infantry . . . : A Diary* . . . (cited hereafter as Thompson, *13th New Hampshire*) (Boston, 1888), 435–36.

Camp before Petersburg, Va., August 7th 1864

My dear Ellen,

This has been a nice quiet day in camp for us. But few guns fired until after dark. It is near 1 a.m., and there is some considerable firing now.

I told you in a former letter that I was planning to have divine service at these Headquarters at 11 a.m. every Sabbath. So today we had seats arranged in front of my tents and the band in attendance. The pioneer corps & provost guard were all present, as well as all my aides, servants, and a large number of officers, making in all quite a large congregation. Chaplain [Samuel T.] Moore of the 6th New Jersey gave us a most excellent and eloquent discourse. Other chaplains were present and opened and closed with prayer. . . . Everything went handsomely, and I may say that our service has becom an established fact as long as we lay here in camp. God grant that grate good may come from it.

Mr. Fay and Miss Gilson visited us today and took dinner. I was very glad to see them. They are at City Point. Miss Gilson gives her time to a colored hospital. Ain't she good? Mr. Fay devotes his time to the Sanitary Commission. . . .

The army never lived better. We have all kinds of vegetables, furnished both by the Government and the Sanitary Commission. We have everything that we want on our table. . . .

Camp before Petersburg, Va., August 8th 1864

My dear Ellen & family,

I had not been favoured with a letter from you for two or three days until just now. The postmaster entered with a letter from little Hennie dated the 5th. I assure you that it is a welcom visitor. One of the greatest comforts I have is my home letters. Come, send them on daily. I write you every day except when on the march or in battle, when you can not expect me to write. . . .

We see in the papers that the Rebs are making another raid into Pennsylvania. You have no idea, and can not immagine the extent of, the feeling of disgust manifested in this army against the poor, miserable, unmanly unpatriotick, young, able-bodied men in Pennsylvania and the North who have not courage and bravery enough to take arms and defend their own firesides, their homes and their families, in this trying hour of this country's history. Instead of organizing, arming, and defending their homes, wifes & children, and all that is dear to them, they become panic stricken at the approach of a few armed men in the character of plunderers and spread the alarm to others. They mount their firy steeds, drive off the stock, load down the cars, and call to their wifes, children, aged parents, and feeble ones to come on in the great skidadle which they lead with tremendous strides. And soon their town is in a blaze of fire, and all is lost.

Three hundred clerks alone left Chambersburg in this disgraceful manner. All of them ought to have been armed, together with a thousand more who could have saved the town. The historian will record this scene with a blush for our country, and thousands of unborn Americans will cry out: "Shame! Shame!"

Oh! Is there no chord that can be touched that will arrous the young and able-bodied men to duty and save this country? Is there no appeal that can be made that will breathe in them the love of civil and religious liberty, that the martial fires may again burn brightly on every hilltop, all over our Northern plains, and along our valleys? Young men of the North, hold not back. Your country needs your services. She is calling you in tones of thunder from the far-off plains of the South to our quiet homes of the North. Can you, in the language of Patrick Henry, "lay supinely on your backs, huging the relusive Phantom of hope until your enemies will have bound you hand and foot"? God forbid. . . .

Many of these men are crying out: "What is the Army of the Potomac doing? Why don't they defend us?"

We answer: why don't you arm and make an effort to fill our ranks? We will help you and you will know what we are doing and will have no complaints to make. . . .

Camp before Petersburg, Va., August 9th 1864

My dear Ellen,

It is now bed time. The mail is not yet in and, of course, no letters from you yet. This has been a very quiet day but a very warm one. We have delightful shade here, but the woods are rather too thick to be cool. The want of a current of air is the difficulty here. These headquarters were located here in the time of the greate dust to get clear of that greate annoyance. Though we have not had much rain, it is not quite so dusty as heretofore. Still the ground is quite dry. . . .

Today we heard a tremendous explosion away down on our right. This evening we learn that a terable explosion took place at City

Point.[34] A large amount of artillery ammunition lay piled up there at the railroad depot, and several hundred persons were at the spot. A negro carrying a shell from a vessel to this large pile let it fall and, bursting, it caused the pile of ammunition to explode, killing and wounding a large number of persons and a greate number of horses and mules. The particulars I have not got. You will see it in the papers before this reaches you. My friend, Mr. Fay, is among the wounded. He and Miss Gilson took dinner here on Sabbath last. I am realy sorry to hear of the disaster.

There is some appearance of rain tonight. So you have a fine garden. I hope you are not hoeing in it yet. I would enjoy your potatoes very much, but fear I shall not have that pleasure very soon. . . . I hope by this time Sarah and Wilson [Lloyd], with little Robert, are with you. One thing: don't spoil that namesake of mine by peting him too much. Don't let it have things as he pleases, or he will not turn out well. It is so easy to spoil children. . . .

We have first rate boarding here. We have several kinds of vegetables every day and watermelons plenty. The army never lived better than it does now. We can get all we want at the commissary's and at our sutler's, but it costs us a grate deal to live, as things are so very high here—much more so than with you. No comparison—perhaps $40 per month for self and servant. An officer's pay is not sufficient for these extravagant times. . . .

Camp before Petersburg, Va., August 10th 1864

My dear family,

. . . Another quiet day but, as usual, the firing is now going on at the front. It always begins at dark and continues all night long. It is the last sound we hear on going to sleep and the first sound we hear on awaking in the morning. I think that there is more mining going on; it is to cover that, or prevent our pickets from communicating with the enemy. We will learn by & by.

The band of the 120th New York has just been here and give me a serinade. They play well. They played "Rally Round the Flag, Boys" splendidly. . . .

34. A Confederate secret service agent claimed to have set off the explosion, which killed 58 persons, wounded 126, and caused $4,000,000 damage to Grant's principal supply base. Grant maintained that an explosion on one of the ordnance boats set off a chain reaction. *OR,* Vol. XLII, Pt. 1, pp. 17, 954–56; Pt. 2, pp. 2, 94–95, 112; Horace Porter, *Campaigning with Grant* (New York, 1907), 273–75.

The dispatches from Mobile are cheering,[35] and news from Sherman is quite good. Lete us persevere and work on, hope, and pray, and all will be right. . . .

The explosion yesterday at City Point was a sad affair. Many lives were lost. It is not known, nor never will be, what caused the explosion. The report of a negro droping a shell is mear supposition. It was a boat load of shells that blew up, throwing a part of the vessel on to the land. The express office was blown to pieces. One man, a quartermaster's clerk, was standing there with $2000 in his hand, about to express it, when the explosion took place. He was killed, and no money was found beside him. One of our Surgeons[36] went down and was about to express $700. He was badly wounded, the money lost, &c. A large portion of the lifes lost were contrabands. . . .

Bivouac at City Point, Va., August 13th 1864

My dear Ellen,

My Brigade and the whole Corps was ordered here on short notice last evening. We arrived here after dark and went into bivouack. A great deal of speculation exists as to our destination. As yet nothing is known. Some say we embark for Washington, some say North Carolina, others that we are going across the James, others that we go across the Appomattox River. But all is as yet in the dark. We are going somewhere for an important purpose with bag & baggage. You will hear of us. . . .

I received your letter of the 10th this morning. Kiss Sarah and the baby for me. The weather is exceedingly dry and very, very dusty. Terrible marching, water very scarce.[37] . . .

---

35. Five days earlier Adm. David Farragut's fleet had blasted its way past shore batteries, repelled an attack by a small Confederate naval force, successfully steamed through mine-infested waters, and entered Mobile harbor. It was on this occasion that Farragut issued his now-famous cry: "Damn the torpedoes! Full speed ahead!"

36. Probably Surgeon Edward K. Hogan of the 120th New York, who was discharged from service shortly thereafter. Van Santvoord, *120th New York*, 236.

37. The weather at this time was unbearably hot. Before noon on the following day, Mott reported to Hancock that a total of 105 men from two small regiments had collapsed from heatstroke. "The rays of the August sun," a staff officer added, "smote the heads of the weary soldiers with blows as palpable as if they had been given with clubs." Bruce, *20th Massachusetts*, 416; Walker, *Second Army Corps*, 572.

North side of the James River, August 14th 1864

My dear family,

I wrote you yesterday from City Point. We embarked and went down the river until nightfall, then turned up and disembarked about daylight. We are now at the enemy's front line of works, or rather those we took from them the last time we were here. I suppose we are going to storm the next line. Some day we are going to Richmond.

I don't like to use God's Holy Day for fighting. God forgive our sins. . . .

North side of the James River, August 15th 1864

My dear Ellen,

I wrote you a short letter saying that a charge was to be made. Well, it was made by Genl. Barlow's men and some of Genl. Gibbon's. I was ordered to report with my Brigade to Genl. Barlow, but not until the fighting had ceased for the night. Barlow made two attempts to storm the works, but unfortunately he was repulsed and with considerable loss. We are now within sight of the enemy's fortifications; and from all appearances, we are ready to make another charge. I do not know what part we are to take in it; we are looking for orders any minute. The 2nd Brigade that Captain Lloyd is in will be in it. That Brigade has reported to Genl. Birney, and Birney, I think, will make the charge. Birney is now in command of the 10th Corps. . . .

We had a fine shower last evening, the first we have had. How refreshing it was. I was on horseback in the pine woods at the time and waiting for orders. It was not unpleasant to get wet. This day is fine. God grant us success. . . .

Hdqrs., 3rd Brigade, 3rd Division, 2nd Corps [38]
August 22nd 1864

Major [John Hancock, Asst. Adjt. Genl., 3rd Division]:

In pursuance to orders from Division Headquarters of the 21st instant, I have the honor to submit the following report of operations

---

38. One, possibly two, letters that McAllister wrote in the Aug. 16–18 period have been lost. It (or they) contained his account of operations on the north bank of the James River. As compensation for this void, McAllister's official report of the expedition has been inserted. The report, slightly edited, is in *OR*, Vol. XLII, Pt. 1, pp. 390–91.

of this command north of James River, Va., from the 13th to the 20th, inclusive:

August 13th 1864. At 5 p.m. this command embarked on board of the steamboats *Periet, Sedgwick,* and *Collins,* and was landed at Deep Bottom Bridge at 5:30 a.m. the next morning.

August 14th. At 9:30 a.m. we marched forward from the river up to New Market Road. At 7 p.m. that evening the Brigade was ordered to report to Genl. [Nelson A.] Miles, who ordered us to take position on his right near New Market in front of the enemy's works, where we remained in line until 4 o'clock the next morning, the 15th, when we were ordered to rejoin our Division in the rear. At 9 a.m. we were again advanced to the front on the left of Four Mile Creek. We massed in the woods and remained there all day. Towards evening the 11th New Jersey was ordered to proceed to Malvern Hill road to support our cavalry.

At 2 p.m. on August 16th, one of our regiments (the 6th New Jersey) was ordered to make a demonstration on our left to draw the enemy's attention, while at the same time two regiments (the 8th New Jersey and 11th Massachusetts) made a demonstration on the right of our picket line to feel the enemy's strength. A heavy line of skirmishers was thrown out, consisting of the 8th New Jersey, and ordered to advance, while the 11th Massachusetts remained in reserve. Our skirmish line was at once exposed to an enfilading fire of the enemy. The enemy's force being apparently weak in our front, yet it was found that his works were too strong to be surprised by a small force. After one hour's heavy skirmishing, in which the officers of the 8th New Jersey and all the men, with very few exceptions, behaved in a very gallant and creditable manner, we fell back to our former position, with the loss of 15 in killed, wounded, and missing.[39]

On the 17th and most of the 18th, we remained quiet in bivouac. About 6 p.m. on the 18th the enemy made a demonstration in our immediate front and then turned to our right, in consequence of which the Brigade was ordered to take position between the New Market and Malvern Hill roads to protect the Pontoon bridges, as an attack of the enemy was expected. At 10 p.m. orders were received to rejoin our Division then crossing the James River. We crossed Pontoon bridges at 11 and marched back to the front of Petersburg, where we arrived on the 19th at 8 a.m. At 3 p.m. we relieved the 2nd Brigade,

39. For other accounts of the action, see *ibid.,* 341, 936, 939–40; Marbaker, *11th New Jersey,* 207–9; Walker, *Second Army Corps,* 568–80. In his *New Jersey and the Rebellion,* 147, Foster erroneously gave Col. John Ramsey credit for the assault of the 8th New Jersey. Maj. Virgil Healy should have received the praise.

4th Division, 9th Corps, U.S. Colored Troops, in the works on the Norfolk and Suffolk Railroad, and took position in the trenches.[40]

At the demonstration of the 16th, I wish to mention the efficient and gallant conduct of two of my staff officers who accompanied me to the scene of action, viz, Capt. J. P. Finklemeier, Acting Adjt. Genl., and Capt. R. T. Lombard, Acting Aide-de-Camp, and also Major [John] William of Genl. Mott's staff, who assisted me most bravely and effectually in the midst of the enemy's fire. . . .

Bivouack on New Market Road, Va., August 18th 1864

My dear Ellen,

Yesterday was rather a quiet day for our Corps. We had a flag of truce for one hour to bury the dead between our lines.[41] I had three dead bodies brought in and decently buried. They fell in that fatal charge I made day before yesterday. We lost 16 out of less than 100 men.[42] These three, as well as the one we brought off the day of the charge, were shot right in the head. One of them lived in your county at Andersonburg. Poor fellows, they done and served their country faithfully and died as heroes on the field of battle. If there is any one thing I dislike, it is to be a "forelorn hope"—to be shot at and cannot effectively return it.

The 2nd Brigade has reported back to us again. They lost 256 men. Col. Craig is dead. He was in command of a Pennsylvania regiment.[43] He was from the west of the mountains. He told me that he was not related to our Craigs in Shippensburg. He was a gallant officer. Capt. Lloyd was in the midst of the fight and came out safely. He was here this morning, and all is well. He is very brave and does his duty wherever he is placed. Col. [Daniel] Chaplin received a mortal wound yesterday while on picket. He commanded the 1st Maine Heavy Artillery. He was a good officer and a gentleman. We have now but few Colonels left.

Birney lost the works after having gained them. He has now forti-

---

40. McAllister's division, the strongest in the II Corps, was recalled from Deep Bottom to relieve the IX Corps and allow it to assist the V Corps in operations against the Weldon Railroad.

41. See *OR,* Vol. XLII, Pt. 1, p. 243.

42. McAllister's losses were 15 men, including 2 members of the 11th New Jersey wounded. *Ibid.,* 119.

43. Col. Calvin A. Craig of the 105th Pennsylvania was killed in the Aug. 16 fighting. He was commanding the 2nd Brigade, 3rd Division, II Corps. That unit's losses in the Aug. 13–20 period were 234 men. *Ibid.,* 51, 118, 218–19.

fied and holds a line in front of the enemy. There was very heavy cannonading last night on our left. I have not yet learned the cause of it. We have got [General A. Powell] Hill's Corps on our front and expect an attack any day.

No letters from you for two days.

Love to all, kisses for all. . . .

Camp before Petersburg, Va., August 20th 1864

My dear family,

I have not written you for two days. You know that we were on the march and in the battles of Deep Bottom on the north side of the James River. On the evening of the last day I wrote you (day before yesterday), the enemy tried to turn our right and succeeded in driving the cavalry back. But our infantry under Genl. Birney repulsed them handsomely. It proved a failure on the enemy's part. They tried all our line but found that the Yanks, as they call us, were ready to receive them.

Then they started off towards our right again. I was ordered to take my Brigade, go down the river, and protect our Pontoon bridges. It was now dark. Off I went, threw out pickets towards Malvern Hill, and waited for the Rebs. But they did not come. All was now quiet. We were ordered to join my Division, already on the march for this place. We arrived here yesterday morning and relieved a part of the 9th Corps, who were hurried off to our left to assist the 5th Corps in holding and destroying the Weldon Railroad. You can now see that one of the objects of our expedition was to draw off the Rebels from here so that the 5th Corps could tear up the railroad, cuting the Rebels' southern connections. This is accomplished. There has been a good deal of fighting there. We got the road and, at last accounts, we still hold it.

Now I will tell you what kind of a place we have got. We have only one division; the other two divisions of this Corps have not yet returned to this side of the river. With our Division we have relieved a whole Corps. I hold the right, resting on the 18th Corps. At this point we are fired on all day by the enemy's sharpshooters; but along the ballance of our front there is no firing in the day time, only at night. They open all their cannon on us and shell us for hours at a time. This they did for two nights before we came here, and they continued all last night. They can not do us so much harm in the fortifications by shelling us as they can outside. My Headquarters are in the rear of the works, and the shells fly all around us. I have some logs and earth for protection; but the enemy change their batteries, and it is hard to protect ourselves in this way. Today I am at work making it more secure.

Just think of us laying asleep or awake, as the case may be, and the shells rolling, flying, and bursting all around, cracking and breaking the timber in their mission of destruction. Yet I have not had a casualty. One man was killed a half mile further to the rear. You would be astonished at how little damage is don by these storms of iron hail. I have greate reason to thank God for His protecting care over me. For one whole week I have been more or less under fire, with a fair prospect of continuing in these dangerous positions. But do not be alarmed. God will take care of me. . . .

The papers will tell you all about these movements. One thing I am certain of: this movement was in part to prevent the Rebels from reinforcing their army farther south. This we have don, as well as cut the Weldon Railroad. So grate good will result from the flying visits of this flying Corps.

Oh! Let the North give us 50,000 more men and Richmond is ours! Then we would not have to run here and there. . . .

Camp before Petersburg, Va., August 22nd 1864
My dear Ellen & family,

I wrote you a family letter and also a business letter on Saturday night, which you no doubt will get before this reaches you. That night at 1 a.m. the Rebel batteries opened upon us a terrific shell fire. They fell in all directions around us, but fortunately no one was hurt. I must confess that it did somewhat disturb my repose. They kept it up some two or more hours. Then about 9 a.m. they opened on us again in the same style. Only one man was wounded.

We were now ordered to make a demonstration, which I did, similar to that on the day of the blowing up of the mine. I found the Rebels in a fair line of battle, as well as a strong picket line. On Sunday morning [August 21] the enemy attacked [General Gouverneur] Warren on our left to drive him from the railroad. But it resulted in their defeat, as it did on Saturday. Yet they still kept sending troops to our left (their right). Grant thought that they would make another attack this morning, so we were relieved and sent down here to hold this position.

We arrived here at dark and found ourselves just in rear of the place where we were the latter part of June and first part of July —before we leveled our old works and shortened our lines. We worked all night and are now finishing a long, strong line of rifle pitts. We were expecting an attack to take this place this morning, but as yet (4 p.m.) all is quiet. 5 p.m. is the Rebel time to attack, and it may come this evening.

We are holding the railroad and connecting our lines with it. Consequently, they are very long. Send us recruits and not only Petersburg but Richmond will soon be ours. Grant is a good General and a great man. I am satisfied that if the Rebels come against us here, we will, by the help of God, whip them. We have a good position. We are not with our Corps just at present. We left the James sooner than the other two divisions did and then arrived here yesterday morning. They were hurried off to the left, but we will soon be with them again. Capt Lloyd is well.

I received a letter from Ellen last night, dated the 17th, and was glad to receive it. Another letter came to me written by Sarah to her sister-in-law Tamaqua. I see the mistake and remail it back to you. Well, it will be better perhaps for having visited the army. I rather think one written to me at the same time may by the same mistake have gone to the coal regions. If so, it may be improved by its traveling experience. I received Henrietta's letter, giving me a drawing of little Robert's hand. By looking at it I must conclude he has a very large hand. I see Sarah, in writing to her friends, calls my namesake "Baby." She must quit that at once, or I will not consider him called after me. So quit it and get out of the abominable habit. . . .

While in the fortifications the other day, I learned from a Rebel deserter that a Colonel McAllister commanded a Brigade right opposit to me. I was fighting against him. But I do not think it could be Thompson for these reasons: he commanded North Carolina troops, he was supposed to be about 35 years old, and rather fat and full in the face.[44] This description will not suit Thompson, nor would it suit any of his sons. The Colonel McAllister killed in the cavalry raid on the Rebel side I do not think could have been Thompson either, for he, I think, came from Georgia.[45] . . .

Many of our Jersey troops go out of service in a few days, and my Brigade will be small. . . .

44. Reference is to Lt. Col. Alexander C. McAlister, who commanded the 46th North Carolina in Gen. John R. Cooke's brigade of Henry Heth's division. *Ibid.,* Pt. 3, p. 1230.
45. McAllister was confused on this point. The only person from Georgia who could have fit his description was Lt. Col. J. L. McAllister of the 7th Georgia Cavalry. Yet this officer was then commanding a troop in the South Carolina-Georgia military department. Compiled service records of Georgia Confederate soldiers, Georgia Department of Archives and History.

THE SIEGE BEGINS ♣ [487]

Camp before Petersburg, Va., August 24th 1864

My dear Ellen,

Last evening I wrote you a few lines on Mr. Wilson's letter and also sent you my official report of the 1st epoch of this greate campaign from the 4th to the 9th day of May last. The second epoch, including the battles of Spotsylvania Court House, I will have ready in a day or two. This will include the 13th of May and will report the events of the 12th, the greate and successful charge, and the 14 hours of hard fighting. This will end my connection with that Brigade at that time. Then I have a Brigade report to make out for the short time I was in command of the 2nd Brigade, including hard fighting and three different charges around the Hare House. I then came back and took command of this Brigade for two days. Next I went back to my regiment until Genl. Birney went to take command of the 10th Corps. Since that time I have been in command of this Brigade. . . .

Today has passed off rather quietly, though we anticipated a battle. We still hold the Weldon Railroad and hope to do so. Yet it extends our lines very much. I told you in one of my letters, "Give us 50,000 men, and Richmond will soon be ours."

Think of our thin, stretched-out, long lines, in order to hold this road. Think of the flying infantry corps, here and there and everywhere, and ask why it is. The answer comes back to you from the battlefields of the South: *You replenish not our depleted ranks.* You require us to do double duty and then blame us for not sending you victory on every breese that wafts to the North. If we lose that road and don't get Richmond, don't blame our Generals and our army. Put the blame where it ought to be: on those who stay at home and won't raise a helping hand to save our country. They cry "Peace! Peace!" when there is and can be no peace. They are willing to lay still and see the good old flag of our country trailing in the dust. . . .

Camp before Petersburg, Va., August 26th 1864

My dear Ellen,

I did not get time to write you yesterday evening. For some days, as you are aware, we held the Weldon Railroad. We still hold it. The Rebs are doing everything to retake it. The 5th Corps has fortified across it, from which all the efforts by the Rebels to retake it have proved a failure. Genl. Hancock, with two divisions (1st and 2nd) of this Corps, has been at Ream's Station and destroying the road. He has made some breastworks. But the distance between him and the 5th Corps was considerable, and connected only by a thin picket line.

Yesterday the Rebels took all of their spare troops, leaving their lines very bare of men, and hurled them against Hancock.[46] Hancock repulsed them. The Rebels made another attack and were again repulsed. Fearing that they would flank his position, Hancock ordered us to leave only a picket line and come to his help. I received orders to take my Brigade and also the 2nd Brigade, leaving a slim picket line. I now set about reducing the pickets and calling them in. I had my two brigades on the move when the Rebels, seeing us, opened fire. Then Genl. Mott, who was still in command of the line and the 1st Brigade, ordered that the pickets about to be relieved should remain, as well as those that had just went out. I had to move with my command less 700 men. I was joined on the road by 40 cavalrymen[47] who reported to me, as well as a battery of artillery—6 Parrott guns. I now had quite a command and had to play Division Commander with an independent command all to myself.

My orders were to march up the plank road to the intersection with the Ream's Station road, halt, and report to Genl. Hancock at Ream's Station. I arrived at the designated point at 5 p.m. and immediately sent two aides to report to Genl. Hancock, who was four miles distant at the Station and then engaged in the fight. In a few minutes Genl. Meade came along and gave me the orders to advance along the plank road towards the Blackwater, throw out my cavalry well to the river, and take up a good position for defence. He said that the enemy had sent around a brigade and that I would likely be attacked.

I rode forward and took a survey of the ground, selected my position, formed my line of battle, advanced my cavalry (another regiment reported to me), and planted my artillery. As dark closed in on us, I was ready for action. During all this time Hancock was fighting.

---

46. The Weldon Railroad, linking Richmond with Wilmington, N.C., and points farther south and west, was a vital key to the endurance of the Confederacy in general and Richmond in particular. Its destruction, therefore, became one of Grant's primary objectives. Hancock's corps spent two days tearing up trackage. But on Aug. 25, while destroying rails and roadbed near Ream's Station, Hancock's men received sudden and vicious assaults from Confederate troops under A. P. Hill and Wade Hampton. The Federals were almost overrun, and for them the battle bordered on a disaster. A staff officer subsequently wrote of the Weldon line: "It is touching a tiger's cubs to get on that road!" *OR*, Vol. XLII, Pt. 1, pp. 942–44; Lyman, *Meade's Headquarters*, 217; Illinois Commandery, M.O.L.L.U.S., *Military Essays and Recollections*, III (1899), 125–40; Walker, *Second Army Corps*, 581–606. McAllister's short official reports of the action are in *OR*, Vol. XLII, Pt. 1, pp. 391, 392–93.

47. This was a detachment of the 3rd Pennsylvania Cavalry under Capt. Frank W. Hess.

[General Orlando B.] Wilcox's Division hurried to his support, but unfortunately it did not reach him in time.[48] Hancock was driven back from his slight earthworks. He again advanced and retook some of them. The slaughter of the Rebels was terrible. But they got rather the best of Hancock and captured 9 pieces of artillery after having shot all the horses. As Willcox did not get up in time, Hancock with two divisions consequently fought the whole available force of the Rebel army and held them till night. He then fell back, and I covered the retreat.

Our loss does not reach 1,000, while the Rebel loss is five times that much.[49] One Rebel prisoner says that they lost nine men to our one. But they will call it a greate victory. But a few more such victories would destroy them. Genl. Hancock says that if he had had my command there, he would have whiped them handsomely.[50] But my orders were different and I could not go. Besides, they expected a flank movement and it was necessary for me to guard against it.

Our Corps is growing small by these continued battles. We were somewhat discouraged this morning but feel better now, as what seemed to be our defeat is realy a victory. We still hold the Weldon Railroad. . . .

As soon as it was dark last night, Lee drew off his forces and sent them down to strengthen their lines along here. The cannonading along these lines last night was terrifick.

I am well. Capt. Lloyd has not been well for a day or two, but he is better now. I seen him this evening and took tea with him. . . .

Camp before Petersburg, Va., August 28th 1864

My dear Ellen,

I have just received a nice letter from Sarah. I am glad your party turned out such a success, and I am pleased that you all enjoyed yourselves. . . .

In the late battle day before yesterday at Ream's Station on the

---

48. For explanations and criticisms of Willcox's tardiness, see *OR*, Vol. XLII, Pt. 1, pp. 31, 391, 591–92.

49. Here McAllister was grossly in error. The Confederates suffered 720 casualties. Hancock's losses were 2,742 men (including 2,150 captured), 19 cannon, 32 horses and 12 stands of colors. So staggered was Hancock by the large sacrifices that he placed his hand on an aide's shoulder and cried out: "I pray God I may never leave this field!" *Ibid.*, 129–31, 851, 940; Bruce, *20th Massachusetts*, 422.

50. Hancock's official mention of McAllister's role in this engagement is in *OR*, Vol. XLII, Pt. 1, pp. 226–27.

Weldon Railroad, Col. [James] Beaver was badly wounded.[51] His leg was amputated high up. I called to see him today at the 1st Division Hospital. He is doing well and has strong hopes of his recovery. You know that but few live when the amputation is so high up. He is a man of temperate habits, and that is greatly in his favour. I hope he will get well. This evening I wrote Brother Nelson all about him.

Col. Beaver is considered one of the best officers in the army. He was wounded in the first battle before Petersburg. He had went home and just returned. When this battle was raging, he reported to Hancock, who told him that he was the ranking officer of his Brigade. Beaver took command and, in less than half an hour, was shot.

Dr. [John D.] Heritage, our Asst. Surgeon, disappeared that night.[52] He must have road into the enemies' lines and was taken prisoner. I saw him while I was forming my line of battle. I heard this evening that his horse was seen, but it needs confirmation.

Two New Jersey regiments—the 5th and 6th—left my Brigade this evening. Their going leaves only those veterans that have reinlisted. I have lost nearly all my fine staff. Some members of these regiments have gone home, and some are detailed to Division Headquarters. I have lost some that are hard to replace. . . .

Ellen, I want you to get my namesake Robert a carriage as agreed upon. . . . Send Robert out riding; it will do him good. It is now very late and I must close. . . .

Camp before Petersburg, Va., August 29th 1864

My dear Ellen,

It is now 9:30 p.m. and late. Today was rather quiet until towards evening. We then had some artillery firing. One shell of the enemy went into Fort Crawford,[53] where I have 700 men, and bursted. Though the fort is somewhat crowded, the shell only slightly wounded one man—a sutler, not a soldier. This fort has been built for some time. But having a screen around it made of brush—and that brush not removed until today, the enemy did not know that such a fort was

---

51. Beaver's valor in the Ream's Station fight earned him promotion to brigadier. *Ibid.*, 245; Pt. 2, pp. 558, 594; Pt. 3, p. 483.

52. For Heritage's own account of his capture and imprisonment, see Marbaker, *11th New Jersey*, 211–19.

53. Fort Crawford (or Fort Warren, as it was later called) was not a well-excavated bastion of the caliber of Forts Stedman, Morton and Alexander Hays. Rather, it was a shallow earthwork—but of such size as to accommodate easily an entire brigade. *Ibid.*, 220.

there. My men are in this fort and along the front line of works right and left. This is one of the largest forts we have here. There is quite a distance between the fort and the right of my line of battle on the left of the fort, but it is protected by a heavy slashing of brush & timber. Our guns can sweep it so that there is no danger.

We are now in possession of the Weldon Railroad, and the enemy will make—as they have made—every effort to brake our lines. So we are strengthening our works to be ready for them. Just now very heavy firing, cannonading and musketry, is going on and has been for some hour or more to our right. It is either on the lines of the 10th or 18th Corps. But this is nothing. The sound of the roaring artillery is heard by us all hours of day and night. A greate big noise and but little damage, as all are behind forts or breastworks. The Rebs will now have to bump up against us, instead of us against them, for they want that Railroad. . . .

Camp before Petersburg, Va., August 31st 1864

My dear Ellen,

It is now very late, and time will not let me write you but a few lines. All is well—nothing new.

I have had some company here, and they have just gone. Mr. Fay & Miss Gilson, with Dr. Welling, a few of our military friends, and two chaplains, were present. The Band discoursed fine music, speeches were made, and Miss Gilson sang beautifully. The entertainment passed off handsomely, and all were highly delighted. Some said that they never enjoyed themselves so much in the army. Our repast was quite good and passed off well. I wish you could have been here to enjoy it—and all this right under the enemy's guns!

Miss Gilson called today to see Col. Beaver. She said that he is very weak. I fear that he will not live, though the Doctor says he is doing well. Yet remember that but one in twenty get well with amputations as high up as his is. I do hope some of his friends will be here soon. . . .

Camp in front of Petersburg, Va., September 1, 1864

My dear family,

Inclosed you will please find a rough copy, the original one, of my report of the opperations of my Brigade around Spotsylvania

Court House up to May 13th, when the old Division was consolidated and Genl. Mott came back to the Brigade. It embraces nearly all of the 2nd Epoch. I was really in command of the Brigade long after that, and Genl. Mott desires that I should make out the report. But I don't feel like doing it; and besides, I have lost my notebook. I have time and again risked my life in command of this Brigade when [Mott] should have been to the front himself and I with my Regiment. But let this all go. I am now in command of it, and am willing to take the responsibility and share the dangers and honours.

The clerks have copied this report; we have sent it up to Headquarters and also copied it in the Copy Book. I wish Henrietta to copy this nicely like the other, writing on only one page, tie them together with red tape, and file away as usual. You can read these reports to confidential friends only. *On no account must they get into the papers.* The losses are not stated because that has been given before.

I was to have given you a discription of my headquarters, but time will not permit it tonight. Reports tonight are that the enemy are geting into our rear. But all is right now. They were driven back —just a skirmish line of cavalry. We are building new fortifications and connecting them with rifle pitts. The work is hard.

Col. Beaver, I fear, will not live. At my request Miss Gilson has gon to give him some attention. I hope his friends will arrive soon. Poor man, I do pity him. . . .

Camp before Petersburg, Va., September 2nd 1864

My dear family,

As usual, it is now very late and I can not write but a line or two.

Brother Nelson came today to see Col. Beaver. He came up to see me and is looking quite well. He was here but a short time and returned to the Hospital where Col. Beaver is laying. He will come up again.

I am the President of a court marshall that is trying an important case—Lt. Col. Benjamin Butler for stragling,[54] &c.

All is quiet here. There was a little fuss last evening on our left and rear, but all is quiet again. I am very well. Inclosed is a delicate flower I gathered this evening in our fortifications near where the

54. During the Aug. 15–16 operations some straggling did occur in Lt. Col. Benjamin C. Butler's 93rd New York. Butler admitted it in his official report. Apparently nothing came of the hearing, for Butler remained in command. *OR,* Vol. XLII, Pt. 1, p. 375.

Rebel fort was blown up. Real battle ground cannonading occurs all the time. . . .

                        Camp before Petersburg, Va., September 4th 1864
My dear family,
    No home letters for two days. Why is it? Do you write them? It is now 9 p.m.; and before retiring, I thought I would write you a line or two.
    We have received additional telegrams that confirm that Atlanta is ours.[55] This and the taking of Fort Morgan,[56] and the prospect that Mobile will soon be ours, is cheering news. And then what is first rate is that we still hold the Weldon Railroad. Give us the men, and Richmond will soon be ours.
    We have been building a new fort on my left and runing a new line of rifle pitts to connect the two forts. This line is a little in front of the old one. We have all been working very hard to get it completed before Early gets back from the Valley.[57]
    Brother Nelson was here yesterday. We called at Genl. Birney's, Hancock's, &c. He returned in the evening to the 1st Division Hospital where Col. Beaver is lying. The Colonel is thought by his physician to be doing well. . . . I fear the worst. Nelson will stay here until there is a change. This he ought to do. Miss Gilson is doing all she can for him. She went at my request.
    I had divine service at these Headquarters today, and a good sermon. Chaplain Clark Cline is looking miserable. A report says he is lovesick. Is anything wrong with his lady love in your town?[58] Say nothing about it, but he does look bad. . . .

                        Camp before Petersburg, Va., September 5th 1864
My dear Ellen & family,
    This evening I received three letters from home written by Ellen, Sarah & Henrietta. They were welcom visitors.

    55. Atlanta, as previously mentioned, fell Sept. 2 to Sherman's forces.
    56. Fort Morgan had been the Confederates' principal defense for Mobile Bay.
    57. Although Confederate Gen. Jubal Early's forces were campaigning in the Shenandoah Valley and had no orders to rejoin Lee, Federal troops in the Petersburg trenches were certain of an attack by Early along the Jerusalem Plank Road. *OR*, Vol. XLII, Pt. 2, pp. 635, 676, 688.
    58. On Oct. 24, 1865, Chaplain Cline married Mary Hutchinson of Oxford Furnace. *Minutes of the . . . Synod of New Jersey of the Presbyterian Church . . .* , XCIV (1916), 46.

I am very tired and sleepy tonight. I was up all last night expecting the enemy to attack us. But they did not do so. I expect that they will very soon, as Early's forces are arriving. Also, as they have lost Atlanta, they will fight still harder for this position. I would not be surprised if the greate battle of the war would be fought here and that within a few days.

Brother Nelson was here this evening. Rev. Mr. [A. D.] White and Dr. [John K.] Davis were with him. Col. Beaver is doing as well as could be expected, but the case is doubtful.

Our guns opened all along the line last night in honor of the greate victory achieved at Atlanta. . . .

Camp before Petersburg, Va., September 6th 1864

My dear Ellen,

It is now late and I can write but a line or two.

Early has returned and is now trying to get on our flank and rear. We are ready for him and are expecting a battle every day—I may say almost every hour. We will give him a warm reception and, by the help of God, we hope to drive him back. Oh, how we want men! A few thousand more and Richmond would be ours. Convalesents and some recruits are arriving daily. No doubt in a short time we will have them, but it is now that we need them. . . .

Brother Nelson was up here today. He has bid me goodby and leaves tomorrow morning. Col. Beaver is better and there is a prospect of his recovering. . . .

Camp before Petersburg, Va., September 7th 1864

My dear Ellen,

All is quiet here yet, but we are looking for Early and geting ready for him. We have now fortifications front and rear, all connected with lines of breastworks some twenty-five miles in length—from the James River to the Weldon Railroad and bending around to our rear so that the rear line runs nearly parallel to our front line. The redoubts are constructed so as to give the enemy a raking fire when they advance on our lines. I road around today and am satisfied that we can hold the enemy in check and give them a good drubing too if they attempt to dislodge us.

Most of my force is placed in Fort Crawford, and part of it is on the Jerusalem Plank Road. This is a very important position and one where most fear is entertained of an attack, as well as where the enemy can shell us handsomely if they choose to do so. They do often amuse themselves in this way. But we can do the same to them.

I told you that Brother Nelson was to leave this morning. I suppose that he has. He and I called on Genl. Hancock yesterday. But the General was out the first time and asleep on our second call. We did not see him, as we had to leave because Nelson wished to get to the 1st Division Hospital before night and it was then late in the evening. When the General got awake and found that we had been there, he wrote a very polite note to me, saying he was disappointed in not seeing us. He wished to know if Nelson was still here. My Adjt. Genl. answered that we had both just started to the Hospital. I only went as far as Genl. Mott's Headquarters. Genl. Hancock, on hearing this message from my Adjt. Genl., went to the Hospital and called on Nelson. It was after dark and raining at that. Quite a compliment. The General told me that he expected to see me there, &c.

I have not heard how Col. Beaver is today. Yesterday he was decidedly better.

I am quite disappointed tonight that I have received no home letters from you. Well, we will expect them tomorrow, if I am spared. This day was more quiet than usual. Some firing is down on our right now. Last night there was a greate deal.

The nomination of McClellan is not well received in the army, from the fact that they pute that abominable traitor, Pendleton, on as Vice President.[59] The ticket has no chance here. McClellan's friends here have abandoned him.

Rebel deserters come into our lines every night. Everything looks well now for our cause and country. Send on the men, and the day is ours. We want to stretch out Grant's army clear across all these railroads. If we do so, Richmond falls to our lot and the Rebellion is ended. . . .

59. By 1864 the Democratic Party had hopelessly split into "war" and "peace" factions. The former succeeded in getting Gen. George B. McClellan nominated as the party's presidential candidate—largely by granting second place on the ticket to a representative of the latter group. Thus, the vice-presidential nominee was "Gentleman George" H. Pendleton. Known to his enemies as "Peace and Surrender at Any Price" Pendleton, the Ohio congressman was a definite liability to the ticket. One politician sneered: "Pendleton is as rank a traitor and secessionizer as Vallandigham himself." Strong, *Diary of the Civil War*, 498, 504. See also Wainwright, *Diary of Battle*, 476–77.

12

Lines of Endeavor

THE AUTUMN MONTHS of 1864 passed slowly for the men in the trenches around Petersburg. Each day seemed a repetition of its predecessor. Daily fusillades of Minié "balls" and cannon shells were constant nuisances—so much so that on many sectors of the 40-mile siege line opposing troops agreed to informal truces in order to gain relief from the noise and danger. Moreover, as McAllister pointed out in two letters, woe befall the side that violated such truce arrangements!

During the long periods of inactivity, McAllister took heart from the victories elsewhere by Sherman and Sheridan. He manifested an active interest in the presidential election of 1864. Although elated over Lincoln's victory, the Colonel was disappointed at the Democrats' carrying New Jersey. He also found time to comment at varying length on conscription, local inhabitants, Confederate desertions, and such general officers and friends as Hancock, Birney, Humphreys, and the flamboyant Frenchman Philippe Régis de Trobriand.

The jockeying for better geographical position by one side or the other occasionally exploded into full combat. In less than two months McAllister and his brigade took part in four such engagements: the Chimneys (September 10), Poplar Spring Church (October 1–2), Boydton Plank Road (October 27), and Fort Morton (November 5).

For McAllister the third of these actions—the October 27 collision on the Boydton Plank Road—was the most important. To tighten the noose around Lee's army, Grant dispatched 43,000 men to cut both the plank road and the Southside Railroad. But once again mismanagement and disorder marked a Federal offensive. Two wings of the advance became lost in swampy, timbered country; and when Confederate General A. P. Hill characteristically took advantage of the Federal confusion and attacked, a good portion of the Union line broke apart. McAllister's brigade was caught with its flanks unsupported and was assailed from all four sides. Its commander succeeded in extricating his regiments—with such credit to himself that the long-awaited promotion to brigadier was forthcoming.

♣

Camp before Petersburg, Va., September 9th 1864
My dear Ellen,
It is now late (10 p.m.); but as I expect to go up to the lines tonight and do not intend going to bed, I may as well write you a few lines. At 1 a.m. we expect to drive in the enemy's picket line so that we can ocquipy and hold the crest of the hill in front of our forts. We will no doubt have a little brush with the enemy, but no general engagement at all is anticipated.

Early has not yet made his appearance and we have not had the greate battle expected. But we may have it yet. One thing I have not told you: we have got a railroad right past my headquarters. We have had the Rebel City Point Railroad brought to a point near Petersburg, a distance of some seven or more miles. We have now extended it up past this place and expect to continue it up to the Weldon Railroad or near to it. This will be a greate help to us in geting our supplys up. The Rebels see our cars runing along and fire at them occasionly. The inhabitants here must be astonished to see this road built so rapidly—to wake up in the morning and see a railroad runing past their house, and a fortification built in a single night. . . .

[498] ✗ THE McALLISTER LETTERS

Camp before Petersburg, Va., September 11th 1864

My dear Ellen,

It is now late Sabbath evening. When I wrote you Friday night, I told you that we were going out to drive in the Rebel picket line and capture some of them if we could.[1] This part of the Rebel line which we wished to drive in was too close to our lines and give them the advantage of the crest of a hill. To give you a better idea: the Jerusalem Plank Road runs along here to Petersburg. On this side and to the left of this road is a large fort which I have 700 of my Brigade in. It is sometimes called Fort Warren, but its real name is Fort Crawford. Higher up this road is another fort, now nearly completed, and close to the Rebel line. To the left of it is a short line of rifle pitts.

This fort and these short pitts are manned by my men and cover the head of this road facing towards Petersburg. In front of this and on the left is our line of pickets, with the Rebel line of pickets close by. Fort Crawford is a little to the left and rear. To the left of Fort Crawford we have a strong line of rifle pitts connecting a chain of forts as far as the Weldon Railroad. The Jerusalem Plank Road is considered a very important point, and my Brigade has the honor of guarding it—with instructions to hold this point at all hazards, cost what it may. Genl. De Trobrean's[2] Brigade is on my right, Genl. Pierce's on my left. All of the Division is on the front line.

On Friday night I was to hold this point while Genl. de Trobriand sent one regiment under Col. Biles[3] to the right and two regiments under Lt. Col. Michael[4] to the left. They were to drive in and

1. McAllister is about to describe here the Sept. 10 action at a point on the Jerusalem Plank Road known as "The Chimneys." Confederate pickets had pushed forward too close to the Federal lines, and Mott's division was ordered to drive them back. McAllister's short report of the affair is in *OR*, Vol. XLII, Pt. 1, p. 392. See also de Trobriand, *Army of the Potomac*, 641–43; Walker, *Second Army Corps*, 606–7.

2. Philippe Régis de Trobriand was the son of a French baron. He attended the finest schools in Europe, graduated in law in 1834 but "promptly occupied himself with duels and literature." In 1841, on nothing more than a dare, he came to the United States. De Trobriand married an heiress, settled in New York City, and devoted most of his labors to a local literary society. Soon after the outbreak of civil war he was elected colonel of the 55th New York. Valorous service brought him a brigadier's stars in the summer of 1864. De Trobriand was noted as a stern disciplinarian of soldiers, but a gracious host to any and all camp visitors. Ella Lonn, *Foreigners in the Union Army and Navy* (Baton Rouge, 1951), 206–7, 588–89, 651.

3. Col. Edwin R. Biles was officially in command of the 99th Pennsylvania, though he served occasionally as a brigade leader.

4. Lt. Col. George W. Meikel then commanded the 20th Indiana.

goble up the Rebel pickets. At 1 o'clock all was ready. They moved forward and, without firing a shot, pounced on the Rebels, many of whom were sleeping. They captured nearly 100 Rebels. The ballance of the Rebels run back and fired on our men, but only hit one or two. We had plenty of shovels. We soon dug little rifle pitts and I advanced my picket line which, with the regiments before mentioned, made a very strong picket line.

The enemy got over their panick and, with reinforcements, pounced on us. But we soon repulsed them handsomely and continued our work till dawn of day, up to which time we all regarded it as a complete success. However, in the darkness of the night Col. Biles had mistaken a wrong tree from the one to which he had been ordered to advance; and in his eagerness to push far out, he went too far. When daylight came, the Rebels saw his position, attacked his flank, and captured fifty of our men. They caused us to come very near loosing all that we had gained. But our artillery and infantry lines opened up and drove them back. I had a large reserve that could fire over the heads of the pickets, and we held our ground.

Firing continued all day long. My staff and I were right up to the front and under fire all day, but we were protected by rifle pitts. Yet when walking we would have to carry ourselves quite low or we would be hit. Night closed in on us, but the firing still continued. We finished our works worn out with fatigue. Finding all now pretty safe, I came in and had a good sleep.

We lost ten men in my Brigade yesterday; I do not know how many in de Trobriand's.[5] Firing continued all last night, all day today, and it continues to this hour. We have lost ten or a dozen men today in killed and wounded. I have just come in from under this fire. Balls fly rapidly. We hold the new line and the Rebs can't take it from us without their loosing heavily. So they are disappointed in loosing the game and seem determined to keep firing on us constantly to pay us back. So the sound of musketry is constantly ringing in my ears. All night and day the same crackling of small arms, mingled occasionally with booming artillery, can be heard. How long we are to be thus anoyed with this fire I know not. I hope that it will soon stop.

Capt. Morehouse [6] of the 11th New Jersey was wounded in this fight while we were protecting what we had gained.

I have received several nice letters from home. I am much

---

5. Casualties in Mott's division were 8 killed, 14 wounded and 59 missing. *OR,* Vol. XLII, Pt. 1, p. 343n.
6. Benjamin F. Morehouse of Co. B was not wounded seriously, for he continued as captain of his company. *N.J. Record,* I, 547.

obliged to Sarah for telling me all the news and also for Robert's hair. It is real pretty. . . .

                        Camp before Petersburg, Va., September 13th 1864
My dear Ellen,

I have just come in from Fort Crawford, where I witnessed a splendid battle—much noise but little execution. It is still going on at a rapid rate. The roar of musketry goes far out on the evening air, the whizzing minie balls fly thick and fast, and my boys are engaged heart and hand in throwing lead into the enemy's lines.

In my last I told you that we advanced our lines in front of this Division. We took the crest of the hill and not only drove the Rebels from their line of pickets but held all the ground we took. We threw up rifle pitts, afterwards connected them into a continuous line, and manned it with about a half a line of battle. This provoked the Rebels and they determined to drive us out. But all their efforts have thus far failed. They have kept up a constant fire for three days and nights. Several times the Rebels have called upon our boys to cease firing, and we did as they desired.[7] The boys jumped up, shook their blankets, walked around—as well as talked across to the Rebels, who don the same thing. Each time a Rebel officer would come along and order his men to fire, they would yell to our boys to keep down, as they were ordered to fire again. And when they relieved the pickets in the evening, they would beg of us not to fire. We complied with this request for two evenings, and the firing ceased until they had their pickets relieved. But when our relief would come, they would keep up a constant fire. Our boys determined that this evening they would not be deceived. So when the Rebels came along to relieve their pickets and said for us to "stop firing," our men, instead of ceasing to fire, rolled volley after volley until a Rebel could not show his head.

They cried out: "Cease firing!"

Our men then marched and relieved without any difficulty.

It is now 10 p.m. and the firing still continues. No doubt it will go on all night. My Brigade has fired *60,000 rounds of cartridges.*

    7. The long periods of inactivity at Petersburg led to many and widespread instances of fraternization between opposing troops. For example, see James H. Clark, *The Iron Hearted Regiment* . . . (Albany, N.Y., 1865), 157–58; Robert Tilney, *My Life in the Army* (Philadelphia, 1912), 137–39; Thompson, *13th New Hampshire,* 449–50, 452, 491–92. For efforts by commanders to stop such practices, see *OR,* Vol. XLII, Pt. 3, p. 752; Thompson, *13th New Hampshire,* 456–57; Rauscher, *Music on the March,* 212–13.

I hold an important point, the Jerusalem Plank Road, and the brunt of the matter comes on me. You see by the papers that Genl. de Trobriand gets the credit for capturing the pickets. He did so; but my own men were on the picket line at the time, I strengthened the line, and this line advanced with de Trobriand's and assisted in the capture of the pickets, throwing up the works, and holding the line. The latter I have, and am now holding, myself. The first day I lost 12 men; the second day, 14; the third, 2. Today I don't think I have lost any. Our works are completed and our men better protected. Except for the prisoners that de Trobriand lost, my loss is much heavier than his.

Inclosed you will please find a minnie ball that the Rebels fired at long range. It hit the ground and bounded over into the fort at the Jerusalem Plank Road. You see how it wore off as it passed the ground, then rose like a bird in its flight, passed over the redoubt, and fell into the fort. This is one of thousands of the same kind. With my compliments, I wish you to give this ball and its history to my friend, the Rev. Mr. Osborn. Do not say that this ball hit me or came near me, for it did not pass very close. Thousands of others of the same character have come much closer to me than this one. But it is a Rebel ball, fired to hit a Yankee, and, like thousands of balls, it don no harm.

I am going to write to Stocks in Philadelphia to make and send me a blouse and pants. In the meantime, I wish you to send me by express my plain blouse that I sent home last spring. It will do me some service yet. I need it now very much. . . . Dr. Welling has sent to New York for two good woolen overshirts for me—nice ones that cost $7–8 each. The shirts that we buy here . . . all get too small after washing. . . . Do not delay, as my blouse is looking very mean and I do not wish to wear my dress coat. . . .

Camp before Petersburg, Va., September 14th 1864
My dear Ellen,
I was very tired and sleepy—worn down with fatigue—when I wrote you last night. I fear I give you a very poor discription of the events of the last days. The firing continued all night long. My boys on the picket line fired 17,000 rounds of cartridges. The Rebels got the worst of it for their treachery the two evenings previous. I think, when all agree to stop firing hereafter, that they will be more careful. Last night we lost 1 killed and 3 wounded. We think the enemy lost

considerable, as quite a number of ambulances came out this morning to haul them away. Picket firing is still going on, but only a few shots—principally telescope rifles, long range.

I have just now had a man wounded through the lungs at these rear breastworks, ¾ of a mile from the Rebel lines. We have some of these improved rifles in the hands of sharpshooters and have compelled the Rebs to move their camp back. I dred these rifles in the hands of the enemy more than I do shot & shell. They will send a ball over a mile with a certainty of hiting, if the object is not moving.[8] A good marksman is handling the piece. I have always made it a point, if possible, to keep moving around.

Genl. Birney told me that he sent the Rebels word today that if they did not stop firing, he would open on the town. And so he did. He belched away with a large number of batteries and riddled Petersburg.[9] What amount of damage we don't know. The Rebs have not fired so much since. They don't like our cars runing along here, and they try to hit them. The first passenger train passed here today. The road is now finished to the Weldon Railroad.

In one of the knapsacks left by the Rebs in their pits the night of the surprise was found a letter written by a Rebel to his brother but not yet mailed. The Reb said that Genl. Grant was a smart old fellow, that he had out-generaled Lee, that he was now runing his cars right along his camps and supplying our army with everything, that the Rebellion was gon up, and that there was no use fighting longer, &c.

Col. Beaver is geting along finely, and hopes are entertained of his recovery. . . .

Sarah's long letter of little things was quite interesting. Time permiting, I will have to write her one of the same character. Poor Uncle Washington [McAllister], it will go hard for him to pay $1000 for a substitute. Well, it is good for him if he won't come out and fight like

---

8. McAllister was probably referring to one of several types of heavy, cumbersome rifles equipped with a telescopic sight longer than the weapon's barrel. Many sharpshooters compared the rifles to clubs and preferred the lighter, more usable Sharps carbine. Stevens, *Berdan's Sharpshooters,* 205, 451, 460.

9. A few weeks earlier Birney and his command had been assigned that portion of the Federal siege line closest to Petersburg. Birney immediately let it be known that no sharpshooting was to take place in his sector. If it did, he warned the Confederates, he would bombard everything in his front. For ten days the informal truce held. On Sept. 13 Confederate pickets inexplicably opened fire on the Federals. Birney kept his word: in one day his batteries fired over 1,740 rounds into the city and its defenses. *OR,* Vol. XLII, Pt. 2, p. 849; Page, *Letters of a War Correspondent,* 255.

a man ought to in this time of our country's trials. Why, let him pay for it.

Love to all, kiss the baby, and don't spoil it. . . .

Camp before Petersburg, Va., September 15th 1864

My dear Ellen,

. . . I feel the necessity of having some sleep tonight, as I had but little last night. The Rebs were rather troublesome to us and would not cease firing. Our men retaliated. About midnight we was about to run out of cartridges and had almost stoped firing. I was informed of the fact, and a mesenger came and told me that the enemy were creeping up towards our works to try to take possession of some old rifle pitts close to ours.

Knowing how fatal this would be to us, I sprang out of my bed, put on my clothes in a hurry, and, with an aide and orderly, galloped out to the Plank Road. I reached Fort Crawford and ordered Col. Schoonover to send us ammunition at once or all would be lost. He had some in the magazine. Then onto my horse and up the Plank Road at a rapid rate amid the whizzing bullets, for the enemy were sending their lead at a rapid rate. I arrived at my reserves, where we have a bomb proof, ordered all the cartridges that could be spared from the reserves to be sent on at once to the front line, and for the reserves to continue their firing. Soon boxes of ammunition came up and our boys paid the Rebs home pretty well till morning and all was safe.

There has been some firing all day, all evening, and at this time. It is like a greate battle. How long this firing is going to be kept up I don't know. It is one of the strangest scenes I have witnessed in campaigning. There is an immense amount of firing; but as both parties are so well protected, there is but little destruction of life on either side. Our casualties yesterday were four.

We had 148 recruits arrive here this evening for the 6th New Jersey. Almost every day some arrive so that, notwithstanding so many going home at the expiration of their terms of service, we are increasing. In the whole army the increase is very large, though there are thousands that desert before they arrive here. In many cases more than one half desert. Bounty jumpers [10] are very numerous. Greate

---

10. Bounty jumpers were known to enlist as many as twenty times and, by their subterfuge, to amass more than $8,000 in bounties. James Barnett, "The Bounty Jumpers of Indiana," *Civil War History*, IV (1958), 431.

scamps, ain't they? But we are geting some good men now. . . .

Hark! What is this? The sweet strain of music rolls far out on the evening air. It is the band of the 120th New York, come to give me a serenade. Well, I must stop and say a word of welcome to them. I have don so, and now pick up my pen to talk to you. The night is beautiful. The moon shines in its usual splendor, and the music enlivens everything around us. The band is now playing "Rally Round the Flag, Boys." But how strange these sounds mingle with the rattle of musketry that is now roaring along our lines. Close to our rear is the whistle of the locomotive and the rumbling of the cars. Now they are playing "Old Hundred" for the benefit of our Brigade Inspector, Capt. [Isaac] Starbird. He was raised down in Maine, in the land of steady habits, and thinks that there never was or ever will be a tune like "Old Hundred." Well, he is pretty near right. So you see we have musketry, "Old Hundred," and locomotive whistles all together.

. . . Tell little Robert that his grandpa is well and would like to see him, but can't leave these active scenes of campaigning to visit now. Kiss the boy for me, and teach it to love and venerate the flag of our country.

When I set down, I did not intend to write you so much; and though I have run to the end of the sheet, I fear I have not been interesting to you. . . .

Camp before Petersburg, Va., September 16th 1864

My dear Family,

The firing on my front today has not been so strong. But this evening it was again like a greate battle. Relieving the pickets is the time when we have such spirited firing. We lost no men for the last 24 hours, our men being so well protected. It is reported that the enemy have lost quite a number. Last night and this morning the enemy drove in our cavalry pickets and drove off our beef cattle— it is said a large number.[11] But like all other stories, it gathers strength

11. The Sept. 14–16 "Beefsteak Raid" by Confederate cavalry was an attempt to secure meat for hungry Southern troops. Gen. Wade Hampton's troopers bagged 2,486 cattle and 304 prisoners at a loss of only 10 killed, 47 wounded and 4 missing. When the Confederates successfully herded their cattle back through the Federal lines, Lincoln grudgingly termed the raid "the slickest piece of cattle stealing I ever heard of." *OR*, Vol. XLII, Pt. 1, pp. 287–88, 944–47; William Child, *A History of the Fifth Regiment, New Hampshire Volunteers* . . . (Bristol, N.H., 1893), 282–83. A popular account of the affair is Edward Boykin, *Beefsteak Raid* (New York, 1960).

as it travels. I hope it is not so bad as reported. We heard the firing but did not know what it was. I suppose the cattle were out there pasturing.

Genl. Mott has received information today that he is made a Brevet Major General. I called down and congratulated him on his promotion. He seems pleased. He said he would write me a letter of recommendation tonight. . . .

I have just learned that the number of cattle lost is 4,500 head. A big loss. Our cavalry and some infantry have gon out to recapture them. I don't know as to their success. We have captured 75 wagons from the enemy. . . .

Camp before Petersburg, Va., September 17th 1864

My dear Ellen & family,

. . . The picket firing was kept up all last night. But today the Rebs beged our boys to quit firing and they would not breake their promise to our boys again. What answer our boys give them I don't know, yet there is but little firing this evening. Some few shots now, but none of that continuous roar we have had for several days past. Quietness once more reigns here.

Recruits are arriving here in large numbers. My Brigade is geting its share, and my regiment quite a number. Many that are sent never reach here. They desert somehow. We are all rejoicing over the coming draft, and are glad that it was ordered.[12] The ordering has made Lincoln many friends here. We are all in favour of the draft. Lincoln's stock has gone up above par.

My long looked for box has at last arrived. Butter spoiled, jumbles good for nothing, cake will or can be eaten, dried fruit good, canned fruit I have not yet tried but no doubt it is good, handkerchiefs a bit soiled but can be washed, spool of thread all right, soap nice. We get and have canned fruit almost every meal. Dried fruit always comes good.

I must close and retire. Love to all. Kiss the boy. Remember me

---

12. With the three-year terms of service of approximately 380,000 Federal soldiers about to expire, Lincoln asked Congress for authority to initiate a new draft. This was a dangerous move for Lincoln to make on the eve of national elections. Nevertheless, he pushed the measure through the Congress and then issued a call for 500,000 recruits. See Page, *Letters of a War Correspondent*, 259–61.

kindly to all. Tell them to vote for Abreham Lincoln and our country, and hang Valandingham [13] and all traitors, and all will be aright. . . .

Camp before Petersburg, Va., September 18th 1864

My dear family,

The mail has not come in yet. I hope I may have a letter or two tonight.

Today has been very quiet and but little firing until just now, 9 p.m. They have commenced it again. I do not think it will last long. I suppose it is firing on working parties from one or the other side.

We had a nice church service at my headquarters today, and a good sermon by Chaplain Hamilton.[14] The Chaplains all attend and take turns to preach. They prepare, and as a result we get good sermons.

A report says that we have recaptured nearly all our cattle. But there is some doubt about this being true. I hope that it is. Recruits are arriving daily. The 7th [New Jersey] Regiment goes home in a few days —or about one half of them that have not reinlisted. . . .

Camp before Petersburg, Va., September 19th 1864

My dear Ellen,

Some picket firing occurred last night and today, but not much. Yet today I have had 1 man killed and 2 wounded in the Brigade.

Recruits are coming in pretty rapidly. If we could only get all that is sent to us, we would have a much larger force. My regiment, the 11th, has got quite a number. So has the 5th, 6th & 8th New Jersey Battalions.[15] If the draft is successful, we will be filled up without consolidating them. This is what ought to be don. If not, there will be consolidation and some of the old organizations will become extinct in all but name.

I told you that Genl. Mott has got a brevet promotion and now ranks as a Major General. He has not only given me a strong letter in favour of my promotion, but he has also handed in my name to Genl.

---

13. Clement L. Vallandigham of Ohio was the epitome of the Copperhead spirit in the North. He was opposed to the Civil War in general and to President Lincoln in particular. In May, 1863, Federal officials arrested Vallandigham on charges of "treasonable sympathy." Lincoln, realizing that Vallandigham's very presence was a threat to the war effort, shrewdly banished the Copperhead from the North.

14. Edward J. Hamilton was chaplain of the 7th New Jersey.

15. These three regiments numbered at the time less than the normal complement of ten companies. Hence, McAllister referred to them as battalions.

Hancock, who has endorsed it and today sent it forward for my promotion. I may only get Brevet Brigadier at first, as Genl. Mott has Brevet Major General, or I may get a full promotion. The brevet is more of a compliment than a full promotion, as it is not given unless it is thought—or known—that the officer geting it merits it. Once that is reached, others soon follow. Genl. Birney has promised me a letter, but I have not yet received it. No doubt I will in a day or two. I will be all right. If I am spared, my promotion will come sooner or later. When it does come, it will be because I deserve it. I have letters and promises of letters from all the Generals I have served under, showing that my record is clear, and no one can doubt it. I have the proud satisfaction to know—and others know—that I have thus far done my duty. By the help of God, I will continue to do it.

I believe that a person with a brevet rank draws the pay of that rank and has the title of the promotion. For a large portion of this campaign I have commanded a Brigade with only a Colonel's pay. But I don't care for that. That is a small matter. In fact, I care but little for the promotion—only to show my friends that I deserve it. It will also be a satisfaction to my family. . . .

Camp before Petersburg, Va., September 23rd 1864
My dear Family,

Inclosed you will please find an ordinance receipt which shows that my ordinance account has passed the secretary of the first auditor and is in the hands of the second auditor, which is equivalent to a final passage and shows that it is all right. Keep this, as so many officers can't get their pay because their ordinance accounts are not right. If I would die and any difficulty would occur, you have this receipt to show.

You will also find a communication to Genl. Mott in answer to an inquiry as to how many battles I have been in in this campaign. I, with others, have been recommended for promotion, and I presume they are hunting up our history. If I had given them all the skirmishes I have been in, it would have been a long list. This is only for this campaign. I have no doubt of my promotion to at least a brevet Brigadier General. When Congress meets I may get full promotion. All admit that my record is a good one and that I deserve it. Hancock will do what is right. I have many very warm friends here. Neither myself or my Brigade have got justice in this last little affair of moving and holding this picket line. De Trobriand deserves credit but not all of it. I fought more and lost more men than he did. I told Genl.

Hancock that for myself I did not care, but I wanted the credit due my officers & men, as they had acted nobly. He desired me to send up the facts and said he would do me justice. I have not don so nor don't think that I will. Genl. Mott is to blame and not Genl. Hancock. As they are both recommending me so highly, I did not want to get into a mess. Genl. Hancock has not only endorsed Genl. Mott's letter of recommendation to the Secretary of War but had nominated me before I spoke to him.

My Brigade feel that they have been slighted. This evening I told McGregor,[16] the New York *Herald* corrispondent, that the press had not don justice to my Brigade in this affair, that as for myself I did not want any credit—I wanted my officers & men to have what they deserve, to incourage them to noble deeds hereafter. He said that he was sick and knew nothing about it, &c. Well, it is a small matter anyhow, so I will let it go.

I was told today that Maj. [John] William of Genl. Mott's staff, who was always at the front during these trying times through this campaign, was last evening called upon to write the facts concerning my gallantry. He recorded the fact that I "had acted nobly" and said that "it was not only on one occasion but that my conduct all through the campaign, either as a regimental or brigade commander, was a succession of heroic acts and deeds of bravery."

I am glad that he was called on to do it, for he knew more about me in these trying scenes than any one man living. He was always at the front with me and had a good right to know. His report will go up to Corps Headquarters and will be a part of my history. They are collecting these facts from, and for, all Colonels commanding brigades so as to know who is the most worthy of promotion. I am proud of my record, and have no fears on that score.

I had a very unpleasant duty to perform last evening: to give the battles that Col. [John] Ramsey of the 8th New Jersey was in and the facts relative to his conduct, &c. He, you know, was one of Genl. Mott's pets and no friend of mine. He was an officer that wanted a greate deal of credit for doing very little. He acted badly in the Wilderness battles—went to the hospital and also to Washington.[17]

16. William D. McGregor was a capable field reporter for three New York newspapers and the Associated Press.
17. In the Wilderness fighting of May 5 the 8th New Jersey bolted to the rear in panic. Only Capt. George M. Stelle managed to rally a portion of the regiment. In addition, its casualties in that day's action comprised one third of the losses in the nine-regiment brigade. *OR*, Vol. XXXVI, Pt. 1, pp. 122, 488. For a biographical sketch of John Ramsey, see Foster, *New Jersey and the Rebellion*, 835–36.

He was ordered back to his regiment by the Provost Marshall of Washington. He got command of the Irish Brigade for *gallantry* in the Wilderness battles that he never earned. The command should have been given to Capt. [George M.] Stelle of his [8th New Jersey] regiment. He done the fighting after Col. Ramsey ran back. [Ramsey] was slightly wounded in another battle, went home, and is not here yet. I told the truth; and if it gets to Genl. Hancock, he will not have him appointed. . . .

Camp before Petersburg, Va., September 24th 1864

My dear Ellen,

. . . We have received the glorious news of Sheridan's two greate victories.[18] It gives our boys more spirit. We are increasing by recruits coming. But we have too many foigners. Some of them are not true to our country and desert. Two Frenchmen deserted from my regiment night before last, making in all five that have deserted from the 11th —a thing unheard of with our old troops.[19] Bounty jumpers are of no use. Let the young men come themselves and not send us such trash who have no interest in our country and its laws. The drafting is the only true way to keep up an army and get good men. The large bounties are demoralizing. Also, they give us a class of worthless men. . . .

Camp before Petersburg, Va., September 28th 1864

My dear family,

Although I head my letter as before—i.e., before Petersburg, I have moved camp and have come down about 1½ or 2 miles to the right. I am now quite near to the place where the exploded mine is. The cause of this change is not known to any of us.[20] The 10th Corps

18. Sheridan's campaign in the Shenandoah Valley against Early's Confederates had just resulted in Federal victories at Opequon Creek (Sept. 19) and Fisher's Hill (Sept. 22).

19. The two deserters were Pvts. Edward Gastineau and August Genot of Co. H. A majority of the replacements at this time were either substitutes or immigrants who were lured into the army by bounties. Generally speaking, such men made unreliable soldiers. In the summer and fall of 1864, 341 of them deserted from the ranks of the 11th New Jersey. Ten of them deserted en masse. *N.J. Record,* I, 574; Marbaker, *11th New Jersey,* 224; *OR.* Vol. XLII, Pt. 3, p. 733.

20. Federal commanders were merely alternating units between the first and second lines of battle.

(Birney's) has moved back from the front and our Corps had to fill up the space. What Birney is to do we of course don't know. Perhaps what the 2nd [Corps] has so often don—make a dash somewhere.

One day the Rebels hollered over to our boys and wanted to know: "Why don't we fight some other corps? If we go to the right, we meet and fight the 2nd Corps. If we go to the left, we meet and fight the 2nd Corps. If we come to the center, we meet you again."

So you see the Rebels understand that the 2nd Corps does considerable fighting.

My new headquarters are on one of the leading roads to Petersburg. We have breastwork barricades and bombproofs and all sorts of protection. The minie birds fly along and all around here day and night. A few shells came along this evening. I was walking alone along the road from the line of battle at a time when one of our fatigue details came to camp. The enemy opened on them. The first shell fell on my right, the second to my front, and the third to my left. But none of them, thank God, came near enough to hurt me. One man in camp was wounded. There is considerable firing now. It will continue all night.

The carpet bag arrived this evening with the coat you sent me. The chicken is spoiled and can't be saved. Don't send anything that will spoil. The cake is first rate. The pies come fine. So does all the other things—just what I wanted. I have not got the package from Stocks yet, but I received the bill: a dress blouse coat, double-breasted, $45; a pair of pants, $25; 2 yards of storm cloth to cover my overcoat, $1.50; I pair of silver eagles, $1.50. This is a good deal of money for very few clothing. . . .

Camp before Petersburg, Va., September 29th 1864

My dear Ellen,

I wrote you last night. We have not yet moved. We were ready at 4 a.m. It is now 4:30 p.m. I expect that we will move this evening after dark. Everything is kept a profound secret—very few know anything about the intended move. God grant that it may be a successful one and that victory may perch on our banner.

Dr. Welling, Col. Schoonover and myself have just been enjoying your cake. It is real nice. I have just now cut it.

I have bought a note book. You need not send me one. You know that I lost my old one. I am sorry to say that Alice's picture was in it and was lost with it. . . .

October 2nd 1864

My dear Ellen,

We are here on the west side of the Weldon Railroad and are about moving on the enemy to turn their flank. I expect a hard fight. My Brigade are half raw recruits—never fired a gun. I don't know how we will get along. . . .

Bivouac near Poplar Grove Church, Va.
October 3rd 1864

My dear Ellen,

I wrote you a short note yesterday morning, telling you of our intended advance. In about ½ hour from that time our Division moved towards the enemy lines and soon came across the skirmish line. We deployed and drove in their pickets, reached their new line of works, and captured them. One of my regiments captured a redoubt. The 120th New York has that honor. We also assisted in capturing parts of the line. The enemy seemed to have but a small force in this line. We now drew in our extended lines, advanced again about one mile and run up against another line of works. These works are within 1½ miles of the Southside Railroad. The enemy opened an enfilade fire on us and defended these works stoutly—so much that we did not take them. Our men fought well, but we had to fall back—especially as the enemy were making a demonstration on our left, with the intention of taking us on our left flank. We came to this place after dark and are here yet—12 noon.

This was a line of works that was thrown up after we took the enemy's Poplar Grove Church works. We are in the advance of that line. The enemy have not retaken the line we captured yesterday morning from them. Our pickets held it last night and this morning. Whether we shall advance again or not I don't know. It is possible that we may. I think, however, that this is only a demonstration to hold the enemy to this point while others are opperating at other points. My men did well yesterday. I am sorry to say that I lost some first rate men and officers, though my loss was small compared to Genl. Pierce's, the General commanding the 2nd Brigade.[21] He massed some two or three regiments and made a charge, while I made a demonstration with one regiment. The fire of grape and can-

21. McAllister erred on this point. His brigade lost 12 killed, 65 wounded and 12 missing; the brigade of Gen. Byron R. Pierce suffered casualties of 4 killed, 39 wounded and 11 missing. *OR,* Vol. XLII, Pt 1, p. 139.

ister concentrated on him, and he lost some fifty men in killed and wounded. The dead were left on the field and, I fear, some of the wounded. But of the latter I am not certain. My loss yesterday was but 14 men.

One brave veteran Sergeant [22] had his leg blown off by a solid shot. As he was going off the field on a blanket, he said to me, "Goodbye, Colonel, I have done my duty and have lost my limb in a good cause."

"Yes, Sergeant," I replied, "you have done your duty. Boys, handle him tenderly. He is a brave soldier!"

He bore his wound like a hero and was in fine spirits as he left the field. I am sorry to say that he died in the Hospital last night. This I did not expect. It must have been from the loss of blood.

Another good and brave soldier right by his side was killed by the same shot. This was close by where I was. But this is the fate of war. Both of these men were members of the 11th Massachusetts. It is the loss of such brave men that we feel so much.

One half of my Brigade are raw recruits, some of whom have never been in battle nor even fired off a gun. Some of them do not understand the English language. We have a great number of Dutch, some French—all nations but the Hottentots. Our Patriots stay home and send us these to save our country. They entrust all to them and stay home and attend to making money. I hope, however, that they may do better than I expect.

Day before yesterday, the day we came up here, it rained all day. As I had nothing on but a pair of shoes, I got my feet very wet. But as soon as we arrived here, I got a dry pair of stockings on and don't feel the worse for it. My health is good. . . .

Bivouac west of Weldon Railroad, October 4th 1864

My dear Ellen,

I wrote you a long letter yesterday. We are still here and are busy at work building forts and breastworks for defence. How long we shall remain on the defence I don't know—perhaps until we get our works completed. Then we shall stretch out again. The Army of the Potomac have now about 28 miles of works thus built and thus defended. Then

---

22. This soldier was George Dunham, a 29-year-old farmer from the vicinity of Lowell, Mass. Dunham was originally a member of the 16th Massachusetts. He was promoted to sergeant on the day before his fatal wounding. Mass. Adj. Gen., *Massachusetts Soldiers*, I, 781.

add Butler's lines and we have about 40 miles—and are now extending them. Can it be possible the Rebels can stretch much more?

Recruits are coming in rapidly. Last evening we received 135 for the 11th New Jersey. My Brigade now has 2,100 for duty, nearly 4,000 altogether, including sick, wounded, and detached men. If I had time to drill them, I would like it. But there is no time for this. March, fight, and dig is all we can do at the present. . . .

I hear some firing and must close. . . .

Old camp before Petersburg, Va., October 6th 1864

My dear Ellen,

We are back here again right in my old camp—the one we were in when we moved to the right, before we went to the left of the Weldon Railroad. I wrote you two penciled letters while I was on the extreme left and told you nearly all. On the last two days we were there, we were all engaged cuting slashings and building forts and breastworks, both front and rear. We are advancing our lines on to the left just as fast as we have troops to hold them, by thin lines. As we advance we fortify both front and rear, so that if the enemy attack us in the rear, we strike across and meet him. . . .

We don't take more from the enemy at a time than we can hold and then fortify. Had we not have don so, we could not have held what we took. You can now easily see that by a few more successful moves we will cross and hold the Southside Railroad. Then Lee will be compelled to leave Richmond. When persons talk of Grant doing nothing, it shows how little they know. Richmond will be ours. All is right. You can now see how necessary it is to have men to man this long line of works. And I am rejoiced to say that we are geting them. Every day our army is increasing in numbers. If they were only drilled, we could walk right into Richmond.

I told you this Division went out to the left and took a new line of works, then advanced up against another line that we did not take. I don't think that it was intended that we should take it, for we were too far out to hold it. So we got orders to fall back—even past what we did take. But our cavalry holds that line now. One of these days we will go out again, make another advance, fortify again, &c.

You know this Corps is called "Hancock's Cavalry" from the fact that it is flying around everywhere. A good anacdote is told of this Division on one of its marches. When moving on rapidly one day, a bystander asked what these troops were.

One of our boys replied, "Don't you know Hancock's Cavalry? We have just stopped for the officers to change horses!" [23]

Wherever we go, all eyes are turned towards us, and a feeling of security prevails. The other day a lot of cavalry were picketing along the Bond and Squirrel Level Road, where we were on the left.

"What troops are these?" they inquired.

We replied: "The 2nd Corps."

"We are safe," they said.

As we were passing the Yellow Tavern on our way up last Saturday, a very gentlemanly looking man, on hearing that we were the 3rd Division of the 2nd Corps, spoke out: "3rd Corps! 3rd Corps! I must see these brave men!"

Out he came in the storm to look at us trudging along in the mud. Just as he was looking, with eyes wide open, along came the 5th and 7th New Jersey, which had that day 140 raw recruits added to their number—men who had never seen or fired a gun. No doubt this gentleman thought that he was gazing on the old tried veterans of scores of battles. He will tell the story that he has seen the heroes of the 3rd Corps. I was amused at thinking how nicely he was sold.

We arrived here very late last night and had to relieve a brigade of darkeys (Russell's brigade).[24] I reported to the Headquarters of that Brigade that I was ready to relieve them, and I asked the Colonel commanding how many pickets he had out.

"Five hundred," he replied, "but as you are a part of the 2nd Corps, you will only want half that number."

"Why?" I asked.

The Colonel blushed and said nothing. I knew well what he meant.

Well, I have bragged enough tonight and I will stop. You will excuse me, as I have not said anything about myself. I was only talking about Hancock's old 3rd Corps Cavalry, now called a part of the 2nd Corps. . . .

23. A slight variation of this anecdote is in Lyman, *Meade's Headquarters,* 221.

24. Col. Charles S. Russell and his 28th U.S. Colored Troops belonged to Gen. Edward Ferrero's division of the IX Corps. For a humorous incident that occurred when a portion of the II Corps relieved these troops, see *ibid.,* 269–70.

Headquarters, 3rd Brigade, 3rd Division,[25]
2nd Corps, Before Petersburg, Va.
October 7th 1864

Captain [J. P. Finklemeier, Assistant Adjutant General]:

In compliance with circular from Headquarters, 3rd Division, of this date, I have the honor to make the following report of the part taken by this Brigade in the recent operations on the left of the Army.

On the morning of the 1st instant, I received orders to hold the Brigade in readiness to move to the trestle bridge as soon as relieved from the works I held near the Avery House. At a later hour in the morning (4 a.m.), I was instructed to commence the movement without waiting for the troops sent to relieve me. I arrived at the trestle bridge soon after daylight, remaining there until 3 p.m. I was then ordered to place my Brigade aboard the cars and proceed to the Peeble House southwest of the Weldon Railroad. Arriving at the Yellow House, the Brigade again took up the line of march at 4:30 p.m., arriving at the Peebles House at 6:30 p.m., where we bivouacked for the night.

During the night I received orders to be ready to move at daylight. At 6 a.m., October 2nd, I moved forward with my command and ordered it to close en masse. We moved up the road following Genl. Pierce's orders to form regiment after regiment on the left of him, as he was to swing around his left to the right. I was ordered also to deploy regiment after regiment as a very strong line of skirmishers. The regiments deployed—the 120th New York, Lieut. Col. [John R.] Tappen, and the 5th & 7th New Jersey, Col. [Francis] Price—marched up towards the enemy's redoubts through the slashing, driving the enemy from the redoubt and breastworks. Col. Price was ordered to support Genl. Pierce's advance at the same time my left stretched out past the white house (Smith's house) and far into the woods, driving the enemy before them.

After our forces had got possession of the works, we were ordered to move by the right flank, having all my Brigade but two regiments deployed as skirmishers. I closed them all up, leaving a sufficient number of skirmishers to more than cover my Brigade, and followed Genl. Pierce by the right and left flank until we came in sight of the Rebels' second line of defences near the Boydton road, where we halted and pushed the skirmishers forward. They were hotly engaged and under a sharp fire from the Rebel sharpshooters together with an

---

25. This official report, with some grammatical changes, is in *OR*, Vol. XLII, Pt. 1, pp. 393–94. It is included here because of McAllister's rather skimpy account of the affair in his letters home.

enfilading fire from the Rebel batteries in earthworks. I was ordered to make a demonstration in front of Genl. de Trobriand's Brigade, while Genl. Pierce charged on the works on my right. I ordered Major [Charles C.] Rivers to make a demonstration, which he did with the 11th Massachusetts. This regiment marched under a galling fire and did all that was asked of them.

After the demonstration the enemy moved on my left flank and made it very unpleasant for this regiment, as well as my whole Brigade, together with a portion of Genl. Pierce's. Late in the afternoon Col. Biles of the 1st Brigade informed me that he was taking his regiment from my left and that I must look out for my left flank. I soon received orders to move my whole command back. My first effort was to get the 11th Massachusetts out of its critical position, which was accomplished by Major Rivers in a manner highly creditable to himself and his command. The manner in which the officers and men during the transactions of the day performed their duty is alike creditable to themselves and the Brigade. All showed a willingness to obey every order. Col. Tappen and Major Rivers deserve particular mention. Capt. Snyder,[26] in charge of my picket line, showed himself a brave, efficient officer. He was badly wounded.

I returned and took position in the rifle pits on the right of Squirrel Level Road. Large details were made to slash in our front, and from that time on details were kept slashing and building new works until 10 p.m., October 5th, when I received orders to march my Brigade to occupy the works connecting between Fort Davis and Fort Alexander Hays. On arrival I found that the only troops occupying the works were the 19th U.S. Colored Troops, whom I relieved at the breastworks and on the picket line at 11 p.m., at the same time placing 575 men in Fort Davis and massing three regiments in rear of Genl. Pierce's old Headquarters, my Brigade being in position as ordered at 12 midnight.

I cannot close my report without mentioning favorably Major William of [Mott's] staff. He was always where he was needed, regardless of danger. My own staff did all that I asked or desired of them, and they deserve my warmest thanks.

Very respectfully, your obedient servant,
R. McAllister
Colonel, 11th New Jersey Vols., Comdg. Brigade

26. Jacob L. Snyder was a captain in the 120th New York.

Camp before Petersburg, Va., October 8th 1864
My dear Ellen & family,

I wrote you a long letter night before last. I did not write last evening, as I was very much engaged in making reports and had not time to write. I am now through with them.

Nothing of particular note has occured on this part of the line since our return from the left. There was some fighting on our extreme right in Genl. [Benjamin F.] Butler's department yesterday morning. We have not heard the particulars. Some reports say that our cavalry was badly whipped, and others say that we whipped the enemy. We have nothing official. Before this reaches you, you will see it in the papers. Very little has been said in the papers about our movement to the left. I don't know why it is so. But it is a small matter and we don't care for newspaper talk. The cause of it was that we were detached and acting with the 9th Corps, and some newspapers are jealous of the 2nd Corps. Hancock says that he did not expect them to notice us—rivalries, you know, between Corps.

Brevet Maj. Genl. Mott starts in the morning for home on a leave of absence. He was all ready to go when we were ordered to move, and his leave was recalled for the time being.

I don't know when my time will come. It is not likely until this campaign ends and the winter sets in. How I would like to visit you all. If spared, I hope to have that pleasure in the winter. I am glad that Captain Lloyd got his leave through. I hope that he will enjoy himself, recover, and soon join us again. It is probable that he will receive a promotion before long.

My Brigade is filling up rapidly. I received 109 recruits just now for the 120th New York. I now number 2,300 men for duty and, on paper, present and absent, between 4–5,000 men. My Brigade looks like a Division. I only wish that they were drilled.

Within the last 24 hours I had two deserters come in through my pickets—one last evening and one this morning. Both were from Florida and heartily tired of the war. They wish to take the oath of allegence and stay in the Union.[27] They told me that a good meal in Petersburg will cost them $36 in their money. They only get $11 a month, which, in our money, is about ten cents on the dollar. One dollar of our greenbacks will buy $10 of their worthless trash; and in many parts of their so-called Confederacy, it will buy $15. Think of working three months for one meal!

---

27. Prisoners of war were sometimes offered an oath of allegiance, which was simply a parole on their promise not to bear arms again.

I wonder how the Copperheads would like this currency for one week in politicks.

You may ask how the Army is going to vote. You will be astonished when I tell you that I have not come across an officer or a man that will vote for McClellan and Pendleton. Why, we don't touch the Chicago platform! The former friends of George B. McClellan have abandoned him because he has got in *such bad company*. Tell our friends that if our New Jersey troops were alowed to vote, our little state would be all right for Lincoln. Some New Yorkers are here now, receiving votes for some of their districts. One gentleman told me that he never was so much astonished as he was when arriving here— having been lead to believe that the army vote would go largely for McClellan. He finds that it will go 6 to 1 for Lincoln and thinks that it will go 10 to 1 for him. All that do go for McClellan are foreigners, no native-born.

. . . The mail just came in. No letter for me tonight nor last night. I am sorry that I can't hear from home. I have just heard that we have captured a gunboat up the James. I hope it is true. . . .

Camp before Petersburg, Va., October 11th 1864

My dear Ellen,

I am at a loss to know what is the matter at home. I have not received a letter from you for almost a week. I have been very much disappointed for several evenings when the postmaster would come to my tent and say, "No letter for you tonight, Colonel." Evening after evening this same unwelcom news came ringing in my ears. What this evening may bring I know not. I shall be more disappointed if the same unwelcom sound shall greet me tonight.

Last evening I wrote you a few lines, introducing Capt. [Richard T.] Lombard, who started today to visit his far off home in the Bay State. He was on my staff for a considerable time. He is one of the most active, enijetick men I have ever met, a soldier every inch of him. He will call and tell you all. He is a young man but is married and is going on to see his family. I sent with him for you some Rebel bullets that was shot at us the 22nd day of June. I thought that they might be interesting to you. . . . Lombard is a lawyer by profession and a splendid officer. I was very sorry to loose him from my staff. But my policy is to help good men to promotion. He went up to the Division, and I give him a strong letter to [Massachusetts] Governor [John A.] Andrew. I have no doubt but that he will receive the promotion to Major in a few days. He richly deserves it.

Many of our officers are now being mustered out on the strength of a new order alowing those that have served three years that privilege. Many are taking advantage of it, and it is weaking our army very much. They ought not to take advantage of it at this time but wait till the close of the campaign. It is very unfortunate for us who stay. We want good men and good officers to push this thing through.

We have just received the good news of another victory for Sheridan.[28] Genl. Torbert has don well as a cavalry commander. We had the telegram read to the different regiments, and three hearty cheers followed. The Rebel pickets report to our boys that [General John B.] Hood has whiped Sherman, and they had a little cheering on the strength of this report. But we don't believe it. It is a report got up to cheer their drooping spirits. Sherman is all right.

. . . This is the day of the Pennsylvania and Ohio elections. I hope to hear cheering news of our success in those states. Col. Beaver has gone home. I met Miss Mary Wilson's brother here yesterday. (Miss Wilson of Bellefonte.) He was procuring votes for his district. Inclosed you will find Capt. Layton's photograph. He was killed on June 16th before Petersburg.[29] . . .

We have had quite a cannonading this evening. I think we must have fired some in honor of our victory. The Rebels threw over their mortar shells quite lively in response. They keep up musketry fire nearly all night. We go to sleep with firing and get awakened with a constant rattle. Often at night I jump up and run out expecting an attack. But they are afraid to advance on us. They can't get their men to charge against our works. . . .

Camp before Petersburg, Va., October 12th 1864

My dear Ellen,

I wrote you last evening and said that I felt uneasy, as I had not received a letter from you for nearly a week. One came this morning from Hennie. But as is often the case with her letters, there was

---

28. On Oct. 9, under orders from Sheridan "to whip the rebel cavalry or get whipped," Torbert's cavalry division attacked the Confederate troopers of Thomas L. Rosser and Lunsford L. Lomax at Tom's Brook near Fisher's Hill. The gray-clad horsemen were defeated in what one Confederate commander termed "the greatest disaster that ever befell our cavalry during the whole war." *OR*, Vol. XLIII, Pt. 1, pp. 51, 431; *Southern Historical Society Papers*, XIII (1885), 134.

29. Capt. Sidney M. Layton of Co. D was buried in the City Point National Cemetery. *N.J. Record*, I, 555; Marbaker, *11th New Jersey*, 100, 363.

no date but the month, October. The postmark was so dim that it did not show the date. . . .

All is quiet here except the usual amount of picket firing, which is kept up all night long. We had a fine officer killed on picket the other night, Lieut. [George C.] Boice of the 11th New Jersey. He had placed his pickets and was standing by the fire. No doubt a Rebel sharpshooter aimed at him. He fell and died in a few minutes. For a long time he was our Quartermaster Sergeant. He accepted a commission and went into the line. He was from the neighbourhood of New Brunswick. He is a loss to the regiment, and we all regret his death.

. . . I send you a little work called "American Melodies." The author of this work is Cassius C. Cullen, a private in the 6th New Jersey,[30] and it is entirely his own composition. It has cost him considerable to get it published, and he has given 200 copies to the Christian Commission. These poems are very patriotic and will do good. The author seems to have been a sailor at one time. . . .

Camp before Petersburg, Va., October 15th 1864

My dear Ellen,

. . . Election news is good. No doubt Mr. Lincoln will be elected. This Division voted—those that could vote—7 to 1 in favour of the Administration. And the Corps voted 10 to 1 the same way. This decides how the Army votes. This has always been considered the Democratic Corps. If this is the way it goes here, dear help the Democrats in the other parts of the Army that McClellan never had anything to do with—Butler's army and the Western army. He can't win at all. The soldiers know what they are fighting against, and they know who their friends are.

Here comes the band. They have just struck up a martial air after playing a couple of tunes. I went out and welcomed them in a very short speech. They come over very frequently and serenade me. This is the 120th New York Vols. Band.[31] We have another new band, the Brigade Band, just formed. But it is detailed at Division Headquarters. It has about 30 members and one of the best leaders in

---

30. Cullen initially joined the 6th New Jersey but served for most of the war in Ramsey's 8th New Jersey. He remained a private throughout his military service. *N.J. Record,* I, 282, 393.

31. See Van Santvoord, *120th New York,* 236; Lyman, *Meade's Headquarters,* 317.

the country. They are coming over here one of these evenings. So, you see, we have plenty of this kind of music. We hear it all hours of the day while in camp, and the 120th New York Band plays church music for us on Sabbaths.

Has Capt. Lombard called on you yet? He is a brave and gallant soldier. I expect he will return a Major. Here comes the mail, but no letter for me—nothing but papers. I have read them; nothing new. Elections are all right. It is said that the 6th Corps is on its way here. If so, we will have stirring times soon. . . .

Camp before Petersburg, Va., October 17th 1864

My dear Ellen,

Yesterday we had the Rev. Mr. Stevenson, the Secretary of the American Tract Society,[32] to preach for us. He preached in the 11th New Jersey and in the 120th New York. He is one of the finest speakers I have yet heard. I was delighted with him. Today I rode around our fortifications with him and showed him everything of interest, but keeping away from danger.

There was a very solom funeral here today and Mr. Stevenson spoke at the grave. The deceased was a young lady 16 years of age. We are encamped on the farm of a Mr. Jones.[33] Division Headquarters are at his house—a very fine building, just new, and on very large property. It is said that since the war began he has been offered $40,000 in gold for it. He was very wealthy, owns several houses in Petersburg, as well as farms between this place and Richmond, with perhaps a half a million in all. He has a son, married and living with him, and two daughters. The youngest was the one buried today. The old man is very aged—say 70 years old—and quite feeble.

When our army first came here, his son was taken prisoner and is still in our hands. The family tell the story thus. The son and his family went to town in a carriage about the time our first cavalry

---

32. The Rev. J. M. Stevenson was a leading official in the American Tract Society, which published and distributed evangelical literature. Moss, *Annals of the U.S. Christian Commission,* 84–85, 698–99.

33. William Jones owned a 740-acre farm southeast of Fort Sedgwick and alongside the U.S. Military Railroad. The elder Jones had once been a wealthy man, de Trobriand observed, but within a month "everything was swallowed up at once before his eyes." Nevertheless, "the old man bore misfortunes with a philosophy somewhat callous . . ." It was the youngest of his granddaughters who died Oct. 15 of typhoid fever. *Official Atlas,* Plate LXXVII, Map 2; de Trobriand, *Army of the Potomac,* 653–54.

came here. The Rebs compelled this Mr. Jones to get out of the carriage and put a gun in his hands. When our party came here, they took him a prisoner because of the gun in his hands. He has been a prisoner ever since, and we have held possession of his place. His fences are all gone, together with all his barns, &c. Nothing is left but this fine house, in which the family reside, and it is used as a headquarters for the Division now. Although the family have been wealthy, they now have not had anything to live on but what they get from the Government and from the Headquarters table. The General & staff furnish them with everything that they have.

This young lady took sick and died. Our doctors gave her every attention, but all was in vain. She left this world of trouble on Saturday. Here the family was, surrounded by the Yankee army, with no communication with sympathizing friends, and the father a prisoner. All the officers around Headquarters wanted to be kind and offered to do all in their power. Chaplain Barbour [34] of the U.S. Sharpshooters, known as the "Fighting Chaplain," offered his services in any and every way he could aid them. It was repugnant to them to have a Yankee chaplain to perform the funeral ceremony. They rather declined it, alleging that Mr. Barber was a Methodist. But the secret was that he was a Yankee chaplain. Yet after more deliberations, they concluded to have our Chaplain hold some little service. The young officers on the staff purchased a nice coffin for $50 to have her decently interred.

Mr. Stevenson and I were about to take the ride. He expressed a wish to call at the funeral house, which we did just as the funeral was about to leave. He was asked to perform the funeral ceremony. He don it in a very feeling manner and to the satisfaction of all. The Band played as we marched to and returned from the grave. I thought the poor mother and sister would breake down with grief, especially when, in Mr. Stevenson's prayer, he alluded to the absent father. It was indeed a solom scene—so much poverty amidst so much wealth. Officers carried and deposited the remains in the grave in the family graveyard near the house. Mr. Stevenson said afterwards that he could not help thinking about that funeral and all the circumstances attending it.

Here comes the mail with two letters from home. . . . Why [one] letter should have went wrong I can not see. It was directed right and very plainly, and yet it went to the 106th Pennsylvania Vols. just like the other one. . . .

34. Chaplain Lorenzo Barber of the 2nd U.S. Sharpshooters also performed the duty of writing his unit's official reports. See *OR,* Vol. XLII, Pt. 1, pp. 355–57.

Camp before Petersburg, Va., October 19th 1864

My dear Ellen,

Two of your lost letters has come around to me . . . I did not write you last evening for the want of time. We seem to have a renewal of the old picket firing every night. Sometimes it is heavy and we have quite a number of casualties. This morning 5 were reported —1 killed and 4 wounded. Last night the artillery fire was heavy, also that of mortars. This latter is practised all most every night. It is a splendid sight to see these balls of fire fly through the air—but not so pleasant to be where they fall and burst.

A report says that the 6th Corps are coming.[35] Some say they have gon up to Deep Bottom, but we don't know the facts. One thing I believe: we are on the eve of very active and important operations. But I know not where the blow is to be struck, or which Corps are to make the attack.

We have had quite an increase in our army in the way of substitutes. But many of them have deserted to the enemy, and many more to the rear. They came out for the bounty and are worthless creatures. We can't trust them on picket duty—or, indeed, any place.

We are all very sorry to hear of the death of Genl. [David B.] Birney.[36] His death is a greate loss to the country. Notice of his death has been read to every regiment in the Division. He was a very hardworking and active officer. . . .

Camp before Petersburg, Va., October 22nd 1864

My dear Ellen,

I am just preparing to go to bed, but thought I would write you a line or two. Capt. Lloyd is back and brought me a pair of stockings sent by Sarah, and four pair of white gloves. Much obliged. The Cap-

---

35. The VI Corps was not ordered back to Petersburg until the second week of December.

36. Birney died in Philadelphia, Oct. 18, 1864, "of disease contracted on the field in the line of his duty." In the eyes of many soldiers, Birney "was one of the bravest, most faithful and conscientious officers of the national army, whose qualities and worth will be cherished with tenacious devotion by all whose fortune it was to know him or to serve under his command." *OR*, Vol. XLII, Pt. 3, pp. 275, 276, 298; Isaiah Price, *History of the Ninety-seventh Regiment, Pennsylvania Volunteer Infantry* . . . (Philadelphia, 1875), 326–27. See also George Lewis, *The History of Battery E, First Rhode Island Light Artillery* . . . (cited hereafter as Lewis, *1st Rhode Island Light Artillery*) (Providence, 1892), 382–84; Luther S. Dickey, *History of the Eighty-fifth Regiment, Pennsylvania Volunteer Infantry, 1861–1865* (New York, 1915), 397–98.

tain's commission will be on in a few days as Major in the 7th New Jersey. [Uriel B.] Titus has come for 1st Lieutenant.[37] You can congratulate Mrs. Welling, his sister, on his promotion.

I am glad you are holding so many nice large Lincoln Union Meetings. Keep on, go on, redeem the State, and we in the army will give you three hearty cheers. You must make a vote for me, as I do not think I can go home to vote. We can not well leave, though I would like to very much. You must work for me and make a vote.

Glorious news from Sheridan.[38] More and better. All is right here. . . .

Camp before Petersburg, Va., October 23rd 1864

My dear Ellen,

Your kind letter giving me a discription of some of the amusing things that were said at the Union Meeting came today. I am glad that things look so well for Lincoln. How I do wish you could carry New Jersey for the Administration. It would end the war. Let us all do our duty and leave the results to Providence. I think things look cheering.

. . . I did not say that old Mr. [William] Jones was a prisoner, but his son. These two girls are his son's children, the old gentleman's granddaughters. Only one of them is left now. The old man is a good Union man; I have no doubt about it. He took dinner with us yesterday. . . . The granddaughter was his pet.

Today we had a nice church service here at these Headquarters. Chaplain Hamilton preached. Genl. de Trobriand honored us with his presence. It is geting rather cold for outdoors congregations. I do not think I can get home for the Elections. It is rumoured around here that we are to have a move in a day or two.

Our Chaplain Cline is in miserable health. With great difficulty we have at last got him to consent to taking a sick leave and go home for a time. He is unable now to preach much. It was his turn to preach here today, but while he was here he could not preach. I have asked him to visit you and to make himself at home there. He is such a good

37. Titus became ordnance officer for the 3rd Division, II Corps. Marbaker, *11th New Jersey*, 164, 272–73, 364.

38. On Oct. 19 Early's numerically inferior army delivered a surprise attack against Sheridan's forces at Cedar Creek. The Federal troops broke in disorder. Sheridan arrived on the field at an opportune time, rallied his command, and counterattacked successfully. Although forced to retire, Early took with him 1,500 Federal prisoners.

man that I am willing to do anything for him. His father and mother are dead, but he has a sister living near Harmony in your county. If he goes up to Belvidere, ask him to stay a few days, or as long as he desires to stay. He is a very diffident man. Col. Schoonover thinks that he is love sick, disappointed, or something of the kind. But be this as it may, he has the chills and fever. He is loved by all who know him and is considered among the best chaplains in the army. . . .

Bivouac before Petersburg, Va., October 25th 1864

My dear Ellen,

Last evening we received orders to move. We packed up as soon as it was dark and left our comfortable camp to try the realities of bivouacking and campaigning once more. The 1st Division of our Corps was left to hold the works. They stretched out and relieved us.

We marched with the 2nd Division back here, arrived on this ground at 11 p.m., lay down on the ground, and had a good sleep. It is now 12 noon and we are still here. I don't know what is up, but think that there is an important movement on hand. No doubt we will move one way or the other as soon as night closes upon us. By being massed up in this way out of sight of the enemy, we can move without being noticed. . . .

Dr. Welling has received a 20-day leave of absence from the War Department. He has left today and will go right to electioneering.[39] He will call and see you. Call a meeting and he will make a speech for the Union and Abraham. Chaplain Cline leaves for home today on a sick leave of 20 days. One good vote for our side, and he will help Col. Scranton, as he hails from Warren County. Do all you can for him. I don't think there is any chance for me to get home at all, so don't look for me. You will have to make a vote in my place. If you can get one Democrat to vote the Union side, it will count as two votes. . . .

---

39. One of the ambiguities of the American system during the 1860's was that when a man left his state he lost his vote. This was particularly unfair to soldiers who, while fighting for their country, were denied the ballot box. During the Civil War several states remedied this shortcoming with laws empowering soldiers to vote in the field. However, New Jersey Democrats succeeded in beating down such a bill in their state. Many soldiers were therefore granted furloughs, sick leaves, etc. in order to return home and vote in the national elections. Josiah H. Benton, *Voting in the Field: A Forgotten Chapter of the Civil War* (Boston, 1915), 5, 270–78, 311–12.

[526] ✗ THE McALLISTER LETTERS

Bivouac as yesterday, October 26th 1864

My dear Ellen,

We are still here but we will move in an hour. We don't know where, yet it is a very important move and you will soon hear of it. The weather is very fine. Hancock commands the expedition—two divisions of our Corps, one or two of the 9th, and one or two of the 5th. I have just time to say good by. God bless you, and don't be disappointed if you don't hear from me for several days. . . .

Camp before Petersburg, Va., October 29th 1864

My dear Ellen & family,

My last letter was written to you in bivouac just on the eve of our starting to the left for march and battle.[40]

At 5 p.m.[41] [October 26] we moved and marched rapidly until we reached the Weldon Railroad. Then we bivouacked for the night. At 3:30 a.m.[42] the next morning, October 27th, we resumed our march. After having marched about two miles, we struck the enemy's picket lines and drove in the pickets. The 1st Division remained in the works to hold them. The 2nd Division and ours (the 3rd) were all that marched on our road. Brig. Genl. [Thomas W.] Egan was in command of the 2nd Division and was in the advance. After driving in the pickets, he again moved forward and captured some small Rebel rifle pitts at Hatcher's Run. We now moved on, meeting but little or no opposition, until we reached the Boydton Plank Road within a mile of the Southside Railroad.

Here the enemy showed themselves in greate force. The cavalry struck the Plank Road to the left of the infantry and swung around, with the aid of Genl. Egan's division. The Plank Road was now in our possession.

At this time I was bringing up the rear. The head of my Brigade had reached the field where we were massing. One regiment had turned in to the massing line, quite close to the plank road, when an aide came to me from Genl. [George] Meade with his compli-

---

40. McAllister's narrative-letter to Ellen of the Boydton Plank Road battle is a fuller account of his participation than his official report. For the latter, see *OR,* Vol. XLII, Pt. 1, pp. 394–96.
41. In his official report McAllister placed the time of departure at 3 P.M. *Ibid.,* 394.
42. The Colonel was again inconsistent as to time. His official report stated 4 A.M. *Ibid.*

ments and orders that I should stop and defend the rear—that the enemy were coming up in that direction. I halted, road back, and found Genl. Meade and staff coming up. The General directed me to throw a line across the road, put pickets far out, and send a company to reconnoiter, all of which I did. I reported to Genl. Mott what I had don. The cavalry firing now ceased in our rear, and we could find nothing of the enemy. But there was heavy firing in our front and shells flying all around and bursting among us without doing any damage. I was now ordered forward and passed in the field spoken of. Genl. Egan had now advanced up the plank road a considerable distance—about one mile.

I had just got my Brigade all in the field when I received an order to report to Genl. Egan, as he was nearly out of ammunition. He had arrived at a stream—a small run and a large mill pond. He had driven the enemy before him and had taken the hill on this side of the stream and held all up to it. This hill is a beautiful place, falling off all around and with small springs, runs and streams all around it. The hill was all cleared. On the left side ran the plank road; on the front, next to the enemy, were the streams and dam spoken of; in the rear was a smaller stream and narrow belt of flat swampy land; on the right was something similar. You have now a discription of this part of the battle field, which I wish you to notice. In front of this and the stream & dam was another hill, even higher than ours. A narrow bridge crossed the stream and connected the two hills.

I have told you that Genl. Egan's division was along this front in rifle pitts captured from the enemy and facing the last hill. He had a small division. The two Brigades of my own Division lay along the plank road, swinging around to the rear. These troops were not engaged when I left to report to Genl. Egan. I marched up the plank road with about 2,000 muskets and reported to Genl. Egan without having a shot fired at me.

He ordered me to form two lines of battle on the crest of this hill—facing the enemy on the opposit hill. Genl. [Thomas A.] Smyth had his brigade along the stream in those rifle pitts. Genl. Egan informed me that he wanted me to cross the narrow bridge and the stream and take the opposit hill from the enemy. I was then ordered to extend my left with the rear line of battle, making but one line. I had just completed this, preparatory to taking the opposit hill, when we were all surprised at the roar of musketry and artillery in our rear. The two Brigades of my Division under Genl. Mott were attacked. Our ambulances and artillery were all exposed and liable to be captured. These had to be protected. These Brigades had to change front and fight the enemy on the very road we had just come in on. This left our rear and the plank road exposed, and the enemy pushed right up towards us on the hill. A few minutes more and we could be surrounded.

The enemy's artillery and musketry poured in upon us on every side. Our communication with the ballance of the 2nd Corps was entirely cut off; and what was worst than all, a connection had not been made between the 5th and 2nd Corps. We had secured the road, and the 5th Corps was to have connected with us. This they failed to do. The enemy's column passed through the gap thus left. And what was still worse, we had no ammunition except sixty rounds to a man in the cartridge boxes and on the persons of the men. We were to have received a new supply of ammunition along the lines from the 5th Corps, but the want of a connection prevented this.

You now understand our critical condition. Cut off from the ballance of our own Corps, as well as the 5th, were Egan's small division and my Brigade, nearly as large as his division, but ¾ of them new men, some of which had never fired a gun and had had but very little drill.

The enemy, flushed with apparent victory, ran madly forward and captured one piece of artillery. Balls, shells, and musketry rolled in upon us from every side. It was enough to shake the courage of our old veterans. Genl. Egan ordered me to about face and charge the enemy. I gave the order, and off on the charge we went—down the hill, through the hazel brush and swamp. We met the enemy, drove them back pell mell, and captured over 100 prisoners. We met a heavy fire from two brigades in our rear (of which we knew nothing). This and the enemy's fire on my left—now the right—were too severe for my new troops. My line faltered and broke as we rose up the hill on the opposit side.[43] But on recrossing the swamp, I reformed them again. The enemy, encouraged by our falling back, re-attacked. My men opened on them with a terrific fire and drove them back once more. The day was ours. Our communication was opened and the enemy passed from our rear. The artillery lost was recaptured after I had drove the enemy back as above described.

This charge not only saved Egan's division and my Brigade, but saved the Corps. Just as we were making it, the enemy was planting a battery in my rear (now my front). My left regiment, the 120th

---

43. An artilleryman recollected in later years that "a body of infantry" which he designated as part of McAllister's brigade "came falling back through the guns. We remonstrate[d] with them, but all to no purpose." Billings, *10th Massachusetts Battery*, 359.

New York, had nearly come up to it. But on seeing us come down the hill, the enemy limbered up and pulled out just as we were reaching it.

The enemy were now foiled in their attempt to brake my front.[44] They pushed on by us, by the 1st & 2nd Brigades, moved off by the right, and made an attack on our left flank. I was ordered by Genl. Egan to form a second line, protecting that flank. I also strengthened the front lines so that the enemy's attack on us there proved a failure. The darkness of the night closed in around us. A few pickets firing, an occasional shot, was all that was left of the sound of battle. Stillness reigned throughout the field. The rain poured down rapidly. The men lay down on the cold, wet ground and fell fast asleep.

On the plank road stood two houses. Here our wounded were carried—those that were taken back. With an aide I road and called to see them. In one house were 50 men from my Brigade. They were badly wounded, many of them mortally. In another house were about a dozen men. Poor fellows. They would take me by the hand and say, "Colonel, did I do my duty?"

"Yes! Yes!" I would reply. "You did it nobly. You did it nobly."

They would say, "I fought for my country, and I die for my country."

Oh, how my heart thrilled for these poor, dying soldiers! They were far from home and friends; and they were soon to be left in the hands of the enemy, for our ambulances were but few and all full. The ambulances could not make a second trip, and our part of the battlefield was so far in the advance—right in on the enemy.

Only one Surgeon made his appearance at these hospital houses. There were no nurses, no chaplains, no consolation, no relief. There was hardly a candle to light up the rooms even while we were there to see the wounded. Capt. [David A.] Granger, an old veteran captain and a brave and gallant officer, commanded the 11th Massachusetts that day. He fell mortally wounded and was laying on the floor of one of the houses, suffering intense pain. He was so anxious to be taken to the ambulances that I ordered his regiment to carry him and as many others as they could down to the ambulances, about a mile distant. We had no stretchers, and it was pitch dark and raining. Some were carried, some were not. Some died while being carried. On arriving at the designated place, they found the ambulances gone. The wounded had to be left. Capt. Granger died. I had the greatest regard for him. He was so brave, so gallant, and he always did his duty. He

---

44. McAllister sent his battle narrative home in two installments. The second section, beginning with this sentence, was mailed Nov. 1 with no accompanying letter.

belonged to the same regiment (11th Massachusetts) that Capt. Lombard does. The 16th Massachusetts is consolidated with it.

About 10 p.m. orders came for me to move and report my Brigade back to Genl. Mott. I did; and after some delay, we moved out, though at a very slow march. We moved on a very narrow road, along which for miles was a thick woods. I need not say that we were all tired, sleepy, and hungry. We had not had time the whole day to make coffee or eat anything. We had started at 3:30 that morning. After the battle was over, we could not—in our advanced position—have any fires. After marching several miles, we bivouacked for the night and remained there till about noon the next day [October 28]. When the rear [elements] had all come up, we moved homeward inside our works. Thus ended the "reconnaisence," as it is called.

I shall never forget that day or that battle—surrounded on all sides, cut off from the ballance of our Corps, no connection with the 5th Corps. The victorious yells of the Rebels sounded in our ears. Our fate seemed to be sealed without a hope of escape. It was a time of suspence and doubt. But add to all this what was still worse: some of Genl. Egan's men were about out of ammunition and none could be had. There was not a spade or shovel to throw up breastworks. But God pute it in our hearts to work on and trust in Him. We charged down the hill; the enemy became panic-stricken and gave way. We rushed on and received the enemy's front and flank fire. We wavered and fell back. The enemy took courage and followed. We reformed and rolled in the musketry upon them. They faltered and retreated. The day was ours, and we were masters of the field.

Inclosed you will please find a copy of Genl. Egan's congratulatory order. He does full justice to myself and Brigade. You will also find mine to my Brigade.[45] . . . There is no objection to the orders being published, for they are public. But don't let this letter or narrative reach the press. . . .

My Brigade—officers and men—behaved most gallantly, and all bestow upon them the praise due. Genl. Egan thanked me time and again and said I saved his division.[46] He tells all the same story. But God alone saved us all and spared our lives at that critical moment.

---

45. Egan's praise of McAllister is in *OR*, Vol. XLII, Pt. 1, p. 300. McAllister's congratulatory order to his troops is in *ibid.*, 400.

46. Egan wrote his official report on Oct. 31, when his enthusiasm had cooled somewhat. Yet he did state that "Colonel McAllister arrived most opportunely, and his gallantry and the steadiness of his men rendered him and them of vital importance until the withdrawal of the troops." Then, in the list of officers whom Egan recommended for brevet promotion, McAllister's name headed the list. *Ibid.*, 297, 299.

Let the praise go to Him. When it seemed almost certain that we would be captured or destroyed, He rolled back the tide of battle and we were saved. Oh, what reason we have to thank Him for His goodness to us!

I met Genl. Hancock this morning and he complimented my Brigade and myself handsomly. He was highly pleased. You will find that Genl. Egan gets greate credit. Well, he deserves it, and he seems to do me full justice. Remember that I was with the 2nd Division of this Corps in this fight instead of the 3rd, my own. . . .

Maj. Lloyd was on Genl. Pierce's staff in the 2nd Brigade down on our rear and is severely wounded. I told you that the attack there was sudden and unexpected. His wound is severe but not considered dangerous. He will get well. I have got his leave and will send it to him tomorrow. I expect Chaplain Moore to accompany him. His wound is in the hip. He can't set up. The ball is still in him. You need not feel uneasy about him. All will be right . . .[47]

Camp before Petersburg, Va., October 31st 1864

My dear Ellen,

. . . I have had so much to do, fixing up camp and Headquarters on the rear line. Then yesterday came orders that we must move on the front. So last night and this morning we changed again. I am now in my old Headquarters, not the real old headquarters on the Jones farm, but where I was before we went to the left the first time. In other words, we are where the Rebels throw shot, shells, and bombs just to amuse us and them—and where we throw back the same.

Yesterday I had to write out my official reports [of the battle] . . . I feel so tired and worn out now with marching, fighting, making out reports, and moving . . .

Maj. Lloyd started today for home under the care of Chaplain Moore. He has a leave of absence that I procured for him for the purpose of accompanying Maj. Lloyd home. I have not seen Lloyd since I wrote you last, but I heard from him. He was quite lively this morning. He will be at home tomorrow. He is pretty badly wounded, but, it is thought, not dangerously. I hope not.

Your letter of the 28th came this evening. So you heard that we had a battle and were back. The 2nd Corps had done well, which is true. Egan gets great credit, and he is by no means selfish. He comes

47. For more on the wounding of Lloyd, see Marbaker, *11th New Jersey*, 231–32, 357.

out boldly and declares that I saved him and his command from being gobbled up, which is true. All acknowledge that it saved the whole army. Genl. Egan issued a congratulatory order, giving me grate credit, and sent it to Headquarters. It is acknowledged by all to be splendid. In my next [letter] I will send you a copy of it, and also my congratulatory orders to my command. My Brigade, composed of a few old veterans and largely of new recruits, stands A No. 1 in the Corps. We hear of it everywhere we go. All give us praise. Had it not been for the timely aid of my Brigade, and the bold and daring charge we made, all would have been lost. As Genl. Hancock stood below and saw the charge, he cried out: "General Egan is making a charge with one of his brigades. The day is ours!"

He did not know at the time that it was my Brigade. I was under Egan's command. Had Genl. Egan been as too many Generals are—selfish, he would have taken all the credit for himself. But he told Genl. Hancock that I made the charge, saved him, and deserve the credit. He has given it to me.

I have fought many battles but was never so completely surrounded before. It was a miracle that we got out of it. But as I said before, God alone saved us. I was His instrument. The charge broke the enemy's lines and threw them in confusion, and the victory was ours.

One more remarkable thing: my staff and all the field officers remained mounted, rushed into the very thickest of the fight in all parts of the field, and not one of them was killed or wounded. I did not dismount, but I was all the time right up in the line of battle. I personally led the charge down the hill.

I see the papers have this move a "reconnaisance force." Well, all right, it was a big force to make a reconnaisance with. One thing is certain: it was a big thing for the 2nd Corps, but not so with the 5th. Had the latter done its duty, the Rebels would not have gotten through the gap and we would not have been surrounded as we were. . . .

Camp before Petersburg, Va., November 2nd 1864

My dear Ellen,

I finished my long narrative last night and it went into the mail this morning. You have now got most of the particulars of the last march and battle. I wish brother Nelson and Sarah to have a copy. I would also like Lucian Wilson to have a copy. He does so much for us and would take it well to have these facts. [William D.] McGregor of the Associated Press, I see, give us credit. Well, he is about right. He calls mine the Jersey Brigade and says that by that charge I saved the day. He is right again. . . . Had it not been for my Brigade, it is hard telling what might have been the result. I lost over 200 killed, wounded & missing. . . .

It rains today. I had a long ride this afternoon way up to the Yellow House [48] at the Weldon Railroad. By order of Army Headquarters,[49] I am on a commitee of three from this Corps to decide what battles are to be placed on regimental flags. Genl. Miles, commanding the 1st Division, Capt. [R. Bruce] Ricketts, and myself are the three that are to decide for this Corps. Today we met with a similar commitee from the 5th Corps to have an understanding as to what engagements are to be considered a battle. We met Genl. [Samuel W.] Crawford, Genl. [Henry] Baxter, Genl. [Edward] Ferrero, and others in counsel and decided. Now, if spared, Genl. Miles, Capt. Ricketts and myself will meet from time to time and decide what regiments are entitled to that honor. It is a delicate matter; some will be disappointed and dissatisfied. But we will, by the help of God, do our duty. . . .

We are geting all our soldiers home to vote that will not be fit for duty in fifteen days. This will help to swell the vote for Lincoln. We are sending all such to hospitals. An order has come from Corps Headquarters for us to send home veterans only. . . . I think it doubtful about my geting home for election. I hear nothing of a leave of absence for me. Well, I will send a sick man in my place. Tell them that we in the army send our bullets and ballots the same way—against our enemies and in favor of law, order, Constitution, and Union. Let us hear a good report from New Jersey next Tuesday.

My quarters here is right under the enemy's fire. They shell us occasionally. Today the enemy threw a good many. None struck here, but they fell all around us. . . .

Camp before Petersburg, Va., November 5th 1864
My dear Ellen & family,

Last evening I received Hennie's nice long letter of the 1st. No wonder that she, as well as the rest of you, were uneasy on hearing of

48. Known also as the "Blick House," "Globe Tavern," and "Six-Mile House," Yellow Tavern was "a large yellow brick building standing directly on the public road, and was used as a tavern, no doubt, before railroads came in and destroyed all these wayside inns." Wainwright, *Diary of Battle*, 452.

49. See *OR*, Vol. XLII, Pt. 2, p. 968.

the [battle] dispatches before you got the facts. I told you before that Genl. Egan give me full justice as to what I don in that battle—saving him from entire capture. McGregor's Associated Press dispatches told the truth. But [Finley] Anderson, the *Herald* corrispondent, as well as the correspondent of the *Times,* does not give either myself or our Division the credit due us.[50] They are more interested in the 2nd Corps than they are for the old 3rd Corps. You know our Division is all that is left of the old 3rd Corps. While they bestow so much praise on Egan's 2nd Division, they leave out of sight my Brigade and the 3rd Division. We lost about 600 men; Egan's Division lost only about 200. My Brigade alone lost more than Egan's whole Division did.[51] The 2nd and 9th Corps did but little and lost but very few men. But be this all as it may, the official reports give me the deserved credit and the facts are well known here.

I will not be home for the election. I am sorry for it, but no leave came for me and I cannot go. I did not expect that I could. Well, you must make a vote to offset the loss of mine.

It is thought that the enemy may make an attack on us within three or four days. But we are wide awake for them and say, "Let them come." We are massing troops for their reception. . . .

Camp before Petersburg, Va., November 6th 1864
My dear Ellen & family,

Last night, in closing my letter to you, I said that it was rumoured that the enemy would attack us. I closed the letter and looked at my watch, which told me that it was 11:30. Picket firing was very brisk. I had given all the necessary instructions in case of an alarm, and directed that I must be awakened at 5 a.m. I lay down and thought I would take a little sleep.

50. Possibly McAllister was unduly upset over newspaper articles relative to the Boydton Plank Road fight. But it must be remembered that newspapers of the day were the only broadcasters of events. Their reporting and/or opinions carried heavy weight. Moreover, wrote one correspondent, "everybody in the army depends upon the New York papers for knowledge of what the army does. Even corps commanders have no other means of learning details of movements wherein their own corps do not participate." Page, *Letters of a War Correspondent,* 237. The Washington *Chronicle* gave high praise to McAllister for his role in the battle. Foster, *New Jersey and the Rebellion,* 182n. See also *OR,* Vol. XLII, Pt. 1, p. 240.

51. McAllister was slightly in error on comparative casualties. Mott's 3rd Division suffered 712 losses, of which 247 were in McAllister's brigade. Egan's 2nd Division lost 346 men. *OR,* Vol. XLII, Pt. 1, pp. 153–55.

I had not more than five minutes in bed when I heard the *Rebel yell*. I knew the enemy were charging our picket line.[52] Up and out I went, calling aides & orderlies as I sprang out. On reaching the line I found that the Rebels had charged and broken a portion of it. I soon learned that they advanced in line of battle against us. The dash was so sudden that about 40 picket posts gave away. But our brave boys turned on the enemy, recaptured about one half the number, and turned the enemy's flank. A desperate fight ensued—a hand-to-hand contest over the breastworks. Bullets, bayonets, and butts of muskets were used. The battle raged fearfully and terably.

I now sent 50 more men to the assistance of our gallant boys. After a strugle of a short time, we recaptured some more of our pitts. But in the ballance the enemy fought with a stuborness unparallelled. I sent 50 more men to our assistance, and on the battle raged. It was now near dawn. I knew the necessity of recapturing those works before daylight. I sent 50 more men; but before they reached the scene of action, the day was ours. It resulted for us in nearly 50 prisoners, one a Lieutenant.

The slaughter of the enemy, this Lieutenant says, was terrific. They lost terably from our enfilade fire. They carried back the wounded and dead, but some lay on the ground where they fought. The Lieutenant says they had brought picks & shovels, also a cross-cut saw to cut the timbers in the breastworks and turn our works. Of course they had to leave all these tools.

Here comes an order for me to make up a full report of this affair at once—yes, tonight. Oh, I am so sleepy and tired. My report is not interesting. . . .

Camp before Petersburg, Va., November 7th 1864

My dear Ellen,

My time has been so fully ocqupied with the Brigade constantly on the alert and making out my reports that I could not write you.

---

52. On the night of Nov. 5 Confederate Gen. Bushrod R. Johnson's divisions made simultaneous attacks against Forts Haskell and Morton. (McAllister's men guarded the latter.) The purpose of the assaults, stated Johnson, was "to force the enemy's picket-line farther back at points very near our line." The Confederates suffered defeat and lost 60 men. Federal casualties numbered 20 soldiers. *Ibid.*, 23, 909–10, 933; Pt. 3, p. 1205; Marbaker, *11th New Jersey*, 239–45; Lewis, *1st Rhode Island Light Artillery*, 388–89. McAllister's cursory report of the engagement is in *OR*, Vol. XLII, Pt. 1, p. 397.

The enemy fell back with greate loss from our rifle pitts on the night of the 5th, leaving behind their dead, guns, cartridge boxes and intrenching tools. The prisoners say they came to stay but were badly whiped. I managed the whole affair without orders or assistance from any superior officers. My own Brigade alone—indeed, only a part of them—were engaged and don the fighting. It was a complete success and a greate triumph for us. We fought two or three times our number and beat them after they had taken our pitts from us.

The prisoners we took are all South Carolinians. They fought desperately and long before they would give up. The bravery, gallantry, and determination of my men and officers in this contest merits my warmest praise. I kept Headquarters posted as to my progress during this fight. At one time it looked squally; their spirits were down, thinking that my line was gone. But by dawn of day I sent a dispatch that the day was ours, my lines were reestablished, and the enemy had fallen back. Joy beamed on every countenance, and Genls. Mott & Hancock were in ecstasies. Compliments thick and fast came in upon me. Hancock took me by the hand and thanked me, congratulated me on my glorious victory, and afterwards sent it in writing.[53] Generals, as well as newspaper reporters, came and sent up to get the facts. The *Tribune* reporter was here, also McGregor. The Brigade . . . is now considered the best fighting brigade in the Division. The fact is, I consider this last a greater victory than the celebrated charge at [the Boydton Plank Road].

My loss in killed, wounded and missing was only 29 men. A prisoner that came in to Headquarters told Genl. Hancock that they lost 200, and I have every reason to believe that it is true. This evening the enemy sent in a flag of truce to bury the dead. But it was too late; we will have a truce in the morning. They must have lost heavy or they would not have asked for it. Perhaps a general officer is killed.[54] We will see. . . .

They made another attack that night on Genl. Egan on my right at the same time they did on me. They captured from him seven picket posts and a number of prisoners, and he was not able to take them back again.

The enemy are in a state of fiendish excitement. We have reason to believe that they wish to disturb us so that we in the army can not hold our elections tomorrow. They are working in favour of the Copperheads. . . . There are some appearances that the enemy are pre-

53. See *ibid.*, Pt. 3, pp. 532, 535, 548.
54. No general officer on the Confederate side was a casualty in the battle. One Southern lieutenant was captured. *Ibid.*, Pt. 1, p. 397; Pt. 3, p. 530.

paring for an attack on our lines along the river. We may have a brisk time tomorrow.

Genl. Hancock is about leaving us.[55] He goes, it is said, to raise another Corps of troops that have seen service. *I am real sorry that he is going.* Inclosed you will find a farewell song. . . .

Camp before Petersburg, Va., November 8th 1864

My dear Ellen,

I told you at the close of my letter last night that the enemy asked for a flag of truce. This morning at daylight Maj. [William G.] Mitchell of Hancock's staff and I went to the lines and arranged to have it from 9 to 10 o'clock. At the appointed time we met our enemy. Sixteen dead bodies were handed over to them. They were all shot right over the works, most of them in the head. They no doubt carried off many more that lay next to their works. They acknowledge to us that they lost 200 in killed and wounded, besides the prisoners, which amounted to 42 in our hands. In all, they have lost no less than 300, while our loss is only 29 men.

We have gathered up 50 muskets & rifles. That many more are lying there yet, as well as 50 shovels and picks, spades, a crosscut saw, and various other tools. They came to stay. They had commenced turning their pitts; in doing so, many of them lost their lives.

A reporter from the *Tribune* came here today to get the particulars. But on account of the election news, the papers will say but little about it. . . .

I forgot to say to you that the flag of truce today took place right on the large, long grave containing the remains of the large number of men who fell on the day that the mine was exploded. Some thousands of our men in Burnside's Corps fell in that terrible charge. Truly we may say that this is Historic ground.

The brigade that I was fighting with here is a South Carolina brigade of [Gen. Richard H.] Anderson's Corps (formally Longstreet's). So you see I had a fair chance with the hot spurs of that Rebel state.

I have a very hard and hot place here—all the time under fire. . . . We are under arms every morning at 5 o'clock.

The band of the 120th New York is serenading me and has been here for the last two hours. . . .

55. On Nov. 28 Hancock was assigned to command of the newly formed I Corps, to be composed entirely of veterans of two years' service. The corps was to perform guard duty in Washington. *Ibid.,* Pt. 3, pp. 713–14, 728.

Camp before Petersburg, Va., November 9th 1864

My dear Ellen,

It is now 9 p.m. and I have just come in from the lines. Heavy musketry fire, artillery, and bomb shells commenced off to the left and was carried all along the lines. But the Rebels did not break our lines. I think that they opened from their pits alone. Here I am disturbed again and may not be able to finish this letter tonight.

November 10th. It is now 9 o'clock at night. We have had another scare, and I had my Brigade all under arms. It is not a real attack, but we are expecting an attack tonight. The enemy may attempt to capture our picket works. We are ready for them. We are losing men every day in this hot place—always under the shells and bullets. The enemy is in a state of feverish excitement. I do not know what they are driving at. My men are now lying on their arms.

The telegrams here report Lincoln elected. Good for that! Glorious news! But McClellan has carried our little state.[56] Bad for that. But all is right nevertheless.

. . . I have received one of the strongest and best recommendations for promotion from Genl. Egan that I have yet received. I forwarded it to Governor Newell this evening. The General is very generous to me indeed. All the Generals here say I must have the promotion. If I live, I will get it. . . .

Camp before Petersburg, Va., November 11th 1864

My dear Ellen,

I have made inquiry of Col. Schoonover relative to Jacob Sapp and have learned that he has never been seen since we made the charge on the 27th at [Boydton Plank Road].[57] No one saw him fall, or do they know of his being wounded. The probabilities are that he is a prisoner in the hands of the enemy. He is known to have been in the charge. As he is a brave soldier, and as he was not seen to fall, we all think he was taken prisoner. If so, he will no doubt write to his father. As I was not in command of the Regiment, I was not aware of this

---

56. The political views of McClellan and Lincoln were not as contrasting as is generally supposed. As late as September, 1864, McClellan seemed virtually assured of election—a fact even Lincoln conceded. Yet the fall of Atlanta, the cementing of the Republican party, and the Democrats' insistence on peace swung the tide to Lincoln. He won by a popular majority of 400,000 votes and carried all Northern states except New Jersey, Delaware and Kentucky.

57. Pvt. Jacob Sapp of Co. A was not wounded or reported missing at this time.

as soon as I would have been had I commanded the 11th New Jersey. I wish you to give my kind regards to his father and tell him all about it—or read him this letter. I have received his letter and will write him all the facts as soon as I can. Also, I will write some members of his company and get all the information I can in regard to him. It was my intention to try and get a furlough for him to take his brother's remains home.[58]

We have been in such a constant state of excitement since our return from the left that I have had but little chance to get facts and incidents. We are now under a constant fire night and day. And as you are aware, we have fought quite a battle on the picket line. . . .

Camp before Petersburg, Va., November 12th 1864
My dear Ellen & family,

Inclosed you will please find a letter to Charles Sapp, which I wish you to read and hand over to him. I am inclined to think his son is a prisoner, though he may be dead. I have always said we lost more men in that charge than have been reported, and I still think so. It was a gallant charge. I rode at the head of it. God spared my life. We ought all to thank Him for it.

McGregor's Associated Press dispatches has done me justice and told the truth, so far as the charge and battle of October 27th was concerned. But they fell very far from the truth in this late picket affair of November 5th. That, of the two, was the most brilliant. I do not think that McGregor wanted to do us justice at that time, for he is a great Copperhead and would rather see things looking blue around election time. I met him yesterday and told him he did not do us justice. He at once acknowledged it but excused himself by saying that when he made the first dispatch, he had not all the facts. He said that he had sent another one that does us full justice. If so, I have not seen it.

Just think, the enemy admit of a loss of 200 in killed and wounded, besides the 42 we took prisoners, as well as 100 stands of arms, picks and shovels, &c. It is certainly the nicest affair that has come off yet on this line. It is so regarded by Hancock and all that know the facts. Genl. Hancock called to see me today and said that he had recommended me for promotion and that "my appointment would be right along."

58. The only other Sapp in the 11th New Jersey was musician William C. Sapp, who died July 31, 1864, in a Washington hospital. *N.J. Record*, I, 546.

... The roar of musketry is still sounding in my ears. It is almost one continual battle. We lost today a very fine, young Lieutenant in the 7th New Jersey,[59] and also one other man. Not a day goes over our head that we don't lose one or two killed beside the wounded. My headquarters is right under the enemy's fire. We have a stockage to keep the minnies from hitting us. The shells burst all around us but have not hurt us yet, for which we thank God.

A brigade of the 1st Division is lying in reserve here. The other day a youthful looking officer called on me. He said, "I don't suppose you know me."

"No," I answered.

He then said he was James Patterson,[60] John's and Ellen's son. He is a Captain in the 148th Pennsylvania, Beaver's regiment, and lives in Bellefonte. I think he told me he is married. He is a very nice young officer and has the very movements of his father. He made me think of days that are past. Oh, how fast time rolls us towards the grave! . . . Capt. Patterson was astonished to see me look so young. I never looked better than I do now, My health is first rate. . . .

Tell my friends that I rejoice with them over the results of the election. It is a greate triumph and will have very much to do with puting down the Rebellion. All here seem to be pleased with the results.

I have received Hennie's short letter in which she gives three cheers for "Father Abraham." Good for Hennie. Hang out your banner—the Stars and Stripes forever! . . .

59. The officer was Lt. Alfred H. Austin of Co. E, 7th New Jersey. Until a month before his death Austin had been a member of the 5th New Jersey. *Ibid.,* 330.

60. Patterson temporarily commanded the 148th Pennsylvania during the October, 1864, operations. See Muffly, *148th Pennsylvania,* 693–711.

13

Unbuilding a Railroad

CONFEDERATE SORTIES and camp church services occupied McAllister's attention through most of November, 1864. Persistent rumors of a pending movement continued and, early in December, became reality. McAllister's division was placed in readiness for an advance. Simultaneous with marching orders came another development, for a note among McAllister's papers states: "On the morning of Dec. 7, 1864, just as we were ready to move, I received my promotion as Brevet Brigadier General for gallantry at Boydton Plank Road, October 27, 1864."

The December 7–12 expedition on which the new Brigadier embarked was designed to cripple the Weldon Railroad to a point of rendering it useless to the Confederates. The Federal elements involved in the raid were Gouverneur K. Warren's V Corps, Gershom Mott's division of the II Corps, and David Gregg's cavalry. With McAllister himself demonstrating a quick and sure method of destruction, the men ripped up some twenty miles of railroad. A Federal chaplain who accompanied the expedition observed: "The sight presented by the burning road, bridges, piles of wood, and fences, was sad and grand in the extreme—a terrible comment on the waste and ravages of war." [1]

1. *OR*, Vol. XLII, Pt. 1, p. 356.

[542] ✗ THE McALLISTER LETTERS

In spite of hard marches and guerrilla menaces, the raiding party returned with but light casualties. McAllister secured a fifteen-day furlough and enjoyed Christmas at home with his family. In January, 1865, he returned to the Petersburg lines. There he discovered to his disgust that a fellow New Jersey officer had been scheming to secure command of his highly regarded brigade. The ruse failed, much to McAllister's satisfaction.

His letters for the next four weeks are loquacious commentaries on a body servant, brigade chapels, officers' pay, military successes elsewhere, Confederate peace commissioners, and "a snake in the grass" named General John Ramsey.

♣

Camp before Petersburg, Va., November 14th 1864

My dear Ellen,

. . . I am Corps Officer of the Day. I have had a long ride and feel very tired. I have nothing new or interesting to write. Last night Genl. Egan was pretty severely wounded by a sharpshooter.[2] He went out to the picket line to give some orders relative to fixing it up. A Rebel heard him; and as it was a beautiful moonlight night, they could see him. They shot him in the arm. The ball has run along the arm and shattered the bone a little. I am real sorry. Today I was shot at by a sharpshooter near the same place. I was riding along our lines. The ball struck a tree and did not hit me. We lost a fine young officer on Saturday by a sharpshooter. He was giving some instructions to the men on the picket line when he was killed. . . .

Dr. Welling has arrived. I have not seen him. He is at the Hospital, and I will see him tomorrow. All officers are ordered back. I suppose by this that there is going to be a move. I look for a movement soon. If I am spared until after it takes place, I will ask for a leave of absence and go home for a few days. . . .

2. Egan was shot while standing in the trenches. The gunshot wound ended his active service in the field. Floyd, *40th New York,* 236.

Camp before Petersburg, Va., November 18th 1864

My dear Ellen,

We are again under marching orders. What the move is to be no one seems to know. Suppositions are that the move is a contingent one, depending on some other movements—most likely Sherman's army. I think that the powers that be are expecting the Rebels to leave our front and go down to help keep Sherman from going where he pleases. All seems to be in uncertainty. We may move from here tonight, we may not move for several days, or we may not move at all. . . .

I have just subscribed to the Newark *Daily*. This paper has always spoken so favorably of me and I have never patronized it. It has said and done more for the 11th New Jersey and this Brigade than any other New Jersey paper. So a number of us concluded to support it. I intend to give up the Trenton *State Gazette*. I have taken it since the war broke out, and it has don very little for me. In fact, the Belvidere *Intelligencer* is not much better. I think it is a poor investment. Of course, you ought to take it, but it is of no use to me.

This is a dark, rainy night. Troops are moving past here preparatory, I suppose, to relieving us. It is said that some of Butler's troops are to take this line and that the Army of the Potomac is to strike out and fight. Butler's Army of the James don't do much fighting; our army and our Corps has that to do.

Genl. Hancock has not left us yet. He will hardly go until this movement is made. . . .

Camp before Petersburg, Va., November 19th 1864

My dear Ellen,

We are still here. The enemy remains on our front. We may move as contemplated, but I think our moving depends very much on some other movements outside the Army of the Potomac.

Col. Schoonover has received the sad news that Mrs. Schoonover is not expected to live. He has got a leave of absence for ten days and leaves in the morning for home. . . . I sincerely hope he will find Mrs. Schoonover better on his arrival at home. I can well immagine how he feels; as you know, I had a similar treat when you were ill and I was on the Peninsula. But there was one difference: he has got a leave and I could not get one. But things are better now. A wiser and better policy is adopted. Both officers and men can get leaves and furloughs at any time in extreme cases. . . .

Camp before Petersburg, Va., November 20th 1864

My dear Ellen,

. . . I can not say when I will be home. Just as soon as we are settled in camp, I will ask for the leave of absence. But you know that we are under marching orders and could not go. I think that, if I am spared, I will be home for the Holidays. . . . As to Mr. [Henry S.] Osborn, you and Hennie coming down just now, I would be very, very pleased to see you all. But there is no authority as yet to let ladies come down here. They may let them come before long. I can accommodate Mr. Osborn very well; but if you and Hennie come, I must get another tent. There is no trouble about boarding, only sleeping. When we get into winter quarters, we will fix up for you—if Grant lets us go into winter quarters.

We don't know what are to be our movements. To us they are mysterys. The enemy seem to be pressing on our lines, and we have to be very watchful. . . .

Camp before Petersburg, Va., November 23rd 1864

My dear Ellen,

Yours of the 17th came to hand last evening. The weather blew up cold last night, and the ground is frozen. It will freeze much harder tonight. Tomorrow is Thanksgiving. Our boys are looking anxiously for the turkeys & chickens, and with appetites well whet for the good things expected. It is now 8 p.m. and they have not arrived. The teams went to the railroad for them this morning; no poultry yet. I hope the boys will not be doomed to a disappointment. It would be nice for them to have them, it would be quite encouraging to them, and they would say, "After all, the people of the North do think something of us poor soldiers."

My Brigade has had a hard time of it in the trenches. It has rained for three days and nights. There they had to stand all night long, without sleep, and fire away. The enemy try to advance their line and we to prevent them. For two mornings I have had no casualties to report. But all other mornings I have had killed and wounded. The enemy have lost heavily every morning. I have seen them carry them off. A deserter came in this morning and told me that they lost killed and wounded every day—quite a number of them.

We have been expecting an attack from them at this point ever since their defeat on the night of the 5th, and we have been prepared for them. This deserter told me that the other night they intended to attack us in front of their crater fort—the same place they did before, but that they could not get the men to do it. I had strengthened my pickets at that very place. I asked him if he knew anything about Sherman's operations. He said that he did not but that something was going on, as the privates could not get any papers. They placed a guard between their lines and the town to prevent the newsboys from selling their papers. I am in hopes that we will all hear good news from Sherman very soon. If so, the Rebs will have to move, and so will we.

. . . I hope you may all enjoy your delightful church service and Thanksgiving dinner. I wish I could be with you. . . .

Camp before Petersburg, Va., November 24th 1864

My dear Ellen,

. . . Last night I told you how our boys' appetites were whetted up for a Thanksgiving dinner. Well, what do you think? Neither turkeys, nor chickens, nor anything else came. The boat [stuck] fast, rail cars did not come, and all sorts of difficulties. The fact is that it was most miserably managed by somebody. I don't know who. But this afternoon two carloads of poultry and two of apples arrived for our Division. But the apples had to be run on up the road to Warren Station—in order to be switched off, so it is said. As to the poultry, nobody was here to divide it out, notwithstanding wagons and commisaries ready to attend to it. The day is gone, the night is closed, and no distribution yet. So our poor soldiers' Thanksgiving dinner is either in the cars, or just loaded in the wagons, and Thanksgiving is gone. Tomorrow morning, if nothing happens, the boys will get their good things—if those who ought not to have it don't get it first. The citizens of the North have managed well in collecting the articals together, but the ballance of the operations has been miserable.

We had a turkey for dinner today that we bought and which we all enjoyed. But I would willingly have don without it if the boys could have got theirs. But it is better late than never. I have not got my box yet. It has arrived at City Point, and I will get it perhaps tomorrow. . . .

Camp before Petersburg, Va., November 25th 1864

My dear Ellen,

The Thanksgiving dinner did not arrive until 12 midnight last night. It was not distributed until this morning. We had for this Brigade ¾ pound of poultry per man, besides 3 donuts each, also some nice pies, and about 4 or 5 aples to a man. I tell you our boys enjoyed it. It would have don you good to have seen them. It may seem to some a little thing, but it was a greate thing for our brave boys. They had a good dinner. Then they know you care for the soldier in the field. It makes them better soldiers, and they will do their duty more faithfully. The poultry seemed to be nicely cooked; everything was in good order. I think you people in the North deserve a greate deal of credit for your thoughtfulness and energy in this matter. Accept then our hearty thanks for your donation and rest assured that the soldiers feel under lasting obligations for this Thanksgiving dinner, although it did (through no fault of yours) arrive a day too late.

It was interesting to read some of the notes tied to turkeys and to cans—some written to the soldiers by the loyal ladies, and some by little girls which were quite amusing and pretty good. One little girl writes that this was her chicken and quite a pet. She fed it and raised it, but give it freely to the soldiers, &c. This note was from Essex County. Another lady wrote: "This turkey was raised by a full-blooded Copperhead, but purchased by a loyal lady, who gives it freely to the soldiers of her country."

. . . Here is a letter from Patterson, N.J., telling me that the ladies of that place have sent the Brigade a Thanksgiving dinner: turkeys, chickens, pies, preserves, donuts, dried beefe, pound cake, sponge cake, apples, ginger snaps, and lots of good things, all for the Jersey Brigade. Why, how kind they are to think of us. Their boxes are all marked and numbered in large letters for "The Jersey Brigade in Genl. Grant's Army." They also added tobaco & cigars and many delicecies I have not mentioned—all regularly invoiced.

Well, what has become of them is the question now to be asked. I have called my Commisary to hunt them up. We guess, however, that they were sent to New York to Mr. Blunt,[3] Chairman of the Soldiers' Thanksgiving Dinners. He attended to the shipping, &c. The boxes were tumbled in all together. Some other brigade has got our good things, while we got from the general pile. . . .

3. George W. Blunt was a publisher, advocate of the free-soil cause, and active member of the Union League Club in New York City. Late in October he suggested that the people of New York provide all soldiers in the field with "a grand Thanksgiving dinner." The plan captured popular sentiment. That the dinners were happily received is borne out in Bartlett, *12th New Hampshire,* 252–53; Tilney, *My Life in the Army,* 154–56; de Trobriand, *Army of the Potomac,* 685–86. New York *Daily Tribune,* Oct. 31, 1864; James J. Heslin to James I. Robertson, Jr., May 21, 1964.

At City Point there was such a pulling and hauling and breaking open of boxes, &c. Regiments near that place got three times their share of things, which is always the case. We must conclude that the Petterson ladies' donation has gon somewhere else. We will try and find out, then write and thank them whether we get it or not. We got a good supply of turkey—over 2,000 pounds for my Brigade, besides the things before mentioned. Everybody was pleased.

Today I was Corps Officer of the Day. I have a report to write in the morning, so I must retire. . . .

Camp before Petersburg, Va., November 26th 1864

My dear Ellen,

Thanksgiving is not over with us. Today we received for this Brigade 800 more pounds of turkey besides other eatables. They was distributed among the men. I have not come across the Patterson donation. I guess that it was thrown into the big pile at City Point. Well, all right, just so the soldiers gets their donations.

My box arrived this evening. All is in good condition. I will cut the cake tomorrow for dinner and also use some of the nice butter. . . . One thing I would like to have had: a couple of nice red flannel bandages. These that I have are worn so that they are not comfortable. But you can have them for me when I get home, if I get there in any reasonable time.

Genl. Hancock has left us today. We are real sorry to part with him. In bidding good by to me, he said, "Colonel, you will have the star in a few days."

"Thank you, General," was my reply.

Major General Humphreys takes his place.[4] In congratulating him on taking command of this Corps, I was told by Humphreys: "Colonel, you have the star."

"No," said I. "General, you see the eagle yet."

"Well," he said, "you may say that you have it, for it is coming."

Of course, I thanked him. You know that he is a good friend of mine and a year ago give me a strong letter of recommendation for promotion. While I am sorry to loose Genl. Hancock, I am glad to have Genl. Humphreys.

4. Of Humphreys assuming command of the II Corps, Col. Lyman stated: "He is in high glee at going, and will be in despair if a big fight is not got up for his special benefit." *Meade's Headquarters,* 279.

I have just received a letter from Col. Schoonover, telling me that his wife is geting better and that he will be back at the end of his leave of absence. I am truly glad that she is better. . . .

All night long the sound of musketry sounds in my ears. We have to keep up firing all night to prevent the Rebs from taking the line at this place. It is an important point and the enemy want it. We are determined that they shan't have it. We lose men every day, but not near as many as the enemy do. We frequently see them carrying off their wounded. . . .

Camp before Petersburg, Va., November 27th 1864

My dear Ellen,

This is the Sabbath night; and before I retire, I thought I would write you a few lines.

This morning I concluded I would go over and hear the Chaplain of the 120th New York, Mr. Hopkins,[5] preach. The time was 11 a.m. Just as I was starting, the church bells of Petersburg commenced ringing. They have been silent for a long time. But as we don't shell the town anymore, they hold church and ring their bells. I marched along on the Baxter road, leading towards the town. But I did not go far till I came to the 120th New York. I thought it most prudent not to go to Petersburg to church but to stop and hear Chaplain Hopkins, which I did. He commenced; and as he got fairly started, the Rebs opened up their long-range guns in this direction. This was answered by our forts with compound interest. During our whole service there was a lively cannonading kept up. But as there was nobody hurt, it did not disturb us. The Chaplain finished and closed as though nothing was the matter. I call that holding Divine Service under fire. I was wondering how you would like to come to church here?

We have had more firing today than usual—and a greate deal at this hour. They are mad at us, and we don't give them much rest. We have them pretty well down and intend to keep them down, if it is possible. They would like to have our picket line so we could not anoy them so much with our fire. But I don't intend that they shall have it. . . .

---

5. Henry Hopkins was the 27-year-old son of Mark Hopkins, president of Williams College. As McAllister implied in a subsequent letter, Chaplain Hopkins tended in battle to substitute martial for spiritual ardor. He was unquestionably one of the most patriotic zealots in the army. See Van Santvoord, *120th New York,* 143, 159–61.

Camp before Petersburg, Va., November 28th 1864

My dear Ellen,

... Nothing new here but firing away in the front. Nothing indicates a move yet, though the order may come when we least expect it. ... I think I shall, if spared, get home sometime before Christmas—if we don't have to pull up stakes and go into active campaigning. If so, I may not be able to get off. If we settle down in winter quarters, it is most likely I will be able to visit you. Only one Brigade commander from a division can leave at a time, and I think I can get the first chance. I will try for it at any rate when the time comes for leaves & passes to be granted. They are only granted in extreme cases now—sickness and very important business. ...

Three Rebel deserters came in last night. All tell the same story: they are tired of the war, &c. These were Alabamians. Desertions from the enemy are very numerous now since the election. And I am sorry to say we lose a good many from our army deserting to the enemy. Poor miserable conscripts, bounty jumpers, and forigners who have no interest in our Government, country or cause. One native-born is worth a dozen of them. ...

Camp before Petersburg, Va., November 29th 1864

My dear Ellen,

This is the last letter I will write you from this place. We have orders to move tonight. We are to be relieved by the 9th Corps. I think it is nothing more than to change places with the 9th Corps. They had the extreme left of this army—from the Yellow House to the left, all beyound the Weldon Railroad. This is, and has been, a very hard place and very severe duty for the men. The 9th Corps had it easy. Now I think it is a change to give us a little rest and time to drill. We will see. It may turn out to be some kind of move, but I think not.

I am very glad to get out of this place. We are under fire all the time and have lost quite a number of men. I am sorry to say a large number of deserters (the bounty jumpers) have gone to the enemy. ...

Col. Schoonover has not come back yet, but I expect him tomorrow. ... I have nothing new to tell you. I think, if I am spared, I will get a leave to be home on Christmas. ... But we must not expect too much or we may all be disappointed. ...

[550] ✗ THE McALLISTER LETTERS

Poplar Spring Church,⁶ Va., December 1st 1864

My dear family,

My last letter told you we were about to move. We came up here yesterday but did not settle down until about the middle of the day, having located two or three different places. But we seemed so crowded that we were crying: "More room!"

So this morning I brought my Brigade out in front of the works and am getting it nicely fixed. I have my Headquarters in front of the Brigade. If we stay, I will soon be fixed up very nicely. My tent is right up beside a house—an old house with a very nice family living in it by the name of Tucker.⁷ It is on the Vaughan Road. The old gentleman, his wife, three girls (young ladies), and two small boys constitute the family. They own this property but are poor, of course, as all in Virginia are poor. But they are good Union people. The old gentleman has taken the Oath of Allegiance and gets his living for himself and family from our Commisary. They have two or three cows, have no feed for them, and, of course, can't get any milk. They are not of any use to us or the family. . . .

We received orders today to be in readiness to move at a moment's notice to . . . support Genl. Gregg, who has gone out on a cavalry reconnaisance.⁸ We have not been called on yet, but it is possible that we may.

Col. Schoonover has not arrived yet. He is behind time. Dr. Welling is writing and shaking the table. He sends his kind regards. . . .

Camp Poplar Spring Church, Va., December 3rd 1864

My dear Ellen,

This is Saturday night and very late. I write to inform you that there were no letters from home for two or three evenings. What is the matter? You know I want letters daily from your Headquarters. . . .

Genl. Gregg did well at Stony Creek—170 prisoners, 30 mules, a large amount of corn, feed, &c., 2 guns captured—all with little or no loss. This is a good haul. Stony Creek is a station on the Weldon

---

6. Poplar Springs Church lay four miles southwest of Petersburg between the Squirrel Level and Vaughan roads. *Official Atlas,* Plate XCIII, Map 1.

7. The Tucker farm, three-fourths of a mile southeast of Poplar Springs Church, is clearly marked in *ibid.,* Plate LXVII, Map 8.

8. On Dec. 1 Gen. David M. Gregg's cavalry division attacked and captured Stony Creek Station. Gregg reported taking 190 prisoners, 8 wagons, 30 mules, and large quantities of corn and hay. *OR,* Vol. XLII, Pt. 1, pp. 610–11, 854.

Railroad below here, where the Rebels tranship their supplies to feed their army at Petersburg.

The Misses Tucker, our close neighbors, were out riding today. Three young officers came up today with three horses and side saddles. While the ladies were getting ready, three more came with horses and saddles. But as they could not all have them, the first three got the prize. Where the side saddles came from I don't know. This family, like all Virginia families since the war, are very poor. They have all got the jaundice from eating army hardtack and salt pork. They are looking badly. I was glad to see the poor things out riding to get a little fresh air.

I was Corps Officer of the Day and have had quite a ride. I feel somewhat tired, so you must excuse this dull letter. Everything is dull here just now.

I have just got a chimney built to my tent without stones or brick—with mud and mortar. I have a nice cozy fire in it that makes me quite comfortable. No stone is in this country, and very few bricks are to be had. We get brick only when we tear down a house that has been deserted by the inhabitants. Many such houses have been used to make our officers & men comfortable. . . .

Camp Poplar Spring Church, Va., December 5th 1864
My dear Ellen,
. . . This evening the Division Band came down and give me a fine serenade. It is a splendid band. I wish you could hear it.

There is not much news here, only that the 6th Corps has arrived, except one division, and that is on the way. They have relieved the 5th Corps. What the 5th is going to do I don't know. But I suppose we will have an important move soon. If there is a move and a fight, of course the 2nd Corps will have a hand in it.

Our men are geting nicely fixed. They have good huts and comfortable quarters. I do hope they will enjoy them, for we need rest. . . .

Camp Poplar Spring Church, Va., December 6th 1864
My dear Ellen,
We are again under marching orders. We break camp and move off at daylight tomorrow morning. We are the only division of our Corps that moves at this time. You know that we are the cavalry division—always on the trot. Where we are going I don't know, but

I understand we are going with the 5th Corps. So we fight with it this time. Before this reaches you, you will hear from us. We are as yet in the dark as to our movements, and it is best that we are.

Mr. & Mrs. Fay, together with Miss Gilson, our friends in the Sanitary Commission, were here today. They came all the way from City Point to see us. They intended to stay a couple of days; but as we are about to move, they have left and are on their way back down to City Point. . . .

Camp near Weldon Railroad, December 14th 1864

My dear Ellen,

The evening of our return from the greate raid [9] I wrote you a hasty penciled note and said among other things that we had just received new marching orders, &c. The next morning we received orders to go into camp and make ourselves comfortable, which we are trying to do. But it is not the new camp which we had just built and left. We have laid out a new camp here and are at work lower down towards the Yellow House. It is very discouraging to men to build a camp, get comfortable, then leave and return to a new place to fix up. But such is life in the army, and we must not complain.

I wrote to Sarah last night and could not write you. I am now sitting in my tent beside a nice cozy fire, with a new chimney just pute up, and I will try to tell you something about our long march. But whether I will be interesting is for you to judge. It depends much on how I feel before retiring to the slumbers of the night.

On the morning of December 7th, at 1:30 a.m., our column was in motion. The 5th Corps was in the advance of us, with the cavalry in front of them. I brought up the rear. After a march of a few miles, it began to pour down rain. This made the marching hard. We struck the Jerusalem Plank Road with our faces towards Weldon in North Carolina. Our march was very rapid; the road was lined with straglers.[10] We were soon through our outposts, far in the enemy's country, cut off from our communications, with guerillas all around us. We had but few halts, and short ones at that. After dark we arrived

9. This was the Dec. 7–12 expedition against the Weldon Railroad. McAllister wrote his long account of the expedition in the Dec. 14–17 period, in lieu of his regular letters home.

10. A member of the 11th New Jersey recollected: "We had not marched many miles before it began to rain heavily, making the marching extremely tiresome. The march was a very rapid one, and the halts few and short. Heavily loaded as the troops were with blankets, overcoats and extra clothing necessary in winter, the rapid marching told heavily upon them, and the roadway was soon lined with stragglers." Marbaker, *11th New Jersey*, 252.

at the Nottoway River and crossed it. We crossed on a pontoon bridge laid by the head of the column before we reached the river. We bivouacked on the opposite bank. We had now marched about twenty miles through rain and mud. The storm now ceased, the dark clouds broke away, and the stars made their appearance. We closed in mass and laid down as tired soldiers to enjoy the sweet slumbers of the night—to dream of home and friends far away, regardless of the danger around us.

December 8th. All were up before daylight, with campfires burning brightly. Breakfast over, at 6:30 the column was in motion. All had crossed the river except a large number of straglers. They were then taken back by some of our cavalry, who had orders to gather up all who had not crossed the river and take them back to camp to prevent them from falling into the hands of the enemy. Pontoons were taken up, loaded, and moved with us. The day was fine—beautiful country with some fine houses, women & children, no men, the latter all either in the army or acting the part of guerillas. They would flee to the woods and swamps until we passed, then rob and murder our soldiers and strip them of every stitch of clothing, while the women would plead for safeguards to protect their property.

You ought to have seen the poor slaves—old and young, men and women—running out to meet us and hobbling along to the "land of liberty." When asked where they were going, they would answer: "Going with the Union Army!" They know that our flag is the flag of liberty and not oppression. One man and all his family (except one little girl) were fleeing from their masters and had reached the road. But the thought of leaving the child behind caused the old man to cry out: "God bless you! God bless you! Oh, get my daughter, my daughter! I will pay you for it! I will do anything! Get her! Get her! God help you!"

One of my aides rode up to the house, procured the child, and delivered it to the parents. I cannot describe to you the happiness of that family, some nine in number, and a happy group. They stood in the road as our column was passing, with a fair prospect of soon geting to the land of liberty.

What was still more amusing to me was the deep interest taken by Col. [Francis] Price of the 7th New Jersey to have them cared for and got into a wagon. You know the Colonel is a son of Ex-Governor Price [11] of our state. His father and family are greate Copperheads.

11. Rodman M. Price was governor of New Jersey from 1854 to 1857. He also represented the state in the unsuccessful Peace Conference of 1861. His son, Francis Price, Jr., commanded the 7th New Jersey.

The Colonel is a Democrat but not a Copperhead. In fact, I think he leans to our side. He is a good clean man, a fine officer, and very brave. I like him very much.

After a long, hard march, we arrived at Jarratt Station on the Weldon Railroad and learned that our cavalry had already driven the Rebs away, burnt the station and bridge, cut the telegraph, and were busy destroying the road. We now bivouacked for the night so as to be ready for hard work in the morning. The north wind blew fierce and very cold; the ground froze hard. Large fires were built, the light of which, together with that of the burning [rail]road, aluminated the country around us as well as the clouds above. All this made the scene grand and sublime. But we were soon all fast in the arms of slumber. To be continued. . . .

December 9th, Friday morning. As I awoke from the sweet slumbers of the night, before the dawn of day, I heard the cold north wind blowing at a fearful rate. The campfires had all been rebuilt at an early hour, as the soldiers could not sleep well for the cold. A cup of hot coffee and breakfast was over. As soon as daylight appeared, we were formed and moving down the railroad past that portion already torn up and destroyed. After moving a couple of miles we came to the track not yet touched, and I was ordered to commence work.

As we were moving to take our place to destroy the railroad, Genl. Mott rode to me to give me instructions as to how I could best accomplish it. After this I gave him my plan. As I was a builder of railroads, I thought I ought to know how to demolish them, to which he consented. I then placed my whole Brigade in single file, with here and there a small reserve to assist in case of necessity. I then gave an order not known in tactics and not taught at West Point: "Take hold!"

All the Brigade stooped down and took hold of the end of the [cross]ties. The next order was: "Turn over!" And in a few minutes the road was lying upside down, with the ties on top of the rails. A few minutes more and the road was torn up, piled up, and on fire. In a little while longer we had the rails bent and twisted.[12]

The cavalry, who had been pounding away all night, making but little progress, was utterly astonished and looked on in wonder. I need

---

12. "Never was a railway more completely destroyed," a young soldier stated. "As far as the eye could see down the road were men in blue, divested of weapons and accoutrements, prying and wrenching and tearing at iron rails and wooden ties." Harry M. Kieffer, *The Recollections of a Drummer-Boy* (Boston, 1883), 316–17.

not say that all adopted this plan, and the work was soon accomplished.

During this time our pickets brought me 1 prisoner, 19 head of cattle, and 2 mules.

In my rear stood the nice house of a Mrs. Greggs.[13] (No men, of course.) She complained of the cavalry stealing thousands of dollars in gold from her, besides robbing her of everything. I stopped this plunder by giving her a safeguard. In a short time one of her outbuildings was in flames; and as I looked up, I heard the firing of small arms and supposed that the enemy were on us. But it turned out that arms had been deposited in this outhouse and, for this reason, it was burnt. While burning, the arms went off. These were the arms used by these people when they acted the part of guerillas. After this I give myself very little trouble about a safeguard for her.

We now moved on further down the road. I deployed my Brigade once more along the Railroad for its destruction. In about three minutes I had over a quarter of a mile upside down, and in half an hour it was entirely destroyed. Then we took another piece and don the same with it. Thus we worked, and thus the whole Division, as well as all the 5th Corps, worked until about 9 p.m., when we received orders to bivouac for the night. We did, and all laid down to rest.

We were then informed that the object of our movements had been completed and that at daylight we would commence our return. The order of our march was given. [General Samuel] Crawford's division of the 5th Corps, with one brigade of cavalry, would bring up the rear. We were now far in the enemy's country, within nine miles of the North Carolina state line. To return all this distance without meeting the enemy seemed almost impossible. Our preparations were made to fight in the rear, flanks and front. All except the pickets were soon wrapped in sleep. It began to rain and [sleet]. Large fires were kept up to keep the men warm. As we awoke from the slumbers of the night, we beheld a strange scene for the Sunny South. The trees and bushes were loaded with icesecles; the ground was covered with ice. Here we were in the South, but a Northern climate was around us. It was truly a hard morning to start an army on its long return march. There was mud, water, and ice, and some of our men were almost barefooted, shoes having given out as they often do on a long march—even though new when we started.[14]

13. The Grigg farm was one of two properties by that name a mile south of Jarratt's Depot. *Official Atlas,* Plate XCIII, Map 1.
14. "Many men were badly frostbitten," wrote a Massachusetts artilleryman, "and I saw some, whose shoes had been worn out, marching with bleeding

But a hot cup of coffee and breakfast is over. Then all began to move. We passed the house of Rev. Mr. Bailey,[15] owner of the cotton that was set afire by our troops when we marched past before. Then we struck out from the Railroad. We had gone but a short distance when we heard cannon and musketry in our rear. The enemy were hanging on Genl. Gregg's rear. But he managed them handsomely and repulsed all their attacks. We made short halts and continued to march, though our artillery sunk deep in the mud. The ice still hung on the trees, and it continued cold.

As we were passing a plantation owned by a Mr. Level [16] (who with his son was somewhere in the woods, no doubt with arms in their hands), I beheld a sight which I wish could be seen by every man in the North. Slaves were running off in squads to have the protection of the Union army—old men, young men, old women, young women, and even babys—seventeen from this one house. . . . These slaves, hearing of the Union army coming and soon seeing our glorious old flag—the emblem of union and liberty—floating to the breezes along their highways, snatched up their little all and came running to the road to join our moving column and to march to the land of freedom. They were all either very thinly or very poorly clad. The house girls had old threadbare summer clothes and shawls, given to them by their mistress. They were all colors from the very dark to almost white. One girlie of about sixteen was very pretty, nearly white. You would hardly know there was negro blood in her veins. Another one, a little older, was rather dark. Both called the same woman their mother. The latter had two little children, one at the breast. In their flight across the field to reach us, one of these children was left behind. On hearing this, the darkest girl dropped her bundle and run back to get the child, saying she would carry it herself before she would leave it behind.

Very soon she returned with this child, who had nothing on to protect it from the cold . . . In fact, neither of these children had anything on but a very short, thin, calico dress—no shoes, no stockings. The mother carried the youngest child, and the other small children walked. At this time we had no wagons with us. They were ahead. On marched the veteran troops, and on pushed these contra-

---

feet tied up in old rags." A. S. Roe and Charles Nutt, *History of the First Regiment of Heavy Artillery, Massachusetts Volunteers* . . . (cited hereafter as Roe and Nutt, *1st Massachusetts Heavy Artillery*) (Worcester, 1917), 201.

15. The Bailey residence was on the west side of the Weldon Railroad, six miles south of Jarratt's Depot. *Official Atlas*, Plate XCIII, Map 1.

16. McAllister was probably referring to the Leaville farm, about ten miles by road east of Jarratt's Depot. *Ibid.*

bands to keep up, yet buoyed up by the hope of liberty and freedom. Barefooted, on they trudged through the mud and ice, with smiling faces and with the thought of liberty.

The girls carrying these helpless children soon fagged. We came to a creek. Here my aides each took a child in their arms before them on horseback as they crossed the stream. It was indeed an amusing scene for these military men having in their arms little children with their bare legs hanging down. But a sympathy for suffering humanity required them to do it, and I give them credit for it.

After marching about one mile further, we came to a halt and camped for the night. We built a large fire, put up a tent for the contrabands, give them something to eat, and also blankets to prevent them from freezing. But while their hearts rejoiced at the thought of freedom, a sadness hung around them at the thought of an absent sister.

They told us this story. Some week or more before we passed along, this girl was tied to the whipping post and received 100 lashes from her mistress, after which she fled to the woods and had not returned to the home. Her brother attended to her by carrying her food in the darkness of the night. After seeing the family safe in our hands, the father and brother devoted that night to getting the lost sister, notwithstanding the dangers of the undertaking with the Rebels on our rear. To the joy of this family, before the dawn of day the lost and abused one was restored to this contraband household. The night was very stormy, with a greate deal of rain. But it was not so cold as it had been, and the morning found them quite comfortable.

We will now for a few minutes make a call at this mansion and plantation occupied by Mrs. Leaville and her daughter. It was rather a comfortable looking establishment—hay and grain stalks all around. The father and son had fled to the woods for fear that they would be taken prisoners because they belonged to the home guard, or rather guerilla band. Our soldiers had visited the house and, in their search for liquor, had turned things upside down very considerably, much to the anoyance of Mrs. Leaville. She declared that her husband was "a first rate Union man," &c., and she begged the boys not to touch her smoke house. She insisted on having a guard. But as none of us who could give her one was present, she did not receive a guard to protect her. Lieuts. [Charles F.] Bowers and [William] Plimley, my aides, were at the house and gave these facts. They represent the lady of the house as very ugly, crosseyed, and anything but pleasing in her manner. Her daughter took after the mother in looks. I suppose, however, that the aides did not see this family under very advantageous circumstances, and due alowances must be made. Their slaves

[558] ✕ THE McALLISTER LETTERS

ran off, their horses were taken, and their house was visited by a bad class of soldiers. But such is life now in the South. They rebelled against this, the best of all other Governments, and they are reaping the bitter fruits. . . .

December 11th. All were up and ready for the march at an early hour, and we soon moved off. We had not gone far on the road leading to Sussex Court House when I was informed that the bodies of six or seven of our murdered soldiers lay close together in the woods not far from the road. I went to the spot. It was a sad sight. From appearances they had been stripped of all their clothing and, when in the act of kneeling in a circle, they were shot in the head—murdered in cold blood by the would-be "Chivalry of the South." Oh, what a story for historians to tell! It is a story that will make the blood run cold in the veins of those who read it. It holds up to light the true character of those who are pushing the rebellion to the destruction of our glorious Union. Need I now tell you why our boys burnt buildings? [17] I ordered the men to bury the bodies.

Towards evening we reached the Nottoway River and then halted. Genl. Mott ordered me to throw out two regiments, one on each flank, to protect us from the guerillas that were hanging around us. This order I obeyed. I then took the balance of my Brigade to meet Genl. Crawford, relieve him, and protect our crossing. I was among the last to cross, as I was anxious to see all our men safely over the river. When I crossed, our artillery was firing a parting salute to the Rebels. All was now safe. We marched a short distance and camped for the night.

December 12th, Monday. At 7 a.m. we moved along the Jerusalem Plank Road, reached our lines, and went into camp. Thus ended the Weldon Railroad Campaign.[18]

17. A Pennsylvania infantryman remembered in later years that the discovery of these bodies "had a peculiar effect upon the soldiers. Up to this time there had been no destruction of private property . . . but now, either with or without orders, the men began to burn and destroy every thing within their reach. Even the fences were fired when it could be done. Not a single ablebodied man could be seen along the route; they had fled from the wrath to come." E. E. M'Bride, *In the Ranks* (Cincinnati, 1881), 128–29. See also Lyman, *Meade's Headquarters,* 295–96; Floyd, *40th New York,* 238–39; Craft, *141st Pennsylvania,* 232.

18. McAllister overlooked two final aspects of the campaign. First, the return march through rain and mud was so strenuous that one veteran regiment was subsequently declared unfit for duty. Secondly, and as a result of McAllister's good work in neutralizing the Weldon Railroad, Humphreys recommended the new brigadier for promotion to brevet major general. Lyman Jackman (ed.), *History of the Sixth New Hampshire Regiment in the War for the Union* (Concord, 1891), 353; *OR,* Vol. XLII, Pt. 3, pp. 1000, 1028, 1095.

Camp near Weldon Railroad, December 18th 1864

My dear Ellen,

It is Sabbath evening and I thought I would write you a few lines before retiring. Tomorrow morning I will put in for a leave of absence.[19] I don't know what success I will meet with. Genl. Mott will endorse it favourably, but I do not know what Genl. Humphreys will do. He is very conscientious about going against orders; and according to orders, no leaves can be granted except in urgent cases—sickness, &c. But I will try at any rate. They can but refuse it. . . . There don't seem to be any end to this campaign.

Maj. Genl. Humphreys has made an application to have me assigned to this Brigade. In a few days I have no doubt the President will announce the fact. It has to be approved by the War Department. I am all right on that score. Genl. Mott give a good endorsement in favour of it. Genl. Humphreys is very friendly to me. . . .

Camp near Weldon Railroad, December 20th 1864

My dear Ellen,

I put in for a leave of absence yesterday morning. It was approved by Genl. Mott at Division Headquarters and also by Genl. Humphreys at Corps. I expected it would go to Army Headquarters and be approved by Genl. Meade and come down here last night in time for me to leave for home this morning. But I was disappointed; it did not come. It is now dark and another day past and no leave yet. I begin now to think it will not pass Army Headquarters approved, and that I will not have the pleasure of visiting you. If so, I will be as much disappointed as any of you. The fact is that there are no leaves granted except in cases of emergency, sickness, or important business requiring immediate attention. In order to get home, many men certify to having one or another of these when they do not. I will not do this. It is thought, however, that regular leaves of absence will soon be granted, but I do not think that we are permanently fixed for the winter. We are very likely to pack up and move any hour.

As long as we have Lee's greate army where it is, we will no doubt remain. But the movements in the South may cause that army

---

19. In his request for a leave of absence McAllister stipulated that Brig. Gen. John Ramsey would be in temporary command of the brigade. McAllister, as subsequent letters attest, came to regret this interim assignment given to Ramsey. See McAllister to Maj. William R. Driver, Dec. 18, 1864, McAllister's service file.

to move. If so, we will have to push against them in order to let Sherman have a fair sweep over the South. So I do not feel that we are settled. If I do not get home at this time, it is because important movements are expected. Under the circumstances we must not complain but submit to what is thought best.

. . . I have got a beautiful camp for my Brigade. The boys have got the greate portion of their huts up—and nice comfortable ones at that. I will be sorry on their account if we have to break camp and move again. We want rest and drill so much. . . .

Camp near Weldon Railroad, December 21st 1864

My dear Ellen,

This is a dark, dreary, rainy day. Roads are muddy; everything is dragging, especially my leave of absence, as it has not come down yet. My prospects for geting home at Christmas is very poor. . . . If I do not get home, have Sarah, Wilson and Robert, together with the Major [William H. Lloyd], for dinner, as though I were there. I hope you will all enjoy yourselves and have a Merry Christmas. I long to be with you, but you know that soldiers cannot have what they want or go where they please. We have no time that we can call our own, especially those of us at the front. Bummers in the rear and about Washington can suck the public crib, do nothing, and wonder "why the Army of the Potomac don't move." They get leaves of absences and enjoy themselves generally. But not so with us out here.

All are anxous that I get my leave, and all depends on Genl. Meade. If he says no, "not at this time," I have to stay and give up the pleasure of a Christmas with you.

The glorious news of Thomas and Sherman makes us believe that the end is not far off.[20] God grant that it may be so! If we hold Lee and his large and powerful army here, we are doing a greate deal towards accomplishing the desired end. As long as Lee and all his forces remain here watching us, Sherman and Thomas can go where they please. So you see that we are not idle. In fact, the Army of the Potomac has had much harder fighting than any of our armies. We have lost two to their one in battle. These are facts that few understand.

20. Gen. George H. Thomas inflicted a disastrous defeat on the Confederate Army of Tennessee in the Dec. 15–16 battle of Nashville. The day after McAllister's letter, Gen. Sherman culminated his now-famous March to the Sea by presenting to Lincoln as a Christmas present the seaport of Savannah, Ga.

If my leave comes tonight I will be off for home in the morning. . . .

(Between December 21 and January 5 McAllister was home on leave.)

Eutaw House, Baltimore, Md., January 5th 1865

My dear Ellen,

I arrived here at 5 o'clock this morning and had to remain here until 4 this evening. I could have come in the train from Philadelphia this morning in time and am sorry that I did not do so. I would have had that much more of your company.

This is a first rate house [21] and I have had some sleep. I got my passes and transportation, &c. What is better than all, I have got it free through the kindness of the transportation agent. I can now go from here without paying fair. If I succeed in geting a stateroom on the boat, I will be all right and can have a good night's rest. . . .

Headquarters, old camp, January 7th 1865

My dear Ellen,

I arrived here safely last evening and received a warm welcom from all at these Headquarters. Just a short time since I called at Col. Schoonover's. In a few minutes I was surrounded by several hundred soldiers, and cheer after cheer went far out on the evening air. I said a few words to them of a politick character. It was unexpected to me.

Genl. Ramsey was not at all popular with either officers or men. While I was at home he was doing his best to get command of this Brigade. The President has assigned both him and me to commands, but not to any particular brigade. So Ramsey took advantage of this.[22] Yet I arrived in time to set things right again and have no doubt but all will be right. . . .

21. Built in 1835, the Eutaw House was a six-storied structure which *Leslie's Illustrated Weekly* described as an "extensive and splendid establishment . . . capable of accommodating 300 guests . . . [and] replete with every convenience." It was a favorite stopover for Federal soldiers. Information supplied James I. Robertson, Jr., by the Maryland Historical Society. See also Thompson, *13th New Hampshire,* 441–42; Wainwright, *Diary of Battle,* 493.

22. On Jan. 4 Mott recommended Ramsey—"an efficient and energetic officer"—for permanent command of McAllister's brigade. Humphreys vetoed the recommendation a week later and assigned Ramsey to head the 4th Brigade, 1st Division, of the II Corps. *OR,* Vol. XLVI, Pt. 2, pp. 33, 95, 118.

Camp before Petersburg, Va., January 10th 1865

My dear Ellen,

I have been so much engaged since my return that I have not written to you daily. But I hope to have that pleasure hereafter.

As I told you in my last, Genl. Ramsey was working a high game to get himself assigned to this Brigade. But I am happy to say that he did not succeed. His application returned disapproved by Genl. Humphreys, who said that "General McAllister was in command."

I told you that I called on Genl. Humphreys the day after my return and was satisfied then that all was right. I expect to be asigned soon. You know that the President has asigned both Ramsey and myself but not to particular Brigades. That is left to the Corps commanders. The paper that Genl. Ramsey sent up, no doubt favourably endorsed by Genl. Mott, has not come back—as it should have don —through these Headquarters. They evidently don't want me to see it. But I know from reliable sources that it has been disapproved. Their game is foiled and their plans knocked higher than a kite. So much for intrigue when my back is turned.

It is raining very hard—has been all night and all today. Quite a flood, and it is still raining. Roads are in a terable condition. . . . I am now living in a nice little log house built for me when I was absent. I am very comfortable and have a nice open fire which I enjoy so much. I think of you all frequently and often wish I were home again to enjoy the society of my family. Sunday [23] never gets don talking about you all and what a great place Belvidere is. He tells me that he thought Ginny was a white girl. He wants me to remember him kindly to you all. I forgot to give the servants something as a New Year's present. Ellen, I wish you to do it for me. Don't forget it, also a present to Bridget's boy,[24] my namesake.

I had a very handsom pair of shoulder straps with stars presented to me by a Mr. Taylor, a sutler of the 120th New York. He said he presented them to me as a Jersey man to a Jersey General who, he said, deserved it. I took them and thanked him for his remembrance of me.

I had a much more pleasant trip back here than my homeward one was. I had quite a rest at the Eutaw House, got a fine stateroom

---

23. "Sunday" was the nickname of Tom Anderson, a contraband servant who had accompanied McAllister on his Christmas leave to Belvidere.

24. Bridget was another in a series of house servants employed by Mrs. McAllister.

on the *Bay Steamer,* and had a very pleasant time. It is much more pleasant than to come by Washington. . . .

Camp near Weldon Railroad, Va., January 14th 1864

My dear Ellen,

. . . Well, Brevet Genl. Ramsey has not accomplished his purpose in geting this Brigade. The powers that be thought proper to give it to me. So it is mine, not his. He has, however, been assigned to the 4th Brigade, 2nd Division, of this Corps and has left to take command. I am glad of it, for he is a snake in the grass. There is a greate deal of low cunning about him.

Both officers and men of the Brigade are perfectly rejoiced that I remain in command. Col. Price, who is a warm friend of mine, was just in and told me that this Brigade would have went down if Ramsey had the command and that all are highly pleased that I am retained. Ramsey has got the brigade that Col. Beaver was in—Genl. [John R.] Brook[e]'s brigade, one of the best in that Division. I suppose that he will do his best. His military career has not been very briliant thus far, and he will have to do something to retrieve his past conduct.

I am very comfortable fixed now in a nice little house with a splendid fireplace and walls nicely papered. There is a wall tent in the rear, and a door into it, giving me plenty of room. I have a nice headquarters and, if we stay here, will be very comfortable.

Last night I was Corps Officer of the Day. Ten deserters from the enemy came into our line. We have them com in every night. They will average 50 a week in this Corps alone. Since we have hung and shot some of our deserters, ours have quit going over to the enemy. So the desertions are pretty much on the one side.

We have finished a large chapel in the Brigade and will dedicate it tomorrow. Another one is in the progress of completion. . . .

Camp before Petersburg, Va., January 15th 1865

My dear Ellen,

This is Sabbath evening. We had our chapel dedicated today.[25] We find it very comfortable compared to outdoors. In fact, it is quite

---

25. A description of the brigade chapel is in Marbaker, *11th New Jersey,* 275–76. The same writer observed: "A melodeon had been procured, the music of which, added to that of the choir of male voices, carried us in fancy back to the peaceful Sabbath services that we had enjoyed at our far-away Northern homes." *Ibid.,* 263.

comfortable. It is large and will seat a good congregation. We will have preaching tonight and will have prayer meeting every night except one night for singing and one for a literary society which we have in contemplation to form. The chapel at the other end of the Brigade is not yet finished but will be in a week.

Now I wish Rev. Mr. [Henry] Osborn and Rev. Mr. [William H.] Kirk to make us a visit and preach for us. I can assure them of good congregations. Give them my kind regards and say to them that I shall be happy to have them come and make me a visit. And I will do all in my power to make them comfortable. I have room to sleep and eat them and will be glad to entertain them. Tell Mr. Osborn that I was indeed very much pleased and under obligation to him and Mrs. Osborn for the kindness in coming to see me off in the cars. I have borne in mind the text he give me: Psalm 119, Verse 117, "Hold thou me up and I shall be safe, and I will have respect unto thy statutes continually." It is indeed very appropriate and I shall remember it continually. . . .

8 p.m. I have just returned from church. We had a fine congregation, 300 strong. I think our chapel will prove a greate blessing, and I hope and pray that it may be the means of doing greate good. . . .

Camp on Weldon Railroad, January 17th 1865

My dear Ellen,

I am feeling well this evening and in fine spirits. We had a review today by Brigades and I carried off the palm. My Brigade looked the best and marched better than either of the other brigades. It was highly complimented by Maj. Genl. Humphreys, as well as all the Generals present. . . . In fact, all officers said the same thing, and a very large number were present. Genl. Humphreys said it is the finest brigade he has yet inspected. Quite a compliment, I can assure you. My Brigade did look splendid. Genl. [Thomas A.] Smyth complimented me on the fine appearance of the Brigade. I said that three-fourths of them were recruits. He replied that he would like to see the old veterans, for the marching was perfect. I am proud of my Brigade. The boys learned to fight first and came off with high honors. They are now learning to drill and are not behind, but take the lead in appearance as well as marching. I have issued a complimentary order to my Brigade, and Genl. Mott sent one to all the Division, except for two regiments (neither of them mine, by the way) which he deprives of furloughs for not looking better. My officers and men all go into their drills with a spirit, and they are determined not to be outdone by any other brigade.

We have also received the glorious news of our success in capturing Fort Fisher.[26] This is a very heavy blow for the Rebels and tells greatly in our favour. On, on, the tide of victory runs in our favour. God grant that it may thus continue, and may we all give Him the Glory.

Desertions from the enemy to us are very heavy, while we lose none. Let the draft be filled and we will soon have an honorable peace. . . .

We have formed a literary association in this Brigade. Dr. Welling is now writing a speech sugested by me. The subject: "Our Country Past, Present and Future." I told him that I wanted to stir up the hearts of our men to a higher degree of patriotism, more love for country, and a knowledge of the greate contest in which we are involved. We have too little of this both in the Army and at home. . . .

Camp near Weldon Railroad, January 18th 1865

My dear Ellen,

Until the time I went home, one of the F.F.V.'s lived in my front one mile from us. It was a large family by the name of Wyatt.[27] It consisted of husband, wife, two sisters of Col. Wyatt (married ladies), a married daughter or two, the daughter of his second wife, in her teens, and one or two small children, besides two sons in the Rebel army. The Colonel was very wealthy, a large landowner with many slaves. His home was quite new and large, much better than what are called fine mansions here in Virginia, though they do not come up to our style in the North. This house was very handsomly furnished. The parlour was very large, with a couple of dozen very handsome damask cushioned chairs—the best I have ever seen. There were also two sofas of the same material, two excellent pianos in good order and, in a word, everything else to corrispond. From what we could see,

26. In December, 1864, Gen. B. F. Butler led an expedition against Fort Fisher, N.C., which guarded the river entrance to Wilmington. Butler's offensive was pathetic in its failure. On Feb. 13, 1865, 60 ships under Adm. David D. Porter and 8,000 men under Gen. Alfred Terry loosed a land-sea attack on the fort. Some 2,100 of the fort's 2,500 defenders were captured. The fall of Fort Fisher signaled the end of the last great Confederate seaport.

27. The Wyatt estate was four miles west of the Weldon Railroad, midway between Stony Creek and Jarratt's Depot. See *Official Atlas,* Plate XCIII, Map 1. For other comments on the Wyatt family, see Lyman, *Meade's Headquarters,* 301; Roe and Nutt, *1st Massachusetts Heavy Artillery,* 204.

wealth seemed to be stamped on everything in and out of doors. It had a fine yard, trees, shrubery, roses, flowers, &c. Out buildings and negro huts were the best I have seen in the state.

The first time I saw the place was going to Boydton Plank Road. On our return from there, we halted near this place and sent out pickets. This was the first time I saw the Colonel—a very polite gentlemanly man, showing more than ordinary refinement, and perhaps sixty years of age. He looked much younger, but I am told that he was over that. Some time in the early part of December last, our pickets were advanced and his house came in our lines. He, like all others similarly situated, said he was Unionist. But the family were decidedly *Secesh*. All the inhabitants living in our lines have to take the oath of allegince or go over to the enemy. He pute it off and showed a reluctance in taking it. He assigned as the reason that if he should take it and we should fall back, and the Rebs found that he had taken the oath, he would be hung at his own door. But the stern rules of war never argues the question long. He had the offer to take the oath and declined.

On one of the cold bitter days of this month came the order for he and his family to leave and be placed over the lines. He was alowed only one wagon. A few cavalrymen with the Provost Marshal came and executed the order. The Colonel was sick, but the order had to be obeyed. You may now well immagine the scene in that house. This family were now to turn their backs on their comfortable home and leave all to be confiscated—negroes, houses, lands & furniture. They loaded in the wagon their wardrobes and such articals as they could get in, and bid adieu to that home and its comforts. The wagon was so full that they could not ride. So all walked except the little children, who were carried by the cavalrymen on the horses. They cried "Mama! Mama!" after their old darky nurse who was left behind. She was the only one who desired to go with the family but was not permitted. The day was stormy and snowing. The scene must have been one of sadness and speaks volumes against the folly and madness of the Secesh leaders. But sad as this was, it is nothing to what I have witnessed on fields of battle when *life,* not property and comfortable homes, were sacrificed. They cry out: "Vengeance! Vengeance on the traitors of our land!" What thoughts for reflection.

The Provost Marshal pute a guard on the property and in a few days afterwards commenced packing it. They now have it ready for shiping. It is to be taken to Northfolk [Norfolk] and sold by the Government. I was at the house the other day when they were packing. (The thread I sent you was laying on the burough in the room which had been ocquipied by the Colonel's sister. I remarked to the Provost that it would be a relic that someone in the North would like. He told me to take it. This was a fine large room, with a splendid, large mahogany bed in it.) Everything looked as though the house had been on fire and they had gathered up their clothes in a hurry and left. Feather beds, mattresses and blankets in large numbers were left in the house.

One thing struck me very favorably. In the parlour on the walls hung many fine large pictures, handsomly framed, of the two Mrs. Wyatts. (I told you the Colonel was married twice.) There was also one of his mother. I was told that the family started to carry them but found that they were too heavy and left them. The negroes wanted them and said they would take care of them. I told the Provost Marshall not to let them have them, as they would certainly get into the hands of some soldiers and would be lost, but rather to box them up, mark them well, and keep them for the family. He promised me that he would do so. I hope someday these children will get them.

I have another relic made of little shells in plaster of paris which has been very pretty. It was made years ago by someone in the family perhaps long since departed. It was no doubt designed to hang a watch in—made in the form of a clock case. It was also given to me. It is now on my mantle. It is probable that I may send it to you, if we don't pull up stakes and move in too much of a hurry.

When I look over this land and see the desolation, and see the poverty and misery around me, I can't help thinking how much you in the North are blessed and how much you owe to good government. How thankful we ought to be to God that our lot has been cast there in that happy land. . . .

Camp on Weldon Railroad, January 19th 1865

My dear Ellen,

I wrote you a very long letter last evening about the Wyatt family. Mr. Davis of your town knows all about them. He once owned a farm near this and lived here. He says that the Colonel was Union. The Colonel says that he was the Union candidate at the time the state voted for secession. I have no doubt but that was the case. Yet like all others afterwards, he went against the Union.

Yesterday I sent 250 men to gather corn outside of our picket line from the Wyatt farm, deployed a skirmish line, and advanced beyound the cornfield. They did not meet a single Rebel. They brought in nine loads of corn in the husks and three of oats in the sheaf. Today Capt. Bowers of my staff with two officers went out to the same place. A poor white woman at the house near the cornfield crawled on hands and knees towards them and waved a handkerchief, warning them of danger. Had it not been for this poor woman, they would all have been taken prisoner. The Rebs had deployed out to catch them. She belongs to what is called the "white trash." Our officers sent her some coffee and sugar. Was she not good? She was Union of the right stripe. There are but few like her here. Her poor children are barefooted in this cold weather and suffering for the want of the necessities of life.

Deserters come in still more rapidly. Last night seventeen came into the 1st Division of this Corps—twelve in one squad, with two sargeants among them. We have no desertions from us now. That seems to be stoped and I am glad of it.

All talk of our fine Brigade and its splendid appearance on review. Genl. Humphreys tells all that it is the best Brigade in this Corps. I am proud of it. . . .

Camp near Weldon Railroad, January 23rd 1865

My dear Ellen,

I have just returned from a meeting of our brotherhood or Brigade Church. We had a very interesting meeting and fondly hope to have an outpouring of God's Holy Spirit as we had a year ago at Brandy Station. God grant that it may be so.

There is now very heavy cannonading going on in the direction of Petersburg.[28] We don't know what it is. It sounds to us as if it was about the old place where we used to fight daily. It is now quite brisk. You will see by the papers.

It has rained here for two or three days. The roads are very bad. I am well. No mail for two days. . . .

Camp near Weldon Railroad, January 24th 1865

My dear Ellen,

I wrote you a very short letter last night after coming from a meeting of our religious association. I wish Mr. Osborn and Mr. Kirk

28. What McAllister heard was an artillery duel between Federal batteries and Confederate gunboats at Fort Brady in the Bermuda Hundred area. Cannon fire sank one of the Southern warships. *OR,* Vol. XLVI, Pt. 1, pp. 128, 139, 165–66, 608.

would come down now, as we have such fine opportunities of holding meetings. We have a good, large chapel finished and another one nearly completed. We are having large attendances. Let them come to Philadelphia and the Christian Commission can procure them passes. Or they can get their passes at Washington or Baltimore from the Provost Marshall. They will have no trouble. But if they desire it, I can go to Army Headquarters, procure them passes, and send them to them. But this takes time and I cannot say when passes would come. Yet I will cheerfully do so if they prefer it. I would indeed be very happy to have them both here. You can not come along, as ladies are not permitted to come to the Army of the Potomac. Some women came to the Army of the James, but you know Genl. Butler has his own way about things. How it is now I don't know. . . .

Here comes the mail: two letters from Mrs. McAllister and one from Sarah. Welcom, welcom visitors. I have read them over once and will read them again. You seem to have sleighing; we have rain and mud. . . .

The firing last night, it is reported here, was caused by the Rebel rams coming down to Dutch Gap. Two of them is said to be grounded and are now laying under our guns. We are not yet assured of the facts. The firing kept up all night. . . .

It is cold tonight and freezing hard. I have just returned from a very pleasant prayer meeting.

Dr. Welling was all right on the Ramsey question. He was my very real friend, met me at the depot, and told me all. He was rejoiced at my return. The letter I received he wrote before Ramsey showed the cloven foot. The letter he wrote to his father was written after he had written to me. I have no truer friend than the Doctor —and none more so than Maj. [J. P.] Finklemeier, my Adjutant Genl. . . .

Camp near Weldon Railroad, January 27th 1865

My dear Ellen,

Your letters mailed the 23rd & 25th came to hand this morning. I am truly sorry to hear of Robert's illness. I hope he is well again. You must take good care of him; he is my boy as well as yours, and I feel a greate interest in him. Let me know how he is.

. . . The weather is very cold here today and yesterday. It remains froze all the time—real winter, and this is called the Sunny South.

Brevet Genl. Ramsey plays hob and turning up Jack in his Brigade in the 1st Division—tieing up men, refusing them furloughs, and all kinds of cousin measures to knock the manhood out of them. He calls it discipline, but I call it brute force.[29] He has rendered himself very unpopular. He has native Americans to deal with there, among them Col. Beaver's old [148th] Regiment from Pennsylvania.

The latest news now is that this Corps is going to Wilmington. But I think it is only a rumour.

The Rev. Mr. Rinker from Morristown, who visited the 11th New Jersey last winter, has written a letter to me. He desired to join the 11th as a Private.[30] Fearing the draft, he prefers volunteering. Then he can choose his company and regiment. I have answered him. I told him that I admired his patriotism and that, if he came, I would do the best I could for him. I said I thought I could get a chaplaincy for him in this Brigade, as the 11th Massachusetts has no Chaplain. I would see the officers, then write Governor Andrew, &c. If not, I would get him a clerkship either in the Regiment or Brigade. He is a most excellent preacher.

Next Sabbath we are to have the chapel at the other end of the Brigade dedicated. Myself and staff are invited to be present. Of course we go, if spared. You may think it strange, but we don't hear a profane word uttered in a week—and, I may add, in a month—here in this camp. So much for our morals. Your little boys in Belvidere can beat us in swearing. You have wrong impressions about the morals in our army. We have a moral tone here that is good. I think that my Brigade is a modle one. . . .

Camp near Weldon Railroad, January 28th 1865

My dear Ellen,

I have just finished a letter to Alice, the first one I have written to her [since my return].

I have received the picture of yourself. It is very good except for the eyes. But that is the trouble of taking my picture. . . .

It is exceedingly cold here, a real Northern winter. We have no snow but very, very cold weather. Nothing new here; mails are very irregular. We don't get news until it is old with you.

Ellen, I think that the prospect of Brevets geting full pay is very

---

29. Ramsey was not as stern a commander as McAllister alleged. See Muffly, *148th Pennsylvania,* 160–61.

30. Probably the same Henry Rinker mentioned in footnote 15, Chap. IX.

dull. We are all geting very scarce of money here in the army, as the paymaster has not come along yet. We pay up our month's boarding at the beginning of every month. As I had more to pay for the past month than I calculated on, and as another month's boarding ($40) is due, I am afraid that I will run out before I get more. I will call on you for some. If you send me ten or twenty dollars by letter, it will come good. I will pay it back again. My funds are geting very low. We have many officers here who don't send one cent home.

If passed, the bill now before Congress will help us. It takes off the tax and increases the commutation for rations from 30¢ to 50¢. I am entitled to four rations per day, which will make 80¢ per day more to my pay besides the tax off. This will help. No officers above Brevet Brig. Genl. will get the advance if it passes in this shape. And if we stay in the army until this war is over, we will get three months' extra pay without commutation for rations or forage.[31] . . .

Camp near Weldon Railroad, January 29th 1865

My dear Ellen,

This is Sabbath evening; and before I go to evening service, I thought I would write you a short letter.

We had divine service and a dedication service today in the new chapel at the other end of this Brigade. Genls. Mott and McAllister with their staffs were present. The attendance was not so large as it was two weeks ago at our chapel. The house is not near so large, but it is more comfortable. Chaplain Simpson [32] was here. You remember me writing you last fall of a clergyman who had charge of a congregation somewhere in New Jersey and who was drafted. He came here to this Brigade and played Private soldier untill we got him in the 40th New York as its Chaplain. He is now nicely dressed up and looks well, and he is a good speaker. . . .

The weather is very cold—freezing all day long as well as night. It is almost as much as we can do to keep warm. However, I have very comfortable quarters and have much to be thankful for. My mens' quarters were never better. If they can get wood enough, they can make themselves comfortable.

31. For a concise discussion of the officers' salaries, deductions, etc., see Lord, *They Fought for the Union,* 123–24.
32. The Rev. Benjamin F. Simpson was a 29-year-old Methodist minister who, in October, 1864, became chaplain of the 40th New York. Phisterer, *New York in the War of the Rebellion,* III, 2233.

No mail for me last night or this morning. Our papers have not been up for several days. We feel as though we are out of the fold. I hope I will have the pleasure of reading a home letter this evening. Drums are beating for church. I must go and will finish this when I come back.

8 p.m. I have just returned from preaching and prayer meeting. We had an excellent sermon by Mr. Cline. . . . There is a good state of religious feeling in this Brigade. The morals are first rate. . . .

Camp near Weldon Railroad, February 1st 1865

My dear Ellen,

Your kind letter of the 29th came to hand this morning. I need not repete what I have so often said—that I was truely glad to receive it. I feel much better contented when I hear from you daily.

We are again under marching orders and are likely to move at a very short notice. What is in the wind now we know not. Many are the rumours that are in circulation. It is reported that the enemy are preparing to evacuate Petersburg and contract their lines. If so, we have to follow them right up and may have some fighting soon. But it may only be rumours.

One hundred and eighteen Rebel deserters came into our lines night before last in the 6th Corps alone, and eleven came into this Corps, making 129 in one night. These desertions from the Rebels must tell heavily on their ranks and dampen their spirits.[33] The Rebel Vice President, Stevens, and their old Secretary of State, Hunter, came into our lines on the 6th Corps the same night. They have gone to Washington, but what the object is I don't know.[34] You will hear all about it.

It is very hard for our men to break up the comfortable camp in the middle of winter and bivouac in the cold and wet. But if by so

---

33. During February, 1865, morning reports in Lee's army "became a sickening and bewildering story of desertion." In one ten-day period, no less than 1,094 Confederates disappeared from the Petersburg trenches. Freeman, *Lee's Lieutenants,* III, 623–24.

34. This was the prelude to the Feb. 3, 1865, Hampton Roads Conference held aboard a steamboat and attended by Lincoln and Seward for the North, and by Alexander H. Stephens, Robert M. T. Hunter, and John A. Campbell for the South. The purpose of the meeting was to discuss a possible termination of the war. Lincoln's insistence that a full and unconditional restoration of the Union be the first agreement caused the conference to come to naught. *OR,* Vol. XLVI, Pt. 2, pp. 471–73; *Southern Historical Society Papers,* III (1877), 168–76; Porter, *Campaigning with Grant,* 381–85.

doing we bring the war to a nearer close, we will then have sacrificed to some purpose. . . .

9 p.m. I have just come in from a meeting of our Literary Association and find no new order for me, so I may have a comfortable night's rest. . . .

Camp near Weldon Railroad, February 2nd 1865

My dear Ellen,

Yours of the 29th of January was received last night after I had retired to bed. But notwithstanding the fact that I was asleep, the mail was brought in to me. I wakened up and read your letter. I am always so anxous to hear from home. I am glad that Robert is well again, and sorry that Sarah has gone away. I fear the child will take cold in traveling in such weather.

We are still here; no additional orders yet, though we may get a moving order any hour. We are all ready. There seems to be a very considerable uneasiness manifested on the enemy's picket line—as though they wanted to do something but don't know what. They seem to move away and then come back again. This morning, in the front of our 1st Division, they had pulled up stakes and left. At 2 p.m. they came back again. Our movements depends entirely on the enemy's— or at least I suppose so. . . .

One of my aide-de-camps, Lt. [William] Plimley from Catskill, N.Y., has just come in from a leave of absence of 20 days. He has taken himself a wife since he left. He went for that purpose. He is looking well and, of course, is feeling happy. I am glad that he has got back before we moved, as he is a very brave officer. He was just telling me that so many young men in his town who are laying around doing nothing ought to be in the army. He urged them to come out but they could not see it. He was very handsomly received by the citizens and had a splendid serenade given him. He came in as a Private and by his merits reached his present position. . . .

It is quite cold tonight. We had had very cold weather for this country. . . .

Camp near Weldon Railroad, February 3rd 1865

My dear Ellen,

We are still here, although we are under marching orders. There does not seem to be as many signs of moving as there was for a few days past. The enemy that had disappeared from our front have come back again. All seems as usual. I was Officer of the Day today.

There were no desertions from the enemy last night, and I am sorry to say that three from ours went to the enemy—two from the 2nd Division and one from ours. All were bounty jumpers, just come out to the army. Our friends at home pay big bounties, tax themselves heavily to send these scoundrels out here to fight our battles. They intrust the greate interests of the nation, and free government throughout the world, to *these poor, mean, contemptable scoundrels* whom you can never get into a battle. Oh! When will our people understand the principles of this contest and learn wisdom by their past folly?

. . . I had my Brigade out at dress parade this evening. It looked splendid. After this I had a Brigade drill. I desire to have it continue the best Brigade in the Corps, and I am trying to do everything to bring it up to a high state of discipline. If we remain here to spring (which is very doubtful), and if I am spared and all goes well, I will have a Brigade that can't be beat. Genl. Mott witnessed the dress parade and drill this evening. He seemed to be highly pleased, though his pet, Ramsey, did not command it. Genl. Ramsey himself says that this is the best brigade in the Corps. Now a large portion of this Brigade is composed of new troops, and the question looms up: who drilled and disciplined them? Certainly neither Genl. Mott or Genl. Ramsey—only what Ramsey done with the 8th New Jersey, his own regiment. But if these men do not understand this, others do and give me the credit. . . .

14

The Path to Peace

FEBRUARY, 1865, marked the beginning of the end for Lee's strained defenses at Petersburg. Another attempt by Grant "to grasp with the left hand of the army some of Lee's lines of communication with the South" brought on the February 5–6 engagement of Hatcher's Run (or Dabney's Mill).[1] Federal success here did not come cheaply. Confederates counterattacked violently in futile efforts to prevent this new strangle hold. Three times, a Pennsylvania officer recalled, Southern troops "charged with headlong fury upon McAllister's position"; but the veteran commander's "steady and firm bearing checked the enemy's advance and compelled him to withdraw." In the eyes of many, "Gen. McAllister was the hero of the battle."[2]

No one seconded this sentiment more than the General himself. McAllister fumed when newspapers failed to give proper credit to his command, and he personally berated one field correspondent for his lack of reportorial accuracy.

In the meantime, "demoralization of the opposing force was plainly apparent," a member of McAllister's brigade wrote. "Daily, squads of Confederates would come in and be passed to the rear, this being so common as to excite little or

---

1. Marbaker, *11th New Jersey*, 266.
2. Craft, *141st Pennsylvania*, 236; Roe and Nutt, *1st Massachusetts Heavy Artillery*, 205.

no comment."³ Sergeant Marbaker of the 11th New Jersey added: "Even to the dullest mind the fact was plain that the Confederacy was falling to pieces."⁴

McAllister's command played a minor role in repulsing a March 25 attack by Confederates in the Fort Stedman area. Four days later the Federals launched an offensive of their own. The II and V Corps fought their way to the vicinity of Five Forks, where, on April 1, Lee's overextended lines crumbled. McAllister's long narrative of the Appomattox campaign is a vivid and dramatic chronicle of the Union march to victory.

Following Lee's surrender the II Corps camped for several days near Burkeville, Va., then joined the rest of the Army of the Potomac in Washington for the Grand Review. McAllister's last letter, dated June 12, 1865, was written shortly before he returned to Belvidere and the loved ones who had shared—day by day—his Civil War experiences.

♣

Camp near Weldon Railroad, February 4th 1865

My dear Ellen,

Things had settled down rather quietly, and all seemed to think that the move was off. But about one hour since, we got orders to be ready to move. All are buisey in making the necessary arrangements. We expect to be off tonight. Where I don't know. . . . There is a good deal of cannonading. I don't know what is up. . . .

Battlefield of Hatcher's Run, Va., February 6th 1865

My dear Ellen,

We have had another hard battle.⁵ Yesterday we left camp and came out here. The enemy, as usual, massed and fell on us—nearly the whole force against my Brigade. Thank God we three times rolled

---

3. Hutchinson, *11th Massachusetts*, 74.
4. Marbaker, *11th New Jersey*, 274.
5. McAllister's official report of the Hatcher's Run engagement, dated Feb. 13, 1865, is in *OR*, Vol. XLVI, Pt. 1, pp. 238-40.

back the tide of battle. They charged against us with their lines of battle; each time, by the help of God, we sent them hurling back. The slaughter on the enemy's side was terrible. Our loss was light. All are loud in the praise of my Brigade. Let us all thank God for the victory. Firing has commenced again. I will give you the particulars later. . . .

Bivouack, Hatcher's Run, Va., February 7th 1865

My dear Ellen,

I wrote you yesterday about our fight and battle on the 5th. I was stopped short by some firing. It did not amount to anything— only a small party sent out on a reconnaisance. So yesterday was a quiet day for our Corps. But not so with the cavalry and 5th Corps on our left. They advanced on the enemy, swung around, and had a big fight with alternate victory and defeat. But finally they drove the Rebels back and now hold the position. The 2nd Division of the 5th Corps is said to have done badly. I never did think Genl. Crawford a good officer. It is reported that he commands that Division.[6]

All officers and men are loud in their praise of my Brigade for the gallant manner in which it fought on the 5th in rolling back the combined forces of the Rebels six or eight times my numbers, and rolling them back with great slaughter. It was a victory that few win. All praise to my gallant Brigade, and all are willing to award it to us; and well they may, for it saved our army.[7] Had the Rebels succeeded, it would have been a terrible blow to us. . . . When I give you the full history, you will see the hand of God in that battle in saving us and that important position. I am happy to say that not an officer or man shrunk from duty in that desperate struggle on that day, but all fought with great gallantry in this Brigade. I need not add that I am proud of them. Its gallantry is the theme of conversation. . . .

I don't know what is the next move on the board, but I hope it may be successful. Pray for me and the success of our army and our country's cause.

6. Gen. Samuel W. Crawford commanded the 3rd Division of the V Corps. Although Crawford filed no official report of the action, Gen. Henry A. Morrow of his division stated that one brigade gave way before the Confederates. Another brigade succeeded in stemming the Confederate attack, but at a cost of 23 killed and 180 wounded. *Ibid.,* 66–67, 287–88.

7. Gen. Mott wrote: "The conduct of General McAllister and his troops deserves special mention, having repulsed successfully the vigorous attack of the enemy . . . without any protection; yet all bravely stood firm and inflicted severe loss on their assailants." *Ibid.,* 225. See also *ibid.,* 193–95; Pt. 3, p. 541; Earl Fenner, *The History of Battery H, First Regiment, Rhode Island Light Artillery* . . . (Providence, 1884), 58.

I am well. It is now storming—sleet and rain. We are all out in the pelting storm. But I have got a tent up, in which I am writing, and a fire in the front, around which we are warm. . . .

Bivouack, Hatcher's Run, Va., February 8th 1865

My dear Ellen,

We are still here on this ground rendered memorable by our late achievements. . . . Yesterday was a rather quiet day with us as a Corps. The 5th had some skirmishing but not much. All is quiet up to this time (1 p.m.) today. We have now extended our lines to Armstrong Mill, well onto the battle ground of the Boydton Plank Road. This has been so far a grand success. When time will permit, I will give you full details of our battle, which lasted 2½ hours on the 5th. I will tell you of the coolness of my men and officers and the heroism thus displayed.

One thing I must tell you for the benefit of our friends. The enemy moved on us three times, with three lines of battle. Each time we repulsed them. As I rode along the lines, our boys were singing at the top of their lungs "Rally Round the Flag, Boys," and in the finest spirits imagenable. At the same time they were loading and firing away. It was a splendid sight, highly interesting, and the results proved exceedingly satisfactory. . . . I need not say that we are all feeling well over the victory thus gained.

There is an old lady, living just outside of our lines, on whose farm the Rebels massed their troops before making the charge. Col. Schoonover asked her how many troops they had.

"Oh, they had a million!" she replied. "Never saw so many people in my life!"

They buried the officers in her graveyard and men all over her farm. The enemy's loss was very heavy.

As we have now extended our lines, we are strengthening our works and are going to build more forts and hold this position. We will not go back to our old, comfortable camp. We are once more out in the cold. Well, all right; this Rebellion must be put down. . . .

Hatcher's Run, Va., February 10th 1865

My dear Ellen,

I have been astonished to see the papers today giving all the credit of this battle of the 5th to Genl. Smyth's Division and not mentioning my name or Brigade. Everyone is astonished.[8] Genl. Smyth's Division was not attacked at all and is not entitled to any particular credit. The truth is, he had two regiments on my left on this side of the reserve, a short distance from my left. But they ran back very disgracefully as soon as the enemy approached.[9] I have not seen Genl. Smyth today but can't think he will wish to take the credit of what is not his. McGregor, the Associated Press corrispondent, was just here and says he will correct it. I expect him to do it. . . .

Camp Tucker House,[10] Hatcher's Run, Va.
February 11th 1865

My dear Ellen,

I have but a few minutes to write you. Officers in this and other brigades and divisions are indignant at the press reporters relative to this battle. They all say it is my battle and that I ought to have the credit for it. Genl. Smyth says so himself. I hope he will have the manliness to come out and say so.

You know that the corrispondent of the Philadelphia *Inquirer* lauded Genl. Smyth to the skies when it was not Smyth at all but me that did all that. The New York *Times* copied it, as you no doubt have seen. The *Inquirer* now says that I saved the day "by coming up in time." Why, the battle was mine and mine only, from first to last, and *all* the time. The enemy's whole force was hurled against me, and I sent them flying back three different times. Genl. Humphreys is in a bad humour about it. He will call the reporters together and have it corrected. All cry out: "Shame!" But all agree about one thing: the reporters stay so far behind [the lines] that they don't know the facts and gather up scraps from skedadlers. As I had no such cattle this time, and as Genl. Smyth had plenty of them, I was not mentioned.

Here comes Genl. de Trobriand and Genl. [George W.] West with Mr. [William J.] Stark, the *Herald* corrispondent. We talk over the matter. I pitch into Mr. Starks, backed up by de Trobriand and

---

8. A copy of Col. John Schoonover's strong refutation of these newspaper reports is in the McAllister Papers.

9. Naturally Gen. Thomas A. Smyth, who commanded the 2nd Division, gave an entirely different version of his unit's role in the battle. All of his regiments saw action and allegedly performed with valor. *OR*, Vol. XLVI, Pt. 1, pp. 212–13.

10. The Tucker House was ten miles due south of Petersburg, near the point of a neck of land between the Weldon Railroad and Hatcher's Run. *Official Atlas*, Plate LXXVII, Map 2.

West. Mr. Starks acknowledges the mistake and has promised to rectify it in my favour. . . . Mr. Starks says that the *Herald* of the 8th gives me the credit and says he will send me one. . . .

Camp at Tucker House, Hatcher's Run, Va.
February 11, 1865

My dear Ellen,

On the morning of [February] 5th, according to orders received the previous evening, we broke camp and were soon on the march towards the left. All were anxous to know where and what was the move on the board. Genl. de Trobriand, with the 1st Brigade, lead our Division. Brevet Brig. Genl. West, in command of Genl. Pierce's Brigade (the 2nd), was next, and the old 3rd, under my command, brought up the rear. On arriving at the picket line, we were joined by our several picket details except for a very few left to guard the old line. Here we discovered that the 2nd Division was formed and ready to fall in and take the lead, which they did. These two Divisions, the 2nd and 3rd of this Corps, were now on the march for Hatcher's Run. The 1st Division was left on the old lines and did not march with us.

After going a very short distance the 1st Brigade, Genl. de Trobriand, took the lead of the whole and moved forward towards the ford. Here this Brigade encountered the enemy. Their resistance was but slight to what he expected, and this Brigade was soon across and in possession of the enemy's works at the ford. The 2nd Division moved to the ford but did not cross the stream. It wheeled to the right and moved forward in line of battle with their left on [Hatcher's] Run. At the same time, I was ordered to wheel my Brigade to the right and take up a position in line of battle at the Tucker House (this place where we now are) and throw forward a skirmish line well to the front. I was to keep a sharp lookout for the enemy, and also to have my skirmishers connect with those of Genl. Smyth's 2nd Division.

All this was soon accomplished and my line of battle established across the road leading past this house. After riding around and reconoitering, I returned to my command. In the meantime, I had made a connection with the 2nd Division skirmishers but not with the line of battle, as there was more than a half a mile distance between Genl. Smyth's line of battle and mine. You now see that I was separated from the other two Brigades of this Division by Smyth's Division being placed between us. And long intervals it was at that. Genl. Mott was down at the ford with the other two Brigades.

Our men were now resting. All was now quiet with us, with only a few shots down in front of the ford. At 12 noon Genl. Humphreys and staff came and took a survey of our position. He ordered me to put up breastworks at once. On giving the order to my men, they jumped at it with a will. Rails and timber were carried with dispatch and dirt was thrown up with an unparaleled rapidity. I never saw work go on more satisfactory. My men had now been formed in line of battle (two ranks). But finding that the works for our safety ought to be extended down to a swamp, I had them placed in single rank. A bystander could see our lines growing further and further to the right every time he passed his eyes in that direction.

About 2 p.m. I received an order from Genl. Mott to throw our regiment across a road that crossed our lines a considerable distance from my left and which ran down to Armstrong Mill. I at once repaired to the spot. I found it a very important point and one that the Rebels could come through without much difficulty. The woods and roads afforded them every facility. I ordered Col. Price to move his [7th New Jersey] Regiment and pute up works. He had his Regiment placed in position and works nearly completed when I took a ride along the line. I was speaking to my Adjutant General [Finklemeier] relative to the time the troops were thus engaged and how well they worked—only three and one half hours from the time they commenced work.

A few minutes after this, an aide from Genl. Ramsey rode up to me with a telegram from Corps Headquarters that Ramsey's Brigade was to relieve me. It did not say that I should move to the left, only that he was to relieve me. To obey this order, I had to take out my troops and let Ramsey go in. I well knew that Genl. Ramsey could not ocquipy my whole line, and I was fully aware of the danger of the enemy braking the gap between Genl. Ramsey and the 2nd Division. I at once ordered my Adjt. Genl. to go and see Genl. Mott, tell him all, and receive orders. During his absence I massed my Brigade and awaited orders.

Maj. Finklemeier, my Adjt. Genl., soon returned with orders to go into line of battle on the left of Genl. Ramsey. He could not fill much over half of the works I built. I had command of the movement. It was 4:30 p.m. when I heard the firing in my front by the pickets. These pickets were not mine, for I had moved from the rear of my pickets. The pickets in my new front belonged to the 2nd Division. The firing was coming very rapidly towards my front. Our pickets were not firing as they should have don, but were running back with the Rebs after them.

I ordered: "Double quick, and on the right by file into line!" I moved with a rapidity not usual and formed my line along the works that I built but not occupied by Ramsey—all under the fire of the advancing lines of the enemy. All my regiments were now behind breastworks except the 8th New Jersey, commanded by Maj. [Henry] Hartford. The first few companies of it had also filed in. But the works run out, and the [rest of the] men had to be placed in line of battle without works and under a most gauling fire. They faltered for a moment; myself, Adjt. Finklemeier, and aides rushed in and urged them to stand fast and extend their line to the left.[11]

A little to the left of my now extended line were two regiments of the 2nd Division (Genl. Smyth's), which had been placed there to support the pickets. I depended on these two regiments to stand fast and help to fill up the long gap between myself and Smyth. But to my utter astonishment they give way on the approach of the enemy and left me to fight the battle alone.

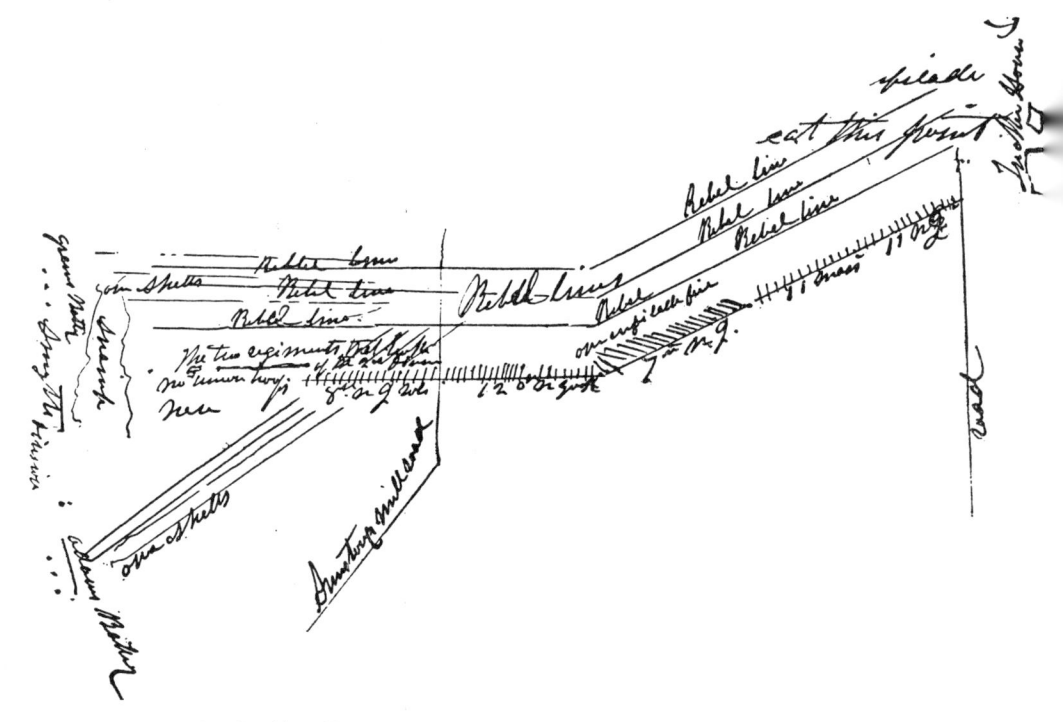

[11]. In his official report McAllister stated that Hartford's men "had no works and were exposed to a terrible fire in this unprotected position, but they stood nobly and fought splendidly; not a man of this regiment . . . left for the rear." *OR*. Vol. XLVI, Pt. 1, p. 239.

I at once saw that here the battle must be fought with energy or all would be lost and a terable disaster to our army would follow. The distance now between my Brigade and Genl. Smyth's 1st Brigade on my left across the swamp was at least 300 yards. Through this the enemy might sweep with their heavy columns. I rode along the line towards the center, encouraging the men to "stand firm and the day will be ours." I talked to them as I rode along. I passed the first two regiments on the left, the 8th New Jersey and the 120th New York. I reached the 7th New Jersey (Col. Price) and ordered him to give an oblique fire so as to enfilade the enemy's lines. My works turned here and gave me a splendid chance.

[I have drawn] a rough sketch which may enable you to get a better idea of the position. You can see the 7th New Jersey pouring in a terable enfilade fire and the artillery across the swamp helping me to keep the enemy from passing into and through the open space. Adams's Battery crosses my 7th New Jersey fire at nearly right angles, while Green's Battery was considerably more of an enfilade.[12] You can now see what a terable fire we concentrated on the enemy. You may suppose that our artillery would strike my line. It did to some extent, but not to damage.

The Rebels recoiled under our deadly fire and the firing ceased in a measure. This give our boys courage. In a few minutes more the well known Rebel Yell rolled out on the evening breeze and on rushed their massed columns. My line now opened a most destructive fire, so much so that it is said to be unequeled since the Wilderness battles. Again the enemy were repulsed. The first slacking some, I rode again along the lines, encouraging the men to stand firm and the day would be ours. They all struck up the song, "Rally Round the Flag, Boys." The Rebels replied: "We will rally round your flag, boys!"

The heavy firing had now ceased for the time being, but the pause was of short duration. The Rebel Mahone, with his famous fighting division, made a rush for the gap in our lines.[13] Once more we heard that unwelcome yell resounding, which told us plainly that they were again charging our lines. But our boys were ready for them. As the darkness of night had closed in upon us, the discharge of musketry and burning, flashing powder illuminated the battle scene. This, together with the roaring of small arms and the loud thundering of

12. Lts. J. Webb Adams and Milbrey Green commanded sections of the 10th Massachusetts Battery.
13. Actually the main Confederate assaults at Hatcher's Run came from troops under Gens. John B. Gordon and John Pegram. The latter was killed in the fighting. Gen. William Mahone's veteran division did not arrive on the field until late in the afternoon of Feb. 6. *OR,* Vol. XLVI, Pt. 1, p. 381; Pt. 2, p. 423.

artillery, made the scene one of more than ordinary grandue. We thus rolled back the Rebel columns for the last time, and the victory was ours. Cheer after cheer resounded along our lines. . . .

As I rode along the line during the battle, I seen Chaplain [Henry] Hopkins of the 120th New York loading and firing away.[14] He don much to encourage the men during this engagement. He is a very brave and gallant officer. I have mentioned him formally in my official report. My Adjt. Genl. and aides acted very bravely.

Some twenty or more prisoners came in that were gathered up by our pickets. All of them said they had advanced in three lines of battle and that we repulsed them every time with greate loss. These prisoners represented 4 different divisions of the Rebel army, showing that they had a very large force in my front. They were at their old game of trying to break our lines. But they were foiled in this attempt by the undaunted bravery of this Brigade. I have never fought a battle that was so highly satisfactory to me in regard to good conduct of both officers & men—all having don nobly, splendidly, and fought gallantly, not an officer or man having left his post during the whole engagement.

The Rebels threw out pickets until they carried away most of their wounded and dead. They then retreated back to their works. We buried over thirty of their dead, including one commissioned officer, that they did not carry off. The next day we discovered many graves that they had made in the rear. My loss was only 53, and the larger portion of these were in the left wing of the 8th New Jersey that was without works and were so much exposed.[15] The Rebel loss must have been quite heavy.[16]

We now hold the position and have thrown up a splendid chain of works. It was a successful move.

I have now given you a plain statement of the facts connected with this battle, and my friends can judge whether Genl. Smyth, or myself and Brigade, ought to have the credit. I fought the battle alone Genl. Smyth had nothing to do with it but to look on. I may truely say that he has "stolen my thunder." . . .

14. It was Hopkins who began singing "The Battle Cry of Freedom," the song which the whole brigade sang at one point in the action. Hopkins received the Congressional Medal of Honor for his valor at this battle. *Ibid.*, Pt. 1, pp. 239, 248; Marbaker, *11th New Jersey,* 272; Phisterer, *New York in the War of the Rebellion,* IV, 3411, 3418.

15. McAllister's brigade lost 12 killed, 41 wounded and 1 missing. Eleven of the killed and 37 of the wounded were members of the 8th New Jersey. *OR,* Vol. XLVI, Pt. 1, p. 65.

16. Lee reported only "small" Confederate losses at Hatcher's Run. *Ibid.,* 381.

Camp at Tucker House, February 12th 1865

My dear Ellen,

. . . I think that the reports of this battle of mine will be corrected. All officers in this Division and Corps have taken an interest to have me placed right. They say that the honor belongs to me alone, so far as we poor mortals are concerned. God, of course, guides and overrules everything. The idea that Ramsey's Brigade saved the day! Ramsey was on my right and did not fire a gun. No attack was made on him at all. And the two pieces of artillery which I planted on my first rear, and which I left Ramsey when I moved, could have helped me by firing into the enemy's massed troops in my front. Although they were ready to do so, he ordered them not to fire. He showed himself a poor commander. Everyone here conversant with the facts are astonished at his want of thought in this matter and condemn him for his stupidity.[17] The fight was on my front alone, and I drove back the columns every time their hosts advanced against me. Justice will be don yet. . . .

Our men and officers are without tents and protection, having to work so hard in building breastworks and redoubts, and cutting slashings in front of the lines. We have also to place abattis in front of these works. I don't know when we will be done. The weather is bitter cold. Tonight is windy and very, very cold. The ground is frozen very hard. But such is the life of a soldier. The Rebels must suffer much more than we do, for they have not so many overcoats and blankets as we have.

I have a large, nice, comfortable room in this house for my Headquarters. I have a good fireplace in it, so I am all right. The men are preparing to build log huts. But it takes some work to make all comfortable, especially if they are kept on details so long. . . .

Hatcher's Run, Va., February 14th 1865

My dear Ellen,

I have just finished my long narrative of the late battle [18] and would have mailed it tonight, but Dr. Welling wished to take a copy and I will defer sending it until tomorrow night.

17. While it is true that Ramsey's brigade took little part in the battle, Ramsey used his official report to fire a barb at McAllister. He was "satisfied" that McAllister "could not have held" his position alone. "My arrival," stated Ramsey, "under the circumstances, was very portentous and opportune." *Ibid.,* 207. See also *ibid.,* 81, 192, 224; Marbaker, *11th New Jersey,* 270–71.

18. McAllister began his Hatcher's Run narrative on the evening of Feb. 11 (under which date it is herein published). He worked on the account over a period of three days.

I have just received the congratulatory order of Genl. Humphreys to us, all officers and men. . . . This order gives me the credit. You can show it to all you please and, if you choose, have it published. It is public and can be used. . . .

I am very sorry to hear of the illness of my dear little namesake. I hope he is well by this time. Write and let me hear all about how he is geting along. I wish you to send my letters to Sarah, as I have not had time to write her since the battle. . . . The mail boy is here for the letter, and I must close it. . . .

Hatcher's Run, Va., February 15th 1865

My dear Ellen,

I have not received my letters from home for several days. . . . I hope little Robert is better by this time.

I see by the Washington *Chronicle* of the 13th that McGregor, the Associated Press corrispondent, has rectified his greate mistake and given my Brigade the credit for the successful battle of the 5th. This correction will be published in all the papers, and all will be right. Well, my Brigade deserves the credit. It would be an injustice if we did not get it.

We have had and are having a greate deal of work to do in building breastworks, redoubts, cutting slashings, and puting in abattis. And besides all that, the men are building their third winter quarters. . . .

Genl. Mott told me yesterday that he had recommended me for full promotion. I am satisfied that Genl. Humphreys will [endorse it]. If I am spared, I will have a full promotion very soon. . . .

This day is rainy and the frost is coming out. It has been very, very cold. Now we will have *mud, mud,* for some time.

Within sight of this place lives a man that they call "Captain Smith." [19] He is one of the F.F.V.'s, a very remarkable looking old man, and has rather an intelligent look. He told me that he has lived here all his life and that he has never been to Richmond, Petersburg, or City Point, and never traveled on a railroad. I told him one of these fine mornings he would waken up and see the steam horse passing his door and that he must take a ride. The road is coming up fast; and in a few days we will have it here. . . .

19. Reference is to one of two Smith families who lived a mile north of Hatcher's Run. See *Official Atlas,* Plate LXXVII, Map 2.

THE PATH TO PEACE ♣ [587]

Hatcher's Run, Va., February 16th 1865

My dear Ellen & family,

. . . Genl. Humphreys has gone on leave of absence, so I suppose we will not move very soon—though I do not expect that we will be long here. Yet we are again fixing up winter quarters. As the Rebels seem determined to fight it out, we must cross swords again and again until the Rebellion is ended.

Tomorrow we are to witness the execution of one of those poor miserable deserters.[20] I hope it will have the effect of preventing others from commiting the like crime. What a miserable death—to die the death of a traitor, false to his solom oath, false to his country, false to all that is high and holy, false to his friends and all that is near and dear to man on earth.

We have a thaw here now and mud is the order of the day. No mail tonight, and no letter for three days from any of you. No doubt it is the fault of the mail. . . .

Camp Tucker House, Va., February 19th 1865

My dear Ellen,

This is Sunday and a very remarkable quiet one for us in the army. But little or nothing is doing. I am glad that our men can have some rest, for they have been kept buisey since the battle.

One thing, however, was done today. The bodies of those that fell in the battle of this place on the 5th and were temporarily buried were taken up, placed in rough coffins, and hauled down to our Division burying ground, there to be deposited in the ground thus set apart for that purpose. Two of them had been taken up last week and sent to their homes. The remainder, ten in number, were taken up today. Brave and gallant men, they gave their lives for their country. Some others, I understand, died at the Hospital of their wounds. There is an order to gather up all the scattered remains of fallen soldiers buried here and there, all over this great battlefield from here to the James, and have them buried in their respective burying grounds. I am sorry to say that it has not yet been carried out. But preparations are in progress for doing it.

Yesterday the Rebels came in under a flag of truce and received

20. The condemned man was a member of the 11th Massachusetts. (Mass. Adj. Gen., *Massachusetts Soldiers* does not list those men from the Bay State who were executed.) Roe and Nutt, *1st Massachusetts Heavy Artillery,* 206; de Trobriand, *Army of the Potomac,* 694–95.

three bodies of officers killed in front of my Brigade. . . . They did not take their privates. They now lay in unknown graves, buried where they fell. We see sad scenes in war. On the morning after the battle I saw 4 or 5 Rebels laying together, all killed by one shell. Who is to answer for the sacrifice of life in this war God only knows. If we could get the leaders of this uncalled for rebellion and hang them, what a blessing this would be to our country and the world.

The weather is now quite mild and pleasant. I hope Dr. Welling will call and make you a visit. Tell him that I am quite lonely since he left, and that there is nothing new here. Genl. Mott has gon home on a ten day's leave of absence, with the understanding that he must return at once if wanted. Our winter quarters are no more permanent than the old ones.

Tell the Doctor that Genl. Mott has recommended me for promotion, saying in his report that he recommended me once before and now takes pleasure in doing it again. He tells Genl. Humphreys in his report that he sent an aide during the battle to aske me how I was geting along. My reply was: "I am doing first rate, can take care of myself, and can whip the enemy with or without works!" [21]

Genl. Mott seems to have been highly pleased with my answer. He told it to his staff and all officers present. It is now known all through the army. . . .

Hatcher's Run, Va., February 21st 1865

My dear Ellen,
 . . . The possession of Charleston and Columbia has given greate joy throughout the army.[22] One hundred guns were fired today in honor of the victory. Bands are playing and the boys are cheering.

This morning at early dawn, as Corps Officer of the Day, I was on picket line and had orders to advance it in order to take in a nice piece of woods to make corderoy roads. I ordered the line forward, and on we went through the woods. We ran against the enemy pickets; they left and run in and we soon found ourselves up close to a very strong picket line. We then halted and built our picket post. The Rebels did not fire on us at all. This is unusual for them.

21. According to Mott's report, McAllister "was most gallantly encouraging his command, and sent me word that he was fighting with and without breast-works; also, that he could whip the rebels away." *OR*, Vol. XLVI, Pt. 1, p. 225.

22. Sherman bypassed Charleston in his northward march through the Carolinas. Only his "bummers" entered the city. Columbia fell on Feb. 17; hours later, it was destroyed by fire.

Deserters are coming in rapidly. Last night we received 9 in this Corps. Today I hear that 15 came in on the 2nd Division in broad daylight and brought their arms with them. They all seem to be heartily sick of the war and say that they are starving. The Rebellion cannot last long. What Lee will do I don't know. It is rather thought that he will make an attack on us here—concentrate all his forces and fight the final battle. We are all on the alert.

Here come six more deserters, and they say more are coming in tonight. They are all North Carolinians. The dissatisfaction amongst them is astonishing. . . .

Camp Tucker House, Va., February 22nd 1865

My dear Ellen,

This evening we have received orders to be ready to move at a moment's notice. What is up I don't know. We may be off before morning. I suppose it is owing to some movement of the enemy. . . .

Camp Tucker House, Va., February 23rd 1865

My dear Ellen,

I wrote you a very short note last night that we were again under marching orders, that we might move before morning, &c. We did not have to move. Whatever caused the order does not just now exist, as the order has been revoked. But we must "be ready at short notice." The Army of the Potomac is always ready to move, and we may well say that we have no winter quarters. We may remain a few days longer here, perhaps weeks, but we are liable to move at any hour—I suppose depending on the movements of the enemy.

One tenth of our troops, besides what are on picket, are kept up all night to be on the watch. Why this additional dilligence I do not understand, unless it is expected that Lee is receiving reinforcements from the South in order to attack our lines, breake them, and retrieve their lost fortunes in that direction. If so, we are fully ready to receive him and would much rather that he attack us than for us to attack him. Time will develop all these plans.

. . . I have reason to believe that I will receive the full appointment [to Brigadier General] soon. I don't see anything to prevent it. Then the question of pay will be settled. Although I am confirmed as a Brevet Brig. General and asigned, I only get a Colonel's pay. Instead of puting our pay on a level with the Regulars by raising ours, they have brought the Regulars to the same pay that we get. So the thing is settled. But there is no doubt that all officers' pay below a Brigadier will be raised. A Colonel will get $50 a month more than he gets now, and that will make a Brigadier General $50 more than a Colonel. As it now stands, a Brigadier gets $100 more than a Colonel. Every thing is so high here that it takes much to live on. Our board and candles cost us $50 per month, and it is still raising. At Corps Headquarters they agreed to give $40 a month to a purveyor to run the mess. He did so for a while and then asked a raise in price. They give him $60; then he give it up and left them without anyone to carry it on.

I have just been talking to our paymaster, Maj. [Moses] Webb. He boards at Willard's in Washington with his wife and daughter. He has two rooms and pays $16 a day, or $480 a month. I said he boards there; I should have said that they asked him that price, but it was more than his salary came to and he went elsewhere. His is a Major's salary and, of course, it is not large. . . .

Camp Tucker House, Va., February 24th 1865

My dear Ellen,

I have received my pay and find that I can let you have $100 and the $10 you sent me . . .

I settled with Sunday. I owed him $40. It is necessary that someone take care of his money. The last time he was paid, he foolishly loaned an orderly by the name of Gibson $10, and that is the last Sunday has seen of his money. I have arranged with Sunday as follows: you are to be his cashiere. I will send to you all the money he has and will get. You are to deposit it in the Belvidere Bank. When it gets up to $50, you are to purchase for him a U.S. $50 Bond, so that when the war is over or he leaves the service, he will have something to show for it. I now send you $35 additional [which] you will at once deposit for Sunday. As soon as he earns it, you will get more. When it amounts to $50, you make the purchase. . . .

Sunday says that he is going to stay with me all the time, go home with me when I leave the service, and do whatever you want. He says that if I get killed, he will see that my body is taken home and remains with you. He thinks the world of you all, and there is no place for him like Belvidere. He is as good as ever. I never seen a better servant. He is a prize for anyone to have. In depositing his money, remember that his name is not Sunday but "Tom Anderson."

THE PATH TO PEACE ♣ [591]

The Chaplain has taken an interest in him. He has a school for all our darkeys. Before we moved, he had them together every day. [Chaplain Cline] says that Sunday learns very fast. The school will commence again as soon as the chapel is finished—and if we don't move. . . .

Glorious news! The capture of Wilmington! A cause of general joy!

The Band is now serenading me. I do not think it likely that we will be here long. We are liable to move any time. . . .

Camp Tucker House, Va., February 25th 1865

My dear Ellen,

. . . We have reports of the Rebels vacating Petersburg from day to day, that we are cannonading to see if they are there, &c. But as yet it is all camp rumor. It is probable that they may be compelled by the movements of Sherman to leave soon, but I don't think that Genl. Grant wants them to leave. The longer they stay here, the better it is for our cause.

. . . The weather is very dull and rainy, and the ground very soft. Our men are now quite comfortable. I hope that they may enjoy their new quarters for a while and until the weather becomes more favourable for movements. . . .

Camp Tucker House, Va., March 6th 1865 [23]

My dear Ellen,

I have but a moment to write you, as the mail will leave soon. I received your letter saying that you were to leave home on Friday for Juniata and Hennie for New Brunswick. I hope that you . . . may have a pleasant time. Give my love to all our friends in Juniata, and say to them all that I would love to see them. While I am in the army, it seems impossible. But if I am spared to the close of this war, I will go up, have a long talk, and spend some time.

We are still here, yet it is probable that we may move soon. In fact, we may move any hour. I am very well. Dr. Welling has returned from his leave of absence.

23. McAllister's letters of Feb. 27, Feb. 28 and Mar. 2 all treat primarily of the financial setback suffered by his son-in-law, Wilson Lloyd. Since these letters have no bearing on McAllister's military or personal life, they have been omitted.

Rev. Dr. [John] Hall is now here and will remain some time. He enjoys it very much. We have some interesting prayer meetings. I have just come from one. Uncle John Vasser [24] is hard at work. He has just left. He never leaves without a word of prayer. He is the most remarkable man I have ever seen. He is doing a greate amount of good.

Reports here say that Sheridan has captured Early and a large part of his army.[25] But these reports need confirmation. We will soon know positively. Perhaps it is too good to be true. I hope not. . . .

Camp Tucker House, Va., March 9th 1865

My dear Ellen,

. . . We have nothing very interesting here except *rain, rain,* every other day. Roads are very bad. We have our quarters for the men quite comfortable, if we can only enjoy them awhile. But this is very uncertain; we are likely to move any day. We are very busy drilling. I had my fine Brigade out this evening on dress parade and drill. They looked very fine, as they always do.

So Early has been well whipped by Sheridan. The news is good from there. I hope that it will continue so. . . .

Hatcher's Run, Va., March 11th 1865

My dear Ellen,

This is Saturday night and I have just returned from prayer meeting—quite a good meeting. We had a review today of the 2nd and 3rd Divisions. Everything went very nicely. Genls. Grant and Meade were both present, also Mrs. Grant and Genl. Meade's daughter. Mrs. Genl. Grant [26] is rather small, not particularly good looking,

---

24. John E. Vassar was an energetic minister and zealous worker for the American Tract Society. "Though never ordained, he was an eloquent preacher and an indefatigable 'fisher of men.' " *National Cyclopaedia of American Biography,* V, 252.

25. At Waynesboro on March 2, Sheridan's forces struck what was left of Early's army and routed the Confederates. Sheridan then started eastward, destroyed the Virginia Central Railroad and James River Canal, and on March 19 rejoined Grant's army. Sheridan's report of the campaign is in *OR,* Vol. XLVI, Pt. 1, pp. 474–81.

26. Grant first met Julia Dent through a close friend and fellow officer of prewar days, James Longstreet. Though the two men became generals on opposite sides, their friendship remained unbroken and genuine. Julia Dent Grant to most people was "a simple-mannered, plain, quiet woman." Longstreet, *From Manassas to Appomattox,* 17–18, 677; Strong, *Diary of the Civil War,* 453.

but she has a fine expression and is rather interesting—very much like other people. The whole party came up in the cars, witnessed the review, looked at the breastworks and redoubts, then went to the cars and left for City Point. . . .

Hatcher's Run, Va., March 13th 1865

My dear Ellen,

. . . We have just received the intelligence of Sheridan's great success in destroying the railroads and canals around Richmond. A report this evening says that he has reached the White House [Landing]. You may now look for some great movements before long. Things are well for our country and cause, and I fondly hope the war will soon be brought to a close. . . .

Camp Tucker House, Va., March 15th 1865

My dear Ellen,

. . . We are under marching orders, and all are ready to move. We may go at any hour. When, I don't know, but we may now expect active movements.

The enclosed letter of Genl. Humphreys was caused by a misunderstanding as to Genl. Mott's recommendation for my promotion. Genl. Humphreys thought Genl. Mott asked that I be made a Brevet Major General. Mott only intended that I should be made a full Brig. General. When this was fully explained, Genl. Humphreys endorsed the recommendation of Genl. Mott as stated in the letter.

Rev. Dr. Hall left this morning. Dr. Welling says that he has gone by way of Washington to urge my full promotion, though I said nothing to him about it.

I have been sick for several days but am now better. Bad cold and a slight billious attack. I intend, God willing, to move with the army. If I can not command, I will be on hand. But if we don't move for a day or two, I will be well again. . . .

Hatcher's Run, Va., March 16th 1865

My dear Ellen,

. . . We are still here but all ready to move at a moment's notice. . . .

I told you in my last that I had been sick. I am much better now and expect to resume command day after tomorrow. If we move sooner, I will take command at once. I took a bad cold that brought on a billious attack. This one was but light. I am all right now, the fever is broke, and I am moving forward. . . .

I may not be able to receive your letters regularly when on a move, but send them on and, if I am spared, I will get them sooner or later.

May God spare us and hold us in His keeping, guide us in our thoughts, and direct us in our actions. . . .

Hatcher's Run, Va., March 17th 1865

My dear Ellen,

. . . You need not feel so uneasy about my health. I am all right now.

This is St. Patrick's Day. In the evening they had the usual races, &c. One Colonel got nearly killed by his horse failing to make the jump. The Colonel fell off and the horse fell on him. I always did think, and do still, that these races are not only dangerous but redicalous. Of course I was not there; I never have attended one in my life. But nearly all officers go to see, as they say, the fun. In reality, it is only to see somebody hurt. . . .

Camp Tucker House, Va., March 18th 1865

My dear Ellen,

Nothing new here today. As you see, we have not yet moved. . . . I have felt quite well today. I walked out a little but found it tired me very considerably. On returning I lay down until I got rested again. I now feel quite bright.

The weather is fine here now, and the roads have dried up nicely. It has the appearance of spring. The rose buds are expanding on the sunny side of the house.

I have never given you a discription of the [Tucker] Mansion and have hardly a disposition to do it now. It is a story and a half high, set up on brick pillars so that a dog can run under the house. There is no cellar. This room is the parlour, quite large, through which everybody must go to get to the upper story. It has a very good fireplace, the only good and comfortable arrangement about the establishment. Next to this is the dining room, some smaller, and a large fireplace. Next to it is the kitchen, large with a real old fashioned fireplace of a very large size. No ceiling or loft, you see the roof. This and two small rooms in the upper story of this part of the house makes up the whol mansion. I forgot to say that there is a very large door in front and one in the rear of this parlour room, making it quite airy for a summer residence.

There are no comforts and no conveniences whatever here. I had forgotten to say that there is a porch in front. The ceiling of this room is very high. You can barely reach to the top of the mantle. . . .

Camp Tucker House, Va., March 22nd 1865

My dear Ellen,

You see by this letter we are still here. But, of course, we are all ready for a move at a moment's notice. Lee sticks well; he seems to hold onto Richmond. Deserters come in even more rapidly than ever. Every night there are quite a number. It is their old soldiers that are now deserting. They come in with their arms and very often by squads. If we lay here long enough we will have a large part of Lee's army on this side.

I am quite well again and am in command. Tomorrow it is said that we will have a Corps review. But it has not been ordered yet. Yesterday it rained. Today we had a very high wind. It is now quite calm and moderate.

Last evening I received a letter from you—the last one written at Brother Washington's. I suppose it was detained by the high water. The day before I had received the one you wrote from Belvidere. I feel very much obliged to our friends in Juniata for their high opinion of me, and I fondly hope that it will continue. You know that when persons are rising, they will have plenty of friends. But if a reverse takes place, or a misfortune happens, only *the precious few* stick to you. You well remember 1857. After all, I do not regret having come to New Jersey, though I might have done better as well in a military way in Pennsylvania as I have in New Jersey. But perhaps not any better, for I have had good fighting regiments to command. I still love Juniata and some of the people, who I shall never forget. But we owe a good deal to New Jersey in the way of business. I like the state very much and am now fairly identified with it. . . .

Camp Tucker House, Va., March 26th 1865

My dear Ellen,

Yesterday was to us an exciting day. From early morning till long after dark the roaring of artillery and rolling of musketry was heard along our lines. Now we have another battle and heroic deeds to record, other families to mourn their dear ones . . . and our nation will rejoice over a new victory.[27]

Unexpected to us all, about 5 a.m. [March 25] we were aroused from our slumbers by heavy cannonading to our right, down on the 9th Corps. It sounded like a battle. What was it? we all asked. Soon an aide rode up to these Headquarters and said, "General Mott's compliments, sir. Get ready to move at once. The enemy have broken through the 9th Corps!"

Soon written orders came and added: "Strike your tents and load your wagons."

All was now a scene of bustle and excitement. Soon tents were striped of their canvas, blankets rolled and knapsacks packed, wagons loaded and lines formed, muskets stacked.

Now came an order: "Send out a party in front of your lines to reconnoiter and report what is in your front."[28] This order was executed at once by Capt. [James K.] Holmes with his company from the 120th New York. He drove in the enemy videttes, faced the enemy picket line, and found them strong with a line of battle in the main works. He reported the facts. He was ordered now to "send one regiment and drive in the picket line." I ordered Col. Schoonover to "take the 11th New Jersey and feel the enemy; ascertain their strength without driving in the pickets, if you can. If not, storm their picket posts and see what the enemy has in the works."

I left my command in our main line of works and went out with the Colonel. On arriving on the ground and reconnoitering, I ordered the 120th New York out to assist Col. Schoonover. I was now ordered to leave these regiments under the command of Col. Schoonover and

---

27. The Mar. 25 Confederate assault against Fort Stedman was a last-ditch effort by Lee to break Grant's siege lines. Lee hoped to pierce the Federal positions and flank Grant from his City Point supply base—or at least force the Federal commander to shorten his lines. McAllister's report of the day's action is in *OR*, Vol. XLVI, Pt. 1, pp. 240–42.

28. "As soon as information of Gordon's assault on Fort Stedman was communicated to General Humphreys, that resolute and sagacious commander, without waiting for orders, rapidly got his corps under arms and proceeded to search the Confederate lines in his front. Reconnaissances were made by each division commander; and these were pushed with so much vigor that the entire entrenched picket line of the enemy was captured." Walker, *Second Army Corps*, 651.

report to Genl. Mott, who was waiting at my Headquarters to see me. I give my order to the Colonel, left him in command of the two regiments, and rode off to receive new orders.

I seen Genl. Mott. He told me to order Col. Schoonover to charge the picket line and drive it in, for me not to send any more regiments out, and to hold my command well in hand, as it was reported that the enemy was coming round on our left. On receiving these orders, I made some alteration in the disposition of troops and placed myself in a position to see the picket line.

I now heard our boys give a cheer. I looked out to the picket line and saw the 11th New Jersey and the 120th New York charge across the open field to the Rebel picket line. It was an exciting moment for us all. On, at double quick, went these two regiments, amidst the cross fire of artillery and musketry, and success crowned their efforts. They captured the works and about 50 prisoners.[29]

I reported this to Headquarters. Genl. de Trobriand on my right did the same and also captured the picket line in front of him. We now had the Rebs back in their main line of works. Things now seemed to move in our favor. An official report arrived that the 9th Corps had defeated the Rebs, drove them back, captured 1,900 prisoners, recaptured the lost fort, and punished the enemy very severely.[30] This was good news for our army.

From the course of things now, the idea, I suppose, was to try the enemy's main line. I had took out two more regiments to where Col. Schoonover was, as a report had reached me that the enemy had driven him out of the works; and on receiving this I hastened to his assistance. But on reaching there, I found that he had retaken it from the Rebels and all was right.

I now formed these two regiments for a support and to protect Col. Schoonover's flank. Genl. Smyth came up with his Brigade on my left. Had he been up sooner, we would not have been flanked and driven out of these works. Things were looking all right on this part of the field. Then I received orders to take my two remaining regiments—the 7th and 8th New Jersey—to the right, where they were preparing for a charge. I took these two regiments as ordered to the right of this Division and massed them preparatory to a charge, in the rear of Genl. de Trobriand, who I found in line of battle and ready to move. Genls. Mott and Humphreys were both there.

29. McAllister reported officially that Schoonover's two regiments captured 100 Confederates. *OR,* Vol. XLVI, Pt. 1, p. 240.
30. The IX Corps recaptured Fort Stedman after bitter fighting; it then launched a counterattack that drove the Confederates from the field.

To our surprise, and before we commenced the movement, the Rebels came out of their works on our right and in front of the 1st Division of our Corps and attacked us. This Division, under Genl. [Nelson] Miles, fought splendidly and held their ground, although the Rebels did their best to break their lines. This battle lasted for some time. I think it caused a change in the intended program and prevented our charging their works.

A little before dark fighting commenced on our left. A message came to me that my regiments under Col. Schoonover were driven out of the works again. I was ordered back there to their support. On arriving there, I found things in rather a bad condition. I hurried my men in line and moved them forward up to the first line taken from the Rebels that morning. I established it more securely, adding to the strength of the force that had fallen back from the more advanced line—the balance of the 120th New York and the 11th New Jersey.

The enemy opened on us again, but we were able to hold our ground. The fire became for a short time quite brisk all along the line. But as the darkness of the night soon closed in upon us, the fighting ceased. It was too late to advance and retake the advanced line. On my left Genl. Smyth drew back his lines, as he was across Hatcher's Run. This I was opposed to, as it would expose my left to another surprise. It was by Genl. Smyth not geting up in time to make a connection with Col. Schoonover's left that cause the surprise of the picket line. However, I drew back my left a little, and all was safe.

We lay on our arms that night until 1 a.m. I had orders to leave a strong picket line and come into camp. With two regiments, the 120th New York and 11th New Jersey, I captured 150 Rebels. I lost 147 men, including two officers, in killed, wounded and taken prisoner. About 80 of these were captured by the enemy in taking the pitts from us.[31] Our killed was small, considering the length of time we were fighting.

We now hold our position and have put up a strong line of picket posts all along and in full view of the enemy's main works, so that we can see their movements. We had some very good fighting and on the whole don very well. The whole thing was a success. Everybody seems to be highly pleased. I see Genl. Grant says that this Corps captured 500 prisoners. Of course, he ought to know.

You can easily see that the object of our becoming the attacking

31. Confederate casualties in the March 25 fighting exceeded 4,500 men, including 2,734 captured. McAllister's losses were 9 killed, 52 wounded and 92 missing. *OR,* Vol. XLVI, Pt. 1, pp. 52, 241n; Freeman, *Lee's Lieutenants,* III, 651.

THE PATH TO PEACE ♣ [599]

party was to draw the troops from the 9th Corps. It had the desired effect. One thing we settled that day, the newspaper corrispondents to the contrary: *the enemy are here in strong force.*

All my regiments done well. The 7th New Jersey was under the command of Col. Price. He wheeled his big battalion—raw recruits —into line and don very well. Genl. de Trobriand's Brigade had quite a hard fight and captured a large number of Rebels. Genl. Pierce had some fighting, but not as much as de Trobriand and myself. If I had not had so long a front, or if I could have remained to support Col. Schoonover, the Rebels would not have recaptured the advanced line. As it was, our line was too thin to resist a heavy line of battle.

March 27th. The 6th Corps pickets were attacked this morning. We were all out of bed in a hurry, but no damage was don. Sheridan is now marching up this way with his cavalry. Something is up! . . .

Camp Tucker House, Va., March 28th 1865

My dear Ellen,

I sent you a full narrative of the battle of the 25th. In the morning we are to brake camp and move off. No doubt it is to be a greate move. Sheridan is here with his cavalry force. We will have stirring times. God grant that we may be successful. . . . It is very probable that we will have no communication and that you will not receive any letters for a long time. I will, if spared, write every opportunity. . . . Pray for me and my Brigade. . . .

Bivouack, Boydton Plank Road, April 1st 1865

My dear Ellen,

Having time to write you for the first time since we broke camp, I avail myself of the opportunity.

The 5th Corps on our left has had considerable fighting. But yesterday Miles's Division, the 1st Division of this Corps, and my Brigade had a hard time of it.[32] The enemy was pressing the 5th Corps very hard. Miles was ordered to attack on the left of the Boydton Road and

32. This was the beginning of Grant's grand drive against Lee's overextended lines. The II and V Corps were ordered to mass on the extreme Federal left. Their object was to get in a position whereby they could strike first the Southside and then the Richmond & Danville Railroad, Lee's two remaining supply lines. Both corps had literally to fight their way into position. The conflict on Mar. 30 is known as the battle of White Oak Road. On Apr. 1, after heavy losses, G. K. Warren's V Corps reinforced Sheridan at Five Forks. Both elements then attacked and broke Lee's right flank.

I was ordered to attack on the right with two or more regiments. I took out four regiments, leaving the 7th New Jersey in camp. I went out into the woods in my front, formed, and moved forward towards the enemy lines. He poured his grape and canister and musketry into us rapidly as we advanced, cutting down our men. My boys still advanced with their usual bravery and reached the enemy rifle pits. But a cross fire of both cannon and musketry rendered them untenable. They came back again, losing 123 men and 2 officers in killed, wounded and taken prisoner.[33] After this I was ordered back to our breastworks.

I have, thank God, been protected once more from the arrows of death. I wish I could say the same for all of my brave comrades in battle. A number of my brave boys were left on the battlefield to the tender mercies of the enemy. Most of them, however, were gotten off. It was not intended that I should take and hold the works—only to make a demonstration, "a forlorn hope" to draw the enemy from pressing the 5th Corps. Genl. Miles lost heavily but drove the enemy a considerable distance.[34] He had no works to bump up against as I had.[35] I was a considerable distance from the 1st Division on my own hook. We have got a strong hold on the Boydton Road and a continuous line down to our old camp.

Orders to move again. Good by, my dear. . . .

McALLISTER'S NARRATIVE OF THE APPOMATTOX CAMPAIGN [36]

March 29th. As per orders, we broke camp at the Tucker House and moved by the left flank across Hatcher's Run about two miles on the Vaughan Road. All the Corps was here. Our connection was kept up with the old works by some of the Army of the James. The 2nd Brigade of this Division was with Genl. Pierce on my right, the 1st Brigade in the reserve. The 1st Division was on my left. At 10 a.m. we halted, faced to the right, and built breastworks. No enemy appearing, we moved forward in line of battle, with our skirmishers in the

33. Casualties in McAllister's brigade were 12 killed, 88 wounded and 49 missing. *OR,* Vol. XLVI, Pt. 1, p. 584.
34. Miles's division suffered losses of 139 killed, 823 wounded and 334 missing. *Ibid.,* 582.
35. Cf. *ibid.,* Pt. 3, p. 406.
36. McAllister's report of this campaign, submitted April 15, 1865, is in *ibid.,* Pt. 1, pp. 788–90.

advance, and passed over some old Rebel breastworks. When darkness set in, we moved by the left flank as we did in the morning. We passed a deserted Rebel camp. It now commenced raining; and to the darkness of the night was added the thick underbrush in the forest through which we had to pass, rendering it almost impossible to march. We now halted in line of battle, threw out our pickets for the night, and lay down to sleep.

March 30th. At 6 a.m. all were up. Breakfast over, we advanced in line of battle through a very heavy forest, encountering difficulties with swamps. We soon crossed the old plank road leading from Dabney Sawmill to the Boydton Plank Road at about equal distance from the two places. The rain increased its fury, poured down in torrents, and made it exceedingly unpleasant for the troops. Our skirmishers now encountered the enemy and drove them back. We advanced to the Grow House and in great haste threw up a line of breastworks. At dark we bivouacked for the night, as we supposed. Though the storm continued, all those not on duty were soon asleep.

March 31st. At 1 a.m. we were ordered to fall in. About 2 a.m. we found ourselves moving slowly along by the left flank in rear of this new line of works. It had now ceased raining, but the mud was so deep that it was almost impossible to travel. But we moved our column. The whole army was going in the same direction. When my left touched the Boydton Plank Road, it was daylight.

We halted and faced the enemy, whose works were frowning down on us. They told us by shot and shell that thus far shalt thou come and no farther. At the left of my Brigade stood the old white oak tree known as Genl. Hancock's Headquarters. It was under this tree that he stood on October 27th last when we fought the Boydton Plank Road battle, and from which he was driven by the enemy when we were surrounded. The enemy guns which were now playing upon us were concealed from our view by redoubts and breastworks built by the enemy upon the very ground on which I fought that day and where my Brigade so nobly drove back the enemy. . . . As I gazed upon that beautiful spot, I could not help thinking that it must and shall be ours—consecrated as it is by the blood of my brave boys who so heroically gave their lives upon the altar of their country.

10 a.m. The 5th Corps and the 1st Division of our Corps now became hotly engaged. It was needful that we should demonstrate against these works, develop the enemy's force, and draw them off from these points of attack. I was ordered to send out one company to demonstrate against their pickets. This I did, and found the enemy strongly posted in our front. Nothing but a heavy force could drive

them away. I was then ordered to take out one or more regiments and attack at another point. I took 4 regiments: the 120th New York, 11th New Jersey, 11th Massachusetts, and 8th New Jersey. I took them under cover of the roads and deployed in line of battle the 120th New York, 11th Massachusetts, and one wing of the 8th New Jersey, retaining the ballance as a support.

They went forward under a terrific fire of musketry, canister and shell. They drove the enemy from their rifle pits and occupied them for about a half an hour, when we found them untenable by the enemy's concentrated fire. We had to abandon the pits the best way we could. It was more dangerous to get out than to go in. On some parts of the line one man at a time ran the gauntlet and made good his escape. Others were cut down in their attempts to get back, and quite a number were taken prisoner. Our loss was considerable. I did not abandon the position until ordered to do so. It was not the intention to capture the works but just to demonstrate. We did more than was expected or desired. It had the desired effect in drawing the enemy towards this point, which enabled Genl. Miles to swing around on the enemy's right. My men and officers acted bravely. Col. Schoonover, although on the reserve, had no less than 15 men wounded by shells. This was remarkable.

4 p.m. I moved to the left with the Corps and erected more works. You see that as we could not attack the enemy's works with success, we pursued Grant's old plan of moving to the left to weaken their lines. This at last was the downfall of Genl. Lee. We remained in this position all night.

April 1st. At daylight we moved back to our old works on the plank road again and remained all day. There was no firing; all was quiet. Late in the evening we went into the same position we had left in the morning and demonstrated on the enemy's lines until daylight Sunday morning [April 2]. This first night of April I shall never forget. It seemed as if the Demons of War had all been let loose. The roar of artillery and musketry all night long, from the Appomattox River below Petersburg to our extreme left, was the most noisy and terrific I have ever heard.[37] Not one moment's rest did we get all night. No language can give you any idea of the noise of musketry and cannon on that battle night. The enemy weakened their left in order to strengthen their right. They expected that the greate attack would take place on our front. While their troops were massing on our left to

---

37. This was the softening-up bombardment for Grant's major assault the following morning.

defend their right, we were massing on our right to break their left.[38] This Genl. Lee did not expect.

April 2nd. The Sabbath morning dawned with all its beauty, calm and serene; and the gray light of dawn cast its lovely rays far over the battlefield, disclosing the battling hosts of those two greate armies arrayed in their full power for the last time in the greate and final strugle of the war. The sacredness of this Holy day was not in this sinful world of ours a barrier to the continuance of the contest, for the battle had already begun, and the dark clouds of war were bursting here and there all along our lines.

It was necessary that another demonstration be made on my front. At 8 a.m., according to orders to attack, I not only sent out one regiment (the 8th New Jersey, Maj. Hartford) but also went out in person to superintend it.[39] We advanced on the enemy's picket line amidst a terrific fire of musketry, canister and shell. Though the dead and wounded fell around us, the regiment advanced and captured the whole picket line in our front—165 prisoners and over 200 muskets. The enemy still continued their fire upon us, and we in return poured a raking fire into the redoubt in front and silenced their guns.

I now sent back for two more regiments, the 11th Massachusetts and 11th New Jersey. I was preparing to charge their main line of works when the enemy ran back their guns and commenced a retreat. We advanced rapidly; and as I rode up to the works, I found quite a number of white flags hung out for protection of those who remained behind on the enemy's leaving. We took possession of the redoubt and a long line of works, gathered up a large number of prisoners, and had the pleasing news from all quarters that the day was ours—not only here but all along the lines. Maj. Hartford had the honor of planting the Star Spangled Banner on the captured redoubt, and well he merited the honor.

It was yet very early in the morning, and what a glorious triumph had crowned our army! For nine long months we had been battling to accomplish this end. For miles along this line the ground had been consecrated by the best blood of our army. Thousands of our brave comrades had fallen on this battlefield and were mouldering to dust

---

38. Apparently McAllister was unaware that elements of the 11th New Jersey were stationed that night in such swampy terrain that "the men had to cut brush with which to build a staging to keep themselves out of the water." Marbaker, *11th New Jersey*, 291.
39. At this point McAllister, who was wearing a dress sword that day, raised the blade over his head and shouted: "Attention! Draw your swords and beat those fellows back!" John L. Parker to McAllister, Aug. 7, 1889, McAllister Papers.

beneath this sod. Thousands more were maimed for life, to say nothing of the slightly wounded and those who died of diseases. What a change had come over us! Our stubborn enemy was fast retreating. We ocquipied the long line of works. Every soldier well knew that Petersburg was virtually ours.[40]

At 9:30 a.m. we moved forward along the Boydton Plank Road, crossed over Hatcher's Run, and passed on our right the battle ground of October 27th last. After traveling a couple of miles, we found that the 6th Corps had come to their left and our front and were driving those of the enemy that had gone in that direction. A number of prisoners and cannon were captured, the enemy still making some resistance. We soon reached close to Petersburg. I remained in reserve with my Brigade, the troops in our front threw up works, and all bivouacked for the night.

April 3rd. There was little or no firing during the night. At dawn of day this morning the Mayor of the town [41] came out and surrendered the city to the 6th Corps. Our boys cheered heartily. It was now ascertained that Lee was retreating southward. At 8 a.m. we were on the march after him. We took the river road and picked up a number of prisoners who had deserted and hid in the woods—as well as some left in the Rebel hospital. We crossed the Southside Railroad. Nothing of particular note having happened today, we marched to a late hour (11 p.m.) and, after throwing out pickets, camped for the night.

April 4th. 6 a.m. We resumed the march and heard of the evacuation of Richmond, which was not officially announced to the troops. It was not expedient to have cheering on so long a line of troops, the design of our movement being to capture Lee. We now traveled on the Danville road and had to stop and repair it, as it was almost impassable in some places. We went into camp before night, expecting rations to be up. But they failed to reach us and our men were entirely out. We were now in Amelia County, Virginia.

April 5th. At 2:15 a.m. we moved, marched a short distance, and ran against our cavalry. We halted to let them pass. Daylight dawned. We waited for the supply wagons to come up. At 8:15 a.m. rations came and were distributed. At 10 a.m. we moved in the direction of the [Richmond &] Danville Railroad, crossed it, and found the

---

40. The fighting of Apr. 1–2 cost the Confederates 5,000 troops, 11 regimental flags and at least one cannon. Grant's casualties totaled 634 men. For the Confederates, Five Forks "was a more costly day than . . . any since May 12 of the preceding year at the Bloody Angle." *OR,* Vol. XLVI, Pt. 1, pp. 54, 836, 1105; Freeman, *Lee's Lieutenants,* III, 671.

41. W. W. Townes was then the mayor of Petersburg. See *OR,* Vol. XLVI, Pt. 1, pp. 913, 1048.

5th Corps encamped with good works thrown up. The cavalry had captured a large haul of prisoners, artillery, and horses. At 8 p.m. we bivouacked for the night.

April 6th. Orders came that our Corps, in conjunction with others, would move on the enemy at Amelia Court House. Our Division was on the left of the railroad. After moving a short distance, we discovered the enemy retreating towards Lynchburg. We then advanced to Amelia Springs. Genl. Mott, in command of the Division, was wounded while driving the enemy by skirmishes.[42] The command then devolved on Genl. de Trobriand. The 1st Brigade had the advance. I was ordered to protect the left. In doing so I threw forward a regiment (the 11th Massachusetts, Col. Rivers) that went on the skirmish line and rendered valuable service in keeping up the connection.

The country is very rolling; every crest and hilltop was contested by the enemy, who threw up little breastworks to protect their rear and cover their retreat. But on for miles rolled our forces, driving the Rebels back over hill and dale, swamp and upland, field and forest. It now became very interesting as well as exciting. The skirmish line ahead fought with greate courage and bravery and was the admiration of all beholders. Our lines of battle followed up as it advanced. The former charged and captured a large number of Rebels in a roadway. The roads were now strewn with Rebel arms, military accoutrements, camp fixings, wagons, and everything needful for an army, clearly showing how hard the enemy was pressed. When the enemy gave way at this point, we moved on without opposition for nearly two miles. The cavalry, that we had not seen all day, came and crossed to our right. It was now evening. The 1st Brigade, which had the advance, was now placed in the reserve and rear, and the 2nd Brigade was placed on our right.

Soon our skirmishers encountered the enemy, who planted artillery on the crest of a hill to enable their infantry to hold us in check until they crossed a small stream with their wagon train. On the road leading to this train Genl. Pierce, with the 2nd Brigade, was passing. I was ordered to make a connection on his left and at once sent the 11th Massachusetts and 120th New York. In a few minutes they were sweeping along near the road.

Then I ordered an advance of the whole Brigade. We soon reached the crest of the hill overlooking the bridge and wagon train. This made it impossible for the enemy to take away the latter, and it fell into our hands—100 wagons loaded with a little of everything.

42. Mott received a bullet wound in the leg while reconnoitering. *Ibid.,* p. 778; de Trobriand, *Army of the Potomac,* 735.

This was quite a haul. The day closed as ours and we camped for the night. A number of prisoners were taken, and deserters came in. During this engagement we heard firing on our left and rear. It was then that the cavalry and 6th Corps made the large capture of prisoners, Genl. Ewell among them.[43]

April 7th. Orders came to move at 1:30 a.m. in line of battle. After moving a very short way in this manner, we changed by the right flank. It was not long before we came in sight of the high bridge of the Danville Railroad that crosses the Appomattox River. The 2nd Division was in advance of us at this point and had some fighting there. On leaving, the enemy fired this splendid structure; but when we arrived, we put it out by cutting four spans loose from the bridge. The bridge is at least 60 or 70 feet to the top of the piers and is very long—1200 or 1500 feet.

Here we crossed the river and moved on, leaving Farmville to our left. Once more we came up with the enemy, who made a stubborn resistance and threw up works. The 2nd Division sent in a brigade on a charge and was repulsed with considerable loss. Night now came; after throwing up works, we camped. I am satisfied that Genl. Grant did not want to drive them further but to hold them there, as Sheridan had been sent to head them off.

This night Genl. Grant sent his first dispatch to Genl. Lee for his surrender.[44] It was sent through our lines at this point. Our pickets had considerable firing up until the middle of the night.

April 8th. At 6:30 a.m. we commenced moving. The enemy had left. We passed their works that they had thrown up the evening previous. The road was now strewn as before mentioned with everything that belonged to an army—caissons blown up and wagons left behind. A number of artillery pieces were found in the woods. We had traveled but a short distance when we were halted. A flag of truce appeared from the enemy. It was answered, after which we resumed our march. About the middle of the day Genl. Grant, Genl. Meade and their staffs

43. Ewell's corps and a part of Richard H. Anderson's corps tried on Apr. 6 to beat back Federal assaults at Sayler's Creek and High Bridge. Yet Grant's men poured in on the Confederates from three sides. Numbered among the 8,000 Confederates taken prisoner were Ewell and Custis Lee, the latter a son of the Confederate commander. See Rauscher, *Music on the March,* 235-38; Miller, *Photographic History,* III, 311; Freeman, *Lee's Lieutenants,* III, 698-711.

44. Grant's message, dispatched at 5 P.M., Apr. 7, stated: "General: The result of the last week must convince you of the hopelessness of further resistance on the part of the Army of Northern Virginia in this struggle. I feel that it is so, and regard it as my duty to shift from myself the responsibility of any further effusion of blood by asking of you the surrender of that portion of the C. S. Army known as the Army of Northern Virginia." *OR,* Vol. XLVI, Pt. 3, p. 619.

passed, and we were informed that they were going out to receive Lee's surrender. There were many stories afloat. Many of them were far from the truth, some bordered on it, and all helped to enliven the scene and raise the spirits of the boys who were weak and hungry, having had no rations to eat. (Wagons could not get up; our march was too rapid for them and roads so bad.)

We now reached the old stage road, called the Buckingham Road, that led from Richmond to Lynchburg. Here we halted a short time and then resumed our march. About sundown we passed New Store. After passing it we halted until rations came up. Here the ground was covered with Rebel ammunition that they had thrown away to lighten their caissons and help speed their march. One of these shells exploded and killed a man in my Brigade. About 10 p.m. the supply train came up and rations were distributed. Then we moved forward. Since Genl. Grant said this would cause Lee's surrender much sooner, we marched all night.

April 9th. At 3 a.m. we arrived on the heels of Genl. Lee and camped. After daylight some firing was heard towards Appomattox Court House. This turned out to be Lee trying to break the lines of Sheridan's cavalry and the 24th Corps that had gone to head him off. Lee was caught fast; there was no chance for his escape. We were all around him.

At 8:30 a.m. we moved on. Our Crops was the first, the 6th Corps next. We marched only a short distance, then halted for a considerable time. I heard that Lee would surrender and that preparations were in the making. All was excitement, all were anxious to hear. Genl. Meade rode along our lines towards Genl. Lee's. The men cheered him as they never did before. The woods between our forces and Lee's prevented us from seeing anything that was going on. Soon Genl. Ould [45] and some other officers came along from our rear. Ould had left Richmond and was captured by our forces. He was not permitted to pass into Lee's lines so as to surrender with the rest.

At 3:30 p.m. it was announced officially that Lee had surrendered.[46] What a scene followed! The excitement is beyound my discription. Why, officers and men were perfectly wild! Greeting, con-

45. Judge Robert Ould was Confederate commissioner for the Exchange of Prisoners.
46. The men in McAllister's brigade spent the early part of Apr. 9 "torn with hopes and fears." The hours dragged by until shortly after 3:30 P.M. "Then from the direction of Lee's army came, at a rapid gallop, a group of officers. As they drew near, Meade, bare-headed, with his hair streaming in the wind and wildly waving his cap, was seen in the advance. Every man was quickly on his feet. As the commander of the Army of the Potomac dashed past, he cried out: 'Lee has surrendered! Lee has surrendered!'" Marbaker, *11th New Jersey*, 296.

gratulations and cheering beggars description. Shoes and hats flew high in the air. Speeches were made, called for loudly, but could not be heard for the cheering at every sentence. The Star Spangled Banner waved high in triumph—high and low, back and forward, over a sea of upturned faces. No picture can be drawn, no language can describe, that interesting scene. You may paint, draw, write and talk over it and about it, and you have but a faint idea of what it was.

But we need not ask why it was. For four long years our armies had been battling for these glorious results, the accomplishment of which thousands had been cut down and thousands more wounded and maimed for life. All knew that by the surrender of Lee and his army the greate contest was over. The war was ended, and we could return to our homes with the proud satisfaction that it has been our privilege to live and take part in the struggle that has decided for all time to come that Republics are not a failure.

May the Glory be given to God! May God be praised for His goodness to us as a nation. . . .

Camp near Burkeville Station, [47] Va., April 14th 1865
My dear Ellen,

I have been able to write but one letter to you and one to Sarah since I wrote you at Petersburg. We have not had mail communications until now. After the surrender of Lee, the command commenced coming back towards this point. We have been from the 10th to this evening in reaching here. The roads were miserable; I never seen them worse. It was almost impossible to haul the artillery. For two days I have had my Brigade with the artillery of the Corps and have just reached this place. The artillery horses are completely worn out. Many of them were left on the road. They will need long rest before we can move again. We are, I understand, to remain here a few days to get rations and clothing, &c. We need a greate deal. Hundreds of our men are now barefooted. It was a rapid and hard march for us. But we have done the work and feel satisfied.

We have not received any late papers and are in the dark as to what is going on, even in our own army. The paroled Rebels, both officers and men, are returning to their homes. Today I conversed with the Rebel General [Clement A.] Evans. He thinks it is all over

---

47. Burkeville Station "was a sort of tank station with an apology for a hotel; two log barns and a rough station near the watering tank, from which the rickety locomotives took long drinks in passing." Roe and Nutt, *1st Massachusetts Heavy Artillery*, 215.

with them—that they are completely whipped and will have to submit. He was returning to his home in Georgia. I can learn nothing of either Thompson or his sons.[48]

I inclose [for] you [$14 in] Rebel money. It is very plentiful here now and not worth a cent. You can keep it for a show. One woman, as we passed her house today, was selling it at 10¢ for $10. This I got for nothing. Some of our officers use it for lighting their cigars. . . .

Burkeville Station, Va., April 15th 1865

My dear Ellen,

Last night we heard the sad and terable news of the assassination of President Lincoln and the Sewards.[49] Oh, what a loss to the country and the world! What a crime before God and Heaven! Who are the guilty parties, and what was their object? We all feel miserable. The Army was and is united for Lincoln and the administration. The soldiers loved him. The South will face worse than if the President had lived. But God's ways are not our ways. Oh, may He lead us as a nation in safety. May peace and tranquility once more reign over our unhappy land. We await with trembling anxiety for further news, with a faint hope that they are not yet dead.

News and everything else arrives here slowly. The Southside Railroad is in a miserable condition. They have been runing at the rate of two miles per hour. It is about fifty miles to Richmond. . . .

Burkeville Station, Va., April 17th 1865

My dear Ellen

Lt. Schoonover,[50] a brother of the Colonel, has got a leave of absence and is about starting for home. He is an active aide on my staff. He will call and tell you all. I will write you more fully after

48. Thompson McAllister was not with Lee's army; rather, he was still commanding Covington's "Alleghany Home Guard." McAllister, *Thompson McAllister,* 23–24.

49. Both Sec. of State William H. Seward and his son Frederick narrowly escaped death at the hands of Lewis Paine, one of John Wilkes Booth's co-assassins. In the chaotic hours immediately following the murder of Lincoln, rumors were paramount that the Sewards also were dead. For example, see Meade, *Letters of George G. Meade,* II, 273.

50. Lt. Amos Schoonover was the brother of the 11th New Jersey's commander. For an incident involving him at this time, see *OR,* Vol. XLVI, Pt. 1, pp. 606–7.

all my reports are finished. I am very well; but like all others in the army, amidst our rejoicing over our success we are sad—very sad—on the confirmation of the death of our President. The army as well as the people loved him.

We are still laying here. I can't see how we are to get away until our artillery horses are recruited up. They are completely worn out. . . .

Burkeville Junction, Va., April 18th 1865

My dear Ellen,

I received Alice's letter last evening. The reason you don't receive my letters is as follows. After leaving Petersburg, all communications with the North was lost, and of course I did not write. On the 9th, the day of Lee's Surrender, I wrote you, as I seen our Postmaster for the first time. He told me that he was going back to Burke[ville] Station.

We were several days geting here. On my arrival I was astonished to find that the letter of the 9th had but just gon. Communications had only just been opened. I am now writing you short notes every day. I can't write long ones. I had many reports to write, which I am happy to say are finished, and I am now at my narrative for your benefit. You will excuse my short letters for the present.

It is not likely that I will get home very soon—perhaps not before July or August. The fighting, I think, is all over. . . .

We are not geting the daily papers and know nothing as to what is going on. Keep a file of these for me.

Burkeville Junction, Va., April 19th 1865

My dear Ellen,

. . . Today is the funeral of our President. No work is to be don in the army, and flags are at half-mast. Guns are to be fired. I have divine service for the Brigade. I have no doubt that it will be interesting. If we only had crepe to tie up our flags, I would like it. But in this out of the world place, we must do as we can. It is a sad day for our nation. God grant that [President Andrew] Johnson may do his duty and pilot the ship in safety. . . .

This is a beautiful morning; everything is lovely. Were it not for the sad news of the President's death, we could all feel happy.

I am very busy on my narrative and hope that it may prove interesting to you. It will be quite lengthy. I hope that it will not tire you to read it. I presum that it will be the last of the kind that I will write, as I only write marches connected with battles, and I have but little doubt that I have fought the last battle of the Rebellion. . . .

Burkeville Junction, Va., April 21st 1865

My dear family,

. . . We had a very interesting service yesterday for the Brigade. Chaplain [Samuel] Moore and Chaplain [Edward] Hamilton give us splendid eulogies on the late President. The colors are all draped in mourning. All felt sad, very sad.

The news of the surrender of [General Joseph E.] Johnston's army just reached us.[51] The war is over and will soon be closed up. Then we can all return to our homes. It may take a little while yet, but it can't be very long. I feel like going home to enjoy the ballance of my life with my dear family. Thank God for this blessed privilege. I did not expect to enjoy it so soon, if at all. I rather thought it more likely that I would fall on the battlefield. How good God has been to me and all of us. God be praised! . . .

Burkeville Junction, Va., April 23rd 1865

My dear Ellen,

Lt. Col. Schoonover left this morning for home and took with him my narrative of [the Appomattox] action, other papers, and also a hasty note to you. I hope that you get them all right and in due time.

Early this morning the 6th Corps left and went in the direction of Danville.[52] They moved very suddenly and unexpectedly. We are the only Corps at this place, and it is rumoured here this evening that

51. After a five-day conference (Apr. 13–18), Gen. Joseph E. Johnston agreed to Sherman's proposed surrender terms. Yet President Andrew Johnson vetoed the terms as being too lenient. The two generals resumed negotiations; on Apr. 26 Johnston surrendered his Army of Tennessee under terms similar to those granted Lee's men.

52. Danville, Va., lying close to the North Carolina border, contained six military prisons, ironworks, an arsenal and a military hospital. In addition, it was an important rail junction between Richmond and points south. Gen. Horatio Wright's VI Corps occupied the city on Apr. 27. *OR*, Vol. XLVI, Pt. 1, pp. 1315–16.

we are also to move very soon—perhaps tomorrow—in the same direction of the 6th Corps. But there is nothing known as a certainty. We can't conjecture what is up. It is rather thought that Johnston has refused to surrender and that Grant is going to compell him by sending aid to Sherman. Our troops are well rested now and are in fine spirits. We have been thinking that the fighting is over. We would be taken by surprise if we were yet to go down and fight Johnston. . . .

Burkeville Junction, Va., April 26th 1865

My dear Ellen,

Yesterday was ushered in by the firing of 13 guns, and one every half hour until sundown. They fired 36 in all. Troops were paraded, and the order of the observance of the day was read to them. All officers are to wear a badge of mourning on their left arm and swords for six months. We had observed one day before as [Lincoln's] funeral day, the same as you did. The soldiers loved Abraham Lincoln and feel his loss deeply.

This is very forlorn country, uninteresting, with nothing to relieve the eye or mind. Rolling hills and hollows are badly cultivated; scracely a green field is to be seen. Old lands are growing up with pines. Fences are bad; buildings are miserable, dilapidated, and few and far between. The farms are large with but very small portions under cultivation. Every year they are growing less. The lazy planter draws in his lines; the pine forest extends his pickets, followed by his line of battle, until the planter finds himself pushed back, flanked, surrounded, and ocquipying only a small portion of the farm for himself, family and negroes. Here he stays. I would not say "lives," for he does not. He is deprived of all the comforts that makes home delightful in the North.

The change from a very active campaign to the inactivity of the camp and the necessity for exercise cause me to stroll far out over this dilapidated country—sometimes on foot for a walk, other times on horseback. It is often said that in our intercourse with the world there are no persons from whom we cannot learn something. I have found this to be true. The other day Dr. Welling and I walked slowly along the railroad towards Farmville. We had gon but a short distance when we met three men, careworn and tired, walking down the road. We soon entered into conversation with them and learned that they had been conductors on this railroad and that they had just come from

Lynchburg. We asked them how they ran the cars on this miserable road. They answered that lately they had had a greate deal of trouble to keep the cars on the track and that they ran very slowly. At the commencement of the war they run at the rate of 25 miles per hour. Then they had to reduce it to 10 miles; and before we took possession, they could only run about 8 miles per hour. The rails were worn out and the ties are completely rotten. All that has been said and more is true in regard to the worn out condition of the railroads. I may well add that, like the land, they are run out. These men lived in Richmond and Petersburg. They were hurrying home to their families and hoped to get into business again. They are heartily sick and tired of the war and expressed a wish to turn back to the Union.

The next party we met was two darkeys. We came up with them while they were resting. We asked them where they were going.

"Home, massa, home," they replied. "We hab been down to de Junction to buy horses."

"What?" said the Doctor. "Buy horses?"

"Yes," one answered. "We went to see if you'uns would gib us a horse so dat we could make some corn. If we'uns could only get de horse, we could turn up de ground, plant de corn, and hab some bread for to keep our families."

"That is a capital idea," I said. "Show yourselves to be men. Plant corn, hoe potatoes, and make an honest living for your families. You are free, but show to us, and to the world, that you are worthy of that freedom. But tell us, where are you going to get the land to work?"

A cunning smile played over their broad faces. "Why, you'uns own de land," they said. "We'uns will work it for you. Your army got it."

"But where is your master?" we asked.

"Massa tell us to get horses and go to work. Massa will work too, and all will share alike."

We told them that they could not make a better bargain than that one and to go to work at once and lose no time, as the season was advancing rapidly. They seemed to fully understand this. All they wanted was the horses to "make corn." They had left one of their number down at the Junction to do what he could to get a horse while they were walking home—twenty-five miles above here—to attend to their work.

I liked the spirit of these men. They seemed anxious and determined to do something to make a living. They were laboring under many difficulties to accomplish their object. They were fully aware that they were free. They seemed to realize their new position and the responsibility resting upon them relative to supporting their families. The next party we met were colored men also on the hunt for horses. They seemed to evince the same spirit as the first.

A short distance further on we came upon a Rebel soldier laying and resting himself under the shade of a small tree. He was a youth 19 years old, of rather delicate make, dressed in a Rebel uniform careworn and very despondent. On approaching him I said, "Well, sir, where are you going?"

He answered, "Home, sir, home—way down on the York River below Gloucester Point."

We then asked him if he was paroled, to which he replied in the affirmative. He belonged to Lee's army and was captured with the rest. He was an artillery man and belonged to a battery. Though a Private, he had been well raised. His manners were good, showing education and culture. He had been raised in easy circumstances and knew nothing of hardships until he entered the Rebel army. He was reserved at first, but kind words caused him to open his heart. He talked freely of their army and their difficulties. He said that we had outnumbered them and out generaled them, that their army had become completely demoralized, deserted and threw away their guns.

Then, with tears in his eyes, he said, "What could General Lee do with such an army?"

He admitted that they were completely whipped and that there was nothing left for them but to submit. He told us that we pushed them so hard that they had not time to cook or bake their bread—that we had an advantage over them in having hardtack, which we could eat as we were marching, while they had only the flour that they would have to bake before using. He further said that their horses were worn out and starved, while ours were strong and hearty, and that they were compelled to leave their artillery behind. The night before the surrender, he said, they hard-marched to a late hour. After halting, a quartermaster officer rode up and told them to move on or they would be captured, as the Yankees were in their front. The men and officers were completely exhausted, and the horses were unable to move. They all refused to move and said they would rather die on the spot than move that night.

So they remained till morning and then started. They had moved but a very short distance when they found our men across the road. A battle followed—as I have already described to you. After this followed the *greate surrender of the War.*

We now returned to camp and walked down the road in company

with the Rebel soldier, who seemed very reluctant to part with us. But he finally did so with many thanks for our kindness to him.

What a subject for reflection! What a mountain of responsibility is resting on the shoulders of the leaders of this Rebellion, North and South. The cry is against them for their deception. . . .

Burkeville Junction, Va., May 1st 1865

My dear Ellen,

I have just received your kind letter of the 27th of April. It has come through quick.

We are again under marching orders. We are going to Manchester, which place, you know, is on this side of the [James] River at Richmond. So we are going to Richmond—not forward, as last year, but back to Richmond. I do not suppose that we are going to stop there. But where our destination is I don't know. We are to leave here as soon as a [pontoon] bridge train arrives here from the Roanoke River. I think we are going to abandon this part of the country. There are no guerillas here. We can ride out any place with perfect safety. The people are all well disposed and glad to cease this war on our Government.

I cannot tell you when I will be home or how long I will stay in the army. There are so many regiments going out in August that we may not be discharged until that time. My [11th New Jersey] Regiment goes home on August 18th; the 120th New York goes on August 21st. However, we may be discharged sooner. The war is no doubt over, but the country has no government yet. Until such time the military will have to be on hand. I am anxious to go home but will hold on until I am discharged.

I hope to have my full appointment soon. I want to look around for some time after I get home with an eye to business. When I get home, we will talk about it.

Papers have just arrived, and the order relative to reducing the army gives us reason to believe that we may go home the 1st of June. But we don't know.

I will write as often as I can and let you know where I am. . . .

The shell I sent you was the one I was struck with on that memorable Sabbath morning. It had been almost spent and I had my heavy coat on. It did not hurt me in the least. When it hit me, I caught it in my hand before it fell to the ground. I give you a history of it in a letter sent by Lt. Schoonover. . . .

Bivouack on the bank of the Appomattox River
May 3rd 1865

My dear Ellen,

We broke camp yesterday afternoon, came down nearly to Jetersville on the Danville Railroad, and halted for the night. Today our Corps alone have crossed the Appomattox River and have just halted for the night. We are going to Manchester. If God spares us, we move again at 6 a.m. tomorrow. We will arive at Manchester day after tomorrow. It is rumoured that after resting there a few days we go to Alexandria, and possibly to Washington, to be mustered out. But as to this I can't say. If this is so, we will go home the 1st of June. It will take to nearly that time to reach Washington. If we stay in Alexandria any length of time, I will write for you and Hennie to come down. We will see.

This is Amelia County. I like the country much better than the one we left (Prince Edward County). But still the cultivation of the soil is poorly done. We passed Amelia Court House, where we saw the remains of over 100 cannon carriages and caissons that Genl. Lee destroyed on his retreat. We had gathered up the guns—or what we could find of them—and sent them to Petersburg, or perhaps Washington. They had buried some of them. Amelia Court House is rather a pretty little village, but with only a few houses.

It is amusing to hear the Rebels talk about their once would-be Confederacy. They all say that "the Confederacy has gone up the spout." They all talk for the Union now, except a few rabid ones. I am very well. . . .

Bivouack, 5 miles from Wolf Run Shoals, Va.
May 12th 1865

My dear Ellen,

We have just arrived at this place. The Postmaster says that letters will go out this evening, so I hasten to write you a few lines sitting beside my bivouack fire in the twilight of the evening.

Last evening we had a terrible storm of rain and hail before we reached our camp, and we had a wet night of it. This morning was very cold and unpleasant. But it cleared up and became more pleasant.

We will reach Alexandria in about two days' march. When we reach there I will write you again. We have not received any papers for several days and know but little as to what is going on. You know more about it than we do. I am very well and feel like geting towards home. . . .

Bivouack on Little River Turnpike
8 miles from Alexandria, Va.
May 15th 1865

My dear family,

We came here on Saturday evening and rested yesterday. We have just received our first mail for many days—lots of nice letters from home and elsewhere.

Your best plan is to get ready, fix up (don't mind the cost), look nice (becoming your position), and I will telegraph you of the time to come here. We are just packing up to move towards Washington. We are to encamp at Roach's Mill on this side of the [Potomac] River, 4 miles from Washington, 4 from Alexandria, and about 3 from [A. M.] Roberts's [mill]. I will write you this evening or tomorrow morning and tell all.

. . . There is no house near to where we encamp that I know of, but I will see and let you know. Don't start until I telegraph or write you. I will go into Washington tomorrow. Love to friends and say that I will be happy to see them. Many are coming down from the North to see the Army. It will be a great sight to see those two greate armies together.

Mr. & Mrs. Roberts were here yesterday. They are looking very well and send lots of love to you and an invitation to come and see them. The bugle is sounding and I must go. Yes, I do get 3 months' pay proper at the end. . . .

Camp at Arlington Heights, Va., May 16th 1865

My dear Ellen,

We arrived here yesterday and are now fixing ourselves up in camp. We are up on these hills. The ground has been chopped over and is growing up thick in brush. We are clearing it off. There are no houses near us. I am sorry for this, as I would like you and Hennie to come and spend some time with me. Roberts's is about 4 miles from here, and that is about as near as you can get a place to stay. I will,

I think, go to Washington today. I will let you know when the [Grand] Review is to come off as soon as we learn the time. . . .

Camp at Arlington Heights, Va., May 17th 1865

My dear Ellen,

Yesterday I went down to town, called at the paymaster's office and received one month's pay—for the month of March. There is due me from the month of March to this time. It will soon be two months. Last evening I sent $100 to you by Adams Express. No doubt you will receive it before this letter reaches you. My pay is increased about $56 per month. This is by the last act of Congress relative to the pay of officers. When mustered out, we will also get three additional months' pay. But that is only the pay proper—without alowances for horses, servants and rations—say $90 a month. And of course the increase of pay don't help me, only from the first of March to the time that I am mustered out. Had this increased pay been a year sooner, it would have been a nice thing for us, for everything was so high. Living must come down one half in price now. When I get all my pay, besides pay for the lost horses, we can get along.

This summer I want to visit with you and Hennie, Juniata, Bellefonte, Shippensburg, &c., before I go into business. I have never before had time to enjoy this pleasure.

We know nothing more about the coming review, but I will let you know in time. Dr. Welling and I have arranged as follows. If you, his mother, and Hennie come down, and if agreeable to you, we will have a tent for you ladies beside ours. There is no difficulty in boarding; we are living first rate now. We think it will be a pleasant time and place for you. We are up high on a knoll and overlook Washington. I don't want Hennie to come down without you. You write to Mrs. Welling whether you will come. If you do come, arrange with her and come together. Stop at Willard's; we will go down for you and bring you up with us at once. The Doctor has written to his mother on the subject. She will wait to hear from you. . . .

Camp at Arlington Heights, Va., May 18th 1865

My dear Ellen,

I have just seen the notice in the papers that the review will take place on Tuesday and Wednesday of next week. I have just written a telegram for you to come at once. You can telegraph Mrs. Welling to meet you in Trenton. . . . Bring a pillow in your trunk and we will furnish the rest of your bedding. Tell our friends in your town. Perhaps Mr. & Mrs. [Israel] Harris will come down. We will do all we can to make it pleasant for you. Let the hired girls take care of the house. I hope to see you on Monday evening.[53] . . .

                                    Headquarters, 3rd Brigade
                                       3rd Division, 2nd Corps
                                              June 2nd 1865
General Order No. 10
   To the Officers and Soldiers of the 3rd Brigade:
   As we are about to separate, allow me once more to congratulate you on your past and brilliant career, which now becomes a matter of history. The war is over, the contest is ended. The glorious old flag of our country—consecrated by the blood of our fallen heroes—under the folds of which you have so often, so long, and so gallantly fought and bled—and to defend which your comrades have died—now floats in triumph over our land. The war brought us to the field. Peace returns us to our homes. Our work is done, and we go to enjoy the fruits of our victories with our friends in the several States represented in this command. New Jersey, New York, and Massachusetts have an interest in you as their representatives and will do justice to the old 3rd Brigade.
   In parting with you, I feel more than I can express or than language can convey. We shared each other's dangers, toils, and fatigues —on the march, in battle, in the charge, whether attended with victory or defeat. Ties of more than an ordinary kind bind us together.
   Goodbye, Comrades in Arms. God bless you, and the widows and orphans of those of our number who have fallen by our side. And if we never meet again on earth, may we meet in a brighter and better world.

                                            Robert McAllister
                                            Brevet Brig. Genl.

   53. Ellen and Henrietta McAllister journeyed to Washington for the May 25–26 Grand Review of the Federal armies. McAllister's brigade was the last unit in the first day's parade. Then, Henrietta wrote, "we went up to Father's Headquarters at Bailey's Cross Roads, four or five miles from Washington, where Mother remained a week or two. . . . It was thrilling to see those armies returned from their campaigns victoriously ended." Undated note in the McAllister Papers; Baldwin MS., 30–31.

Trenton House, Trenton, N.J., June 12th 1865

My dear Ellen,

Today they will commence paying my Regiment. I think that I will get home tomorrow evening; if not, Saturday morning. I am invited out to Dr. [John] Hall's for dinner today. They are having a party for us. They expected you here to be one of the number.

I am well.

Your devoted Husband
Robert

INDEX

♣ ♣ ♣

Abbott, John S. C., 122
Ackerman, Andrew H., 333–35
Adams, J. Webb, 583n
Addams, Lydia M., 177
ALABAMA INFANTRY—
 6th: 180n
 8th: 180
Aldie, Va., 326n, 328
Alexander, Robert, 124–25, 133
Alexandria, Va.: army life at, 12, 27, 41–42, 60–122, 125–30, 133–35, 136, 196, 203–20, 234, 235; mentioned, 42n, 136, 137, 192, 203, 204, 206, 225, 237, 243, 250, 251, 254, 259, 616–17
Allen, Emory D., 319
Allentown, Pa., 17, 19
Allison, Thomas, 79, 169
Alvord, J. W., 287
Ambrose, Thomas L., 329
Amelia, Va., 605, 616
American Tract Society, 287n, 521, 593n
Amputation, 490–91
Anderson, Edmund, 424n
Anderson, Finley, 534
Anderson, John V., 223
Anderson, Richard H., 537, 606n
Anderson, Tom, 562, 590–91
Anderson farm, 424
Andersonburg, N.J., 483
Andrew, John A., 518, 570
Annandale, Va., 60n, 120
Annapolis, Md., 128, 198
Antietam Creek, Battle of, 4, 208–9, 210n

Appomattox Campaign, 16, 576, 600–8
Aquia Creek, Va., 79, 126, 227, 238, 266, 325
Archibald, James, 211
Arlington, Va., 46, 49–61, 199–205, 617–19
Arms, 209, 502
Armstrong Mill, Va., 578, 581
Army & Navy Journal, 438, 464
Arrowsmith (USN), 135
Ashland, Va., 166n
Associated Press—*see* McGregor, William D.
Atlanta, Ga., 466, 468, 493, 494, 538n
Atlantic Monthly, 464
Atrocities, 48–49, 126, 553, 558
Austin, Alfred H., 540n
Averell, William W., 466n

Bacon, Miss, 361, 362
Bacon, Joseph R., 291
Bailey, Rev., 556
Bailey's Crossroads, Va., 71, 95–96, 619n
Baird, S. J., 87, 88
Baker, Edward D., 42n, 88n
Baker, Henry M., 62n, 63, 70
Baker, Isaac H., 30n, 218
Baldwin, James, 336
Baldwin, Johnson H., 18n
Baldwin, Joseph C., 421, 422
Balloons, 165, 259
Ball's Bluff, Battle of, 88n
Baltimore, Md., 36, 198, 345n, 561, 562, 569

Bank's Ford, Va., 296
Banks, Nathaniel P., 121, 122, 158, 167
Banks, William, 106
Bannister, George H., 270
Baptists, 389, 405
Barber, Lorenzo, 522
Barcastle, N.J., 246
Barcliff, Miss, 103n
Barker's Mill, Va.: 433–41
Barksdale, William, 395
Barlow, Francis C.: background of, 432n; mentioned, 415n, 418n, 432, 433, 435, 449, 481
Barnard, John G., 457n
Barnard, William C., 155, 158
Barry, John, 365
Bartlett, George W., 434, 439–40
Bartlett, Joseph J., 172
Battles and Leaders of the Civil War, 23
Baxter, Henry, 533
Bealeton, Va., 349
Beam, John E., 290n
Beaufort, N.C., 146n
Beauregard, P. G. T., 146
Beaver, James A.: wounded, 490–95, 502; mentioned, 34n, 267, 313, 433, 435, 519, 563
Beck, Charles A., 393
Beck's Mill, Va., 41, 45
"Beefsteak Raid," 504–5
Belle Plains, Va., 236, 249
Bellefonte, Pa., 34n, 433n, 448, 519, 540, 618
Belvidere, N.J., 14–19, 28, 32, 47n, 88n, 100, 114, 159, 169, 178, 183, 192, 222, 240, 241, 246, 252n, 262n, 272, 274n, 276n, 295, 296, 311, 314–15, 320, 322, 328, 330n, 359, 376, 385, 396, 399, 417, 422, 447, 453, 466, 525, 570, 576, 590, 595, 619
Belvidere *Intelligencer,* 272, 543
Bender, Daniel, 415n
Benedict, LeGrand, 245, 259, 270, 334, 339, 340, 399
Benedict, Mrs. LeGrand, 270–71, 277, 280, 339
Benton's Tavern, Va., 83, 97–99, 113–14, 117
Berdan, Hiram, 140, 308n
Berdan Sharpshooters, 139–40, 308, 522
Bermuda Hundred, Va., 442n, 568n
Berry, Hiram G.: background of, 280n; death of, 304, 306n; praised, 280, 300, 313; quoted, 301; mentioned, 91n, 253n, 271n, 280, 289, 317
Bethlehem, Pa., 8, 178
Beverly Ford, Va., 323–24, 334, 342
Biedeman, John, 45n
Bigelow, James R., 402
Bigelow, Thomas H., 319n
Biles, Edwin R., 498–99, 516
Birney, David B.: background of, 383n; criticized, 404; death of, 523; praised, 300, 383, 484, 523; mentioned, 270, 274, 365, 384, 389, 390, 406, 407, 418n, 423n, 424, 432, 435, 442, 443n, 444n, 452, 453n, 467, 481, 483–84, 487, 493, 496, 502, 507, 510
Birney, William, 44, 45, 64–65, 73, 84, 129, 170, 249
Blackwood, Thomas, 376
Blair, John I., 28, 47, 211
Blairstown, N.J., 28n
Blaisdell, William: background of, 259n; criticized, 258–59, 385, 387, 400–4; death of, 453; mentioned, 302, 339, 353, 360–61, 366, 368, 374, 385n, 398
Blake, Henry N., 402
Blenker, Louis, 47n, 52, 54, 56, 283n
Blick House, 533n
"Bloody Angle"—*see* Spotsylvania Campaign
Bloomfield, Lott, 299, 310
Blunt, George W., 546
Bodine, Robert L., 390
Boice, George C., 393, 520
Bonham, Milledge L., 44n, 49n
Bonney, Thomas S., 85n
Boonton, N.J., 288n
Bordentown, N.J., 30
Boston, Mass., 305n, 385n, 387, 393n, 402, 406
Bottom Bridge, Va., 161
Botts, John Minor, 357–59, 383, 386
Bounties, 454, 461, 503–4, 509, 523, 549, 574
Bowers, Charles F., 468, 557, 568
Bowling Green, Va., 414, 425–27, 429
Boydton Plank Road: battle of, 4, 16, 496–97, 526–34, 538–39, 541, 578, 601; mentioned, 515, 566, 599–601, 604
Branch, Lawrence O., 166n
Brandy Station, Va.: army life at, 355–63, 371–412, 568; mentioned, 15, 338
Brentsville, Va., 126

Index ♣ [623]

Brewster, George, 28, 66–68, 84, 93, 111, 154, 185, 188, 192, 203
Brewster, William R., 350, 354, 403, 404
Brighton, Isaiah, 119n
Bristoe Station, Va., 130, 133, 136, 343n, 346–47
Bristol, Pa., 38n, 104
Brooke, John R., 563
Brower, Daniel H., 74n
Brown, Henry W., 404, 410
Buckland Mills, Va., 346
Buckley, John T., 336
Bull Run: *1861* battle of, 12, 27–28, 46–58 *passim,* 69, 70, 76, 124, 133, 144n, 145, 198, 300; *1862* battle of, 196, 199n, 200–1, 203, 204n, 210n
Burials, 319, 354, 380–81, 420, 483, 521–22, 536–37, 578, 587–88
Burk, Peter, 246
Burk Station, Va., 123
Burkeville, Va., 576, 608–15
Burkitsville, Md., 330
Burnett, George, 246
Burnside, Ambrose E.: comments on, 219, 220, 259, 260n, 261, 262, 403n; criticized, 470n; praised, 243, 244, 256; removed from command, 260n; mentioned, 40n, 113, 126, 146, 197, 204, 218n, 227n, 245, 263, 269n, 410, 411, 430, 435, 448, 457, 459, 471
Butler, Benjamin C., 492
Butler, Benjamin F., 411, 430n, 442, 513, 517, 520, 543, 565n, 569
Byington, Edward, 217, 262, 271, 275, 281
Byington, Roderick, 262n, 287

Calhoun, John T., 406
"California Regiment," 42
Cambridge, Mass., 280
Camden, N.J., 103, 251n
Cameron, Simon, 79, 84
Cameron Riflemen, 81–82, 99
Camp, Norman W., 102, 119
Camp Advance, Va., 61n, 62
Camp Edgehill, Va., 61–65
Camp Ellsworth, Va., 196, 213–20, 224
Camp Fairfax, Va., 72
Camp Fitzhugh Farm, Va., 248, 253–92, 299–322, 325
Camp Grover, Va., 207–11
Camp Lincoln, Va., 181–82, 185
Camp Monmouth, D.C., 36–40, 62

Camp Olden, N.J., 11, 27, 29–36, 119
Camp Perrine, N.J., 199n
Camp Princeton, Va., 54–61
Camp St. John, Va., 66–70
Camp Seward, Va., 198
Camp Trenton, Va., 41–42, 45, 62
Camp Tucker House, Va., 579–99
Camp Windfield, Va., 144
Camp life, 34–36, 56, 64, 73, 75, 92, 131–32, 194, 212–13, 224, 227, 231, 232, 236, 237, 255, 256, 265–66, 277, 285, 315–16, 324–26, 340, 356–57, 378–79, 385–86, 388n, 392–93, 434, 436–37, 474
Campbell, Edward L., 200
Campbell, John A., 572n
Campbell, Samuel, 68
Campbell, William, 68, 97, 185–86, 188
Canada, 107
Carr, Joseph B.: background of, 221n; praised, 221, 258, 279, 281, 300, 313, 354; quoted, 316, 324n; transferred, 279–80, 339–40, 409, 411–12; mentioned, 221–22, 224, 228–29, 237, 238, 244–46, 251, 253, 255, 259, 262, 270, 273–74, 277, 280, 282, 289, 302–3, 306, 311, 317–19, 334, 337, 341–42, 346, 348, 354–55, 360–61, 367, 383–87, 400, 402, 404–5, 410, 455, 476
Carr, Mrs. Joseph B., 276–77, 280, 282, 314, 339, 342, 383–84, 406
Cartwright, Bingham, 258n
Casey, Joseph, 122, 199, 205
Casey, Mrs. Joseph, 215–16
Casey, Silas, 161, 168, 173, 179, 180, 198, 199
Castle Cuff, Lord, 360n
Catlett's Station, Va., 130–34, 136, 346–52
Catskill, N.Y., 573
Cedar Creek, Battle of, 524n
Cedar Run, Va., 130–31, 226, 324, 347, 349
Centreville, Va., 12, 28, 47, 49n, 50–51, 53–56, 58, 109, 123–26, 133, 150, 199, 201, 221, 222, 325–27, 337, 343n, 347
Chafey, Reading, 217n
Chain Bridge, 196, 199, 201, 202
Chambersburg, Pa., 221n, 325, 471n, 478
Chancellorsville, Va.: battle of, 4, 13–14, 23–24, 249, 268n,

Chancellorsville, Va. (*cont.*)
  293–313, 318, 319, 322, 327n,
  351, 398, 411, 415; mentioned,
  369, 370, 415
Chantilly, Va., 200n
Chaplains, 33–34, 108, 217–18, 226,
  252, 258, 266, 286, 287, 291,
  329, 368, 373, 375, 380, 382,
  386, 393, 405, 434, 435, 440, 471,
  474, 477, 506, 522, 531, 548,
  570, 584, 611
Chaplin, Daniel, 446, 483
Charles City, Va., 441n
Charleston, S.C., 92, 588
Charlestown, Mass., 305n
Charley (horse), 81, 82, 91–92,
  111–12, 135, 136, 284, 296, 329,
  344, 416, 423, 428, 431
Chase, Salmon P., 79
"Chatham," 269n
Chimneys, Battle of the, 496, 498–500
Christian Commission—*see* U.S.
  Christian Commission
Christmas, 105–6, 249, 371, 376, 542
Churches, Army, 381, 392–93, 401,
  403, 405, 411, 563–64, 569, 570
City Point, Va.: explosion at, 478–80;
  mentioned, 186, 471, 477, 481,
  497, 519n, 545, 547, 593, 596n
Civil War: comments on, 22, 31, 38,
  82, 98, 106, 107, 117, 144, 147,
  159–60, 163, 200n, 204, 207, 216,
  220, 256–57, 357, 434, 458–59,
  464–65, 475, 477–78, 485, 495,
  517–18, 558, 575–76, 589,
  614–16
Clark, A. Judson, 290n
Clark, Samuel, 262
Cline, E. Clark, 375, 382, 386, 475,
  493, 524–25, 572, 591
Cloud's Mill, Va., 60, 100
Cobb, Howell, 166
Coffins, 74–75, 381, 522
Cold Harbor, Va.: battle of, 16, 171n,
  414, 431–33; mentioned, 162–65
Cole, Nathaniel, 421n
Collett, Mark W., 233
Columbia, S.C., 588
Congregationalists, 405
CONNECTICUT ARTILLERY—
  2nd: 388n
CONNECTICUT INFANTRY—
  14th: 199
Conrad, Holmes, 70
Conrad, Tucker, 70
Conscription, 505–6, 509, 549, 565,
  570

Convalescents, 213, 228, 234, 236, 494
Cooke, John R., 486n
Coplay, N.J., 16
Copperheads, 272–73, 280, 288, 294,
  313–15, 318, 321, 325, 354n,
  463, 487, 506, 518, 539, 553–54
Corinth, Miss., 146, 174
CORPS, ARMY (U.S.)—
  I: 295, 318, 323, 332, 391, 399n,
    537n
  II: 4, 15–16, 338, 343, 367, 374,
    391, 399–619
  III: 4, 13–15, 148–399, 404, 408,
    423, 514, 534
  IV: 295
  V: 396, 399n, 415n, 430, 432, 435,
    457, 460, 463–65, 468, 483n,
    484, 487–88, 526, 528, 530,
    532–33, 541, 551–52, 555,
    576–78, 599–601, 605
  VI: 260, 307, 342, 355–56, 365,
    375, 391, 396–97, 399, 407,
    415n, 417, 432, 435, 448–49,
    454, 457–58, 461–63, 466–67,
    521, 523, 551, 572, 599, 604,
    606–7, 611–12
  IX: 262, 410, 417n, 430, 435, 448,
    457, 463–65, 468, 483–84, 517,
    526, 534, 537, 549, 596–97, 599
  X: 467, 487, 491, 509
  XI: 293, 300n, 301, 305, 307, 313,
    320, 349, 481
  XVIII: 430n, 457n, 470, 475, 476n,
    484, 491
  XIX: 458n, 469n
  XX: 411n
Cory, Ira W., 336, 395
Couch, Darius N., 161, 260n, 269
Courts Martial, 207–8, 223, 234,
  459–60, 464, 492
Covington, Va., 10, 17, 144n, 145,
  242n, 609n
Coxe, Lorenzo L., 78
Craig, Calvin A., 483
Crater, Battle of the, 452, 470–71,
  537
Crawford, Samuel W., 533, 555, 558,
  577
Crockett, Mr., 140–41
Crook, George, 466
Cudworth, Warren H., 388, 406
Cullen, Cassius M., 520
Culpeper, Va., 337, 339–42, 343n,
  355, 357, 360
Cumberland, Va., 156, 159
Currituck (USN), 157n
Curry, Mary E., 72n

Curtin, Andrew G., 73, 90, 348
Custer, George A., 3

Dabney's Mill, Battle of—*see* Hatcher's Run, Va.
Dahlgren, Ulric, 397n
Dana, Charles A., 417n
Dangerfield farm, Va., 117
Danville, Va., 604, 611
Darrow, George R., 108
Davies, Thomas A., 91–92
Davies, William H., 91n, 92
Davis, George, 241, 246
Davis, J. B., 458
Davis, Jefferson, 110n, 119, 151n, 180, 317n, 359n
Davis, John K., 494
Davis, Thomas H., 310n
Davis, Uriah Q., 269n
Dead, The, 15, 49, 74, 126, 176, 179–80, 184, 247, 255, 300, 319, 358, 365, 415, 416n, 420, 422, 434, 445, 446, 536–37, 558, 584, 587–88
Deep Bottom, Va.: campaign of, 452, 481–84; mentioned, 469, 523
DELAWARE INFANTRY—
 1st: 439n
Delaware & Lackawanna Railroad, 8–9
Democrats, 30, 63, 249, 272n, 273, 288, 354n, 495–96, 518, 520, 525, 538n, 554
De Peyster, J. Watts, 18–19, 342n
Desertions, 156, 158, 171, 174, 177, 267–68, 382, 384, 387, 495–96, 505, 509, 519, 523, 544, 549, 563, 565, 568, 572, 574–75, 589, 595, 604
De Trobriand, Philip Régis: background of, 498n; praised, 507; quoted, 20–21, 251n, 280n, 521n; mentioned, 496, 498–99, 501, 516, 579–80, 597, 599, 605
Dever, James, 258n
Dick, Alice R., 38, 144, 163, 178, 376, 399, 453, 464, 511, 570, 610
Dick, John T., 57, 80, 203
Dickinson, Joseph M., 238, 257n
Doctors, 48, 52, 217, 234, 319, 338, 358, 363n, 491, 529
Dodge, William E., 211
Donnelly, James, 83
Doremus, Daniel, 267n
Doubleday, Abner, 200n, 404n
Doubleday, Thomas D., 200–2
Dowd, Olney B., 209

Drake, Simeon, 202n, 207n
Dranesville, Va., 105n
Drewry's Bluff, Va., 177n
Drill, 77, 89, 90, 110, 272
Duffie, Alfred N., 327n
Dumfries, Va., 227, 230–31, 352
Dunham, George, 512n
Dunning, William B., 315, 333n, 335
DuPont, Samuel F., 92n
Du Puget, Albert, 297
Dupuy, David A., 14, 99, 100, 176
Dupuy, Eliza, 99
Dupuy, T. Harkins, 8, 102

Early, Jubal A., 355n, 458n, 462n, 471n, 493–94, 509n, 524n, 592
Eayre, Thomas W., 419
Edge, Frederick M., 146, 164
Edsall's Hill, Va., 81
Egan, Thomas W., 426, 526–32, 534, 536, 538, 542
Egan, William H., 421
Einstein, Max, 56
Elizabeth, N.J., 36n, 83, 315, 343
Ellsworth, Thomas, 103
Elm City (USN), 135
Ely's Ford, Va., 370
Emancipation Proclamation, 22, 212, 272n, 389n
England, 94n, 107, 360
Episcopal Seminary, Va., 12, 60, 65–97, 100–22, 125–30, 133–34, 206
Episcopalians, 110, 119
Eshelman, Mr., 145
Ettringham, Joseph B., 183
Eutaw House, 561–62
Evans, Augustus O., 69
Evans, Clement A., 608–9
Evans, G. H., 100
Ewell, Richard S., 350, 458, 606
Excelsior Brigade, 211n, 297n, 350, 367, 399, 411n, 448
Executions, 101, 382, 386, 403, 404, 563, 587

Fagan, Henry M., 275
Fair Oaks, Va.: 178–86. *Also see* Seven Pines, Battle of
Fairfax, Va., 42, 44, 53, 54n, 62, 65, 124–26, 129, 133, 136, 221, 222, 228–29, 329, 343
Falmouth, Va.: 13, 228–322
Farmville, Va., 612
Farnum, Mrs. J. Egbert, 271, 280, 283n
Farragut, David G., 480n

Fausett, Orrin B., 223
Fay, Frank B.: background of, 290n; praised, 390; mentioned, 290–91, 296–97, 316, 325, 387, 406, 477, 479, 491, 552
Ferrero, Edward, 514n, 533
Finklemeier, John P., 483, 515, 569, 581–82, 584
Fisher's Hill, Battle of, 509n
Fitzer, Jonathan R., 267–68, 271, 274, 422
Fitzhugh Farm, Va.—*see* Camp Fitzhugh Farm, Va.
Five Forks, Battle of, 576, 599n, 603–4
Food—*see* Rations
Forrest, George, 402–3
Fort Albany, Va., 46–50, 54, 198
Fort Alexander Hays, 490n, 516
Fort Brady, Va., 568n
Fort Crawford, Va., 490–91, 494, 498, 500, 503
Fort Darling, Va., 177–78
Fort Davis, Va., 516
Fort Ellsworth, Va., 212n, 213, 254, 256
Fort Ethan Allen, Va., 202
Fort Fisher, N.C., 565
Fort Haskell, Va., 535n
Fort Lyon, Va., 203–5
Fort Macon, N.C., 146–47
Fort Marcy, Va., 199–203
Fort Morgan, Ala., 493
Fort Morton, Va., 490n, 496, 535n
Fort Runyon, Va., 54, 203n
Fort Sedgwick, Va., 521n
Fort Stedman, Va., 445n, 490n, 576, 596–97
Fort Taylor, Va., 105
Fort Warren, Va., 490n, 498
Fort Worth, Va., 105–6
Fortress Monroe, Va., 95, 137, 141–42, 146n, 193, 299
Foster, John Y., 21, 23, 26
Foster, Reuben, 255n
Foster, William L., 254n
Fowler, A. D., 188
Franklin, William B., 12, 85, 86, 89, 91, 93–94, 98n, 101, 105–6, 110–11, 128, 133–35, 148, 153–55, 159, 168, 179, 192, 210, 227n, 236, 245, 260
Fraternization, 171, 184, 249, 284, 439n, 441, 500; 502n, 505, 510, 583
Frazee, Joseph H., 376
Frederick, Md., 121n, 330–31

Fredericksburg, Va.: army life at, 228–34; battle of, 13, 197, 233, 239–47, 275; mentioned, 126, 158n, 222, 227, 255, 260n, 286, 295, 307, 320, 424
Freeman's Ford, Va., 342
French, William H.: background of, 345n; criticized, 345, 364n; mentioned, 111, 345–46, 357, 365n, 389
Funerals—*see* Burials

Gaines, William G., 164–65
Gaines's Mill, Battle of, 12, 28n, 36n, 97n, 149, 164n, 185–90, 191n, 194n
Gainesville, Va., 346n
Gammell, Albert M., 305
Gastineau, Edward, 509n
Genot, August, 509n
GEORGIA INFANTRY—
  2nd: 189
Germantown, Pa., 17, 173
Germantown, Va., 48n, 50
Gettysburg, Battle of, 4, 14, 24, 235n, 274n, 294, 330–37, 342, 344, 345, 376, 385, 395, 398, 404n, 453n, 455, 456, 475, 476
Gibbon, John, 435, 449, 481
Gill, Sarah A., 276, 385
Gilson, Helen Louise: background of, 290n; praised, 290, 316–17, 325, 390, 406, 477; mentioned, 290–91, 297, 384, 387, 391, 405, 479, 491–93, 552
Glendale, Battle of, 13, 187n
Globe Tavern, Va., 533n
Gloucester, Va., 137–38, 614
Gordon, Charles C., 67, 122
Gordon, John B., 180n, 583n, 596n
Gordonsville, Va., 123
Gosline, John M., 152
Gould, Edward K., 23
Graham, Mrs. Charles K., 271
Graham, Christopher, 241, 246
Grand Review, 576, 618–19
Granger, David A., 529–30
Grant, Julia D., 592–93
Grant, Ulysses S.: comments on, 403n, 408, 416n, 430, 441, 455, 457, 467n, 502, 513, 544, 591, 592, 598, 606; criticized, 431n; praised, 434, 441, 458, 465, 486; quoted, 457; mentioned, 275n, 374, 403, 410n, 411, 413–14, 425, 426n, 429, 430n, 440n, 442n, 443, 451, 457n, 458, 460,

Grant, Ulysses S. (*cont.*)
    462n, 463, 465, 468, 469n,
    470–71, 479n, 485, 488n, 497,
    546, 575, 596n, 599n, 602,
    606–7, 612
Grear, Valentine, 376n
Greeley, Horace, 128n
Green, Milbrey, 583n
Green, Warren, 246
Greenvillage, Pa., 203
Greenwich, Va., 343, 347
Gregg, David M., 368, 541, 550, 556
Gridley, Mr., 295
Grigg family, 555
Grover, Cuvier: background of, 204n;
    praised, 204, 211, 212;
    mentioned, 206, 210, 213
Grover, John H., 223, 234, 235, 269
Guiney's Station, Va., 310n
Gum Springs, Va., 326–29
Gunn, Neil K., 319n
Gurowski, Adam, 110

Hall, John, 35, 592–93, 620
Halleck, Henry W., 129
Halsey, Thomas J., 287–88, 398
Halsted, N. Norris, 72
Hamilton, Edward J., 506, 524, 611
Hamlin, Charles, 352, 399
Hamlin, Mary I., 117n
Hampton, Wade, 154, 488n, 504
Hampton Legion, 154
Hampton Roads Conference, 572n
Hancock, John, 481
Hancock, Winfield S.: illness of, 453;
    incidents of, 532, 536; praised,
    401n, 537; quoted, 489, 532, 539,
    547; transferred, 537, 543, 547;
    mentioned, 401, 415n, 426n,
    430n, 462, 467, 469n, 480n,
    487–90, 493, 495–96, 507–9, 519,
    526, 531, 537, 601
Hanover, Va., 166n, 427
Hardee's *Tactics*, 55
Harden, John S., 220n
Hare, Otway P., 445–47, 454, 487
Harmony, N.J., 525
Harper's Weekly, 464
Harpers Ferry, W. Va., 207n, 411
Harris, Israel, 14, 47, 471, 476, 619
Harris, John, 102
Harris, Mrs. John, 107, 117, 127, 174,
    192, 256, 269, 274–75, 288, 291,
    473
Harris' Farm, Battle of, 424
Harrisonburg (Pa.) *Telegraph*, 402

Harrison's Landing, Va.: army life at,
    188–95; mentioned, 13, 441
Hart, Daniel, 272, 273
Hart, Orson H., 378
Hart, Mrs. Orson H., 406
Hartford, Henry, 582, 603
Hartranft, John F., 18
Hatch, William B., 111
Hatcher's Run, Va.: battle of, 4,
    575–86; mentioned, 526, 598, 600,
    604
Hatfield, David: death of, 36n; illness
    of, 73, 75, 87; incidents of,
    115–16, 129, 138; reminiscences
    of, 36n, 94, 168n, 173n; wounded,
    186–87, 190–93; mentioned,
    36–37, 47–48, 52, 80, 86, 96, 99,
    376, 381
Hatfield, Mrs. David, 121–22, 281
Havelock Association, 87, 113
Healy, Virgil, 482n
Heintzelman, Samuel P., 111, 127,
    146n, 154, 167, 203–4, 208, 244
Henry, Joseph, 120–21
Henry, William, Jr., 48, 53, 64, 73, 84,
    97, 99, 138, 154, 170–71, 176,
    186–87, 192, 198, 232, 375,
    432–33
Herbert, Charles M., 79, 188, 199,
    204, 338, 351
Heritage, John D., 464, 490
Hero (USN), 135–38, 141, 147, 149
Hess, Frank W., 488n
Hexamer, William, 173
High Bridge, Battle of, 606
Hill, A. Powell, 343n, 415n, 484,
    488n, 497
Hill, John, 288n
Hill, John T., 207, 215, 217, 229, 241,
    245, 250, 253, 255, 257, 275,
    286–88, 310
Hinks, Edward W., 184
Hogan, Edward K., 480n
Holmes, James K., 596
Hood, John B., 466n, 519
Hooker, Joseph: as army commander,
    260n, 263, 266, 283, 293, 295,
    296, 298–300, 307, 409; incidents
    of, 238, 271, 283n, 298, 315;
    praised, 238, 285, 300, 311, 321,
    326, 403n; quoted, 315; removed
    from command, 294; mentioned,
    183, 204, 215, 227, 232–33, 237,
    249–51, 253, 257, 272–73, 279,
    307, 312, 317, 319–20, 325, 375,
    411
Hopkins, Henry, 548, 584

Hopkins, Mark, 548n
Hospitals, 48–49, 66, 68, 119, 213, 219–20, 228, 269, 315, 319n, 321, 407, 416, 429, 539n
Howard, Oliver O., 64, 111, 305
"Hugh's Fancy," 6–8
Hume, William H., 448
Humphreys, Andrew A.: background of, 317n; praised, 547, 596n; quoted, 386n, 547, 562, 564; mentioned, 317, 337, 339, 348, 351, 385, 387, 476, 496, 558n, 559, 561n, 564, 568, 579, 581, 586–88, 593, 597
Hunter, David, 438, 458n
Hunter, Robert M. T., 572
Hutchinson, Mary, 493n
Hutchinson family, 115–16, 122

ILLINOIS CAVALRY—
8th: 119n
INDIANA INFANTRY—
20th: 498n
Ingalls, Rufus, 377n
Ingham, Mrs. John, 117
Intoxicants, 6, 13, 14, 63, 98n, 111, 120, 225n, 248, 251, 259, 262n, 345n, 358, 364n, 382, 400n.
See also Temperance Society
Ironton Railroad Co., 16, 18
Irwin, W. H., 61–62, 67

Jackson, Thomas J., 13, 145, 158n, 167n, 177, 185, 200–1, 204, 207n, 241–42, 293, 297n, 310, 322
Jacob's Ford, Va., 363
James City, Va., 342, 344
Janeway, John L., 197
Jarratt, Va., 554, 555n, 556n, 565n
Jenkintown, Pa., 8
Jerusalem Plank Road, 493n, 495, 498, 501, 503
Jetersville, Va., 616
Johns, John, 110
Johnson, Adolphus, 159
Johnson, Andrew, 610, 611n
Johnson, Bushrod R., 535n
Johnson, George H., 365
Johnson, Philip, 433n
Johnson, Thomas, 336
Johnson, William H., 101
Johnston, Joseph E., 124n, 148, 150n, 151n, 167n, 180n, 185n, 611–12
Jones, Peter, 219n
Jones, William, 521–22, 524, 531, 552, 558

Juniata County, Pa., 6–7, 106, 114n, 178, 240, 591, 595

Kearny, Philip: background of, 60n; criticized, 59, 74–76, 138; death of, 200n; discipline of, 74, 76, 116; illnesses of, 104, 110; praised, 93n, 124, 158, 168, 179, 215; mentioned, 4–5, 12, 60, 77, 82, 85, 86, 92–94, 109, 111–12, 115, 122–23, 126, 129, 133, 135, 146, 155, 159, 161, 167, 183, 189, 192, 235n, 347
Kearny, Philip J.: death of, 333; praised, 245, 309, 333; mentioned, 24, 198n, 223, 234–35, 310, 318
Kelly, Edward, 299, 310
Kelly's Ford, Va., 285, 355–56, 358
Kennedy, Edward D., 241, 253, 255, 257, 287, 296, 422
Kennedy, Robert L., 16, 18
Kent County Courthouse, Va., 155–56, 159
Kernstown, Battle of, 145
Key, Philip B., 211
Keyes, Erasmus D., 167
Kilpatrick, Judson, 4, 342, 397n
King's Courthouse, Va., 183n
Kirby, John W., 194n
Kirk, William H., 564, 568–69
Kitching, J. Howard, 424n
Kniten, Miss, 99
Knighton, Frederick: background of, 191n; criticized, 206–8, 217–18, 223–24, 252, 254, 256, 266, 286; described, 191n; praised, 210; resigns, 291, 310; mentioned, 191, 197, 223, 226, 227, 237, 251, 255, 257, 281, 287, 312, 383
Knighton, Mrs. Frederick, 251–52

Labort, John, 399n, 474
Lacy House, 269, 288
Ladies Aid Society, 102n, 103, 107n, 276
Land mines, 150
Lay, George W., 44n
Layton, Sidney M., 310, 442, 519
Leaville family, 556–57
Lee, Fitzhugh, 326n
Lee, G. W. Custis, 606n
Lee, Robert E., 149, 151, 156–57, 180n, 185n, 199n, 204n, 207n, 208n, 260n, 293, 295n, 307n, 320, 322, 325–26, 338, 341n, 343n, 344, 373, 413–14, 415n,

Lee, Robert E. (*cont.*)
  416n, 424–29, 431n, 440n, 442n, 445, 447, 458n, 469n, 474, 489, 493n, 497, 502, 513, 559–60, 572n, 575–76, 584n, 589, 595, 596n, 599n, 602–4, 606–8, 614, 616
Lee, William H. F., 156–57, 165
Leesburg, Va., 41n, 70–71, 326, 327n
Leger, Mary, 29
Lehigh Valley Railroad, 8, 16
Leslie, James H., 470n
Lewis family, 214
Lexington, Va., 438n
Lincoln, Abraham: and conscription, 505; death of, 609–10, 612; in 1864 election, 496, 505n, 506, 518, 520, 533, 538; pardons condemned soldiers, 387; praised, 129, 540, 609, 612; quoted, 504n; visits army, 249, 282–83; mentioned, 11–12, 29n, 37n, 40n, 53, 57, 79, 93, 96, 159, 212n, 218n, 244n, 263n, 279, 348, 361, 389n, 403n, 405n, 454, 466, 474, 506n, 559–62, 572n
Lindley, George, 299, 311
Litsworth, Martin, 333n
Little, Mrs. Amos R., 99
Livingston, N.J., 246
Lloyd, Robert M., 446–48, 452–54, 456, 476, 479–80, 486, 490, 500, 504–5, 560, 569, 573, 586
Lloyd, Mrs. William, 215, 262
Lloyd, William H.: comments on, 390, 438, 517; illness of, 250, 253, 255; incidents of, 231–32, 433, 489; praised, 206, 210, 228, 269, 309, 334, 336, 428, 483; promoted, 269n, 523–24; wounded, 334–35, 531; mentioned, 87, 217, 222–23, 246, 257, 262, 274, 288, 298, 304, 315, 328, 345, 362, 380, 386, 432, 448, 450, 456, 461, 481, 486, 523, 560
Lloyd, Wilson, 87n, 123, 215n, 440, 455, 479, 560, 591n
Logan, Dorastus B., 220, 275, 287, 333–35
Lomax, Lunsford L., 519n
Lombard, Richard T., 468, 472, 483, 518, 521, 530
London *Times,* 51, 58n, 146
Long Bridge, 40, 54n, 56, 198
Longstreet, James, 14, 154n, 415n, 416n, 428, 537, 592n

Loudoun & Hampshire Railroad, 41n, 42n, 43
Loudoun County, Va., 328–29
Lowe, T. S. C., 165n
Lynchburg, Va., 605, 607, 613
Lyon, Nathaniel, 102

McAlister, Alexander C., 486n
McAlister, Hugh, 6
McAllister, Elizabeth, 6n
McAllister, G. Washington, 6n, 106, 502–3, 595
McAllister, Henrietta G.: quoted, 8–9, 14n, 17, 18, 23n, 28–29, 72n, 619n; mentioned, 5n, 7–8, 14, 23–25, 28, 36, 73–74, 89–91, 94n, 100, 116, 118, 169, 172–73, 188–89, 192, 202, 204, 207, 235, 237, 249, 255, 274n, 284, 310, 312–13, 322, 339, 407, 453, 456, 463, 477, 486, 492, 519–20, 533, 544, 591, 616–19
McAllister, Hugh Nelson, 6n, 17, 34, 67, 79, 144, 310, 339, 348, 407, 433n, 490, 493–95, 532
McAllister, J. L., 486n
McAllister, Jane T., 6n
McAllister, Mary, 443
McAllister, Nancy, 6n
McAllister, Robert: birth of, 6; burial of, 19; criticized, 235n; death of, 19; described, 20–24; discipline of, 13; family antecedents of, 5–6; family of, 6–7; postwar career of, 16–19; praised, 4–5, 19–26 *passim,* 160n, 187n, 306, 314–15, 318, 348n, 508, 530–32, 536, 538, 561, 564, 577n; prewar career of, 5–10; promoted, 11, 13, 16, 32–33, 497, 541; proclamation of, 619; wounded, 4, 14, 15, 330n, 333, 414, 416, 427, 429
McAllister, Mrs. Robert, 6–8, 14, 17, 19, 38n, 29–620 *passim*
McAllister, Sarah E., illness of, 216, 220–22, 237–38, 249; marriage of, 284, 311, 318; mentioned, 7–8, 15, 17, 28, 33n, 35, 73–75, 87n, 89–90, 94n, 123, 169, 192, 197, 204–7, 215, 219, 256, 262, 270, 274–75, 289, 313, 317, 322, 339, 343, 345, 363, 376, 381, 407, 440, 447, 453, 456, 473, 476, 479–80, 486, 500, 502, 523, 560, 573, 586, 608

McAllister, Thompson, 6n, 7, 8n, 10, 17, 31, 144–45, 156, 177, 242, 486, 609
McAllister, William, 6
McCall, George A., 105, 185, 263
McClay, John, 203
McClellan, George B.: as presidential candidate, 495, 518, 520, 524–25, 538; criticized, 128–29, 131, 141n, 160, 176–77, 224; illness of, 128; incidents of, 125, 127, 164; letter to, 94n; praised, 110, 128–29, 137–38, 159–60, 163, 165, 167, 177, 182–83, 199, 201, 204, 207–9, 218–19, 243, 248, 256, 261; removed from command, 197, 218, 223; mentioned, 12, 79, 82, 86, 93–96, 100n, 109, 116, 120–21, 125n, 128, 133–34, 138–45, 148, 154–55, 158, 162n, 168–69, 171n, 173, 175, 184, 185n, 187n, 193, 201, 204n, 233, 401n, 403n, 434, 436
McClellan, Mrs. George B., 127
McDonald, Angus, 242n
McDonald, Benjamin, 219n
McDowell, Irvin: criticized, 57–58, 133, 167, 208; mentioned, 12, 28, 47, 51–52, 54, 56n, 129, 158–59, 162, 165, 172
McGowan, Samuel, 419n
McGregor, William D., 508, 532–34, 536, 539, 579, 586
McKean, William R., 113n
McLaughlin, Napoleon B., 302–3, 321, 364
McLean, George W., 42, 47–48, 50, 52, 57, 72n
Mahone, William, 449n, 583
Mail, 38, 91, 142, 193, 203, 233–34, 250, 328, 406–7, 441, 445, 464, 477, 569, 610, 616–17
MAINE ARTILLERY—
  1st: 424n, 430, 435n, 444, 446, 483
  2nd: 222
MAINE CAVALRY—
  1st: 434
MAINE INFANTRY—
  3rd: 64n
  4th: 64n, 280n
  5th: 64n, 152n, 172n
Manassas, Va., 42–45, 47, 50, 95, 120, 123–26, 130, 150, 324–25, 410n
Manchester, Va., 615–16
Mansfield, Joseph K. F., 38–40
Marbaker, Thomas D., 23

Marches, 53, 159, 227–32, 260–61, 322–24, 415n, 416n, 434n, 552–53, 555, 558n
Marston, Gilman, 279
Martin, Luther, 241, 245, 333–35
Martinsburg, W. Va., 70n
Maryland: comment on, 330
Mason, James M., 94
Mason's Hill, Va., 78
MASSACHUSETTS ARTILLERY—
  1st: 388n, 435n, 442n
  2nd: 222
  10th: 583
MASSACHUSETTS INFANTRY—
  1st: 142n, 221n, 297n, 302–3, 319, 321, 341, 344, 388, 399, 406, 418, 430
  6th: 36n
  11th: 221n, 230, 259n, 302, 305, 339, 374, 389, 392–93, 399, 402, 468, 482, 512, 516, 529–30, 570, 582, 587n, 602–3, 605
  16th: 178n, 221n, 280, 339n, 399, 418–19, 512n, 530
  19th: 184
  33rd: 206
  34th: 206–7, 213n
Massey, Mrs., 378, 382
Meade, George G.: and D. B. Birney, 404; comments on, 403n, 607; criticized, 404; mentioned, 294, 331–32, 337, 343n, 373, 397n, 409n, 411, 416n, 417n, 443n, 457n, 462, 526–27, 559–50, 592, 606
Meade (servant), 62–63
Meadow Bridge, Va., 175
Meagher, T. Francis, 4, 205n
Mechanicsville, Va.: army life at, 172–78; battle of, 149, 185; mentioned, 166, 171, 181, 431
Meeker, William H., 245, 274, 278–79, 300
Meikel, George W., 498
Mercersburg, Pa., 6
Merriam, Waldo, 419
Methodists, 35, 405, 522, 571n
Meves, Charles, 191n
MICHIGAN INFANTRY—
  3rd: 443n
  4th: 164, 165n
Middleburg, Va., 326n, 327n, 328
Middletown, Md., 330
Mifflintown, Pa., 106n
Miles, Nelson A., 482, 533, 598–600, 602
Milford, Del., 72n

Miller, Matthew, Jr., 30n
Milroy, Robert H., 341
Mine Run Campaign, 15, 337–38, 345n, 363–73, 376n, 381, 398
Mitchell, Robert B., 102n
Mitchell, William G., 537
Mobile, Ala., 480, 493
Moffett, Samuel G., 431
Monmouth *Democrat,* 276
Montgomery, William R.: background of, 11, 32n, 33n; dismissed from service, 405; relations with McAllister, 11n, 61; mentioned, 12, 27, 32–33, 35, 38, 41–42, 44, 47–48, 50–58, 60, 62–63, 68–75, 79–80, 84, 86, 91, 94, 100, 104, 120, 128–29, 178, 259
Moore, Samuel T., 477, 531, 611
Moore, Stephen: comments on, 217, 234, 310, 328–29; criticized, 234; family of, 220n, 234, 316; illness of, 310, 312, 333; praised, 193; mentioned, 223, 235, 251–54, 261, 263, 270, 280–83, 305, 308, 314, 318, 320
Moore, Mrs. Stephen, 218, 220
Morale, 37–38, 44, 163, 186, 202, 261n, 263, 414, 432, 441, 475, 479, 588
Morehouse, Benjamin F., 499
Morford, Henry, 22
Morris, Louis M., 468n
Morristown, N.J., 383, 570
Morrow, Henry A., 577n
Morton's Ford, Va., 390n
Mosby, John S., 380
Mott, Gershom: and Winfield Hancock, 467; background of, 251n; criticized, 417n, 425–27, 436, 492, 508; illness of, 400; letter to, 417–18; praised, 399; promoted, 505–7; wounded, 306n, 605; mentioned, 251, 262n, 276, 289, 303, 341, 344, 350, 354, 367, 388, 399, 403, 407, 409, 411–13, 415n, 416n, 422–25, 428–29, 435, 437, 442, 449n, 452, 454, 467–68, 475, 480n, 483, 488, 492, 495, 498n, 499n, 507–8, 516–17, 527, 530, 534n, 536, 541, 554, 558–59, 561n, 562, 564, 570, 574, 581, 586, 588, 593, 596–97
Mount, John D. P., 191
Mount Vernon, Va., 88, 90, 93–94, 97, 215
"Mud March," 248, 258–62

Munson's Hill, Va., 61n, 75–76, 78, 96
Music, 265, 280, 283, 319, 339–40, 474, 479, 491, 504, 520–22, 537, 551, 563n, 578, 583, 584n, 588, 591
Mutchler, Samuel B., 186
Mutchler, Valentine, 101, 174, 181, 198, 230
Mystic (USN), 135

Naglesville, N.J., 192
Nashville, Tenn., 560n
Negroes: comments on, 22, 61, 141, 212, 279, 300, 307, 313, 348, 351, 361–62, 379–80, 395–98, 442, 447, 472, 480, 553, 556–57, 562, 590, 613–14
Nelson, Edward D., 241, 246, 422
Nelson, Sarah, 6
New Bridge, Va., 164–66, 171, 184
New Brunswick, N.J., 49n, 246, 382, 520, 591
NEW HAMPSHIRE INFANTRY—
2nd: 229–30, 246, 268, 279
12th: 327, 329, 341
NEW JERSEY ARTILLERY—
1st: 280
NEW JERSEY INFANTRY—
1st: 4, 11–13, 27–196, 198, 210, 218, 232–33, 249n, 375, 432
2nd: 37n, 41, 42n, 45, 47, 48n, 50–52, 56–57, 60n, 72n, 77, 93, 95, 99, 104, 115n, 119, 135, 186–87, 191n
3rd: 37n, 41, 45n, 56–57, 60n, 77, 78n, 81, 97n, 106, 108, 119, 125, 135, 146, 159, 186–87, 191, 200n, 404, 410
4th: 44n, 77–78, 84–85, 119, 135, 176n, 191n, 249n
5th: 180, 251, 290n, 306, 350n, 418, 474n, 490, 506, 514–15, 540
6th: 159, 180, 225n, 350n, 418, 437, 468, 477, 482, 490, 503, 506, 520
7th: 225n, 272–73, 306n, 324n, 350n, 418, 506, 514–15, 540, 581, 583, 597, 599–600
8th: 150n, 159, 350n, 418, 427, 482, 506, 508–9, 520n, 574, 582–84, 597, 602–3
9th: 112
10th: 260, 410
11th: 4, 13–16, 87n, 101n, 188, 191–570 *passim,* 582, 596–98, 602–3, 615, 620
12th: 207n, 288–89, 310, 387n

New Jersey Infantry (cont.)
    15th: 200, 203, 289
    24th: 272n
    25th: 255n
    30th: 197n
New Jersey legislature, 272–73, 277, 287–88, 354
New Orleans, La., 145, 147
New York, N.Y., 17, 42n, 103n, 209n, 211n, 277n, 286, 341, 344, 381, 436, 498n, 501, 546
NEW YORK ARTILLERY—
    1st: 229n, 230
    2nd: 388n, 435n
    6th: 105n
    7th: 388n, 435n
    8th: 435n
NEW YORK CAVALRY—
    1st: 126
    5th: 342n
New York *Citizen,* 23
New York *Herald,* 56, 174, 406, 508, 534, 580
NEW YORK INFANTRY—
    2nd: 221n
    4th: 200n
    8th: 47n, 52
    15th: 66, 93n, 152
    16th: 91–92, 93n, 172n
    18th: 93n, 152n
    26th: 56n, 93n
    27th: 56n, 93n, 172n
    29th: 47n, 52
    31st: 93n, 152–53, 215, 219
    32nd: 93n, 152–53
    40th: 426n, 571
    45th: 98n
    55th: 498n
    68th: 81–82
    70th: 350n
    71st: 350n
    72nd: 350n
    73rd: 350n
    74th: 350n, 364
    93rd: 492n
    120th: 206, 208, 210, 237, 258, 344, 350n, 418, 469n, 474, 479, 480n, 504, 511, 515–16, 520–21, 528–29, 537, 548, 562, 582–84, 596–98, 602, 605, 615
New York *Times,* 77, 116, 129, 160, 534, 579
New York *Tribune,* 62–64, 69, 116, 128–29, 160, 310, 406, 536–37
Newark, N.J., 80n, 246, 276n, 376
Newark *Advertiser,* 188
Newark *Daily,* 543

Newell, William A., 49, 53, 339, 348, 351, 361, 374, 377, 538
Newkirk, Rodney B., 468
Newport News, Va., 194n, 263n
Newton, John, 85, 93, 152, 154
Nichols, Alphonso I., 83
Nixon, John, 348, 361–62
Norfolk, Va., 146, 566
Norristown, Pa., 18
North Anna River Campaign, 414, 426–29
NORTH CAROLINA INFANTRY—
    46th: 486n
North Penn Railroad, 8
Northumberland, Pa., 8
Nurses, 103, 107, 120, 269, 276, 291

Oak Grove, Va., 183n
Oakley, Lewis W., 115–16, 122, 375
OHIO INFANTRY—
    1st: 42n, 43–44, 61
Olden, Charles S., 11, 13, 29n, 30n, 32–33, 63, 72n, 73–74, 80, 90, 100, 104, 188, 192–93, 205, 223
Oldershaw, John, 235
O'Neil, John, 176n
Opequon Creek, Battle of, 509n
Orange, Va., 366
Orange & Alexandria Railroad, 81, 117n, 123, 130–31, 262n, 323, 325, 347, 349n, 373
Osborn, Henry S., 121n, 321, 395, 501, 544, 564, 568–69
Osborn, Mrs. Henry S., 121, 564
Osborn, Thomas W., 229–30, 303
Osborne, Joseph D., 375
Ould, Robert, 607
Oxford Furnace, N.J., 8–9, 14n, 28, 30n, 43, 45, 53, 68, 84, 97, 121, 191n, 205, 214, 252, 493n

Paine, Lewis, 609n
Parades—*see* Reviews
Parisen, Samuel H., 33n
Parker, Joel: incidents of, 289–90; praised, 290; mentioned, 251n, 269, 287–88, 318, 321, 377, 386, 473
Parker's Store, Va., 368
Paterson, N.J., 546–47
Patriotism: expressions of, 38, 72, 106–7, 117, 166, 205, 216, 220, 224, 226, 249, 278, 280, 312–13, 396, 455–56, 459, 464–65, 512, 529, 544–46, 607–8; lacking in the North, 32, 248, 256–57,

Patriotism (*cont.*)
  272–73, 280, 461, 477–78, 487, 512, 560, 574
Patterson, Carlisle P., 104–5, 204–5
Patterson, Mrs. Carlisle P., 104–5, 204–5
Patterson, Francis E., 225–26
Patterson, James, 540
Paul, Charles R., 375, 454, 462
Paul, J. Marshall, Sr., 88
Paul, Miss Sidney, 466
Pay, Army, 67, 89, 91, 114, 253, 281, 338, 358–59, 392, 394–95, 438–39, 455, 471–72, 479, 571, 589–90, 618
Payne's Farm, Battle of—*see* Mine Run Campaign
Peace Democrats—*see* Copperheads; Democrats
Pearson, Mrs. Eleanor B., 104, 204–5
Pearson, Joseph, 104n
Peebles House, 515
Peele, Capt., 360n
Pegram, John, 583n
Pendleton, George H., 495, 518
Peninsular Campaign, 12–13, 109–10, 127, 134–95, 204n, 225n, 401n, 430n, 434, 449n, 543
PENNSYLVANIA CAVALRY—
  3rd: 488n
PENNSYLVANIA INFANTRY—
  23rd: 383n, 448n
  26th: 221n, 222, 245, 280, 339n, 364, 382, 389–90, 393, 399, 402, 418, 430–31
  48th: 457n
  71st: 42n
  84th: 339n, 341, 399
  88th: 327
  96th: 152n, 153, 172n, 173
  99th: 498n
  105th: 483n
  107th: 203n
  115th: 350n
  123rd: 203
  127th: 199
  148th: 269, 313, 433, 540, 570
Pennsylvania Railroad, 7–8
Pequosin Bay, Va., 110, 135–46, 226
Perrine, Lewis, 80, 290, 371
Perry, Nehemiah, 80
Perry County, Pa., 6
Perth Amboy, N.J., 103n
Peters, Mrs. Bernard, 99
Petersburg (Va.) Campaign, 16, 365n, 414, 440–604
Pettigrew, Johnston J., 184

Philadelphia, Pa., 14, 33n, 36, 42n, 72, 76, 78, 79n, 87, 89, 102n, 103n, 107n, 169, 192, 194, 215n, 222n, 262, 275, 291n, 333, 377, 389, 398–99, 410–11, 419, 440, 501, 523n, 569
Philadelphia *Inquirer,* 579
Philipsburg, Pa., 101, 117n, 273
Picket duty, 65, 71–72, 112, 169–71, 175–76, 182–83, 185, 273, 280, 320, 342–43, 433, 440–603 *passim*
Pierce, Byron R., 443, 452, 498, 511, 515–16, 531, 580, 599–600, 605
Pierce, Mary A., 37n
Pioneer Corps, 307, 333n, 474, 477
Pittsburgh, Pa., 17
Pitzer, James, 351
Pleasants, Henry, 457n
Pleasonton, Alfred, 326n
Plimley, William, 557, 573
Point Lookout, Md., 279n
Poland, John S., 303n
Pollard, Edward A., 359n
Pope, John, 196, 199n, 200n, 201, 208–9, 219
Poplar Church, Va., 107
Poplar Spring Church: battle of, 496, 511–16; mentioned, 550–52
Port Royal, S.C., 92n
Porter, David D., 565n
Porter, FitzJohn, 128, 166, 168, 184–85
Potts, Mrs. Robert B., 103
Pratt, Calvin E., 153–54, 215
Presbyterians, 7, 18–19, 33, 35, 88n, 102, 121n, 191n, 252n, 262n, 277n, 383, 405
Price, Francis, Jr., 515, 553–54, 563, 581, 583, 599
Price, Rodman M., 553n
Prince, Henry: background of, 349n; incident of, 372; praised, 350; mentioned, 349, 352, 361–62, 386, 393
Princeton Theological Seminary. 191n, 375n, 383n
Prisoners, 177, 352, 355, 358, 422, 517, 536, 584
Proudfit, John, 95n
Proudfit, Robert B., 95, 102, 108
Provost, William S., 223
Provost Marshal, 509, 566–67, 569
Punishments, 267, 332n, 570. *See also* Executions
Purdy, E. Sparrow, 193

Rafferty, John C., 371, 395
Railroads: destruction of, 130–32, 347, 349, 541, 554–55, 606; travel on, 36, 377, 387, 399, 561, 613
Rains, Gabriel J., 150n
Ramseur, S. Dodson, 466n
Ramsey, John: criticized, 425, 427–28, 435–36, 508–9, 542, 561–63, 569–70, 585; praised, 436, 561n; mentioned, 482n, 570n, 574, 581–82
Rapidan River, 337, 359, 362–71, 373, 390–91, 413, 415n
Rappahannock River, 337–38, 342–43, 347, 353, 356, 375
Rappahannock Station, Va., 322–23, 355–56
Rations, 217, 227, 230–32, 243, 254, 271, 324–25, 362, 379, 382, 389–90, 396, 434n, 465, 474–75, 477, 505, 510, 544–46
Raum, Green B., 19n
Ream's Station (Va.) Campaign, 452, 487–90
Rectortown, Va., 380n
Religion: in the army, 20, 35, 69, 84, 95, 103, 108, 136, 210, 226, 258, 281, 286–88, 312, 324, 329, 354, 379, 381, 383, 385, 389, 392–93, 400–1, 405, 410–11, 440, 459, 463, 474, 477, 493, 506, 521, 524, 541, 548, 563–64, 568, 570–72, 592, 611
Republicans, 17, 33, 49n, 273, 288, 538
Revere, Joseph W., 306
Reviews, 93–96, 253, 281–83, 289–91, 360, 388n, 395, 400, 407–8, 564, 568, 618–19
RHODE ISLAND CAVALRY—
1st: 327
RHODE ISLAND INFANTRY—
1st: 40
Ribble, George T., 262–63, 265, 271, 316, 384, 386, 395
Richardson, Frank, 88n
Richardson, Israel B., 183, 222
Richardson, Johanna, 88
Richardson, Samuel W., 280n
Richardson, Mrs. Samuel W., 280, 384
Richmond, Va., 131, 137, 148–50, 156, 159–66, 169, 172–81, 184, 188, 201, 222, 263, 285–86, 293, 296, 299, 497, 413–604 *passim,* 607, 613, 615

Richmond & Danville Railroad, 599n, 604, 606
Richmond *Examiner,* 359
Richmond, Fredericksburg & Potomac Railroad, 440n
Ricketts, R. Bruce, 533
Ridgeway, Henry, 473
Rinker, Henry, 383, 570
Rivers, Charles C., 516, 605
Roach's Mill, Va., 41n, 617
Roanoke Island (N.C.) Campaign, 113n, 120
Roberts, A. M., 206, 214n, 215–16, 219, 223, 254, 299, 617
Robertson's River, 341n, 342n
Robertson's Tavern, Va., 366
Robeson, Andrew, 272
Robeson, James, 272n, 348
Rosecrans, William S., 347
Rosser, Thomas L., 519n
Runyon, Theodore, 41, 56
Rusling, William J., 468
Russell, Charles S., 514
Russell, William H., 50–51, 58n
Ryerson, Henry O., 99, 186, 410

St. Patrick's Day, 594
Salem Church, Va., 307n
Salm-Salm, Mrs. Felix, 283
Sangster's Station, Va., 125–26
Sanitary Commission—*see* U.S. Sanitary Commission
Sapp, Charles, 539
Sapp, Jacob, 538–39
Sapp, William C., 539n
Sargeant, Frank, 259–60
Saturday Evening Post, 100
Savannah, Ga., 560n
Sayler's Creek, Battle of, 605–6
Schenck, Garret, 206n, 224, 228, 231, 374
Schoonover, Amos, 24, 609, 615
Schoonover, John: background of, 229n; marriage of, 278–79; praised, 288, 309, 334; report of, 334–36; wife of, 543, 548; wounded, 229n, 437–38; mentioned, 229, 270–71, 283, 296, 305, 308, 316, 359, 362, 374–75, 387, 421, 466, 503, 510, 525, 538, 543, 548–50, 561, 578, 579n, 596–99, 602, 609n, 611
Scott, Winfield, 44, 55, 96
Scranton, Charles, 30n, 31–32, 80, 90, 121, 313–14, 318, 525
Scranton, Mrs. Charles, 101, 313
Scranton, Seldon T., 62, 186, 205, 214

Scranton, Pa., 9, 28n, 72
Searing, A. B., 363n
Sedgwick, John, 4, 307n
Seeley, Francis W., 476
Sellers, Cornelius G., 311n, 321
Seven Days Campaign, 12–13, 149, 185–87
Seven Pines, Battle of, 148, 167–69, 173, 179–80, 184, 198n
Seward, Frederick W., 609
Seward, William H., 244, 291, 572n, 609
Sewell, William J., 251, 306, 311, 425
Sharp, John C., 223n
Sharpe, George H., 210n, 237, 258
Sheridan, Philip H., 4–5, 469n, 496, 509, 519, 524, 592–93, 599, 606–7
Sherman, William T., 466, 468, 496, 509, 543, 545, 560, 588n, 611n, 612
Shimersville, Pa., 8
Shippensburg, Pa., 101, 178, 399n, 483, 618
Shooter, Mrs., 212
Shumate, Dr., 349n
Sickles, Daniel E.: background of, 211n; criticized, 14, 211–12, 244, 294, 404; described, 244n; incidents of, 250–51, 271, 283; loss of leg, 345–46; quoted, 5, 24, 300n, 306n; praised, 298, 300–1, 304, 313, 345, 404; mentioned, 4, 13, 213–15, 221–22, 224, 229–30, 233, 237, 239, 243, 253, 257, 276, 282, 289–91, 293, 296, 297n, 299n, 303n, 312, 317, 327n, 339, 346, 348, 361, 374, 387, 389, 399, 404n
Sickness: 66, 68, 142, 160, 176, 182, 192–94, 197, 213, 216–17, 219, 220n, 222–23, 228, 233, 236, 248–50, 252–58, 264–65, 269, 319, 321, 337, 358, 371, 380, 389–90, 451, 480n, 551
Sidgraves, Mrs. Charles, 101
Sigel, Franz, 221
Silvers, Jordan, 82–83
Simpson, Benjamin F., 571
Simpson, James H., 111, 129, 170, 176n
Six-Mile House, 533n
Slavery: 122, 126, 132–33, 143–44, 178, 212, 556–58
Sleeper, Samuel T., 335, 388, 401, 421, 459

Slidell, John, 94
Slocum, Henry W., 85n, 93, 151, 179, 192–93
Smith, Alfred, 376
Smith, Charles A., 33–34, 120
Smith, David, 30, 463
Smith, Mrs. E. A., 277–78, 376
Smith, Ira, 382, 386–87
Smith, J. Hyatt, 389, 392
Smith, J. W., 458
Smith, John H., 281, 283, 316, 321–22
Smith, Walter N., 402
Smith, William F.: criticized, 430n, 442n; mentioned, 159, 169, 171, 263n, 430, 441, 447, 457n
Smith's Point, Va., 136
Smyth, Thomas A., 439, 527, 564, 579–80, 582–84, 597–98
Snicker's Gap, Va., 466
Snooks, Wilson, 439
Snyder, Jacob L., 516
SOUTH CAROLINA INFANTRY—
1st: 42n, 419n
South Mountain, Battle of, 4, 207
Southside Railroad, 456n, 511, 513, 526, 599n, 604, 609
Sovereign, Thomas, 474
Spear, Samuel T., 277
Spettigue, Emma I., 117n
Spohn, Henry, 176n
Spotsylvania Campaign, 4, 16, 23, 401n, 414, 417–23, 426, 432n, 459, 487, 491–92, 604n
Stafford, Va., 227, 232
Stagg, Theodore, 223, 234, 363
Stahel, Julius H., 47n
Stanton, Edwin M., 148–49, 159, 162n, 168n, 169, 193, 267n, 407n
Starbird, Isaac W., 504
Starks, William J., 579–80
Staunton, Va., 438
Steams, Thomas, 145
Stedman, Griffin A., 476n
Steele, Jerry, 379–80, 395, 397–98
Steinwehr, Adolph von, 47n
Stelle, George M., 508n, 509
Stephens, Alexander H., 572
Stephenson's Depot, Battle of, 341n
Steuart, Henry, 348, 351
Stevensburg, Va., 391
Stevenson, J. M., 521–22
Stewart, Kensey J., 119n
Stockton, Robert F., Jr., 29n, 72, 75, 290, 318
Stone, Charles P., 87, 88n

Stoneman, George, 155, 157, 159, 161, 163–65, 172, 253, 255, 257, 262, 281, 296, 299, 374
Stonewall Brigade, 31n, 318n
Stony Creek, Va., 550, 565n
Stoughton, Homer R., 308
Stragglers, 236, 370–71, 552–53
Stratton, John L. N., 56
Street, George E., 276, 281, 287
Stryker, Thomas J., 79–80
Stryker, William, 79n
Stuart, George H., 275, 287
Stuart, James E. B., 105n, 176, 221, 341
Stuart, John, 252
Sumner, Edwin V., 4, 98, 126, 167, 227n, 233, 269n
Sunbury & Erie Railroad, 8
"Sunday"—*see* Anderson, Tom
Sutlers, 181n, 209, 295, 405, 479, 562
Sweeney, John, 181
Sydnor farm, 169–70

Taneytown, Md., 330–31
Tannatt, Thomas R., 442
Tantum, William H., 81, 190
Tappen, John R., 515–16
Taylor, Archibald S., 78
Taylor, Edward F., 48–49, 52–53, 67–68, 233
Taylor, George W.: criticized, 158, 274; praised, 146; mentioned, 45, 56, 77, 97, 106, 125, 129, 179, 186n, 187, 192–93, 195
Temperance Society, 383, 385, 388–90, 394
Tents, 131–32, 217, 224, 228, 231, 236–37, 250, 256, 260–61, 270, 340, 356, 551
Terry, Alfred H., 565n
Thanksgiving, 227, 232, 363, 544–47
Third Corps Union, 341–42, 381, 388, 410, 475
Thomas, Edward C., 402
Thomas, George H., 560
Thomas, Lorenzo, 79
Thompson, Sarah, 6, 123
Thompsontown, Pa., 7
Tiffany & Co., 381
Titus, Uriel B., 524
Todd's Tavern, Va., 417
Tom's Brook, Battle of, 519n
Torbert, Alfred T. A.: criticized, 59–60, 100–1, 134, 187; illness of, 123, 148, 182, 187, 190, 192–93; praised, 77, 101n, 519;
mentioned, 12, 72–73, 75, 86, 94, 102, 111, 135, 142, 146, 152, 154, 159, 162, 193–94, 233, 274, 374–75, 404, 425n
Totten, Jonathan, 119n
Townes, W. W., 604n
Townsend, George A., 164n
Trent Affair, 94n
Trenton, N.J., 11, 13, 27, 29–31, 79n, 80, 102, 112, 140, 181n, 191–93, 197, 199n, 218, 241, 251n, 253, 371, 377, 399, 439, 619–20
Trenton *Star Gazette,* 543
Trimble, Mrs. Joseph, 103
Tripp, Porter D., 389
Tronton, John H., 223n
Troy, N.Y., 270, 277
Truces, 49, 445–46, 448, 483, 536–37, 587, 606
Tucker, Isaac M., 72, 76–77, 111, 186
Tucker family, 550–51, 594–95
Tunis, Daniel W., 191
Tunstall's Station, Va., 158n, 162
Tuscarora Academy, 203
Tuttle, William W., 217n
Tyler, Robert O., 424n, 435
Twichell, Joseph, 406

Uniforms, 176, 181–82, 222, 236, 325, 398, 474, 501, 510
Union Mills, Va., 343
Unitarians, 393
U.S. ARTILLERY—
  2nd: 60n
  4th: 334, 476
U.S. CAVALRY—
  2nd: 60n
U.S. Christian Commission, 87n, 100n, 275, 281, 286–88, 291, 375n, 392–93, 396, 401, 403, 458, 520, 569
U.S. COLORED TROOPS—
  19th: 516
  28th: 514n
U.S. Military Academy, 404, 554
U.S. Military Railroad, 497, 521n, 586
U.S. Sanitary Commission, 73, 264, 465, 477, 552
U.S. Sharpshooters—*see* Berdan Sharpshooters
Utz's Ford, Va., 341n

Vallandigham, Clement L., 495n, 506
Van Cleve, Aaron, 253, 255–256
Van Ness Gap Tunnel, 8–9, 211n
Vassar, John E., 592

VERMONT INFANTRY—
  2nd: 64n
Vests, Bulletproof, 181
Vicksburg, Miss., 321, 403n
Vienna, Va., 12, 27, 41–45, 55, 61
Vill, Michael, 469n
Virginia: comments on, 48n, 91, 109, 131–33, 140, 143, 156, 163, 166, 178–79, 205n, 224–25, 230, 274, 323, 328–31, 350, 357, 433, 441, 458–59, 462, 550–51, 555, 569, 612
Virginia Central Railroad, 592n
VIRGINIA INFANTRY—
  11th: 61n
  27th: 31n
Virginia Military Institute, 438n
Vroom, Peter D., Jr., 232

Wagner, Orlando G., 139n
Wainwright, Charles S., 22, 282n, 283n
Wannan, George, 74n
Warner, Charles B., 184
Warner, Henry C., 28, 29n, 66–68, 84, 97, 193
Warren, Gouverneur K., 366, 368, 390n, 426n, 485, 541, 599n
Warren County, N.J., 10–11, 47, 191, 272, 314–15, 317, 375n, 525
Warren Railroad, 8, 211n
Warren Station, Va., 545
Warrenton, Va., 130, 132, 346–48, 351–54
Washington, D.C.: army life at, 11–13, 36–40, 59, 196, 388n; 1864 raid on, 458n, 461–63, 469n; mentioned, 27, 41, 47n, 51, 54n, 56–57, 73, 77, 79, 101–2, 104, 107, 117, 121n, 122n, 137, 158n, 162, 178, 193, 198–99, 201, 203–4, 214, 225, 230, 238, 243–44, 263, 272–73, 287, 311–12, 321–22, 328, 338–39, 343, 347, 371, 377, 384, 386, 389, 395, 399, 404, 424, 430, 435, 480, 508, 537n, 539n, 560, 562, 569, 572, 576, 590, 593, 616–19
Washington *Chronicle,* 586
Washington *Star,* 115n
Watson, Elisha F., 393n
Waynesboro, Va., Battle of, 592n
Weaversville, Va., 352
Webb, Alexander S., 367
Webb, Moses F., 286, 359, 392, 590

Weldon Railroad: army life near, 559–74; expedition against, 541–42, 552–58; mentioned, 483n, 484–85, 487–91, 493–94, 497–98, 511–13, 515, 526, 533, 549–51, 579n
Welling, Edward F., 14n, 38n, 122, 194–95, 233–34, 315–17, 374–76, 387, 394, 399, 406, 458, 466, 499, 501, 510, 525, 542, 550, 565, 569, 585, 588, 591, 593, 612–14, 618
Welling, Mrs. Edward F., 216, 218, 524, 619
Wells, George D., 207, 219
West, George W., 579–80
West Point, Va.: battle of, 12, 151–55 157, 160, 165, 176; mentioned, 148, 150–51, 238
West Pointers, 404
Whipple, Amiel W., 327
Whiskey—*see* Intoxicants
White, Ansley D., 102, 494
White, Morris, 362, 379–80
White House, Va., 156–60, 162, 165, 174, 181–82, 430, 593
White Oak Road, Battle of, 599–602
Whitehead, Charles, 103
Whiting, W. H. Chase, 152n
Whittier, John G., 115n
Wiestling, George B., 9–10, 31, 38, 40, 46–48, 54–55, 62–63, 80, 82, 84, 100, 115, 122, 144, 171, 183, 191–92, 198, 200, 204–6, 209, 213, 475
Wiestling, John, 40
Wilcox's Landing, Va.—*see* Windmill Point, Va.
Wilderness, Battle of the, 4, 15, 410n, 413–18, 427–29, 467n, 508, 583
Wildrick, James B., 47
Willard's Hotel, 36, 39, 57, 68, 198, 203–4, 214, 399, 590
Willcox, Orlando B., 489
Willetts, J. Howard, 310n
William, John, 483, 508, 516
Williams, Dr., 44
Williams, A. Seth, 260n
Williamsburg, Va., 150n, 154n, 155n, 158, 179
Williamson, John H., 242n, 246
Wilmington, N.C., 488n, 565n, 570, 591
Wilson, Ellen J.—*see* McAllister, Mrs. Robert
Wilson, James H., 456

Wilson, James M., 129, 155, 158
Wilson, Lucian, 9, 114, 310–11, 487, 532
Wilson, Mary, 519
Wilson's Creek, Battle of, 102
Winchester, Va., 145, 167n, 341, 466n
Windmill Point, Va., 136, 440–41
Winter, George, 44
Wolf's Shoals Ford, Va., 222–26, 229–30, 616
Women: Northern, 97, 99, 101, 103, 107, 212, 218, 220, 269–71, 277–78, 280, 290–91, 327, 354, 383–84, 386n, 388n, 405, 546, 569; Southern, 88, 106, 124, 229–30, 459, 521–22, 551, 555, 557, 568, 578, 609
Woodward, Jethro B., 113n, 119
Wool, John E., 146, 198
Wright, Horatio G., 466, 611n
Wyatt family, 565–67
Wynne, Mr., 140, 143

Yard, Robert B., 35, 62, 95, 113n, 131, 154, 160–61, 163, 165, 182, 187, 233, 375
Yellow Tavern, 514–15, 533, 549, 552
Yorktown, Va., 12, 110, 133, 135, 137–38, 141, 144, 148–50, 299n, 397n
Young, Edwin B., 262